Tenth Workshop on NLP for Similar Languages, Varieties and Dialects (VarDial 2023)

Dubrovnik, Croatia
5 May 2023

ISBN: 978-1-7138-7389-1

Printed from e-media with permission by:

Curran Associates, Inc.
57 Morehouse Lane
Red Hook, NY 12571

Some format issues inherent in the e-media version may also appear in this print version.

Association for Computational Linguistics
209 N. Eighth Street
Stroudsburg, Pennsylvania 18360

Phone: 1-570-476-8006
Fax: 1-570-476-0860

acl@aclweb.org

Additional copies of this publication are available from:

Curran Associates, Inc.
57 Morehouse Lane
Red Hook, NY 12571 USA
Phone: 845-758-0400
Fax: 845-758-2633
Email: curran@proceedings.com
Web: www.proceedings.com

ACL 2023

The Tenth Workshop on NLP for Similar Languages, Varieties and Dialects

Proceedings of the Workshop

May 5, 2023

Preface

These proceedings include the 23 papers presented at the 10th Workshop on NLP for Similar Languages, Varieties and Dialects (VarDial), co-located with the 17th Conference of the European Chapter of the Association for Computational Linguistics (EACL). Both EACL and VarDial were held in Dubrovnik, Croatia, in a hybrid format, allowing participants to attend on-site or to participate virtually.
This edition marks VarDial's ten-year anniversary. We are pleased to see that the workshop continues to serve the community as the main venue for researchers interested in the computational processing of diatopic language variation. The papers accepted this year address a wide range of topics, such as corpus building, part-of-speech tagging, and machine translation. This volume once again showcases the great linguistic diversity that VarDial embodies, including work on dialects and varieties of many different languages, such as Arabic, Cantonese, Croatian, Finnish, German, Irish, Italian, Mandarin, Occitan, Serbian, and Spanish.
The VarDial evaluation campaign continues to be an essential part of the workshop. In VarDial 2023, three shared tasks were organized: Slot and intent detection for low-resource language varieties (SID4LR), Discriminating Between Similar Languages – True Labels (DSL-TL), and Discriminating Between Similar Languages – Speech (DSL-S). All three tasks were organized for the first time this year. This volume includes the system description papers prepared by the participating teams, as well as a report written by the task organizers summarizing the results and the findings of the evaluation campaign.
Finally, we would like to take this opportunity to thank all the shared task organizers and the participants for their hard work. We further thank the VarDial program committee members for being an important part of the workshop's success over these ten years.

The VarDial workshop organizers:

Yves Scherrer, Tommi Jauhiainen, Nikola Ljubešić, Preslav Nakov, Jörg Tiedemann, and Marcos Zampieri

http://sites.google.com/view/vardial-2023/

Organizing Committee

Organizers

Tommi Jauhiainen, University of Helsinki
Nikola Ljubešić, Jožef Stefan Institute
Preslav Nakov, Mohamed bin Zayed University of Artificial Intelligence
Yves Scherrer, University of Helsinki
Jörg Tiedemann, University of Helsinki
Marcos Zampieri, George Mason University

Program Committee

Program Committee

Noëmi Aepli, University of Zurich
Željko Agić, Unity Technologies
César Aguilar, Universidad Veracruzana
Laura Alonso Alemany, Universidad Nacional de Cordoba
Eric Atwell, University of Leeds
Jorge Baptista, University of Algarve
Eckhard Bick, University of Southern Denmark
Johannes Bjerva, Department of Computer Science, Aalborg University
Francis Bond, Palacký University
Aoife Cahill, Dataminr
David Chiang, University of Notre Dame
Paul Cook, University of New Brunswick
Jon Dehdari, Fidelity Investments
Liviu P. Dinu, University of Bucharest
Stefanie Dipper, Ruhr-Universität Bochum
Sascha Diwersy, Université Paul-Valéry Montpellier 3
Mark Dras, Macquarie University
Tomaž Erjavec, Dept. of Knowledge Technologies, Jožef Stefan Institute
Pablo Gamallo, CITIUS, University of Santiago de Compostela
Cyril Goutte, National Research Council Canada
Nizar Habash, New York University Abu Dhabi
Chu-ren Huang, The Hong Kong Polytechnic Universiy
Radu Tudor Ionescu, University of Bucharest
Surafel M. Lakew, Amazon.com, Inc
Ekaterina Lapshinova-koltunski, Stiftung Universität Hildesheim
Lung-hao Lee, National Central University
John Nerbonne, Albert-Ludwigs Universität Freiburg
Kai North, George Mason University
Maciej Ogrodniczuk, Institute of Computer Science, Polish Academy of Sciences
Petya Osenova, Sofia University St. Kl. Ohridskiand IICT-BAS
Santanu Pal, Wipro
Barbara Plank, LMU Munich
Taraka Rama, Walmart Global Tech
Francisco Manuel Rangel Pardo, Universitat Politècnica de València
Reinhard Rapp, University of Mainz
Paolo Rosso, Universitat Politècnica de València
Rachel Edita Roxas, Ideacorp
Fatiha Sadat, UQAM
Tanja Samardžić, University of Zurich
Kevin Scannell, Saint Louis University
Serge Sharoff, University of Leeds
Miikka Silfverberg, University of British Columbia
Kiril Simov, Artificial Intelligence and Language Technologies Department, IICT, Bulgarian Academy of Sciences
Milena Slavcheva, Institute of Information and Communication Technologies, Bulgarian Academy of Sciences

Marko Tadić, University of Zagreb, Faculty of Humanities and Social Sciences
Liling Tan, Amazon
Joel Tetreault, Dataminr
Francis Tyers, Indiana University
Rob Van Der Goot, IT University of Copenhagen
Pidong Wang, Google
Taro Watanabe, Nara Institute of Science and Technology
Çağrı Çöltekin, University of Tübingen

Keynote Talk: Bridging the Dialect Gap with Modular Transfer Learning?

Ivan Vulić
University of Cambridge
2023-05-05 14:00:00 –

Table of Contents

Program

Friday, May 5, 2023

09:00 - 09:10 *Opening remarks*

09:10 - 10:30 *Oral presentations*

Findings of the VarDial Evaluation Campaign 2023
Noëmi Aepli, Çağrı Çöltekin, Rob Van Der Goot, Tommi Jauhiainen, Mourhaf Kazzaz, Nikola Ljubešić, Kai North, Barbara Plank, Yves Scherrer and Marcos Zampieri

Two-stage Pipeline for Multilingual Dialect Detection
Ankit Vaidya and Aditya Kane

Fine-Tuning BERT with Character-Level Noise for Zero-Shot Transfer to Dialects and Closely-Related Languages
Aarohi Srivastava and David Chiang

10:30 - 11:00 *Coffee break*

11:00 - 12:15 *Oral presentations*

Analyzing Zero-Shot transfer Scenarios across Spanish variants for Hate Speech Detection
Galo Castillo-lópez, Arij Riabi and Djamé Seddah

Optimizing the Size of Subword Vocabularies in Dialect Classification
Vani Kanjirangat, Tanja Samardžić, Ljiljana Dolamic and Fabio Rinaldi

Comparing and Predicting Eye-tracking Data of Mandarin and Cantonese
Junlin Li, Bo Peng, Yu-yin Hsu and Emmanuele Chersoni

12:15 - 12:40 *Poster Boosters I*

12:40 - 14:00 *Lunch break*

14:00 - 14:50 *Keynote Talk by Ivan Vulić: Bridging the Dialect Gap with Modular Transfer Learning?*

Friday, May 5, 2023 (continued)

14:50 - 15:40 *Round Table: VarDial in the Era of Large Language Models*

15:40 - 16:15 *Coffee break*

16:15 - 16:40 *Poster Boosters II*

16:40 - 18:00 *Poster Session*

Murreviikko - A Dialectologically Annotated and Normalized Dataset of Finnish Tweets
Olli Kuparinen

Exploring Enhanced Code-Switched Noising for Pretraining in Neural Machine Translation
Vivek Iyer, Arturo Oncevay and Alexandra Birch

Does Manipulating Tokenization Aid Cross-Lingual Transfer? A Study on POS Tagging for Non-Standardized Languages
Verena Blaschke, Hinrich Schütze and Barbara Plank

Temporal Domain Adaptation for Historical Irish
Oksana Dereza, Theodorus Fransen and John P. Mccrae

Variation and Instability in Dialect-Based Embedding Spaces
Jonathan Dunn

PALI: A Language Identification Benchmark for Perso-Arabic Scripts
Sina Ahmadi, Milind Agarwal and Antonios Anastasopoulos

Get to Know Your Parallel Data: Performing English Variety and Genre Classification over MaCoCu Corpora
Taja Kuzman, Peter Rupnik and Nikola Ljubešić

Reconstructing Language History by Using a Phonological Ontology. An Analysis of German Surnames
Hanna Fischer and Robert Engsterhold

Friday, May 5, 2023 (continued)

BENCHić-lang: A Benchmark for Discriminating between Bosnian, Croatian, Montenegrin and Serbian
Peter Rupnik, Taja Kuzman and Nikola Ljubešić

A Measure for Linguistic Coherence in Spatial Language Variation
Alfred Lameli and Andreas Schönberg

Spelling convention sensitivity in neural language models
Elizabeth Nielsen, Christo Kirov and Brian Roark

Dialect and Variant Identification as a Multi-Label Classification Task: A Proposal Based on Near-Duplicate Analysis
Gabriel Bernier-colborne, Cyril Goutte and Serge Leger

Lemmatization Experiments on Two Low-Resourced Languages: Low Saxon and Occitan
Aleksandra Miletić and Janine Siewert

The Use of Khislavichi Lect Morphological Tagging to Determine its Position in the East Slavic Group
Ilia Afanasev

DiatopIt: A Corpus of Social Media Posts for the Study of Diatopic Language Variation in Italy
Alan Ramponi and Camilla Casula

Dialect Representation Learning with Neural Dialect-to-Standard Normalization
Olli Kuparinen and Yves Scherrer

VarDial in the Wild: Industrial Applications of LID Systems for Closely-Related Language Varieties
Fritz Hohl and Soh-eun Shim

Using Ensemble Learning in Language Variety Identification
Mihaela Gaman

SIDLR: Slot and Intent Detection Models for Low-Resource Language Varieties
Sang Yun Kwon, Gagan Bhatia, Elmoatez Billah Nagoudi, Alcides Alcoba Inciarte and Muhammad Abdul-mageed

Friday, May 5, 2023 (continued)

Analyzing Zero-Shot transfer Scenarios across Spanish variants for Hate Speech Detection

Galo Castillo-López[1,2*] and **Arij Riabi**[1,3] and **Djamé Seddah**[1]
[1]INRIA Paris, France
[2]Université Paris-Saclay, France
[3]Sorbonne Université
galo.castillo@upsaclay.fr
{firstname.lastname}@inria.fr

Abstract

Hate speech detection in online platforms has been widely studied in the past. Most of these works were conducted in English and a few rich-resource languages. Recent approaches tailored for low-resource languages have explored the interests of zero-shot cross-lingual transfer learning models in resource-scarce scenarios. However, languages variations between geolects such as American English and British English, Latin-American Spanish, and European Spanish is still a problem for NLP models that often relies on (latent) lexical information for their classification tasks. More importantly, the cultural aspect, crucial for hate speech detection, is often overlooked.

In this work, we present the results of a thorough analysis of hate speech detection models performance on different variants of Spanish, including a new hate speech toward immigrants Twitter data set we built to cover these variants. Using mBERT and Beto, a monolingual Spanish Bert-based language model, as the basis of our transfer learning architecture, our results indicate that hate speech detection models for a given Spanish variant are affected when different variations of such language are not considered. Hate speech expressions could vary from region to region where the same language is spoken.

1 Introduction

Hate speech detection is a task that has gained much attention from the NLP community due to the exponential spread of social media platforms[1]. This task aims to identify whether a piece of text contains hateful messages against a person or a group based on characteristics such as color, ethnicity, race, sexual orientation, religion, and others (John, 2000). Gender and nationalities are no exceptions to this. According to the Pew Research Center report in 2021, 33% of women under 35 report having been sexually harassed online, compared with 11% of men under 35 (Vogels, 2021). Misogyny is harm against women due to gender, which might result in psychological, reputational, professional, or even physical damage (Ging and Siapera, 2018). On the other hand, xenophobia is "*attitudes, prejudices, and behavior that reject, exclude and often vilify persons, based on the perception that they are outsiders or foreigners to the community, society or national identity*"[2]. An online manifestation of such behaviors may include hostility, social exclusion, threats of violence, and other forms of discrimination. As a result, the Internet becomes a less equal, less safe, and less inclusive environment for targetted groups.

Online hate speech detection in social medias platforms has been tackled in several studies (Pamungkas et al., 2018; García-Díaz et al., 2022; Pamungkas et al., 2020; Ahluwalia et al., 2018; Muaad et al., 2021; Shushkevich and Cardiff, 2018; Díaz-Torres et al., 2020). However, most studies have been carried out using English language data or limited Spanish data. For example, the significant morphosyntactic variations between Spanish variants (Bentivoglio and Sedano, 2011) make considering the Spanish language homogeneous challenging for language models. According to Ethnologue[3] in 2022, Spanish is currently declared as the official language in 22 countries, being the fourth language with the most significant number of countries. Due to the numerous regions where Spanish is the spoken language, expressions associated with hate speech may differ across various locations. For example, in the variation of the Spanish language from Spain, the word *"fregar"* only means *"scrub"* while at the same time, the same word in the Span-

*Work conducting during an internship at Inria Paris.

[1]Please be aware that this paper contains some examples of offensive slurs that may be considered upsetting.

[2]https://home-affairs.ec.europa.eu/pages/glossary/xenophobia_en

[3]https://www.ethnologue.com/ethnoblog/gary-simons/welcome-25th-edition

Tenth Workshop on NLP for Similar Languages, Varieties and Dialects (VarDial 2023), pages 1–13
May 5, 2023 ©2023 Association for Computational Linguistics

ish Ecuadorian variant can also mean *"annoy"* or *"having fun"*. We note the different connotations of that term across various Latin American regions provided by the Royal Spanish Academy[4] (RAE in Spanish). Thus, the phrase *"Anda a tu casa a fregar"* can only be interpreted as *"Go home to scrub (the dishes)"* by people from Spain, which can contain a misogynous connotation. On the other hand, for people speaking Spanish in Ecuador, it may be mostly interpreted as *"Go home to have some fun"* or *"Go home to annoy (other people)"*, which are not related to discriminatory connotations. Despite these scenarios, studies proposing models for hate speech detection towards women and immigrants in Spanish generally do not include information about the language or cultural variation of the text.

Due to the previously described challenge, other difficulties emerge when developing hateful content detection systems for online platforms.
Current state-of-the-art pre-trained language models (LM), such as the "multilingual" version of BERT (mBERT) (Devlin et al., 2018; Pires et al., 2019), are widely used in several NLP tasks and achieve impressive results. However, mBERT might not help to detect hate speech against women or immigrants when language-specific variants appear. It has been proven to perform worse than monolingual implementations of BERT under certain circumstances (Martin et al., 2020; Wu and Dredze, 2020). mBERT is trained on only Wikipedia data, particularly the entire Wikipedia dump for each language, excluding user and talk pages. However, this is problematic for the Spanish language as according to Wikipedia's *Spanish Wikipedia* article (Spanish Wikipedia, 2021) by September 2017, 39.2% of the Spanish Wikipedia edits come from Spain, being the country with the largest edits, while the rest come from other countries located in regions such as the Americas and others. It is important to note that Spain is the fourth country with the most prominent Spanish language native speakers, whereas Mexico is the first according to Statista (2021). Therefore, language models trained on Wikipedia data may not represent the differences between Spanish variants (Hershcovich et al., 2022). Thus, in this study, we aim to address the following research questions:

- **RQ1**: How does language-specific language models' performance differ from multilingual LM to detect online hate speech against women and immigrants in Spanish corpora?
- **RQ2**: Is zero-shot transfer effective for hate speech detection when different language variants of the same language are considered?

To do so, we compare mBERT with a Spanish version of BERT, named BETO (Canete et al., 2020), for binary classification in two different hate speech domains using various datasets on xenophobia and misogyny. We analyze the effects of Spanish language variants on model performance in both domains using a xenophobia detection corpus we created for this purpose as no other corpora include language variant metadata at the tweet level. Finally, an error analysis conducted with the SHAP interpretability framework (Lundberg and Lee, 2017) highlighted the *vulnerability* to cultural-specific hateful terms of language models fine-tuned on another geolect. In an era where cross-cultural issues in NLP become of increasing and welcome importance (Hovy and Yang, 2021; Nozza, 2021; Hershcovich et al., 2022) , our work and methodology constitute an interesting step in this process. This is why we release our datasets[5], models, and guidelines to the community, hoping to enrich a burgeoning ecosystem.

Our main contributions may be summarized as follows:

- The compilation and annotation of HaSCoSVa-2022, a new corpus of tweets related to hate speech towards immigrants written in Spanish. This corpus contains information regarding the language variant. The dataset is subdivided into two subsets according to the language variant: (1) Latin American and (2) European. The dataset is released to the research community.
- Experiments on zero-shot transfer between European and Latin American Spanish language variants on hate speech detection towards women and immigrants to investigate how the performance of the models vary when used on different variants of the same language.

2 Related Work

Automatic hate speech detection in online platforms has been previously studied across different hate speech domains such as misogyny (Fersini et al., 2022; Plaza-Del-Arco et al., 2020), xenopho-

[4] https://dle.rae.es/fregar

[5] https://gitlab.inria.fr/counter/HaSCoSVa

bia (Romero-Vega et al., 2020; Benitez-Andrades et al., 2022), homophobia (Karayiğit et al., 2022; Arcila-Calderón et al., 2021) and others (Davidson et al., 2017; Lozano et al., 2017). Nevertheless, a limited number of works focus on Spanish data to develop ML-based systems for online hateful content identification.[6] Most of the research developed with Spanish corpora posted on micro-blogging platforms are related to participation in a few recent shared tasks, namely AMI 2018 (Fersini et al., 2018), HatEval 2019 (Basile et al., 2019) and others. In addition, there is a lack of studies considering different variations of the Spanish language and how state-of-the-art language models such as BERT perform in hate speech detection when used for cross variants over the same language (Zhang et al., 2021; Hershcovich et al., 2022).

In (Plaza-del Arco et al., 2021), multilingual and monolingual pre-trained language models were compared to Deep Learning architectures (CNN, LSTM, and Bi-LSTM) and traditional ML models (SVM and Logistic Regression) for detecting hate speech on tweets written in Spanish. The authors used two datasets to conduct the comparison. The first corpus, HaterNet (Pereira-Kohatsu et al., 2019), has no information about the hate speech domain or the location where the tweets were posted. The second dataset is the HatEval corpus which contains only information about the target for hate speech against women and immigrants. They used BETO (Canete et al., 2020), a Spanish language implementation of BERT trained on Wikipedia articles, movies and TED Talks subtitles, scientific documents, and others written in Spanish. Results obtained in (Plaza-del Arco et al., 2021) showed that BETO, a monolingual LM outperforms multilingual pre-trained models such as XLM and mBERT as well as the rest of the models they evaluated for hate speech detection in Spanish. Results in line with Plaza-del Arco et al. (2021) have also been achieved in other similar studies on hate speech detection (Benítez-Andrades et al., 2022; Tanase et al., 2020).

Nozza (2021) studied hate speech detection against women and immigrants across three languages: Spanish, English, and Italian. She investigated the limitations of zero-shot cross-lingual approaches using mBERT. Her results suggest that hate speech targets –i.e. different languages– should be studied separately as transfer learning in zero-shot scenarios is ineffective for misogyny detection. In addition to her findings, we aim to investigate whether such nuances can be extended to cross-variants within the same language.

[6]Many of these works can be found via the IberLEF annual shared tasks.

3 Datasets

In this section, we describe the datasets we use for training the misogyny detection models and the procedure we follow to compile and annotate the HaSCoSVa-2022 corpus, which is later used to train and evaluate our models to detect hate speech against immigrants. In Table 1, you can find a summary of the datasets we used in this work.

3.1 Misogyny existing datasets

3.1.1 MisoCorpus-2020

The MisoCorpus-2020 dataset (García-Díaz et al., 2021) compiles tweets written in Spanish, which are grouped into three categories: **VARW** (Violence Against Relevant Women), which refers to violent tweets directed to women with a significant social relevance; **SELA** (Spanish from Europe vs. Spanish from Latin America), which consists of tweets charged of misogynistic content written in Spanish from Europe – i.e., Spain – and posts with the same type of content written in a Latin America's variation of Spanish; and **DDSS** (Discredit, Dominance, Sexual harassment, and Stereotype), which comprises Twitter posts subdivided into different types of misogynistic attacks, such as derailing, rape, gender violence, and others. The dataset contains 10,244 tweet IDs in total. However, as the tweets were posted some years ago, we could find only 7,575 tweets in total (74% from the original dataset), where 49.2% is labeled as misogynistic.

3.1.2 Detección Misoginia (DetMis)

The Detección Misoginia (DetMis) dataset (Vera Lagos et al., 2021) contains 35K tweets geo-located in Mexico. The corpus is based on keywords related to sexism, stereotyping, and discrimination towards women from (Fisher et al., 2013). The authors used such keywords to search and filter tweets geo-located in each of the 32 states of Mexico. Since tweets were filtered based on keywords, a maximum of 5 tweets per keyword and label (misogynous and non-misogynous) were selected for annotation. Finally, 1K tweets were obtained per label after annotation. It is important to note that only one annotator participated in the annotation process.

Domain	Dataset	Nb tweets	% Hate speech	Variation
women	MisCorpus-2020	7575	49.2%	Europe, LatAm
women	DetMis	2000	50%	LatAm
women	IberEval 2018	3307	49.9%	Europe, LatAm*
immigrants	HaSCoSVa-2022	4000	13.9%	Europe, LatAm

* This dataset does not distinguish between both variations of Spanish — i.e. we cannot identify which tweets correspond to Europe or LatAm variations.

Table 1: Description of Spanish language corpora used for training the binary classification models.

3.1.3 IberEval 2018

The dataset is from the Automatic Misogyny Identification shared task at IberEval 2018 (Fersini et al., 2018). The corpus contains misogynous tweets in English and Spanish, and we only use the Spanish data. There are two main steps in the annotation process: First, part of the dataset was labeled by two annotators to define a gold standard. Next, the rest of the tweets were labeled through a majority voting approach on the CrowdFlower[7] platform based on the standard defined in the first step.

3.2 New Dataset: HaSCoSVa-2022

We reviewed the publicly available data for hate speech against immigrants in Spanish. However, to the best of our knowledge, there are no tweets corpora containing information about different language variations. Therefore, we create the HaSCoSVa-2022 corpus (**Ha**te **S**peech **Co**rpus with **S**panish **Va**riations) to conduct our experiments in the immigration domain. We focus on two immigration cases: immigration from Latin America and certain African countries to Spain and immigration from Venezuela to its surrounding countries where Spanish is their official language. Both cases carry a strong discriminatory online discourse due to religion, stereotypes, and other factors that concern a fraction of the local population.

3.2.1 Data Extraction

We define two geographical coordinates and radius to obtain geo-located tweets from Spain and Latin American regions. Tweets from Spain were extracted from a 520 Km radius surrounding latitude: 40.416705, longitude: -3.703583. The area from where we extracted geo-tagged tweets about immigration coming from Venezuela is centered on latitude: -3.976015, longitude: -79.225102, considering a radius of 1,200 Km. Note that the defined region for obtaining the European tweets is the same as the one defined by García-Díaz et al. (2021). However, since the Latin American region the authors proposed includes Venezuelan territory, we slightly changed it to exclude tweets produced in Venezuela as we need tweets from neighboring countries[8]. The regions we determine to extract the posts can be visualized in Figure 2 in Appendix A. We define three lists of keywords related to immigration and hate speech towards immigrants. Two sets of keywords contain 72 and 18 terms regarding European and Latin American immigration, respectively. In addition, the third set of keywords comprises 26 generic terms related to immigration – i.e., such terms are not region-specific. The terms are mainly demonyms, country names, and nicknames (offensive or not) related to such regions. The tweets were collected in two-time frames: from June 6th to June 28th and July 21st to August 4th. As a result, 75,834 tweets were obtained in total.

3.2.2 Data Annotation

To perform the data annotation, we randomly sampled 2,500 and 1,500 tweets produced in Europe and Latin America. We describe in detail the sampling strategy we follow in Appendix A.4. Two annotators, native Spanish speakers from Latin America, carry out the manual annotation. Both annotators tag each tweet into one of the three labels: xenophobic, non-xenophobic, or ambiguous. Whether a tweet is difficult to manually classify by an annotator, then the label provided by the annotator is "*ambiguous*". Otherwise, a tweet is classified as "*xenophobic*" if it matches **all** following conditions:

1. The content of the tweet primarily targets immigrants as a group, or even a single individual, if they are considered to be a member of that group (and NOT because of their individual characteristics).
2. The content of the tweet propagates, incites, promotes, or justifies hatred or violence to-

[7]https://figure-eight.com/

[8]Note that our aim is to analyze xenophobia against Venezuelan immigrants in regions surrounding Venezuela.

wards the target or a message that aims to dehumanize, hurt or intimidate the target.

We used the guidelines proposed by Basile et al. (2019) with minor modifications. A third annotator participated in the annotation campaign to provide a final label for tweets labeled as "*ambiguous*" by both previous annotators and posts previously tagged with different labels (i.e. one annotator tagged as "*xenophobic*" and the other as "*non-xenophobic*"). This annotator did not have access to the other annotations. Finally, 554 tweets were tagged as xenophobic, while 3,446 were labeled non-hateful towards immigrants. Thus, 13.9% tweets belong to the label of interest. The resulting corpus contains the tweet ID, the full text of the post, its label, and the language variation (LatAm or Europe). The inter-rater agreement reliability between both initial annotators according to Cohen's Kappa (Cohen, 1960) is 0.443 (88% agreement), which can be interpreted as a moderate agreement according to its author. The resulting HaSCoSVa-2022 dataset, keywords used for tweets extraction, and annotation guidelines are freely available to the research community[9].

4 Experimental Settings

Language Models. For the multilingual language model, we use mBERT (Devlin et al., 2019), the multilingual version of BERT, trained on Wikipedia data from 104 languages. We also experiment with BETO (Canete et al., 2020), a monolingual Spanish Bert, trained on the whole Spanish Wikipedia dump combined with the Spanish language texts of the OPUS Project (Tiedemann, 2012) without any differentiation between the Spanish variants. Others models for Spanish exist and are posterior to BETO (Gutiérrez-Fandiño et al., 2021; la Rosa et al., 2022), we decided to focus on BETO because of its pretraining data that makes it more comparable to mBERT. It would be of course interesting to conduct a large-scale Spanish monolingual models study on that topic but we leave it for future work.

Data Preprocessing. We replace all URLs and mentions with the same tokens, *url* and *@user*, respectively. In addition, since hashtags' segmentation has been shown to improve the results for certain tasks (Rosa et al., 2011; Declerck and Lendvai, 2016; Gromann and Declerck, 2017), we segment all hashtags into words to enrich tweets' messages with actual words. To develop such hashtags segmentation, we use Python's package *wordsegment*[10]. We randomly split the dataset into 70% for training and 30% for testing to ensure that each set's class distribution remains balanced. Also, we randomly pick 20% of the previously selected training set as the development set.

Evaluation. All fine-tuned models are trained over 5 different seeds, and all reported performance metrics are averaged over such runs to ensure evaluation robustness. Moreover, we select the best model out of 5 epochs after each training process according to the macro-F1 score on the development sets.

4.1 Multilingual vs. Language-specific

We use all the data described in Section 3 to compare the performance of the two models, mBERT and BETO. We aim to evaluate the differences between mBERT and BETO to detect hate speech in Twitter posts written in Spanish.

4.2 Spanish Language Variations

We use BETO to evaluate the performance of a monolingual model across Spanish variants. For this set of experiments, the Spanish variant of the tweet is relevant. Then, we exclude tweets that do not contain information about the region of origin. As a result, we keep 6,082 tweets for the misogyny experiments, where 3,596 posts correspond to the LatAm variant and 2,486 to the European. More details on the misogyny dataset used for this set of experiments can be found in Table 6 in Appendix A. All tweets on the immigration corpus are kept for this set of experiments.

The Latin American and European variation datasets sizes are not comparable according to the hate speech target. Therefore, we randomly undersample the largest variation dataset depending on the hate speech domain to set both variations to the same size and ensure the comparability of the transfer setting. As a result, the misogyny corpus for this set of experiments ends up with two sets of 2,486 tweets each –i.e., one set per variation. Therefore, each variation contains 1,392 tweets for training, 348 for development, and 746 for testing the models. Similarly, each variation subset in the immigration dataset includes 840, 210, and 450 records for training, development, and testing. An

[9]https://gitlab.inria.fr/counter/HaSCoSVa

[10]https://pypi.org/project/wordsegment/

overview of the train-dev-test splits can be found in Table 7 in Appendix A.

5 Results

Results obtained from the comparison between mBERT and BETO over the whole corpora are shown in Table 2. Results suggest that BETO outperforms mBERT in both hate speech domains. Specifically, BETO macro-F1 score is 11 points higher than mBERT on misogyny detection, whereas 4 points higher on xenophobia-related tweets classification. High standard deviations in both mBERT models compared to BETO suggests that BETO shows more stable and consistent performance across different runs. In line with previous works (Martin et al., 2020; Plaza-del Arco et al., 2021; Benítez-Andrades et al., 2022; Tanase et al., 2020), we find that using a language-specific LM where much more Spanish data is used for training and no other languages are considered, results in a better performance for detecting hateful posts written in Spanish.

Model	women	immigration
mBERT	74.4 (± 7.0)	69.6 (± 2.8)
BETO	**84.9** (± 0.3)	**73.1** (± 0.8)

Table 2: Models' average macro-F1 scores obtained on the test split over five runs. We select the best model out of 5 epochs for each run according to the macro-F1 score on the development set. The standard deviation computed over the 5 runs is inside parenthesis.

The second set of experiments aims to compare mono-lingual and cross-lingual settings across Spanish variants. Table 3 shows that the BETO model performance is significantly higher when trained and tested on the same language variant in both hate speech domains. For instance, the score of the misogyny model trained on European Spanish is 18 points higher when tested on European Spanish than on Latin American Spanish. On the other hand, the difference is 8 points for the xenophobia model, when the model is trained on Latin American Spanish and tested on tweets from Europe. We can also note that in all cases, macro-F1 scores present a higher standard deviation when the source data comes from Latin America.

6 Error Analysis

In this section, we analyze and compare errors in cross variants evaluation. We briefly examine the reasons that might lead to poor performance when the model is trained and tested on different language variants. Part of our analyses is inspired by the error analysis carried out in (Plaza-del Arco et al., 2021). First, we analyze the errors obtained by BETO. Such analysis is detailed in Table 4. Regarding the misogyny models, we can observe that models tend to wrongly classify non-harmful tweets from LatAm as misogynous, as 59.5% errors in common by both models are false positives. Moreover, in the xenophobia-related errors, we can see that 81.5% of the errors obtained in common by both models on European tweets correspond to false negatives. Similarly, a higher rate of false negatives is obtained by both models on the LatAm target since 65% of errors obtained in common are actual xenophobic tweets tagged as non-hateful by both models. We can attribute these results to the class imbalance in the immigration dataset (13.9% of the tweets are xenophobic), which might result in a difficult task for models to detect the minority class.

Moreover, in Table 5, we summarize the vocabulary coverage by the training sets on the test sets. In other words, we display the proportion of terms from the test sets included in each training set. We use a Spanish POS tagger to only consider nouns and adjectives for this analysis. For instance, in the case of the xenophobia dataset, we found 1,095 terms appearing in the LatAm test set and excluded in the Europe train set. As expected, for a given test set, a more significant proportion of terms found in the training set of the same variation than the other one. For instance, in the case of misogyny data, 50.3% of terms from Europe's test set can be found in Europe's training set, while only 39.6% is found in LatAm's training set. On average, test sets include 9.2% more terms in the training sets of the same variation than the others for both hate speech domains. Although we do not only consider hate-speech-related terms for this analysis, we found that various of the most frequently excluded terms correspond to derogatory words associated with a particular variant. For instance, the word "cerda" (which means *pig*) is found in the misogyny Europe set of tweets, but it does not appear in the Latin America tweets. Such a term is more used in Spain as an insult than in Latin America. The same happens with the term "vieja" (which might mean *old woman*), appearing in LatAm tweets but not in the European dataset. This term is mainly used in

	Target	women		immigrants	
		Europe	LatAm	Europe	LatAm
Source	Europe	**89.6** (± **0.6**)	70.5 (± 0.5)	**69.6** (± **0.9**)	64.9 (± 1.7)
	LatAm	71.4 (± 5.0)	**81.8** (± **0.5**)	62.8 (± 5.6)	**73.3** (± **2.7**)

Table 3: BETO's average macro-F1 scores obtained on the test splits over 5 runs. We select the best model out of 5 epochs for each run according to the macro-F1 score on the development set. The standard deviation computed over the 5 runs is inside parenthesis. Scores in **bold** indicate which source outperforms the other for a given target.

		women		immigrants	
Target	Source	False Pos.	False Neg.	False Pos.	False Neg.
Europe	Europe	38 (50.7%)	37 (49.3%)	31 (53.4%)	27 (46.6%)
	LatAm	108 (45.2%)	131 (54.8%)	13 (27.7%)	34 (72.3%)
	Common	15 (50.0%)	15 (50.0%)	5 (18.5%)	22 (81.5%)
LatAm	Europe	117 (55.7%)	93 (44.3%)	32 (43.2%)	42 (56.8%)
	LatAm	68 (55.7%)	54 (44.3%)	23 (43.4.%)	30 (56.6%)
	Common	44 (59.5%)	30 (40.5%)	12 (34.3%)	23 (65.7%)

Table 4: Number of tweets mislabeled per setting for each hate speech domain. In parenthesis, we show the percentage of mislabels on each type of error (False Pos. and False Neg.) from all the mislabels of a given domain and setting. Common mislabels correspond to errors obtained by both models (sources) on the same target.

Mexico for referring to women and can contain a derogatory connotation.

Finally, we use SHAP (Lundberg and Lee, 2017) to study the behavior of BETO in terms of explainability. SHapley Additive exPlanations, also known as SHAP, is a well-known model explainability technique used to interpret the models' decisions. SHAP is based on Game Theory and assigns importance scores to features for a given example classification. Such scores indicate how much a feature influences the model toward its final output. In NLP tasks, it can assign importance scores to terms. Thus, we use SHAP to examine how the models behave when the word *tonta* (which means *idiot*, female gendered, in English) appears in a text. Such an insult is an example of how the same term can be interpreted differently in two variations of Spanish. In Spain, that insult is much more aggressive than how it may be interpreted in Latin America. We take one misogynous tweet containing the word *tonta* from our corpus and classify such text by the misogyny Europe and LatAm models. A colored representation of the scores computed by SHAP on both classifications is shown in Figure 1. We can observe both models provide different classifications, where the model trained on European data performs correctly. SHAP finds the word "*tonta*" highly influences the model trained on European tweets to classify the tweet as misogynous, as shown in Figure 1b. In contrast, the same term provides almost no influence on the LatAm model's final decision according to SHAP in Figure 1b. We can note the analyzed term slightly contributes towards the wrong (non-misogynous) class when the LatAm model is used.

7 Conclusions

In this study, we showed how BETO, a Spanish version of BERT, as expected, performs significantly better than Multilingual BERT for classifying tweets as hateful for two hate speech domains: misogyny and xenophobia. Our outcomes align with previous studies mostly conducted with corpora proposed in popular shared tasks on hate speech detection. This does not mean that Multilingual BERT is not useful since findings in (Wu and Dredze, 2020) suggested that mBERT is remarkably useful on low-resource language tasks, in contrast to monolingual BERT implementations that use a significant amount of data.

Moreover, we demonstrated that variants of a language, for instance, due to its use in different countries or cultures, affect the performance of hate speech detection models. In other words, we found that whether we train a model using data derived from only one variant of Spanish, the model's per-

	women				immigrants			
	Europe Test		LatAm Test		Europe Test		LatAm Test	
Train	Included	Excluded	Included	Excluded	Included	Excluded	Included	Excluded
Europe	50.3%	49.7%	38.5%	61.5%	45.3	54.7%	40.3%	59.7%
LatAm	39.6%	60.4%	47.7%	52.3%	36.4%	63.6%	48.1%	51.9%

Table 5: Proportion of terms on the testing sets included and excluded on each training set.

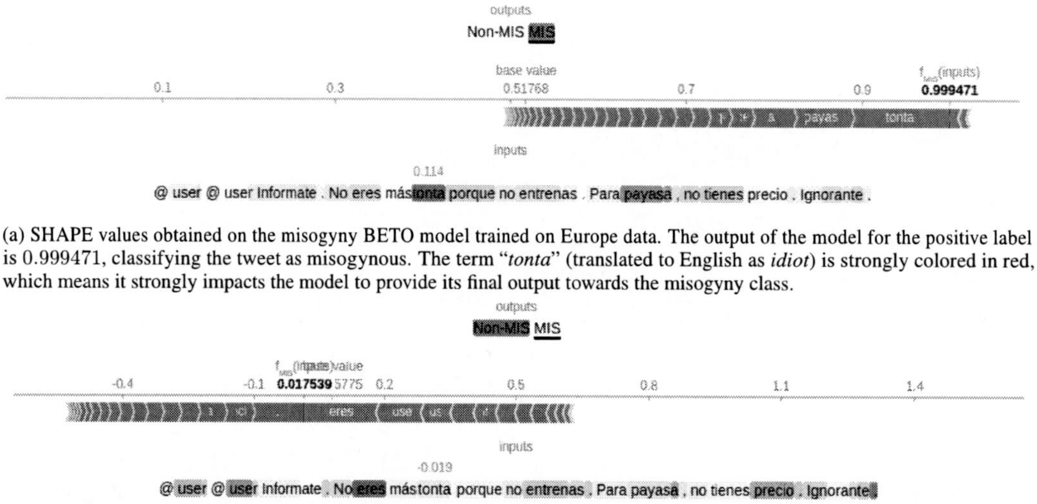

(a) SHAPE values obtained on the misogyny BETO model trained on Europe data. The output of the model for the positive label is 0.999471, classifying the tweet as misogynous. The term "*tonta*" (translated to English as *idiot*) is strongly colored in red, which means it strongly impacts the model to provide its final output towards the misogyny class.

(b) SHAP values obtained on the misogyny BETO trained on LatAm data. The model's output for the positive label is 0.017539, classifying the tweet as non-misogynous. The term "*tonta*" (translated to English as *idiot*) is almost not colored, which means it does not provide any relevant impact on the model to provide its final output.

Figure 1: SHAP values obtained from the misogyny BETO trained on European tweets 1a and LatAm data 1b classifying the same misogynous tweet from our corpus. The model trained on LatAm data detects no misogyny, whereas the European model is capable of identifying hateful content. The final output of the models towards the misogyny class is written in **bold**. Red colored terms influence the final decision towards the misogyny label, while blue colored terms provide influence the model classification towards the non-misogyny class. The tweet can be translated to English as "*@user @user Get informed, you can't be more of an idiot because you don't train, for a clown, you're priceless, ignorant.*"

formance may decay if it is used on data derived from another variant of the same language. An explanation for this may be the usage of terms, which in some regions where Spanish is spoken as a native language may denote hate, could be unrelated to hate speech in other regions where Spanish is also an official language. Thus, the terms used for denoting misogyny in countries where the same language is spoken might differ from one place to another. In our work, we used data produced in Spain, compared to data produced in Latin America, considering various countries such as Mexico (North America), Colombia, Ecuador (South America), and others. Our results extend the findings obtained by Nozza (2021) to transfer cross variants within the same language, demonstrating that different language variants from the same language for a given hate speech domain might also need to be studied separately to develop hate speech detection systems. Additionally, if different variants in the same language are not treated as separate cases but as one single scenario, we should consider using examples from as many variants as possible during the training phase to obtain models capable of dealing with data collected from different regions where hateful expressions may vary from each other. Finally, we followed a structured data extraction and annotation scheme to build a new hate speech towards immigrants corpus in Spanish, considering different language variants. Our dataset will help advance the state-of-the-art in hate speech detection for language variation and contribute to a better understanding of the dynamics of hate speech towards immigrants in online environments. We release this corpus for use by the scientific community.

8 Limitations

In order to perform this work, we had to use simplified assumptions regarding the Spanish variants we worked on. We considered both variants as homogeneous geolects by themselves, whereas, of course, those geographical differences may constitute different dialects (cf. Wikipedia's world map of Spanish dialects, reproduced in Figure 3 in Appendix A.5).

The other limitation of our work is tied to the annotation biases eventually found in our dataset. Indeed, three annotators worked on the annotation of tweets forming the HaSCoSVa-2022 dataset, a new corpus we introduced for hate speech detection in two Spanish variants. Nevertheless, all annotators are from Latin America. Thus, some interpretations of tweets from the European Spanish variant might be questionable, given a potential lack of knowledge of certain hate-speech-related expressions used in Spain. To mitigate this issue, we included extensive observations regarding potentially confusing expressions from the European variant in the guidelines we provided. Additionally, the adjudicator (i.e. the annotator resolving the conflicts) in our annotation campaign has an academic background in political science and discrimination towards minorities and has lived in Spain for a significant amount of time. We thus believe that this problem has been properly handled. Nevertheless, as we will publicly release this dataset, including the guidelines and the seed words we used, within an open-source license, we will welcome any concurrent annotation and bug reports.

9 Ethical Considerations

This paper is part of a line of work aiming to investigate the effect of language variation on hate speech detection, fight the spread of offensive and hateful speech online, and have a positive global impact on the world. It has been approved by our institutional review board (IRB), and follows the national and European General Data Protection Regulation (GDPR). All our experiments were executed on clusters whose energy mix is made of nuclear (65–75%), 20% renewable, and the remaining with gas (or, more rarely, coal when imported from abroad).

Acknowledgments

We warmly thank the reviewers for their very valuable feedback. This work received funding from the European Union's Horizon 2020 research and innovation programme under grant agreement No. 101021607.

References

Resham Ahluwalia, Himani Soni, Edward Callow, Anderson Nascimento, and Martine De Cock. 2018. Detecting hate speech against women in english tweets. *EVALITA Evaluation of NLP and Speech Tools for Italian*, 12:194.

Carlos Arcila-Calderón, Javier J Amores, Patricia Sánchez-Holgado, and David Blanco-Herrero. 2021. Using shallow and deep learning to automatically detect hate motivated by gender and sexual orientation on twitter in spanish. *Multimodal Technologies and Interaction*, 5(10):63.

Valerio Basile, Cristina Bosco, Elisabetta Fersini, Debora Nozza, Viviana Patti, Francisco Manuel Rangel Pardo, Paolo Rosso, and Manuela Sanguinetti. 2019. Semeval-2019 task 5: Multilingual detection of hate speech against immigrants and women in twitter. In *Proceedings of the 13th international workshop on semantic evaluation*, pages 54–63.

José Alberto Benítez-Andrades, Álvaro González-Jiménez, Álvaro López-Brea, Jose Aveleira-Mata, José-Manuel Alija-Pérez, and María Teresa García-Ordás. 2022. Detecting racism and xenophobia using deep learning models on twitter data: Cnn, lstm and bert. *PeerJ Computer Science*, 8:e906.

José Alberto Benitez-Andrades, Álvaro González-Jiménez, Álvaro López-Brea, Carmen Benavides, Jose Aveleira-Mata, José-Manuel Alija-Pérez, and María Teresa García-Ordás. 2022. Bert model-based approach for detecting racism and xenophobia on twitter data. In *Research Conference on Metadata and Semantics Research*, pages 148–158. Springer.

Paola Bentivoglio and Mercedes Sedano. 2011. Morphosyntactic variation in spanish-speaking latin america. *The handbook of Hispanic sociolinguistics*, pages 168–186.

José Canete, Gabriel Chaperon, Rodrigo Fuentes, Jou-Hui Ho, Hojin Kang, and Jorge Pérez. 2020. Spanish pre-trained bert model and evaluation data. *Pml4dc at iclr*, 2020:2020.

Jacob Cohen. 1960. A coefficient of agreement for nominal scales. *Educational and psychological measurement*, 20(1):37–46.

Thomas Davidson, Dana Warmsley, Michael Macy, and Ingmar Weber. 2017. Automated hate speech detection and the problem of offensive language. In

Proceedings of the international AAAI conference on web and social media, 1, pages 512–515.

Thierry Declerck and Piroska Lendvai. 2016. Towards the harmonization and segmentation of german hashtags. *Bochumer Linguistische Arbeitsberichte*, page 10.

Jacob Devlin, Ming-Wei Chang, Kenton Lee, and Kristina Toutanova. 2018. Bert: Pre-training of deep bidirectional transformers for language understanding. *arXiv preprint arXiv:1810.04805*.

Jacob Devlin, Ming-Wei Chang, Kenton Lee, and Kristina Toutanova. 2019. BERT: Pre-training of deep bidirectional transformers for language understanding. In *Proceedings of the 2019 Conference of the North American Chapter of the Association for Computational Linguistics: Human Language Technologies, Volume 1 (Long and Short Papers)*, pages 4171–4186, Minneapolis, Minnesota. Association for Computational Linguistics.

María José Díaz-Torres, Paulina Alejandra Morán-Méndez, Luis Villasenor-Pineda, Manuel Montes, Juan Aguilera, and Luis Meneses-Lerín. 2020. Automatic detection of offensive language in social media: Defining linguistic criteria to build a mexican spanish dataset. In *Proceedings of the Second Workshop on Trolling, Aggression and Cyberbullying*, pages 132–136.

Elisabetta Fersini, Giulia Rizzi, Aurora Saibene, and Francesca Gasparini. 2022. Misogynous meme recognition: A preliminary study. In *International Conference of the Italian Association for Artificial Intelligence*, pages 279–293. Springer.

Elisabetta Fersini, Paolo Rosso, and Maria Anzovino. 2018. Overview of the task on automatic misogyny identification at ibereval 2018. *Ibereval@ sepln*, 2150:214–228.

Terri D Fisher, Clive M Davis, and William L Yarber. 2013. *Handbook of sexuality-related measures*. Routledge.

José Antonio García-Díaz, Mar Cánovas-García, Ricardo Colomo-Palacios, and Rafael Valencia-García. 2021. Detecting misogyny in spanish tweets. an approach based on linguistics features and word embeddings. *Future Generation Computer Systems*, 114:506–518.

José Antonio García-Díaz, Salud María Jiménez-Zafra, Miguel Angel García-Cumbreras, and Rafael Valencia-García. 2022. Evaluating feature combination strategies for hate-speech detection in spanish using linguistic features and transformers. *Complex & Intelligent Systems*, pages 1–22.

Debbie Ging and Eugenia Siapera. 2018. Special issue on online misogyny.

Dagmar Gromann and Thierry Declerck. 2017. Hashtag processing for enhanced clustering of tweets. In *Proceedings of the International Conference Recent Advances in Natural Language Processing, RANLP 2017*, pages 277–283.

Asier Gutiérrez-Fandiño, Jordi Armengol-Estapé, Marc Pàmies, Joan Llop-Palao, Joaquin Silveira-Ocampo, Casimiro Pio Carrino, Aitor Gonzalez-Agirre, Carme Armentano-Oller, Carlos Rodriguez-Penagos, and Marta Villegas. 2021. Maria: Spanish language models. *arXiv preprint arXiv:2107.07253*.

Daniel Hershcovich, Stella Frank, Heather Lent, Miryam de Lhoneux, Mostafa Abdou, Stephanie Brandl, Emanuele Bugliarello, Laura Cabello Piqueras, Ilias Chalkidis, Ruixiang Cui, Constanza Fierro, Katerina Margatina, Phillip Rust, and Anders Søgaard. 2022. Challenges and strategies in cross-cultural NLP. In *Proceedings of the 60th Annual Meeting of the Association for Computational Linguistics (Volume 1: Long Papers)*, pages 6997–7013, Dublin, Ireland. Association for Computational Linguistics.

Dirk Hovy and Diyi Yang. 2021. The importance of modeling social factors of language: Theory and practice. In *Proceedings of the 2021 Conference of the North American Chapter of the Association for Computational Linguistics: Human Language Technologies*, pages 588–602, Online. Association for Computational Linguistics.

T Nockleby John. 2000. Hate speech. *Encyclopedia of the American Constitution (2nd ed., edited by Leonard W. Levy, Kenneth L. Karst et al., New York: Macmillan, 2000)*, pages 1277–1279.

Habibe Karayiğit, Ali Akdagli, and Çiğdem İnan Aci. 2022. Homophobic and hate speech detection using multilingual-bert model on turkish social media. *Information Technology and Control*, 51(2):356–375.

Javier De la Rosa, Eduardo G. Ponferrada, Manu Romero, Paulo Villegas, Pablo González de Prado Salas, and María Grandury. 2022. Bertin: Efficient pre-training of a spanish language model using perplexity sampling. *Procesamiento del Lenguaje Natural*, 68(0):13–23.

Estefanía Lozano, Jorge Cedeño, Galo Castillo, Fabricio Layedra, Henry Lasso, and Carmen Vaca. 2017. Requiem for online harassers: Identifying racism from political tweets. In *2017 Fourth International Conference on eDemocracy & eGovernment (ICEDEG)*, pages 154–160. IEEE.

Scott M Lundberg and Su-In Lee. 2017. A unified approach to interpreting model predictions. *Advances in neural information processing systems*, 30.

Louis Martin, Benjamin Muller, Pedro Javier Ortiz Suárez, Yoann Dupont, Laurent Romary, Éric de la Clergerie, Djamé Seddah, and Benoît Sagot. 2020. CamemBERT: a tasty French language model.

In *Proceedings of the 58th Annual Meeting of the Association for Computational Linguistics*, pages 7203–7219, Online. Association for Computational Linguistics.

ABDULLAH Muaad, Channabasava Chola, Bibal Benifa JV, J Hanumanthappa, et al. 2021. Detection of misogyny from arabic levantine twitter tweets using machine learning techniques. -.

Debora Nozza. 2021. Exposing the limits of zero-shot cross-lingual hate speech detection. In *Proceedings of the 59th Annual Meeting of the Association for Computational Linguistics and the 11th International Joint Conference on Natural Language Processing (Volume 2: Short Papers)*, pages 907–914, Online. Association for Computational Linguistics.

Endang Wahyu Pamungkas, Valerio Basile, and Viviana Patti. 2020. Misogyny detection in twitter: a multilingual and cross-domain study. *Information Processing & Management*, 57(6):102360.

Endang Wahyu Pamungkas, Alessandra Teresa Cignarella, Valerio Basile, Viviana Patti, et al. 2018. Automatic identification of misogyny in english and italian tweets at evalita 2018 with a multilingual hate lexicon. In *Sixth Evaluation Campaign of Natural Language Processing and Speech Tools for Italian (EVALITA 2018)*, volume 2263, pages 1–6. CEUR-WS.

Juan Carlos Pereira-Kohatsu, Lara Quijano-Sánchez, Federico Liberatore, and Miguel Camacho-Collados. 2019. Detecting and monitoring hate speech in twitter. *Sensors*, 19(21):4654.

Telmo Pires, Eva Schlinger, and Dan Garrette. 2019. How multilingual is multilingual bert? *arXiv preprint arXiv:1906.01502*.

Flor-Miriam Plaza-Del-Arco, M Dolores Molina-González, L Alfonso Ureña-López, and M Teresa Martín-Valdivia. 2020. Detecting misogyny and xenophobia in spanish tweets using language technologies. *ACM Transactions on Internet Technology (TOIT)*, 20(2):1–19.

Flor Miriam Plaza-del Arco, M Dolores Molina-González, L Alfonso Urena-López, and M Teresa Martín-Valdivia. 2021. Comparing pre-trained language models for spanish hate speech detection. *Expert Systems with Applications*, 166:114120.

Raúl R Romero-Vega, Oscar M Cumbicus-Pineda, Ruperto A López-Lapo, and Lisset A Neyra-Romero. 2020. Detecting xenophobic hate speech in spanish tweets against venezuelan immigrants in ecuador using natural language processing. In *International Conference on Applied Technologies*, pages 312–326. Springer.

Kevin Dela Rosa, Rushin Shah, Bo Lin, Anatole Gershman, and Robert Frederking. 2011. Topical clustering of tweets. *Proceedings of the ACM SIGIR: SWSM*, 63.

Elena Shushkevich and John Cardiff. 2018. Misogyny detection and classification in english tweets: The experience of the itt team. *EVALITA Evaluation of NLP and Speech Tools for Italian*, 12:182.

Spanish Wikipedia. 2021. Spanish wikipedia — Wikipedia, the free encyclopedia. [Online; accessed 8-March-2022].

Statista. 2021. Countries with the largest number of native spanish speakers worldwide in 2021.

Mircea-Adrian Tanase, George-Eduard Zaharia, Dumitru-Clementin Cercel, and Mihai Dascalu. 2020. Detecting aggressiveness in mexican spanish social media content by fine-tuning transformer-based models. In *IberLEF@ SEPLN*, pages 236–245.

Jörg Tiedemann. 2012. Parallel data, tools and interfaces in opus. In *Lrec*, volume 2012, pages 2214–2218. Citeseer.

Valeria Vera Lagos et al. 2021. Detección de misoginia en textos cortos mediante clasificadores supervisados. B.S. thesis.

Emily A Vogels. 2021. The state of online harassment. *Pew Research Center*, 13.

Shijie Wu and Mark Dredze. 2020. Are all languages created equal in multilingual bert? *arXiv preprint arXiv:2005.09093*.

Sheng Zhang, Xin Zhang, Weiming Zhang, and Anders Søgaard. 2021. Sociolectal analysis of pretrained language models. In *Proceedings of the 2021 Conference on Empirical Methods in Natural Language Processing*, pages 4581–4588, Online and Punta Cana, Dominican Republic. Association for Computational Linguistics.

A Datasets Details

A.1 Misogyny Dataset Description

	Europe			LatAm		
Dataset	Nb MIS	Nb non-MIS	% MIS	Nb MIS	Nb non-MIS	% MIS
MisCorpus-2020	1289	1197	51.9%	1218	378	76.3%
DetMis	-	-	-	1000	1000	50.0%
All	1289	1197	51.9%	2218	1378	61.7%

Table 6: Misogyny corpora descriptions after removing tweets without a variation tag (i.e. no information about the Spanish variation). Information about classes MIS (Misogyny) and non-MIS (non-misogyny) is disaggregated, as well as the percentage of misogyny instances per dataset and variation. The IberEval 2018 dataset is not included because it does not provide information about language variations.

A.2 Subset Splits

	women			immigrants		
Variant	train	dev	test	train	dev	test
Europe	1392	348	746	1400	350	750
LatAm	2014	503	1079	840	210	450
Comparable size	1392	348	746	840	210	450

Table 7: Number of tweets per dataset split on each hate speech domain with comparable data size. The comparable data size is obtained on each hate speech domain by randomly undersampling observations to ensure the comparability of the transfer settings among language variants.

A.3 HaSCoSVa-2022 Tweets Geolocation

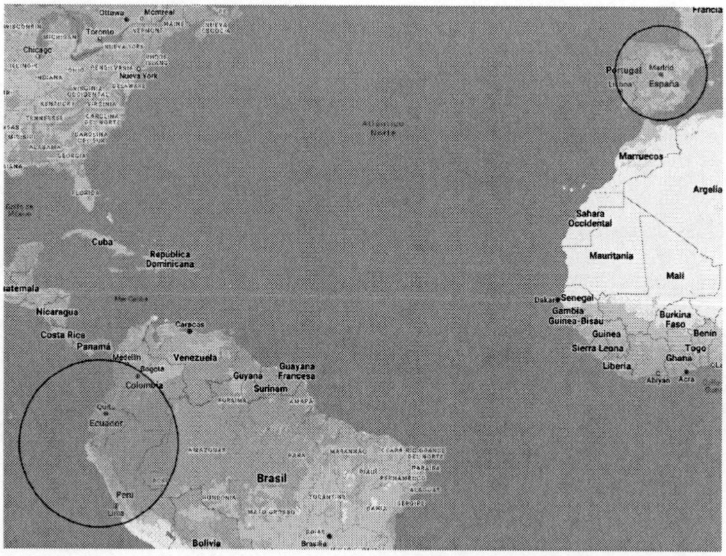

Figure 2: Boundings used to create the HaSCoSVa-2022 dataset by geo-locating European and Latin American tweets.

A.4 HaSCoSVa-2022 Sampling Strategy

In order to collect the data, we used keywords related to hate speech to extract subsets of tweets from Europe and Latin America (LatAm). For each keyword, we randomly sampled up to 50 tweets from Europe and 200 tweets from LatAm. We use a higher maximum number of tweets for LatAm due to the lower number of keywords related to hate speech we used for this region. This initial sampling strategy aims to avoid missing tweets containing non-frequent keywords. We also set a maximum number of tweets per keyword to avoid overrepresenting or underrepresenting some keywords in our final dataset.

After the initial sampling, we obtain 11,298 tweets in total. We then randomly sampled 2,500 tweets for Europe and 1,500 for LatAm from this subset. The decision to use different numbers of tweets for the two regions was based on a review of the datasets, which revealed a higher rate of hate speech in the European dataset. Therefore, we choose to annotate more European tweets to ensure an adequate number of hate speech-related tweets. This selection resulted in 231 negative examples for LatAm out of 1,500 tweets and 323 for Europe out of 2,500 tweets.

A.5 World Map of Spanish Dialects

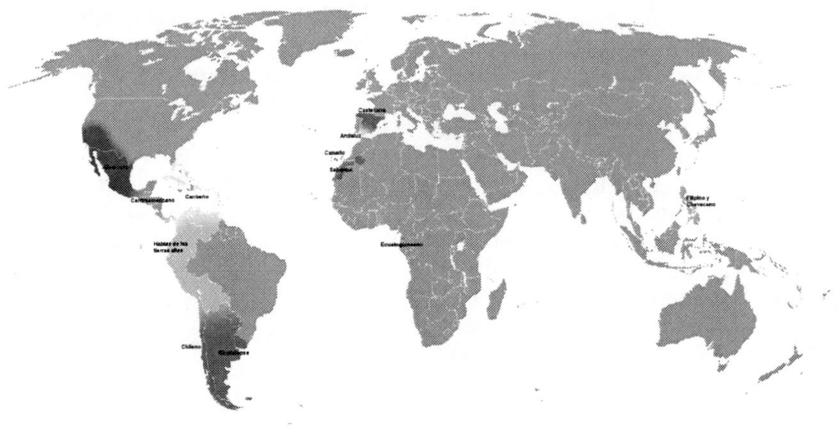

Figure 3: World map of Spanish Dialects (source Wikipedia).

Optimizing the Size of Subword Vocabularies in Dialect Classification

Vani Kanjirangat
IDSIA-USI/SUPSI, Switzerland
vanik@idsia.ch

Tanja Samardžić
URPP Language and Space, UZH
tanja.samardzic@uzh.ch

Ljiljana Dolamic
armasuisse S+T, Switzerland
Ljiljana.Dolamic@armasuisse.ch

Fabio Rinaldi
IDSIA-USI/SUPSI, Switzerland
fabio.rinaldi@idsia.ch

Abstract

Pre-trained models usually come with a predefined tokenization and little flexibility as to what subword tokens can be used in downstream tasks. This problem concerns especially multilingual NLP and low-resource languages, which are typically processed using cross-lingual transfer. In this paper, we aim to find out if the right granularity of tokenization is helpful for a text classification task, namely dialect classification. Aiming at generalizations beyond the studied cases, we look for the optimal granularity in four dialect datasets, two with relatively consistent writing (one Arabic and one Indo-Aryan set) and two with considerably inconsistent writing (one Arabic and one Swiss German set). To gain more control over subword tokenization and ensure direct comparability in the experimental settings, we train a CNN classifier from scratch comparing two subword tokenization methods (Unigram model and BPE). For reference, we compare the results obtained in our analysis to the state of the art achieved by fine-tuning pre-trained models. We show that models trained from scratch with an optimal tokenization level perform better than fine-tuned classifiers in the case of highly inconsistent writing. In the case of relatively consistent writing, fine-tuned models remain better regardless of the tokenization level.[1]

1 Introduction

The change from word to subword tokenization opened a large space of tokenization possibilities: any substring of a word (subword) is potentially a good token, but some might be more useful than others. In contrast to this, pre-trained models usually come with a predefined tokenization and little flexibility in input preprocessing.

This problem is even more important in a multilingual setting, where, for many languages, only a little data is available, often written in a non-standard writing (e.g. transcriptions of spoken language, social media posts) with pronounced regional differences. Fine-tuning pretrained models (with cross-lingual transfer) has become the primary approach to processing such languages. Predefined tokenization, which is part of this research framework, is likely not to be suitable for the level of inconsistency that is typical for target low-resource languages.

In this paper, we study the benefits of optimal subword tokenization in one of the basic tasks in multilingual NLP — dialect classification. This task can be seen as a stand-alone task (e.g., for tracing the source of media posts) or a step in other end-user tasks such as machine translation or natural language understanding (NLU). We choose this task as an especially challenging case of text encoding bridging the work on language modelling and text classification. Although it is a classification task, it does not rely on an abstract semantic representation of the whole sentence (as in usual text classification) but on surface features of the text, such as distinctive suffixes or prefixes of words, phonetic clusters, and order of tokens, closer to language modelling. These features show up occasionally in the text, which otherwise might look the same in two different dialects (Zampieri et al., 2017; Tiedemann and Ljubešić, 2012). The right level of tokenization can be expected to help identify these features and thus encode the text better for other purposes too.

Aiming at generalizations beyond the studied cases, we work with four data sets (two Arabic, one Indo-Aryan, and one Swiss German) representing two levels of writing consistency (transcribed speech vs. originally written text) and three different types of languages. We consider three levels of tokenization (character, subword, word) testing two main subword tokenization methods: one example of a probabilistic model (Unigram model (Kudo,

[1]We will release our code for replication of our results.

Tenth Workshop on NLP for Similar Languages, Varieties and Dialects (VarDial 2023), pages 14–30
May 5, 2023 ©2023 Association for Computational Linguistics

2018)) and one example of a bottom-up compression algorithm (BPE (Sennrich et al., 2016), also implemented by Kudo and Richardson (2018)). To gain flexibility with varying the level of tokenization, we train our own classifiers (one Bidirectional Long Short Term Memory (BiLSTM) and two Convolutional Neural Networks (CNNs)), which we also evaluate against comparable fine-tuned classifiers with BERT-based pre-trained models. Our findings are expected to generalize to other tasks similar to dialect classification and, to a certain degree, to NLU tasks.

2 Related Work

Dialect identification replaces language identification whenever a language has many regional variants as in the case of Arabic, Chinese or (Swiss) German. Such cases are mostly covered in a series of shared tasks (Zampieri et al., 2017, 2018, 2019; Chakravarthi et al., 2021; Gaman et al., 2020). The solutions submitted to the shared tasks range from traditional machine learning to state-of-the-art deep learning models. Traditional machine learning classifiers such as Support Vector Machines (SVM), Logistic Regression (LR), and Naive Bayes (NB) utilizing character or word level n-gram features were found to perform quite well across different languages and dialects (Çöltekin and Rama, 2016; Jauhiainen et al., 2018b; Zirikly et al., 2016; Bestgen, 2021; Jauhiainen et al., 2021). For instance, a version of a character-level n-gram language model with a domain adaptation technique is the state of the art for identifying Swiss German (F-score 0.75) and Indo-Aryan (F-score 0.96) dialects without acoustic features (Jauhiainen et al., 2018a,b, 2019). This approach, however, requires numerous model retraining iterations, which is not suitable for larger models.

Neural networks have been used for this task too including CNN, LSTM, and pre-trained Transformers models, in which are currently prevailing (Bernier-Colborne et al., 2019; Ceolin, 2021; Zaharia et al., 2020; Butnaru, 2019). The performance of these models varies depending on the datasets. Ensembles of neural and traditional models are also utilized (Popa and Ștefănescu, 2020; Hu et al., 2019; Yang and Xiang, 2019).

Character-level tokenization proves useful for capturing the relevant features, but previous studies do not address specifically the question of input granularity.

Outside of dialect identification, Domingo et al. (2018) suggest that tokenization could impact neural machine translation (NMT) quality. They compared tokenizers such as Moses, SentencePiece, OpenNMT, Stanford, and Mecab on Japanese, Russian, Chinese, German and Arabic translations to English. They found that Moses tokenizer gave the best result for Arabic, Russian and German; Mecab for Japanese; and Stanford for Chinese. Uysal and Gunal (2014) studied the effect of pre-processing in the English and Turkish languages and they observed that using appropriate domain and language dependant pre-processing can improve the performance. Gowda and May (2020) propose a general optimization method for finding subword tokens for machine translation. Mielke et al. (2019) find that the surprisal of a language model is minimised cross-linguistically at a particular level of subword segmentation with the resulting size of the input vocabulary being the word-level vocabulary multiplied by 0.4. Gutierrez-Vasques et al. (2021) find that much smaller vocabularies minimize text redundancy and lead to a converging text entropy across 47 languages.

Quite a few solutions have been proposed for unsupervised subword segmentation (Creutz and Lagus, 2005; Schuster and Nakajima, 2012; Poon et al., 2009; Narasimhan et al., 2015; Sennrich et al., 2016; Bergmanis and Goldwater, 2017; Grönroos et al., 2020; Kudo, 2018). The SentencePiece library (Kudo and Richardson, 2018) implements two very popular methods: BPE, a general data compression algorithm (Gage, 1994) first applied to text by Sennrich et al. (2016) and Unigram model (Kudo, 2018), similar to Morfessor (Creutz and Lagus, 2005; Grönroos et al., 2020) in that it considers multiple possible subword splits at the same time. Some related works on fine-tuning vocabulary sizes for NLP applications include (Cherry et al., 2018; Xu et al., 2021; Ding et al., 2019; Li et al., 2021).

The work on comparing subword tokenization algorithms reports rather inconsistent outcomes. For instance, Vania and Lopez (2017) find that BPE gives better results than Morfessor on the task of language modeling, but Ataman and Federico (2018) show that linguistically motivated vocabulary reduction (LMVR), which is an extension of Morfessor, gives better results in the context of machine translation. The benefit of using LMVR increases with increased morphological richness.

A similar conclusion is reached in a wide-scope multilingual comparison with language modeling as the downstream task is performed by Park et al. (2021). A study on English by Bostrom and Durrett (2020) compares BPE preprocessing with the Unigram method by Kudo and Richardson (2018), again on the task of language modeling, obtaining lower results with BPE tokenization, which also gives a slightly larger vocabulary than the competing method.

For our study, we select representative examples of neural models for dialect classification and subword tokenization methods, which are detailed in the next section.

3 Data and Methods

Four datasets used in the main study have been selected so that they represent different language types and different levels of consistency in writing. Table 1 shows the sizes of four datasets expressed as the number of utterances, the number of unique characters (character-level vocabulary) and the number of unique word types (word-level vocabulary). Three of the datasets were released as a part of the VarDial workshop shared tasks (Zampieri et al., 2017, 2018, 2019): the German Dialect Identification (**GDI**)[2], Indo-Aryan Language Identification (**ILI**) [3] and the Arabic Dialect Identification (**ADI**) datasets[4]. The fourth is the Arabic Online Commentary (**AOC**) (Zaidan and Callison-Burch, 2011) dataset.

The GDI dataset is compiled from the ArchiMob corpus of Spoken Swiss German and covers four areas, namely Basel, Bern, Lucern, and Zurich (Samardzic et al., 2016). We used the GDI-2018 dataset for our experiments and worked in a 4-way classification setting.

The ILI dataset includes five closely related Indo-Aryan language dialects: Hindi, Braj Bhasha, Awadhi, Bhojpuri, and Magahi. For each language, 15,000 sentences are extracted, mainly from the literature domain.

The ADI VarDial task (Malmasi et al., 2016; Ali et al., 2016) includes five Arabic dialects: Modern Standard Arabic (MSA), Egyptian (EGY), Gulf (GLF), Levantine (LAV), Moroccan (MOR), and North-African (NOR). MSA is the modern variety of language which is used in news and educational articles. It differs lexically, syntactically, and phonetically from the actual communication language of native speakers. The VarDial ADI dataset is both speech transcribed and transliterated to English from Arabic.

AOC constitutes a large-scale repository of Arabic dialects extracted from reader commentary of three Arabic online newspapers. It covers MSA and the dialectal varieties, viz., Egyptian (EGY), Gulf (GLF), Levantine (LEV), and Moroccan (MOR).

The languages and dialects represented in these four datasets belong to two language families (Indo-European and Semitic). Two of the data sets (GDI and ADI) are created by transcribing spoken language and show a high level of inconsistency in writing. The other two (ILI and AOC) are originally written texts with lower level of inconsistency.

In addition to these four datasets used in the main study, we perform additional experiments on the data from the Nuanced Arabic Dialect Identification (NADI) shared task, which deals with country-level and province-level Arabic dialect identifications (Abdul-Mageed et al., 2020, 2021). NADI 2022 shared task covers 18 country dialects with a training set of $\approx$ 20K tweets (Abdul-Mageed et al., 2022).

3.1 Levels of Tokenization

Dialect classification is usually performed at the level of utterance (loosely structured sentence): each utterance in a dataset is assigned a label. Classification features (typically n-grams) are typically either word-level or character-level. We introduce subword-level features and compare them to both character and word-level ones.

Word Level The most common tokenization is at the word level, mainly using white spaces and punctuation as delimiters. However, this approach is not convenient for languages lacking clear word boundaries (e.g., Chinese and Japanese). This type of tokenization produces large vocabularies, but shorter sequences, which are both important concerns for memory and time complexity.

Character Level Character level tokenization is the simplest way of segmenting the text using Unicode characters as tokens. This level is good for generalizing across languages (many languages share alphabets). It also helps solving some problems of word-level tokenization, such as out-of-

[2] https://drive.switch.ch/index.php/s/DZycFA9DPC8FgD9

[3] https://github.com/kmi-linguistics/VarDial2018

[4] https://arabicspeech.org/resources/

	GDI	ILI	ADI	AOC	NADI
Train	14647	68453	14591	86541	20398
Dev	4659	8286	1566	10820	4871
Test	4752	9032	1492	10812	4871
Word vocabulary (Train)	15041	115766	43150	171184	56163
Character vocabulary (Train)	30	209	52	158	445

Table 1: The size of datasets expressed as the number of utterances. The character (Character vocabulary) and word vocabulary (Word vocabulary) sizes (unique number of characters and words in the training set) is also given.

vocabulary (OOV) symbols. However, representing single characters is hard (too general) and sequences of character-level tokens are very long. Both of these factors have a negative impact on the performance on downstream tasks.

Subword Level The main idea behind the subword-level tokenization is to balance generalization and specificity so that frequently used words are considered a single token (as in word-level tokenization) and rare words are split into smaller units (as in character-level tokenization) called *subwords*. For instance, the word *lowest*, may be split into *low* and *est* depending upon the vocabulary sizes or merge operations. This helps in creating smaller vocabularies while preserving some of the lexical meaning.

3.2 Subword Tokenization Methods

Among many possibilities listed in Section 2, we select two methods, which represent two main approaches to finding subword units. We select **BPE** (Gage, 1994; Sennrich et al., 2016) as a bottom-up algorithm that goes from single characters to subwords by a sequence of merges. As an alternative approach, we select the **Unigram** model (Kudo, 2018), which considers all possible splits of a word gradually discarding some of them.

For BPE, text input is first tokenized at the word level. Each word is then split into a sequence of characters to which a special "end of the word" symbol is appended. The base vocabulary is created from the unique characters in the training corpora. The algorithm iterates through the data many times merging the most frequent pair of symbols into a single symbol every time. The new symbol is added to the vocabulary for the next iteration. The procedure is repeated until the desired vocabulary size, or a specific number of merge operations is obtained, which are the hyperparameters to be tuned.

Unlike the BPE algorithm, the Unigram model can be viewed as a probabilistic mixture model, where the likelihood of the whole data is computed under a given subword split hypothesis. The algorithm starts from a large vocabulary that contains many possible subword splits (a "reasonably" big seed vocabulary). It then reduces the vocabulary gradually by discarding a percentage of vocabulary entries. The decision on what entries to discard relies on a loss function: for each vocabulary entry, measure the difference in the overall likelihood of the data with and without that entry. Those entries that result in the smallest difference are discarded. A threshold $\eta\%$ is set to decide the percentage of vocabulary entries to be discarded. The process is repeated until the desired vocabulary size is reached, which is the hyperparameter to be tuned.

3.3 Optimizing the Size of the Subword Vocabulary

We optimize vocabulary sizes (vocab_sizes) for word-level and subword-level tokenization and take the character-level vocabularies from the data as the only option.

In case of the word-level tokenization, we conducted experiments with different vocab_sizes (2000-20000) and selected the vocab_size that yielded maximum performance on the dev set. Based on the experiments, we found the preferred word level vocab_size is 2000 for the dialect classification task on the specific languages tested. The unknown tokens are represented by *UNK*.

To find the range of vocab_sizes for subword level experiments, we consider different sizes from the character set to a limit identified by Mielke et al. (2019), who find that a BPE vocabulary corresponding to a proportion of the size of all word types $|V|$ minimizes the negative log-likelihood on the data (dev sets) across 21 languages from the Europarl dataset [5]. This proportion is the same for all languages: $0.4 * |V|$. Given this measure,

[5] `https://www.statmt.org/europarl/`

we consider all the subword vocab_sizes ranging from character level vocab_size to $0.4 * |V|$. These ranges for each dataset are reported in Table B1.

For finding the BPE and Unigram model vocabularies, we use the Google SentencePiece library[6], which is an unsupervised tokenizer-detokenizer that accepts raw input (no pre-tokenizations) with predefined vocabulary sizes as arguments. It adopts the BPE algorithm by Sennrich et al. (2016), but unlike specifying the required number of subword merge operations, here the desired final vocab_size has to be given (both approaches yield similar results). We start from the character vocab_size and increment the size by 100 if vocab_size $\leq$ 1000 and then by 1000 if vocab_size $\leq$ 10000. The process is repeated until the merge_size (number of merges) $\leq$ optimal_merge_size ($0.4 * |V|$).

3.4 Models for Classification

For selecting the classification models, we consider two kinds of neural networks with shared parameters: convolutional (CNNs) and recurrent (specifically LSTM RNN). On the side of CNNs, we evaluate two concrete architectures: Kim_CNN (Kim et al., 2016) and Zhang_CNN (Zhang et al., 2015), which are known to perform well on the task of text classification and are widely used. On the side of RNNs, we evaluate the architecture Lin_SA_BiLSTM (Lin et al., 2017), which has been shown to give good results on the task of dialect classifications (Goswami et al., 2020). We manipulated the tokenizers of these models using different granularity levels without changing the overall architecture. The model architectures are briefly described in this section.

Lin_SA_BiLSTM This is a BiLSTM architecture with a self-attention component (Lin et al., 2017), where the sentence embeddings are computed by multiplying the hidden states from BiLSTM with the attention weights obtained across multiple attention hops. If $S = (w_1, w_2, ..., w_n)$ represents a sentence with n tokens, where w_i represents a d dimensional word embedding, then the sentence is represented by a 2D matrix of the shape $n \times d$. The BiLSTM component is used to compute the hidden state matrix H and further, the attention module takes the H vector and outputs the attention matrix A using the Equation 1:

$$A = softmax(W_{s2} tanh(W_{s1} H^T)) \quad (1)$$

[6]https://github.com/google/sentencepiece

Here, W_{s1} and W_{s2} represent the weight matrices. The final embedding is computed as $M = AH$. A penalization term is also used to ensure diversity among multiple attention hops. These embeddings are then to be used as input for a downstream task, such as dialect classification in our case.

Zhang_CNN Zhang et al. (2015) proposed a simple character level model for text classification utilizing a 1D convolution followed by max pooling layers. The model has six CNN layers and three fully connected layers.

Kim_CNN The architecture used by Kim et al. (2016) is originally a neural language model (NLM) used for several NLP tasks. We adapted it in particular for dialect classification. The original architecture uses a CNN with a highway network whose output is given to a recurrent neural network (RNN) neural language model. In the original Kim_CNN model, the input is segmented at the character level and hence a word token of length k is represented as $c_1, c_2, ..., c_k$. A filter F of width m is used to produce the feature maps. The main idea is that a filter captures the n-grams and the filter width corresponds to the n-gram size. Then a max-pooling layer is used to extract the important features. Since, our task is a classification problem, we utilized only the encoder part of the model with CNN, while the RNN layers were replaced by dense layers to perform softmax over the classes. The model has four convolutional layers and two fully connected layers.

4 Experimental Settings

We train and test on the task of dialect classification each of the architectures described in Section 3.4 on each version of the data produced with the tokenizers (one version of the data for each vocab_size). The vocabulary size that gave the best performance on the development set is chosen as the optimal vocabulary size. We compare these results to find out if optimizing the input vocabulary improves the classification performance. In addition to this, we compare the performance achieved with the best performing models trained from scratch with the performance achieved by fine-tuning respective pre-trained models.

In the remainder of this section, we describe the hyperparameters of the neural models trained from scratch, the vocabulary settings, and the fine-tuning settings, which we consider to be the state of the art.[7]

4.1 Hyperparameters

For all the models trained from scratch, we used a *batch_size* of 128 and maximum input length (*max_len*) of 1014 (decided after repeated experiments). The number of epochs is decided by early stopping criteria, monitoring the validation loss with patience value set to 2. The optimal number of epochs ranged between 5-10. For initialization, we used the Keras embedding layer[8], which takes integer encoded vocabulary and learns the vectors during training.

Table A1 in the Appendix reports the parameters for each model as described in the original implementations. In Lin_SA_BiLSTM, the main parameters are the LSTM hidden dimensions, dense layers dimension, and the number of attention hops in the self-attention mechanism. For Kim_CNN and Zhang_CNN, the main parameters include the number of CNN layers and fully connected neural network (FCNN) layers with their corresponding dimensions. The Kim_CNN uses a global max pooling layer, which is common in NLP applications. Zhang_CNN uses a 1D max pooling with specific pool sizes except for layers 3, 4, and 5. The *Kernel_size* represents the n-gram width, and the n-grams will be based on the granularity of the tokenizers.

4.2 Pre-trained Models and Fine-tuning

For comparisons, we use transformer based pretrained models. We evaluate Vanilla BERT (English BERT) and multilingual BERT (mBERT) (Devlin et al., 2019) for all the datasets. The language-specific BERT models are as follows: German BERT[9] and Swiss-German BERT [10] were used for the GDI dataset; IndicTransformers [11] (Jain et al., 2020) for ILI; AraBERT[12] (Antoun et al., 2020) and Multi-dialect-Arabic-BERT [13] (Talafha et al., 2020) for AOC, ADI and NADI datasets. German BERT is pretrained on the latest German Wikipedia dump (6GB of raw text files), OpenLegalData dump (2.4 GB), and news articles (3.6 GB). Swiss-German BERT is fine-tuned on the Swiss German data of the Leipzig Corpora Collection[14] and SwissCrawl[15] on the top of German BERT. IndicTransformers is a BERT model trained with 3 GB of data from the OSCAR corpus[16] covering three Indo-Aryan languages, Hindi, Bengali, and Telugu. AraBERT is pretrained on Arabic news articles and two publicly available large Arabic corpora covering 24 Arab countries on the top of a BERT-based model. Multi-dialect-Arabic-BERT initializes the weights from Arabic BERT and is further pretrained on 10M Arabic tweets from Nuanced Arabic Dialect Identification (NADI)[17] shared task.

For all the BERT based experiments, we used the pretrained models from HuggingFace library[18]. We trained each model for four epochs with Adam optimizer using a learning rate of 2e-5 on the corresponding training set using 1 Tesla K80 GPU. Since all these baselines are BERT based, the default tokenizer is WordPiece.

5 Results and Comparisons

Since the Kim_CNN model gave the best results in all the from-scratch settings, we report only its performance in Table 2, in the test sets with the best vocab_sizes obtained. The detailed experimental results of all the models are reported in Appendix C, Tables C1 and C3.

From Table 2, it can be observed that subword level tokenizer performs better than their character and word level counterparts across all four datasets. Except for ILI and NADI, the Unigram model yields better results than BPE. Comparing the F1 scores, we noted an improvement of 3.9 points in GDI, 9.7 points in ILI, 5.2 points in AOC, 10.2 points in ADI and 3.4 points in NADI compared to the character level tokenizers. Similarly, comparing the subword level tokenizers with word level,

[7]We consider fine-tuned models the state of the art, despite the fact that simpler models can give better performance when combined with domain adaptation techniques. We note that domain adaptation can be combined with any model and should be evaluated separately.

[8]https://keras.io/api/layers/core_layers/embedding/

[9]https://www.deepset.ai/german-bert

[10]https://github.com/jungomi/swiss-language-model

[11]https://huggingface.co/neuralspace-reverie

[12]https://huggingface.co/aubmindlab/bert-base-arabert

[13]https://huggingface.co/bashar-talafha/multi-dialect-bert-base-arabic

[14]https://wortschatz.uni-leipzig.de/en/download/

[15]https://icosys.ch/swisscrawl

[16]https://oscar-corpus.com/

[17]https://sites.google.com/view/second-nadi-shared-task/home

[18]https://huggingface.co/models

Dataset	Number of Classes	Vocabulary Size				F-score (%)			
		Char	Uni	BPE	Word	Char	Uni	BPE	Word
GDI	4	30	2030	3030	15041	58	**61.9**	59.7	57
ILI	5	209	709	309	115776	78	84.8	**87.7**	85
AOC	4	158	8058	4058	171184	68	**73.2**	72.4	70
ADI	5	52	9052	952	43150	37	**47.2**	44.2	45
					Additional Experiment				
NADI	18	445	20045	7045	56163	13.3	16.2	**16.7**	16

Table 2: Performance of the Kim_CNN model at different tokenization levels. Char: Character-level, Uni: Unigram, BPE: Byte Pair Encoding, Word: Word-level. Kim_CNN gave the highest performance among the experimented non-pretrained neural models. The best result in each dataset is bolded.

Dataset	Best Model		F-score (%)	
	Pre-trained	Kim_CNN	Pre-trained	Kim_CNN
GDI	BERT-base-cased	Unigram	61.1	**61.9**
ILI	Indic Transformers	BPE	**88.1**	87.7
AOC	AraBERT	Unigram	**77.1**	73.2
ADI	AraBERT	Unigram	41.1	**47.2**
		Additional Experiment		
NADI	Multi-dialect-Arabic-BERT	BPE	**26.1**	16.7

Table 3: Comparison of the non-pretrained model with best tokenization level with the top performing baseline models in each dataset.

the F1 score was observed to increase by 4.9 points in GDI, 2.7 points in ILI, 3.1 points in AOC, 2.2 points in ADI and 0.7 points in NADI dataset. The optimal vocab_sizes are also reported, corresponding to vocab_size that gave the maximum F-scores. The variation with respect to different vocab_sizes in each dataset for the Kim_CNN with the Unigram model tokens is shown in Appendix D, Figure D1.

From these results, we conclude that optimized subword-level tokenization gives better dialect classification performance across all data sets (different languages, different levels of consistency) when working with a CNN architecture trained from scratch. Similar observations hold for all the non-transformer neural models in Table C1 in Appendix C.

5.1 Comparison with Fine-tuned Models

Table 3 shows the comparison between the results obtained in the trained (from scratch) setting and the best results obtained in the fine-tuned settings (with pre-trained models). The models that achieve the best results on each dataset are presented. The detailed results for all the models are given in Appendix C Table C3.

This comparison shows an interesting interaction between the writing consistency and performance on the classification task. For the two datasets with inconsistent writing (GDI and ADI, see Section 3 for details), the best scores are achieved with one of our models trained from scratch on optimized subword vocabulary (Kim_CNN with the Unigram model vocabulary). We note also that the best pre-trained setting in the case of GDI is BERT-base-cased and not the German BERT (see Table C3 in Appendix C for more details). In the case of ADI, Kim_CNN with the Unigram model tokenization improves the classification F1 score by 6.1 points compared to the best performing fine-tuned setting, which is the language-specific AraBERT model.

On datasets with more consistent writing (ILI and AOC), we see an opposite pattern: the best classification score is achieved in the fine-tuned settings using a language-specific pre-trained model (Indic Transformers and AraBERT respectively).

These results show that finding an appropriate level of tokenization granularity is especially important when datasets contain a considerable level of noise. Using pre-trained models does not bring the expected benefits unless one can count on a reasonably consistent writing. This conclusion is additionally reinforced by the scores obtained on

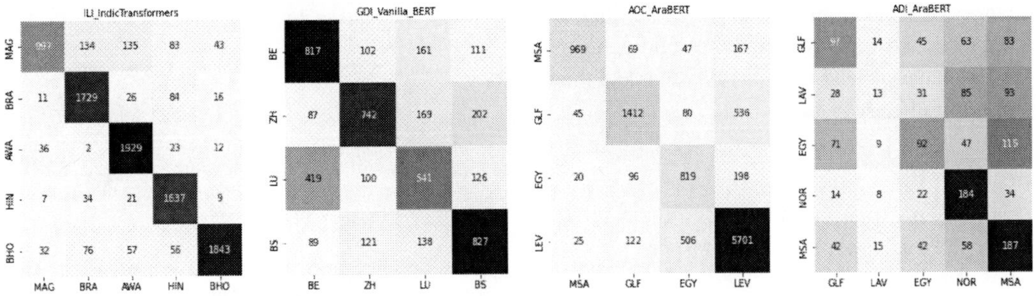

Figure 1: Confusion matrices for the best performing fine-tuned models on the ILI, GDI, AOC and ADI datasets

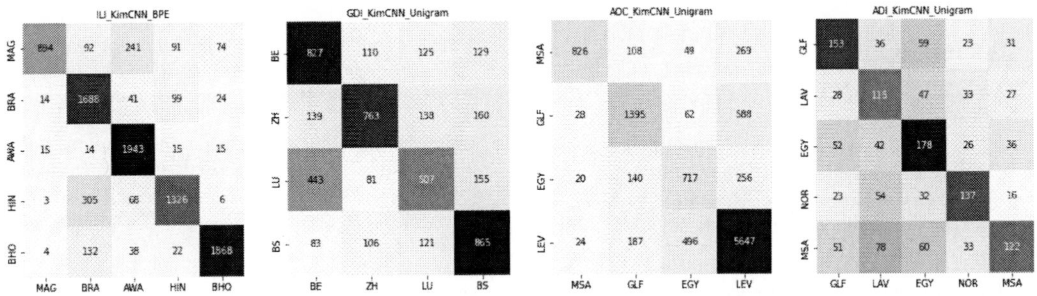

Figure 2: Confusion matrices Kim_CNN models (without pre-training) on the ILI, GDI, AOC and ADI datasets

the NADI dataset, where the fine-tuned classifier with a language specific pre-trained model achieves the best result. Even though the overall results are rather low in this case (likely due to the difficulty of distinguishing between 18 labels), they are better with fine-tuning. In this sense the NADI dataset, which also consists of originally written texts, patterns with ILI and AOC.

We also note the fact that BPE tokenizer gave better results than the Unigram model on 2/3 datasets with consistent writing. This observation is in line with previous research pointing out the sensitivity of BPE to noise in the data.

5.2 Per-class Comparison

To understand better the differences between Kim_CNN and the competing fine-tuned classifiers (results in Table 3), we plot two confusion matrices: Figure 1 shows the best performance with pre-trained models and Figure 2 shows the best performance with Kim_CNN. [19]

The matrices look very similar in all the cases except ADI. In this case, the fine-tuned classifier seems to have learned two classes well, while the success of Kim_CNN are more spread across different classes. The matrices for the AOC data set show that one class is much easier to identify for both approaches than the other classes. The GDI case shows one particularly confusing distinction (BE for Bern vs. LU for Luzern), which is almost equally hard for both approaches to distinguish. Finally, the class (MAG for Magahi) seems to be the most difficult for both approaches on the ILI dataset.

6 Conclusion

We have shown in this paper that optimizing subword vocabulary size is beneficial to text classification tasks, such as dialect classification, when the datasets contain relatively inconsistent writing (transcribed speech). With an optimized vocabulary as input, a CNN model trained from scratch outperforms fine-tuned models on such datasets. On the other hand, fine-tuning large language-specific pretrained models seems to be the best approach when datasets are relatively consistent (originally written, even if not edited). In this case, vocabulary size does not seem to matter much. Regarding the question of which kind of neural architecture is best to use without pretraining, our results point to the CNN architectures, which seem to capture the relevant surface features effectively.

Established on a relatively diverse sample (three

[19] We do not report the visualizations for NADI results here.

language types from two language families), our findings are especially relevant to multilingual NLP, where datasets tend to be inconsistent and the use of pre-trained models tempting.

7 Limitations

One of limitations of our work is the fact that we have not tried manipulating the tokenizers in BERT based models, which will be the focus of future work. In subword level tokenizers, we plan to explore other tokenizers such as WordPiece.

References

Muhammad Abdul-Mageed, Chiyu Zhang, Houda Bouamor, and Nizar Habash. 2020. NADI 2020: The first nuanced Arabic dialect identification shared task. In *Proceedings of the Fifth Arabic Natural Language Processing Workshop*, pages 97–110, Barcelona, Spain (Online). Association for Computational Linguistics.

Muhammad Abdul-Mageed, Chiyu Zhang, AbdelRahim Elmadany, Houda Bouamor, and Nizar Habash. 2021. NADI 2021: The second nuanced Arabic dialect identification shared task. In *Proceedings of the Sixth Arabic Natural Language Processing Workshop*, pages 244–259, Kyiv, Ukraine (Virtual). Association for Computational Linguistics.

Muhammad Abdul-Mageed, Chiyu Zhang, AbdelRahim Elmadany, Houda Bouamor, and Nizar Habash. 2022. NADI 2022: The Third Nuanced Arabic Dialect Identification Shared Task. In *Proceedings of the Seven Arabic Natural Language Processing Workshop (WANLP 2022)*.

Ahmed Ali, Najim Dehak, Patrick Cardinal, Sameer Khurana, Sree Harsha Yella, James Glass, Peter Bell, and Steve Renals. 2016. Automatic dialect detection in arabic broadcast speech.

Wissam Antoun, Fady Baly, and Hazem Hajj. 2020. Arabert: Transformer-based model for arabic language understanding. In *Proceedings of the 4th Workshop on Open-Source Arabic Corpora and Processing Tools, with a Shared Task on Offensive Language Detection*, pages 9–15.

Duygu Ataman and Marcello Federico. 2018. An evaluation of two vocabulary reduction methods for neural machine translation. In *Proceedings of the 13th Conference of the Association for Machine Translation in the Americas (Volume 1: Research Track)*, pages 97–110, Boston, MA. Association for Machine Translation in the Americas.

Toms Bergmanis and Sharon Goldwater. 2017. From segmentation to analyses: a probabilistic model for unsupervised morphology induction. In *Proceedings of the 15th Conference of the European Chapter of the Association for Computational Linguistics: Volume 1, Long Papers*, pages 337–346, Valencia, Spain. Association for Computational Linguistics.

Gabriel Bernier-Colborne, Cyril Goutte, and Serge Léger. 2019. Improving cuneiform language identification with bert. In *Proceedings of the Sixth Workshop on NLP for Similar Languages, Varieties and Dialects*, pages 17–25.

Yves Bestgen. 2021. Optimizing a supervised classifier for a difficult language identification problem. In *Proceedings of the Eighth Workshop on NLP for Similar Languages, Varieties and Dialects*, pages 96–101.

Kaj Bostrom and Greg Durrett. 2020. Byte pair encoding is suboptimal for language model pretraining. In *Findings of the Association for Computational Linguistics: EMNLP 2020*, pages 4617–4624.

Andrei Butnaru. 2019. Bam: A combination of deep and shallow models for german dialect identification. In *Proceedings of the Sixth Workshop on NLP for Similar Languages, Varieties and Dialects*, pages 128–137.

Andrea Ceolin. 2021. Comparing the performance of cnns and shallow models for language identification. In *Proceedings of the Eighth Workshop on NLP for Similar Languages, Varieties and Dialects*, pages 102–112.

Bharathi Raja Chakravarthi, Mihaela Gaman, Radu Tudor Ionescu, Heidi Jauhiainen, Tommi Jauhiainen, Krister Lindén, Nicola Ljubešić, Niko Partanen, Ruba Priyadharshini, Christoph Purschke, et al. 2021. Findings of the vardial evaluation campaign 2021. In *Proceedings of the 8th VarDial Workshop on NLP for Similar Languages, Varieties and Dialects*. The Association for Computational Linguistics.

Colin Cherry, George Foster, Ankur Bapna, Orhan Firat, and Wolfgang Macherey. 2018. Revisiting character-based neural machine translation with capacity and compression. In *Proceedings of the 2018 Conference on Empirical Methods in Natural Language Processing*, pages 4295–4305.

Çağrı Çöltekin and Taraka Rama. 2016. Discriminating similar languages with linear svms and neural networks. In *Proceedings of the Third Workshop on NLP for Similar Languages, Varieties and Dialects (VarDial3)*, pages 15–24.

Mathias Creutz and Krista Lagus. 2005. Inducing the morphological lexicon of a natural language from unannotated text. In *In Proceedings of the International and Interdisciplinary Conference on Adaptive Knowledge Representation and Reasoning (AKRR'05*, pages 106–113.

Jacob Devlin, Ming-Wei Chang, Kenton Lee, and Kristina Toutanova. 2019. Bert: Pre-training of deep bidirectional transformers for language understanding. In *Proceedings of the 2019 Conference of the*

North American Chapter of the Association for Computational Linguistics: Human Language Technologies, Volume 1 (Long and Short Papers), pages 4171–4186.

Shuoyang Ding, Adithya Renduchintala, and Kevin Duh. 2019. A call for prudent choice of subword merge operations in neural machine translation. In *Proceedings of Machine Translation Summit XVII: Research Track*, pages 204–213.

Miguel Domingo, Mercedes Garcıa-Martınez, Alexandre Helle, Francisco Casacuberta, and Manuel Herranz. 2018. How much does tokenization affect neural machine translation? *arXiv preprint arXiv:1812.08621*.

Philip Gage. 1994. A new algorithm for data compression. *C Users Journal*, 12(2):23–38.

Mihaela Gaman, Dirk Hovy, Radu Tudor Ionescu, Heidi Jauhiainen, Tommi Jauhiainen, Krister Lindén, Nikola Ljubešić, Niko Partanen, Christoph Purschke, Yves Scherrer, et al. 2020. A report on the vardial evaluation campaign 2020. In *Proceedings of the 7th Workshop on NLP for Similar Languages, Varieties and Dialects*, pages 1–14.

Koustava Goswami, Rajdeep Sarkar, Bharathi Raja Chakravarthi, Theodorus Fransen, and John Philip McCrae. 2020. Unsupervised deep language and dialect identification for short texts. In *Proceedings of the 28th International Conference on Computational Linguistics*, pages 1606–1617.

Thamme Gowda and Jonathan May. 2020. Finding the optimal vocabulary size for neural machine translation. In *Findings of the Association for Computational Linguistics: EMNLP 2020*, pages 3955–3964, Online. Association for Computational Linguistics.

Stig-Arne Grönroos, Sami Virpioja, and Mikko Kurimo. 2020. Morfessor EM+Prune: Improved subword segmentation with expectation maximization and pruning. In *Proceedings of the Twelfth Language Resources and Evaluation Conference*, pages 3944–3953, Marseille, France. European Language Resources Association.

Ximena Gutierrez-Vasques, Christian Bentz, Olga Sozinova, and Tanja Samardzic. 2021. From characters to words: the turning point of bpe merges. In *Proceedings of the 16th Conference of the European Chapter of the Association for Computational Linguistics: Main Volume*, pages 3454–3468.

Hai Hu, Wen Li, He Zhou, Zuoyu Tian, Yiwen Zhang, and Liang Zou. 2019. Ensemble methods to distinguish mainland and taiwan chinese. In *Proceedings of the Sixth Workshop on NLP for Similar Languages, Varieties and Dialects*, pages 165–171.

Kushal Jain, Adwait Deshpande, Kumar Shridhar, Felix Laumann, and Ayushman Dash. 2020. Indic-transformers: An analysis of transformer language models for indian languages. *arXiv preprint arXiv:2011.02323*.

Tommi Jauhiainen, Heidi Jauhiainen, and Krister Lindén. 2018a. Iterative language model adaptation for indo-aryan language identification. In *Proceedings of the Fifth Workshop on NLP for Similar Languages, Varieties and Dialects (VarDial 2018)*, pages 66–75.

Tommi Jauhiainen, Krister Lindén, and Heidi Jauhiainen. 2019. Discriminating between Mandarin Chinese and Swiss-German varieties using adaptive language models. In *Proceedings of the Sixth Workshop on NLP for Similar Languages, Varieties and Dialects*, pages 178–187, Ann Arbor, Michigan. Association for Computational Linguistics.

Tommi Jauhiainen, Tharindu Ranasinghe, and Marcos Zampieri. 2021. Comparing approaches to dravidian language identification. In *Proceedings of the Eighth Workshop on NLP for Similar Languages, Varieties and Dialects*, pages 120–127.

Tommi Sakari Jauhiainen, Heidi Annika Jauhiainen, Bo Krister Johan Linden, et al. 2018b. Heli-based experiments in swiss german dialect identification. In *Proceedings of the Fifth Workshop on NLP for Similar Languages, Varieties and Dialects (VarDial 2018)*. The Association for Computational Linguistics.

Yoon Kim, Yacine Jernite, David Sontag, and Alexander M Rush. 2016. Character-aware neural language models. In *Thirtieth AAAI conference on artificial intelligence*.

Taku Kudo. 2018. Subword regularization: Improving neural network translation models with multiple subword candidates. In *Proceedings of the 56th Annual Meeting of the Association for Computational Linguistics (Volume 1: Long Papers)*, pages 66–75, Melbourne, Australia. Association for Computational Linguistics.

Taku Kudo and John Richardson. 2018. SentencePiece: A simple and language independent subword tokenizer and detokenizer for neural text processing. In *Proceedings of the 2018 Conference on Empirical Methods in Natural Language Processing: System Demonstrations*, pages 66–71, Brussels, Belgium. Association for Computational Linguistics.

Jiahuan Li, Yutong Shen, Shujian Huang, Xinyu Dai, and Jiajun Chen. 2021. When is char better than subword: A systematic study of segmentation algorithms for neural machine translation. In *Proceedings of the 59th Annual Meeting of the Association for Computational Linguistics and the 11th International Joint Conference on Natural Language Processing (Volume 2: Short Papers)*, pages 543–549.

Zhouhan Lin, Minwei Feng, Cícero Nogueira dos Santos, Mo Yu, Bing Xiang, Bowen Zhou, and Yoshua Bengio. 2017. A structured self-attentive sentence embedding. In *5th International Conference on Learning Representations, ICLR 2017, Toulon, France, April 24-26, 2017, Conference Track Proceedings*. OpenReview.net.

Shervin Malmasi, Marcos Zampieri, Nikola Ljubešić, Preslav Nakov, Ahmed Ali, and Jörg Tiedemann. 2016. Discriminating between similar languages and arabic dialect identification: A report on the third dsl shared task. In *Proceedings of the third workshop on NLP for similar languages, varieties and dialects (VarDial3)*, pages 1–14.

Sabrina J. Mielke, Ryan Cotterell, Kyle Gorman, Brian Roark, and Jason Eisner. 2019. What kind of language is hard to language-model? In *Proceedings of the 57th Annual Meeting of the Association for Computational Linguistics*, pages 4975–4989, Florence, Italy. Association for Computational Linguistics.

Karthik Narasimhan, Regina Barzilay, and Tommi Jaakkola. 2015. An unsupervised method for uncovering morphological chains. *Transactions of the Association for Computational Linguistics*, 3:157–167.

Hyunji Hayley Park, Katherine J. Zhang, Coleman Haley, Kenneth Steimel, Han Liu, and Lane Schwartz. 2021. Morphology matters: A multilingual language modeling analysis. *Transactions of the Association for Computational Linguistics*, 9:261–276.

Hoifung Poon, Colin Cherry, and Kristina Toutanova. 2009. Unsupervised morphological segmentation with log-linear models. In *Proceedings of Human Language Technologies: The 2009 Annual Conference of the North American Chapter of the Association for Computational Linguistics*, pages 209–217, Boulder, Colorado. Association for Computational Linguistics.

Cristian Popa and Vlad Ştefănescu. 2020. Applying multilingual and monolingual transformer-based models for dialect identification. In *Proceedings of the 7th Workshop on NLP for Similar Languages, Varieties and Dialects*, pages 193–201.

Tanja Samardzic, Yves Scherrer, and Elvira Glaser. 2016. Archimob-a corpus of spoken swiss german. In *Proceedings of the tenth international conference on language resources and evaluation (LREC 2016)*. European Language Resources Association (ELRA).

Mike Schuster and Kaisuke Nakajima. 2012. Japanese and korean voice search. In *2012 IEEE International Conference on Acoustics, Speech and Signal Processing (ICASSP)*, pages 5149–5152.

Rico Sennrich, Barry Haddow, and Alexandra Birch. 2016. Neural machine translation of rare words with subword units. In *Proceedings of the 54th Annual Meeting of the Association for Computational Linguistics (Volume 1: Long Papers)*, pages 1715–1725, Berlin, Germany. Association for Computational Linguistics.

Bashar Talafha, Mohammad Ali, Muhy Eddin Za'ter, Haitham Seelawi, Ibraheem Tuffaha, Mostafa Samir, Wael Farhan, and Hussein Al-Natsheh. 2020. Multi-dialect arabic bert for country-level dialect identification. In *Proceedings of the Fifth Arabic Natural Language Processing Workshop*, pages 111–118.

Jörg Tiedemann and Nikola Ljubešić. 2012. Efficient discrimination between closely related languages. In *Proceedings of COLING 2012*, pages 2619–2634, Mumbai, India. The COLING 2012 Organizing Committee.

Alper Kursat Uysal and Serkan Gunal. 2014. The impact of preprocessing on text classification. *Information processing & management*, 50(1):104–112.

Clara Vania and Adam Lopez. 2017. From characters to words to in between: Do we capture morphology? In *Proceedings of the 55th Annual Meeting of the Association for Computational Linguistics (Volume 1: Long Papers)*, pages 2016–2027, Vancouver, Canada. Association for Computational Linguistics.

Jingjing Xu, Hao Zhou, Chun Gan, Zaixiang Zheng, and Lei Li. 2021. Vocabulary learning via optimal transport for neural machine translation. In *Proceedings of the 59th Annual Meeting of the Association for Computational Linguistics and the 11th International Joint Conference on Natural Language Processing (Volume 1: Long Papers)*, pages 7361–7373.

Li Yang and Yang Xiang. 2019. Naive bayes and bilstm ensemble for discriminating between mainland and taiwan variation of mandarin chinese. In *Proceedings of the Sixth Workshop on NLP for Similar Languages, Varieties and Dialects*, pages 120–127.

George-Eduard Zaharia, Andrei-Marius Avram, Dumitru-Clementin Cercel, and Traian Rebedea. 2020. Exploring the power of romanian bert for dialect identification. In *Proceedings of the 7th Workshop on NLP for Similar Languages, Varieties and Dialects*, pages 232–241.

Omar Zaidan and Chris Callison-Burch. 2011. The arabic online commentary dataset: an annotated dataset of informal arabic with high dialectal content. In *Proceedings of the 49th Annual Meeting of the Association for Computational Linguistics: Human Language Technologies*, pages 37–41.

Marcos Zampieri, Shervin Malmasi, Nikola Ljubešić, Preslav Nakov, Ahmed Ali, Jörg Tiedemann, Yves Scherrer, and Noëmi Aepli. 2017. Findings of the vardial evaluation campaign 2017. In *Proceedings of the fourth workshop on NLP for similar languages, varieties and dialects*.

Marcos Zampieri, Shervin Malmasi, Preslav Nakov, Ahmed Ali, Suwon Shon, James Glass, Yves Scherrer, Tanja Samardžić, Nikola Ljubešić, Jörg Tiedemann, et al. 2018. Language identification and morphosyntactic tagging. the second vardial evaluation campaign.

Marcos Zampieri, Shervin Malmasi, Yves Scherrer, Tanja Samardžić, Francis Tyers, Miikka Silfverberg, Natalia Klyueva, Tung-Le Pan, Chu-Ren Huang, Radu Tudor Ionescu, et al. 2019. A report on the third vardial evaluation campaign. Association for Computational Linguistics.

Xiang Zhang, Junbo Zhao, and Yann LeCun. 2015. Character-level convolutional networks for text classification. *Advances in neural information processing systems*, 28.

Ayah Zirikly, Bart Desmet, and Mona Diab. 2016. The gw/lt3 vardial 2016 shared task system for dialects and similar languages detection. In *COLING*, pages 33–41. The COLING 2016 Organizing Committee.

A Model Hyperparameters

Model	Model Parameters	Parameter Values
Lin_SA_BiLSTM	LSTM hidden_dim	50
	Dense_layer_ dim	50
	Number of attention hops	10
Kim_CNN	Number of CNN layers	4
	Number of Filters	256
	Kernel_size	(10,7,5,3) respectively in each CNN layer
	Number of FCNN	2
	FCNN_dim	1024
Zhang_CNN	Number of CNN layers	6
	Number of Filters	256
	Kernel_size	7 in first two layers, 3 in other layers
	Pool_size	3 in first two layers and last layer (no pooling in other layers)
	Number of FCNN	3
	FCNN_dim	1024

Table A1: Parameter settings for the experimented neural models

B Subword Vocabulary Ranges

Dataset	vocab_size range (char_vocab_size - 0.4*|V|)
GDI	30-6016
ILI	209-46306
AOC	158-68473
ADI	52-17260
NADI	445-22465

Table B1: Subword vocabulary ranges considered in the experimental set-up for each dataset

C Detailed Experimental Results with Neural Models and Comparisons

From Table C3, it can be observed that between the three neural models experimented at different tokenization schemes, the subword level Kim_CNN model outperforms the Zhang_CNN and Lin_SA_BiLSTM models. Kim_CNN unigram model performs the best in GDI, AOC, and ADI with 61.9, 73.2, 47.21 % F1 scores, while the Kim_CNN BPE model presents the maximum performance in the ILI and NADI dataset with 87.79% and 16.7% F-scores. Compared with BERT based models, it can be noted that in GDI and ADI datasets, Kim_CNN performs slightly better than BERT models. In ILI, the subword level models surpass the vanilla BERT and mBERT. The NADI results were obtained from the official evaluation site [20].

Table C1 reports the performance based on accuracy, and F1 macro scores[21] and the vocab_sizes at which the peak performances are obtained (the best performances are bolded). It can be observed that in all the datasets except ILI, the best classification performance is obtained with the Kim_CNN Unigram model. In ILI, Kim_CNN BPE presented the best performance. During the analysis, we also observed that in all datasets except ADI, the vocab_sizes that presented the best performances were overlapping. The overlapping values are between 1000-6000 for GDI, 200-600 for ILI, and 700-5000 in AOC.

D Experiments on Vocabulary Sizes for Subword Tokenziers

Figure D1 depicts the variation of accuracy in Kim_CNN unigram model with respect to the different vocabulary sizes.

E Details of Experimental Runs

The BERT models trained on 1 Tesla K80 GPU took about 40-60 minutes training time and an inference time of 10-20 minutes. For the subword level experiments, the training of different subword level models took $\approx$ 50-60 minutes in HPC cluster and an inference time of 5-10 minutes.

[20] https://codalab.lisn.upsaclay.fr/competitions/6514#participate-submit_results

[21] Accuracy and Fmicro represent the same value for multi-class classification

Dataset	Model	Subword Tokenizers	Acc	F1	optimal vocab_size
GDI	Lin_SA_BiLSTM	BPE	28.5	28	830
		Unigram	59.18	59.2	4030
	Kim_CNN	BPE	59.53	59.73	3030
		Unigram	62.4	**61.9**	2030
	Zhang_CNN	BPE	56.25	55.19	4030
		Unigram	57.3	56.7	4030
ILI	Lin_SA_BiLSTM	BPE	81.3	79.4	20009
		Unigram	81.4	79.8	9009
	Kim_CNN	BPE	88.48	**87.79**	309
		Unigram	85.6	84.8	709
	Zhang_CNN	BPE	84.94	84.33	309
		Unigram	84.2	83.5	409
AOC	Lin_SA_BiLSTM	BPE	55.35	27.77	458
		Unigram	77.69	70.66	9058
	Kim_CNN	BPE	79.5	72.4	4058
		Unigram	79.4	**73.2**	8058
	Zhang_CNN	BPE	75.87	69.34	5058
		Unigram	79.4	73.2	8058
ADI	Lin_SA_BiLSTM	BPE	21.3	11.18	852
		Unigram	23.79	14.33	852
	Kim_CNN	BPE	45.37	44.2	952
		Unigram	47.25	**47.21**	9052
	Zhang_CNN	BPE	31.97	30.68	6052
		Unigram	32.8	31.2	6052
NADI	Lin_SA_BiLSTM	BPE	32.9	15.3	20045
		Unigram	16.1	5.6	845
	Kim_CNN	BPE	33.5	16.7	20045
		Unigram	31.4	16.2	7045
	Zhang_CNN	BPE	29.1	5.1	20045
		Unigram	29.2	4.9	9045

Table C1: Model performances (Accuracy and Fmacro%) with BPE and Unigram subword tokenizers and the optimal vocabulary sizes

Dataset	Model	Tokenization Levels	F1(%)
GDI	Lin_SA_BiLSTM	Character Level	49.4
		Subword_BPE	28
		Subword_Unigram	59.2
		Word Level	58
	Kim_CNN	Character Level	56.9
		Subword_BPE	59.7
		Subword_Unigram	**61.9**
		Word Level	57
	Zhang_CNN	Character Level	47
		Subword_BPE	55.2
		Subword_Unigram	56.7
		Word Level	25
ILI	Lin_SA_BiLSTM	Character Level	64.4
		Subword_BPE	79.4
		Subword_Unigram	79.8
		Word Level	84.6
	Kim_CNN	Character Level	76.9
		Subword_BPE	**87.8**
		Subword_Unigram	84.8
		Word Level	84.3
	Zhang_CNN	Character Level	80
		Subword_BPE	84.3
		Subword_Unigram	83.5
		Word Level	85
AOC	Lin_SA_BiLSTM	Character Level	63.3
		Subword_BPE	27.8
		Subword_Unigram	70.6
		Word Level	75.5
	Kim_CNN	Character Level	73.3
		Subword_BPE	**72.4**
		Subword_Unigram	**73.2**
		Word Level	65.6
	Zhang_CNN	Character Level	66.7
		Subword_BPE	69.3
		Subword_Unigram	73.2
		Word Level	66
ADI	Lin_SA_BiLSTM	Character Level	13.4
		Subword_BPE	11.18
		Subword_Unigram	14.33
		Word Level	15.6
	Kim_CNN	Character Level	36.6
		Subword_BPE	44.2
		Subword_Unigram	**47.2**
		Word Level	45
	Zhang_CNN	Character Level	23
		Subword_BPE	30.7
		Subword_Unigram	31.2
		Word Level	31
NADI	Lin_SA_BiLSTM	Character Level	14.5
		Subword_BPE	15.3
		Subword_Unigram	5.6
		Word Level	14
	Kim_CNN	Character Level	13.4
		Subword_BPE	16.7
		Subword_Unigram	16.2
		Word Level	16.1
	Zhang_CNN	Character Level	7.2
		Subword_BPE	5.1
		Subword_Unigram	4.9
		Word Level	2.6

Table C2: Comparisons(F1%) of the neural models analyzed using different tokenization levels

Dataset	Model	F1(%)
GDI	**Bert-base-cased**	**61**
	mBERT	59
	German BERT	60
	Swiss-German BERT	60
ILI	Bert-base-cased	80
	mBERT	87
	IndicTransformers	**88**
AOC	Bert-base-cased	75
	mBERT	76
	AraBERT	**77**
	multi-dialect-ArabicBERT	76
ADI	Bert-base-cased	40
	mBERT	23
	AraBERT	**41**
	multi-dialect-ArabicBERT	40
NADI	**Bert-base-cased**	4.8
	mBERT	4.9
	AraBERT	20
	multi-dialect-ArabicBERT	**26**

Table C3: Comparisons(F1%) of the different pre-trained models in each dataset

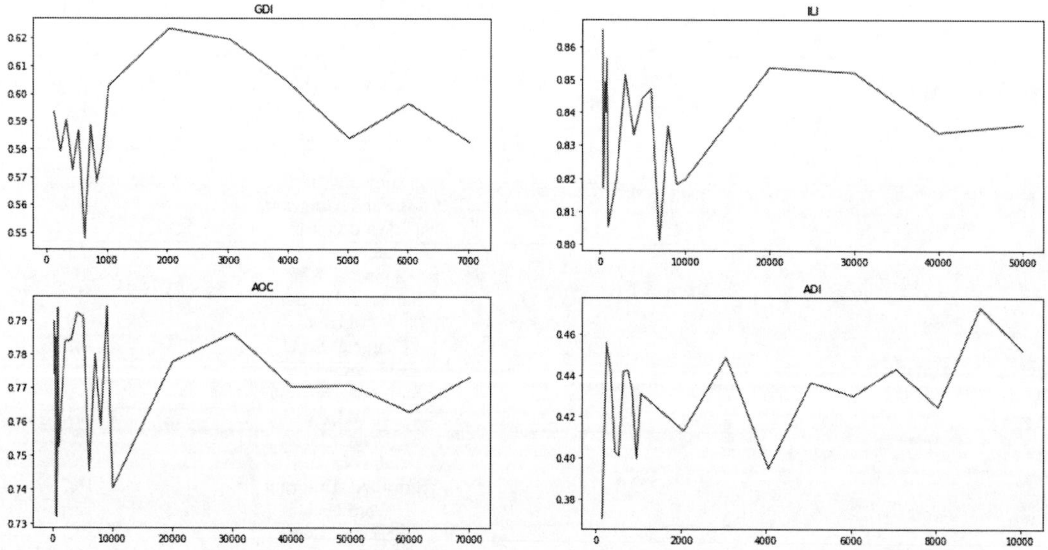

Figure D1: Variation of performances with respect to vocabulary sizes in Kim_CNN subword level unigram models across GDI, ILI,AOC and ADI datasets

Murreviikko – A Dialectologically Annotated and Normalized Dataset of Finnish Tweets

Olli Kuparinen
Department of Digital Humanities
University of Helsinki
olli.kuparinen@helsinki.fi

Abstract

This paper presents Murreviikko, a dataset of dialectal Finnish tweets which have been dialectologically annotated and manually normalized to a standard form. The dataset can be used as a test set for dialect identification and dialect-to-standard normalization, for instance. We evaluate the dataset on the normalization task, comparing an existing normalization model built on a spoken dialect corpus and three newly trained models with different architectures. We find that there are significant differences in normalization difficulty between the dialects, and that a character-level statistical machine translation model performs best on the Murreviikko tweet dataset.

1 Introduction

Dialectal variation is typical of user-generated content on social media, alongside other types of variation such as misspellings and emojis. Such language can be challenging for Natural Language Processing tools that are trained on standard language.

We present a dataset of dialectal Finnish tweets which have been manually annotated by dialect and normalized to standard Finnish spelling. The dataset can be used as a test set for further work in, for instance, dialect identification or dialect-to-standard normalization.

We further experiment with the latter, testing four different methods to normalize the tweets automatically: the publicly available RNN-based Murre normalizer (Partanen et al., 2019), a statistical machine translation system, a Transformer-based neural machine translation system, and a normalizer based on the pre-trained ByT5 model. To give an example of the task, the original dialectal text *oonko mää nähäny* should be replaced with the standard form *olenko minä nähnyt* ('have I seen').

The main contributions of the paper are:

- We collect a tweet dataset spanning three years.
- We manually annotate the dialects and normalize the tweets to be used in further work.
- We train three new normalization models on transcribed dialect data with different model architectures.
- We evaluate the normalization performance of our three models, as well as an existing normalization model, on the dataset.

2 Related Work

2.1 Collection of Dialectal Content from Social Media

There have been a lot of efforts in recent years to collect dialectal content from social media. Ljubešić et al. (2016) describe TweetGeo, a tool to collect data from Twitter with restrictions on geography, language and features. They use the tool to collect tweets from the language continuum of Bosnian, Croatian, Montenegrin, and Serbian. Likewise, Huang et al. (2016) collect tweets originating in the United States to study dialectal variation on social media.

Hovy and Purschke (2018) collect over 16 million Jodel posts from German-speaking areas and use the data for dialect clustering. Barnes et al. (2021) collect a dataset of Norwegian tweets and annotate them by language (Bokmål, Nynorsk, dialect, and mixed). The dataset is further annotated with POS tags in Mæhlum et al. (2022).

The MultiLexNorm (van der Goot et al., 2021) dataset includes data from social media in 12 languages or varieties and is collected mostly from Twitter. Even though the collection does not directly aim for dialectal content, it includes dialectal variation in addition to, for instance, orthographic variation.

Tenth Workshop on NLP for Similar Languages, Varieties and Dialects (VarDial 2023), pages 31–39
May 5, 2023 ©2023 Association for Computational Linguistics

	Tweets	Dialect	Standard	Swedish	English
2020	181	143	37	1	-
2021	203	142	55	3	3
2022	76	59	16	-	1
Total	460	344	108	4	4

Table 1: Distribution of the tweets by year and language. Dialect and standard refer to Finnish. Five dialectal tweets from 2020 were deemed abusive and were excluded from the dataset.

2.2 Normalization

Lexical normalization has been used especially in the domain of historical texts (e.g., Pettersson et al., 2014; Bollmann, 2019). The recent MultiLexNorm shared task addressed the normalization of a multilingual dataset of user-generated content (van der Goot et al., 2021), and some work has also been conducted on dialect normalization (Scherrer and Ljubešić, 2016; Abe et al., 2018; Partanen et al., 2019).

Methodologically, character-level statistical machine translation models have been proposed for normalization tasks (e.g., Pettersson et al., 2014; Scherrer and Ljubešić, 2016; Hämäläinen et al., 2018). More recently, neural machine translation models have been used, either based on recurrent networks with attention (e.g., Abe et al., 2018; Partanen et al., 2019), or on the Transformer architecture (Tang et al., 2018; Wu et al., 2021; Bawden et al., 2022). Finally, the best performance in the MultiLexNorm shared task (Samuel and Straka, 2021) was obtained by fine-tuning byT5, a byte-level pre-trained model (Xue et al., 2022).

3 Murreviikko

Murreviikko ('dialect week') is a Twitter campaign initiated at the University of Eastern Finland which aims to promote the use of dialects in Finland on social media. The campaign has run for three years (2020, 2021, 2022) and lasts for one week in October.

3.1 Data Collection from Twitter

We collected tweets that included the keyword *murreviikko* or *#murreviikko* via the Twitter API. Our data comes from all three years (2020–2022). The yearly and language-wise distribution of the tweets is presented in Table 1. Future augmentation of the dataset is possible if the campaign is continued.

3.2 Dialectal Annotation

The collected tweets were first annotated with the language they include (dialectal Finnish, standard Finnish, Swedish or English; see Table 1).[1] After this initial stage, the dialectal tweets were checked for abusive content and five such tweets were removed from the dataset, leaving 344 dialectal tweets in total.

The dialectal Finnish tweets were annotated on two levels: following the two-way division of Finnish dialects (Eastern–Western) and the seven-way division traditionally used in Finnish dialectology, based on Kettunen (1940). An eighth dialect area is often distinguished between South-West and Häme[2], called transitional Southwestern dialects. Since it shares many features with South-West and Häme, it would be hard to discern it from these in a single tweet. It is thus left out of this study. The dialect areas are presented in Figure 1.

The traditional division is based mostly on morphological and phonological features. The annotation of the tweets is based on these same features. The features include, for instance, several diphthong changes and different gemination cases, as well as case markers, elision, consonant gradation variation, and personal pronouns. For most cases the annotation is straightforward based on these features. Tweets that are not recognizable or include mixed features are deemed to their own class.

The traditional division does not account for the capital Helsinki due to its history as a Swedish-speaking city. There are however nine tweets written in Helsinki slang (a mainly Häme dialect with a wealth of Swedish loanwords). Another dialect group (Helsinki) was thus added to the annotation to accommodate these tweets.

Table 2 presents the dialectal distributions of the tweets, which mostly follows the population densities of the areas, except for the city of Helsinki, which is seriously underrepresented. The Savo dialect is also overrepresented, which might be explained by the fact that the University of Eastern Finland, where the campaign is initiated, is located in Savo and the official tweets of the campaign are written in that dialect.

[1]The annotation and normalization is performed by the author, who holds a PhD in Finnish with a special focus on language variation.

[2]Häme is sometimes referred to with its Swedish name Tavastia.

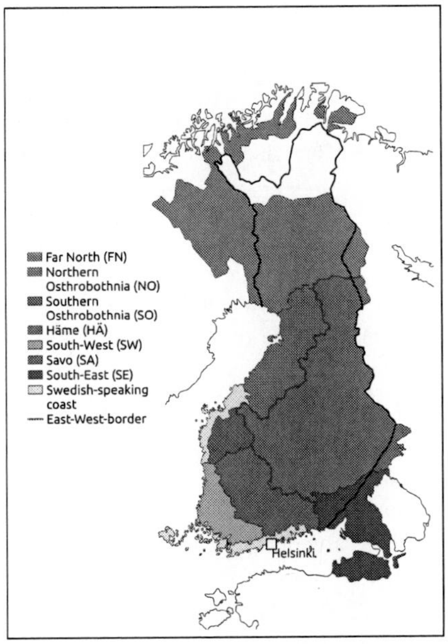

Figure 1: The seven dialect areas of Finnish, the East-West border (blue line) and the capital Helsinki. The dialect areas presented reflect the situation before World War II, when data was collected comprehensively (Kettunen, 1940). Modern-day dialects are mostly spoken inside the current borders of Finland, presented in black. The Northern Ostrobothnia in the map also includes Central Osthrobothnia which shares the dialect. The Northernmost areas are Sámi-speaking.

West	SW	74
	HÄ	58
	SO	17
	NO	33
	FN	14
	HE	9
	NA	12
	Total	217
East	SA	95
	SE	14
	NA	1
	Total	110
Unknown/Mixed		17

Table 2: Distribution of the tweets dialect-wise. The abbreviations are the same as in Figure 1 and HE=Helsinki. NA refers to tweets which contain dialectal language but are not distinguishable due to conflicting or scarce dialectal features. There might also be cases where the two-way division is distinguishable, but more fine-grained annotation is not possible.

3.3 Normalization

The dialectal tweets were manually normalized, following mostly the same principles as in the Samples of Spoken Finnish corpus (see Section 4.1). In essence, the tweets are normalized to a phonological and morphological standard, but word order is not altered, nor grammar rules of standard Finnish followed otherwise.

To give some examples of the phonological and morphological normalization, open or reduced diphthongs are returned to the standard alternative (*nuari* > *nuori* 'young', *koera* > *koira* 'dog'), weak grade alternatives of *t* are substituted with the standard *d* (*tehrä* > *tehdä* 'to do') and inessive case endings are presented with the standard *-ssa* or *-ssä* (*talos* > *talossa* 'in a house').

The principle has been to not distance the normalizations too far from the original dialects with insertions or word substitutions. An example of the principle is that possessive suffixes (*minun kirja**ni***, 'my book-my') are not added if they are not present in the original tweet (*mun kirja*, 'my book'), even though they are a part of standard Finnish. Likewise, dialect words are not corrected to the standard alternative, even if such words would exist, but instead normalized phonetically and morphologically (*seki diggaa fisuist* > *sekin diggaa fisuista* instead of *hänkin pitää kaloista* 's/he likes fish also').

The tweets include emojis, URLs, user mentions and hashtags. For the normalization experiments, emojis and URLs are removed from both the original and normalized side, user mentions are replaced with @@, and hashtags are normalized with the same rules as plain text.

The original text and normalization are aligned on tweet level. The dataset is accessible in compliance with the rules of the Twitter API, and the European Union's Digital Single Market directive (2019/790). This means that the tweet IDs, dialect annotations and corresponding normalizations are publicly available on Github.[3] The original tweets can be shared non-publicly for scientific use.

4 Normalization Experiments

4.1 Training Data

We use the Samples of Spoken Finnish (Institute for the Languages of Finland, 2021), hereafter SKN, for training. The corpus consists of 99 transcribed

[3]The public data is available at `https://github.com/Helsinki-NLP/murreviikko`. Licence: CC-BY-SA 4.0.

interviews from the 1960s that represent the dialects of Finnish comprehensively.[4] There are 50 Finnish-speaking locations in the corpus, with two speakers always representing a location (with one exception). The speakers are old and rural men and women, who have been born in the end of the 19th century (thus 70 to 90 years old at the time of the interview). The utterances of each interview have been randomly sampled and split to training (80%), development (10%) and test sets (10%).

The SKN corpus includes two transcription layers: one with very high precision, and a simplified version. Both rely on the Uralic Phonetic Alphabet (UPA), but the simplified transcriptions use almost exclusively standard Finnish characters and no diacritics. We use this version for training our own models. In contrast, the detailed transcriptions have been used to train the Murre normalizer (Partanen et al., 2019), which we will also experiment with. The transcriptions have been normalized to a phonetic standard manually by linguists. The principles of the normalization procedure are explained in the corpus, and they have been used as a guideline for the normalization of the tweet dataset (see Section 3.3).

Even though the simplified transcriptions use the same alphabet as the tweets, there are differences in, for instance, sandhi phenomena, which are marked in the transcriptions (*tehdäs se*) 'to do it', but often not in written dialectal Finnish (*tehdä se*). Likewise, the lexis used in old, rural interviews is naturally very different from the one used in the tweets. These are both issues that could affect the performance of the trained models.

Since the dialect transcriptions do not include any characters typical of social media, we add a set of 130 Finnish tweets to the training set. The tweets are collected from the OOD test set for Finnish Universal Dependencies[5], and added as such on both the original side and the normalized side. Such a small dataset makes the models aware of the special characters, but does not affect the normalization quality. The key figures of this dataset, along with those in the test set, are presented in Table 3.

4.2 Methods and Tools

We treat normalization as a character transduction problem. This means that we split the sequences into individual characters and treat the characters as tokens, as has been standard practice in normalization tasks before (e.g., Scherrer and Ljubešić, 2016; Wu et al., 2021).

	Sequences	Words	Words/Seq	Chars/Seq
Murreviikko	344	8269	24.04	175.25
SKN+UD_{tweets}	38,982	699,902	17.96	92.52

Table 3: Key figures of the datasets. Sequences refer to tweets on Murreviikko and UD_{tweets} and utterances on SKN. Words/Seq = mean sequence length in words. Chars/Seq = mean sequence length in characters.

We experiment with four models:[6]

- **Murre.** The publicly available Murre normalizer[7] is based on a recurrent neural network (RNN) architecture and trained on the detailed transcriptions of the SKN corpus (Partanen et al., 2019). The Murre normalizer splits the data into non-overlapping trigrams and returns them to sentences in the output.

- **SMT.** Our statistical normalizer uses the Moses SMT toolkit (Koehn et al., 2007) with a character 10-gram KenLM language model trained on the training set. We do not use an additional language model on the target side. We use eflomal (Östling and Tiedemann, 2016) for character alignment. The model weights are tuned with minimum error rate training (MERT), with word error rate as the objective. Note that since we are working on characters, the word error rate is essentially character error rate.

- **NMT.** Our neural model follows standard Transformer architecture (Vaswani et al., 2017). It has 6 Transformer layers in the encoder and the decoder, with 8 heads each. There are 512 embedding and hidden layer dimensions. We use a batch size of 5000 tokens with an accumulate gradient of 4, and an initial learning rate of 4. The dropout is set to 0.1. We use position representation clipping with a value of 4 (Shaw et al., 2018). We train for 50,000 steps with checkpoints every 1000 steps. The model is trained with the OpenNMT-py toolkit (Klein et al., 2017).

[4] http://urn.fi/urn:nbn:fi:lb-2021112221, Licence: CC-BY.

[5] https://github.com/UniversalDependencies/UD_Finnish-OOD/, Licence: CC-BY-SA 4.0

[6] The training time and the number of parameters for each model are presented in Appendix A in Table 9.

[7] https://github.com/mikahama/murre, Licence: CC-BY-NC-ND 4.0

- **ByT5.** ByT5 (Xue et al., 2022) is a multilingual pre-trained sequence-to-sequence model which encodes all text as UTF-8 byte sequences (instead of subword tokenization), and uses the Transformer architecture. The model is pretrained on a masked language modeling task, where the model is asked to predict the content of a masked span. The data for pre-training is the multilingual m4C corpus (Xue et al., 2021), with 1.35% of the data being in Finnish. We use the `byt5-base` model and fine-tune it with our training data for 5 epochs, with maximum training sequence length of 512 bytes and a batch size of 4 sequences.

Our models are trained on sentence-level, whereas the tweets are left as they are and could thus include several sentences.

4.3 Evaluation

We evaluate the models on two metrics: character n-gram F-score (chrF2) and character error rate (CER). The former is typically used when evaluating machine translation models, and it calculates the F-score over character n-grams (Popović, 2015). CER is the Levenshtein distance between the model prediction and the correct target, normalized by the length of the target.[8]

We compare the systems to a **leave-as-is** (LAI) baseline, which evaluates the original sentences as they are, i.e., what would the scores be if the source was left untouched. For our own models, we also report the corresponding performance on a test set of the SKN corpus. This is not calculated with the Murre normalizer, since it is likely that some sentences in our test set were part of the training data for the model.

5 Results and Discussion

The chrF2 scores for the complete datasets are presented in Table 4. The statistical model performs best on the tweets (Murreviikko), with ByT5 achieving a very similar score. On the original dialect data (SKN) however, the best performance is obtained with the ByT5 model. The NMT model performs well on the original data, but does not generalize to the tweet dataset, as it barely outperforms the baseline. Likewise, the Murre normalizer does not produce a comparable score.

Model	Murreviikko	SKN
LAI	71.2	61.8
Murre	78.5	–
SMT	**84.4**	93.4
NMT	74.3	95.5
ByT5	83.6	**95.8**

Table 4: Character n-gram F-scores for complete datasets (↑).

Partanen et al. (2019)	5.73
SMT	7.95
NMT	5.32
ByT5	6.47

Table 5: Comparison of our models and Partanen et al. (2019) on the SKN corpus on word error rate (↓).

Partanen et al. (2019) present their results on the SKN dialect corpus on word error rate, which means the results presented in Table 4 are not directly comparable. To see how our models' performance relates to theirs, we present the word error rates of the models in Table 5, along with the score from Partanen et al. (2019). We calculated the word error rate with the same implementation as in the original work.[9]

Table 5 shows that our NMT model and the Murre normalizer (Partanen et al., 2019) offer very similar performance. The ByT5 model, which achieved the best chrF2 score, performs slightly worse when measured on word error rate. The models trained for this work are thus functioning on par with previous work for the dialect normalization task, but the performance does not translate to the tweet dataset.

To further analyze the difficulty of the tweet normalization task, we scrutinize the normalization performance on the different dialect groups to see if some dialects are inherently harder to normalize, or if some models fail on some dialects. The chrF2 scores broken down by dialect are presented in Table 6.

The baselines reflect that the South-Eastern (LAI 67.3) and especially South-Western dialects (LAI 59.3) are further from standard Finnish than the other dialects. Both dialects include for instance eli-

[8]We calculate chrF2 with the *sacrebleu* tool (Post, 2018), available at `https://github.com/mjpost/sacrebleu`, and CER with `https://github.com/nsmartinez/WERpp`.

[9]`https://github.com/nsmartinez/WERpp`.

Model	SW	HÄ	SO	NO	FN	HE	SA	SE	NA
LAI	59.3	71.7	73.1	74.9	75.6	73.9	74.2	67.3	83.7
Murre	75.1	78.8	79.1	81.1	77.2	70.4	80.4	78.3	79.6
SMT	**77.3**	85.4	**86.5**	87.5	**85.6**	73.2	**87.2**	**84.7**	88.8
NMT	62.9	75.8	76.7	78.1	77.1	73.6	77.8	68.9	83.5
ByT5	71.7	**85.9**	85.8	**87.6**	84.5	**83.4**	86.9	83.7	**91.0**

Table 6: Character n-gram F-scores dialect-wise (↑). SW = South-West, HÄ = Häme, SO = Southern Osthrobothnia, NO = Northern Osthrobothnia, FN = Far North, HE = Helsinki slang, SA = Savo, SE = South-East, NA = Not discernible.

Model	Murreviikko	SW	HÄ	SO	NO	FN	HE	SA	SE	NA	SKN
LAI	11.58	17.13	11.42	9.93	9.65	9.65	10.12	10.22	13.18	6.29	14.25
Murre	11.09	13.50	12.18	9.96	9.36	10.95	13.01	9.72	10.31	10.21	–
SMT	**7.64**	**11.13**	7.43	**6.91**	6.16	7.37	11.23	6.20	7.16	5.52	3.93
NMT	10.92	16.3	10.39	9.09	8.93	9.35	10.31	9.46	12.63	6.79	**1.84**
ByT5	7.72	13.49	**6.58**	11.06	**4.99**	**6.71**	**6.50**	**5.86**	**6.19**	**4.18**	2.37

Table 7: Character error rates for the complete datasets and dialect-wise. (↓).

sion and influence from other languages (Swedish and Estonian for the South-Western dialects, and other Finnic languages and Russian for the South-Eastern dialects). The rest of the dialect groups (disregarding NA) tend to have very similar baselines.

Regarding model performance, the Helsinki slang (HE) offers an interesting challenge. All models except ByT5 perform worse than the baseline. This is somewhat to be expected, as the training data does not include the slang. ByT5 on the other hand has been trained on web data by Common Crawl (Xue et al., 2021), which could include text written in the Helsinki slang. It could also be that the Swedish training data is helpful for the normalization task, since Helsinki slang is characterized by Swedish loanwords.

The difficulty of the South-Western dialects is reflected in the model scores, with all models achieving F-scores below 80. Given this is the second largest dialect group in the dataset, it also affects the overall performance quite significantly.

The character error rates for the complete datasets and dialects separately are presented in Table 7. The results follow mostly the same lines as the chrF2 scores presented in Table 4 and Table 6, but ByT5 achieves a better score on most dialects. However, it struggles with Southern Ostrobothnian and South-Western dialects so much that the statistical model achieves the best overall score on the whole dataset. Likewise for SKN, the NMT model performs better than ByT5 when evaluating on character error rate, whereas for chrF2 ByT5 achieved a better score.

5.1 Error Analysis

Table 8 presents an example sentence from a tweet with the predictions of each model. The example highlights common errors the models make. As South-Western dialects proved to be the hardest to normalize, the example is chosen from this dialect.

Murre fails to insert the hashtag and punctuation altogether. It has not seen the # in training (unlike our own models which were trained with the small tweet dataset added), and thus can not produce it. Likewise, it normalizes the *f* to *v* which is sometimes necessary in dialectal Finnish, but does not work well with the tweets which include a lot of loanwords from Swedish (such as the one in the example, *fundera* 'to think') and English.

However, Murre normalizes the morphological elements well, for instance managing to insert the correct adessive case ending *-lla* in *viikolla*, which is not achieved with any other model, as well as the ablative case ending *-ltä* in *sieltä*. Further finetuning of the model with modern text might thus produce comparable results.

The statistical model produces the hashtag and punctuation correctly, and also makes several correct substitutions and insertions (e.g., *päättys* >

Source	#Murreviikko päättys viime viikol, mut täsä muutmi fundeerauksi siält.
Target	#Murreviikko päättyi viime viikolla, mutta tässä muutamia fundeerauksia sieltä.
Murre	**M**urreviikko päättyi viime viikolla mutta tässä muu**tmin** **v**undeerauks**i** sieltä
SMT	#Murreviikko päättyi viime viiko**l**, mutta tässä muutam**i** fundeerauksia siel**t**.
NMT	#Murreviikko päätty**s** viime viiko**l**, **mut** täsä muu**tmi** fundeerauks**i** sieltä
ByT5	#Murreviikko päättyi viime viiko**l**, mutta tässä muu**tmi** fundeerauks**i** siel**t**.
Gloss	'#Dialectweek ended last week, but here are some thoughts on it.'

Table 8: An example sentence from a tweet, with the source and correct target on top, and the corresponding normalizations of each model below. An English gloss is provided on the bottom. Errors of each model are presented in bold.

päättyi, mut > mutta, täsä > tässä, fundeerauksi > fundeerauksia), but fails to insert word-final characters in *viikol, muutami, sielt*.

The Transformer-based NMT consistently undernormalizes, producing predictions very close to the original source. The only difference in the example is the correctly normalized *siält > sieltä*. The prediction is also missing the final punctuation mark.

ByT5 has been originally trained on web crawled data, which enables the model to produce sensible output on the tweets. The errors are very similar to the ones produced by SMT, such as failing to insert word-final characters.

6 Conclusions

In this paper, we present a dataset of dialectal Finnish tweets which have been manually annotated by dialect and normalized to a standard form. The dataset will be made accessible to the scientific community for further testing and fine-tuning of models in the fields of dialect-to-standard normalization and dialect identification, for instance.

We furthermore evaluate four automatic normalization methods, which have been trained with transcribed spoken dialect data. Three of the models have been purpose-built for this paper, while a fourth model has been made publicly available (Partanen et al., 2019).

Character-level statistical machine translation provides the best normalization quality of the evaluated models on the Murreviikko-dataset, with the pre-trained and fine-tuned ByT5 model achieving very similar scores. Meanwhile, the ByT5 and a Transformer-based neural model perform best on the test set of the dialect transcriptions (SKN). The NMT model fails to transfer the performance to the tweets, however, consistently undernormalizing and barely outperforming the baseline. The RNN-based Murre normalizer struggles with the special characters typical of social media, while providing a reasonable performance on dialectal morphological features.

Dialect-wise, the South-Western dialects provide the lowest baseline and worst scores for the models. In the context of this work, it is thus the hardest to normalize from the traditional Finnish dialects. Helsinki slang, traditionally not seen as one of the dialects, is also difficult for the models but this is mostly due to a lack of training data.

Limitations

The size of the dataset is modest, and it is not possible to sensibly split it to train, development and test sets, for instance. We thus endorse it as a test set for future work.

We have not executed exhaustive hyperparameter tuning for our normalization experiments. It is likely that, for example, the neural machine translation model could perform better with further tuning and development. Likewise, we focus on character-level normalization and do not experiment with byte-pair encoding, found to enhance performance in recent normalization tasks (e.g., Bawden et al., 2022).

Acknowledgments

This work has been supported by the Academy of Finland through project No. 342859 "CorCoDial – Corpus-based computational dialectology".

References

Kaori Abe, Yuichiroh Matsubayashi, Naoaki Okazaki, and Kentaro Inui. 2018. Multi-dialect neural machine translation and dialectometry. In *Proceedings of the*

32nd Pacific Asia Conference on Language, Information and Computation, Hong Kong. Association for Computational Linguistics.

Jeremy Barnes, Petter Mæhlum, and Samia Touileb. 2021. NorDial: A preliminary corpus of written Norwegian dialect use. In *Proceedings of the 23rd Nordic Conference on Computational Linguistics (NoDaLiDa)*, pages 445–451, Reykjavik, Iceland (Online). Linköping University Electronic Press, Sweden.

Rachel Bawden, Jonathan Poinhos, Eleni Kogkitsidou, Philippe Gambette, Benoît Sagot, and Simon Gabay. 2022. Automatic normalisation of early Modern French. In *Proceedings of the Thirteenth Language Resources and Evaluation Conference*, pages 3354–3366, Marseille, France. European Language Resources Association.

Marcel Bollmann. 2019. A large-scale comparison of historical text normalization systems. In *Proceedings of the 2019 Conference of the North American Chapter of the Association for Computational Linguistics: Human Language Technologies, Volume 1 (Long and Short Papers)*, pages 3885–3898, Minneapolis, Minnesota. Association for Computational Linguistics.

Mika Hämäläinen, Tanja Säily, Jack Rueter, Jörg Tiedemann, and Eetu Mäkelä. 2018. Normalizing early English letters to present-day English spelling. In *Proceedings of the Second Joint SIGHUM Workshop on Computational Linguistics for Cultural Heritage, Social Sciences, Humanities and Literature*, pages 87–96, Santa Fe, New Mexico. Association for Computational Linguistics.

Dirk Hovy and Christoph Purschke. 2018. Capturing regional variation with distributed place representations and geographic retrofitting. In *Proceedings of the 2018 Conference on Empirical Methods in Natural Language Processing*, pages 4383–4394, Brussels, Belgium. Association for Computational Linguistics.

Yuan Huang, Diansheng Guo, Alice Kasakoff, and Jack Grieve. 2016. Understanding u.s. regional linguistic variation with twitter data analysis. *Computers, Environment and Urban Systems*, 59:244–255.

Institute for the Languages of Finland. 2021. Samples of Spoken Finnish, VRT Version.

Lauri Kettunen. 1940. *Suomen murteet. 3, A, Murrekartasto*. Suomalaisen Kirjallisuuden Seuran toimituksia ; 188. Osa. Suomalaisen kirjallisuuden seura, Helsinki.

Guillaume Klein, Yoon Kim, Yuntian Deng, Jean Senellart, and Alexander Rush. 2017. OpenNMT: Open-source toolkit for neural machine translation. In *Proceedings of ACL 2017, System Demonstrations*, pages 67–72, Vancouver, Canada. Association for Computational Linguistics.

Philipp Koehn, Hieu Hoang, Alexandra Birch, Chris Callison-Burch, Marcello Federico, Nicola Bertoldi, Brooke Cowan, Wade Shen, Christine Moran, Richard Zens, Chris Dyer, Ondřej Bojar, Alexandra Constantin, and Evan Herbst. 2007. Moses: Open source toolkit for statistical machine translation. In *Proceedings of the 45th Annual Meeting of the Association for Computational Linguistics Companion Volume Proceedings of the Demo and Poster Sessions*, pages 177–180, Prague, Czech Republic. Association for Computational Linguistics.

Nikola Ljubešić, Tanja Samardžić, and Curdin Derungs. 2016. TweetGeo - a tool for collecting, processing and analysing geo-encoded linguistic data. In *Proceedings of COLING 2016, the 26th International Conference on Computational Linguistics: Technical Papers*, pages 3412–3421, Osaka, Japan. The COLING 2016 Organizing Committee.

Petter Mæhlum, Andre Kåsen, Samia Touileb, and Jeremy Barnes. 2022. Annotating Norwegian language varieties on Twitter for part-of-speech. In *Proceedings of the Ninth Workshop on NLP for Similar Languages, Varieties and Dialects*, pages 64–69, Gyeongju, Republic of Korea. Association for Computational Linguistics.

Robert Östling and Jörg Tiedemann. 2016. Efficient word alignment with Markov Chain Monte Carlo. *Prague Bulletin of Mathematical Linguistics*, 106:125–146.

Niko Partanen, Mika Hämäläinen, and Khalid Alnajjar. 2019. Dialect text normalization to normative standard Finnish. In *Proceedings of the 5th Workshop on Noisy User-generated Text (W-NUT 2019)*, pages 141–146, Hong Kong, China. Association for Computational Linguistics.

Eva Pettersson, Beáta Megyesi, and Joakim Nivre. 2014. A multilingual evaluation of three spelling normalisation methods for historical text. In *Proceedings of the 8th Workshop on Language Technology for Cultural Heritage, Social Sciences, and Humanities (LaTeCH)*, pages 32–41, Gothenburg, Sweden. Association for Computational Linguistics.

Maja Popović. 2015. chrF: character n-gram F-score for automatic MT evaluation. In *Proceedings of the Tenth Workshop on Statistical Machine Translation*, pages 392–395, Lisbon, Portugal. Association for Computational Linguistics.

Matt Post. 2018. A call for clarity in reporting BLEU scores. In *Proceedings of the Third Conference on Machine Translation: Research Papers*, pages 186–191, Brussels, Belgium. Association for Computational Linguistics.

David Samuel and Milan Straka. 2021. ÚFAL at MultiLexNorm 2021: Improving multilingual lexical normalization by fine-tuning ByT5. In *Proceedings of the Seventh Workshop on Noisy User-generated Text (W-NUT 2021)*, pages 483–492, Online. Association for Computational Linguistics.

Yves Scherrer and Nikola Ljubešić. 2016. Automatic normalisation of the Swiss German ArchiMob corpus using character-level machine translation. In *Proceedings of the 13th Conference on Natural Language Processing (KONVENS)*.

Peter Shaw, Jakob Uszkoreit, and Ashish Vaswani. 2018. Self-attention with relative position representations. In *Proceedings of the 2018 Conference of the North American Chapter of the Association for Computational Linguistics: Human Language Technologies, Volume 2 (Short Papers)*, pages 464–468, New Orleans, Louisiana. Association for Computational Linguistics.

Gongbo Tang, Fabienne Cap, Eva Pettersson, and Joakim Nivre. 2018. An evaluation of neural machine translation models on historical spelling normalization. In *Proceedings of the 27th International Conference on Computational Linguistics*, pages 1320–1331, Santa Fe, New Mexico, USA. Association for Computational Linguistics.

Rob van der Goot, Alan Ramponi, Arkaitz Zubiaga, Barbara Plank, Benjamin Muller, Iñaki San Vicente Roncal, Nikola Ljubešić, Özlem Çetinoğlu, Rahmad Mahendra, Talha Çolakoğlu, Timothy Baldwin, Tommaso Caselli, and Wladimir Sidorenko. 2021. MultiLexNorm: A shared task on multilingual lexical normalization. In *Proceedings of the Seventh Workshop on Noisy User-generated Text (W-NUT 2021)*, pages 493–509, Online. Association for Computational Linguistics.

Ashish Vaswani, Noam Shazeer, Niki Parmar, Jakob Uszkoreit, Llion Jones, Aidan N Gomez, Ł ukasz Kaiser, and Illia Polosukhin. 2017. Attention is all you need. In *Advances in Neural Information Processing Systems*, volume 30. Curran Associates, Inc.

Shijie Wu, Ryan Cotterell, and Mans Hulden. 2021. Applying the transformer to character-level transduction. In *Proceedings of the 16th Conference of the European Chapter of the Association for Computational Linguistics: Main Volume*, pages 1901–1907, Online. Association for Computational Linguistics.

Linting Xue, Aditya Barua, Noah Constant, Rami Al-Rfou, Sharan Narang, Mihir Kale, Adam Roberts, and Colin Raffel. 2022. ByT5: Towards a token-free future with pre-trained byte-to-byte models. *Transactions of the Association for Computational Linguistics*, 10:291–306.

Linting Xue, Noah Constant, Adam Roberts, Mihir Kale, Rami Al-Rfou, Aditya Siddhant, Aditya Barua, and Colin Raffel. 2021. mT5: A massively multilingual pre-trained text-to-text transformer. In *Proceedings of the 2021 Conference of the North American Chapter of the Association for Computational Linguistics: Human Language Technologies*, pages 483–498, Online. Association for Computational Linguistics.

A Experimental Details

We trained the NMT model and ByT5 on a single NVIDIA V100 GPU. The CSMT model is trained on a Xeon Gold 6230 CPU. Table 9 presents the training time and number of parameters for the training data.

Model	Runtime (hh:mm)	Parameters
SMT	72:00	—
NMT	16:26	25.4 M
ByT5	9:56	581 M

Table 9: Training runtime and number of parameters for the training data.

Does Manipulating Tokenization Aid Cross-Lingual Transfer? A Study on POS Tagging for Non-Standardized Languages

Verena Blaschke **Hinrich Schütze** **Barbara Plank**
Center for Information and Language Processing (CIS), LMU Munich, Germany
Munich Center for Machine Learning (MCML), Munich, Germany
blaschke@cis.lmu.de inquiries@cislmu.org bplank@cis.lmu.de

Abstract

One of the challenges with finetuning pretrained language models (PLMs) is that their tokenizer is optimized for the language(s) it was pretrained on, but brittle when it comes to previously unseen variations in the data. This can for instance be observed when finetuning PLMs on one language and evaluating them on data in a closely related language variety with no standardized orthography. Despite the high linguistic similarity, tokenization no longer corresponds to meaningful representations of the target data, leading to low performance in, e.g., part-of-speech tagging.

In this work, we finetune PLMs on seven languages from three different families and analyze their zero-shot performance on closely related, non-standardized varieties. We consider different measures for the divergence in the tokenization of the source and target data, and the way they can be adjusted by manipulating the tokenization during the finetuning step. Overall, we find that the similarity between the percentage of words that get split into subwords in the source and target data (the *split word ratio difference*) is the strongest predictor for model performance on target data.

1 Introduction

Transformer-based pre-trained language models (PLMs) enable successful cross-lingual transfer for many natural language processing tasks. However, the impact of tokenization and its interplay with transferability across languages, especially under-resourced variants with no orthography, has obtained limited focus so far. Tokenization splits words into subwords, but not necessarily in a meaningful way. An example with a current PLM is illustrated for Alsatian German in Figure 1a. This problem is especially pronounced for vernacular languages and dialects, where words tend to be split at a much higher rate than the standard. This has been observed on, e.g., informally written Algerian Arabic (Touileb and Barnes, 2021). As poor

a.	M'r	redd	alemànnischi	Mundàrte	.
	M, ', r	red, ##d	al, ##em, ##à, ##nn, ##isch, ##i	Mund, ##à, ##rte	.
b.	Wir	sprechen	alemannische	Mundarten	.
	Wir	sprechen	al, #emann, ##ische	Mund, ##arten	.
c.	W(r	sprechen	alemaInische	Mundarten	.
	W, (, r	sprechen	al, ##ema, ##In, ##ische	Mund, ##arten	.

Figure 1: "We speak Alemannic dialects", tokenized by GBERT. Compared to Standard German (*b.*), the quality of the Alsatian German (*a.*) tokenization is poor, making cross-lingual transfer hard. Noise injection (*c.*) often improves transfer from standard to poorly tokenized non-standardized varieties.

subword tokenization can lead to suboptimal language representations and impoverished transfer, it becomes important to understand if the effect holds at a larger scale. We are particularly interested in challenging setups in which, despite *high language similarity,* comparatively low transfer performance is obtained.

A recent study proposes an elegant and lean solution to address this 'tokenization gap,' without requiring expensive PLM re-training: to *manipulate tokenization* of PLMs post-hoc (Aepli and Sennrich, 2022), i.e., during finetuning by injecting character-level noise (Figure 1c). Noise injection has been shown to successfully aid cross-lingual transfer and is an appealing solution, as it is cheap and widely applicable. In this work, we first provide a reproduction study and then broaden it by a systematic investigation of the extent to which noise injection helps. We also show how it influences the subword tokenization of the source data vis-à-vis the target data. We hypothesize that, while not emulating dialect text, injecting noise into standard language data can raise the tokenization rate to a similar level, which aids transfer.

The importance of token overlap between source

Tenth Workshop on NLP for Similar Languages, Varieties and Dialects (VarDial 2023), pages 40–54
May 5, 2023

and target is an on-going debate (to which we contribute): Prior research has found that subword token overlap between the finetuning and target language improves transfer (Wu and Dredze, 2019; Pires et al., 2019), although it might neither be the most important factor (K et al., 2020; Muller et al., 2022) nor a necessary condition for cross-lingual transfer to work (Pires et al., 2019; Conneau et al., 2020b).

To enable research in this direction, we contribute a novel benchmark. We collected under-resourced language variants covering seven part-of-speech (POS) tagging transfer scenarios within three language families. This collection enables also future work to study cross-lingual and cross-dialect transfer.

Our contributions are:

- We investigate the noise injection method by Aepli and Sennrich (2022) with respect to the ideal noise injection rate for different languages and PLMs.
- To the best of our knowledge, this is the broadest study that focuses specifically on transfer to closely related, non-standardized language varieties with languages from multiple linguistic families. We convert several dialect datasets into a shared tagset (UPOS) and share the conversion scripts.
- We compare the effect of noise injection on the subword tokenization differences between the source and target data, and the effect of these differences on the model performance, and find that the proportions of (un)split words are a better predictor than the ratio of seen subword tokens.

2 Method

We make our code, including scripts for reproducing the benchmark, available at `github.com/mainlp/noisydialect`.

2.1 Injecting Character-Level Noise

We follow the approach by Aepli and Sennrich (2022) to add noise to the finetuning datasets. Given a noise level $0 \leq n \leq 1$ and a finetuning dataset F with a grapheme inventory $\mathcal{I}$,[1] we inject noise into each sentence $S \in F$ as follows: we randomly select $n|S|$ words,[2] and for each of these words, we randomly perform one of the three following actions:

- delete one randomly chosen character
- replace one randomly chosen character with a random character $\in \mathcal{I}$
- insert one random character $\in \mathcal{I}$ into a random slot within the word.

Aepli and Sennrich (2022) investigate transferring POS tagging models to five target languages (Swiss German, Faroese, Old French, Livvi and Karelian) and compare set-ups with no noise ($n = 0$) to adding noise with $n = 0.15$. They find that, when the source and target languages are closely related, the configuration with noise consistently performs better. We additionally experiment with adding noise at higher levels: to 35 %, 55 %, 75 % and 95 % of each sentence's tokens.

2.2 Comparing Datasets via Subword Tokenization

We consider several simple measures of comparing the subword tokenization of the source data with that of the target data:

- *Split word ratio difference:* The (absolute) difference between the ratios of words that were split into subword tokens in the source and target data. (We additionally considered the average number of subword tokens per word, but found that that measure yielded very similar results to the split word ratio difference.)
- *Seen subwords* and *seen words:* The ratios of the target subword tokens and target words,[3] respectively, that are also in the source data. (We also included type-based versions of these measures, but found that they behaved similarly to their token-based counterparts.)
- *Type–token ratio (TTR) ratio:* The subword-level type-token ratio of the target data divided by that of the source data. This is similar to the TTR-based measures used by Lin et al. (2019) and Muller et al. (2022).

[1]Unlike Aepli and Sennrich (2022), we also include non-alphabetic characters in $\mathcal{I}$, as some of the orthographic differences are punctuation-based (see Figure 1).

[2]Excluding words that only contain numerals or punctuation marks.

[3]We consider words here as the annotated units provided by the datasets.

3 Experimental Set-up

3.1 Data

We analyze transfer between eight source and 18 target datasets in the following language varieties (see Appendix A for details):

- Modern Standard Arabic (MSA) (Hajič et al., 2009) → Egyptian, Levantine, Gulf and Maghrebi Arabic (Darwish et al., 2018)
- German (Borges Völker et al., 2019) → Swiss German (Hollenstein and Aepli, 2014), Alsatian German (Bernhard et al., 2019)
- German (Borges Völker et al., 2019), Dutch (Bouma and van Noord, 2017) → Low Saxon (Siewert et al., 2021)
- Norwegian (Nynorsk) (Velldal et al., 2017), Norwegian (Bokmål) (Øvrelid and Hohle, 2016) → West, East and North Norwegian (Øvrelid et al., 2018)
- French (Guillaume et al., 2019) → Picard (Martin et al., 2018)
- French (Guillaume et al., 2019), Spanish (Taulé et al., 2008) → Occitan (Bras et al., 2018)
- Finnish (Pyysalo et al., 2015) → six Finnish dialect groups (University of Turku and Institute for the Languages of Finland)

This list includes varieties from three language families (Afro-Asiatic, Finno-Ugric and Indo-European), written in two types of writing systems (alphabetical and abjad). It also covers a range of different degrees of linguistic relatedness (e.g., the Norwegian dialects are much more closely related to each other and to the standardized varieties than can be said of the Arabic group) and text genres (including tweets, Wikipedia articles, and professionally transcribed interviews). While orthographies for some of our target languages (e.g., Low Saxon) have been proposed, none of these languages have a sole orthography that is used by virtually all speakers.

Many of these corpora are from the Universal Dependencies (UD) project (Zeman et al., 2022), or annotated according to UD's POS tagging scheme (UPOS). For some language varieties, we first make the data compatible with UPOS: We convert the tagsets used for the Arabic dialects and the Finnish dialects to UPOS (Appendix B). To process the Occitan data, we separate contractions (ADP+DET), similarly to the way these cases are handled in other Romance UD treebanks.[4] For the Norwegian dialects, we merge parallel data from the original corpus (dialect vs. orthographic transcriptions) with the orthography-only treebank to get a treebank with dialect transcriptions.[5]

3.2 PLMs

We use two multilingual PLMs: mBERT (Devlin et al., 2019) and XLM-R (Conneau et al., 2020a). Additionally, we include one monolingual model per source language. Both multilingual PLMs included all of our source languages in their pretraining data, and mBERT also contains two of our target languages (Low Saxon and Occitan). Details on the PLMs we used can be found in Appendix C.

We use *base*-size, cased versions of all models, and finetune the PLMs on the default training data subsets. We perform a simple grid search to choose one set of hyperparameters to be used for all experiments. This grid search was performed on the German (and Swiss German), Arabic (and Egyptian), and Finnish (and Savonian Finnish) data, using XLM-R and the respective monolingual models. Table 5 in Appendix C contains details on the hyperparameters.

4 Results and Discussion

All results we report are averaged over five different random initializations. Table 1 shows the accuracy scores of the inferred POS tags. We observe similar trends for the macro-averaged F1 score as well.

Zero-shot transfer. Performance on the unseen test languages/dialects is much lower than on the test partitions of the corpora on which the models were finetuned. This is expected, as there are not only orthographic and stylistic differences between the corpora, but also some grammatical differences between the language varieties.

The extent to which performance drops is language-dependent: For instance, the best results for the Finnish dialects are 12–17 percentage points below the best results for the Finnish standard language (XLM-R), whereas the best results for the

[4]E.g., `universaldependencies.org/fr/tokenization.html`

[5]The resulting scripts are available at `github.com/mainlp/{convert-qcri-4dialects, convert-la-murre, convert-restaure-occitan, UD_Norwegian-NynorskLIA_dialect}`.

Source	Target	Monolingual PLM						mBERT						XLM-R					
	Noise:	0	15	35	55	75	95	0	15	35	55	75	95	0	15	35	55	75	95
German	Alsatian G.	44	71	76	77	78	77	58	76	78	78	77	76	46	71	76	78	77	77
German	Swiss German	55	78	80	80	79	78	62	78	78	79	78	77	56	77	79	79	79	78
German	*German*	*98*	*98*	*98*	*98*	*98*	*98*	*98*	*98*	*98*	*98*	*98*	*98*	*98*	*98*	*98*	*98*	*98*	*98*
German	Low Saxon*	18	35	48	51	58	60	36	61	66	68	67	67	26	44	58	71	71	71
Dutch	Low Saxon*	52	62	63	64	64	63	73	75	75	75	73	72	63	71	73	73	73	72
Dutch	*Dutch*	*98*	*97*	*97*	*95*	*93*	*83*	*97*	*97*	*97*	*96*	*95*	*92*	*98*	*98*	*97*	*96*	*96*	*94*
Bokmål	East N.	35	60	67	65	62	60	57	60	58	57	56	54	66	63	63	62	61	59
Bokmål	North N.	36	63	69	67	65	62	61	61	61	60	60	58	70	66	66	65	64	62
Bokmål	West N.	33	59	66	63	61	59	58	57	56	55	54	53	67	62	61	60	59	57
Nynorsk	East N.	64	69	67	65	62	59	59	59	56	56	55	53	67	66	64	62	60	57
Nynorsk	North N.	67	72	69	68	65	63	62	61	59	60	59	57	71	68	67	66	64	62
Nynorsk	West N.	65	69	66	64	63	60	58	58	56	56	56	54	68	64	63	61	60	58
Bokmål	*Bokmål*	*99*	*98*	*98*	*97*	*96*	*91*	*98*	*98*	*97*	*97*	*96*	*92*	*99*	*98*	*98*	*98*	*97*	*93*
Nynorsk	*Nynorsk*	*98*	*98*	*97*	*97*	*95*	*90*	*97*	*97*	*96*	*96*	*94*	*90*	*98*	*97*	*97*	*96*	*95*	*92*
French	Picard	48	52	52	52	51	48	68	73	74	73	73	72	67	74	76	76	75	75
French	*French*	*89*	*88*	*86*	*83*	*78*	*66*	*98*	*98*	*97*	*97*	*96*	*93*	*98*	*98*	*98*	*98*	*97*	*94*
French	Occitan*	41	44	45	45	45	44	86	87	86	85	85	83	77	81	83	83	82	82
Spanish	Occitan*	62	69	70	69	69	69	83	84	83	82	81	79	72	79	78	79	78	77
Spanish	*Spanish*	*99*	*99*	*97*	*97*	*96*	*89*	*99*	*99*	*98*	*96*	*96*	*91*	*99*	*99*	*98*	*98*	*97*	*93*
MSA	Egyptian A.	67	70	66	62	57	50	59	61	60	58	54	47	64	66	65	62	57	50
MSA	Gulf Arabic	66	69	65	61	56	49	65	65	62	60	55	49	66	66	65	61	57	49
MSA	Levantine A.	64	65	62	58	53	47	56	57	55	53	50	45	59	61	60	57	53	46
MSA	Maghrebi A.	51	54	53	50	46	42	50	51	49	48	46	42	51	53	52	50	47	42
MSA	*MSA*	*94*	*93*	*89*	*83*	*78*	*67*	*96*	*95*	*91*	*85*	*79*	*69*	*96*	*95*	*91*	*86*	*80*	*70*
Finnish	Ostroboth. F.	81	80	79	77	78	75	78	78	76	74	73	70	81	85	86	86	86	84
Finnish	SE Finnish	81	79	77	75	76	73	75	75	73	70	69	66	81	84	84	84	84	82
Finnish	SW Finnish	75	73	72	71	71	70	68	68	67	64	63	61	76	80	80	81	81	79
Finnish	SW trans. area	79	78	77	76	76	74	72	72	70	68	67	65	79	84	84	85	84	83
Finnish	Savonian F.	82	80	78	76	76	73	77	79	76	73	72	69	81	84	85	85	85	83
Finnish	Tavastian F.	81	80	79	78	78	75	76	77	76	73	72	69	81	85	86	86	86	84
Finnish	*Finnish*	*98*	*98*	*98*	*97*	*96*	*94*	*96*	*96*	*96*	*95*	*94*	*93*	*98*	*97*	*97*	*97*	*96*	*94*

Table 1: **Accuracy scores (in %) by language combination, language model and noise level.** Scores are averaged over five initializations. Target languages marked with an asterisk* appear in the training data for mBERT. Rows *in italics* contain scores on the test splits of the datasets used for finetuning. The best accuracy for each language pair and PLM combination is underlined.

Norwegian dialects are 26–29 percentage points below the standard language accuracy (Nynorsk with NorBERT). When we have multiple target dialects for one source language, the target scores tend to be similar to one another across noise levels and PLM choices.

PLM choice matters for low-resource languages. While the models are for the most part indistinguishable in their performance on the source languages, the performance on the target languages can vary substantially. For instance, XLM-R outperforms mBERT and FinBERT on the Finnish dialect data. Similarly, both multilingual models perform much better than the monolingual models on the Low Saxon, Picard and Occitan data, and the reverse is true for the Arabic dialects. Neither the performance on the source languages nor the transfer performance with $n = 0$ reveal which model performs best on the target data when the ideal amount of noise is added.

Effect of noise level on accuracy. The optimal noise level depends on the language pair and on the PLM – there is no universal best noise level choice. In many (but not all) cases, the accuracy rises drastically when increasing the noise level from 0 % to 15 %, and the (positive or negative) differences between subsequent noise levels are less pronounced. The noise level of 15 % used by Aepli and Sennrich (2022) is thus a reasonable choice, although not always optimal. In some cases, the accuracy might be much greater at a different noise level (e.g., in the German→Low German XLM-R set-up the maximum gain compared to using no noise is +42 percentage points; +27 compared to 15 % noise). In other cases, adding any noise at all decreases the performance – most drastically in the case of Bokmål→West Norwegian with XLM-R, where the accuracy drops by 5 percentage points when using 15 % noise instead of no noise at all. However, the general trend is that accuracy as a function of noise has a single global maximum and no local maxima – there is a clear optimum level of noise in almost all cases.[6]

Performance on the standard language test splits from the corpora used for finetuning always decreases when noise is introduced. Whether this is detrimental depends on the language: the accuracy on the German test set only drops very slightly (less than one percentage point) whereas the quality of the tag predictions for MSA deteriorates considerably, independently of the model used.

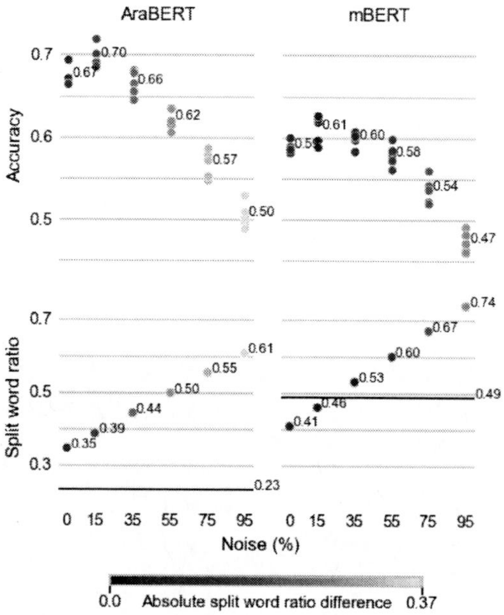

Figure 2: **Transfer from MSA to Egyptian Arabic with AraBERT (left) and mBERT (right).**
Top: Accuracy scores per language model and noise level (five initializations per set-up; the numbers in the scatterplot indicate the mean accuracy per set-up).
Bottom: Split word ratios per language model and noise level for the source data (dots) and the target data (dark blue lines) (five initializations per set-up). The colours indicate the (absolute) difference between the split word ratio of the training and target data (darker = smaller difference).

Effect of noise level on split word ratio difference. The words in the target data tend to be split into subword tokens more often than is the case for the source data.[7] Increasing the noise level during finetuning results in the source data being split into more subword tokens (see the rising sequences of dots in the lower part of Figure 2). In all set-ups, the split word ratio of the source data is higher than that of the target data when $n \geq 0.75$.

[6]The minor exceptions to this are FinBERT's performance on the Ostrobothnian and South-East Finnish data and XLM-R's predictions for the Spanish→Occitan transfer (see Table 1). In all of these cases, a second increase occurs after the maximum accuracy has already been reached and stays below this maximum.

[7]The exceptions to this are the tokenization of the Finnish dialects by the multilingual models and the tokenization of the Arabic dialects with AraBERT. The latter is likely due to AraBERT including a pre-tokenization step that splits words into stems and affixes (Antoun et al., 2020), but MSA and non-standard varieties of Arabic having morphological differences.

Src	Target	Monoling.		mBERT		XLM-R	
		ρ	p	ρ	p	ρ	p
Ger.	Als. G.	−0.84	0.00	−0.58	0.00	−0.68	0.00
Ger.	Swiss G.	−0.82	0.00	−0.74	0.00	−0.31	0.10
Ger.	*German*	−0.69	0.00	−0.74	0.00	−0.70	0.00
Ger.	L. Saxon	−0.75	0.00	0.37	0.05	0.44	0.02
Dutch	L. Saxon	−0.84	0.00	−0.71	0.00	−0.50	0.01
Dutch	*Dutch*	−0.89	0.00	−0.88	0.00	−0.91	0.00
Bokm.	East N.	−0.72	0.00	−0.75	0.00	−0.62	0.00
Bokm.	North N.	−0.69	0.00	−0.70	0.00	−0.68	0.00
Bokm.	West N.	−0.75	0.00	−0.85	0.00	−0.72	0.00
Nynor.	East N.	−0.70	0.00	−0.88	0.00	−0.94	0.00
Nynor.	North N.	−0.68	0.00	−0.79	0.00	−0.94	0.00
Nynor.	West N.	−0.64	0.00	−0.85	0.00	−0.95	0.00
Bokm.	*Bokm.*	−0.95	0.00	−0.96	0.00	−0.96	0.00
Nynor.	*Nynor.*	−0.97	0.00	−0.98	0.00	−0.98	0.00
French	Picard	−0.45	0.01	−0.82	0.00	−0.86	0.00
French	*French*	−0.99	0.00	−0.90	0.00	−0.97	0.00
French	Occitan	−0.76	0.00	−0.45	0.01	−0.40	0.03
Spa.	Occitan	−0.64	0.00	−0.38	0.04	−0.71	0.00
Spa.	*Spanish*	−0.95	0.00	−0.95	0.00	−0.97	0.00
MSA	Egy. A.	−0.88	0.00	−0.91	0.00	−0.90	0.00
MSA	Gulf A.	−0.89	0.00	−0.95	0.00	−0.89	0.00
MSA	Lev. A.	−0.91	0.00	−0.87	0.00	−0.83	0.00
MSA	Mag. A.	−0.72	0.00	−0.70	0.00	−0.82	0.00
MSA	*MSA*	−0.96	0.00	−0.96	0.00	−0.96	0.00
Fin.	Ost. F.	−0.46	0.01	−0.90	0.00	0.30	0.11
Fin.	SE F.	−0.71	0.00	−0.93	0.00	0.21	0.27
Fin.	SW F.	−0.09	0.63	−0.94	0.00	0.29	0.12
Fin.	SW tr.	−0.40	0.03	−0.94	0.00	0.27	0.15
Fin.	Sav. F.	−0.68	0.00	−0.89	0.00	0.24	0.20
Fin.	Tav. F.	−0.71	0.00	−0.89	0.00	0.34	0.07
Fin.	*Finnish*	−0.95	0.00	−0.96	0.00	−0.96	0.00

Table 2: **Correlation between split word ratio difference and accuracy.** Spearman's ρ with p-values for all noise levels and random initializations per language pair and PLM. Negative correlations are highlighted in blue, positive ones in yellow. P-values of 0.05 and above have a grey background.

Effect of split word ratio difference on accuracy. Out of the subword tokenization measures introduced in Section 2.2, the *split word ratio difference* correlates most consistently with the performance: the smaller the difference is (i.e., the more similar the ratios are), the higher the accuracy tends to be (Table 2). Figure 2 shows an example; note that the correlation is stronger for the model on the right-hand side (mBERT) than for the model on the left (AraBERT).

The correlation is strong enough that, if one really wants to avoid including the noise level in a hyperparameter search, only carrying out the cheap calculations needed for the *split word ratio difference* and choosing the noise level with the lowest difference can be a proxy. Nevertheless, the correlation is not perfect and this method does not necessarily pick the best noise level.

4.1 Additional Findings

The role of seen (sub)words. Adding noise to the source data initially increases the word and subword token overlap with the target data for all cross-lingual/cross-dialectal set-ups, regardless of model choice. As the noise level increases, this trend ultimately reverses, although the source and target data still have a greater (sub)word overlap at $n = 0.95$ than at $n = 0$.

The seen word ratio and seen subword ratio are much poorer predictors for the model performance than the split word ratio difference is. They are much less consistent and correlate positively with accuracy for many set-ups but negatively for many others, and the correlations tend to have larger p-values (see Tables 6 and 7 in Appendix D for details). While prior works have come to conflicting conclusions regarding the importance of subword token overlap for transfer between more distantly related (or unrelated) languages (Wu and Dredze, 2019; Pires et al., 2019; K et al., 2020; Conneau et al., 2020b; Muller et al., 2022), we find that it is a very poor predictor for the transfer between very closely related languages when injecting character-level noise. One possibility for this is that the seen target subwords contained in the noisy source data might not necessarily belong to the same POS classes.

The role of TTR ratio. For most set-ups, the TTR ratio initially decreases before ultimately increasing, with no local minima. In all of our experiments, the TTR ratio either always stays above one (the target data's TTR remains higher than that of the source data) or always below one (the source data's TTR stays higher than that of the target data; this is only the case for the cross-dialected Finnish set-ups) – adding noise does not result in bringing the TTRs to a similar level. The TTR ratio correlates positively with accuracy for some set-ups and negatively with others (see Table 8 in Appendix D). This overall very weak predictive capacity of the TTR ratio is similar to what Muller et al. (2022) find for named entity recognition and in line with Lin et al.'s (2019) results for POS tagging – their TTR-based measure is only a useful performance predictor when used in conjunction with other measures.

5 Conclusion

We have confirmed the usefulness of the noise injection method by Aepli and Sennrich (2022) for model transfer between closely related languages. To that end, we have converted additional dialectal datasets to the UPOS standard and make the conversion code available to other researchers. Furthermore, we have shown that the ideal amount of noise that should be injected at finetuning time depends on the languages and PLMs used. We have also investigated the role that subword tokenization plays in this and found that the *split word ratio difference* – the (absolute) difference between the proportion of words split into subword tokens in the source and target data – is a reliable, albeit imperfect, predictor of the performance of the transfer model.

Limitations

We include data from three linguistic families, as we were not able to find additional accessible high-quality dialect datasets manually annotated with POS tags for more linguistic families. This general lack of annotated resources is also why we were only able to focus on one NLP task. The tagsets for the Arabic and Finnish varieties were converted to UPOS by a linguist who is not a specialist of Arabic or Finnish.

We only consider one way of modifying the tokenization. In future research, it would be interesting to also consider BPE dropout (Provilkov et al., 2020), which Aepli and Sennrich (2022) show to have an effect on transfer between related languages that is somewhat similar to that of noise injection. It would also be of interest to investigate token-free models like ByT5 (Xue et al., 2022) or CharacterBERT (El Boukkouri et al., 2020), the latter of which has proven useful for processing data in a non-standard variety of Arabic (Riabi et al., 2021).

Acknowledgements

We thank the members of the MaiNLP research group as well as the anonymous reviewers for their useful feedback. This research is supported by European Research Council (ERC) Consolidator Grant DIALECT 101043235. This work was partially funded by the ERC under the European Union's Horizon 2020 research and innovation program (grant 740516).

References

Noëmi Aepli and Rico Sennrich. 2022. Improving zero-shot cross-lingual transfer between closely related languages by injecting character-level noise. In *Findings of the Association for Computational Linguistics: ACL 2022*, pages 4074–4083, Dublin, Ireland. Association for Computational Linguistics.

Wissam Antoun, Fady Baly, and Hazem Hajj. 2020. AraBERT: Transformer-based model for Arabic language understanding. In *Proceedings of the 4th Workshop on Open-Source Arabic Corpora and Processing Tools, with a Shared Task on Offensive Language Detection*, pages 9–15, Marseille, France. European Language Resource Association.

Delphine Bernhard, Pascale Erhart, Dominique Huck, and Lucie Steiblé. 2019. Annotated corpus for the Alsatian dialects. Version 2.0.

Delphine Bernhard, Anne-Laure Ligozat, Fanny Martin, Myriam Bras, Pierre Magistry, Marianne Vergez-Couret, Lucie Steiblé, Pascale Erhart, Nabil Hathout, Dominique Huck, Christophe Rey, Philippe Reynés, Sophie Rosset, Jean Sibille, and Thomas Lavergne. 2018. Corpora with part-of-speech annotations for three regional languages of France: Alsatian, Occitan and Picard. In *Proceedings of the Eleventh International Conference on Language Resources and Evaluation (LREC 2018)*, Miyazaki, Japan. European Language Resources Association (ELRA).

Emanuel Borges Völker, Maximilian Wendt, Felix Hennig, and Arne Köhn. 2019. HDT-UD: A very large Universal Dependencies treebank for German. In *Proceedings of the Third Workshop on Universal Dependencies (UDW, SyntaxFest 2019)*, pages 46–57, Paris, France. Association for Computational Linguistics.

Gosse Bouma and Gertjan van Noord. 2017. Increasing return on annotation investment: The automatic construction of a Universal Dependency treebank for Dutch. In *Proceedings of the NoDaLiDa 2017 Workshop on Universal Dependencies (UDW 2017)*, pages 19–26, Gothenburg, Sweden. Association for Computational Linguistics.

Myriam Bras, Louise Esher, Jean Sibille, and Marianne Vergez-Couret. 2018. Annotated corpus for Occitan. Version 1.0.

Kristen E. Brustad. 2000. *The syntax of spoken Arabic.* Georgetown University Press, Washington, D.C., USA.

José Cañete, Gabriel Chaperon, Rodrigo Fuentes, Jou-Hui Ho, Hojin Kang, and Jorge Pérez. 2020. Spanish pre-trained BERT model and evaluation data. In *Proceedings of the Practical Machine Learning for Developing Countries Workshop*.

Branden Chan, Stefan Schweter, and Timo Möller. 2020. German's next language model. In *Proceedings of the 28th International Conference on Computational*

Linguistics, pages 6788–6796, Barcelona, Spain (Online). International Committee on Computational Linguistics.

Alexis Conneau, Kartikay Khandelwal, Naman Goyal, Vishrav Chaudhary, Guillaume Wenzek, Francisco Guzmán, Edouard Grave, Myle Ott, Luke Zettlemoyer, and Veselin Stoyanov. 2020a. Unsupervised cross-lingual representation learning at scale. In *Proceedings of the 58th Annual Meeting of the Association for Computational Linguistics*, pages 8440–8451, Online. Association for Computational Linguistics.

Alexis Conneau, Shijie Wu, Haoran Li, Luke Zettlemoyer, and Veselin Stoyanov. 2020b. Emerging cross-lingual structure in pretrained language models. In *Proceedings of the 58th Annual Meeting of the Association for Computational Linguistics*, pages 6022–6034, Online. Association for Computational Linguistics.

Kareem Darwish, Ahmed Abdelali, and Hamdy Mubarak. 2014. Using stem-templates to improve Arabic POS and gender/number tagging. In *Proceedings of the Ninth International Conference on Language Resources and Evaluation (LREC'14)*, pages 2926–2931, Reykjavik, Iceland. European Language Resources Association (ELRA).

Kareem Darwish, Hamdy Mubarak, Ahmed Abdelali, Mohamed Eldesouki, Younes Samih, Randah Alharbi, Mohammed Attia, Walid Magdy, and Laura Kallmeyer. 2018. Multi-dialect Arabic POS tagging: A CRF approach. In *Proceedings of the Eleventh International Conference on Language Resources and Evaluation (LREC 2018)*, Miyazaki, Japan. European Language Resources Association (ELRA).

Wietse de Vries, Andreas van Cranenburgh, Arianna Bisazza, Tommaso Caselli, Gertjan van Noord, and Malvina Nissim. 2019. BERTje: A Dutch BERT model. *Computing Research Repository*, arXiv:1912.09582.

Jacob Devlin, Ming-Wei Chang, Kenton Lee, and Kristina Toutanova. 2019. BERT: Pre-training of deep bidirectional transformers for language understanding. In *Proceedings of the 2019 Conference of the North American Chapter of the Association for Computational Linguistics: Human Language Technologies, Volume 1 (Long and Short Papers)*, pages 4171–4186, Minneapolis, Minnesota. Association for Computational Linguistics.

Hicham El Boukkouri, Olivier Ferret, Thomas Lavergne, Hiroshi Noji, Pierre Zweigenbaum, and Jun'ichi Tsujii. 2020. CharacterBERT: Reconciling ELMo and BERT for word-level open-vocabulary representations from characters. In *Proceedings of the 28th International Conference on Computational Linguistics*, pages 6903–6915, Barcelona, Spain (Online). International Committee on Computational Linguistics.

William Falcon and The PyTorch Lightning team. 2022. PyTorch Lightning.

Kilian A. Foth, Arne Köhn, Niels Beuck, and Wolfgang Menzel. 2014. Because size does matter: The Hamburg Dependency Treebank. In *Proceedings of the Ninth International Conference on Language Resources and Evaluation (LREC'14)*, pages 2326–2333, Reykjavik, Iceland. European Language Resources Association (ELRA).

Bruno Guillaume, Marie-Catherine de Marneffe, and Guy Perrier. 2019. Conversion et améliorations de corpus du français annotés en Universal Dependencies. *Revue TAL*, 60(2):71–95.

Jan Hajič, Otakar Smrž, Petr Zemánek, Petr Pajas, Jan Šnaidauf, Emanuel Beška, Jakub Kracmar, and Kamila Hassanová. 2009. Prague Arabic dependency treebank 1.0. LINDAT/CLARIAH-CZ digital library at the Institute of Formal and Applied Linguistics (ÚFAL), Faculty of Mathematics and Physics, Charles University.

Katri Haverinen, Jenna Nyblom, Timo Viljanen, Veronika Laippala, Samuel Kohonen, Anna Missilä, Stina Ojala, Tapio Salakoski, and Filip Ginter. 2014. Building the essential resources for Finnish: the Turku Dependency Treebank. *Language Resources and Evaluation*, 48:493–531. Open access.

Nora Hollenstein and Noëmi Aepli. 2014. Compilation of a Swiss German dialect corpus and its application to PoS tagging. In *Proceedings of the First Workshop on Applying NLP Tools to Similar Languages, Varieties and Dialects*, pages 85–94, Dublin, Ireland. Association for Computational Linguistics and Dublin City University.

Ernst Håkon Jahr. 1996. Dialektane i indre Troms: Bardu og Målselv. In Ernst Håkon Jahr and Olav Skare, editors, *Nordnorske dialektar*, pages 180–184. Novus forlag, Oslo.

Karthikeyan K, Zihan Wang, Stephen Mayhew, and Dan Roth. 2020. Cross-lingual ability of multilingual BERT: an empirical study. In *8th International Conference on Learning Representations (ICLR 2020)*.

Andrey Kutuzov, Jeremy Barnes, Erik Velldal, Lilja Øvrelid, and Stephan Oepen. 2021. Large-scale contextualised language modelling for Norwegian. In *Proceedings of the 23rd Nordic Conference on Computational Linguistics (NoDaLiDa)*, pages 30–40, Reykjavik, Iceland (Online). Linköping University Electronic Press, Sweden.

Yu-Hsiang Lin, Chian-Yu Chen, Jean Lee, Zirui Li, Yuyan Zhang, Mengzhou Xia, Shruti Rijhwani, Junxian He, Zhisong Zhang, Xuezhe Ma, Antonios Anastasopoulos, Patrick Littell, and Graham Neubig. 2019. Choosing transfer languages for cross-lingual learning. In *Proceedings of the 57th Annual Meeting of the Association for Computational Linguistics*, pages 3125–3135, Florence, Italy. Association for Computational Linguistics.

Fanny Martin, Christophe Rey, and Philippe Reynés. 2018. Annotated corpus for Picard. Version 4.0.

Louis Martin, Benjamin Muller, Pedro Javier Ortiz Suárez, Yoann Dupont, Laurent Romary, Éric de la Clergerie, Djamé Seddah, and Benoît Sagot. 2020. CamemBERT: a tasty French language model. In *Proceedings of the 58th Annual Meeting of the Association for Computational Linguistics*, pages 7203–7219, Online. Association for Computational Linguistics.

Benjamin Muller, Deepanshu Gupta, Siddharth Patwardhan, Jean-Philippe Fauconnier, David Vandyke, and Sachin Agarwal. 2022. Languages you know influence those you learn: Impact of language characteristics on multi-lingual text-to-text transfer. *Computing Research Repository*, arXiv:2212.01757.

Lilja Øvrelid and Petter Hohle. 2016. Universal Dependencies for Norwegian. In *Proceedings of the Tenth International Conference on Language Resources and Evaluation (LREC'16)*, pages 1579–1585, Portorož, Slovenia. European Language Resources Association (ELRA).

Lilja Øvrelid, Andre Kåsen, Kristin Hagen, Anders Nøklestad, Per Erik Solberg, and Janne Bondi Johannessen. 2018. The LIA treebank of spoken Norwegian dialects. In *Proceedings of the Eleventh International Conference on Language Resources and Evaluation (LREC 2018)*, Miyazaki, Japan. European Language Resources Association (ELRA).

Adam Paszke, Sam Gross, Francisco Massa, Adam Lerer, James Bradbury, Gregory Chanan, Trevor Killeen, Zeming Lin, Natalia Gimelshein, Luca Antiga, Alban Desmaison, Andreas Kopf, Edward Yang, Zachary DeVito, Martin Raison, Alykhan Tejani, Sasank Chilamkurthy, Benoit Steiner, Lu Fang, Junjie Bai, and Soumith Chintala. 2019. PyTorch: An imperative style, high-performance deep learning library. In *Advances in Neural Information Processing Systems 32 (NeurIPS 2019)*. Curran Associates, Inc.

Telmo Pires, Eva Schlinger, and Dan Garrette. 2019. How multilingual is multilingual BERT? In *Proceedings of the 57th Annual Meeting of the Association for Computational Linguistics*, pages 4996–5001, Florence, Italy. Association for Computational Linguistics.

Ivan Provilkov, Dmitrii Emelianenko, and Elena Voita. 2020. BPE-dropout: Simple and effective subword regularization. In *Proceedings of the 58th Annual Meeting of the Association for Computational Linguistics*, pages 1882–1892, Online. Association for Computational Linguistics.

Sampo Pyysalo, Jenna Kanerva, Anna Missilä, Veronika Laippala, and Filip Ginter. 2015. Universal Dependencies for Finnish. In *Proceedings of NoDaLiDa 2015*, pages 163–172. NEALT.

Arij Riabi, Benoît Sagot, and Djamé Seddah. 2021. Can character-based language models improve downstream task performances in low-resource and noisy language scenarios? In *Proceedings of the Seventh Workshop on Noisy User-generated Text (W-NUT 2021)*, pages 423–436, Online. Association for Computational Linguistics.

Karin C. Ryding. 2005. *A Reference Grammar for Modern Standard Arabic*. Cambridge University Press, Cambridge, UK.

Manuela Sanguinetti, Cristina Bosco, Lauren Cassidy, Özlem Çetinoğlu, Alessandra Teresa Cignarella, Teresa Lynn, Iris Rehbein, Josef Ruppenhofer, Djamé Seddah, and Amir Zeldes. 2022. Treebanking user-generated content: a UD based overview of guidelines, corpora and unified recommendations. *Language Resources and Evaluation*.

Janine Siewert, Yves Scherrer, and Jörg Tiedemann. 2021. Towards a balanced annotated Low Saxon dataset for diachronic investigation of dialectal variation. In *Proceedings of the 17th Conference on Natural Language Processing (KONVENS 2021)*, pages 242–246, Düsseldorf, Germany. KONVENS 2021 Organizers.

Per Erik Solberg, Arne Skjærholt, Lilja Øvrelid, Kristin Hagen, and Janne Bondi Johannessen. 2014. The Norwegian dependency treebank. In *Proceedings of the Ninth International Conference on Language Resources and Evaluation (LREC'14)*, pages 789–795, Reykjavik, Iceland. European Language Resources Association (ELRA).

Mariona Taulé, M. Antònia Martí, and Marta Recasens. 2008. AnCora: Multilevel annotated corpora for Catalan and Spanish. In *Proceedings of the Sixth International Conference on Language Resources and Evaluation (LREC'08)*, Marrakech, Morocco. European Language Resources Association (ELRA).

Samia Touileb and Jeremy Barnes. 2021. The interplay between language similarity and script on a novel multi-layer Algerian dialect corpus. In *Findings of the Association for Computational Linguistics: ACL-IJCNLP 2021*, pages 3700–3712, Online. Association for Computational Linguistics.

University of Turku and Institute for the Languages of Finland. The Finnish dialect corpus of the Syntax Archive, downloadable VRT version.

Leonoor van der Beek, Gosse Bouma, Robert Malouf, and Gertjan van Noord. 2002. The Alpino dependency treebank. In *Computational Linguistics in der Netherlands 2001*, Language and Computers: Studies in Practical Linguistics, pages 8–22. Rodopi.

Erik Velldal, Lilja Øvrelid, and Petter Hohle. 2017. Joint UD parsing of Norwegian Bokmål and nynorsk. In *Proceedings of the 21st Nordic Conference on Computational Linguistics*, pages 1–10, Gothenburg, Sweden. Association for Computational Linguistics.

Antti Virtanen, Jenna Kanerva, Rami Ilo, Jouni Luoma, Juhani Luotolahti, Tapio Salakoski, Filip Ginter, and Sampo Pyysalo. 2019. Multilingual is not enough: BERT for Finnish. *Computing Research Repository*, arXiv:1912.07076.

Thomas Wolf, Lysandre Debut, Victor Sanh, Julien Chaumond, Clement Delangue, Anthony Moi, Pierric Cistac, Tim Rault, Remi Louf, Morgan Funtowicz, Joe Davison, Sam Shleifer, Patrick von Platen, Clara Ma, Yacine Jernite, Julien Plu, Canwen Xu, Teven Le Scao, Sylvain Gugger, Mariama Drame, Quentin Lhoest, and Alexander Rush. 2020. Transformers: State-of-the-art natural language processing. In *Proceedings of the 2020 Conference on Empirical Methods in Natural Language Processing: System Demonstrations*, pages 38–45, Online. Association for Computational Linguistics.

Shijie Wu and Mark Dredze. 2019. Beto, bentz, becas: The surprising cross-lingual effectiveness of BERT. In *Proceedings of the 2019 Conference on Empirical Methods in Natural Language Processing and the 9th International Joint Conference on Natural Language Processing (EMNLP-IJCNLP)*, pages 833–844, Hong Kong, China. Association for Computational Linguistics.

Linting Xue, Aditya Barua, Noah Constant, Rami Al-Rfou, Sharan Narang, Mihir Kale, Adam Roberts, and Colin Raffel. 2022. ByT5: Towards a token-free future with pre-trained byte-to-byte models. *Transactions of the Association for Computational Linguistics*, 10:291–306.

Daniel Zeman, Joakim Nivre, Mitchell Abrams, Elia Ackermann, Noëmi Aepli, Hamid Aghaei, Željko Agić, Amir Ahmadi, Lars Ahrenberg, Chika Kennedy Ajede, Salih Furkan Akkurt, Gabrielė Aleksandravičiūtė, Ika Alfina, Avner Algom, Chiara Alzetta, Erik Andersen, Lene Antonsen, Katya Aplonova, Angelina Aquino, Carolina Aragon, Glyd Aranes, Maria Jesus Aranzabe, Bilge Nas Arıcan, Þórunn Arnardóttir, Gashaw Arutie, Jessica Naraiswari Arwidarasti, Masayuki Asahara, Katla Ásgeirsdóttir, Deniz Baran Aslan, Cengiz Asmazoğlu, Luma Ateyah, Furkan Atmaca, Mohammed Attia, Aitziber Atutxa, Liesbeth Augustinus, Elena Badmaeva, Keerthana Balasubramani, Miguel Ballesteros, Esha Banerjee, Sebastian Bank, Verginica Barbu Mititelu, Starkaður Barkarson, Rodolfo Basile, Victoria Basmov, Colin Batchelor, John Bauer, Seyyit Talha Bedir, Juan Belieni, Kepa Bengoetxea, Yifat Ben Moshe, Gözde Berk, Yevgeni Berzak, Irshad Ahmad Bhat, Riyaz Ahmad Bhat, Erica Biagetti, Eckhard Bick, Agnė Bielinskienė, Kristín Bjarnadóttir, Rogier Blokland, Victoria Bobicev, Loïc Boizou, Emanuel Borges Völker, Carl Börstell, Cristina Bosco, Gosse Bouma, Sam Bowman, Adriane Boyd, Anouck Braggaar, Kristina Brokaitė, Aljoscha Burchardt, Marie Candito, Bernard Caron, Gauthier Caron, Lauren Cassidy, Maria Clara Castro, Tatiana Cavalcanti, Gülşen Cebiroğlu Eryiğit, Flavio Massimiliano Cecchini, Giuseppe G. A. Celano, Slavomír Čéplö, Neslihan Cesur, Savas Cetin, Özlem Çetinoğlu, Fabricio Chalub, Liyanage Chamila, Shweta Chauhan, Ethan Chi, Taishi Chika, Yongseok Cho, Jinho Choi, Jayeol Chun, Juyeon Chung, Alessandra T. Cignarella, Silvie Cinková, Aurélie Collomb, Çağrı Çöltekin, Miriam Connor, Daniela Corbetta, Marine Courtin, Mihaela Cristescu, Philemon Daniel, Elizabeth Davidson, Leonel Figueiredo de Alencar, Mathieu Dehouck, Martina de Laurentiis, Marie-Catherine de Marneffe, Valeria de Paiva, Mehmet Oguz Derin, Elvis de Souza, Arantza Diaz de Ilarraza, Carly Dickerson, Arawinda Dinakaramani, Elisa Di Nuovo, Bamba Dione, Peter Dirix, Kaja Dobrovoljc, Timothy Dozat, Kira Droganova, Puneet Dwivedi, Christian Ebert, Hanne Eckhoff, Sandra Eiche, Marhaba Eli, Ali Elkahky, Binyam Ephrem, Olga Erina, Tomaž Erjavec, Aline Etienne, Wograine Evelyn, Sidney Facundes, Richárd Farkas, Federica Favero, Jannatul Ferdaousi, Marília Fernanda, Hector Fernandez Alcalde, Jennifer Foster, Cláudia Freitas, Kazunori Fujita, Katarína Gajdošová, Daniel Galbraith, Federica Gamba, Marcos Garcia, Moa Gärdenfors, Sebastian Garza, Fabrício Ferraz Gerardi, Kim Gerdes, Filip Ginter, Gustavo Godoy, Iakes Goenaga, Koldo Gojenola, Memduh Gökırmak, Yoav Goldberg, Xavier Gómez Guinovart, Berta González Saavedra, Bernadeta Griciūtė, Matias Grioni, Loïc Grobol, Normunds Grūzītis, Bruno Guillaume, Céline Guillot-Barbance, Tunga Güngör, Nizar Habash, Hinrik Hafsteinsson, Jan Hajič, Jan Hajič jr., Mika Hämäläinen, Linh Hà Mỹ, Na-Rae Han, Muhammad Yudistira Hanifmuti, Takahiro Harada, Sam Hardwick, Kim Harris, Dag Haug, Johannes Heinecke, Oliver Hellwig, Felix Hennig, Barbora Hladká, Jaroslava Hlaváčová, Florinel Hociung, Petter Hohle, Marivel Huerta Mendez, Jena Hwang, Takumi Ikeda, Anton Karl Ingason, Radu Ion, Elena Irimia, Ọlájídé Ishola, Artan Islamaj, Kaoru Ito, Siratun Jannat, Tomáš Jelínek, Apoorva Jha, Katharine Jiang, Anders Johannsen, Hildur Jónsdóttir, Fredrik Jørgensen, Markus Juutinen, Hüner Kaşıkara, Andre Kaasen, Nadezhda Kabaeva, Sylvain Kahane, Hiroshi Kanayama, Jenna Kanerva, Neslihan Kara, Ritván Karahóğa, Boris Katz, Tolga Kayadelen, Sarveswaran Kengatharaiyer, Jessica Kenney, Václava Kettnerová, Jesse Kirchner, Elena Klementieva, Elena Klyachko, Arne Köhn, Abdullatif Köksal, Kamil Kopacewicz, Timo Korkiakangas, Mehmet Köse, Alexey Koshevoy, Natalia Kotsyba, Jolanta Kovalevskaitė, Simon Krek, Parameswari Krishnamurthy, Sandra Kübler, Adrian Kuqi, Oğuzhan Kuyrukçu, Aslı Kuzgun, Sookyoung Kwak, Veronika Laippala, Lucia Lam, Lorenzo Lambertino, Tatiana Lando, Septina Dian Larasati, Alexei Lavrentiev, John Lee, Phương Lê Hồng, Alessandro Lenci, Saran Lertpradit, Herman Leung, Maria Levina, Cheuk Ying Li, Josie Li, Keying Li, Yixuan Li, Yuan Li, KyungTae Lim, Bruna Lima Padovani, Krister Lindén, Nikola Ljubešić, Olga Loginova, Stefano Lusito, Andry Luthfi, Mikko Luukko, Olga Lyashevskaya, Teresa Lynn, Vivien Macketanz, Menel Mahamdi, Jean Maillard, Ilya Makarchuk, Aibek Makazhanov, Michael Mandl, Christopher Manning,

Ruli Manurung, Büşra Marşan, Cătălina Mărănduc, David Mareček, Katrin Marheinecke, Stella Markantonatou, Héctor Martínez Alonso, Lorena Martín Rodríguez, André Martins, Jan Mašek, Hiroshi Matsuda, Yuji Matsumoto, Alessandro Mazzei, Ryan McDonald, Sarah McGuinness, Gustavo Mendonça, Tatiana Merzhevich, Niko Miekka, Karina Mischenkova, Margarita Misirpashayeva, Anna Missilä, Cătălin Mititelu, Maria Mitrofan, Yusuke Miyao, AmirHossein Mojiri Foroushani, Judit Molnár, Amirsaeid Moloodi, Simonetta Montemagni, Amir More, Laura Moreno Romero, Giovanni Moretti, Keiko Sophie Mori, Shinsuke Mori, Tomohiko Morioka, Shigeki Moro, Bjartur Mortensen, Bohdan Moskalevskyi, Kadri Muischnek, Robert Munro, Yugo Murawaki, Kaili Müürisep, Pinkey Nainwani, Mariam Nakhlé, Juan Ignacio Navarro Horñiacek, Anna Nedoluzhko, Gunta Nešpore-Bērzkalne, Manuela Nevaci, Lương Nguyễn Thị, Huyền Nguyễn Thị Minh, Yoshihiro Nikaido, Vitaly Nikolaev, Rattima Nitisaroj, Alireza Nourian, Hanna Nurmi, Stina Ojala, Atul Kr. Ojha, Hulda Óladóttir, Adédayọ̀ Olúòkun, Mai Omura, Emeka Onwuegbuzia, Noam Ordan, Petya Osenova, Robert Östling, Lilja Øvrelid, Şaziye Betül Özateş, Merve Özçelik, Arzucan Özgür, Balkız Öztürk Başaran, Teresa Paccosi, Alessio Palmero Aprosio, Anastasia Panova, Hyunji Hayley Park, Niko Partanen, Elena Pascual, Marco Passarotti, Agnieszka Patejuk, Guilherme Paulino-Passos, Giulia Pedonese, Angelika Peljak-Łapińska, Siyao Peng, Cenel-Augusto Perez, Natalia Perkova, Guy Perrier, Slav Petrov, Daria Petrova, Andrea Peverelli, Jason Phelan, Jussi Piitulainen, Rodrigo Pintucci, Tommi A Pirinen, Emily Pitler, Magdalena Plamada, Barbara Plank, Thierry Poibeau, Larisa Ponomareva, Martin Popel, Lauma Pretkalniņa, Sophie Prévost, Prokopis Prokopidis, Adam Przepiórkowski, Robert Pugh, Tiina Puolakainen, Sampo Pyysalo, Peng Qi, Andriela Rääbis, Alexandre Rademaker, Mizanur Rahoman, Taraka Rama, Loganathan Ramasamy, Carlos Ramisch, Fam Rashel, Mohammad Sadegh Rasooli, Vinit Ravishankar, Livy Real, Petru Rebeja, Siva Reddy, Mathilde Regnault, Georg Rehm, Ivan Riabov, Michael Rießler, Erika Rimkutė, Larissa Rinaldi, Laura Rituma, Putri Rizqiyah, Luisa Rocha, Eiríkur Rögnvaldsson, Ivan Roksandic, Mykhailo Romanenko, Rudolf Rosa, Valentin Roșca, Davide Rovati, Ben Rozonoyer, Olga Rudina, Jack Rueter, Kristján Rúnarsson, Shoval Sadde, Pegah Safari, Benoît Sagot, Aleksi Sahala, Shadi Saleh, Alessio Salomoni, Tanja Samardžić, Stephanie Samson, Manuela Sanguinetti, Ezgi Sanıyar, Dage Särg, Marta Sartor, Mitsuya Sasaki, Baiba Saulīte, Yanin Sawanakunanon, Shefali Saxena, Kevin Scannell, Salvatore Scarlata, Nathan Schneider, Sebastian Schuster, Lane Schwartz, Djamé Seddah, Wolfgang Seeker, Mojgan Seraji, Syeda Shahzadi, Mo Shen, Atsuko Shimada, Hiroyuki Shirasu, Yana Shishkina, Muh Shohibussirri, Maria Shvedova, Janine Siewert, Einar Freyr Sigurðsson, João Ricardo Silva, Aline Silveira, Natalia Silveira, Maria Simi, Radu Simionescu, Katalin Simkó, Mária Šimková, Haukur Barri Símonarson, Kiril Simov, Dmitri Sitchinava, Maria Skachedubova, Aaron Smith, Isabela Soares-Bastos, Barbara Sonnenhauser, Shafi Sourov, Carolyn Spadine, Rachele Sprugnoli, Vivian Stamou, Steinþór Steingrímsson, Antonio Stella, Abishek Stephen, Milan Straka, Emmett Strickland, Jana Strnadová, Alane Suhr, Yogi Lesmana Sulestio, Umut Sulubacak, Shingo Suzuki, Daniel Swanson, Zsolt Szántó, Chihiro Taguchi, Dima Taji, Yuta Takahashi, Fabio Tamburini, Mary Ann C. Tan, Takaaki Tanaka, Dipta Tanaya, Mirko Tavoni, Samson Tella, Isabelle Tellier, Marinella Testori, Guillaume Thomas, Sara Tonelli, Liisi Torga, Marsida Toska, Trond Trosterud, Anna Trukhina, Reut Tsarfaty, Utku Türk, Francis Tyers, Sveinbjörn Þórðarson, Vilhjálmur Þorsteinsson, Sumire Uematsu, Roman Untilov, Zdeňka Urešová, Larraitz Uria, Hans Uszkoreit, Andrius Utka, Elena Vagnoni, Sowmya Vajjala, Rob van der Goot, Martine Vanhove, Daniel van Niekerk, Gertjan van Noord, Viktor Varga, Uliana Vedenina, Giulia Venturi, Eric Villemonte de la Clergerie, Veronika Vincze, Natalia Vlasova, Aya Wakasa, Joel C. Wallenberg, Lars Wallin, Abigail Walsh, Jing Xian Wang, Jonathan North Washington, Maximilan Wendt, Paul Widmer, Shira Wigderson, Sri Hartati Wijono, Vanessa Berwanger Wille, Seyi Williams, Mats Wirén, Christian Wittern, Tsegay Woldemariam, Tak-sum Wong, Alina Wróblewska, Mary Yako, Kayo Yamashita, Naoki Yamazaki, Chunxiao Yan, Koichi Yasuoka, Marat M. Yavrumyan, Arife Betül Yenice, Olcay Taner Yıldız, Zhuoran Yu, Arlisa Yuliawati, Zdeněk Žabokrtský, Shorouq Zahra, Amir Zeldes, He Zhou, Hanzhi Zhu, Anna Zhuravleva, and Rayan Ziane. 2022. Universal Dependencies 2.11. LINDAT/CLARIAH-CZ digital library at the Institute of Formal and Applied Linguistics (ÚFAL), Faculty of Mathematics and Physics, Charles University.

A Dataset Details

These are the datasets we use in this study:

- Modern Standard Arabic: UD Arabic PADT (Hajič et al., 2009) – CC BY-NC-SA 3.0 – `github.com/UniversalDependencies/UD_Arabic-PADT`
- Egyptian, Levantine, Gulf and Maghrebi Arabic: QCRI Dialectal Arabic Resources (Darwish et al., 2018) – Apache License 2.0 – `alt.qcri.org/resources/da_resources`
- German: UD German HDT (Borges Völker et al., 2019; Foth et al., 2014) – CC BY-SA 4.0 – `github.com/UniversalDependencies/UD_German-HDT`
- Swiss German: NOAH v 3.0 (UPOS-tagged subset) (Hollenstein and Aepli, 2014; Aepli and Sennrich, 2022) – CC BY 4.0 – `github.com/noe-eva/NOAH-Corpus`

- Alsatian German: Annotated Corpus for the Alsatian Dialects (Bernhard et al., 2019, 2018) – CC BY-SA 4.0 – zenodo.org/record/2536041. Like Swiss German, Alsatian German is a variety of Alemannic German. Note that while both NOAH and the Alsatian corpus contain parts of the Alemannic Wikipedia, the corpora do not overlap.
- Dutch: UD Dutch Alpino (Bouma and van Noord, 2017; van der Beek et al., 2002) – CC BY-SA 4.0 – github.com/UniversalDependencies/UD_Dutch-Alpino
- Low Saxon: UD Low Saxon LSDC (Siewert et al., 2021) – CC BY-SA 4.0 – github.com/UniversalDependencies/UD_Low_Saxon-LSDC
- Norwegian (Nynorsk): UD Norwegian Nynorsk (Velldal et al., 2017; Solberg et al., 2014) – CC BY-SA 4.0 – github.com/UniversalDependencies/UD_Norwegian-Nynorsk
- Norwegian (Bokmål): UD Norwegian Bokmaal (Øvrelid and Hohle, 2016; Solberg et al., 2014) – CC BY-SA 4.0 – github.com/UniversalDependencies/UD_Norwegian-Bokmaal
- West, East and North Norwegian: dialect transcriptions: LIA Norwegian—Corpus of historical dialect recordings (Øvrelid et al., 2018) – CC BY-NC-SA 4.0 – tekstlab.uio.no/LIA/norsk; treebank: UD Norwegian NynorskLIA (Øvrelid et al., 2018) – CC BY-SA 4.0 – github.com/UniversalDependencies/UD_Norwegian-NynorskLIA. The Trønder data (Lierne/Nordli) from the same dataset are omitted because their sample size is much smaller than those of the other dialect groups. We group the remaining locations as follows: East Norwegian (Ål, Bardu,[8] Eidsberg, Gol), West Norwegian (Austevoll, Farsund/Lista, Giske), North Norwegian (Flakstad, Vardø).
- French: UD French GSD (Guillaume et al., 2019) – CC BY-SA 4.0 – github.com/UniversalDependencies/UD_French-GSD

[8]The history of the dialects spoken in and around Bardu is complex, as it is a contact point of East and North Norwegian. For more information, see Jahr (1996).

- Picard: Annotated Corpus for Picard (Martin et al., 2018; Bernhard et al., 2018) – CC BY-SA 4.0 – zenodo.org/record/1485988
- Spanish: UD Spanish AnCora (Taulé et al., 2008) – CC BY 4.0 – github.com/UniversalDependencies/UD_Spanish-AnCora
- Occitan: Annotated Corpus for Occitan (Bras et al., 2018; Bernhard et al., 2018) – CC BY-SA 4.0 – zenodo.org/record/1182949
- Finnish: UD Finnish TDT (Pyysalo et al., 2015; Haverinen et al., 2014) – CC BY-SA 4.0 – github.com/UniversalDependencies/UD_Finnish-TDT
- Finnish dialects: The Finnish Dialect Corpus of the Syntax Archive, Downloadable VRT Version (University of Turku and Institute for the Languages of Finland) – CC-BY-ND 4.0 – urn.fi/urn:nbn:fi:lb-2019092001. We use the dialect regions that are indicated in the corpus: South-Western, South-Eastern, Tavastian, Ostrobothnian, and Savonian dialects, as well as dialects from the transition region between the South-Western area and Tavastia.

B Tagset Conversion

B.1 QCRI Dialectal Arabic Resources

To convert the POS tags of the dialectal Arabic dataset, we use the corpus documentation (Darwish et al., 2018), the documentation of the Farasa tagset (Darwish et al., 2014) (on which the corpus's tagset is based), the documentation for Arabic treebanks in general and UD Arabic PADT in particular,[9], grammars of standard and non-standard Arabic (Ryding, 2005; Brustad, 2000), and Sanguinetti et al.'s (2022) tagging recommendations for user-generated content. Table 3 shows how we converted the tags to UPOS. The PART tag is converted to UPOS PART unless the associated word form is one of the subordinating conjunctions tagged as such (SCONJ) in UD Arabic PADT. Tokens tagged with CASE/NSUFF or PROG_PART are fused with preceding ADJ/NOUN or VERB tokens, when possible. When they appear on their own, they are tagged with X. Additional tags from the extended Farasa tagset that are not used in the treebank are: ABBREV, JUS, VSUFF.

[9]universaldependencies.org/ar/index.html; universaldependencies.org/treebanks/ar_padt

UPOS	Farasa (extended)
ADJ	(DET+)ADJ(+CASE/NSUFF)
ADP	PREP
ADV	ADV
AUX	FUT_PART
CCONJ	CONJ
DET	DET
NOUN	(DET+)NOUN(+CASE/NSUFF)
NUM	NUM
PART	PART,* NEG_PART
PROPN	MENTION
PRON	PRON
PUNCT	PUNC
SCONJ	PART*
SYM	EMOT, URL
VERB	(PROG_PART+)V
X	FOREIGN, HASH, CASE* NSUFF,* PROG_PART*

Table 3: **POS tag conversion for the non-standard Arabic varieties.** The treatment of tags marked with an asterisk* is explained in the text.

UPOS	Finnish Dialect Corpus
ADJ	a, a:pron, a:pron:dem, a:pron:int, a:pron:rel, num:ord, num:ord_pron, q*
ADP	p:post, p:pre
ADV	adv, adv:pron, adv:pron:dem, adv:pron:int, adv:pron:rel, adv:q, p:adv
AUX	v*, neg
CCONJ	cnj:coord
DET	–
INTJ	intj
NOUN	n
NUM	num:card, num:murto
PART	–
PROPN	n:prop, n:prop:pname
PRON	pron, pron:dem, pron:int, pron:pers, pron:pers12, pron:ref, pron:rel, q*
PUNCT	punct
SCONJ	cnj:rel, cnj:sub
SYM	–
VERB	v*
X	muu

Table 4: **POS tag conversion for the Finnish Dialect Corpus.** Tags marked with an asterisk* are disambiguated with the help of lexical information.

B.2 Finnish Dialect Corpus of the Syntax Archive

The conversion of the Finnish tags is based on documentation for the Finnish Dialect Corpus,[10] on the UPOS documentation,[11] and on the documentation of the UD Finnish TDT corpus.[12] Table 4 shows the correspondences between the two tagsets. UD Finnish TDT does not use DET or PART. Two tags needed to be further disambiguated: *v* (used for auxiliaries and full verbs) and *q* (used for interrogative words). For these entries, we use the lemma to decide which POS a given word belongs to.

C Language Models

We use the following PLMs:

- mBERT (Devlin et al., 2019)[13] – Apache 2.0 – huggingface.co/bert-base-multilingual-cased. mBERT's pretraining data include all of the source languages from our study. It also includes Low Saxon and Occitan.
- XLM-R (Conneau et al., 2020a) – MIT licence – huggingface.co/xlm-roberta-base. XLM-R's pretraining data also include all of the source languages from our study. The documentation does not specify whether the Norwegian pretraining data are written in Bokmål, Nynorsk, or both. XLM-R was not trained on any of our target languages.
- Arabic: AraBERT v. 2 (Antoun et al., 2020) – custom licence[14] – huggingface.co/aubmindlab/bert-base-arabertv2
- German: GBERT (Chan et al., 2020) – MIT licence – huggingface.co/deepset/gbert-base
- Dutch: BERTje (de Vries et al., 2019) – Apache 2.0 – github.com/wietsedv/bertje

[10] kielipankki.fi/aineistot/la-murre/la-murre-annotaatiot; blogs.helsinki.fi/fennistic-info/files/2020/12/2.-Sananmuodot-morfologia-morfosyntaksi.pdf

[11] universaldependencies.org/u/pos/all.html

[12] universaldependencies.org/treebanks/fi_tdt

[13] The article details the architecture. Information on the multilingual version can be found at github.com/google-research/bert/blob/master/multilingual.md

[14] github.com/aub-mind/arabert/blob/master/arabert/LICENSE

- Norwegian (both Bokmål and Nynorsk): NorBERT v. 2 (Kutuzov et al., 2021) – CC0 1.0 – huggingface.co/ltgoslo/norbert2.
- French: CamemBERT (Martin et al., 2020) – MIT licence – camembert-model.fr
- Spanish: BETO (Cañete et al., 2020) – CC BY 4.0 – huggingface.co/dccuchile/bert-base-spanish-wwm-cased
- Finnish: FinBERT v. 1.0 (Virtanen et al., 2019) – CC BY 4.0 – github.com/TurkuNLP/FinBERT

We also use the *Transformers* (Wolf et al., 2020) and *PyTorch Lightning* (Falcon and The PyTorch Lightning team, 2022; Paszke et al., 2019) libraries for Python. We use the following hyperparameters for finetuning the models:

Parameter	Grid search	Used
Batch size	16, 32	32
Learning rate	3e-5, 2e-5	2e-5
Epochs	1, 2, 3	2
Classifier dropout	(0.1)	0.1

Table 5: **Hyperparameters used during the grid search and for the final experiments.**

D Additional Correlations

Src	Target	Monoling.		mBERT		XLM-R	
		ρ	p	ρ	p	ρ	p
Ger.	Als. G.	0.34	0.03	0.62	0.00	0.69	0.00
Ger.	Swiss G.	0.78	0.00	0.79	0.00	0.64	0.00
Ger.	L. Saxon	0.40	0.01	0.73	0.00	0.86	0.00
Dutch	L. Saxon	0.75	0.00	−0.25	0.19	0.68	0.00
Bokm.	East N.	0.30	0.11	−0.64	0.00	−0.79	0.00
Bokm.	North N.	0.29	0.11	−0.51	0.01	−0.72	0.00
Bokm.	West N.	0.22	0.25	−0.76	0.00	−0.80	0.00
Nynor.	East N.	−0.36	0.05	−0.64	0.00	−0.82	0.00
Nynor.	North N.	−0.42	0.02	−0.56	0.00	−0.80	0.00
Nynor.	West N.	−0.62	0.00	−0.71	0.00	−0.81	0.00
French	Picard	0.82	0.00	0.24	0.21	0.52	0.00
French	Occitan	0.66	0.00	−0.79	0.00	0.48	0.01
Spa.	Occitan	0.69	0.00	−0.87	0.00	0.15	0.44
MSA	Egy. A.	−0.36	0.05	0.27	0.14	0.57	0.00
MSA	Gulf A.	−0.56	0.00	−0.41	0.02	−0.02	0.94
MSA	Lev. A.	−0.58	0.00	−0.30	0.11	0.33	0.11
MSA	Mag. A.	−0.23	0.22	−0.26	0.17	0.27	0.20
Fin.	Ost. F.	0.01	0.98	−0.79	0.00	0.44	0.01
Fin.	SE F.	−0.07	0.71	−0.73	0.00	0.40	0.03
Fin.	SW F.	−0.37	0.05	−0.84	0.00	0.35	0.06
Fin.	SW tr.	−0.12	0.52	−0.83	0.00	0.37	0.05
Fin.	Sav. F.	0.01	0.95	−0.77	0.00	0.47	0.01
Fin.	Tav. F.	−0.06	0.75	−0.73	0.00	0.57	0.00

Table 6: **Correlation between seen subword ratio and accuracy.** Spearman's ρ with p-values for all noise levels and random initializations per language pair and PLM. Negative correlations are highlighted in blue, positive ones in yellow. P-values of 0.05 and above have a grey background.

Src	Target	Monoling.		mBERT		XLM-R	
		ρ	p	ρ	p	ρ	p
Ger.	Als. G.	0.89	0.00	0.77	0.00	0.85	0.00
Ger.	Swiss G.	0.81	0.00	0.76	0.00	0.84	0.00
Ger.	L. Saxon	0.86	0.00	0.72	0.00	0.88	0.00
Dutch	L. Saxon	0.74	0.00	0.26	0.16	0.79	0.00
Bokm.	East N.	0.30	0.11	–0.66	0.00	–0.70	0.00
Bokm.	North N.	0.37	0.04	–0.65	0.00	–0.59	0.00
Bokm.	West N.	0.23	0.21	–0.81	0.00	–0.68	0.00
Nynor.	East N.	–0.48	0.01	–0.76	0.00	–0.86	0.00
Nynor.	North N.	–0.52	0.00	–0.61	0.00	–0.77	0.00
Nynor.	West N.	–0.59	0.00	–0.62	0.00	–0.79	0.00
French	Picard	0.51	0.00	0.62	0.00	0.79	0.00
French	Occitan	0.82	0.00	–0.50	0.00	0.77	0.00
Spa.	Occitan	0.51	0.00	–0.53	0.00	0.44	0.01
MSA	Egy. A.	0.17	0.38	0.39	0.03	0.29	0.12
MSA	Gulf A.	0.01	0.96	0.04	0.85	–0.27	0.19
MSA	Lev. A.	0.07	0.72	0.12	0.54	–0.08	0.69
MSA	Mag. A.	0.30	0.11	0.02	0.93	–0.03	0.90
Fin.	Ost. F.	0.23	0.22	0.41	0.02	0.62	0.00
Fin.	SE F.	–0.11	0.55	0.01	0.94	0.76	0.00
Fin.	SW F.	–0.34	0.06	–0.15	0.42	0.69	0.00
Fin.	SW tr.	0.36	0.05	0.49	0.01	0.44	0.01
Fin.	Sav. F.	0.16	0.41	0.28	0.13	0.75	0.00
Fin.	Tav. F.	0.24	0.20	0.50	0.01	0.61	0.00

Table 7: **Correlation between seen word ratio and accuracy.** Spearman's ρ with p-values for all noise levels and random initializations per language pair and PLM. Negative correlations are highlighted in blue, positive ones in yellow. P-values of 0.05 and above have a grey background.

Src	Target	Monoling.		mBERT		XLM-R	
		ρ	p	ρ	p	ρ	p
Ger.	Als. G.	0.87	0.00	0.37	0.05	0.53	0.00
Ger.	Swiss G.	0.67	0.00	0.11	0.57	0.21	0.26
Ger.	L. Saxon	0.90	0.00	0.62	0.00	0.69	0.00
Dutch	L. Saxon	0.53	0.00	–0.50	0.00	0.15	0.44
Bokm.	East N.	0.16	0.41	–0.80	0.00	–0.49	0.01
Bokm.	North N.	0.15	0.44	–0.67	0.00	–0.45	0.01
Bokm.	West N.	0.13	0.49	–0.73	0.00	–0.56	0.00
Nynor.	East N.	–0.83	0.00	–0.65	0.00	–0.10	0.62
Nynor.	North N.	–0.85	0.00	–0.47	0.01	–0.05	0.80
Nynor.	West N.	–0.92	0.00	–0.61	0.00	–0.06	0.74
French	Picard	–0.14	0.45	0.15	0.42	0.33	0.07
French	Occitan	0.45	0.01	–0.83	0.00	0.39	0.03
Spa.	Occitan	0.36	0.05	–0.95	0.00	–0.41	0.03
MSA	Egy. A.	–0.38	0.04	–0.77	0.00	–0.82	0.00
MSA	Gulf A.	–0.37	0.05	–0.95	0.00	–0.89	0.00
MSA	Lev. A.	–0.31	0.10	–0.91	0.00	–0.84	0.00
MSA	Mag. A.	–0.63	0.00	–0.87	0.00	–0.73	0.00
Fin.	Ost. F.	–0.87	0.00	–0.75	0.00	–0.03	0.87
Fin.	SE F.	–0.87	0.00	–0.76	0.00	–0.17	0.38
Fin.	SW F.	–0.81	0.00	–0.71	0.00	–0.08	0.69
Fin.	SW tr.	–0.81	0.00	–0.69	0.00	–0.10	0.60
Fin.	Sav. F.	–0.87	0.00	–0.77	0.00	–0.09	0.63
Fin.	Tav. F.	–0.87	0.00	–0.80	0.00	0.02	0.90

Table 8: **Correlation between TTR ratio and accuracy.** Spearman's ρ with p-values for all noise levels and random initializations per language pair and PLM. Negative correlations are highlighted in blue, positive ones in yellow. P-values of 0.05 and above have a grey background. The TTR ratio stayed below 1 for all cross-dialectal Finnish set-ups (regardless of PLM choice) and above 1 for all others.

Temporal Domain Adaptation for Historical Irish

Oksana Dereza and **Theodorus Fransen** and **John P. McCrae**
University of Galway
Insight Centre for Data Analytics
firstname.lastname@insight-centre.org

Abstract

The digitisation of historical texts has provided new horizons for NLP research, but such data also presents a set of challenges, including scarcity and inconsistency. The lack of editorial standard during digitisation exacerbates these difficulties.

This study explores the potential for temporal domain adaptation in Early Modern Irish and pre-reform Modern Irish data. We describe two experiments carried out on the book subcorpus of the Historical Irish Corpus, which includes Early Modern Irish and pre-reform Modern Irish texts from 1581 to 1926. We also propose a simple orthographic normalisation method for historical Irish that reduces the type-token ratio by 21.43% on average in our data.

The results demonstrate that the use of out-of-domain data significantly improves a language model's performance. Providing a model with additional input from another historical stage of the language improves its quality by 12.49% on average on non-normalised texts and by 27.02% on average on normalised (demutated) texts. Most notably, using only out-of-domain data for both pre-training and training stages allowed for up to 86.81% of the baseline model quality on non-normalised texts and up to 95.68% on normalised texts without any target domain data.

Additionally, we investigate the effect of temporal distance between the training and test data. The hypothesis that there is a positive correlation between performance and temporal proximity of training and test data has been validated, which manifests best in normalised data. Expanding this approach even further back, to Middle and Old Irish, and testing it on other languages is a further research direction.

1 Introduction

With the increasing digitisation of historical texts, more data becomes available for analysis alongside contemporary documents. However, such data poses a set of challenges for any NLP task as it tends to be both scarce and inconsistent. Apart from natural artefacts of language evolution, such as spelling variation and grammatical changes, working with historical languages is complicated by the lack of a linguistic / editorial standard when this data is being digitised (Piotrowski, 2012; Jenset and McGillivray, 2017; Bollmann, 2019). It is especially true for Early Irish, as Doyle et al. (2018, 2019) and Dereza et al. (2023) have pointed out.

In this work, we explore the possibility of temporal domain adaptation[1] on Early Modern Irish and pre-reform Modern Irish data. Although these are not the oldest stages of the Irish language, they are less resourced and more versatile than Modern Irish, which is itself a minority language. We conduct a set of experiments on the use of out-of-domain data, both later and earlier than the target time period, for pre-training embedding models to improve the quality of a language model at the said period. We also investigate the effect that temporal distance between embedding training data and test data has in such a setting. Finally, we propose a simple and efficient normalisation method for historical Irish.

2 Related Work

The surge of interest in distributional semantics has lately reached historical linguistics. A recently emerged concept of diachronic, or dynamic (Bamler and Mandt, 2017; Rudolph and Blei, 2018; Yao et al., 2018; Hofmann et al., 2020), embeddings transforms the task of language modelling into the task of modelling language change, which most papers in this field focus on (Kulkarni et al., 2015; Fremmann and Lapata, 2016; Hamilton et al., 2016;

[1]We use the term 'temporal domain adaptation' to describe transfer learning between two different stages of the same language. We believe that this is an instance of domain adaptation, where the main difference between source and target domains is associated with the time when the texts were produced, hence 'temporal'.

Tenth Workshop on NLP for Similar Languages, Varieties and Dialects (VarDial 2023), pages 55–66
May 5, 2023 ©2023 Association for Computational Linguistics

Dubossarsky et al., 2017; Rosenfeld and Erk, 2018; Tahmasebi, 2018; Boukhaled et al., 2019; Rodina et al., 2019; Brandl and Lassner, 2019; Hu et al., 2022). In 2018, three comprehensive surveys of detecting and measuring semantic shifts with word embeddings came out (Kutuzov et al., 2018; Tahmasebi et al., 2018; Tang, 2018). In 2020, one of the SemEval shared tasks was dedicated to unsupervised lexical semantic change detection (Schlechtweg et al., 2020). At least two PhD theses on the topic, "Distributional word embeddings in modelling diachronic semantic change" (Kutuzov, 2020) and "Models of diachronic semantic change using word embeddings" (Montariol, 2021), have been defended in the last few years.

Less attention has been paid to addressing the challenges historical languages pose for training a robust embedding model, such as high spelling variation or substantial grammatical change over time. A good example of such a work is a paper by Montariol and Allauzen (2019), who discuss the effectiveness of different algorithms for embedding training in diachronic low-resource scenarios and propose improvements to initialisation schemes and loss regularisation to deal with data scarcity. Di Carlo et al. (2019) are suggesting to use atemporal compass vectors as heuristics while training diachronic word embeddings on scarce data.

On the other hand, the use of closely related languages or language varieties to improve word embeddings and language models in a low-resource setting has been a subject of active discussion. For example, Currey et al. (2016) model a low-resource scenario on Spanish data, using Italian and Portuguese as donor languages for training a statistical machine translation model. Abulimiti and Schultz (2020) work in real low-resource conditions, successfully using Turkish data to improve a language model for Uyghur. Kuriyozov et al. (2020) make another successful attempt at leveraging better-resource Turkic languages to improve the quality of the embeddings for related low-resource languages. Ma et al. (2020) achieve a better performance on the low-resource Tibetan language by training cross-lingual Chinese-Tibetan embeddings. Generally, transfer learning is a popular approach in neural machine translation when it comes to the lack of data, as described in Zoph et al. (2016); Nguyen and Chiang (2017); Kocmi and Bojar (2018); Maimaiti et al. (2019); Chen and Abdul-Mageed (2022). However, the cross-lingual transfer aimed at overcoming data scarcity is not limited to related languages (Adams et al., 2017; Agić et al., 2016). The problem of low-resource scenarios is also discussed in an extensive survey of the cross-lingual embedding models (Ruder et al., 2018).

A few works consider the transfer between different historical stages of the same language as a case of domain adaptation (Yang and Eisenstein, 2015; Huang and Paul, 2019; Manjavacas and Fonteyn, 2022), and we adopt this terminology. Manjavacas and Fonteyn (2022) compare adapting and pre-training large language models for historical English, concluding that pre-training on domain-specific (i.e. historical) data is preferable despite being costly and dependent on the amount of training data.

However, the effect on a language model's performance produced by initialising it with temporarily distant pre-trained embeddings and by using the out-of-domain temporal data at the training stage has not been evaluated yet, to the best of our knowledge. Moreover, the Irish data has never been used in the research on diachronic word embeddings and temporal domain adaptation before.

3 Data

The data for the experiment is a collection of Early Modern Irish and Modern Irish texts spanning over 350 years, from the late 16th to early 20th century.

Irish belongs to the Celtic branch of the Indo-European language family. Like other Celtic languages, it is notable for initial mutations: sound changes at the beginning of a word happening in certain grammatical environments, which are reflected in spelling. These are combined with a rich nominal and verbal inflection at the end of a word. The four types of initial mutations in modern Irish and their effect on spelling is shown in Table 1.

Before becoming a grammatical feature of the language, mutations happened as historical phonetic processes.[2] For instance, a mutation called *lenition* in the intervocalic position turned Old Irish *cride* [ˈkʲrʲiðʲe] 'heart' into Middle Irish *croi**d**(**h**)e* / *cri**dh**e* / *crai**d**(**h**)e* [ˈk⁽ʲ⁾r⁽ʲ⁾iɣʲə] / [ˈk⁽ʲ⁾r⁽ʲ⁾ijə], which later became Modern Irish *croí* [krˠiː].[3]

[2]We apologise for this necessary simplification of historical Irish phonology to our Celticist readers.

[3]Our IPA transcriptions of Middle Irish forms are purely hypothetical. Not enough is known about spoken Middle Irish to say with any authority how things were pronounced, as

Letter	Lenition	Eclipsis	t-prothesis	h-prothesis
b	bh	mb	-	-
c	ch	gc	-	-
d	dh	nd	-	-
f	fh	bhf	-	-
g	gh	ng	-	-
p	ph	bp	-	-
t	th	dt	-	-
m	mh	-	-	-
s	sh	-	ts	-
vowels	-	n-V	t-V	hV

Table 1: Initial mutations in modern Irish.

3.1 Early and Pre-Reform Modern Irish

Early Modern Irish is a term used to describe a vast period in the history of the Irish language between Middle and pre-reform Modern Irish. It spans from the 13th to the 18th century (McManus, 1994) and is marked by multiple religious works (both original and translated), epic tales (both native and adapted from continental material), bardic poetry and historical writing, such as genealogical tracts.

Modern declension and conjugation systems were formed during this period, which makes Early Modern Irish relatively close to what Irish is today, and even closer to what it was before the spelling reform in 1947 and the introduction of the official standard, *An Caighdeán Oifigiúil*, in 1958 (Rannóg an Aistriúcháin, 1958), which is being regularly revised and updated (Tithe an Oireachtais, 2017).

However, both Early Modern Irish and pre-reform Modern Irish texts show considerable spelling variation and unstable grammatical changes, which makes them challenging for NLP tasks (Scannell, 2022).

3.2 Historical Irish Corpus

The data used in the experiments originates in a book subcorpus of the Historical Irish Corpus, or *Corpas Stairiúil na Gaeilge* (hereafter CSnaG), created by the Royal Irish Academy (Acadamh Ríoga na hÉireann; Uí Dhonnchadha et al., 2014). It includes texts from 1581 to 1926 and amounts to $13,599,882$ tokens. It covers a wide variety of genres, such as bardic poetry, native Irish stories, translations and adaptations of continental epic and romance, annals, genealogies, grammatical and medical tracts, diaries, and religious writing. Each text is dated (both creation and publication dates are provided), and the majority of the texts are author-attributed. The data is available in different formats (plain text, TEI, ePub) along with the metadata on the CSnaG website.[4]

For our purposes, the data was continuously split into 10 parts, 99 texts each, except for the last one, which only includes 97 texts. The motivation for splitting the corpus by the number of texts as opposed to the number of tokens comes from the necessity to keep whole texts within a particular corpus subset to avoid the time, author, and genre interference. Cutting a text into several chunks would have created an overlap between the corpus parts and affected the results of the experiments. Table 2 shows the time frame of each corpus subset along with its size.

3.3 Preprocessing

The texts were split into sentences by the end-of-sentence punctuation marks; then, all sentence-level punctuation was removed and the texts were lowercased. No stemming, lemmatisation or part-of-speech tagging was applied.

In addition to that, a normalised (hereafter 'demutated') dataset was created where mutations were removed regardless of their type and position in the word. As a result of such normalisation, *ngrádhmhar* became *grádmar*, *t-ollmhughadh* became *ollmugad*, and so on. Mutations are one of the main sources of spelling variation, especially in the diachronic setting. Although we do lose some grammatical information and sometimes create lexical ambiguities by removing them at the beginning of a word, this change is not critically damaging and is comparable to lemmatisation. Scannell (2020) discusses demutation in modern Irish and the types of errors it can lead to in great detail.

Removing historical mutations that occur in the middle and at the end of a word may, in turn, lead to the conflation of dialectal and standard spellings (standard *d(h)éanfadh* vs. dialectal *d(h)éanfad*), as well as of unrelated words (*óige* 'youth' and *óighe*, 'Gen. sg. Virgin [Mary]'). However, homonymy exists in non-normalised Irish texts too: for instance, *óige* not only means 'youth', but can also be a part of the analytical comparative and superlative forms of *óg* 'young'. A slight increase in homonymy

the writing standard of the period was very archaic. Scribes were following the rules of Old Irish, leaving us with only occasional errors and innovations to conjecture the language they were speaking.

[4] http://corpas.ria.ie/index.php?fsg_function=1

Part	Years	Tokens	Mutated		Demutated		Improvement, %
			Types	TTR	Types	TTR	
0	1581 – 1640	1 669 581	54 748	32.79	42 411	25.40	22.53
1	1640 – 1690	1 524 344	49 658	32.58	39 434	25.87	20.59
2	1691 – 1728	775 412	28 967	37.36	23 425	30.21	19.13
3	1729 – 1771	875 635	33 038	37.73	26 367	30.11	20.19
4	1771 – 1817	688 900	28 708	41.67	22 995	33.38	19.90
5	1817 – 1836	1 094 053	36 048	32.95	28 361	25.92	21.32
6	1836 – 1875	634 692	21 981	34.63	17 468	27.52	20.53
7	1876 – 1908	1 562 576	33 833	21.65	26 185	16.76	22.61
8	1908 – 1919	2 294 943	38 548	16.80	29 132	12.69	24.43
9	1919 – 1926	2 479 746	46 117	18.60	35 501	14.32	23.02

Table 2: Reducing vocabulary size by removing mutations. TTR scores are calculated as $TTR = \frac{types}{tokens} \times 1000$ according to Schlechtweg et al. (2020).

Language	Period	TTR
English	1880 – 1860	13.38
German	1800 – 1899	14.25
Swedish	1790 – 1830	47.88
Latin	−200 – 0	38.24
CSnaG (original)	1581 – 1926	45.50
CSnaG (demutated)	1581 – 1926	33.15

Table 3: TTR scores of Early Modern Irish and pre-reform Modern Irish compared to other historical languages.

Part	Baseline	EX1.1	EX1.2	EX1.3	EX1.4	EX1.5
0	11.25	10.35	14.39	16.62	13.32	19.17
1	8.88	7.97	10.98	13.62	11.20	10.09
2	4.77	3.85	8.30	13.25	8.36	11.96
3	8.27	6.19	10.72	16.95	11.01	12.44
4	8.64	6.77	13.00	19.33	13.55	17.11
5	9.46	9.91	12.70	11.51	11.56	16.37
6	3.85	5.36	10.30	33.02	7.43	20.08
7	9.39	9.60	11.33	16.25	10.38	8.78
8	8.88	9.52	10.68	32.57	10.25	9.97
9	9.52	10.24	11.87	13.88	10.49	26.01
AVG	**8.29**	**7.98**	**11.43**	**18.70**	**10.76**	**15.20**

Table 4: The % of a language model's quality improvement (the decrease in perplexity) achieved by simple orthographic normalisation consisting in the removal of synchronic and historical mutations.

seems to be a justified tradeoff for a significant reduction of vocabulary size unless one is specifically interested in dialectal variation, pronunciation and spelling change, or rhyme patterns in bardic poetry.

Removing mutations from data reduces vocabulary size and type-token ratio (TTR) by 21.43% on average (see Table 2). Moreover, it helps to bridge the gap between Old Irish, where mutations were not marked in writing, and more modern stages of the language. To put these results into context, let us compare TTR scores calculated on the whole CSnaG, containing Early Modern Irish and pre-reform Modern Irish texts, with similar results for historical English, German, Swedish, and Latin provided by Schlechtweg et al. (2020), in Table 3.

Lower TTR has a positive effect on NLP models' performance: in our case, it leads to a notable drop in the perplexity of a language model. Table 4 shows the percent of improvement on demutated texts in comparison to the original ones in each of the experiments, described in more detail in Section 5.1.

4 Methodology

4.1 Embedding Model

We use a FastText (Bojanowski et al., 2017) embedding model that takes subword information into account, which is preferable due to the nature of historical language data. Due to a high degree of variation, which is explained both by the morphological complexity of historical languages and by the lack of standardisation, going down to the subword level is crucial for reducing the vocabulary and effectively dealing with out-of-vocabulary words at the same time. A similar approach is adopted in other works on low-resource data (Kuriyozov et al., 2020; Ma et al., 2020). During our initial set of experiments on non-normalised diachronic Early Irish data, embedding models learned mostly paradigmatic and derivational morphological relations, as well as spelling variation. Some semantic relations were also captured but to a lesser extent (Dereza et al., 2023).

For both experiments described in this paper, all embedding models were trained with the following parameters: embedding size = 100, context window = 10, and minimal count = 2 regardless of vocabulary size. The embedding size is motivated by the experimental results demonstrating that a smaller embedding dimension reduces the model's sensitivity to noise when the data is scarce (Stewart et al., 2017). The low minimal word count is aimed at preserving as much information at each time step as possible.

4.2 Evaluation Scenario

Extrinsic evaluation of embeddings (Schnabel et al., 2015; Bakarov, 2018; Torregrossa et al., 2021) through language modelling seems preferable since it is language-independent and scalable. In addition to that, it does not require manual preparatory work such as dataset creation, unlike other popular downstream tasks, such as bilingual dictionary induction, part-of-speech tagging, or any kind of classification. Hypothetically, using pre-trained embeddings must lower the perplexity score of a language model, even if these were trained on a different period of the language in question.

Perplexity is a standard metric to evaluate language models, which can be defined as the inverse probability of the test set normalised by the number of words. The lower it is, the better.

$$\mathrm{PPL}(X) = \exp\left\{ -\frac{1}{t} \sum_{i}^{t} \log p_\theta \left(x_i \mid x_{<i} \right) \right\}$$

4.3 Language Model

The configuration of our language model is deliberately simple so that it would allow seeing the contribution that the pre-trained embeddings make to its performance more clearly. It is an LSTM (Hochreiter and Schmidhuber, 1997) with one hidden layer trained until convergence with the Adam optimiser using the early stopping technique, starting with the learning rate = 0.001. The minimum word count was set to 2 to match the pre-trained embedding models. The number of neurons on the hidden layer was calculated depending on corpus vocabulary size as $n_{hidden} = V \times 0.01$ regardless of whether pre-trained embedding models were used or not, and of their vocabulary size. The coefficient was devised empirically based on available computational resources. The pre-trained embeddings were not fixed during the language model training to allow for domain adaptation. More information on vocabulary sizes for each experiment can be found in Tables 9 and 8 in Appendix A.

5 Experimental Results

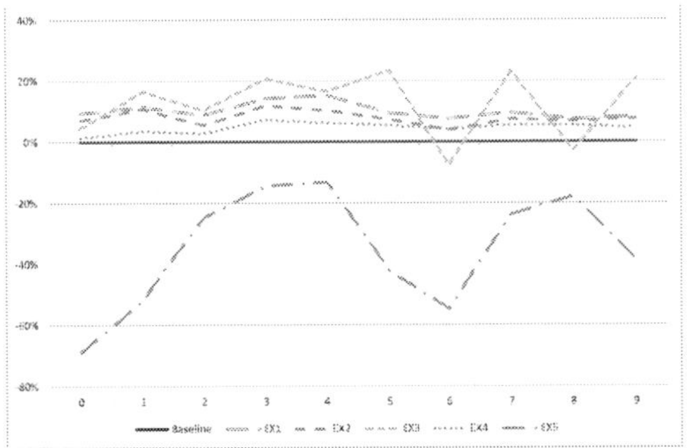

Figure 1: Experiment I: the % of a language model's quality improvement / deterioration in comparison to the baseline, original texts without orthographic normalisation.

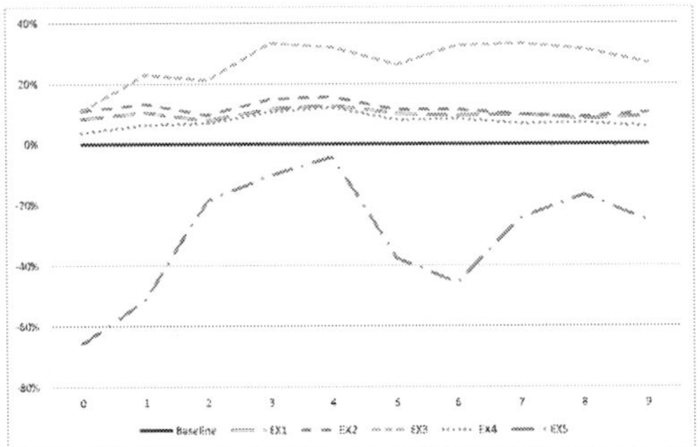

Figure 2: Experiment I: the % of a language model's quality improvement / deterioration in comparison to the baseline, orthographically normalised (demutated) texts.

5.1 Experiment I

Experiment I consisted of 5 tasks summarised in Table 5. Each of these tasks was aimed at answering a particular question about pre-training, such as *"Does the use of an embedding model pre-trained on related data without the target [temporal] domain help to lower the perplexity of a language model at timestamp t_i?"*. The perplexity of a language model trained on a target temporal domain data t_i (i.e. one of the corpus parts № 0-9) without pre-training was taken as a baseline.

№	LM train data	LM test / valid data	Pre-training	Research Question
1.0	t_i	t_i	—	Baseline
1.1	t_i	t_i	t_i	Does pre-training on the target temporal domain t_i help to lower the perplexity of a language model for the timestamp t_i?
1.2	t_i	t_i	T	Does using a bigger pre-trained embedding model, containing more than the target domain, help to lower the perplexity of an LM for the timestamp t_i?
1.3	T	t_i	T	Does the use of out-of-domain data along with in-domain data at both the pre-training and the LM training stages help to lower the perplexity of an LM for the timestamp t_i?
1.4	t_i	t_i	T_{-i}	Does the use of an embedding model pre-trained on related data without the target domain t_i help to lower the perplexity of an LM for the timestamp t_i?
1.5	T_{-i}	t_i	T_{-i}	If we do not have any in-domain data for training, does the use of related data at both the pre-training and the LM training stages help to lower the perplexity of an LM for the timestamp t_i?

Table 5: A overview of Experiment I: t_i refers to a single corpus part from 0 to 9, T stands for the whole corpus, and T_{-i} is the whole corpus excluding a single corpus part from 0 to 9.

Part	EX1.1	EX1.2	EX1.3	EX1.4	EX1.5
0	+9.35	+6.98	+4.43	+1.34	–68.82
1	+11.45	+10.70	+16.49	+3.50	–51.84
2	+8.77	+5.44	+10.40	+2.82	–24.85
3	+14.13	+11.82	+20.67	+7.15	–14.43
4	+15.14	+10.23	+16.49	+6.08	–13.19
5	+9.37	+7.20	+23.27	+5.32	–42.44
6	+7.57	+3.84	–7.69	+4.18	–54.89
7	+9.44	+7.35	+23.03	+5.40	–23.81
8	+7.39	+6.66	–2.80	+5.28	–17.82
9	+8.18	+7.51	+20.64	+4.51	–38.96
AVG	**+10.08**	**+7.77**	**+12.49**	**+4.56**	**–35.10**

Table 6: Experiment I: the % of a language model's quality improvement / deterioration in comparison to the baseline; original texts without orthographic normalisation.

Part	EX1.1	EX1.2	EX1.3	EX1.4	EX1.5
0	+8.25	+10.90	+11.16	+3.76	–65.76
1	+10.36	+13.32	+22.90	+6.21	–51.19
2	+7.72	+9.49	+21.19	+6.85	–18.72
3	+1.60	+14.89	+33.27	+10.46	–10.35
4	+12.83	+15.75	+31.92	+12.10	–4.32
5	+9.92	+11.19	+26.13	+7.82	–37.68
6	+9.29	+11.30	+32.50	+8.19	–45.73
7	+9.69	+9.69	+33.10	+6.57	–24.32
8	+8.15	+8.81	+31.34	+6.89	–16.83
9	+9.04	+10.38	+26.74	+5.64	–25.35
AVG	**+9.68**	**+11.57**	**+27.02**	**+7.45**	**–30.02**

Table 7: Experiment I: the % of a language model's quality improvement / deterioration in comparison to the baseline; orthographically normalised (demutated) texts.

Every corpus part covering a particular period in the history of the Irish language, as shown in Table 2, was split into training (80%), validation (10%), and test (10%) subsets. Validation and test subsets have not been seen by the language model at any stage, including pretraining (i.e. word embeddings were trained only on the training subset of each corpus part).

The results of this experiment are reported in Tables 6 and 7, where each number shows an improvement (marked with a +) or a drop (marked with a –) in the performance of a language model compared to the baseline. For example, in *Experiment 1.3*, the use of additional out-of-domain data both at the pre-training and training stages results in a 11.16% improvement (i.e. the language model's perplexity drops by 11.16%) in comparison to the baseline on the corpus part № 0 with orthographic normalisation. In other words, adding the texts from 1640 – 1926 to those from 1581 – 1640 at both the pre-training and training stages improves the results of the model on the 1581 – 1640 test data by 11.16%. Generally, *Experiment 1.3* demonstrates that providing a model with additional input improves its quality by 12.49% on average on non-normalised texts and by 27.02% on average on normalised texts.

Similarly, in *Experiment 1.5*, pre-training and training a language model on the whole normalised corpus excluding part № 0 and testing its performance on part № 0 makes the resulting score 65.76% worse (i.e. the language model's perplexity rises by 65.76%). Still, it is not as discouraging as it may seem: it means that we are still able to obtain 34.24% of the baseline model quality even if we do not have the target data from 1581 – 1640 in our training corpus at all. This number is even higher for later stages of the language, where using related data for training allows to achieve up to 86.81% of the baseline model quality on non-normalised texts and up to 95.68% on normalised texts.

As expected, both pre-training on the same data and using additional out-of-domain data only at the pre-training stage leads to the improvement of a language model's performance despite the shallow architecture of a language model. Naturally, language models trained on earlier texts or on texts with genre-specific language are more sensitive to the absence of in-domain data. For example, parts 5 and 6 include a substantial amount of poetry, which often exhibits a richer, more archaic vocabulary compared to prose.

Figures 1 and 2 provide a graphical overview of the effect that the pre-training data makes on the performance of a language model in comparison to the baseline. Raw sentencewise perplexity scores for the experiment are given in Tables 10 and 11 in Appendix B.

5.2 Experiment II

The second experiment was aimed at observing the effect of the temporal distance between the pre-training and the training/test data. It consisted in the training of language models on each of the 10 corpus subsets initializing them with embeddings pre-trained on each of these corpus parts in all possible combinations. We hypothesised that smaller temporal distances would result in better performance than bigger ones. Our hypothesis has proven correct, as shown in Figures 3 and 4. This correlation is most pronounced when evaluating orthographically normalised (demutated) texts. Naturally, language models fed with embeddings pre-trained on the same data yield the best results. Table 12 in the Appendix C provides the results of this experiment run on non-normalised texts, where all mutations are preserved, and Table 13 presents similar results for demutated texts. Columns correspond to embedding models, and rows are corpus parts they were tested on. For the reader's convenience, we cite *normalised inverse perplexity* instead of the original sentence-wise perplexity scores. It shows how well a model performed in comparison to the best result, where 100% is the best result.

$$NIP = \frac{best\_score}{score} \times 100$$

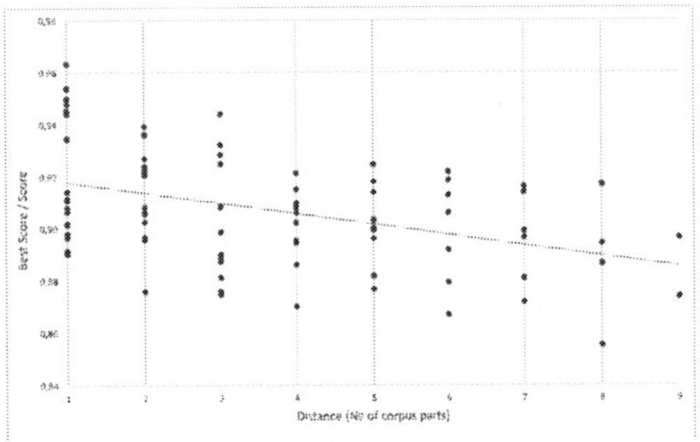

Figure 3: The effect of temporal distance between the pre-training (embedding) data and the language model training and test data; original texts without orthographic normalisation.

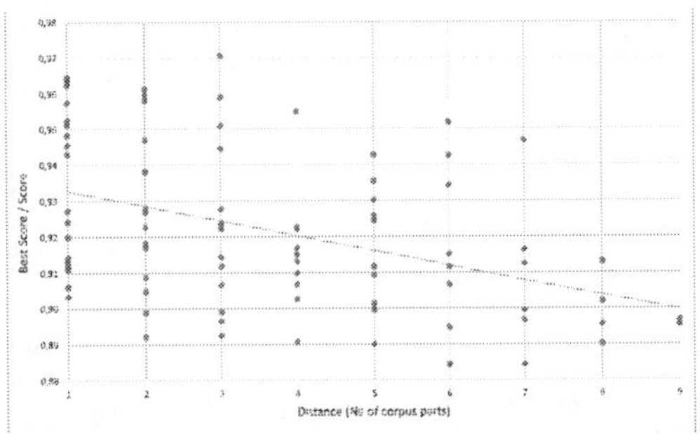

Figure 4: The effect of temporal distance between the pre-training (embedding) data and the language model training and test data; orthographically normalised (demutated) texts.

6 Conclusion

The results cited above testify that using out-of-domain temporal data in the pre-training and training of a language model for a historical language can significantly improve its performance. This is extremely valuable in low-resource scenarios, where we may only have a few texts dating back to a particular period, which would not be enough to train a robust language model. Providing a model with additional input improves its quality by 12.49% on average on non-normalised texts and by 27.02% on average on normalised texts even if this information is retrieved from data covering a different — no matter later or earlier — period in the history of a language. Most importantly, using only out-of-domain data at both pre-training and training stages allows for achieving up to 86.81% of the baseline model quality on non-normalised texts and up to 95.68% on normalised texts without any target domain data.

Our hypothesis that there is a positive correlation between the performance of language models and the temporal proximity of training and test data has been validated. This effect manifests best in orthographically normalised texts. Expanding this approach even further back, to Middle and Old Irish, and testing it on other languages is a further research direction.

Finally, we proposed a simple yet very effective orthographic normalisation method for historical Irish that reduced the type-token ratio by 21.43% on average in our data and allowed for up to 33.02% drop in a language model's perplexity.

7 Acknowledgements

This publication has emanated from research in part supported by the Irish Research Council under grant number IRCLA/2017/129 (CARDAMOM – Comparative Deep Models of Language for Minority and Historical Languages). It is co-funded by Science Foundation Ireland (SFI) under Grant Number SFI/12/RC/2289 P2 (Insight 2). We also wish to acknowledge the Irish Centre for High-End Computing (ICHEC) and our colleague Adrian Doyle for the provision of computational facilities and support.

References

Ayimunishagu Abulimiti and Tanja Schultz. 2020. Building language models for morphological rich low-resource languages using data from related donor languages: the case of Uyghur. In *Proceedings of the 1st Joint Workshop on Spoken Language Technologies for Under-resourced languages (SLTU) and Collaboration and Computing for Under-Resourced Languages (CCURL)*, pages 271–276, Marseille, France. European Language Resources association.

Acadamh Ríoga na hÉireann. Corpas Stairiúil na Gaeilge 1600-1926. Accessed: February 19, 2023. Data downloaded: June 10, 2022.

Oliver Adams, Adam Makarucha, Graham Neubig, Steven Bird, and Trevor Cohn. 2017. Cross-lingual word embeddings for low-resource language modeling. In *Proceedings of the 15th Conference of the European Chapter of the Association for Computational Linguistics: Volume 1, Long Papers*, pages 937–947.

Željko Agić, Anders Johannsen, Barbara Plank, Héctor Martínez Alonso, Natalie Schluter, and Anders Søgaard. 2016. Multilingual projection for parsing truly low-resource languages. *Transactions of the Association for Computational Linguistics*, 4:301–312.

Amir Bakarov. 2018. A survey of word embeddings evaluation methods. *arXiv preprint arXiv:1801.09536*.

Robert Bamler and Stephan Mandt. 2017. Dynamic word embeddings. In *International conference on Machine learning*, pages 380–389. PMLR.

Piotr Bojanowski, Edouard Grave, Armand Joulin, and Tomas Mikolov. 2017. Enriching word vectors with subword information. *Transactions of the association for computational linguistics*, 5:135–146.

Marcel Bollmann. 2019. A Large-Scale Comparison of Historical Text Normalization Systems. In *Proceedings of the 2019 Conference of the North American Chapter of the Association for Computational Linguistics*, pages 3885–3898.

Mohamed Boukhaled, Benjamin Fagard, and Thierry Poibeau. 2019. Modelling the semantic change dynamics using diachronic word embedding. In *11th International Conference on Agents and Artificial Intelligence (NLPinAI Special Session)*.

Stephanie Brandl and David Lassner. 2019. Times are changing: Investigating the pace of language change in diachronic word embeddings. In *Proceedings of the 1st International Workshop on Computational Approaches to Historical Language Change*, pages 146–150.

Wei-Rui Chen and Muhammad Abdul-Mageed. 2022. Improving neural machine translation of indigenous languages with multilingual transfer learning. *arXiv preprint arXiv:2205.06993*.

Anna Currey, Alina Karakanta, and Jon Dehdari. 2016. Using related languages to enhance statistical language models. In *Proceedings of the NAACL Student Research Workshop*, pages 116–123.

Oksana Dereza, Theodorus Fransen, and John P. McCrae. 2023. Do not trust the experts: How the lack of standard complicates NLP for historical Irish. In *Proceedings of the 3d Workshop on Insights from Negative Results in NLP, EACL 2023*. Upcoming.

Valerio Di Carlo, Federico Bianchi, and Matteo Palmonari. 2019. Training temporal word embeddings with a compass. In *Proceedings of the AAAI conference on artificial intelligence*, volume 33, pages 6326–6334.

Adrian Doyle, John P McCrae, and Clodagh Downey. 2018. Preservation of original orthography in the construction of an Old Irish corpus. *Sustaining Knowledge Diversity in the Digital Age*, pages 67–70.

Adrian Doyle, John Philip McCrae, and Clodagh Downey. 2019. A character-level LSTM network model for tokenizing the Old Irish text of the Würzburg glosses on the Pauline Epistles. In *Proceedings of the Celtic Language Technology Workshop*, pages 70–79.

Haim Dubossarsky, Daphna Weinshall, and Eitan Grossman. 2017. Outta control: Laws of semantic change and inherent biases in word representation models. In *Proceedings of the 2017 Conference on Empirical Methods in Natural Language Processing*, pages 1136–1145. Association for Computational Linguistics.

Lea Frermann and Mirella Lapata. 2016. A Bayesian model of diachronic meaning change. *Transactions of the Association for Computational Linguistics*, 4:31–45.

William L. Hamilton, Jure Leskovec, and Dan Jurafsky. 2016. Diachronic word embeddings reveal statistical laws of semantic change. In *Proceedings of the 54th Annual Meeting of the Association for Computational Linguistics (Volume 1: Long Papers)*, pages 1489–1501, Berlin, Germany. Association for Computational Linguistics.

Sepp Hochreiter and Jürgen Schmidhuber. 1997. Long short-term memory. *Neural computation*, 9(8):1735–1780.

Valentin Hofmann, Janet B Pierrehumbert, and Hinrich Schütze. 2020. Dynamic contextualized word embeddings. In *Proceedings of the 59th Annual Meeting of the Association for Computational Linguistics and the 11th International Joint Conference on Natural Language Processing: System Demonstrations*.

Hai Hu, Patrícia Amaral, and Sandra Kübler. 2022. Word embeddings and semantic shifts in historical Spanish: Methodological considerations. *Digital Scholarship in the Humanities*, 37(2):441–461.

Xiaolei Huang and Michael Paul. 2019. Neural temporality adaptation for document classification: Diachronic word embeddings and domain adaptation models. In *Proceedings of the 57th Annual Meeting of the Association for Computational Linguistics*, pages 4113–4123.

Gard B Jenset and Barbara McGillivray. 2017. *Quantitative historical linguistics: A corpus framework*, volume 26. Oxford University Press.

Tom Kocmi and Ondrej Bojar. 2018. Trivial transfer learning for low-resource neural machine translation. *WMT 2018*, page 244.

Vivek Kulkarni, Rami Al-Rfou, Bryan Perozzi, and Steven Skiena. 2015. Statistically significant detection of linguistic change. In *Proceedings of the 24th International Conference on World Wide Web, WWW'15*, pages 625–635, Republic and Canton of Geneva, Switzerland.

Elmurod Kuriyozov, Yerai Doval, and Carlos Gómez-Rodríguez. 2020. Cross-lingual word embeddings for Turkic languages. In *Proceedings of the Twelfth Language Resources and Evaluation Conference*.

Andrey Kutuzov. 2020. Distributional word embeddings in modeling diachronic semantic change. [PhD thesis].

Andrey Kutuzov, Lilja Øvrelid, Terrence Szymanski, and Erik Velldal. 2018. Diachronic word embeddings and semantic shifts: a survey. In *Proceedings of the 27th International Conference on Computational Linguistics, COLING 2018*.

Wei Ma, Hongzhi Yu, Kun Zhao, Deshun Zhao, and Jun Yang. 2020. Tibetan-Chinese cross-lingual word embeddings based on MUSE. In *Journal of Physics: Conference Series*, volume 1453, page 012043. IOP Publishing.

Mieradilijiang Maimaiti, Yang Liu, Huanbo Luan, and Maosong Sun. 2019. Multi-round transfer learning for low-resource NMT using multiple high-resource languages. *ACM Transactions on Asian and Low-Resource Language Information Processing (TALLIP)*, 18(4):1–26.

Enrique Manjavacas and Lauren Fonteyn. 2022. Adapting vs. pre-training language models for historical languages. *Journal of Data Mining & Digital Humanities*, pages 1–19.

Damian McManus. 1994. An Nua-Ghaeilge Chlasaiceach. In K. McCone; D. McManus; C. Ó Háinle; N. Williams; L. Breatnach, editor, *Stair na Gaeilge: in ómós do Pádraig Ó Fiannachta*, pages 335–44. Maynooth: Department of Old Irish, St. Patrick's College.

Syrielle Montariol. 2021. *Models of diachronic semantic change using word embeddings*. Ph.D. thesis, Université Paris-Saclay.

Syrielle Montariol and Alexandre Allauzen. 2019. Empirical study of diachronic word embeddings for scarce data. In *Proceedings of the International Conference on Recent Advances in Natural Language Processing (RANLP 2019)*, pages 795–803, Varna, Bulgaria. INCOMA Ltd.

Toan Q Nguyen and David Chiang. 2017. Transfer learning across low-resource, related languages for neural machine translation. In *Proceedings of the Eighth International Joint Conference on Natural Language Processing (Volume 2: Short Papers)*, pages 296–301.

Michael Piotrowski. 2012. *Natural language processing for historical texts*, volume 5 of *Synthesis lectures on human language technologies*. Morgan & Claypool Publishers.

Rannóg an Aistriúcháin. 1958. Gramadach na Gaeilge agus litriú na Gaeilge: An caighdeán oifigiúil. *Baile Átha Cliath/Dublin: Oifig an tSoláthair*.

Julia Rodina, Daria Bakshandaeva, Vadim Fomin, Andrei Kutuzov, Samia Touileb, and Erik Velldal. 2019. Measuring diachronic evolution of evaluative adjectives with word embeddings: the case for English, Norwegian, and Russian. Association for Computational Linguistics.

Alex Rosenfeld and Katrin Erk. 2018. Deep neural models of semantic shift. In *Proceedings of the 2018 Conference of the North American Chapter of the Association for Computational Linguistics: Human Language Technologies, Volume 1 (Long Papers)*, pages 474–484.

Sebastian Ruder, Ivan Vulić, and Anders Søgaard. 2018. A survey of cross-lingual word embedding models. *Journal of Artificial Intelligence Research*.

Maja Rudolph and David Blei. 2018. Dynamic Bernoulli embeddings for language evolution. In *WWW 2018: The 2018 Web Conference, April 23–27, 2018, Lyon, France*. ACM.

Kevin Scannell. 2014. Statistical models for text normalization and machine translation. In *Proceedings of the First Celtic Language Technology Workshop*, pages 33–40, Dublin, Ireland. Association for Computational Linguistics and Dublin City University.

Kevin Scannell. 2020. Neural models for predicting Celtic mutations. In *Proceedings of the 1st Joint Workshop on Spoken Language Technologies for Under-resourced languages (SLTU) and Collaboration and Computing for Under-Resourced Languages (CCURL)*, pages 1–8.

Kevin Scannell. 2022. Diachronic parsing of prestandard Irish. In *Proceedings of the 4th Celtic Language Technology Workshop within LREC2022*, pages 7–13.

Dominik Schlechtweg, Barbara McGillivray, Simon Hengchen, Haim Dubossarsky, and Nina Tahmasebi. 2020. SemEval-2020 Task 1: Unsupervised lexical semantic change detection. In *Proceedings of the Fourteenth Workshop on Semantic Evaluation*, pages 1–23, Barcelona (online). International Committee for Computational Linguistics.

Tobias Schnabel, Igor Labutov, David Mimno, and Thorsten Joachims. 2015. Evaluation methods for unsupervised word embeddings. In *Proceedings of the 2015 Conference on Empirical Methods in Natural Language Processing*, pages 298–307, Lisbon, Portugal. Association for Computational Linguistics.

Ian Stewart, Dustin Arendt, Eric Bell, and Svitlana Volkova. 2017. Measuring, predicting and visualizing short-term change in word representation and usage in VKontakte social network. 11(1):672–675.

Nina Tahmasebi. 2018. A study on word2vec on a historical Swedish newspaper corpus. In *DHN*.

Nina Tahmasebi, Lars Borin, and Adam Jatowt. 2018. Survey of computational approaches to diachronic conceptual change. In *Computational Linguistics*, volume 1.

Xuri Tang. 2018. A state-of-the-art of semantic change computation. *Natural Language Engineering*, 24(5):649–676.

Tithe an Oireachtais. 2017. Gramadach na Gaeilge. An Caighdeán Oifigiúil. Accessed: February 19, 2023. Data downloaded: July 6, 2022.

François Torregrossa, Robin Allesiardo, Vincent Claveau, Nihel Kooli, and Guillaume Gravier. 2021. A survey on training and evaluation of word embeddings. *International Journal of Data Science and Analytics*, 11(2):85–103.

Elaine Uí Dhonnchadha, Kevin Scannell, Ruairí Ó hUiginn, E. Ní Mhearraí, Máire Nic Mhaoláin, Brian Ó Raghallaigh, Gregory Toner, Séamus Mac Mathúna, Déirdre D'Auria, Eithne Ní Ghallchobhair, and Niall O'Leary. 2014. Corpas na Gaeilge 1882–1926: Integrating Historical and Modern Irish Texts. In *LREC 2014 Workshop LRT4HDA: Language Resources and Technologies for Processing and Linking Historical Documents and Archives-Deploying Linked Open Data in Cultural Heritage*, pages 12–18, Reykjavik, Iceland.

Yi Yang and Jacob Eisenstein. 2015. Unsupervised multi-domain adaptation with feature embeddings. In *Proceedings of the 2015 conference of the North American chapter of the association for computational linguistics: human language technologies*, pages 672–682.

Zijun Yao, Yifan Sun, Weicong Ding, Nikhil Rao, and Hui Xiong. 2018. Dynamic word embeddings for evolving semantic discovery. In *Proceedings of the eleventh acm international conference on web search and data mining*, pages 673–681.

Barret Zoph, Deniz Yuret, Jonathan May, and Kevin Knight. 2016. Transfer learning for low-resource neural machine translation. In *Proceedings of the 2016 Conference on Empirical Methods in Natural Language Processing*, pages 1568–1575.

A Vocabulary Sizes

Part	EX1.1		EX1.2		EX1.3		EX1.4		EX1.5	
	Original	Normalised	Original	Normalised	Original	Normalised	Original	Normalised	Original	Normalised
0	60,042	47,688	60,042	47,688	210,537	161,958	60,042	47,688	183,439	141,804
1	53,202	43,103	53,202	43,103	209,507	161,323	53,202	43,103	187,557	144,540
2	30,847	25,358	30,847	25,358	206,508	159,109	30,847	25,358	197,197	151,883
3	36,141	29,205	36,141	29,205	207,025	159,467	36,141	29,205	195,729	150,838
4	31,829	25,796	31,829	25,796	206,679	159,233	31,829	25,796	196,818	151,708
5	39,330	31,268	39,330	31,268	207,517	159,726	39,330	31,268	194,385	150,004
6	24,738	19,962	24,738	19,962	205,936	158,630	24,738	19,962	198,647	153,164
7	39,286	30,811	39,286	30,811	207,110	159,570	39,286	30,811	194,832	150,355
8	44,870	34,039	44,870	34,039	207,301	159,558	44,870	34,039	190,256	150,169
9	53,400	41,417	53,400	41,417	208,567	160,595	53,400	41,417	189,740	146,577

Table 8: Corpus vocabulary sizes. The data used in the Experiment II is the same as in the Experiment 1.1

Part	EX1.1		EX1.2		EX1.3		EX1.4		EX1.5	
	Original	Normalised	Original	Normalised	Original	Normalised	Original	Normalised	Original	Normalised
0	51,302	41,268					175,325	135,366	175,325	135,366
1	45,554	37,176					181,140	139,403	181,140	139,403
2	26,497	21,909					194,791	150,019	194,791	150,019
3	30,872	25,175					192,775	148,533	192,775	148,533
4	27,073	22,064	204,290	157,402	204,290	157,402	194,493	149,911	194,493	149,911
5	33,609	26,931					190,620	147,236	190,620	147,236
6	21,274	17,298					196,621	151,648	196,621	151,648
7	34,108	26,901					191,514	147,827	191,514	147,827
8	39,220	30,063					190,256	147,416	147,416	147,416
9	46,447	36,260					183,939	142,114	142,114	142,114

Table 9: Vocabulary sizes of the pre-trained embedding models. The models used in the Experiment II are the same as in the Experiment 1.1

B Experiment I

Part	Baseline	EX1.1	EX1.2	EX1.3	EX1.4	EX1.5
0	336.35	307.58	314.40	322.07	331.90	1078.61
1	337.98	303.26	305.32	290.13	326.54	701.80
2	361.98	332.79	343.32	327.89	352.05	481.70
3	412.06	361.04	368.50	341.49	384.55	481.53
4	542.83	471.44	492.45	465.98	511.74	625.31
5	351.83	321.69	328.19	285.42	334.07	611.22
6	266.43	247.67	256.58	288.62	255.75	590.64
7	230.54	210.66	214.76	187.38	218.73	302.57
8	180.49	168.07	169.22	185.69	171.44	219.63
9	222.64	205.81	207.08	184.55	213.03	364.72
AVG	**324.31**	**293.00**	**299.98**	**287.92**	**309.98**	**545.77**

Table 10: Experiment I: sentencewise perplexity scores; original texts without orthographic normalisation.

Part	Baseline	EX1.1	EX1.2	EX1.3	EX1.4	EX1.5
0	298.50	275.75	269.15	268.53	287.69	871.87
1	307.98	279.08	271.79	250.60	289.96	630.99
2	344.70	319.99	314.81	284.44	322.61	424.11
3	377.99	338.7	329.01	283.62	342.20	421.61
4	495.91	439.51	428.44	375.91	442.40	518.32
5	318.56	289.82	286.51	252.56	295.45	511.15
6	256.16	234.39	230.16	193.33	236.76	472.01
7	208.89	190.44	190.43	156.94	196.02	276.00
8	164.46	152.07	151.14	125.22	153.86	197.73
9	201.44	184.74	182.50	158.94	190.68	269.85
AVG	**297.46**	**270.45**	**265.39**	**235.01**	**275.76**	**459.36**

Table 11: Experiment I: sentencewise perplexity scores; orthographically normalised (demutated) texts.

C Experiment II

Part	0	1	2	3	4	5	6	7	8	9
0	100.00	90.65	87.59	87.59	87.02	88.18	86.70	87.19	85.53	87.39
1	91.44	100.00	89.05	89.67	87.48	88.62	87.68	87.94	88.11	88.66
2	93.94	95.00	100.00	93.48	92.71	93.23	90.60	91.41	92.19	91.64
3	88.87	90.26	91.12	100.00	89.81	90.83	88.74	89.54	90.35	91.88
4	90.23	88.13	90.59	89.67	100.00	90.81	90.58	89.01	90.79	91.83
5	90.03	89.45	90.87	92.39	90.18	100.00	90.20	89.57	90.86	90.90
6	92.20	90.30	92.49	94.43	92.24	94.43	100.00	91.15	92.18	92.51
7	89.91	89.19	89.96	91.53	90.83	92.08	89.16	100.00	94.55	93.94
8	91.71	91.43	91.30	92.47	92.15	92.86	92.18	95.40	100.00	96.34
9	89.65	89.43	89.67	90.61	89.63	91.00	89.87	93.62	94.80	100.00

Table 12: Experiment II. Original texts, normalised inverse perplexity scores in %, where 100% is the best score. Columns correspond to embedding models, and rows are corpus parts they were tested on.

Part	0	1	2	3	4	5	6	7	8	9
0	100.00	91.30	89.21	89.24	89.07	89.96	88.44	88.43	89.01	89.55
1	92.42	100.00	91.17	90.88	89.64	90.26	89.01	89.47	89.95	90.20
2	96.14	95.76	100.00	94.55	93.82	95.09	92.22	93.55	95.18	94.68
3	91.19	91.77	92.01	100.00	91.43	92.72	91.44	90.99	92.59	93.42
4	91.69	92.22	91.83	94.29	100.00	92.73	89.88	94.46	92.27	94.28
5	90.94	91.51	90.67	92.79	90.34	100.00	90.62	91.71	92.78	92.22
6	94.25	93.02	95.48	97.06	94.70	96.25	100.00	95.13	95.96	95.90
7	91.64	91.52	91.17	92.25	92.36	92.27	91.10	100.00	96.48	95.82
8	91.31	91.25	91.16	92.46	91.31	92.38	90.49	95.25	100.00	96.38
9	89.68	89.56	89.67	90.67	90.13	90.67	89.91	92.69	94.83	100.00

Table 13: Experiment II. Demutated texts, normalised inverse perplexity scores in %, where 100% is the best score. Columns correspond to embedding models, and rows are corpus parts they were tested on.

Variation and Instability in Dialect-Based Embedding Spaces

Jonathan Dunn
Department of Linguistics and
New Zealand Institute for Language, Brain and Behaviour
University of Canterbury
Christchurch, New Zealand
jonathan.dunn@canterbury.ac.nz

Abstract

This paper measures variation in embedding spaces which have been trained on different regional varieties of English while controlling for instability in the embeddings. While previous work has shown that it is possible to distinguish between similar varieties of a language, this paper experiments with two follow-up questions: First, does the variety represented in the training data systematically influence the resulting embedding space after training? This paper shows that differences in embeddings across varieties are significantly higher than baseline instability. Second, is such dialect-based variation spread equally throughout the lexicon? This paper shows that specific parts of the lexicon are particularly subject to variation. Taken together, these experiments confirm that embedding spaces are significantly influenced by the dialect represented in the training data. This finding implies that there is semantic variation across dialects, in addition to previously-studied lexical and syntactic variation.

1 Dialects and Embedding Spaces

This paper investigates the degree to which embedding spaces are subject to variation according to the regional dialect or variety that is represented by the training data. The experiments train character-based skip-gram embeddings on gigaword corpora representing four regional dialects of English (North America, Europe, Africa, and South Asia). While there is a robust tradition of discriminative modelling of dialects and varieties within NLP (Zampieri et al., 2017, 2018, 2019; Gaman et al., 2020; Chakravarthi et al., 2021; Aepli et al., 2022), there has been much less work on the influence which the dialectal composition of the training data (upstream) has on embedding spaces after training (downstream).

The basic idea in this paper is to train five iterations of character-based skip-gram embeddings on dialect-specific corpora in order to measure both variation (across dialects) and instability (within dialects); this is visualized in Figure 1. In order to find out whether specific parts of the lexicon are especially influenced by the dialect represented in the training data, the lexicon used for comparing embedding spaces is annotated for frequency, concreteness, part-of-speech, semantic domain, and age-of-acquisition.

If the specific dialect represented in the training corpus has no influence on embedding spaces, then variation across regions will be the same as variation within regions. In other words, we must control for instability (operationalized as variation across embeddings from the same dialect) to avoid false positives. However, if the dialect represented in the training data does have an influence on embedding spaces after training, then there will be a clear distinction between variation across dialects and instability within dialects.

The contribution of this paper is to show (i) that dialectal variation in character-based embedding spaces is significantly stronger than the noise caused by background instability and (ii) that this variation remains concentrated in certain parts of the lexicon. To accomplish this, we model the impact of dialect-specific training corpora on embeddings by controlling for background instability and organizing the experiments around the lexical attributes of frequency, concreteness, part-of-speech, semantic domain, and age-of-acquisition.

We begin by reviewing related work on dialectal variation and embedding stability (Section 2), before describing the main experimental questions (Section 3), the data (Section 4), and the methods (Section 5). We then compare variation within and between dialect-specific embeddings (Section 6) before modelling the influence of lexical factors on such dialectal variation (Section 7). Taken together, these experiments confirm that regional dialect or variety has a significant influence on embedding spaces that far exceeds baseline instability.

Tenth Workshop on NLP for Similar Languages, Varieties and Dialects (VarDial 2023), pages 67–77
May 5, 2023

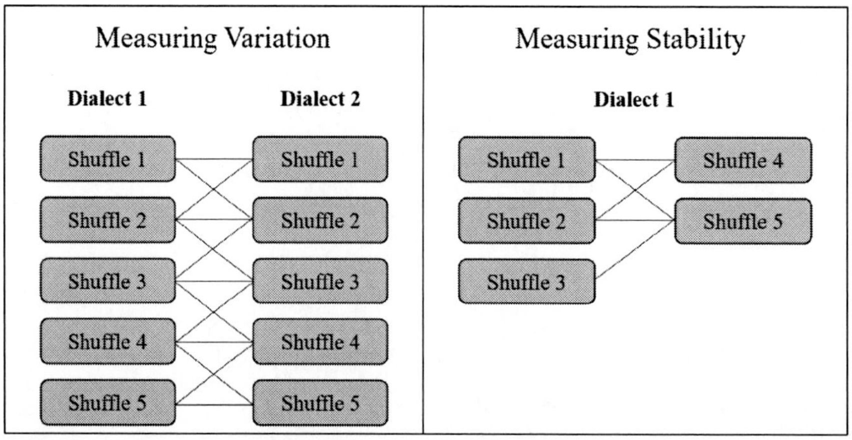

Figure 1: Overview of Comparison Methodology: Variation between dialects is estimated by sampling ten unique pairs of embeddings, where each embedding represents a shuffled version of a dialect-specific corpus. The baseline instability is estimated by sampling ten unique pairs of embeddings from different shuffled versions of a single dialect-specific corpus. Non-geographic factors like time period and random seed are held constant.

2 Related Work

This section discusses previous work in which models trained on data from different varieties (upstream) become significantly different after training (downstream). It also presents previous work on instability in embedding spaces.

Geography and Dialects. The creation of large geo-referenced corpora has made it possible to model variation across dialects, where unique locations represent unique dialect regions. Previous work has described geo-referenced corpora derived from web pages and social media (Davies and Fuchs, 2015; Dunn, 2020). Other work has evaluated the degree to which such corpora represent dialectal patterns found using more traditional methods (Cook and Brinton, 2017; Grieve et al., 2019), and the degree to which these corpora capture population movements triggered by events like the COVID-19 pandemic (Dunn et al., 2020). Further work has shown that geographic corpora from distinct sources largely agree on their representation of national dialects (Dunn, 2021). Building on these corpora, recent work has modelled both lexical variation (Wieling et al., 2011; Donoso and Sánchez, 2017; Rahimi et al., 2017) and syntactic variation (Dunn, 2018, 2019b; Dunn and Wong, 2022) in English as well as in other languages (Dunn, 2019a).

To what degree does dialectal variation influence semantic representations like skip-gram embeddings in addition to lexical and syntactic features? Previous work has shown that there is a significant difference between generic web-based embeddings and web-based embeddings trained using corpora sampled to represent actual population distributions; this difference was observed across 50 languages (Dunn and Adams, 2020). While these previous results lead us to expect dialectal variation across embeddings, there are two remaining questions: First, to what degree is this variation caused by dialectal differences as opposed to random instability? Second, is dialectal variation spread equally across the lexicon, equally influencing nouns and verbs, abstract and concrete, frequent and infrequent words?

Instability in Embeddings. A related line of work focuses on sources of instability in embedding spaces. It has been shown that many embeddings are subject to random fluctuation across different cycles of shuffling and retraining (Hellrich et al., 2019). Such instability has been investigated using word similarities (Antoniak and Mimno, 2018), showing that smaller corpora are subject to greater instability. In this line of work, two embeddings are compared by measuring the overlap in nearest neighbors for a target vocabulary. It has been shown, for example, that even high-frequency words can be unstable (Wendlandt et al., 2018) and that instability is related to properties of a language like the amount of inflectional morphology (Burdick et al., 2021). Other work has focused on the impact of time on embeddings, with variation leading to change (Cassani et al., 2021).

Circle	Region	Country	N. Words, Web	N. Words, Tweets
Inner-Circle	North American	Canada	250 mil	250 mil
		United States	250 mil	250 mil
Inner-Circle	European	Ireland	250 mil	250 mil
		United Kingdom	250 mil	250 mil
Outer-Circle	African	Nigeria	262 mil	100 mil
		Kenya	1 mil	100 mil
		Gabon	100 mil	100 mil
		Uganda	37 mil	100 mil
		Mali	100 mil	100 mil
Outer-Circle	South Asian	India	250 mil	250 mil
		Pakistan	250 mil	250 mil

Table 1: Source of Data by Region, Country, and Register

Other recent work has shown that register variation (Biber, 2012) has a significant impact on embedding similarity across a diverse range of languages (Dunn et al., 2022). This general approach to comparing embedding spaces focuses on aligned vocabulary (using nearest neighbors) rather than aligned embeddings because of instability in such alignment methods themselves (Gonen et al., 2020). As shown by this previous work, the comparison of nearest neighbors provides a robust method for detecting variation across embedding spaces.

This work on instability in embeddings is important because we need to distinguish between (i) variation across dialects and (ii) random fluctuations in embedding representations themselves. In other words, given the finding that embeddings trained on corpora representing different dialects are significantly different, how much of this is noise caused by random instability?

3 Experimental Questions

This paper focuses on two questions: First, are there significant differences in embeddings trained from corpora representing different dialects when accounting for baseline instability in the embeddings? Second, if so, are these dialectal differences specific to a certain part of the vocabulary, such as words belonging to a specific semantic domain?

The basic idea here is to compile four gigaword corpora representing English as used in North America, Europe, Africa, and South Asia. These areas represent different dialect regions. For example, while there are smaller differences between American English and Canadian English, these two dialects are more similar to one another than to other national dialects like Irish English. For example, work on syntactic variation has shown that American and Canadian English, at least in digital contexts, are closely related while UK and Irish English form a separate closely related pair (Dunn, 2019a). Based on the distribution of errors within a confusion matrix, other work has shown that Indian and Pakistani English are likewise more similar to one another than to other dialects (Dunn, 2018).

The dialects included represent both inner-circle and outer-circle varieties. The concept of inner-circle vs outer-circle is based on the historical stages of European colonization (Kachru, 1982). This distinction within the World Englishes paradigm is meant to capture the perceived prestige differences of these dialects rather than to make a distinction between dialects and varieties as linguistic objects. For example, inner-circle populations tend to have a higher socio-economic status and better access to digital technologies, leading to their status as prestige varieties. Both groups can be considered dialects. In some cases speakers of outer-circle varieties could be considered second-language learners; however, regardless of a distinction between native and non-native speakers, the production found in outer-circle varieties remains robust and predictable over time. Thus, we treat both inner-circle and outer-circle varieties as dialects of equal standing but maintain the terminology from the World Englishes paradigm in order to provide a bridge to work in sociolinguistics.

We first train embeddings on each dialect-specific corpus and then measure variation across a lexicon that is annotated for concreteness, age-of-acquisition, semantic domain, part-of-speech, and frequency. We train five sets of embeddings for each dialect-specific corpus, each based on a random reshuffling of the corpus. This allows us to measure the difference between variation (across dialects) and baseline instability (within dialects).

We work with skip-gram embeddings (SGNS: Mikolov et al. 2013) as implemented in the fastText framework (Bojanowski et al., 2017). In particular, we use the skip-gram variant with negative sampling ($n = 50$) trained for 20 epochs with a learning rate of 0.05 and 100 dimensions. The character n-gram sizes range from 3 to 6, with a maximum of 2 million n-gram buckets allowed. Because previous work has shown that different random seeds can cause instability (Gonen et al., 2020), we control for such instability by using the same random seed for each set of embeddings. Thus, variation caused by random seed and by training parameters is taken into account in this experimental set-up.

Several considerations support the use of non-contextual skip-gram embeddings for these experiments. In the first case, the focus here is on semantic variation rather than lexical or syntactic structures and the long-distance co-occurrences captured by the skip-gram task are taken as better representations for such semantic variation. In the second case, the inclusion of low-resource dialects like African English means that the amount of training data available is limited and insufficient for training robust contextual embeddings. Given the dual goals of focusing on semantics while also including low-resource dialects, skip-grams provide the most practical type of embedding for answering these particular experimental questions.

4 Data

The data used here represents different geographic locations which, in turn, represent different dialects. The data itself is drawn from two registers, web pages and tweets, both derived from the *Corpus of Global Language Use* (Dunn, 2020). The experiments train character-based embeddings for these four different regional dialects, as shown in Table 1. Each corpus contains 1 billion words, equally divided between registers (web pages and tweets). Thus, for example, the inner-circle North American corpus contains 500 million words of tweets, equally divided between Canada and the United States. The African web corpus has additional constraints because there is less data per country. As shown in Table 1 this corpus combines five countries into a single regional data set. The even split between web pages and tweets is maintained.

5 Methods

For each regional variety of English, we train embeddings using the fastText framework with the parameter settings described above. Previous work has shown that this family of embeddings can be unstable; in this context, *instability* means that the same training corpus could result in multiple sets of nearest neighbors over different iterations (Hellrich et al., 2019). We control for this by randomly shuffling each corpus and retraining the embeddings five times. Because all comparisons are between two sets of embeddings, we thus obtain ten observations (unique comparisons) to represent each condition, as visualized in Figure 1. We use the same random seed and the same parameters across all sets of embeddings to control for other sources of variation.

Vocabulary Features. The vocabulary for the embedding space is derived from semantic and psycholinguistic resources that provide categorizations for specific lexical items. This source of vocabulary allows us to compare stability and variation across different sub-sets of the lexicon.

Concreteness	N.	POS	N.
1.0 to 2.0	2,426	Adjective	4,130
2.0 to 3.0	5,619	Adverb	189
3.0 to 4.0	4,167	Name	139
4.0 to 5.0	4,599	Noun	9,827
-	-	Verb	2,322
-	-	Other	205
Total	**16,812**	**Total**	**16,812**

Table 2: Distribution of Vocabulary Items Across Concreteness Categories and Parts-of-Speech

The first source of lexical annotations is a participant-based study of concreteness (Brysbaert et al., 2014). This source provides concreteness ratings between 1 and 5 for each lexical item, with higher values reflecting more concrete and lower values reflecting more abstract judgements from participants. This source also provides the most common part-of-speech for each lexical item. The distribution of the vocabulary across concreteness ratings and parts-of-speech is shown in Table 2. An example of an abstract word (1.0 to 2.0) is *belief*; less abstract (2.0 to 3.0) is *famished*; more concrete (3.0 to 4.0) is *galaxy*; and most concrete (4.0 to 5.0) is *fire*. Within parts-of-speech, most words are categorized as adjectives, adverbs, nouns, or verbs.

Because different vocabulary items are generally

Category	N.	Conc	AoA
General & Abstract	2,384	2.4	10.5
Body & Individual	1,268	3.8	9.8
Arts & Crafts	114	3.8	9.8
Emotion	765	2.3	9.9
Food & Farming	586	4.2	8.6
Government & Public	761	2.9	10.9
Housing & Home	336	4.2	8.7
Money & Commerce	531	3.2	10.5
Entertainment	459	3.9	8.7
Life & Living Things	594	4.3	8.3
Movement & Travel	897	3.5	9.1
Numbers & Measures	795	2.8	9.7
Materials & Objects	1,806	3.7	9.0
Education	118	3.3	9.8
Communication	943	3.2	9.9
Social Actions	1,959	2.7	10.2
Time	474	2.7	9.2
World & Environ.	298	3.9	8.6
Psychological	1,255	2.4	9.8
Science & Tech	161	3.3	11.4
Names & Grammar	307	2.9	7.5
Total	**16,812**	**3.1**	**9.7**

Table 3: Distribution of Vocabulary Items Across Semantic Domains with Concreteness and Age-of-Acquisition Information for Each Domain

Word	Stability	Overlap		
	NA	EU	AF	SA
shag	0.53	0.00	0.00	0.03
daft	0.59	0.00	0.00	0.13
posh	0.66	0.00	0.00	0.05
proprietor	0.52	0.10	0.06	0.12
queue	0.63	0.10	0.08	0.08
abolish	0.80	0.22	0.23	0.28
bicker	0.61	0.22	0.03	0.20
isolationist	0.79	0.32	0.17	0.30
justice	0.82	0.32	0.24	0.22
reminisce	0.79	0.42	0.02	0.39
weeping	0.78	0.42	0.38	0.38
dictatorship	0.88	0.68	0.48	0.53
totalitarian	0.88	0.69	0.42	0.51
ten	0.93	0.77	0.57	0.69
twelve	0.94	0.77	0.62	0.70

Table 4: Examples With Different Levels of Overlap, North America Compared to All Other Varieties

learned at different stages of language acquisition, we also include age-of-acquisition ratings for the vocabulary (Kuperman et al., 2012). These ratings are collected via MechanicalTurk but validated against ground-truth age-of-acquisition ratings collected in a laboratory setting. For instance, words like *mom*, *water*, and *yes* are reported to be learned during a child's second year. But words like *constrain*, *confound*, and *thyme* are reported to only be learned at the age of twelve. If more socially-conditioned words are subject to more variation, we might expect, then, that vocabulary learned later in life is subject to more variation as a result. Note that both sets of participant-based ratings (age-of-acquisition and concreteness) depend on inner-circle participants. Thus, these experiments are focused on variation in embedding spaces rather than variation in participant-based lexical features.

The next source of lexical annotations is the UCREL Semantic Analysis system (Piao et al., 2015) which provides a high-level semantic domain for each vocabulary item. For example, there are 586 items belonging to the domain FOOD AND FARMING and 761 to the domain GOVERNMENT AND PUBLIC. The inventory of semantic domains is shown in Table 3 along with the average concreteness and average age-of-acquisition for each. There is a clear relationship between semantic domain and concreteness: for example, the domain that includes PSYCHOLOGICAL STATES is highly abstract at 2.4 while the domain that includes FOOD AND FARMING is highly concrete at 4.2. In the same way, some semantic domains are acquired early (like NAMES AND GRAMMAR at 7.5 years of age) and others much later (like SCIENCE AND TECHNOLOGY at 11.4 years of age).

In addition to these participant-based and semantic-based annotations, each lexical item also belongs to a frequency strata. This is calculated using the entire corpus across all regions and reported in occurrences per 1 million words.

Calculating Overlap. The stability and similarity of word representations are calculated using the overlap of nearest neighbors (Burdick et al., 2021). Given two sets of embeddings (i.e., North America and Europe) we iterate over each word in the lexicon. First, we retrieve the k nearest neighbors using cosine similarity. Second, we calculate the overlap between the two sets of nearest neighbors. For example, if all ten out of ten words appear in both embeddings as nearest neighbors, the overlap is 100%. If only five words out of ten appear as neighbors, the overlap is 50% (five shared words

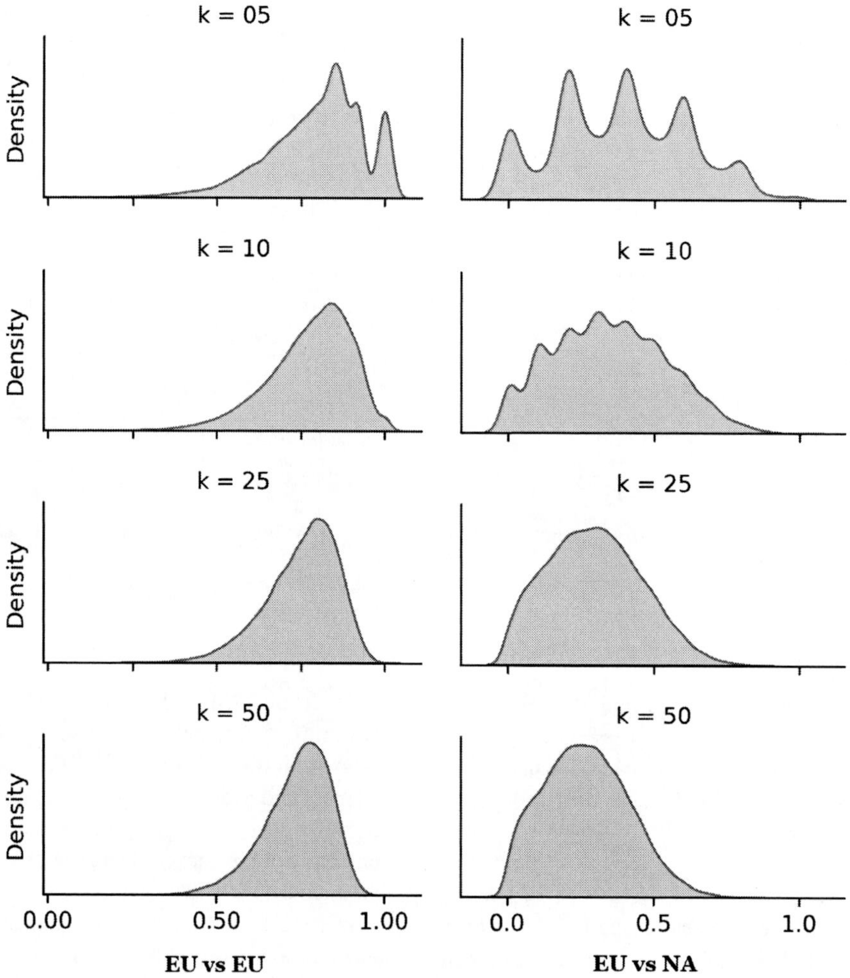

Figure 2: Distribution of Overlap Values Across Settings of k, for Europe-Europe and Europe-America Comparisons

out of 10 possible shared words). This provides a word-specific measure of overlap. This method aligns the vocabulary space rather than aligning the embedding spaces; this approach is taken because alignment methods have previously been shown to be unstable (Gonen et al., 2020) and thus less suitable for identifying variation across dialects.

A selection of example levels of overlap is shown in Table 4, with the North American embeddings compared with all other dialects. The smallest amount of overlap is shown for words like *daft* and *posh* which are used in different senses across these dialects. Culture-specific words like *isolationist* and *justice* provide a mid-level of overlap, with a similar sense but different references across dialects. Finally, a further cultural influence is shown for political words like *dictatorship*, which are more similar in inner-circle dialects than in outer-circle dialects. These examples show the range of overlap levels that are observed.

We measure overlap with values for k of 5, 10, 25, and 50. The distribution of overlap values is shown in Figure 2 for the European and North American model (on the right) and for the European and European model (on the left). Thus, the distributions on the right are across dialects and those on the left are within the same dialect. The impact of k is shown in the plots, with $k = 5$ at top and $k = 50$ at bottom. Smaller values of k lead to ragged distributions simply because the number of possible overlap values is limited. How much impact does the choice of k have on the results? We can see that higher values lead to finer estimates of the distribution of overlap, but overall the val-

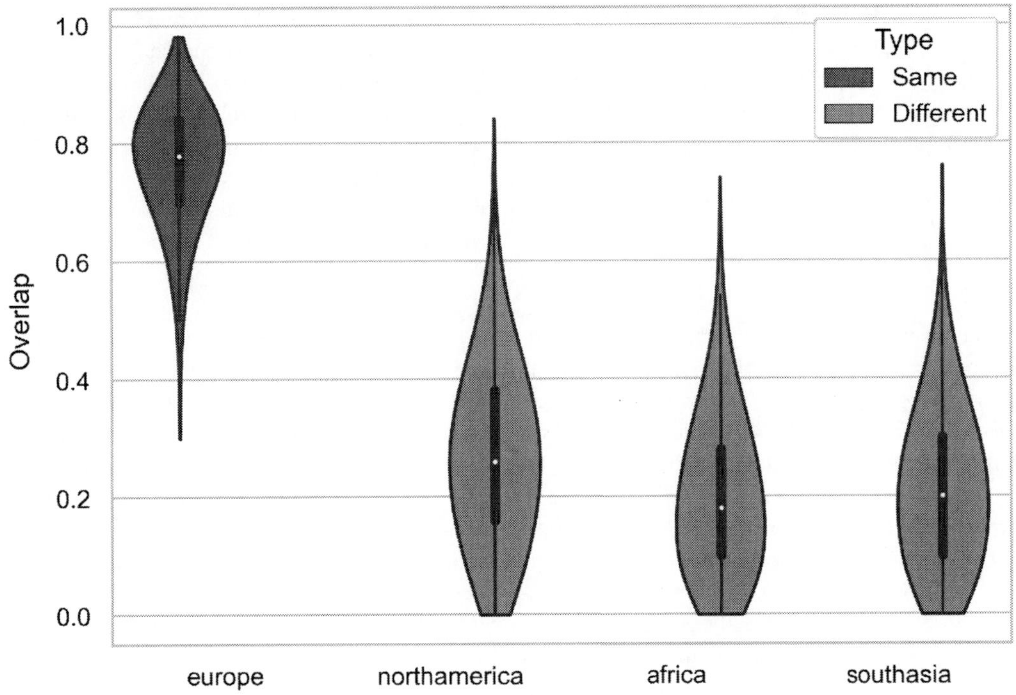

Figure 3: Distribution of Within-Dialect vs Between-Dialect Overlap Values for Europe

ues are much the same once k is above 10. For example, there is a significant Pearson correlation between overlap values at $k = 25$ and $k = 50$ (0.937 on the right and 0.879 on the left, in both cases with $p < 0.001$). We use $k = 50$ for the rest of the analysis, but the choice of k (above 10) has minimal impact on the results. We also see that the overlap within the same dialect (on the left) is greater than the overlap between different dialects (on the right). The figures for all distributions are available in the supplementary material.[1]

6 Overlap Within vs Between Dialects

The first experiment evaluates whether the variation between dialects remains meaningful when compared with baseline instability within a single dialect. The overlap measure described above compares the similarity between two sets of embeddings. We visualize the within vs between dialect condition in Figure 3 for Europe, with each type of comparison a separate violin plot. In blue we see the within-dialect overlap in which we compare European embeddings to other European embeddings. In orange we see between-dialect overlap for each of the other three regions. There is a clear distinction here between variation within the same dialect (baseline instability) and between different dialects (actual variation).

While we measured overlap between ten unique pairs of embeddings for each condition, this figure shows only the first pair for each. The supplementary materials contain the figures for all comparisons. The conclusion remains the same: the variation in embeddings across dialects is not simply a result of instability alone. There is a clear visual distinction between within-dialect and between-dialect overlap in all cases. We test for significance using a paired t-test: for example, are the values for Europe-Europe comparisons actually different from the values for Europe-Africa comparisons? For each comparison, we randomly choose a single pair of embeddings to test (i.e., so that we compare Europe and Africa only once). In each case the difference is significant with $p < 0.001$.

Thus, there is a visually clear and statistically significant difference between baseline instability and variation across dialects. We quantify the magnitude of this difference in Table 5 using a Bayesian estimate of the mean difference across the entire vocabulary and all pairs of embeddings. Within-

[1]https://jdunn.name/2023/03/27/variation-and-instability-in-dialect-based-embedding-spaces/

	EU	NA	AF	SA
EU	**74.1%**	26.8%	19.7%	21.5%
NA	–	**74.0%**	20.3%	22.0%
AF	–	–	**71.5%**	20.7%
SA	–	–	–	**72.8%**

Table 5: Bayesian Estimates of Overall Overlap Within and Between Dialects at 95% Confidence Interval, Across All Comparisons, $k = 50$

dialect overlap ranges from 71.5% to 74.1%, providing a baseline for instability. Between-dialect overlap ranges from 19.7% to 26.8%, showing that the dialect represented by the training corpus has a large influence on downstream embeddings.

There is a slight effect for inner-circle and outer-circle dialects: North America (NA) and Europe (EU) are more similar to one another than to Africa (AF) or South Asia (SA). Compared to the distinction between variation and baseline instability, however, this effect is relatively minor. The outer-circle varieties also have slightly lower stability than the inner-circle varieties.

7 Lexical Factors

We have shown that there is a significant difference in embedding spaces depending on the dialect represented in the training data, a difference that is much greater than baseline instability within dialects (as simulated by shuffling and retraining on the same corpora). This section explores dialectal variation in embedding spaces further by focusing on the impact of the lexical factors described in Section 5. We ask whether this kind of variation is distributed equally across the lexicon or whether it is concentrated in particular types of vocabulary.

We model the relationship between lexical attributes and overlap using a linear mixed effects regression model, with one model for each dialect. Within each model, the region of comparison is a fixed effect: for example, we model variation within the European embeddings using their overlap with North America, Africa, and South Asia as fixed effects. For random effects we include all lexical attributes. We represent each region using the average overlap across all ten pairs of embeddings, using $k = 50$ as before. The means of different regions are independent in the sense that each vocabulary item is modelled independently from corpora representing that region.

The coefficients and p-values for each lexical attribute are shown in Table 6 for all attributes that are significant for at least one dialect ($p < 0.01$). Positive categorical factors are shown above and negative factors below. Columns show results from the four dialect-specific models. While some factors are significant in one dialect but not another, no attributes have opposite effects across dialects (i.e., indicate more variation in one dialect but less variation in another).

Within semantic domains, vocabulary involving BODY AND INDIVIDUAL (e.g., *pain* and *ache*) are more stable across dialects, as are FOOD AND FARMING (e.g., *celery* and *sushi*) and SCIENCE AND TECHNOLOGY (e.g., *biologist* and *geologist*). These terms are less socially-conditioned in the sense that they refer to tangible objects or to specially-defined fields (like biology) that transcend cultural boundaries. On the other hand, vocabulary from semantic domains HOME AND HOUSING (e.g., *guest* or *pew*), MOVEMENT AND TRAVEL (e.g., *turnpike* or *curbside*), and NAMES AND GRAMMAR (e.g., *northwestern* or *roman*) are subject to more variation. These words are more socially-conditioned in the sense that they presume socially-defined concepts: a *guest* requires a definition of family units and a *pew* is a part of the concept CHURCH. Within parts-of-speech, function words (e.g., *of* or *and*) and adverbs (e.g., *hardly* and *exactly*) are much more stable. And named entities (e.g., *Flint*) are much less stable. Verbs are more important to the model than nouns.

Of the three scalar attributes, frequency has a significant effect but the coefficient is so small it is negligible. Concreteness is significant in every region, with more abstract words (e.g., *surreal* and *sanctimonious*) being more stable while more concrete words (e.g., *cookie* and *bug*) are less stable. In this case, the specific instances (the referents) of these more concrete terms are likely to be quite different across dialects (*cookies* are different in different places). Age-of-acquisition is significant in three out of four regions, but it has only a relatively small effect, with words acquired at a younger age being more stable. For instance, *mother* and *grandmother* (learned at age 2) are quite stable while *ethos* and *polarization* (learned at age 15) are subject to variation. The full regression results and the stability/variability values for the entire lexicon are available in the supplementary materials.[2]

[2]https://jdunn.name/2023/03/27/variation-and-instability-in-dialect-based-embedding-spaces/

Positive Factors		Europe		N. America		Africa		South Asia	
Subject to Less Variation		*coef.*	*p*	*coef.*	*p*	*coef.*	*p*	*coef.*	*p*
Domain	Body, Individual	3.97	0.000	4.36	0.000	3.82	0.000	4.56	0.000
Domain	Science, Tech	3.10	0.000	4.19	0.000	2.19	0.000	3.25	0.000
Domain	Food, Farming	2.67	0.000	2.98	0.000	1.87	0.000	3.25	0.000
Domain	Emotion	1.44	0.000	1.67	0.000	0.58	0.002	1.08	0.000
Domain	Arts, Crafts	1.37	0.004	–	–	–	–	1.21	0.008
Domain	Govt., Public	1.28	0.000	1.87	0.000	1.57	0.000	1.60	0.000
Domain	Entertainment	0.84	0.001	0.75	0.004	–	–	–	–
Domain	World, Environ.	–	–	0.91	0.003	–	–	1.22	0.000
Domain	Psychological	–	–	0.65	0.000	–	–	0.46	0.005
Domain	Social Actions	–	–	0.49	0.001	–	–	–	–
POS	Verb	2.58	0.000	2.48	0.000	2.71	0.000	2.26	0.000
POS	Function	12.97	0.000	10.35	0.000	12.14	0.000	10.43	0.000
POS	Adverb	8.83	0.000	7.23	0.000	8.47	0.000	6.55	0.000
Negative Factors		**Europe**		**N. America**		**Africa**		**South Asia**	
Subject to More Variation		*coef.*	*p*	*coef.*	*p*	*coef.*	*p*	*coef.*	*p*
Domain	Communication	-0.59	0.002	–	–	-0.77	0.000	-0.59	0.001
Domain	Money, Com.	-1.07	0.000	-0.88	0.000	–	–	-0.67	0.004
Domain	Life, Living	-1.12	0.000	–	–	-1.72	0.000	–	–
Domain	Materials, Objects	-1.14	0.000	-0.91	0.000	-1.42	0.000	-0.63	0.000
Domain	Movement, Travel	-1.94	0.000	-1.50	0.000	-2.14	0.000	-1.28	0.000
Domain	Housing, Home	-2.19	0.000	-2.38	0.000	-2.39	0.000	-1.54	0.000
Domain	Name, Grammar	-2.24	0.000	–	–	-2.10	0.000	–	–
POS	Names	-5.81	0.000	-6.40	0.000	-4.67	0.000	-6.19	0.000
POS	Noun	–	–	-0.34	0.001	–	–	-0.40	0.000

Scalar Factors		Europe		N. America		Africa		South Asia	
Lower Ratings=Less Variation		*coef.*	*p*	*coef.*	*p*	*coef.*	*p*	*coef.*	*p*
Empirical	AoA	-0.54	0.000	-0.53	0.000	-0.56	0.000	-0.48	0.000
Empirical	Concreteness	-1.66	0.000	-1.72	0.000	-1.69	0.000	-1.74	0.000

Table 6: Coefficients and P-Values from a Linear Mixed Effects Regression Model Using the Mean Overlap Across Dialects as the Dependent Variable. Non-Significant Effects are Not Shown.

8 Discussion and Conclusions

These experiments have shown that embedding spaces are subject to variation according to the dialect represented by the training data. This variation is significantly greater than noise caused by baseline instability in the embeddings themselves. This finding confirms the importance of regional dialects in NLP: while previous work has shown the impact of dialect on lexical and syntactic representations, this paper shows that such variation also extends to semantic representations.

Previous work has focused on distinguishing between dialects or on directly modelling variation over space and time. This paper has taken a different approach by training otherwise comparable models on corpora representing different dialects, controlling for other sources of variation like parameter settings and random seeds. The results show that the dialects represented in the training context have significant downstream impacts on common semantic representations (embeddings). These findings raise important questions for future work. First, is the influence of dialect consistent across languages or is this a result of the colonial history of a few languages like English? Second, do contextual embeddings also manifest this type of variation or is it confined to non-contextual skip-gram embeddings? Third, would a larger inventory of dialect-specific embeddings change the distribution of variation within the lexicon or is this a stable effect? Regardless of such further questions, these experiments show that dialect has a downstream effect on semantic representations, expanding previous work on lexical and syntactic representations.

References

Noëmi Aepli, Antonios Anastasopoulos, Adrian-Gabriel Chifu, William Domingues, Fahim Faisal, Mihaela Gaman, Radu Tudor Ionescu, and Yves Scherrer. 2022. Findings of the VarDial evaluation campaign 2022. In *Proceedings of the Ninth Workshop on NLP for Similar Languages, Varieties and Dialects*, pages 1–13. Association for Computational Linguistics.

Maria Antoniak and David Mimno. 2018. Evaluating the Stability of Embedding-based Word Similarities. *Transactions of the Association for Computational Linguistics*, 6:107–119.

Douglas Biber. 2012. Register as a predictor of linguistic variation. *Corpus Linguistics and Linguistic Theory*, 8(1):9–37.

Piotr Bojanowski, Edouard Grave, Armand Joulin, and Tomas Mikolov. 2017. Enriching word vectors with subword information. *Transactions of the Association for Computational Linguistics*, 5:135–146.

Marc Brysbaert, Amy Beth Warriner, and Victor Kuperman. 2014. Concreteness ratings for 40 thousand generally known English word lemmas. *Behavior Research Methods*, 46:904–911.

Laura Burdick, Jonathan K. Kummerfeld, and Rada Mihalcea. 2021. Analyzing the Surprising Variability in Word Embedding Stability Across Languages. In *Proceedings of the 2021 Conference on Empirical Methods in Natural Language Processing*, pages 5891–5901. Association for Computational Linguistics.

Giovanni Cassani, Federico Bianchi, and Marco Marelli. 2021. Words with consistent diachronic usage patterns are learned earlier: A computational analysis using temporally aligned word embeddings. *Cognitive Science*, 45(4):e12963.

Bharathi Raja Chakravarthi, Gaman Mihaela, Radu Tudor Ionescu, Heidi Jauhiainen, Tommi Jauhiainen, Krister Lindén, Nikola Ljubešić, Niko Partanen, Ruba Priyadharshini, Christoph Purschke, Eswari Rajagopal, Yves Scherrer, and Marcos Zampieri. 2021. Findings of the VarDial evaluation campaign 2021. In *Proceedings of the Eighth Workshop on NLP for Similar Languages, Varieties and Dialects*, pages 1–11. Association for Computational Linguistics.

Paul Cook and Laurel J. Brinton. 2017. Building and Evaluating Web Corpora Representing National Varieties of English. *Language Resources and Evaluation*, 51(3):643–662.

Mark Davies and Robert Fuchs. 2015. Expanding horizons in the study of World Englishes with the 1.9 billion word Global Web-based English Corpus (GloWbE). *English World-Wide*, 36(1):1–28.

Gonzalo Donoso and David Sánchez. 2017. Dialectometric analysis of language variation in Twitter. In *Proceedings of the Fourth Workshop on NLP for Similar Languages, Varieties and Dialects (VarDial)*, volume 4, pages 16–25. Association for Computational Linguistics.

Jonathan Dunn. 2018. Finding variants for construction-based dialectometry: A corpus-based approach to regional CxGs. *Cognitive Linguistics*, 29(2):275–311.

Jonathan Dunn. 2019a. Global syntactic variation in seven languages: Towards a computational dialectology. *Frontiers in Artificial Intelligence: Language and Computation*.

Jonathan Dunn. 2019b. Modeling global syntactic variation in english using dialect classification. In *Proceedings of the Workshop on NLP for Similar Languages, Varieties and Dialects*, pages 42–53. Association for Computational Linguistics.

Jonathan Dunn. 2020. Mapping languages: The corpus of global language use. *Language Resources and Evaluation.*, 54:999–1018.

Jonathan Dunn. 2021. Representations of language varieties are reliable given corpus similarity measures. In *Proceedings of the Workshop on NLP for Similar Languages, Varieties, and Dialects*, pages 28–38. Association for Computational Linguistics.

Jonathan Dunn and Ben Adams. 2020. Geographically-balanced gigaword corpora for 50 language varieties. In *Proceedings of the Language Resources and Evaluation Conference*, pages 2528–2536. European Language Resources Association.

Jonathan Dunn, Tom Coupe, and Ben Adams. 2020. Measuring linguistic diversity during covid-19. In *Proceedings of the Workshop on NLP and Computational Social Science*, pages 1–10. Association for Computational Linguistics.

Jonathan Dunn, Haipeng Li, and Damien Sastre. 2022. Predicting embedding reliability in low-resource settings using corpus similarity measures. In *Proceedings of the 13th International Conference on Language Resources and Evaluation*, pages 6461–6470. European Language Resources Association.

Jonathan Dunn and Sidney Wong. 2022. Stability of syntactic dialect classification over space and time. In *Proceedings of the International Conference on Computational Linguistics*.

Mihaela Gaman, Dirk Hovy, Radu Tudor Ionescu, Heidi Jauhiainen, Tommi Jauhiainen, Krister Lindén, Nikola Ljubešić, Niko Partanen, Christoph Purschke, Yves Scherrer, and Marcos Zampieri. 2020. A report on the VarDial evaluation campaign 2020. In *Proceedings of the 7th Workshop on NLP for Similar Languages, Varieties and Dialects*, pages 1–14. International Committee on Computational Linguistics (ICCL).

Hila Gonen, Ganesh Jawahar, Djamé Seddah, and Yoav Goldberg. 2020. Simple, interpretable and stable method for detecting words with usage change across corpora. In *Proceedings of the 58th Annual Meeting of the Association for Computational Linguistics*, pages 538–555. Association for Computational Linguistics.

Jack Grieve, Chris Montgomery, Andrea Nini, Akira Murakami, and Diansheng Guo. 2019. Mapping Lexical Dialect Variation in British English Using Twitter. *Frontiers in Artificial Intelligence*, 2:11.

Johannes Hellrich, Bernd Kampe, and Udo Hahn. 2019. The Influence of Down-Sampling Strategies on SVD Word Embedding Stability. In *Proceedings of the 3rd Workshop on Evaluating Vector Space Representations for NLP*, pages 18–26. Association for Computational Linguistics.

Braj Kachru. 1982. *The Other tongue: English across cultures*. University of Illinois Press, Urbana-Champaign.

Victor Kuperman, Hans Stadthagen-Gonzalez, and Marc Brysbaert. 2012. Age-of-acquisition ratings for 30,000 english words. *Behavior Research Methods*, 44:978–990.

Tomas Mikolov, Kai Chen, Greg Corrado, and Jeffrey Dean. 2013. Efficient estimation of word representations in vector space. In *arXiv preprint*, volume arXiv:1301.3781.

Scott Piao, Francesca Bianchi, Carmen Dayrell, Angela D'egidio, and Paul Rayson. 2015. Development of the multilingual semantic annotation system. In *Proceedings of the 2015 Conference of the North American Chapter of the Association for Computational Linguistics: Human Language Technologies*, pages 1268–1274. Association for Computational Linguistics.

Afshin Rahimi, Trevor Cohn, and Timothy Baldwin. 2017. A neural model for user geolocation and lexical dialectology. In *Annual Meeting of the Association for Computational Linguistics, Proceedings of the Conference*, pages 209–216.

Laura Wendlandt, Jonathan K. Kummerfeld, and Rada Mihalcea. 2018. Factors Influencing the Surprising Instability of Word Embeddings. In *Proceedings of the 2018 Conference of the North American Chapter of the Association for Computational Linguistics: Human Language Technologies, Volume 1 (Long Papers)*, pages 2092–2102. Association for Computational Linguistics.

Martijn Wieling, John Nerbonne, and R. Harald Baayen. 2011. Quantitative social dialectology: Explaining linguistic variation geographically and socially. *PloS One*, 6:9.

Marcos Zampieri, Shervin Malmasi, Nikola Ljubešić, Preslav Nakov, Ahmed Ali, Jörg Tiedemann, Yves Scherrer, and Noëmi Aepli. 2017. Findings of the VarDial evaluation campaign 2017. In *Proceedings of the Fourth Workshop on NLP for Similar Languages, Varieties and Dialects (VarDial)*, pages 1–15. Association for Computational Linguistics.

Marcos Zampieri, Shervin Malmasi, Preslav Nakov, Ahmed Ali, Suwon Shon, James Glass, Yves Scherrer, Tanja Samardžić, Nikola Ljubešić, Jörg Tiedemann, Chris van der Lee, Stefan Grondelaers, Nelleke Oostdijk, Dirk Speelman, Antal van den Bosch, Ritesh Kumar, Bornini Lahiri, and Mayank Jain. 2018. Language identification and morphosyntactic tagging: The second VarDial evaluation campaign. In *Proceedings of the Fifth Workshop on NLP for Similar Languages, Varieties and Dialects (VarDial 2018)*, pages 1–17. Association for Computational Linguistics.

Marcos Zampieri, Shervin Malmasi, Yves Scherrer, Tanja Samardžić, Francis Tyers, Miikka Silfverberg, Natalia Klyueva, Tung-Le Pan, Chu-Ren Huang, Radu Tudor Ionescu, Andrei M. Butnaru, and Tommi Jauhiainen. 2019. A report on the third VarDial evaluation campaign. In *Proceedings of the Sixth Workshop on NLP for Similar Languages, Varieties and Dialects*, pages 1–16. Association for Computational Linguistics.

PALI: A Language Identification Benchmark for Perso-Arabic Scripts

Sina Ahmadi **Milind Agarwal** **Antonios Anastasopoulos**
Department of Computer Science
George Mason University
{sahmad46,magarwa,antonis}@gmu.edu

Abstract

The Perso-Arabic scripts are a family of scripts that are widely adopted and used by various linguistic communities around the globe. Identifying various languages using such scripts is crucial to language technologies and challenging in low-resource setups. As such, this paper sheds light on the challenges of detecting languages using Perso-Arabic scripts, especially in bilingual communities where "unconventional" writing is practiced. To address this, we use a set of supervised techniques to classify sentences into their languages. Building on these, we also propose a hierarchical model that targets clusters of languages that are more often confused by the classifiers. Our experiment results indicate the effectiveness of our solutions.[1]

1 Introduction

Historically, the territorial expansion of the Arab conquests led to various long-lasting changes in the world, particularly from an ethnolinguistic point of view where the local languages of the time faced existential challenges (Wasserstein, 2003). With Arabic being the language of administration –a *Reichssprache*– many languages were affected and adapted in many ways such as writing or vocabulary. Over centuries the Persian language extended the Arabic script by adding additional graphemes such as <پ> (<p>, U+067E) and <گ> (<g>, U+06AF) to conform to the phonology of the language. Hence, one of the main extended variants of the Classical Arabic script is the Perso-Arabic script which has been gradually adopted by many other languages to our day, mainly in West, Central and South Asia (Khansir and Mozafari, 2014). Some of the languages using a Perso-Arabic script are Urdu, Kurdish, Pashto, Azeri Turkish, Sindhi, and Uyghur, along with many others that historically used the script such as Ottoman Turkish. This said, there are other scripts that were directly adopted from the Arabic script without being affected by the Persian modifications such as Ajami script used in some African languages like Swahili and Wolof, Pegon and Jawi scripts used in Southern Asia and Aljamiado historically used for some European languages.

Language identification is the task of detecting the language of a text at various levels such as document, sentence and sub-sentence. Given the importance of this task in natural language processing (NLP) as in machine translation and information retrieval, it has been extensively studied and is shown to be beneficial to various applications such as sentiment analysis and machine translation (Jauhiainen et al., 2019). This task is not equally challenging for all setups and languages, as it has been demonstrated that language identification for shorter texts or languages that are closely related, both linguistically and in writing, is more challenging, e.g. Farsi vs. Dari or varieties of Kurdish (Malmasi et al., 2015; Zampieri et al., 2020).

Furthermore, some of the less-resourced languages spoken in bilingual communities face various challenges in writing due to a lack of administrative or educational support for their native language or limited technological tools. These result in textual content written unconventionally, i.e. not according to the conventional script or orthography of the language but relying on that of the administratively "dominant" language. For instance, Kashmiri or Kurdish are sometimes written in the Urdu or Persian scripts, respectively, rather than using their adopted Perso-Arabic orthography. This further complicates the identification of those languages, causing confusion due to the resemblance of scripts and hampers data-driven approaches due to the paucity of data. Therefore, reliable language identification of languages using Perso-Arabic scripts remains a challenge to this day, particularly in under-represented languages.

[1] Data and models are available at `https://github.com/sinaahmadi/PersoArabicLID`

Tenth Workshop on NLP for Similar Languages, Varieties and Dialects (VarDial 2023), pages 78–90
May 5, 2023 ©2023 Association for Computational Linguistics

Language	639-3	WP	Script type	Diacritics	ZWNJ	Dominant
Azeri Turkish	`azb`	`azb`	Abjad	✓	✓	Persian
Gilaki	`glk`	`glk`	Abjad	✓	✓	Persian
Mazanderani	`mzn`	`mzn`	Abjad	✓	✓	Persian
Pashto	`pus`	`ps`	Abjad	✓	✗	Persian
Gorani	`hac`	-	Alphabet	✗	✗	Persian, Arabic, Sorani
Northern Kurdish (Kurmanji)	`kmr`	-	Alphabet	✗	✗	Persian, Arabic
Central Kurdish (Sorani)	`ckb`	`ckb`	Alphabet	✗	✗	Persian, Arabic
Southern Kurdish	`sdh`	-	Alphabet	✗	✗	Persian, Arabic
Balochi	`bal`	-	Abjad	✓	✗	Persian, Urdu
Brahui	`brh`	-	Abjad	✓	✗	Urdu
Kashmiri	`kas`	`ks`	Alphabet	✓	✗	Urdu
Sindhi	`snd`	`sd`	Abjad	✓	✗	Urdu
Saraiki	`skr`	`skr`	Abjad	✓	✗	Urdu
Torwali	`trw`	-	Abjad	✓	✗	Urdu
Punjabi	`pnb`	`pnb`	Abjad	✓	✗	Urdu
Persian	`fas`	`fa`	Abjad	✓	✓	-
Arabic	`arb`	`ar`	Abjad	✓	✗	-
Urdu	`urd`	`ur`	Abjad	✓	✓	-
Uyghur	`uig`	`ug`	Alphabet	✗	✗	-

Table 1: Perso-Arabic scripts of the selected languages studied in this paper. Columns 2 and 3 show the codes of the languages in ISO 639-3 and on their specific Wikipedia (WP), if available. The diacritics and zero-width non-joiner (ZWNJ) columns refer to the usage of diacritics (*Harakat*) and ZWNJ as individual characters.

As such, we select several languages that use Perso-Arabic scripts, summarized in Table 1. Among these, the majority face challenges related not only to a scarcity of data but also unconventional writing. Therefore, we define the language identification task for these languages in two setups where a) the text is written according to the script or orthography of the language, referred to as conventional writing, or b) the text contains a certain degree of anomalies due to usage of the script or orthography of the administratively-dominant language. Considering that Perso-Arabic scripts are mostly used in languages native to Pakistan, Iran, Afghanistan and Iraq, we also include Urdu, Persian and Arabic as they are primarily used as administratively-dominant languages. Furthermore, having a more diverse set of languages can reveal which languages are more often confused. Although we also include Uyghur, it should be noted that it is mainly spoken in a bilingual community, i.e. in China, where unconventional writing is not Perso-Arabic; therefore, we only consider conventional writing for Uyghur.

Contributions This paper sheds light on language identification for languages written in the Perso-Arabic script or its variants. We describe collecting data and generating synthetically-noisy sentences using script mapping (§2). We implement a few classification techniques and propose a hierarchical model approach to resolve confusion between clusters of languages. The proposed approach outperforms other techniques with a macro-average F_1 that ranges from 0.88 to 0.95 for noisy settings (§3).

2 Methodology

Given that the selected languages are mostly low-resourced, collecting data and, more importantly, identifying text written in a conventional and unconventional way is a formidable task. To tackle this, we focus on collecting data from various sources on the Web, notably Wikipedia.[2] Then, we propose an approach to generate synthetic data that can potentially reflect and model various types of noise that occur in unconventional writing. To that end, we use a simple technique that maps characters from the script of a language to that of another one, i.e. the dominant language. And finally, we discuss our efforts to benchmark this task and propose a hierarchical model that resolves confusion between similar languages.

[2] `https://www.wikidata.org`

2.1 Data Collection

As Table 1 shows, all languages have their dedicated Wikipedia pages using their Perso-Arabic scripts, except Gorani, Northern and Southern Kurdish, Balochi, Brahui and Torwali. Therefore, we use the Wikipedia dumps as corpora for the available languages.[3] On the other hand, for Northern and Southern Kurdish, Balochi and Brahui, we collect data by crawling local news websites as listed in Table A.2. Additionally, we use Uddin and Uddin (2019)'s corpus for Torwali, Ahmadi (2020)'s corpus for Gorani, Esmaili et al. (2013)'s corpus for Central Kurdish and Tehseen et al. (2022)'s corpus for Punjabi. Regarding Persian, Arabic and Urdu, we use the Tatoeba datasets.[4]

Once the data is collected, we carry out text preprocessing after converting various formats to raw text, use regular expressions to remove special characters related to formatting styles and remove information such as emails, phone numbers, and website URLs. We also convert numerals to Latin ones as a mixture of numerals is usually used in Perso-Arabic texts, namely Persian <۰۱۲۳۴۵۶۷۸۹> and Arabic <٠١٢٣٤٥٦٧٨٩> numerals along with the Latin ones. This is to ensure that a diverse set of numerals are later included in the sentences for the language identification task. As some of the selected languages use two scripts, as in Punjabi written in Gurmukhi and Shahmukhi or Kashmiri written in Devanagari and Perso-Arabic, we also applied a few regular expressions to remove script and code-switched sentences or quoted ones in the corpora. Given the complexity of detecting such alternations, we note that script and code-switched words may still exist in the cleaned corpora.

We finalize text preprocessing by unifying the Unicode encoding of characters. Inconsistencies in Unicode encoding are oftentimes due to the usage of keyboards with different code bindings and are previously included in preprocessing for some languages (Ahmadi, 2019; Doctor et al., 2022). As an example, <ے> (U+06D2) and <ي> (U+064A) may be used instead of <ی> (U+06CC) or <ك> (U+0643) instead of <ک> (U+06A9) in Kurdish. Depending on the usage of zero-width non-joiner character (ZWNJ, U+200C), as shown in Table 1, we also consider its removal in the preprocessing step.[5] Finally, we tokenize the corpora at the sentence level using regular expressions.

Table A.3 presents the 10 most frequent trigrams in the collected corpora among which many affixes and conjunctions are retrieved that can be indicative of a language.

2.2 Script Mapping

Assuming that a noisy text is written using the dominant language's script or orthography, we map the Perso-Arabic script of a given language to that of the dominant language, e.g. Kashmiri script to Urdu or Central Kurdish script to Persian and Arabic. To do so, we rely on the visual resemblance and Unicode encoding of the characters as follows:

- If two graphemes exist in the scripts of the two languages, as in <ھ> (U+06BE) in Sindhi and Urdu or <ٹ> (U+0679) in Saraiki and Urdu, we map them together regardless of their pronunciation in the two languages.
- In absence of an identical grapheme in the dominant script, the most visually similar character is mapped to the source character. For instance, the most similar character in Urdu to <ڷ> (U+06B7) in Brahui is <ل> (U+0644). Similarly, <ۋ> (U+06CB) in Gilaki is mapped to the similar <و> (U+0648) in Persian. This way, a character can be mapped to many other characters in the source language.
- Some mappings follow orthographic rules, particularly for characters that vary depending on the position in a word. For instance, vowels in Kurdish appear with an initial *hamza*, i.e. <ئ> (U+0626) as in <ئۆ> /oː/ and <ئێ> /eː/. We also include such rules.
- Since the numerals are unified in data collection (§2.1), we also map the Latin numerals to those of Persian and Arabic randomly.

Depending on the dominant languages, for each source and dominant language, a script mapping is manually created. It should be noted that along with the non-diacritical characters, diacritical ones are also included if the diacritics, including *Harakat*, are part of the grapheme as in <ڎ> (U+068E) in Gorani and Sindhi, but not <أ>. Detachable Harakat such as *fatha*, *kasra* and *damma* are not included in the script mapping. Table A.1 presents the set of characters used in the selected languages based on their relation with Arabic, Persian, and Urdu as the three major languages using Perso-Arabic scripts.

[3] Dumps of 20 January 2023.

[4] `https://tatoeba.org`

[5] We consult various sources on the Web for information about common writing practices in the selected languages, notably `https://scriptsource.org`.

2.3 Synthetic Data Generation

Using the script mappings, we mimic unconventional writing by generating synthetic sentences based on the 'clean' ones, i.e. sentences in the collected corpora. This is carried out by randomly substituting characters in the clean sentence with an alternative in the target script using our mappings. In order to evaluate the impact of noise on language identification, we synthesize data at various levels starting from 20% noise up to 100%, where a certain level of noise is applied based on the number of possible substitutions. Table 2 shows an example of a clean sentence in Northern Kurdish and its synthetic noisy equivalents based on the level of noise.

Therefore, the datasets are categorized as follows:

1. CLEAN: a dataset containing original sentences from the corpora without injecting any noise. This is equivalent to 0% of noise in the data. This includes all the selected languages along with Urdu, Persian, Arabic, and Uyghur.
2. NOISY: datasets of sentences having noisy characters at various levels, starting from 20% of noise and gradually increasing 20% up to 100%. Regardless of usage, detachable diacritics are removed when the noise level is 100%, including for Kashmiri for which diacritics are strictly used. We combine all data with all levels of noise in a separate dataset called ALL. Given that Persian, Urdu, Arabic, and Uyghur do not face unconventional writing, they are not included in the noisy data.
3. MERGED: the result of merging CLEAN and ALL datasets.

The CLEAN and NOISY datasets contain 10,000 sentences per language, except for Brahui, Torwali, and Balochi, for which only 549, 1371, and 1649 sentences are available in the corpora respectively. Therefore, we included 500 sentences from those languages in the test sets and upsample the remaining sentences with a coefficient of four, i.e. duplicating four times the remaining sentences, and consider them as a train set. Similarly, for Kashmiri and Gorani for which 6340 and 8742 sentences are respectively available, 2000 sentences are added to the test set while the remaining sentences are upsampled to have 8000 sentences in the train set.

To avoid an imbalance of data for dominant languages for which there is no noise, i.e. Urdu, Persian, Arabic, along with Uyghur, 10,000 more instances are added from their respective clean corpora. As such, the MERGED dataset contains 20,000 clean and noisy sentences per language.

Noise %	Sentence
Clean	دووەمین پێشانگەها فۆتۆگرافەرێن کورد ل بەلجیکا Second Kurdish photographers' exhibition in Belgium
20	دووهمین پێشانکهها فۆتۆکرافهرێن کورد ل بهلجیکا
40	دووه مین بشانکه ها فطکرافه رن کورد ل به لجیکا
60	دووة مین بشانکة ها فوتوکرافة رن کورد ل بة لجیکا
80	دووةمین بیشانکةها فؤتؤکرافةرین کورد ل بةلجیکا
100	دووهمین بیشانکهها فوتوکرافهرین کورد ل بهلجیکا

Table 2: A sentence in Northern Kurdish (Kurmanji) along with its synthetically-generated noisy ones based on different levels of noise.

2.4 Benchmarking

We consider language identification as a probabilistic classification problem where each sentence is predicted to belong to a specific class, i.e. language, with a certain probability. We use the 80/20 split of the sentences in the various datasets for the train and test sets as described in the previous sections. Both sets are from the same data.

As a baseline system, we use fastText's pretrained language identification model–`lid.176` that is trained using data from Wikipedia, Tatoeba and SETimes for 176 languages, including all the selected languages except Balochi, Brahui, Gilaki, Gorani, Northern Kurdish (in Perso-Arabic script), Southern Kurdish and Torwali. In addition, we train a model using fastText with word vectors of size 64, a minimum and maximum length of character n-grams of 2 to 6, 1.0 learning rate, 25 epochs and a hierarchical softmax loss.

Other than the fastText-related baseline and our own models, we also report precision, recall, and F_1 scores for benchmarking purposes for state-of-the-art methods such as Google's CLD3 (Salcianu et al., 2020), `Franc`[6] and `Langid.py` (Lui and Baldwin, 2012). We also share two other baselines trained from scratch with character n-gram features of sizes 2 to 4 - Multinomial Naive Bayes model (MNB – non-uniform learned class priors, no Laplace smoothing), and a Multilayer Perceptron (MLP) with maximum iterations of 500, one hidden layer of size 500 and a batch size of 1000.

[6] `https://github.com/wooorm/franc/`

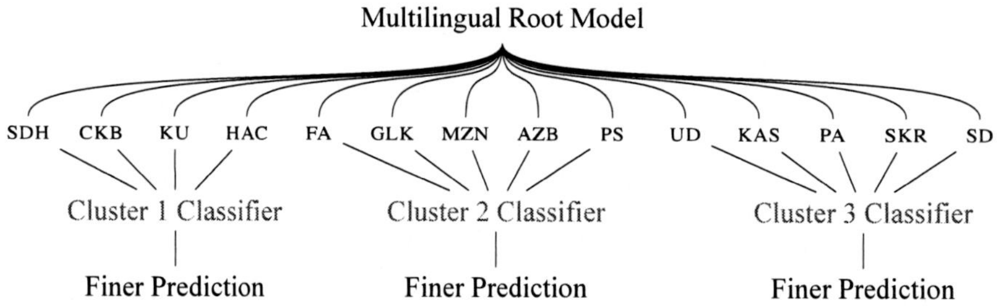

Figure 1: Architecture of our hierarchical model. If the root model predicts Southern Kurdish (SDH), Gorani (HAC), Northern Kurdish (KMR), or Central Kurdish (CKB), the sample gets sent down to a smaller expert classifier that is trained to resolve confusion between these four closely-related languages. Likewise for cluster 2 and cluster 3's languages. If an unclustered language is predicted by the root model, i.e. none of the branches are available, the hierarchical model predicts the same label as the root.

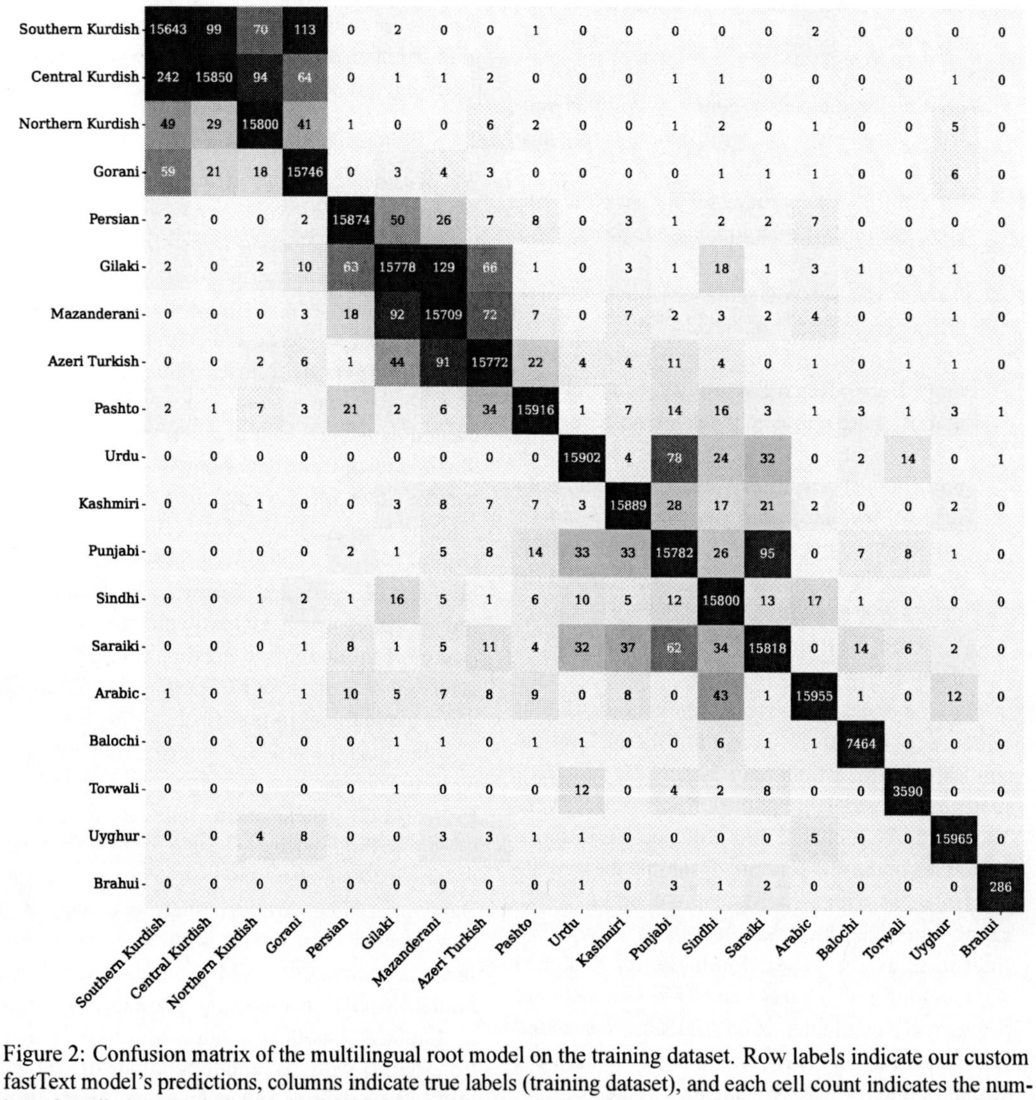

Figure 2: Confusion matrix of the multilingual root model on the training dataset. Row labels indicate our custom fastText model's predictions, columns indicate true labels (training dataset), and each cell count indicates the number of predictions made by the model for a (prediction, true label) pair. From the confusion matrix, we identified three highly-confused language clusters as reported in Section 2.5.

2.5 Hierarchical Modeling

The goal behind hierarchical modeling (Figure 1) is to resolve a model's confusion between highly-related languages by training expert classifiers that specialize in distinguishing between a small set of languages. We achieve this by inspecting the confusion matrix of the best-performing model (on training data) and identifying language clusters that the model shows high confusion in predicting. The custom-trained fastText model described in the previous section serves as the root classifier and we identify three clusters, as mentioned below, from its confusion matrix (Figure 2):

1. Cluster 1 containing Southern Kurdish, Central Kurdish, Northern Kurdish and Gorani
2. Cluster 2 containing Persian, Gilaki, Mazanderani, Azeri Turkish and Pashto
3. Cluster 3 containing Urdu, Kashmiri, Punjabi, Sindhi and Saraiki

Each sub-unit in the hierarchical tree is a fastText model trained from scratch on data from the relevant cluster's languages with the same parameterization as the root model.

3 Results

In Table 3, we report precision, recall, and F_1 scores across all datasets, 6 state-of-the-art and custom-trained baselines, our root fastText model (Root), and a hierarchical confusion-resolution model (Hier). We find that our root fastText model performs well by considerable margins when compared to the pre-trained fastText baseline, Google's CLD3, `langid.py`, `Franc`, MNB and MLP.

3.1 State-of-the-Art vs. Simple Baselines

None of the three state-of-the-art models (CLD3, `langid.py`, `Franc`) get more than 0.15 F_1 score on our test set across all 19 languages and noise settings. In fact, they often get acutely low F_1 scores ($0 \leq F_1 < 0.1$) for mixed noise settings (40% - ALL). This is despite these models' support of Urdu, Persian, Arabic, Sindhi, with `Franc` additionally covering Central Kurdish. This demonstrates the poor quality of language identification in the state-of-the-art pre-trained models despite claims of covering hundreds of languages, further highlighting that language identification is far from solved. Compared to these three models, the MNB and MLP models perform better across all noise levels (except 20% noise), and even outperform fastText's large pre-trained model `lid.176` on 7 out of 8 noise settings, becoming a stronger baseline than the `lid.176` model.

3.2 Hierarchical Modeling with fastText

Coming to our two models, the custom fastText model (Root) and the hierarchical confusion-resolution model (Hier), it is clear that both models perform noticeably better compared to any of the baselines by a huge margin. Since the hierarchical model is trained on the MERGED dataset which contains noisy and clean sentences with four more classes than the clean (0% noise) setting, it is natural that the Root model performs better in the clean setting. However, for any realistic noise level (from 20% to MERGED) the hierarchical model performs better than the Root model.

To test these subtle improvements, we report statistical significance results for each noise level according to a one-tailed Z-test, comparing the root model with the hierarchical model, at a significance level 0.01. We perform a Z-test because the number of samples is greater than 30 and the sample variance can be reliably used as an estimate of the population variance. The null hypothesis is that there is no significant difference between the root and the hierarchical model ($\mu_0 : f_{root} = f_{hier}$) and the alternative hypothesis proposes that the hierarchical model's performance is significantly and strictly greater than the root model ($\mu_1 : f_{root} < f_{hier}$). We compute a one-tailed 99% confidence interval for the root model's F_1 score f_{root}. As per the one-tailed Z-test, we can reject the null hypothesis and conclude that the difference between F_1 scores is statistically significant if the hierarchical model's F_1 score f_{hier} is strictly over this interval's upper bound. In Table 4, we report the results of our hypothesis testing and find that the advantage provided by our hierarchical confusion-resolution approach is statistically significant at the 99% confidence level for all noise settings. Therefore, we establish that a confusion-informed hierarchical approach could be utilized to improve performance on noisy data without re-training the entire model and that it translates well to the test set by bringing statistically significant improvements.

3.3 Language-Specific Performance

In Table 5, we report language-level scores across noise levels for the best two systems: our custom fastText model and our confusion-resolution hierarchical model. Across all languages and noise levels, the hierarchical model only underperforms in

Noise	Metric	Hier	Root	fastText	CLD3	langid.py	Franc	MNB	MLP
0%	Precision	0.72	**0.91**	0.16	0.03	0	0.02	0.43	0.47
	Recall	0.70	**0.89**	0.07	0.05	0	0.02	0.14	0.16
	F_1 Score	0.72	**0.90**	0.10	0.04	0	0.02	0.21	0.24
20%	Precision	**0.92**	0.92	0.30	0.08	0.13	0.13	0.08	0.03
	Recall	**0.89**	0.89	0.32	0.18	0.18	0.18	0.05	0.05
	F_1 Score	**0.91**	0.90	0.31	0.11	0.15	0.15	0.06	0.04
40%	Precision	**0.91**	0.90	0.17	0.04	0	0.01	0.51	0.49
	Recall	**0.88**	0.88	0.07	0.05	0	0	0.09	0.11
	F_1 Score	**0.90**	0.89	0.10	0.05	0	0	0.16	0.19
60%	Precision	**0.91**	0.90	0.17	0.04	0	0	0.45	0.54
	Recall	**0.88**	0.87	0.07	0.05	0	0	0.12	0.09
	F_1 Score	**0.89**	0.88	0.09	0.04	0	0	0.20	0.15
80%	Precision	**0.90**	0.90	0.16	0.03	0	0	0.25	0.33
	Recall	**0.88**	0.87	0.06	0.05	0	0	0.12	0.15
	F_1 Score	**0.89**	0.88	0.08	0.04	0	0	0.16	0.21
100%	Precision	**0.90**	0.90	0.15	0.03	0	0	0.44	0.44
	Recall	**0.88**	0.87	0.06	0.05	0	0	0.08	0.11
	F_1 Score	**0.89**	0.88	0.08	0.03	0	0	0.13	0.17
ALL	Precision	**0.90**	0.89	0.15	0.03	0	0	0.28	0.51
	Recall	**0.87**	0.86	0.06	0.05	0	0	0.16	0.10
	F_1 Score	**0.88**	0.88	0.08	0.04	0	0	0.20	0.17
MERGED	Precision	**0.95**	0.95	0.28	0.06	0.11	0.11	0.15	0.15
	Recall	**0.94**	0.94	0.27	0.16	0.16	0.16	0.08	0.07
	F_1 Score	**0.95**	0.94	0.27	0.09	0.13	0.13	0.10	0.10

Table 3: Comparison of all language identification models' precision, recall, and F_1 scores across noise settings. Our hierarchical (Hier) and Root models perform as the best two models for all noise levels. fastText, Multinomial Naive Bayes (MNB) and Multilayer Perceptron (MLP) take third place for different noise levels. Precision, recall, and F_1 scores are reported for all methods to provide benchmarks. For two values that are the same up to the hundredth decimal place, boldfaced entries indicate strictly better performance.

Noise	Test Samples	Δ	Significant
0	33500	-0.188	✗
20	25500	0.005	✓
40	25500	0.006	✓
60	25500	0.007	✓
80	25500	0.007	✓
100	25500	0.007	✓
ALL	27806	0.007	✓
MERGED	69304	0.002	✓

Table 4: Improvements (positive Δ) in the F_1 scores of our hierarchical modeling approach compared to the Root model are statistically significant for all noise levels at significance level = 0.01, i.e. 99% confidence.

5 out of 128 settings. For all others, it performs either at par or better than the Root model. The boldface entries indicate that the hierarchical model brings the most improvements in the noisy settings (20%-ALL) across all three identified clusters. As expected, for languages that were not part of any highly-confused cluster, i.e. AR, BAL, TRW, UG and BRH, the hierarchical and Root model produce the same predictions, therefore, have the same scores across noise levels. In Table A.4, we also provide a few language identification examples at various noise levels based on the predictions of the pre-trained fastText model in comparison to our model.

	0%		20%		40%		60%		80%		100%		ALL		MERGED	
	M1	M2	M1	M2	M1	M2	M1	M2	M1	M2	M1	M2	M1	M2	M1	M2
Cluster 1																
SDH	0.95	**0.96**	0.95	**0.96**	0.94	**0.95**	0.93	**0.94**	0.93	**0.94**	0.94	0.94	0.94	0.94	0.95	**0.96**
CKB	0.95	0.95	0.94	0.94	0.92	**0.94**	0.91	**0.93**	0.91	**0.93**	0.91	**0.92**	0.92	**0.93**	0.95	0.95
KU	0.95	0.95	0.93	**0.94**	0.93	0.93	0.92	**0.93**	**0.93**	0.92	0.92	0.92	0.92	**0.93**	0.95	0.95
HAC	0.94	0.94	0.94	0.94	0.93	0.93	0.92	0.92	0.92	0.92	0.92	0.92	0.91	**0.92**	0.94	0.94
Cluster 2																
FA	0.97	**0.98**	-	-	-	-	-	-	-	-	-	-	-	-	0.97	**0.98**
GLK	0.92	**0.94**	0.88	**0.89**	0.88	**0.89**	0.88	**0.9**	0.88	**0.89**	0.88	**0.89**	0.92	0.92	0.92	**0.94**
MZN	0.92	0.92	0.85	**0.86**	0.85	**0.86**	0.85	**0.87**	0.85	**0.86**	0.85	**0.87**	0.92	**0.93**	0.92	0.92
AZB	0.91	0.91	0.86	**0.87**	0.85	**0.86**	0.86	**0.87**	0.86	**0.87**	0.85	**0.86**	0.9	**0.91**	0.91	0.91
PS	0.96	0.96	0.94	**0.95**	0.94	**0.95**	0.94	**0.95**	0.94	**0.95**	0.94	0.94	0.96	0.96	0.96	0.96
Cluster 3																
UD	0.96	**0.97**	-	-	-	-	-	-	-	-	-	-	-	-	0.96	**0.97**
KAS	0.94	**0.95**	0.9	**0.91**	0.9	**0.91**	0.9	**0.91**	0.9	**0.91**	0.87	**0.88**	**0.91**	0.9	0.94	**0.95**
PA	0.91	0.91	**0.87**	0.86	0.86	0.86	0.86	0.86	0.85	**0.86**	0.85	0.85	0.87	0.87	0.91	0.91
SD	0.93	**0.94**	0.89	**0.91**	0.88	**0.89**	0.87	**0.89**	0.87	**0.89**	0.87	**0.89**	0.91	0.91	0.93	**0.94**
SKR	**0.92**	0.91	0.85	0.85	0.84	**0.85**	0.84	**0.85**	0.85	0.85	0.84	**0.85**	0.86	**0.88**	**0.92**	0.91
AR	0.98	0.98	-	-	-	-	-	-	-	-	-	-	-	-	0.98	0.98
BAL	0.98	0.98	0.94	0.94	0.94	0.94	0.94	0.94	0.95	0.95	0.95	0.95	0.97	0.97	0.98	0.98
TRW	0.95	0.95	0.87	0.87	0.89	0.89	0.88	0.88	0.88	0.88	0.87	0.87	0.91	0.91	0.95	0.95
UG	0.99	0.99	-	-	-	-	-	-	-	-	-	-	-	-	0.99	0.99
BRH	0.84	0.84	0.7	0.7	0.67	0.67	0.68	0.68	0.68	0.68	0.65	0.65	0.63	0.63	0.84	0.84

Table 5: Language-level F_1 scores for our hierarchical (M1) and Root (M2) models. Our hierarchical model shows improvement in F_1 score for languages in all three clusters (first 3 sections from the top) across noise levels. Dashed cells show that the language only has a conventional script and therefore was not part of the synthetic data settings.

4 Related Work

Modeling Approaches Language identification is generally modeled as a multi-class text classification task and has achieved state-of-the-art performance with straightforward byte, character or word-level n-gram features across languages and language varieties and in limited data settings (Jauhiainen et al., 2017). Model or classifier choice is highly dependent on the source, domain and quantity of data per language, with simple linear classifiers like Support Vector Machines (Ciobanu et al., 2018; Malmasi and Dras, 2015) and Multinomial Naive Bayes (King et al., 2014; Mathur et al., 2017) providing strong baselines with limited data and compute across domains. If large amounts of data are available, aggregated classifiers (Baimukan et al., 2022) and neural models may be used, but have continued to struggle with similar language varieties and dialects and have been prone to overfitting (Medvedeva et al., 2017; Criscuolo and Aluísio, 2017; Eldesouki et al., 2016).

In our paper, we propose a hierarchical approach to language identification that identifies commonly-confusable language pairs in noisy settings and resolves such mispredictions with small classification units. Such a modeling approach can be used to expand language coverage and improve the performance of the existing pre-trained models without retraining large compute-hungry models. In our case, we noticed statistically significant improvements for noisy data settings.

Similar Languages and Varieties Language identification is a well-studied problem, sometimes even considered *solved*; in reality, most of the world's languages are not supported by current systems. This lack of representation affects large-scale data mining efforts and further exacerbates data shortage for low-resource languages. One key bottleneck in improving language coverage in language identification systems is the ability to distinguish between similar languages, language varieties, and dialects. As outlined in this paper, this becomes even more challenging when a language community adopts the unconventional script of a dominant language. Recently, there has been studies in distinguishing between Nordic languages (Haas and Derczynski, 2021),

Arabic dialects (Nayel et al., 2021; Abdul-Mageed et al., 2020; Salameh et al., 2018) and regional Italian and French language varieties (Jauhiainen et al., 2022; Camposampiero et al., 2022). Haas and Derczynski (2021), for instance, experiment with many modeling and featurization approaches to best distinguish between six Nordic languages: Danish, Swedish, Norwegian (Nynorsk), Norwegian (Bokmål), Faroese and Icelandic. They find that skipgram embeddings extracted out of fastText are rich and capable of distinguishing between closely-related languages. It is worth noting that while the paper's approach presented improvements across selected languages, all six selected Nordic languages have a large amount of training data (50K+ sentences) and are already supported by off-the-shelf tools like `langid.py`. This is in contrast to our work where previously unsupported languages and varieties are incorporated into language identification systems and evaluated.

To distinguish between similar languages and dialects, more shallow and linear classifiers such as Naive Bayes and Logistic Regression tend to outperform neural models like MLP or convolutional neural networks (Chakravarthi et al., 2021; Aepli et al., 2022; Ceolin, 2021). This is confirmed by non-neural classical machine learning approaches winning a majority of VarDial 2021 and 2022 shared tasks across typologically diverse languages such as Dravidian languages, Romanian dialects, Italian and French regional varieties (Jauhiainen et al., 2022; Camposampiero et al., 2022), and Uralic languages (Chakravarthi et al., 2021). Neural modeling approaches, due to limited data in similar languages/varieties, may also sometimes under-perform non-neural baselines as reported in the Uralic Language Identification or the Italian Dialect Identification shared tasks (Chakravarthi et al., 2021; Aepli et al., 2022).

5 Conclusion

We focus our study on languages written in bilingual communities where an unconventional dominant Perso-Arabic script is often utilized in place of a conventional and more suitable Perso-Arabic variant writing system. We discuss challenges unique to this scenario, in both data collection and language identification, and consequent performance issues in state-of-the-art systems when faced with data in such unconventional writing systems. This is highlighted by the 20-point performance difference in F_1 scores between noisy and clean/mixed settings. Our proposed hierarchical approach outperforms a custom-trained fastText system, simple MNB and MLP and the state-of-the-art language identification systems of Google's CLD3, `Franc` and `langid.py`. We find statistically significant improvements by using a hierarchical model after analyzing a root multilingual model's confusion matrix.

6 Limitations

Some of the selected languages use more than one script, as in Punjabi or Kurdish. This affects the quality of the collected data which is preprocessed automatically. As such, we believe that our datasets contain a trivial but existing amount of code-switched text. Moreover, having focused on the Perso-Arabic scripts, we did not include texts from other scripts of such languages. Although a language can be affected by more than one dominant language and the synthetic data is generated by considering various script mappings, the impact of individual dominant languages is yet to be analyzed. To this end, a finer-grained classification task should be defined per dominant language.

Additionally, variants such as Dari and Farsi of Persian, and sub-dialects of the selected languages could be included in this task. In the same vein, our hierarchical approach can be applied to other scripts, particularly those that are adopted by many languages, such as Cyrillic and Latin. Finally, other techniques can be implemented and fine-tuned based on our collected data.

Generally, it is expected that the presented models perform better when trained on more data. We also believe that our hierarchical model's improvements over the root model are limited by the size of our training sets. With more genuine noisy data available, it is possible that our performance will improve across all noise setups as well as the clean data setup.

Acknowledgments

This work was generously supported by the National Science Foundation under DEL/DLI award BCS-2109578, and by the National Endowment for the Humanities under award PR-276810-21. The authors are also grateful to the anonymous reviewers, as well as the Office of Research Computing at GMU, where all computational experiments were conducted.

References

Muhammad Abdul-Mageed, Chiyu Zhang, Houda Bouamor, and Nizar Habash. 2020. NADI 2020: The first nuanced Arabic dialect identification shared task. In *Proceedings of the Fifth Arabic Natural Language Processing Workshop*, pages 97–110.

Noëmi Aepli, Antonios Anastasopoulos, Adrian-Gabriel Chifu, William Domingues, Fahim Faisal, Mihaela Gaman, Radu Tudor Ionescu, and Yves Scherrer. 2022. Findings of the VarDial evaluation campaign 2022. In *Proceedings of the Ninth Workshop on NLP for Similar Languages, Varieties and Dialects*, pages 1–13, Gyeongju, Republic of Korea. Association for Computational Linguistics.

Sina Ahmadi. 2019. A rule-based Kurdish text transliteration system. *ACM Transactions on Asian and Low-Resource Language Information Processing (TALLIP)*, 18(2):1–8.

Sina Ahmadi. 2020. Building a Corpus for the Zaza-Gorani Language Family. In *Proceedings of the 7th Workshop on NLP for Similar Languages, Varieties and Dialects, VarDial@COLING 2020, Barcelona, Spain (Online), December 13, 2020*, pages 70–78. International Committee on Computational Linguistics (ICCL).

Nurpeiis Baimukan, Houda Bouamor, and Nizar Habash. 2022. Hierarchical aggregation of dialectal data for Arabic dialect identification. In *Proceedings of the Thirteenth Language Resources and Evaluation Conference*, pages 4586–4596.

Giacomo Camposampiero, Quynh Anh Nguyen, and Francesco Di Stefano. 2022. The curious case of logistic regression for Italian languages and dialects identification. In *Proceedings of the Ninth Workshop on NLP for Similar Languages, Varieties and Dialects*, pages 86–98, Gyeongju, Republic of Korea. Association for Computational Linguistics.

Andrea Ceolin. 2021. Comparing the performance of CNNs and shallow models for language identification. In *Proceedings of the Eighth Workshop on NLP for Similar Languages, Varieties and Dialects*, pages 102–112, Kiyv, Ukraine. Association for Computational Linguistics.

Bharathi Raja Chakravarthi, Gaman Mihaela, Radu Tudor Ionescu, Heidi Jauhiainen, Tommi Jauhiainen, Krister Lindén, Nikola Ljubešić, Niko Partanen, Ruba Priyadharshini, Christoph Purschke, Eswari Rajagopal, Yves Scherrer, and Marcos Zampieri. 2021. Findings of the VarDial evaluation campaign 2021. In *Proceedings of the Eighth Workshop on NLP for Similar Languages, Varieties and Dialects*, pages 1–11, Kiyv, Ukraine. Association for Computational Linguistics.

Alina Maria Ciobanu, Marcos Zampieri, Shervin Malmasi, Santanu Pal, and Liviu P. Dinu. 2018. Discriminating between Indo-Aryan languages using SVM ensembles. In *Proceedings of the Fifth Workshop on NLP for Similar Languages, Varieties and Dialects (VarDial 2018)*, pages 178–184, Santa Fe, New Mexico, USA. Association for Computational Linguistics.

Marcelo Criscuolo and Sandra Maria Aluísio. 2017. Discriminating between similar languages with word-level convolutional neural networks. In *Proceedings of the Fourth Workshop on NLP for Similar Languages, Varieties and Dialects (VarDial)*, pages 124–130, Valencia, Spain. Association for Computational Linguistics.

Raiomond Doctor, Alexander Gutkin, Cibu Johny, Brian Roark, and Richard Sproat. 2022. Graphemic Normalization of the Perso-Arabic Script. *arXiv preprint arXiv:2210.12273*.

Mohamed Eldesouki, Fahim Dalvi, Hassan Sajjad, and Kareem Darwish. 2016. QCRI @ DSL 2016: Spoken Arabic dialect identification using textual features. In *Proceedings of the Third Workshop on NLP for Similar Languages, Varieties and Dialects (VarDial3)*, pages 221–226, Osaka, Japan. The COLING 2016 Organizing Committee.

Kyumars Sheykh Esmaili, Donya Eliassi, Shahin Salavati, Purya Aliabadi, Asrin Mohammadi, Somayeh Yosefi, and Shownem Hakimi. 2013. Building a test collection for Sorani Kurdish. In *2013 ACS International Conference on Computer Systems and Applications (AICCSA)*, pages 1–7. IEEE.

René Haas and Leon Derczynski. 2021. Discriminating between similar Nordic languages. In *Proceedings of the Eighth Workshop on NLP for Similar Languages, Varieties and Dialects*, pages 67–75, Kiyv, Ukraine. Association for Computational Linguistics.

Tommi Jauhiainen, Heidi Jauhiainen, and Krister Lindén. 2022. Italian language and dialect identification and regional French variety detection using adaptive naive Bayes. In *Proceedings of the Ninth Workshop on NLP for Similar Languages, Varieties and Dialects*, pages 119–129, Gyeongju, Republic of Korea. Association for Computational Linguistics.

Tommi Jauhiainen, Krister Lindén, and Heidi Jauhiainen. 2017. Evaluation of language identification methods using 285 languages. In *Proceedings of the 21st Nordic Conference on Computational Linguistics*, pages 183–191, Gothenburg, Sweden. Association for Computational Linguistics.

Tommi Jauhiainen, Marco Lui, Marcos Zampieri, Timothy Baldwin, and Krister Lindén. 2019. Automatic Language Identification in Texts: A Survey. *J. Artif. Intell. Res.*, 65:675–782.

Ali Akbar Khansir and Nasrin Mozafari. 2014. The impact of Persian language on Indian languages. *Theory and Practice in Language Studies*, 4(11):2360.

Ben King, Dragomir Radev, and Steven Abney. 2014. Experiments in sentence language identification with groups of similar languages. In *Proceedings of the First Workshop on Applying NLP Tools to Similar Languages, Varieties and Dialects*, pages 146–154, Dublin, Ireland. Association for Computational Linguistics and Dublin City University.

Marco Lui and Timothy Baldwin. 2012. langid.py: An off-the-shelf language identification tool. In *Proceedings of the ACL 2012 System Demonstrations*, pages 25–30, Jeju Island, Korea. Association for Computational Linguistics.

Shervin Malmasi and Mark Dras. 2015. Language identification using classifier ensembles. In *Proceedings of the Joint Workshop on Language Technology for Closely Related Languages, Varieties and Dialects*, pages 35–43, Hissar, Bulgaria. Association for Computational Linguistics.

Shervin Malmasi, Mark Dras, et al. 2015. Automatic language identification for Persian and Dari texts. In *Proceedings of PACLING*, pages 59–64.

Priyank Mathur, Arkajyoti Misra, and Emrah Budur. 2017. LIDE: language identification from text documents. *CoRR*, abs/1701.03682.

Maria Medvedeva, Martin Kroon, and Barbara Plank. 2017. When sparse traditional models outperform dense neural networks: the curious case of discriminating between similar languages. In *Proceedings of the Fourth Workshop on NLP for Similar Languages, Varieties and Dialects (VarDial)*, pages 156–163, Valencia, Spain. Association for Computational Linguistics.

Hamada Nayel, Ahmed Hassan, Mahmoud Sobhi, and Ahmed El-Sawy. 2021. Machine learning-based approach for Arabic dialect identification. In *Proceedings of the Sixth Arabic Natural Language Processing Workshop*, pages 287–290, Kyiv, Ukraine (Virtual). Association for Computational Linguistics.

Mohammad Salameh, Houda Bouamor, and Nizar Habash. 2018. Fine-grained Arabic dialect identification. In *27th International Conference on Computational Linguistics, COLING 2018*, pages 1332–1344. Association for Computational Linguistics (ACL).

Alex Salcianu, Andy Golding, Anton Bakalov, Chris Alberti, Daniel Andor, David Weiss, Emily Pitler, Greg Coppola, Jason Riesa, Kuzman Ganchev, Michael Ringgaard, Nan Hua, Ryan McDonald, Slav Petrov, Stefan Istrate, and Terry Koo. 2020. Compact Language Detector v3 (CLD3).

Amina Tehseen, Toqeer Ehsan, Hannan Bin Liaqat, Amjad Ali, and Ala Al-Fuqaha. 2022. Neural POS tagging of Shahmukhi by using contextualized word representations. *Journal of King Saud University-Computer and Information Sciences*.

Naeem Uddin and Jalal Uddin. 2019. A step towards Torwali machine translation: an analysis of morphosyntactic challenges in a low-resource language. In *Proceedings of the 2nd Workshop on Technologies for MT of Low Resource Languages*, pages 6–10, Dublin, Ireland. European Association for Machine Translation.

David J Wasserstein. 2003. Why did Arabic succeed where Greek failed? Language change in the Near East after Muhammad. *Scripta Classica Israelica*, 22:257–272.

Marcos Zampieri, Preslav Nakov, and Yves Scherrer. 2020. Natural language processing for similar languages, varieties, and dialects: A survey. *Natural Language Engineering*, 26(6):595–612.

A Selected Languages

Graphemes	Kurdish	Gorani	Uyghur	Arabic	Azeri	Gilaki	Mazanderani	Persian	Urdu	Kashmiri	Punjabi	Saraiki	Torwali	Pashto	Sindhi	Brahui	Balochi
Arabic	ئ ا ب ت ج د ر ز س ش ل م ن و ه ی ح خ ع غ ف ق	ئ ا ب ت ج د ر ز س ش ل م ن و ه ی ح خ ع غ ف ق	ئ ا ب ت ج د ر ز س ش ل م ن و ه ی خ غ ف ق ي ك	ئ ا ب ت ج د ر ز س ش ل م ن و ه ی آ أ إ ؤ ث ذ ح خ ص ض ط ظ ع غ ف ق ة ي ك	ئ ا ب ت ج د ر ز س ش ل م ن و ه ی آ أ إ ؤ ث ذ ح خ ص ض ط ظ ع غ ف ق	ئ ا ب ت ج د ر ز س ش ل م ن و ه ی آ أ إ ؤ ث ذ ح خ ص ض ط ظ ع غ ف ق	ئ ا ب ت ج د ر ز س ش ل م ن و ه ی آ أ إ ؤ ث ذ ح خ ص ض ط ظ ع غ ف ق	ئ ا ب ت ج د ر ز س ش ل م ن و ه ی آ أ إ ؤ ث ذ ح خ ص ض ط ظ ع غ ف ق	ئ ا ب ت ج د ر ز س ش ل م ن و ه ی آ أ إ ؤ ث ذ ح خ ص ض ط ظ ع غ ف ق	ئ ا ب ت ج د ر ز س ش ل م ن و ه ی آ أ إ ؤ ث ذ ح خ ص ض ط ظ ع غ ف ق	ئ ا ب ت ج د ر ز س ش ل م ن و ه ی آ أ إ ؤ ث ذ ح خ ص ض ط ظ ع غ ف ق	ئ ا ب ت ج د ر ز س ش ل م ن و ه ی آ أ إ ؤ ث ذ ح خ ص ض ط ظ ع غ ف ق	ئ ا ب ت ج د ر ز س ش ل م ن و ه ی آ أ إ ؤ ث ذ ح خ ص ض ط ظ ع غ ف ق	ئ ا ب ت ج د ر ز س ش ل م ن و ه ی آ أ إ ؤ ث ذ ح خ ص ض ط ظ ع غ ف ق	ئ ا ب ت ج د ر ز س ش ل م ن و ه ی آ أ إ ؤ ث ذ ح خ ص ض ط ظ ع غ ف ق	ئ ا ب ت ج د ر ز س ش ل م ن و ه ی آ أ إ ؤ ث ذ ح خ ص ض ط ظ ع غ ف ق	ئ ا ب ت ج د ر ز س ش ل م ن و ه ی آ أ إ ؤ
Persian	پ ک چ گ ژ	پ ک چ گ ژ	پ چ گ ژ		پ ک چ گ ژ	پ ک چ گ ژ	پ ک چ گ ژ	پ ک چ گ ژ	پ ک چ گ ژ	پ ک چ گ ژ	پ ک چ گ ژ	پ ک چ گ ژ	پ ک چ گ ژ	پ ک چ گ ژ	پ ک چ گ	پ ک چ گ ژ	پ ک چ گ ژ
Urdu	ھ	ھ	ھ						ھ ے ٹ ں ڈ ڑ	ھ ے ٹ ں ڈ ڑ	ھ ے ٹ ں ڈ ڑ	ھ ے ٹ ں ڈ ڑ	ھ ے ٹ ں ڈ ڑ	ے ں	ھ	ھ ے ٹ ں ڈ ڑ	ھ ے ٹ ڈ
Language-specific	ڕ ە ڤ ڵ ۆ ێ ۊ	ڕ ە ڤ ڵ ۆ ێ ۊ ۋ ۍ ێ ۉ ۮ	ڭ ە ۆ ۈ ۇ ۋ ې		ۏ ێ ۆ ۇ	ۋ ۊ				ٲ ٳ ۄ ۆ ۉ ۍ	ݪ ڼ ݨ	ٻ ڄ ݙ ڳ ݨ	ځ څ ڂ ڂ ڒ ݸ ۈ ݜ	ځ څ ډ ړ ټ ښ ګ ڼ ۀ ې ۍ ی	ڀ ٻ ٺ ٽ ٿ ڃ ڄ ڇ ڊ ڏ ڍ ڌ ڙ ڦ ڪ ڳ ڱ ڻ ي ۽ ؤ	ڵ	ٹ ۏ ٚ
Total/Unique	35/7	40/12	34/7	35/0	41/4	40/3	38/1	37/0	43/0	50/6	46/3	48/5	49/8	52/13	58/21	44/1	32/3

Table A.1: The Perso-Arabic scripts used in the selected languages with a comparative overview of the Arabic, Persian and Urdu scripts. Note that language-specific characters refer to those characters that are unique to a language and not used in Arabic, Persian or Urdu. This is shown in the last row as well.

Language	Website
Balochi	`https://sunnionline.us/balochi/`
Brahui	`https://talarbrahui.com`
Northern Kurdish	`https://badinan.org`
Southern Kurdish	`https://shafaq.com/ku`

Table A.2: Local news websites from which the collected data are crawled.

KMR	CKB	SDH	HAC	UIG	ARB	AZB	GLK	MZN	FAS	URD	KAS	PNB	SKR	TRW	PUS	SND	BRH	BAL
␣و␣	نی␣	لە␣	␣و␣	ئا␣	ال␣	ای␣	␣ان	␣ون	␣ست	␣یں	چھ␣	␣دے	␣اں	␣سی	␣د␣	␣جي	␣نا	␣نت
ێن␣	لە␣	␣لە	بە␣	نىڭ	أن␣	␣یر	ستا	␣نه	می␣	␣ے␣	آ␣	␣اں	␣دے	سی␣	␣په	جي␣	نا␣	␣اں
ان␣	انی	ئە␣	␣نە	␣ىڭ	␣لى	یند	ای␣	␣و␣	است	می␣	مَن	دے␣	␣یں	می␣	په␣	␣ان	␣ان	␣ان
هە␣	ان␣	وە␣	ان␣	ىنى	من␣	␣ین	تان	␣تا	را␣	میں	چھِ	␣وں	␣وں	␣می	او␣	␣۾␣	اس␣	انت
ئە␣	بە␣	ان␣	جە␣	␣نى	الم	␣ده	␣ته	و␣ه	␣را	ہیں	␣ھِ	␣تے	␣تے	مھ␣	␣او	␣۽␣	␣ئی	␣نی
کو␣	ە␣ی	␣و␣	ە␣ی	ىلى	في␣	او␣	␣␣	ا␣ه	اس␣	کی␣	␣ہٕ	␣دی	␣دی	کی␣	د␣ه	جو␣	اٹ␣	␣که
یا␣	ئە␣	ەیل	کە␣	␣ان	␣في	␣ان	ا␣ه	␣ره	به␣	␣ہے	␣کھ	دی␣	دے␣	␣ھی	کې␣	ج␣ن	او␣	ان␣
␣ل␣	ەوە	␣یل	␣جە	␣ئى␣	سا␣	ا␣ی	ایس	ای␣	␣ند	ہ␣ا	مَ␣	وچ␣	␣دا	م␣ی	␣له	آه␣	␣آ␣	انی
نا␣	␣و␣	کرد	انی	ى␣ئ	␣مي	␣و␣	وست	␣له	␣به	ہو␣	آک	␣نے	تے␣	تھ␣	د␣ي	␣ھن	ا␣ن	که␣
دا␣	ئ␣ی	␣یگ	ئا␣	ىرى	␣من	␣دا	␣سه	␣ته	می_	␣نے	کھ	␣وچ	دی␣	بھ␣	␣کې	␣جو	دا␣	␣یں

Table A.3: The 10 most frequent trigrams in the collected corpora of the selected languages. ␣ and _ represent space and ZWNJ, respectively. Among the trigrams, many affixes and conjunctions can be seen, such as ␣و␣ ('and') in Northern Kurdish (KMR), ␣کە ('that') in Gorani (HAC).

Language	Noise %	Prediction (@1)		Sentence
		`lid.176`	Our's	
Punjabi	0	Urdu	Azeri	اور لادینیت واشتراکیت کو جمہوریت کے حسین لبادہ میں پیش کردیا گیا ۔
Saraiki	0	Punjabi	Saraiki	کہیں وی زبان وادب تے تحقیق زیادہ تر کیفیتی
Sindhi	0	Sindhi	Sindhi	گھڻا دفعا هڪ عورت سائياڻي جنهن سان ڪوئي افلاطوني
Balochi	0	Urdu	Balochi	آیانی راہا کہ تئی مہر بوتگ اَنت گنجّ گْوار
Azeri	0	Persian	Azeri	قوزئی و دوغو سوریه موختار ایدارەائتمەسی
Gilaki	0	Persian	Gilaki	شوراب ایسم ایته روستا ایسه جه راستوپی دهستان
Persian	0	Persian	Persian	جوانی زمان فرا گرفتن دانایی است. پیری زمان تمرین کردن آن است.
Uyghur	0	Uyghur	Uyghur	ھەيدەكچىلىك تەرتىپىنى ئاياغلاشتۇرۇش توغرىسىدا كىبسىم چىقىرىدۇ
Southern Kurdish	0	Sorani	Southern Kurdish	ڤایرۆس کۆرۆنا لەڕێ دادوەر و پاریزەرەیل دەوام لە دادگای هەولێر وسان
Kashmiri	20	Urdu	Kashmiri	سودھا رانی چھ اَکھ ہِندوستانٕ اَداکارہ یوس فِلمَن مَنٛز چھ کامٕ کَران.
Kashmiri	100	Urdu	Kashmiri	سودھا رانی چھ اکھ ہندوستانے اداکارہ یوس فلمن منز چھ کام کران.
Sorani	20	Persian	Sorani	ریژهی دهرجوانی ئهمسال له سالی پێشتر زیاتره
Sorani	100	Arabic	Sorani	ريژهي دهرجاني ئهمصال له صالي پيشطر زياطره

Table A.4: A few examples in the selected languages along with the predictions of fastText's pretrained models (`lid.176`) in comparison to those of one of our models trained using fastText on our collected data.

Get to Know Your Parallel Data: Performing English Variety and Genre Classification over MaCoCu Corpora

Taja Kuzman and **Peter Rupnik**
Jožef Stefan Institute, Slovenia
taja.kuzman@ijs.si,
peter.rupnik@ijs.si

Nikola Ljubešić
Jožef Stefan Institute, Slovenia
Center za jezikovne vire in tehnologije
Univerze v Ljubljani, Slovenia
nikola.ljubesic@ijs.si

Abstract

Collecting texts from the web enables a rapid creation of monolingual and parallel corpora of unprecedented size. However, unlike manually-collected corpora, authors and end users do not know which texts make up the web collections. In this work, we analyse the content of seven European parallel web corpora, collected from national top-level domains, by analysing the English variety and genre distribution in them. We develop and provide a lexicon-based British-American variety classifier, which we use to identify the English variety. In addition, we apply a Transformer-based genre classifier to corpora to analyse genre distribution and the interplay between genres and English varieties. The results reveal significant differences among the seven corpora in terms of different genre distribution and different preference for English varieties.

1 Introduction

Collecting text corpora in an automatic manner, by crawling web pages, allows for quick gathering of large amounts of texts. With this approach, the MaCoCu[1] project (Bañón et al., 2022h) aims to provide some of the largest freely available monolingual and parallel corpora for more than 10 under-resourced European languages. However, in contrast to manual text collection methods, the disadvantage of automatic methods is that both the corpora creators and the users do not know what the overall quality of the dataset is, and what type of texts the collections consist of (Baroni et al., 2009). The MaCoCu corpora address this issue by providing rich metadata, including information on source URLs, paragraph quality, translation direction, English varieties, and genres. In this paper, we present two of the text classification methods, used to automatically enrich massive corpora with meaningful metadata: English variety classification and automatic genre identification. We show how they provide a better insight into the differences between corpora.

There is limited research on the use of British and American English in the non-native English-speaking countries. Previous findings show that these English varieties are preferred to a different extent in different educational systems (Forsberg et al., 2019), translation services (Forsyth and Cayley, 2022) and on different national webs (Atwell et al., 2007). However, to the best of our knowledge, there is no freely available classifier between American and British English which would allow easy identification of an English variety in large corpora, and thus allow for a corpus-based research of this phenomenon on a larger scale. To this end, we develop a fast and reliable classifier which is based on a lexicon of variety-specific spellings and words. In addition, we also compare the web corpora in terms of genres. Genres are text categories which are defined considering the author's purpose, common function of the text, and the text's conventional form (Orlikowski and Yates, 1994). Examples of genres are *News*, *Promotion*, *Legal*, etc. In addition to providing a valuable insight into the dataset content, information about the genre of the document was shown to be beneficial for various NLP tasks, including POS-tagging (Giesbrecht and Evert, 2009), machine translation (Van der Wees et al., 2018) and automatic summarization (Stewart and Callan, 2009).

The main contributions of our paper are the following:

1. We present a freely available American-British variety classifier that we make available as a Python package[2]. The classifier is based on a lexicon of variant-specific words and is thus reliable and fast. In contrast to deep neural models that are trained on varying

[1] https://macocu.eu/

[2] https://pypi.org/project/abclf/

Tenth Workshop on NLP for Similar Languages, Varieties and Dialects (VarDial 2023), pages 91–103
May 5, 2023 ©2023 Association for Computational Linguistics

texts, deemed to represent different varieties, the classifier cannot be influenced by any bias in the training data, such as differences in topics or proper names, and its predictions are explainable. The classifier can be applied to any English corpus with texts of sufficient length and could be used for researching which English variety is preferred in different national web domains, official translations, school systems and so on.

2. We introduce a method of comparing large web corpora and obtaining additional insight into their contents based on English variety and genre information. We apply the English variety and genre classifier to 7 parallel web corpora harvested from the following European national webs: Icelandic, Maltese, Slovene, Croatian, Macedonian, Bulgarian and Turkish. The results show that English variety and genre information reveal differences between these datasets. These insights provide useful information to corpora creators and researchers that use the corpora for downstream tasks, such as training language models and machine translation models, as well as performing corpus linguistic studies on these corpora.

The paper is organized as follows. We first present the related work on English variety identification and automatic genre identification in Section 2. In Section 3, we present the web corpora to which we apply the classifiers, described in Section 4. The results in Section 5 show that these approaches reveal important differences between the corpora. The paper concludes with Section 6, where we summarize the main findings and present future work.

2 Related Work

Diatopic variation, that is, variation among national varieties of the same language (Zampieri et al., 2020), can be approached similarly to variation between different languages. Two main approaches in language identification of English varieties are 1) corpus-based text classification and 2) lexicon-based text classification. In corpus-based classification, researchers use datasets which have a known origin of the texts as a reference based on which the classifiers are trained and evaluated, while lexicon-based classifiers identify varieties based on a list of variety-specific words or spelling variants.

Most previous studies on identification of English varieties were corpus-based (Lui and Cook, 2013; Utomo and Sibaroni, 2019; Cook and Hirst, 2012; Dunn, 2019; Simaki et al., 2017; Rangel et al., 2017). The advantage of corpus-based classification is that as the model is trained on actual text collections, it could show the differences in the varieties as they appear "in the wild", and researchers do not need a profound knowledge of lexical differences between the varieties that linguists are aware of. To obtain reference datasets that are large enough to be used for training the model, researchers most often used or constructed web corpora (Atwell et al., 2007; Lui and Cook, 2013), using the national top-level domains as indicators of the text origin (e.g., `.uk` for British English), journalistic corpora (Zampieri et al., 2014), national corpora (Lui et al., 2014; Utomo and Sibaroni, 2019), such as the British National Corpus (BNC) (Consortium et al., 2007) , and/or social media corpora (Dunn, 2019; Simaki et al., 2017; Rangel et al., 2017), consisting of texts from Twitter and Facebook, where the variety is assigned to texts based on the metadata about the post or its author.

However, one of the major drawbacks of this approach is that it is assumed that the texts from a specific top-level domain or posted to social media from a certain location are written by a native speaker of this variety, while this is hard or impossible to verify. In addition, web, national and journalistic corpora can contain cross citations and republications (e.g., a British text that was republished by an American newspaper website and vice versa). This was revealed for the DSL corpus collection, used in the Discriminating between Similar Languages (DSL) shared task 2014, where 25% of texts were discovered to be likely annotated with the wrong English variety (Zampieri et al., 2014). Another drawback of the corpus-based approach is that training on text collections can introduce various bias into the classification task. As no parallel corpus of English varieties exists, the classification is based on two or more separate collections of texts. The datasets which represent each variety do not differ only in language specificities, but also in content and style. This hinders learning truly representative differences between the varieties, and the classification models might learn to differentiate between the datasets based on other differences, unrelated to varieties, such as topic (Kilgarriff and Kilgarri, 2001; Tiedemann and Ljubešić, 2012).

An alternative approach to the corpus-based classification is lexicon-based. It has been used by Lui and Cook (2013) who devised a "variant pair" classifier based on the VarCon lexicon of spelling variants (Atkinson and Titze, 2020). This approach does not introduce any biases, related to the corpora content, and the classification is explainable. However, its disadvantage is that as it relies on a specific list of words, if none of the words occur in a text, its variety is unknown, meaning that some texts in the corpus may remain unclassified.

While research on automatic identification of English varieties is rather limited, automatic genre identification (AGI) has been an established text categorization task ever since the advent of the world wide web. As genre information is very useful for obtaining better hits to a query in information retrieval tools, used on the web, there has been large interest for genre identification in the area of information retrieval (see Roussinov et al. (2001); Vidulin et al. (2007)). In addition, with the emergence of technologies for automatic collection of text corpora, an interest for tools for AGI emerged also in the field of corpora creation and curation. To this end, genre researchers devised sets of genre categories which aim to cover all of the diversity of texts found on the web, and provided manually annotated datasets (see Egbert et al. (2015); Sharoff (2018); Kuzman et al. (2022b)). Classification of genres was shown to be a hard task as texts can display characteristics of multiple genres (Sharoff, 2021), and most genre classification models were not able to generalize outside of the dataset on which they were trained (Sharoff et al., 2010). However, recent advances in deep neural technologies led to a breakthrough in this field, and Transformer-based language models (Vaswani et al., 2017), fine-tuned on manually-annotated genre datasets, showed the ability to identify genres in various web corpora and languages (see Rönnqvist et al. (2021); Kuzman et al. (2022a)). Following encouraging results, Transformer-based genre classifiers have started to be applied to web corpora to provide genre information as metadata. For instance, as part of newly available massive Oscar web corpora, 351 million documents in 14 languages were enriched with genre information (Laippala et al., 2022).

Dataset	Size	Text length
MaCoCu-tr-en	193,782	184
MaCoCu-hr-en	91,619	172
MaCoCu-sl-en	91,459	190
MaCoCu-bg-en	88,544	170
MaCoCu-mt-en	21,376	300
MaCoCu-mk-en	20,108	194
MaCoCu-is-en	11,639	201

Table 1: Comparison of English datasets, extracted from the parallel corpora, in terms of size (number of English texts) and median text length in words.

3 Datasets

In this paper, we compare seven parallel web corpora, created in the scope of the MaCoCu project (Bañón et al., 2022h): Croatian-English MaCoCu-hr-en (Bañón et al., 2022b), Slovene-English MaCoCu-sl-en (Bañón et al., 2022f), Bulgarian-English MaCoCu-bg-en (Bañón et al., 2022a), Macedonian-English MaCoCu-mk-en (Bañón et al., 2022d), Turkish-English MaCoCu-tr-en (Bañón et al., 2022g), Icelandic-English MaCoCu-is-en (Bañón et al., 2022c) and Maltese-English MaCoCu-mt-en (Bañón et al., 2022e) corpus. The corpora were created by crawling the national top-level domains, e.g. the Slovenian top-level domain `.si` for the English-Slovene dataset MaCoCu-sl-en. Important to note is that the crawl primarily focused on the top-level domain crawling, but was allowed to harvest data from generic domains (`.com`, `.net` etc.) if the domain proved to have enough data in the language being crawled. Websites containing the target language and English were identified and processed with the Bitextor[3] tool.

3.1 Preparation of Datasets

The corpora we analyse are available in a sentence-level and paragraph-level format. Based on the information on the URL of the original document and metadata on the position of the sentence in this document, we took English sentences from the sentence pairs in the sentence-level format and created a document-level corpus of English texts from each parallel corpus.

We applied the American-British variety classifier and genre classifier to the documents. Finally, as a post-processing step, we filtered out texts with noisy genre predictions, that is, based on manual

[3] https://github.com/bitextor/bitextor

inspection, we decided to remove texts that were annotated with two less reliable and very infrequent labels – Forum and Other –, and texts with labels where the confidence of the genre classifier was low. This post-processing step amounted to around 10% of documents being discarded from the final corpora. The code for the dataset preparation, enrichment and analysis of the results is published on GitHub for the purposes of reproducibility[4].

3.2 Final Datasets

The final sizes of datasets, used in our comparisons, are shown in Table 1. The Turkish corpus is the largest, consisting of almost 200,000 English texts, followed by the Croatian, Slovenian and Bulgarian corpora with around 90,000 English texts. The smallest corpora are Maltese, Macedonian and Icelandic with 10,000 to 20,000 English texts. Table 1 also shows differences between the median length of texts. While the median text length in most datasets is between 170 and 200 words, the Maltese stands out with longer texts with the median length of 300 words.

4 Enrichment of Datasets

4.1 American-British Variety Classifier

Although there exist numerous English varieties throughout the world, including Indian English, New Zealand English, Irish English, etc., in this paper, we focus on differentiating between American and British English, which are often considered as the main varieties of standard English (Quirk, 2014). To avoid topic-related and other biases that come with training a classifier on any reference corpora, we opted for the lexicon-based approach. At the same time, as the classifier is based on a lexicon of variety-specific words and spellings, it has a limited coverage: it cannot classify texts if they do not contain any of variety-specific words. However, to obtain reliable results, we opted for a high precision approach rather than high recall.

To create our classifier, we used the VarCon lexicon of different spellings and vocabularies (Atkinson and Titze, 2020) which is based on various dictionaries and resources on spelling differences. We extracted British and American variety-specific words from the lexicon. To improve the classifier's performance and reliability, a researcher with a translation background inspected the list. We discarded rare words and words that are specific for one variety solely when used as a certain part-of-speech type, e.g. *can* (noun, as opposed to *tin*, while the verb *can* is used in both varieties), or in a certain context, e.g., *rubber* (as opposed to *eraser*, while the material *rubber* is used in both varieties). Multiple English dictionaries were consulted as a reference, including Oxford Advanced Learner's Dictionary of Current English (Hornby, 1995) and the online Cambridge dictionaries[5].

The final size of the lexicon is 6,041 words. It includes spelling differences, such as "-our" versus "-or" (Br. *behaviour*, Am. *behavior*), "-ll-" versus "-l-" (Br. *bejewelled*, Am. *bejeweled*), "-ae-" versus "-a-" (Br. *anaemia*, Am. *anemia*), "-re" versus "-er" (Br. *theatre*, Am. *theater*). While the great majority of words in the lexicon are spelling variants, there are also some variety-specific words, such as Br. *lorry* and Am. *beltway*.

Since the spelling variant "-ise" (*apologise, criticise*, etc.) is specific for British English, while its alternative "-ize" is used in both American and British English, we included only the British "-ise" variants of these words. Consequently, the lexicon is unbalanced towards British. It consists of 4,368 British words and 1,673 American words. In this paper, we trained the classifier on the unbalanced lexicon. However, we also provide a balanced lexicon by discarding the British "-ise" spelling variants, and allow an option of using the classifier with the balanced lexicon. It consists of 3,268 words: 1,652 American and 1,616 British words. Both lexicons are made available along with the code of the classifier[6].

The American-British variety classifier transforms the input text into lower case and counts the number of variety-specific words from the lexicon that are present in the text. If no variety signal is present, the text is classified as "unknown". If one variety is at least twice as present than the other, the text is classified as the prevalent variety, either as British or American. If both varieties are present in a similar extent, the text is classified as a "mix". The resulting classifier is fast and explainable. It classifies a text of an average length from the MaCoCu corpora (190 words) in 0.25 ms and a text of 1,000 words in 1.2 ms.

We analysed the classifier's reliability by performing a manual analysis of the lexicon it is based

[4] https://github.com/TajaKuzman/Applying-GENRE-on-MaCoCu-bilingual

[5] https://dictionary.cambridge.org/dictionary/

[6] https://github.com/macocu/American-British-variety-classifier

Dataset	Size (texts)	Median length	Coverage	Accuracy	Mix
DSL-TL dev	599	30	12%	94%	0.1%
GloWbE + NOW	1,445	634	66%	90%	4.0%
PAN17 test	800	1,391	78%	94%	12.0%

Table 2: The size of datasets, used for testing the coverage and performance of American-British classifier, in terms of number of texts, and the median length of texts in terms of number of words. The coverage shows what percentage of texts was assigned a variety label (American or British) as opposed to the labels "unknown" or "mix". The accuracy is calculated only for the texts that were assigned a variety label. Mix shows the percentage of texts which include words from both varieties.

on, and by improving the lexicon by using the English dictionaries as a reference. We also evaluated the performance of the classifier on three datasets, annotated with English varieties: 1) the web corpora GloWbE (Davies, 2013) and NOW (Davies, 2016), 2) the manually-annotated news DSL-TL dataset, and 3) the Twitter PAN17 dataset (Rangel et al., 2017). We evaluated the classifier in two criteria: coverage – in what percentage of the texts it recognizes a variety instead of categorizing them as "UNK" (unknown) or "MIX" – and performance, calculated for the texts to which a British or American variety is assigned.

To test the classifier on web-corpus-like content, we applied it over samples of the Corpus of Global Web-based English (GloWbE) (Davies, 2013) and the News on the Web (NOW) corpus (Davies, 2016). The GloWbE corpus is a web corpus, collected by searching frequent n-grams on Google, while the NOW corpus consists of texts from web-based newspapers and magazines. While the corpora consist of texts from around 20 English-speaking countries, we used only texts from United Kingdom and United States. The sample is balanced between the two varieties and consists of around 1,400 texts. As shown in Table 2, our classifier identified a British or American variety in two thirds of texts (66%) and 90% of them were predicted correctly.

Similar results were obtained on the Twitter dataset[7] from the PAN 2017 shared task on author profiling (Rangel et al., 2017). The English part of the dataset comprises tweets, originating from the United States, Great Britain, Ireland, Canada, Australia and New Zealand. However, we used only texts from Great Britain and United States. For each author, 100 tweets were collected and concatenated into one text instance, and the assigned language variety was based on the location from which the author mostly posted tweets. We applied the American-British classifier on the test split of the dataset, which consists of 800 texts with the median text length of around 1,400 words. As shown in Table 2, the American-British variety classifier identified a variety in 78% of texts with accuracy of 94%. Out of the unidentified texts, 12% were revealed to consist of words from both varieties which might point toward lower reliability of this dataset.

In contrast, the classifier performed poorly when tested on the DSL-TL dataset[8]. The dataset is a subset of the DSLCC dataset (Zampieri et al., 2014) that was manually annotated with American and British English variety labels for the VarDial 2023 shared task on discriminating between similar languages. At the time of writing the paper, the test set with labels has not been published yet, so we tested our classifier on the development split. The dataset consists of excerpts from journalistic texts which are rather short – the median text length of the texts in the dev subset is only 30 words. The texts were shown to be too short to provide any signal of English varieties to our classifier. As shown in Table 2, it recognized English varieties in only 12% of texts. However, its accuracy on the labeled texts was high, reaching 94%.

The comparison of results on the three datasets shows a high reliability of the classifier on the texts that were predicted to be British or American. It also nicely shows its limitations, connected with the length of texts. Results in Table 2 show very clearly, but also very expectedly, that the longer the texts are, the bigger is the classifier's coverage.

[7]The PAN17 dataset is available at `https://zenodo.org/record/3745980#.ZBxM3HbMI2w`.

[8]The dataset is available at `https://github.com/LanguageTechnologyLab/DSL-TL`

4.2 Genre Classifier

To obtain information on genres in the corpora, we used the X-GENRE classifier[9], a multilingual classifier which categorizes texts into genres. It uses the following genre categories: *Information/Explanation*, *Instruction*, *News*, *Legal*, *Promotion*, *Opinion/Argumentation*, *Prose/Lyrical*, *Forum* and *Other* (see the description of the labels in Appendix A). The classifier is based on the base size multilingual XLM-RoBERTa Transformer-based model (Conneau et al., 2020). It was fine-tuned on a combination of three datasets, manually annotated with genre labels: English CORE (Egbert et al., 2015), English FTD (Sharoff, 2018) and Slovene GINCO (Kuzman et al., 2022b) dataset. Each of the datasets has their own set of categories, which were mapped into a joint schema. The reason for using multiple datasets instead of just one is to assure better generalization of the model to new datasets and languages.

We manually annotated around 150 English texts from the Slovene MaCoCu-sl-en corpus to analyse the reliability of the genre classifier on the MaCoCu datasets. Based on that, the genre classifier reached macro F1 of 0.73 and micro F1 of 0.88. Analysis showed that we can eliminate some noisy predictions by removing texts, annotated as *Forum* and *Other*, and texts, predicted with low confidence level, obtained from the raw output. As the main goal of this study is to analyse global differences between MaCoCu datasets, we decided to remove less reliably predicted instances, as described in Section 3.1, to perform comparison only on the most reliable data. With this intervention, while sacrificing the model's coverage a bit, we obtained a much higher classifier's performance, reaching 0.92 in terms of micro and macro F1 score.

We applied the genre classifier to each of the seven English datasets from the parallel MaCoCu corpora. Prediction took approximately 6 hours per 100,000 texts which amounted to around 35 hours on one NVIDIA V100 GPU. Afterwards, we post-processed the data, discarding noisy genre predictions. In the next section, we compare the resulting datasets in terms of English variety and genre distribution.

[9]https://huggingface.co/classla/xlm-roberta-base-multilingual-text-genre-classifier

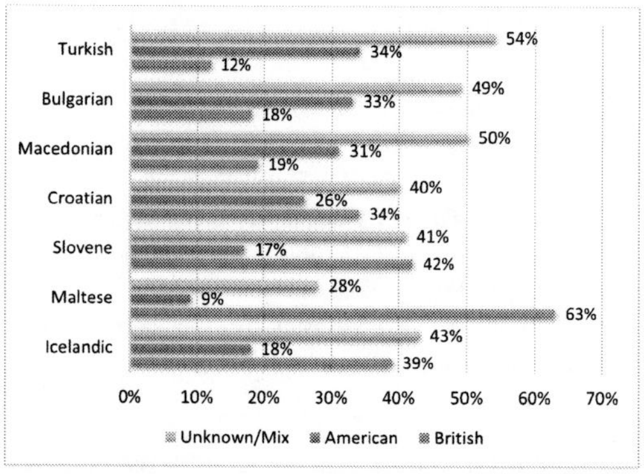

Figure 1: Distribution of American and British English in the English parts of the Icelandic, Maltese, Slovene, Croatian, Macedonian, Bulgarian and Turkish parallel web corpora.

5 Results

5.1 English Variety Distribution

By using our American-British variety classifier, more specifically, the unbalanced version, we identified the predominant English variety in each English text in the MaCoCu parallel corpora. If there were equal amounts of American and British variety-specific words in a text, the text was annotated as a "mix", and if there were no variety-specific words, the text was labeled as "unknown". The results, presented in Figure 1, show the distribution of British and American English in analysed corpora. The analysis shows that a variety was identified in mostly over 50% of texts in a corpus. Rather large amounts of unlabeled texts are not surprising, because most of the texts are quite short, with the median length of 170 to 300 words.

Figure 1 also shows that web corpora, obtained from different national top-level web domains, display different preference towards British and American English variety. The Maltese corpus was shown to have an overwhelming preference towards British English, with 63% texts classified as British, and only 9% classified as American. One of possible reasons for a strong influence of British English is Malta's close connection to the United Kingdom. The country is a former British colony and a member of the Commonwealth of Nations (Busuttil and Briguglio, 2023). Secondly, an inspection of the most frequent domains in the Maltese corpus revealed that half of the 10 most frequent domains are websites from the European Union, e.g. *europarl.europa.eu, eur-lex.europa.eu,*

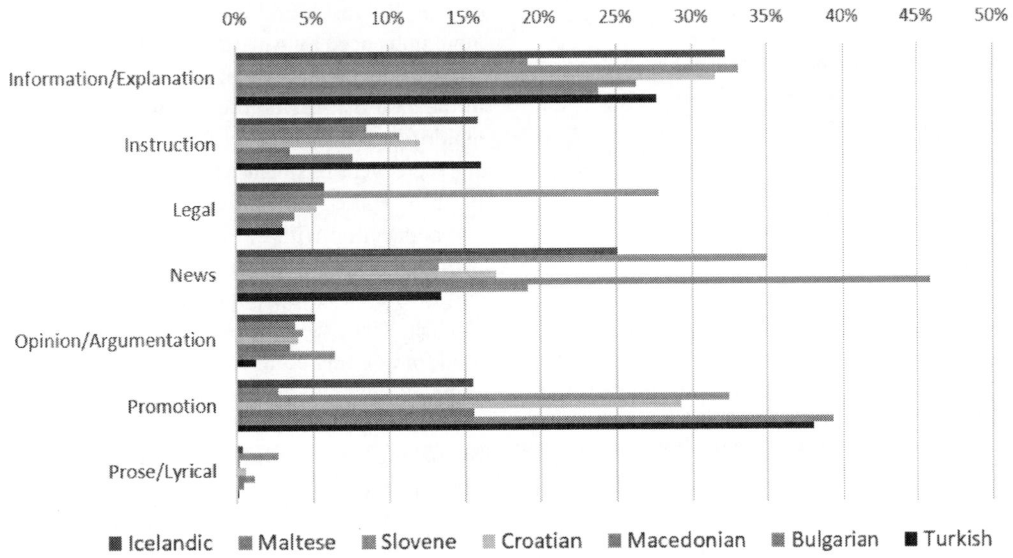

Figure 2: Distribution of genres in Icelandic-, Maltese-, Slovene-, Croatian-, Macedonian-, Bulgarian- and Turkish-English MaCoCu parallel web corpora.

ec.europa.eu, etc., covering 43% of all texts from the corpus. As the translation services in European Union have a preference towards British English (see Forsyth and Cayley (2022)), large amounts of EU texts in the corpus surely impacted the English variety distribution in it. The predominance of British English was also observed in the case of Icelandic, Slovene and Croatian corpora. In contrast, the corpora from the web domains of the countries further to the East, namely Macedonian, Bulgarian and Turkish corpora, show a much bigger influence of American English.

5.2 Genre Distribution

To obtain genre information, we applied the X-GENRE classifier to each text in the English part of the MaCoCu parallel corpora. The analysis of genre distribution, shown in Figure 2, revealed interesting differences between the corpora. The results show that the category *Information/Explanation* is notably present in all corpora, covering 20–30% of all texts. Other two predominant categories are *News* and *Promotion*, mostly covering 15–45% of texts. *News* is especially present in the Macedonian corpus, where it amounts to almost half of all texts, followed by Maltese and Icelandic with 25–35% of texts of this genre. In contrast, *Promotion* represents only up to 15% of texts in these three corpora, while it is much more frequent in Slovene, Croatian, Bulgarian and Turkish corpora, representing 30–40% of texts.

Other genre categories are generally less frequent. *Instruction* represents 5–15% of texts, with the highest frequency in Icelandic and Turkish. *Legal* represents around 5% of corpora. However, legal texts represent 28% of all texts in the Maltese corpus, showing this corpus to be significantly different than the others based on genre distribution as well. *Opinion/Argumentation* is more or less equally represented in all corpora, representing around 5% of texts. This category is the least represented in the Turkish corpus, with only 1% of texts. The least frequent category is *Prose/Lyrical*, representing 0.2–3% of texts, with the largest distribution in the Maltese corpus.

5.3 Genre Distribution in English Varieties

To obtain more information on the interplay of genres and English varieties, we looked at the average distribution of English varieties in each genre across all corpora. The results, shown in Figure 3, reveal that *News* texts and *Legal* texts from the analysed corpora are in average much more frequently written in British English, representing twice as much texts as the texts of these genres written in American English. *News* and *Legal* texts represent 60% of texts in the Maltese corpus, which also provides some explanation on why the Maltese corpus contains so much more British English than the others. In contrast, the category

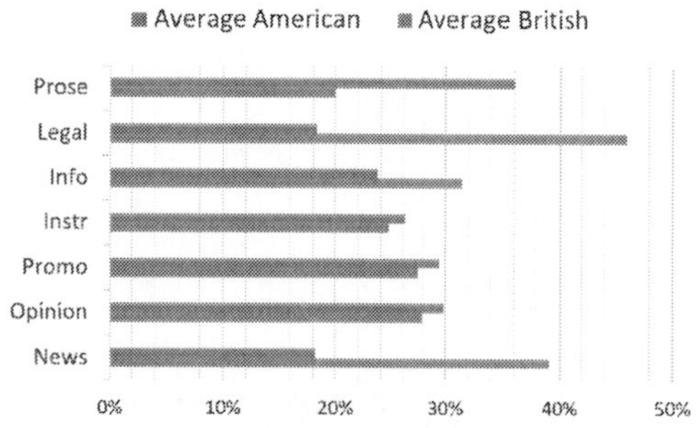

Figure 3: Average distribution of British and American varieties in each genre over all seven corpora. The abbreviated labels represent the following categories: Info – Information/Explanation, Promo – Promotion, Opinion – Opinion/Argumentation, Instr – Instruction, Prose – Prose/Lyrical.

Prose/Lyrical was shown to be more frequently written in American English. An inspection of the domains of the *Prose/Lyrical* texts revealed that in most corpora, a large majority of *Prose/Lyrical* texts come from American religious websites, such as *www.biblegateway.com* and *www.jw.org*, which explains the predominance of American English in this genre. In other genres, namely, *Information/Explanation, Instruction, Promotion* and *Opinion/Argumentation*, the two varieties are more or less equally present.

6 Conclusion

In this paper, we introduce a freely-available English variety classifier for fast and reliable identification of British and American English. The corpus-based approaches to language variety classification can be impacted by topic-related or other biases, occurring due to differences between the corpora on which the model is trained. In contrast, our lexicon-based approach is based on a carefully selected lexicon of words which are confirmed by linguists to be variety-specific, making the results more reliable and explainable. We then show how the classifier can be used to obtain an insight into the characteristics of large parallel corpora, collected with automatic methods. We compare parallel web corpora from European national webs in seven languages. As all languages are paired with English, we obtained meaningful information on the differences between the corpora in terms of English varieties. The results revealed British English is prevalent in Maltese, Icelandic, Slovene and Croatian corpora, while corpora from the Macedonian, Bulgarian and Turkish national webs are more influenced by American English. A stark difference between the use of varieties was observed in the case of the Maltese corpus, where a large majority of texts were written in British English and there were less than 10% of texts in American English. These results reflect the country's historical connection with the United Kingdom, along with a significant presence of EU websites in the corpus, which have a policy of preferring British English. Thus, we show how the classifier can be used for not only comparing corpora, but also obtaining insight into the use of English by native and non-native speaking content writers and translators. By making the classifier freely available, we hope to encourage analyses of the use of English and its varieties among teachers, translators and content creators in the fields of corpus linguistics, translation studies, linguistics and digital humanities.

Furthermore, we extend the comparison by automatically annotating the English texts from the parallel corpora with genre information. The results revealed significant differences between the corpora in terms of genre distribution. Once again, the Maltese corpus was shown to be more different than the others, consisting mostly of *News* and *Legal* texts. *News* is also strongly present in Macedonian and Icelandic corpora, while Slovene, Croatian, Bulgarian and Turkish corpora constitute of large amounts of promotional texts.

With the two classification approaches, we obtained valuable information on the characteristics of the datasets. As such datasets are often used for creation of machine translation systems, various NLP tools, as well as linguistic studies, it is crucial that the users are provided with the information on what types of texts and language varieties the datasets consist of. The MaCoCu project will provide this information for all their datasets, covering 13 European under-resourced languages: Albanian, Bosnian, Bulgarian, Catalan, Croatian, Icelandic, Macedonian, Maltese, Montenegrin, Slovene, Serbian, Turkish and Ukrainian. The datasets will be made freely available by June 2023. As the initial analysis of the English variety and genre distribution in corpora, presented in this paper, revealed that this information highlights important differences between the corpora, in the future, we plan to extend the analysis to all 13 newly available MaCoCu corpora. Furthermore, one important downstream task that we did not tackle in this work is the inspection of the impact of the variation in variety and genre on machine translation and other systems based on these and other datasets, which we also plan to analyse in future studies.

Limitations

In this paper, we describe how we devised a lexicon-based classifier for American and British English. We argue for the lexicon-based approach as a better alternative to the corpus-based approach, as it is rule-based and explainable. However, we are aware that a lexicon-based approach is less feasible or impossible for classification of varieties of other languages or identification between languages. While the corpora-based approaches can be performed on all languages where at least one corpus of appropriate size exists, this approach requires an availability of a lexicon or at least linguistic rules on which a new lexicon needs to be based.

Secondly, by using the lexicon-based approach, we prefer reliability over coverage. If no variety-specific word is present in the analysed text, the text is left unlabeled. This was the case for 30 to 50% of texts in our analysed corpora. Furthermore, our lexicon is based on words only, and does not take account of variety-specific multiword expressions. Consequently, one should be aware that the findings reflect only the characteristics of the texts that were long enough and had any variety-specific word. Furthermore, while the corpora were collected by crawling the national web domains, there might exist texts on the web that were deliberately or not left out of the final datasets. This means that the nature of these corpora does not necessarily reflect the English variety distribution of all texts found on a national web.

Thirdly, in this research, we limit ourselves to the two most recognized varieties of the Standard English. We are aware that numerous other varieties from throughout the world exist. As this analysis has been done on texts from non-native English-speaking European countries, we consider that focusing on the two varieties which are often considered to be the main varieties is appropriate, albeit simplistic. However, we are aware that some of British or American-specific words might overlap with words that are also typical for other English varieties, such as Australian, Canadian, Irish, etc., and could for instance classify Irish English as British. We are aware that our pragmatic approach could be regarded as discriminatory towards other English varieties. While our classifier can be used on any English text, we should be aware that it solely provides information on the frequency of words, defined to be British or American. We leave discussions whether these texts are by that truly British, or whether we are talking about European English with British influence to the linguists, as we are aware that defining how many English varieties are there and what are their key differences is outside of our expertise.

Finally, in contrast to the English variety classifier which can be used only for English, the genre classifier is multilingual and covers all of the languages, included in the XLM-RoBERTa language model (Conneau et al., 2020). On the other hand, while the English variety classifier does not require massive computational resources, genre identification requires the use of a GPU. We are aware that not everyone is privileged to have access to such computational resources to be able to reproduce our research.

Ethics Statement

We are aware that collecting texts from the web can raise questions of respecting the intellectual property and privacy rights of the original authors of the texts. The web corpora, analysed in this paper, have been collected by crawling the national top-level domains. To assure that no sensitive data would be included, only texts that have been freely accessible were included in the corpora. We are aware that the datasets might still include some texts that the authors do not consent to be included. To mitigate this, the datasets are published with a notice, which informs the authors of the text that the texts can be taken out of the corpora upon their request. Secondly, for privacy issues, the sentences in the published corpora that contain personal information are flagged, so that the corpora users can leave them out of their research if the nature of their study would reveal this information. In our paper, we look into and report on the overall characteristics of the texts and do not examine texts more closely or produce systems which could abuse personal information or intellectual property rights. That is why anonymisation or additional filtering was not necessary.

Secondly, as mentioned in Limitations, our English variety classifier labels a text to be British or English based on the counts of variety-specific words. While it is a useful tool for quick inspection of the differences in English between various corpora, it is meant to be used on English texts, produced by non-native English speakers. As the British and American-specific words it detects could overlap with other English varieties, such as Irish, Australian, Canadian, Indian etc., one should not use it with the intention of belittling other varieties or proving that the entire world uses only the two mentioned varieties.

Acknowledgements

This work has received funding from the European Union's Connecting Europe Facility 2014-2020 - CEF Telecom, under Grant Agreement No. INEA/CEF/ICT/A2020/2278341. This communication reflects only the author's view. The Agency is not responsible for any use that may be made of the information it contains. This work was also funded by the Slovenian Research Agency within the Slovenian-Flemish bilateral basic research project "Linguistic landscape of hate speech on social media" (N06-0099 and FWO-G070619N, 2019–2023), the research project "Basic Research for the Development of Spoken Language Resources and Speech Technologies for the Slovenian Language" (J7-4642), and the research programme "Language resources and technologies for Slovene" (P6-0411).

References

Kevin Atkinson and Benjamin Titze. 2020. Variant Conversion (VarCon). `http://wordlist.aspell.net/varcon/`.

ES Atwell, Junaid Arshad, Chien-Ming Lai, Lan Nim, N Rezapour Ashregi, Josiah Wang, and Justin Washtell. 2007. Which English dominates the world wide web, British or American? In *Proceedings of CL'2007 Corpus Linguistics Conference*. UCREL, Lancaster University.

Marta Bañón, Miquel Esplà-Gomis, Mikel L. Forcada, Cristian García-Romero, Taja Kuzman, Nikola Ljubešić, Rik van Noord, Leopoldo Pla Sempere, Gema Ramírez-Sánchez, Peter Rupnik, Vít Suchomel, Antonio Toral, Tobias van der Werff, and Jaume Zaragoza. 2022a. Bulgarian-English parallel corpus MaCoCu-bg-en 1.0. Slovenian language resource repository CLARIN.SI.

Marta Bañón, Miquel Esplà-Gomis, Mikel L. Forcada, Cristian García-Romero, Taja Kuzman, Nikola Ljubešić, Rik van Noord, Leopoldo Pla Sempere, Gema Ramírez-Sánchez, Peter Rupnik, Vít Suchomel, Antonio Toral, Tobias van der Werff, and Jaume Zaragoza. 2022b. Croatian-English parallel corpus MaCoCu-hr-en 1.0. Slovenian language resource repository CLARIN.SI.

Marta Bañón, Miquel Esplà-Gomis, Mikel L. Forcada, Cristian García-Romero, Taja Kuzman, Nikola Ljubešić, Rik van Noord, Leopoldo Pla Sempere, Gema Ramírez-Sánchez, Peter Rupnik, Vít Suchomel, Antonio Toral, Tobias van der Werff, and Jaume Zaragoza. 2022c. Icelandic-English parallel corpus MaCoCu-is-en 1.0. Slovenian language resource repository CLARIN.SI.

Marta Bañón, Miquel Esplà-Gomis, Mikel L. Forcada, Cristian García-Romero, Taja Kuzman, Nikola Ljubešić, Rik van Noord, Leopoldo Pla Sempere, Gema Ramírez-Sánchez, Peter Rupnik, Vít Suchomel, Antonio Toral, Tobias van der Werff, and Jaume Zaragoza. 2022d. Macedonian-English parallel corpus MaCoCu-mk-en 1.0. Slovenian language resource repository CLARIN.SI.

Marta Bañón, Miquel Esplà-Gomis, Mikel L. Forcada, Cristian García-Romero, Taja Kuzman, Nikola Ljubešić, Rik van Noord, Leopoldo Pla Sempere, Gema Ramírez-Sánchez, Peter Rupnik, Vít Suchomel, Antonio Toral, Tobias van der Werff, and Jaume Zaragoza. 2022e. Maltese-English parallel corpus MaCoCu-mt-en 1.0. Slovenian language resource repository CLARIN.SI.

Marta Bañón, Miquel Esplà-Gomis, Mikel L. Forcada, Cristian García-Romero, Taja Kuzman, Nikola Ljubešić, Rik van Noord, Leopoldo Pla Sempere, Gema Ramírez-Sánchez, Peter Rupnik, Vít Suchomel, Antonio Toral, Tobias van der Werff, and Jaume Zaragoza. 2022f. Slovene-English parallel corpus MaCoCu-sl-en 1.0. Slovenian language resource repository CLARIN.SI.

Marta Bañón, Miquel Esplà-Gomis, Mikel L. Forcada, Cristian García-Romero, Taja Kuzman, Nikola Ljubešić, Rik van Noord, Leopoldo Pla Sempere, Gema Ramírez-Sánchez, Peter Rupnik, Vít Suchomel, Antonio Toral, Tobias van der Werff, and Jaume Zaragoza. 2022g. Turkish-English parallel corpus MaCoCu-tr-en 1.0. Slovenian language resource repository CLARIN.SI.

Marta Bañón, Miquel Esplà-Gomis, Mikel L Forcada, Cristian García-Romero, Taja Kuzman, Nikola Ljubešić, Rik van Noord, Leopoldo Pla Sempere, Gema Ramírez-Sánchez, Peter Rupnik, et al. 2022h. Macocu: Massive collection and curation of monolingual and bilingual data: focus on under-resourced languages. In *Proceedings of the 23rd Annual Conference of the European Association for Machine Translation*, pages 301–302.

Marco Baroni, Silvia Bernardini, Adriano Ferraresi, and Eros Zanchetta. 2009. The WaCky wide web: a collection of very large linguistically processed web-crawled corpora. *Language resources and evaluation*, 43(3):209–226.

Salvino Busuttil and Lino Briguglio. 2023. Malta. https://www.britannica.com/place/Malta. Encyclopaedia Britannica.

Alexis Conneau, Kartikay Khandelwal, Naman Goyal, Vishrav Chaudhary, Guillaume Wenzek, Francisco Guzmán, Édouard Grave, Myle Ott, Luke Zettlemoyer, and Veselin Stoyanov. 2020. Unsupervised Cross-lingual Representation Learning at Scale. In *Proceedings of the 58th Annual Meeting of the Association for Computational Linguistics*, pages 8440–8451.

BNC Consortium et al. 2007. British national corpus. *Oxford Text Archive Core Collection*.

Paul Cook and Graeme Hirst. 2012. Do Web Corpora from Top-Level Domains Represent National Varieties of English? In *Proceedings of the 11th International Conference on Textual Data Statistical Analysis*, pages 281–293.

Mark Davies. 2013. Corpus of Global Web-Based English. https://www.english-corpora.org/glowbe/.

Mark Davies. 2016. Corpus of News on the Web (NOW). https://www.english-corpora.org/now/.

Jonathan Dunn. 2019. Modeling Global Syntactic Variation in English Using Dialect Classification. *NAACL HLT 2019*, 660:42.

Jesse Egbert, Douglas Biber, and Mark Davies. 2015. Developing a bottom-up, user-based method of web register classification. *Journal of the Association for Information Science and Technology*, 66(9):1817–1831.

Julia Forsberg, Susanne Mohr, and Sandra Jansen. 2019. "The goal is to enable students to communicate": Communicative competence and target varieties in TEFL practices in Sweden and Germany. *European Journal of Applied Linguistics*, 7(1):31–60.

Angus Forsyth and Mireille Cayley, editors. 2022. *English Style Guide: A handbook for authors and translators in the European Commission*. European Commission.

Eugenie Giesbrecht and Stefan Evert. 2009. Is part-of-speech tagging a solved task? An evaluation of POS taggers for the German web as corpus. In *Proceedings of the fifth Web as Corpus workshop*, pages 27–35.

Albert Sydney Hornby. 1995. *Oxford Advanced Learner's Dictionary of Current English*. Oxford, England: Oxford University Press.

Adam Kilgarriff and Adam Kilgarri. 2001. Comparing corpora. In *International Journal of Corpus Linguistics*. Citeseer.

Taja Kuzman, Nikola Ljubešić, and Senja Pollak. 2022a. Assessing Comparability of Genre Datasets via Cross-Lingual and Cross-Dataset Experiments. In *Jezikovne tehnologije in digitalna humanistika: zbornik konference*, Jezikovne tehnologije in digitalna humanistika: zbornik konference, page 100–107. Institute of Contemporary History.

Taja Kuzman, Peter Rupnik, and Nikola Ljubešić. 2022b. The GINCO Training Dataset for Web Genre Identification of Documents Out in the Wild. In *Proceedings of the Language Resources and Evaluation Conference*, pages 1584–1594, Marseille, France. European Language Resources Association.

Veronika Laippala, Anna Salmela, Samuel Rönnqvist, Alham Fikri Aji, Li-Hsin Chang, Asma Dhifallah, Larissa Goulart, Henna Kortelainen, Marc Pàmies, Deise Prina Dutra, et al. 2022. Towards better structured and less noisy web data: Oscar with register annotations. In *Proceedings of the Eighth Workshop on Noisy User-generated Text (W-NUT 2022)*, pages 215–221.

Marco Lui and Paul Cook. 2013. Classifying English documents by national dialect. In *Proceedings of the Australasian Language Technology Association Workshop 2013 (ALTA 2013)*, pages 5–15.

Marco Lui, Ned Letcher, Oliver Adams, Long Duong, Paul Cook, and Timothy Baldwin. 2014. Exploring methods and resources for discriminating similar languages. In *Proceedings of the First Workshop on Applying NLP Tools to Similar Languages, Varieties and Dialects*, pages 129–138.

Wanda J Orlikowski and JoAnne Yates. 1994. Genre repertoire: The structuring of communicative practices in organizations. *Administrative science quarterly*, pages 541–574.

Randolph Quirk. 2014. *Grammatical and lexical variance in English*. Routledge.

Francisco Rangel, Paolo Rosso, Martin Potthast, and Benno Stein. 2017. Overview of the 5th author profiling task at PAN 2017: Gender and language variety identification in Twitter. *Working notes papers of the CLEF*, 48.

Samuel Rönnqvist, Valtteri Skantsi, Miika Oinonen, and Veronika Laippala. 2021. Multilingual and Zero-Shot is Closing in on Monolingual Web Register Classification. In *Proceedings of the 23rd Nordic Conference on Computational Linguistics (NoDaLiDa)*, pages 157–165.

Dmitri Roussinov, Kevin Crowston, Mike Nilan, Barbara Kwasnik, Jin Cai, and Xiaoyong Liu. 2001. Genre based navigation on the web. In *Proceedings of the 34th annual Hawaii international conference on system sciences*, pages 10–pp. IEEE.

Serge Sharoff. 2018. Functional text dimensions for the annotation of web corpora. *Corpora*, 13(1):65–95.

Serge Sharoff. 2021. Genre annotation for the web: text-external and text-internal perspectives. *Register studies*.

Serge Sharoff, Zhili Wu, and Katja Markert. 2010. The Web Library of Babel: evaluating genre collections. In *LREC*. Citeseer.

Vasiliki Simaki, Panagiotis Simakis, Carita Paradis, and Andreas Kerren. 2017. Identifying the authors' national variety of English in social media text. Association for Computational Linguistics.

Jade Goldstein Stewart and J Callan. 2009. *Genre oriented summarization*. Ph.D. thesis, Carnegie Mellon University, Language Technologies Institute, School of Computer Science.

Jörg Tiedemann and Nikola Ljubešić. 2012. Efficient discrimination between closely related languages. In *Proceedings of COLING 2012*, pages 2619–2634.

Muhammad Romi Ario Utomo and Yuliant Sibaroni. 2019. Text classification of British English and American English using support vector machine. In *2019 7th International Conference on Information and Communication Technology (ICoICT)*, pages 1–6. IEEE.

Marlies Van der Wees, Arianna Bisazza, and Christof Monz. 2018. Evaluation of machine translation performance across multiple genres and languages. In *Proceedings of the Eleventh International Conference on Language Resources and Evaluation (LREC 2018)*.

Ashish Vaswani, Noam Shazeer, Niki Parmar, Jakob Uszkoreit, Llion Jones, Aidan N Gomez, Łukasz Kaiser, and Illia Polosukhin. 2017. Attention is all you need. *Advances in neural information processing systems*, 30.

Vedrana Vidulin, Mitja Luštrek, and Matjaž Gams. 2007. Using genres to improve search engines. In *1st International Workshop: Towards Genre-Enabled Search Engines: The Impact of Natural Language Processing*, pages 45–51.

Marcos Zampieri, Preslav Nakov, and Yves Scherrer. 2020. Natural language processing for similar languages, varieties, and dialects: A survey. *Natural Language Engineering*, 26(6):595–612.

Marcos Zampieri, Liling Tan, Nikola Ljubešić, and Jörg Tiedemann. 2014. A report on the DSL shared task 2014. In *Proceedings of the first workshop on applying NLP tools to similar languages, varieties and dialects*, pages 58–67.

A Appendix

A.1 Genre Categories

Label	Description	Examples
Information/Explanation	An objective text that describes or presents an event, a person, a thing, a concept etc. Its main purpose is to inform the reader about something.	research article, encyclopedia article, product specification, course materials, biographical story/history.
Instruction	An objective text which instructs the readers on how to do something.	how-to texts, recipes, technical support
Legal	An objective formal text that contains legal terms and is clearly structured.	small print, software license, terms and conditions, contracts, law, copyright notices
News	An objective or subjective text which reports on an event recent at the time of writing or coming in the near future.	news report, sports report, police report, announcement
Opinion/Argumentation	A subjective text in which the authors convey their opinion or narrate their experience. It includes promotion of an ideology and other non-commercial causes.	review, blog, editorial, letter to editor, persuasive article or essay, political propaganda
Promotion	A subjective text intended to sell or promote an event, product, or service. It addresses the readers, often trying to convince them to participate in something or buy something.	advertisement, e-shops, promotion of an accommodation, promotion of company's services, invitation to an event
Prose/Lyrical	A literary text that consists of paragraphs or verses. A literary text is deemed to have no other practical purpose than to give pleasure to the reader. Often the author pays attention to the aesthetic appearance of the text. It can be considered as art.	lyrics, poem, prayer, joke, novel, short story

Table 3: Descriptions of genre labels, with examples.

Reconstructing Language History by Using a Phonological Ontology. An Analysis of German Surnames

Hanna Fischer
Institut für Germanistik
University of Rostock, Germany
h.fischer@uni-rostock.de

Robert Engsterhold
Research Center *Deutscher Sprachatlas*,
Philipps-University Marburg, Germany
engsterhold@uni-marburg.de

Abstract

This paper applies the ontology-based dialectometric technique of Engsterhold (2020) to surnames. The method was originally developed for phonetic analyses. However, as will be shown, it is also suited for the study of graphemic representations. Based on data from the *German Surname Atlas* (DFA), the method is optimized for graphemic analysis and illustrated with an example case.

1 Introduction

Engsterhold (2020) introduced an ontology-based dialectometric method aiming at the investigation of the phonological structure of dialects on the basis of phonetic features.[1] The author exemplifies his technique based on the phonetic maps of the *Linguistic Atlas of the Middle Rhine Area* (MRhSA), which are available in IPA notation. The so-called *phonOntology* is a classification of the sounds of the MRhSA data according to their phonetic features, which are automatically matched by means of an inference procedure. At the same time, they are related to a historical reference system, which means that, in addition to the phonetic assignment, a phonological classification is implemented. For example, the long vowel [uː] in Moselle Franconian *gruß* ('big') is assigned the phonetic features [+close, +back, +long, +round] and relates to MHG *ô*.

On this basis, a vector of sound characteristics is created for each location in the study area. Comparing the vectors of all locations in the dataset, data classifications can then be performed that provide information about which locations are maximally similar or distant with respect to the phonetic characteristics of the data. Since the procedure systematically accounts for historical phonological classes (*gruß*, *groß* < MHG. *ô*), the analysis can be restricted to selected subsets, for example, to a single historical reference sound or the combination of historical sound classes.

For historical data, however, phonetic assignment cannot be reliably implemented. Even a phonological classification bears its difficulties since in historical writing, we find a broad variation of graphemes referring to the same sound. What is required is a rough assignment of graphemes to all possible phonemes which leaves room for both, allophonic and allographic variation. In this paper, we present such a modification based on German surname data. Our aim is to show how the ontology-based procedure can be applied to identify regional phonological patterns, even in data that is part of written language.

2 Method

In order to process large amounts of data and, at the same time, apply the inferences based on the ontology, *phonOntology* makes use of semantic web technologies. The data is organized in a TripleStore graph database (*GraphDB*)[2] using the *Resource Description Framework* (RDF) and the *Web Ontology Language* (OWL) as a language for describing the rules that are implemented in the phonetic ontology.

The classification of the data is based on cluster analyses. This needs the transformation of data, which is performed via one-hot encoding into a data set that generates a multidimensional feature vector for all locations and for all sounds. Subsequently, the data are standardized using *z*-transformation. In order to optimize classification results, principal component analysis (PCA) is performed so that the resulting data set has fewer dimensions but still explains most of the variance in the data set.

[1] https://doi.org/10.17192/z2020.0213

[2] https://ontotext.com

Tenth Workshop on NLP for Similar Languages, Varieties and Dialects (VarDial 2023), pages 104–112
May 5, 2023 ©2023 Association for Computational Linguistics

The clustering algorithms used are *k*-means, Ward's agglomerative clustering (Ward), and the Gaussian mixture model (GMM). In our study we added *k*-medoids and spectral clustering (*k*-nearest neighbor, SC-*k*NN). Since no ground truth or verification dataset is available, the evaluation of the cluster analysis is limited to intrinsic metrics. Thus, primarily cluster stability is evaluated. For this purpose, the silhouette coefficient (SC) and the Calinski-Harabasz index (CH) are used. In addition, bootstrapping and *k*-fold methods are used to generate pseudo-ground truths, which can then be used to evaluate classification results (cf. Engsterhold 2020).

In this way, cluster analysis based on the *phonOntology* allows the semi-automated investigation of sound properties across all tokens and phenomena of a given corpus. This provides a deeper insight into the sound-related structure of a study area under discussion.

The method is free of interpretative assumptions and designed for large data sets. It offers the possibility to highlight and evaluate structures in a chaotic-looking data set. The architecture is similar to the built-up of the PHOIBLE database (Moran et al., 2014). The classification methodology is similar to the methods described in Nerbonne et al. (2011).

3 Material

3.1 Background

We chose German surnames as an example of applying the ontology-based dialectometric technique to a data set of graphic representations. Surnames preserve linguistic material which is up to 900 years old. They developed from bynames in the medieval period and became finally fixed in the course of the 16th century. Investigating the current distribution of surnames allows conclusions to be drawn about historical dialects and writing traditions.

Several studies focus on the areal distribution of specific phonological or graphic variants in German surnames (e.g., Kunze and Kunze, 2003; Dammel and Schmuck, 2009). They face the difficulty that most of the surnames are restricted to limited regions. Usually, several surname types are compared in order to be able to investigate the areal distribution of linguistic features in the surnames.

Quantitative approaches as e.g., the isonomy analyses by Cheshire et al. (2011) or Flores Flores and Gilles (2020) are able to determine spatial structures by using big datasets, but they do not inform about the linguistic characteristics of the identified isonymy structures.

In contrast, our technique not only allows to determine spatial structures but also makes it possible to investigate the linguistic features that are crucial for the classification. It is the characteristic of ontologies that they allow a multidimensional access to the data and thus provide the user with different perspectives of analysis.

3.2 Data

The data comes from the *German Surname Atlas* database (cf. DFA), which is an extract from the database of the *Deutsche Telekom AG* as of June 30, 2005. The database comprises > 28 million private telephone connections (= surname tokens) with > 850,000 different names (= surname types). The data set matches the number of tokens of a surname type with the postal code districts comprising five digits each, e.g., *Hausmann* (surname type) | *27628* (postal code) | *5* (number of tokens).

3.3 Preparation

In preparation for the analysis, the historical reference sounds for each surname type were determined via the map commentaries of the DFA volumes as well as via historical and etymological dictionaries. The map commentaries inform about the etymology of the presented surnames, and they collect the relevant variants of a surname group (e.g., the surname types *Groth*, *Grote*, *Grott*, *Groß*, *Gros*, and *Gross* [see Table 1] that can be traced back to the same etymon WG **grauta-*). For vowels the Middle High German (MHG) and for consonants the West Germanic (WG) reference sounds were identified. By aligning the surname types with historical reference sounds we encountered a central problem that comes across when researching the spatial distribution of surnames: Except for a limited number of high frequent surname types, the occurrence of most surnames is restricted to small-scale regions. Applying the historical reference system, these types become aggregated via the annotation.

As surnames are writing-induced data with considerable historical depth, a phonetic classification of the data is hardly possible. Hence the annotation was oriented towards the grapheme-phoneme system of Early New High German (cf. Anderson et al., 1981) which enables to align the graphemes of the surnames with phonological sound types. In this way, we allow for allophonic and allographic variance. Applying the *phonOntology*, we created feature vectors for each postal code district. The feature vectors to be derived here are thus rougher and more strongly typed than in the original use case of *phonOntology*.

Table 1 provides an extract from the annotation table dealing with the variance of the consonant (sound types *t* vs. *s*) in the coda of names which are related to the standard German adjective *groß* 'big' (cf. DFA 2: 448–449). The sound types, as does

Grapheme	Types	Sound	Historical reference
<t>	*Grote*	t	WG *t*
<th>	*Groth*	t	WG *t*
<tt>	*Grott*	t	WG *t*
<ß>	*Groß*	s	WG *t*
<s>	*Gros*	s	WG *t*
<ss>	*Gross*	s	WG *t*

Table 1: Example of the grapheme-phoneme alignment of the surname types.

their graphemic representation, differ with respect to the plosive vs. fricative realization thus referring to the historical process of the High German consonant shift.

In this specific case, the different graphemes <ß>, <s> and <ss> refer to the same idealized sound type *s* whereas <t>, <th> and <tt> refer to the sound type *t*. When the alignment to several sound types is possible, the annotation allows for multiple references. Especially, concerning the length and quality of vowels, multiple reference is the normal case. In the present case, an idealized phonological feature vector as in (1) would be applied to the sound types. This feature vector is the basis of the intended linguistic classification over several family names. The feature vectors consist of the place (postal code district), the corresponding linguistic features and the number of tokens that account for the features.

$$s = [+cont,\ -nas,\ -lab, \ldots] \quad (1)$$

$$t = [-cont,\ -nas,\ -lab, \ldots]$$

Following the choice of linguistic phenomena that are presented in the DFA 1 and 2, the annotated data set comprises 8,197 surname types with more than 2.3 million tokens (= approx. 8 % of the whole dataset). The sounds and graphemes that show oppositions in the surnames were traced back to 36 historical reference sounds. In Table 1, the historical reference sound is West Germanic *t* (= WG *t*).

4 Analysis of a Defined Range of Sound Classes

4.1 Quantitative Analysis

The following analysis focuses on the linguistic structure of surnames that are linked to long vowels in Middle High German. Therefore, the data set is filtered for the historical reference sounds MHG *â, æ, ê, î, ô, œ, û, iu*. This reveals a subsample of 1034 different surname types with a total of 278,689 surname tokens.

Table 2 shows the results of the evaluation of cluster stability performed by *phonOntology* for both a 2-cluster and a 3-cluster solution. Comparing the silhouette coefficients (SC) and the Calinski-Harabasz indexes (CH), we see that for both clusterings – following the silhouette

	2		3	
Clustering	**SC**	**CH**	**SC**	**CH**
GMM	0.20	186.97	0.13	133.60
k-*means*	0.27	251.24	0.23	210.14
k-*medoids*	0.24	235.63	0.23	209.03
SC-k*NN*	0.28	217.73	0.25	198.12
Ward	0.23	207.96	0.23	190.38

Table 2: Evaluation of the clustering algorithms.

coefficients – the SC-*k*NN algorithm shows the best results. Regarding the Calinski-Harabasz index *k*-means leads to the best results. It should be noted that *k*-means still performs well on the SC, while SC-*k*NN only achieves average performance on the CH. In the following, we present the findings of both cluster analyses.

The results of the cluster analyses consist of two parts, a map and an assessment of the individual linguistic features. As regards the maps, the clustering is plotted against the dialect classification introduced by Wiesinger (1983). The clustering is strictly based on the properties of the feature vectors and neither influenced by the geographical proximity of the postal code districts nor by the linguistic information provided by Wiesinger's map. The colors and numbers of the clusters are allotted by chance and have no meaning.

The assessment of linguistic features is no longer binary, as indicated by (1), but metrical according to their impact on the particular clusters found by the classification algorithm under discussion.

Figure 1: SC-*k*NN clustering (2 clusters) for MHG long vowels.

Figure 2: *K*-means clustering (2 clusters) for MHG long vowels.

Comparing the maps in Figure 1 and 2 reveals that both clustering techniques, *k*-means and SC-*k*NN, lead to overall contingent and coherent clusters. In both maps there is a clear north-south divide. However, the northern cluster in Figure 2 (*k*-means) is more widespread than the comparable cluster in Figure 1 (SC-*k*NN). On the other hand, in contrast to Figure 1, there are some regions in the Southwest that are part of the northern cluster in Figure 2.

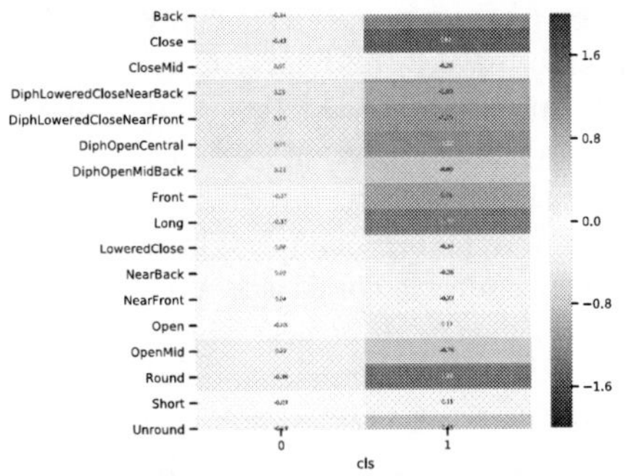

Figure 3: Linguistic features of the SC-*k*NN clustering (2 clusters) for MHG long vowels.

In addition, Figure 3 shows the linguistic features that are relevant for the clusters in Figure 1. In this analysis, the data set is filtered for MHG long vowels. Therefore, Figure 3 shows only the linguistic features of the sounds (in the surnames) that are related to MHG long vowels as reference sounds. The values are presented in contrast for each feature (we have kept Engsterhold's feature names for now out of simplicity). Above-average values are colored in red, low values in blue. Compared to (1), it becomes obvious that, in order to ensure comparability, the phonologically induced binary classification has been resolved. Each category of a binary differentiation is now defined as a separate feature. The same holds for the categorical classification of the vowel space. Figure 3 lists all of the resulting characteristics for all features set for the vocalism.

Since the values per cluster are related and scaled at the relations of all features per cluster, the values across clusters cannot be directly related to each other. Nevertheless, they indicate an inverse relationship in the two-part cluster. Not reported are features with zero realizations as is the case, for example, for [central], [nil], [mid]. These features typically refer to schwa, which seems to be not relevant for the sound class under discussion.

The logic of this procedure can be best explained by focusing on the northern red cluster 1 in Figure 1. The first result from Figure 3 is that this cluster prefers monophthongs over diphthongs, which becomes clear by the fact that features connected to diphthongs are the less frequent ones in cluster 1 (e.g., [DiphLoweredClose-NearBack] refers to *au*).

Second, the most characteristic features of cluster 1 are [close], [long], [round]. Translating these features into sounds, the most frequent features of cluster 1 stand for sounds like *u* and *i*, but also *ü* if assuming that the features do not necessarily have to be linked. Other features of higher impact are [back], but also [front] and [unround] thus referring to the remaining monophthongs.

In this way, for the sound class in focus, not only a spatially definable dominance of monophthongs over diphthongs becomes apparent through cluster 1. In addition, a gradation in the relevance of individual features within the group of monophthongs becomes clear, which characterizes the quantitatively identified cluster. These features, in turn, make it possible to predict which sounds to expect in this cluster.

Examining the characteristic features of the clusters in Figures 4 (*k*-means), a similar picture becomes visible, however, the values are more balanced than in the SC-*k*NN clustering.

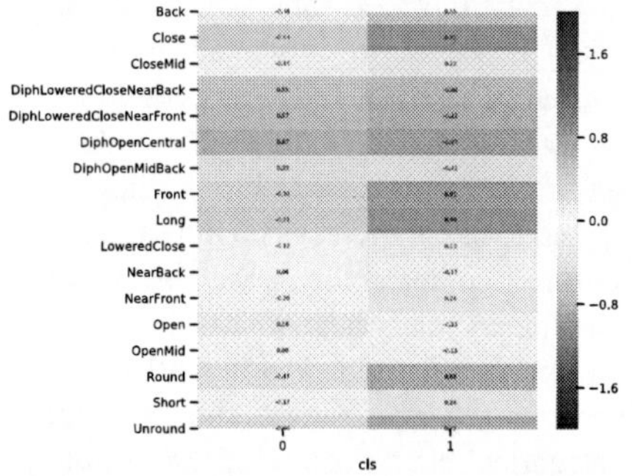

Figure 4: Linguistic features of the *k*-means clustering (2 clusters) for MHG long vowels.

4.2 Linguistic Interpretation

The specific characteristics of the clusters can be interpreted by looking at the historical sound changes that affected the Middle High German long vowels and their Low German equivalents. Here, we recognize the New High German diphthongization that affected the German dialect regions in different extent and in temporal succession (cf. Reichmann and Wegera, 1993: 64–67).

While the diphthongization captured most of the High German area, the Low German and the Alemannic dialects preserved the historical monophthongs. However, the areal distribution of the surname clusters differs from the distribution of the NHG diphthongization in the dialects: the surnames show phonological features of the NHG diphthongization even in areas where the dialects preserve the old monophthongs, for example, in Eastern Low German and in Alemannic (with some exceptions, see e.g., the scattered red postal code districts in Figure 2). This refers to the graphematic basis of surnames. Surnames were part of the regional writing traditions that were severely influenced by the arising NHG written language. In the Low German regions, the strong influence even led to a change from the former Low German writing language of the Hanse to the NHG written language, starting in the Brandenburgish area in the 16th century (cf. Peters, 2015). Thus, the surnames as part of the writing traditions mirror an advanced and medially different development of the NHG diphthongization compared to the dialects; they show "verhochdeutschte" forms.

The influence of the NHG written language was especially high when the source lexemes of the surnames were transparent and could be transferred into High German forms by applying simple transformation rules (e.g., LG/ALEM *u* > HG *au* in LG/ALEM *Husmann* > HG *Hausmann*).

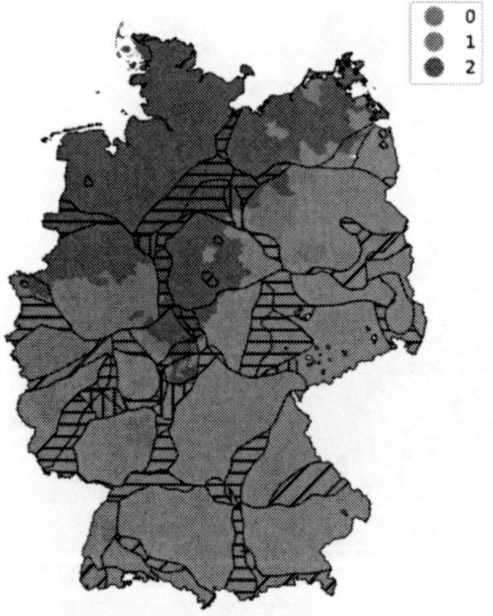

Figure 5: SC-*k*NN clustering (3 clusters) for MHG long vowels.

Looking at the higher clustering in Figure 5, we see that the areas that change their classification between Figures 1 and 2 now create own clusters, together with the adjacent areas.

It thus becomes apparent that the third cluster structure in Figure 5 indicates transition zones (grey cluster, 0). It shows intermediate values for diphthongs and long monophthongs (cf. Figure 6). On the other hand, cluster 0 is characterized by high values for specific features which sets it apart from the two main clusters. The most prominent features are [NearFront] and [OpenMid], pointing at high occurrences of different monophthong sound features and their underlying phonological processes, for example, shortening of long vowels (e.g., *Siffert* < MHG *Sîvrit* 'Siegfried') or umlaut (e.g., *Krämmer* < MHG *krâmære* 'grocer').

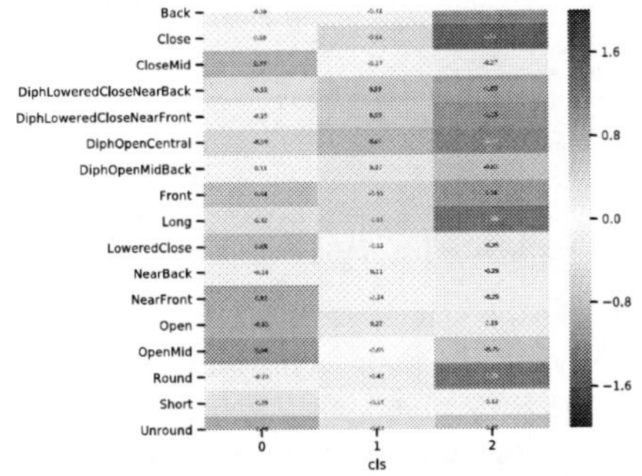

Figure 6: Linguistic features of the SC-*k*NN clustering (3 clusters) for MHG long vowels.

As a result, this example analysis has shown that the cluster structure of the surnames that relate to MHG long vowels depict both, the development of historical sound changes like the diphthongization, and region-specific phonological characteristics. In this way, the spatial structures revealed by our ontology also reflect fundamental cultural events and processes like the change of the writing tradition in the Low German area.

5 Analysis of an Individual Sound Class

5.1 Quantitative Analysis

Focusing on only one sound class, we are able to investigate the outcome of regional specific developments in more detail. As an example, we restricted our data set to surnames that were assigned to MHG û (e.g., *Kruse, Kruss, Krause* < MHG *krûs*). We expect that the spatial structure mirrors the realization of the NHG diphthongization and its regionally different outcomes. In contrast to the analysis of all MHG long vowels we should see more clearly how the historically long monophthong *û* developed depending on the dialect regions. Except from our interest for the diphthongization, we aim at identifying regions with a tendency towards umlaut.

The subsample of our analysis comprises 199 types with 58,708 tokens. We present the cluster solution for four clusters. As Table 3 indicates, *k*-means shows the best results.

	4	
Clustering	**SC**	**CH**
GMM	0.02	167.48
k-*means*	0.47	599.98
k-*medoids*	0.34	418.14
*SC-*k*NN*	0.44	586.25
Ward	0.42	553.89

Table 3: Evaluation of the clustering algorithms.

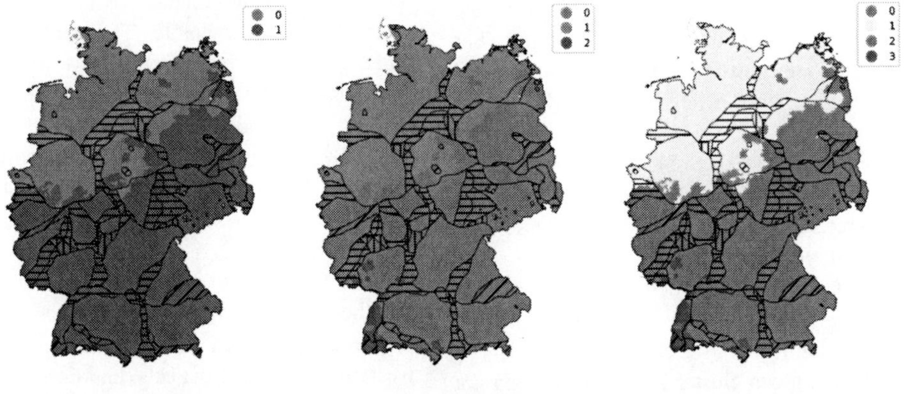

Figure 7: Comparing the *k*-means clusterings (2, 3, and 4 clusters) for MHG *û*.

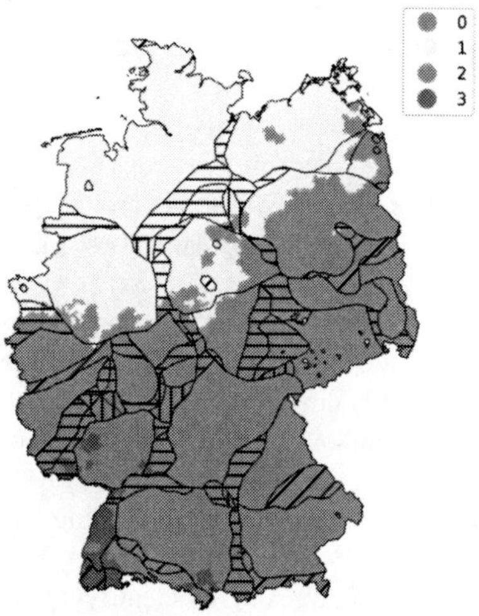

Figure 8: *K*-means clustering (4 clusters) for MHG *û*.

The map in Figure 8 presents the results for the 4-cluster solution for *k*-means. Again, the cluster structures are mostly coherent and consistent. Comparing this map with the 2-cluster solution in Figure 7, it becomes evident that the northern cluster (yellow, 1) is already separated from the other clusters. The 3-cluster analysis then segregates the red cluster (3) in the southwest. Only in the 4-cluster map, the green cluster (2) appears as a substructure of the grey one (0).

Comparing the clusters from Figure 8 with their linguistic features in Figure 9, we see that the clusters are defined by the different outcomes and developments of the historical reference sound MHG *û*.

The main divide in Figure 8 results from the opposition of monophthongs vs. diphthongs. For example, the grey cluster 0 is mainly characterized by the features [DiphLoweredCloseNearBack] and [DiphOpen-Central] which indicate the diphthongized vowel *au*. Similar holds for the green cluster 2, which refers, e.g., to the well-known preference for diphthongs in Hesse (see Birkenes and Fleischer, 2019).

Furthermore, in the Baden area of southeast Germany, it is the short lowered-closed, near-back vowel *u*, that influences the clustering (red, 3).

Finally, the green cluster 2 is characterized not only by diphthong features but mainly by features that indicate the umlaut diphthong *äu/eu* [DiphOpenMidLoweredClose-NearFront].

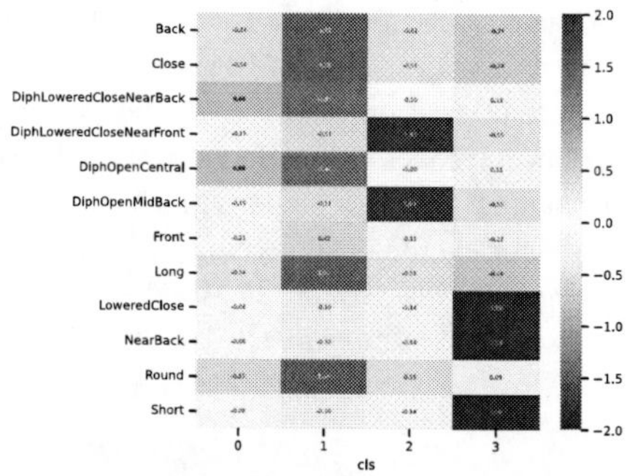

Figure 9: Linguistic features of the SC-*k*NN clustering (3 clusters) for MHG *û*.

5.2 Linguistic Interpretation

Evaluating the spatial structure from a historical point of view, the main north-south divide shows where the NHG diphthongs were adopted in the regional writing traditions. It is remarkable that the diphthongs in the surnames (e.g., *Krause* vs *Kruse*) prevail not only in the regions where the diphthongs occur in the dialects, but also in Baden and Brandenburg where the Alemannic and Low German dialects preserved monophthongs. Here, the surnames are influenced by the regional writing traditions that are more progressive in adopting NHG forms than the dialects.

On the other hand, the higher clusterings show that in cases where the lexical basis is not transparent, the dialectal realizations prevail: In Baden, an example is the surname *Sutter(er)* vs *Sauter* which shows characteristic shortening (*uː* > *u*) in the closed syllable. The profession name *Sutter/Sauter* derives from MHG *sûter* 'tailor, shoemaker'. Other than the competing lexemes *Näher*, *Schneider* and *Schuster*, the lexeme *Sutter/Sauter* was not adopted into the NHG written language. Today, it is only known as a dialect word (cf. *Schweizerisches Idiotikon*[3]) or as a surname.

Thirdly, the analysis shows that there are well-defined areas in which, additionally to diphthongization, umlaut modification took place. Those areas (green cluster 2) are restricted to western and central dialects, and do not appear in

[3] https://www.idiotikon.ch/Register/faksimile.php?band=7&spalte=1477

the Upper German regions, that, significantly, are known for their non-affinity towards umlaut.

In summary, the example demonstrates that the spatial analysis of surnames provides information about regionally specific developments in the graphic and phonological representations of surnames.

6 Conclusion

The paper has shown that the ontology-based analysis technique provides a tool which allows to investigate the regional distribution of phonological characteristics in the German surnames. At the same time, it is possible to detect the spatial extension of historical sound changes that are mirrored in the surnames. We assume that the surnames not only represent fossils of historical spoken language but also developments in regional and transregional writing traditions.

A characteristic of our approach is the multidimensional processing of the surname data, which provides a variety of starting points for further research. Depending on how the data set is filtered, different perspectives are possible. Either the diachronic and diatopic developments of a single historical reference sound are investigated, or the analysis is broadened to describe the major graphemic and phonological features of the surname landscapes of Germany.

Limitations

The presented study was limited by the selection of the surname types for annotation. Following the choice of topics that are presented in the DFA 1 and 2 the historical reference sounds are not represented in a balanced way. Also, our annotation categories cover, at present, neither the phonological nor the morphological contexts of the analyzed sounds.

The greatest challenge was the alignment of graphemes and phonemes. While we managed to cope with multiple references between graphemes and phonemes, we did not yet implement a technique that identifies regionally diverse phonological realizations of the same grapheme (e.g., the grapheme <ue> corresponds to either /y/ or /u:/ depending on the dialect area). We plan to implement this in the future.

Ethics Statement

We declare that our research complies with the ACL Ethics Policy. As surnames are part of personal data, we ensured that data protection was not violated at any time.

References

Anderson, Robert R., Ulrich Goebel, and Oskar Reichmann. 1981. Ein idealisiertes Graphemsystem des Frühneuhochdeutschen als Grundlage für die Lemmatisierung frühneuhochdeutscher Wörter. *Studien zur neuhochdeutschen Lexikographie,* I: 53–122.

Breder Birkenes, Magnus and Jürg Fleischer. 2019. Zentral-, Nord- und Osthessisch. In J. Herrgen and J. E. Schmidt, editors, *Sprache und Raum: ein internationales Handbuch der Sprachvariation. Band 4: Deutsch.* (Handbücher zur Sprach- und Kommunikationswissenschaft 30.4). De Gruyter Mouton, Berlin/Boston, pages 435–478.

Cheshire, James, Pablo Mateos, and Paul A. Longley. 2011. Delineating Europe's Cultural Regions: Population Structure and Surname Clustering. *Human Biology*, 83(5):573–598.

Dammel, Antje and Mirjam Schmuck. 2009. Familiennamen und Dialektologie. In K. Hengst and D. Krüger, editors, *Familiennamen im Deutschen.* Universitätsverlag, Leipzig, pages 271–296.

DFA = Kunze, Konrad and Damaris Nübling, editors. 2009–2018. *Deutscher Familiennamenatlas [German Surname Atlas].* De Gruyter, Berlin/Boston.

DFA 1 = Bochenek, Christian and Kathrin Dräger. 2009. *Deutscher Familiennamenatlas [German Surname Atlas]. Band 1: Graphematik/Phonologie der Familiennamen I: Vokalismus.* De Gruyter, Berlin/New York.

DFA 2 = Dammel, Antje, Kathrin Dräger, Rita Heuser, and Mirjam Schmuck. 2011. *Deutscher Familiennamenatlas [German Surname Atlas]. Band 2: Graphematik/Phonologie der Familiennamen II: Konsonantismus.* De Gruyter, Berlin/New York.

Engsterhold, Robert. 2020. Sprachraumanalyse mithilfe einer phonetischen Ontologie. Dissertation, Philipps-University, Marburg.

Flores Flores, W. Amaru and Peter Gilles. 2020. Die Verlustlisten des Ersten Weltkriegs als historisches namengeographisches Corpus. *Beiträge zur Namenforschung*, 55(2–3):127–167.

Kunze, Konrad and Richard Kunze. 2003. Computergestützte Familiennamen-Geographie. Kleiner Atlas zur Verbreitung der Apokope. *Beiträge zur Namenforschung,* 38:121–224.

Moran, Steven, Daniel McCloy, and Richard Wright, editors. 2014. PHOIBLE Online. Max Planck Institute for Evolutionary Anthropology.

MRhSA = Bellmann, Günter, Joachim Herrgen, and Jürgen Erich Schmidt. 1994–2002. *Mittelrheinischer Sprachatlas [Linguistic Atlas of the Middle Rhine Area].* Max Niemeyer, Tübingen.

Nerbonne, John, Rinke Colen, Charlotte Gooskens, Peter Kleiweg, and Therese Leinonen. 2011. Gabmap – A Web Application for Dialectology. *Dialectologia, Special Issue II,* 65–89.

Peters, Robert. 2015. Zur Sprachgeschichte des norddeutschen Raumes. *Jahrbuch für Germanistische Sprachgeschichte*, 6(1):18–36.

Reichmann, Oskar and Klaus-Peter Wegera. 1993. Frühneuhochdeutsche Grammatik. Max Niemeyer, Tübingen.

Wiesinger, Peter. 1983. Die Einteilung der deutschen Dialekte. In W. Besch et al., editors, *Dialektologie. Ein Handbuch zur deutschen und allgemeinen Dialektforschung.* (Handbücher zur Sprach- und Kommunikationswissenschaft 1.2) De Gruyter, Berlin/New York, pages 807–900.

BENCHić-lang: A Benchmark for Discriminating between Bosnian, Croatian, Montenegrin and Serbian

Peter Rupnik and **Taja Kuzman**
Jožef Stefan Institute, Slovenia
taja.kuzman@ijs.si,
peter.rupnik@ijs.si

Nikola Ljubešić
Jožef Stefan Institute, Slovenia
Center za jezikovne vire in tehnologije
Univerze v Ljubljani, Slovenia
nikola.ljubesic@ijs.si

Abstract

Automatic discrimination between Bosnian, Croatian, Montenegrin and Serbian is a hard task due to the mutual intelligibility of these South-Slavic languages. In this paper, we introduce the BENCHić-lang benchmark for discriminating between these four languages. The benchmark consists of two datasets from different domains – a Twitter and a news dataset – selected with the aim of fostering cross-dataset evaluation of different modelling approaches. We experiment with the baseline SVM models, based on character n-grams, which perform nicely in-dataset, but do not generalize well in cross-dataset experiments. Thus, we introduce another approach, exploiting only web-crawled data and the weak supervision signal coming from the respective country/language top-level domains. The resulting simple Naive Bayes model, based on less than a thousand word features extracted from web data, outperforms the baseline models in the cross-dataset scenario and achieves good levels of generalization across datasets.

1 Introduction

The status of "separate language" for Bosnian, Croatian, Montenegrin and Serbian is frequently discussed and is in academic circles mostly understood as related to the construction of identity (Alexander, 2013) and diverging and converging tendencies throughout history (Ljubešić et al., 2018). While each is an official language in the respective country, with a separate top-level Internet domain (Ljubešić and Klubička, 2014), their mutual intelligibility cannot be disputed. Regardless of the mutual intelligibility, differences do exist (Ljubešić et al., 2018). In this paper, we introduce a discrimination benchmark based on two datasets: a newspaper-based one, covering three out of four languages, and a Twitter-based one, covering all four languages. The publication of this benchmark coincides with the 10th anniversary of the VarDial workshop, in which this language group has been involved from the beginning.

The main contributions of this paper are the following. We introduce two datasets, based on previously collected data, that we now encode with maximal structure and publish in an academic data repository following the FAIR principles (Jacobsen et al., 2020). We introduce a benchmark based on the two datasets, and present baselines for the benchmark. Given the low performance of these competitive baselines on the benchmark, we introduce a new web-dataset-based method that shows to carry specificities of each language across the two datasets much better than any model directly trained on one of the two datasets. We hope that the availability of this benchmark, as well as the introduced strong competitors, will motivate further research in discriminating between similar languages.

2 Benchmark Datasets

The benchmark consists of two rather different datasets, whose selection was made with the aim of fostering cross-dataset evaluation of different modelling approaches. The first dataset is the parallel newspaper dataset from the "South-Eastern Times" (SETimes) website covering news in languages of South-Eastern Europe, including Bosnian, Croatian and Serbian. The dataset has been part of the VarDial shared task since 2014 (Zampieri et al., 2014) as part of the DSLCC collection (Tan et al., 2014), and was present in the following iteration of the shared task as well (Zampieri et al., 2015). Within VarDial, it was available in the form of 22 000 instances per language, each no longer than 100 tokens. We have now published all available content from the SETimes website in the form of 9 258 whole documents (Ljubešić and Rupnik, 2022a).[1] The documents are separated into a train, devel-

[1] http://hdl.handle.net/11356/1461

Tenth Workshop on NLP for Similar Languages, Varieties and Dialects (VarDial 2023), pages 113–120
May 5, 2023 ©2023 Association for Computational Linguistics

opment and test subset in an 8:1:1 ratio. While dividing the documents, we made sure that, given that the dataset consists of the same content in the three languages, there is no leakage of parallel data across these three subsets, especially given the mutual intelligibility of the languages covered. We assume that, given the parallel nature of this dataset, it could be very useful in learning the specifics in which the three close languages differ. The median length of instances (documents) is 627 words, while the arithmetic mean length is 849 words.

The second dataset is based on tweets, harvested with the TweetCat (Ljubešić et al., 2014) tool. This dataset was used as the out-of-domain testing data in the third iteration of the VarDial shared task (Malmasi et al., 2016), but in significantly smaller volume than what we included in this benchmark. We share tweets of 614 users, 394 of which are labeled as tweeting in Serbian, 89 in Croatian, 75 in Bosnian, and 56 in Montenegrin. Each user is represented with at least 200 tweets, merged in our experiments into one single text per each user. Single tweets were not filtered by the language they are written in, which allows for other languages besides the four languages of interest to occur in the dataset, such as infrequent tweets in English. With this decision we wanted to keep the dataset as natural and realistic as possible. The users were split into the train, development and test subset in a 3:1:1 ratio, so that the development and test splits would be large enough. The median length of instances (all tweets of one user) is 5,438 words, while the arithmetic mean length is 7,257 words. The dataset is published as a JSON file, each primary entry representing one user, the label denoting which language the user is tweeting in, and a list of the users' tweets (Ljubešić and Rupnik, 2022b).[2]

The benchmark allows for training on any of the two training datasets, as well as using external data, provided that it does not overlap with texts in the test split. Hyperparameters or model decisions can be chosen with the help of development data. The two official metrics of the benchmark are micro F1 and macro F1, both considered equally important.

The researchers are welcome to add to this benchmark the results achieved on any combination of training and testing datasets (in-domain or out-domain). However, the primary goal of this benchmark is to present results obtained in the cross-dataset scenario, that is, testing the model on test data from a dataset on which the model was not trained on, to prove the general applicability of the resulting model on the task of discriminating between the languages in question. The results of various models can be submitted via the GitHub repository[3] through a pull request.

3 Experiments

We experiment with two approaches: the baseline approach – a linear SVM model with character n-gram representation, described in Section 3.1, and our new approach, presented in Section 3.2: a Naive Bayes model using a text representation based on feature extraction from national web corpora. The classifier selection in each of the approaches is based on best results on the development data, and each of the two classifiers were considered in each of the approaches.

3.1 Baseline: SVM Model with Character N-Gram Text Representation

For the initial baseline of this benchmark, we used a simple approach that has been shown to be very competitive with even much more complex solutions (Malmasi et al., 2016; Zampieri et al., 2017) – a linear SVM model, used with the character n-gram text representation. We implemented the baseline solution inside the sklearn package (Pedregosa et al., 2011), and the only hyperparameter we tuned was the maximum length of the character n-gram, given that the shortest character n-gram is 3.

During hyperparameter tuning on the development data, we first selected the appropriate classifier, comparing the SVM and the Naive Bayes classifier while using character 3-grams as features. The results showed, as expected, that SVMs work better with the significant number of features produced with the character 3-gram feature generator. We next compared character 3-gram and 3–5-gram representations on our development data. The experiments showed that the character 3–5-grams perform slightly better in the in-dataset setup, reaching 1 to 6 points higher micro and macro F1 scores, while in the cross-dataset setup the 3-gram text representation provides slightly better results, outperforming the 3–5-gram representation by 1 to 4 points. This result does not come as a surprise as the character 3-gram model has a higher generaliz-

[2] http://hdl.handle.net/11356/1482

[3] https://github.com/clarinsi/benchich/tree/main/lang

Test data	Train data	micro F1	macro F1
SETimes	SETimes	0.995	0.995
	Twitter (3 class)	0.839	0.672
Twitter (3 class)	SETimes	0.743	0.747
	Twitter (3 class)	0.929	0.875

Table 1: Results of the linear SVM baseline with a character 3-gram text representation, trained either on the SETimes or the Twitter 3-class dataset, and tested in the in-dataset and the cross-dataset setup.

ability, important in the cross-dataset setup, while the 3–5-gram model has more capacity to learn the specifics of a dataset, preferred in the in-dataset setup. In further experiments, we use the character 3-gram text representation, as we are interested in a model which is able to generalize well to be applicable to different downstream datasets.

The method is tested on in-dataset and cross-dataset experiments, using the benchmark datasets: the SETimes and Twitter datasets. The in-dataset experiments consist of training and testing the model on the train and test split from the same dataset, while in the cross-dataset experiments, the model is trained on the train split from one dataset and tested on the test split of the other dataset. The cross-dataset setup was shown to be especially relevant for the task of discrimination between similar languages (Malmasi et al., 2016; Zampieri et al., 2017; Gaman et al., 2020), as well as document classification in general, because it shows the ability of the model to generalize across the datasets, and with that, its usefulness for the real-world applications.

Given that the SETimes dataset covers only three out of the four languages, while the Twitter dataset covers all four languages of interest, we used only languages that occur in both datasets for the baseline experiments, that is, the Bosnian, Croatian and the Serbian language.

Table 1 shows the results of the two baseline models, that is, the SVM model, trained on SETimes, and the SVM model, trained on the Twitter dataset. The models were tested on test splits from both datasets, showing their in-dataset and cross-dataset performance. The results show that, as expected, the in-dataset results are much higher than the cross-dataset results on both datasets. The in-dataset results reached up to 0.995 micro and macro F1 scores in the case of the SETimes model and 0.929 micro F1 and 0.875 macro F1 in the case of the Twitter model. As expected, in the in-domain setup, the SETimes model achieves higher results than the Twitter model. Somewhat unexpected, in the cross-dataset setup both combinations of training and evaluation data result in a very similar micro F1, showing a similar level of per-instance cross-dataset portability. However, on the macro F1 metric, the SETimes dataset shows to be a simpler evaluation dataset than the Twitter dataset, which is quite probably due to the fact that the SETimes dataset is more balanced, while the Twitter dataset is more challenging with its intensive skewness towards the Serbian language.

In the cross-dataset setup, the models scored for 9 up to 25 less points in micro and macro F1 points than in the in-dataset setup. This shows that models trained on any of the two datasets show to be rather incapable of generating predictions in the cross-dataset scenario that would be useful in the downstream, as around 25% of predictions are incorrect.

3.2 Our Approach: Naive Bayes Model and Web Corpora Feature Extraction

Given the rather low results of the proposed baselines in the cross-dataset setup on both datasets, we decided to propose a more robust approach to discriminating between the languages included in this benchmark. Since each of the four languages/countries has a top-level Internet domain (`.hr` for Croatian, `.ba` for Bosnian, `.me` for Montenegrin and `.rs` for Serbian), and since there are crawls of all four top-level domains available (Ljubešić, 2021), we are proposing a weak-supervised approach exploiting the information about the top-level domain from which a text came as our signal of weak supervision. That is, we regard texts from a specific top-level domain as being of the language related to the domain, e.g., texts from `.hr` as texts in Croatian language. Based on this, we perform a feature selection that identifies a small subset of words that are most specific for each language, i.e., top-level domain.

For the experiments, we use web corpora for the

	Feature Extraction		Training	
	paragraph #	word #	paragraph #	word #
Bosnian	943 515	18 503 316	2 102 489	37 681 981
Croatian	959 600	17 536 075	1 970 022	32 639 016
Montenegrin	864 921	35 684 637	999 997	35 677 096
Serbian	952 964	17 954 495	2 868 638	49 577 451

Table 2: Size of the parts of the web corpora used for feature extraction and model training.

four languages, available as part of the BERTić-data (Ljubešić, 2021), a text collection used for training the BERTić transformer model (Ljubešić and Lauc, 2021). We use part of the data for feature extraction and part of the data for training the Naive Bayes model, using the obtained features. Similarly to the baselines presented in the previous step, we have considered both the linear SVM and the Naive Bayes model, but the latter proved to be better performing on this task. The amount of data used for the feature extraction and for the model training is shown in Table 2. We used between 17 and 35 million words for the feature extraction, while we trained the classifier on 100 000 documents from each of the four top-level domains, each consisting of between 33 and 50 million words.

The feature extraction is based on comparing pairs of web corpora: for each pair, we identify features (words) that are the most specific for one language given another language. The weighting function for each language pair is the odds ratio, i.e., how much more probable it is for a word to appear in one language (or web corpus) in comparison to another language. As possible features, we consider words of three or more characters, consisting only of letters.

One hyperparameter that has to be tuned in our approach is the number of features per ordered language pair to be included in the feature set. Our experiments on the development data of both the SETimes and the Twitter dataset showed that using around 100 most prominent features per ordered language pair gives the best results on both test datasets. Since we obtain from each ordered language pair a list of 100 features, we have to calculate a union of 12 lists of 100 features, resulting in 819 final features, due to expected feature repetition. When training a model, texts are represented as vectors based on the 819 features, created with the CountVectorizer tool, available inside the sklearn package (Pedregosa et al., 2011). Preliminary experiments on the development set showed that among various quantifications of feature occurrence (frequency, TF-IDF, binary), the binary values regularly provided the best results.

Our next step is to train our model on web texts, classified into languages based on the top-level domain they are published on. As already reported, preliminary results showed that the Naive Bayes classifier performs better than the linear SVM classifier. It was shown to be much more stable across datasets, which does not come as a surprise given the low number of selected features. This is exactly the opposite from our baseline method, relying on many character n-gram features, where the SVM method showed to perform better. Interestingly, for both classifiers, the optimal number of features per ordered language pair showed to be around 100 features.

SETimes test data		
model	micro F1	macro F1
NB Web	0.957	0.957
SVM SETimes	**0.995**	**0.995**
SVM Twitter	0.839	0.672
Twitter 3-class test data		
model	micro F1	macro F1
NB Web	**0.946**	**0.897**
SVM Twitter	0.929	0.875
SVM SETimes	0.743	0.747
Twitter 4-class test data		
model	micro F1	macro F1
NB Web	**0.870**	0.682
SVM Twitter	**0.870**	**0.732**

Table 3: Results of our Naive Bayes model with web feature-based text representation and trained on web corpora (NB Web), compared to the baseline models: SVM model, trained on SETimes (SVM SETimes), and SVM model, trained on Twitter (SVM Twitter), on test splits of various datasets. The best results are in bold.

We compare our method, hereinafter referred to as "NB Web", with the in-dataset and cross-dataset baseline results, described in the previous section, both on the SETimes and Twitter test splits. The results are shown in Table 3. When the models are applied to the SETimes test dataset, the baseline SVM model, trained on the SETimes dataset, does perform best, reaching almost perfect scores of 0.995 micro and macro F1. This does not come as a surprise given the narrowness of the SETimes dataset (single-source news dataset). However, the NB Web model performs also rather well, micro and macro F1 scores lagging behind only for 4 points. Most importantly, the NB Web model performs drastically better than the baseline SVM model which was trained on the Twitter 3-class training dataset and used here in a cross-dataset setup.

The second section of Table 3 reports on the results on the Twitter 3-class test set where we used only instances from the three classes that are available in the SETimes dataset, that is, instances of Bosnian, Croatian and Serbian. In this setup, our model slightly outperforms even the in-dataset baseline results, i.e., the SVM model trained on Twitter data. It also performs drastically better than the baseline SVM model trained on SETimes, with a difference of more than 20 points.

This model finally allows also for some comparison to the 4-class baseline experiments, results of which we did not show in the previous section, given that the SVM classifier, trained on the SETimes dataset, only contains three out of four classes. The results on the Twitter 4-class test dataset are presented in the final section of Table 3. In this scenario, the NB Web model did not significantly outperform the baseline SVM model, trained on the Twitter dataset, as was the case on the 3-class Twitter test set. On the micro F1 metric, we obtained an equally good result with both methods – micro F1 of 0.87, while on the macro F1 metric, the SVM model, applied in an in-dataset setup, performs better, reaching the score of 0.73, while the NB Web model obtained 0.68 macro F1. However, given the equal result on the micro F1 metric, we assume that the edge of the (in-dataset) SVM Twitter model here is just the knowledge of the class distribution in the test set, information to which the NB web model was not exposed. Given this result, we can even assume that, with a class distribution far from the Twitter 4-class dataset, the NB web model should result in a better per-category performance than the in-domain method, and comparably on the per-instance level.

3.2.1 Impact of Amount of Training Data

Given that we have used a significant amount of data for training the web model (100 000 documents per class), we perform an additional analysis of the dependence of the performance of the NB Web model to the amount of web training data. We investigate how the model performs on all three test datasets (SETimes, Twitter 3-class and Twitter 4-class) if we are to train it on 25%, 50%, or 100% of our training data. The results are presented in Figure 1. The experiments show that we obtain very similar results to the previously presented ones even if we perform parameter estimation on one fourth of the training data. The only argument for using as much data as we are is the stability of the results, especially in the case of the 4-class Twitter problem, while on the SETimes dataset the results on less training data do not vary much.

What we have not explored, and what we leave for future work, is the impact of the amount of data used for feature selection. Given that best results were obtained with only 100 features selected from millions of words of text, we have to assume that these 100 features could have been similarly well extracted on a portion of the text used in our case.

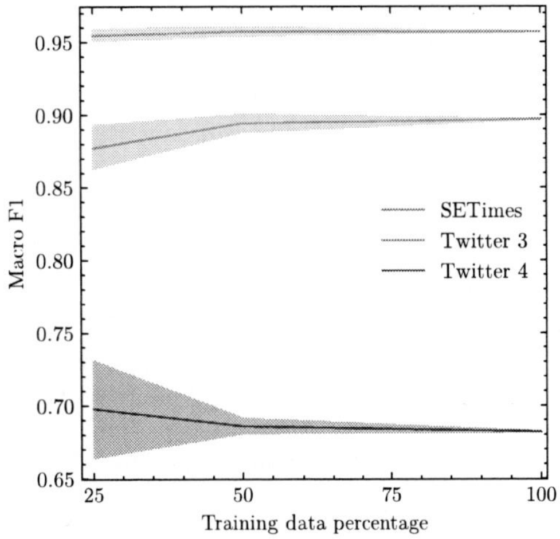

Figure 1: Impact of the size of the training dataset of the NB Web model on its performance on the SETimes and Twitter test datasets. Variation in the results is represented through the standard deviation.

3.2.2 Per-Category Performance

We conclude the results section with an analysis of the per-category performance of both models that are able to discriminate between all four languages, which are the baseline SVM Twitter in-

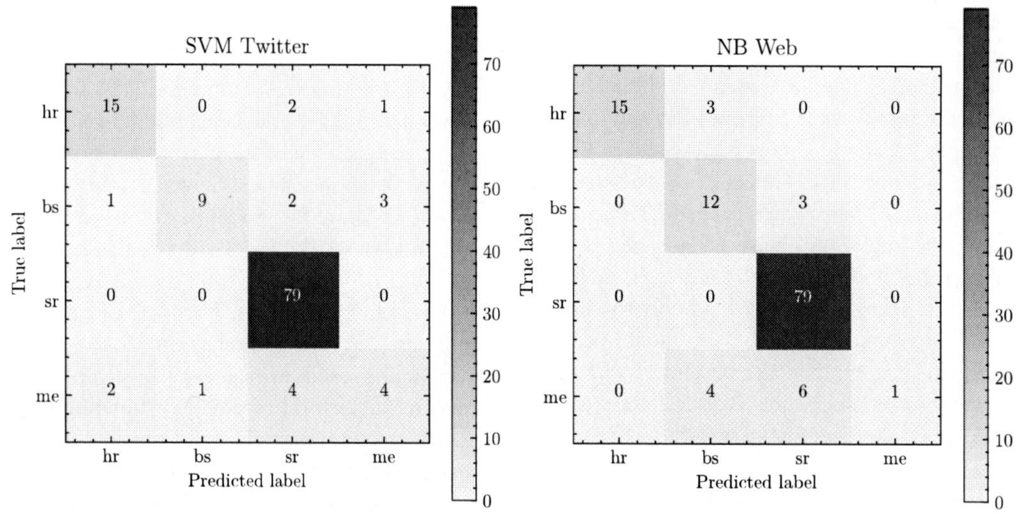

Figure 2: Confusion matrices for the baseline in-dataset SVM Twitter model and the NB Web model. The models are evaluated on the test split of the 4-class Twitter dataset.

dataset model, and the NB Web model. We present the performance via confusion matrices on the Twitter 4-class test split in Figure 2.

We can observe a good performance of both models on Croatian and Serbian, with a decent performance on Bosnian, especially with the NB Web model. However, the performance on Montenegrin is very unsatisfactory in case of both models. While the SVM Twitter in-dataset model correctly classifies only 4 out of 11 test instances in the Montenegrin category, the situation with the NB Web model is even worse. It classifies correctly only one out of 11 instances, others being taken primarily by Serbian and Bosnian. This analysis shows the limitation of our current results – while we do have a robust dataset-independent way of discriminating between Bosnian, Croatian and Serbian, the problem of identifying Montenegrin cannot be considered solved to a satisfactory level.

4 Conclusion

In this paper, we introduce the BENCHić-lang benchmark for discriminating between four very similar languages: Bosnian, Croatian, Montenegrin and Serbian. The benchmark consists of two rather different datasets, providing a good test bed for beyond-model generalizability.

We introduce two methods for discriminating between the languages. The first, a baseline, is a linear SVM model using character n-gram features, showing to perform well in-dataset, but not having generalization power to perform well in the cross-dataset setup. For that reason, we introduce another approach, exploiting only web-crawled data and the weak supervision signal coming from the country/language respective top-level domains. We perform heavy feature selection of less than 1000 word features on one subset of the web data, and train a Naive Bayes model on the remainder of the web data. We show that this model performs much better than the character n-gram models in the cross-dataset setting. What is more, it even outperforms the in-dataset results of the SVM model on one of the Twitter test sets. While we obtain very stable results on Bosnian, Croatian and Serbian, we must put forward that neither the in-dataset SVM Twitter, nor the NB Web model perform satisfactory on discriminating Montenegrin from the three other languages, which is a task to be tackled in future work.

Besides improving the identification of Montenegrin, there are many other directions we hope the community will investigate. One direction is exploiting linguistic features known to vary between the four languages (Ljubešić et al., 2018) and base the classification decision on these features. Another is to investigate transformer models, fine-tuning them either on the training data, or on the weak-supervision web data. We have performed an initial experiment on the latter, fine-tuning the BERTić model (Ljubešić and Lauc, 2021) for one epoch on the 400 000 web documents. During this first epoch we consistently obtained low results, with no tendency of improvement. Additional experimentation, potentially with lower learning rates or more complex loss functions, could be performed here. Finally, additional datasets should be added to the benchmark, especially such datasets that cover all of the four languages of interest.

Limitations

The two datasets included in the benchmark are by no means representative for the four languages we focus in this work. However, the datasets are different enough to serve as an initial test bed for robust discrimination between the four languages through a cross-dataset setup. Furthermore, the definition of these four languages is also rather problematic due to their similarity, and a potentially more viable option would be a linguistically-motivated multidimensional description of the variation among these languages, rather than aiming at the single-dimension 4-level description. The linguistically-motivated methods might be also more reliable, as they would be based on rules and lexicons, defined by linguists, rather than training corpora with unknown biases. We are aware that training the models with our method might introduce some bias to the results, because it is based on identifying words that are specific for each language by comparing the web corpora content. Consequently, some of the identified words might be more connected to topic differences between the corpora than variety differences. For instance, one of the words, specific for Croatian, is "kuna", a former Croatian currency, which is more of a culture-specific than a language-specific word. However, by extracting many features from very large numbers of documents, and then training the model on thousands of texts, we hope that such topic biases are minimized by the massive amounts of texts used.

Finally, using top-level domain information for assuming language labels is a weak-supervision method and is less reliable than manual annotation. With this approach, we presume that the majority of texts, published on the top-level web domain, are written by native speakers of the language that is associated with the respective country and its top-level domain. However, we are aware that it is possible that some texts are mislabeled and actually written in another language. We cannot be sure that the authors of these texts are native speakers, live in the respective country related to the national web domain, or that the text is not a republication from another source in another language, as was shown to be the case for the British-American English dataset in the Discriminating between Similar Languages (DSL) shared task 2014 (Zampieri et al., 2014).

Ethics Statement

We are aware that using web data is inevitably connected with questions of respecting the intellectual property and privacy rights of the original authors of the texts. In this paper, we used web corpora that have been collected by crawling the national top-level web domains. Only freely accessible texts were included in the corpora to avoid inclusion of sensitive data. Since the datasets were collected automatically and are too large to review manually, it is possible that the datasets include some texts whose authors do not consent to be included. However, in our paper, we only use the overall characteristics of the texts by extracting the most frequent language-specific words and do not examine the texts more closely or produce systems that could abuse personal information or intellectual property rights.

Secondly, as mentioned in Limitations, when training our NB Web model on web data, we presume that all texts from a specific national top-level domain are written in the main official language of the country to which the domain is connected. However, we are aware that there are national minorities of each of the analyzed languages that live across the borders of the country where the language is officially spoken, and that we can, for example, find a Serbian minority living in Bosnia and speaking Serbian on the Bosnian national web. By labeling all web texts from the Bosnian domain as Bosnian language, the resulting model could discriminate towards the minorities, equating their language with the language of the majority, publishing on the national domain. We are aware that our weak-supervision approach is a bit simplistic in regards to this issue, and while this is out of the scope of this paper, we plan to analyze this issue further in the future.

Acknowledgements

This work has received funding from the European Union's Connecting Europe Facility 2014-2020 - CEF Telecom, under Grant Agreement No. INEA/CEF/ICT/A2020/2278341. This communication reflects only the author's view. The Agency is not responsible for any use that may be made of the information it contains. This work was also funded by the Slovenian Research Agency within the Slovenian-Flemish bilateral basic research project "Linguistic landscape of hate speech on social media" (N06-0099 and FWO-G070619N, 2019–2023), the research project "Basic Research for the Development of Spoken Language Resources and Speech Technologies for the Slovenian Language" (J7-4642), and the research programme "Language resources and technologies for Slovene" (P6-0411).

References

Ronelle Alexander. 2013. Language and identity: The fate of Serbo-Croatian. In *Entangled Histories of the Balkans-Volume One*, pages 341–417. Brill.

Mihaela Gaman, Dirk Hovy, Radu Tudor Ionescu, Heidi Jauhiainen, Tommi Jauhiainen, Krister Lindén, Nikola Ljubešić, Niko Partanen, Christoph Purschke, Yves Scherrer, and Marcos Zampieri. 2020. A report on the VarDial evaluation campaign 2020. In *Proceedings of the 7th Workshop on NLP for Similar Languages, Varieties and Dialects*, pages 1–14, Barcelona, Spain (Online). International Committee on Computational Linguistics (ICCL).

Annika Jacobsen, Ricardo de Miranda Azevedo, Nick Juty, Dominique Batista, Simon Coles, Ronald Cornet, Mélanie Courtot, Mercè Crosas, Michel Dumontier, Chris T Evelo, et al. 2020. FAIR principles: interpretations and implementation considerations.

Nikola Ljubešić. 2021. *Text collection for training the BERTić transformer model BERTić-data*. Slovenian language resource repository CLARIN.SI.

Nikola Ljubešić, Darja Fišer, and Tomaž Erjavec. 2014. TweetCaT: a tool for building Twitter corpora of smaller languages. In *Proceedings of the Ninth International Conference on Language Resources and Evaluation (LREC'14)*, pages 2279–2283, Reykjavik, Iceland. European Language Resources Association (ELRA).

Nikola Ljubešić and Filip Klubička. 2014. {bs, hr, sr} wac-web corpora of Bosnian, Croatian and Serbian. In *Proceedings of the 9th web as corpus workshop (WaC-9)*, pages 29–35.

Nikola Ljubešić and Davor Lauc. 2021. BERTić - the transformer language model for Bosnian, Croatian, Montenegrin and Serbian. In *Proceedings of the 8th Workshop on Balto-Slavic Natural Language Processing*, pages 37–42, Kiyv, Ukraine. Association for Computational Linguistics.

Nikola Ljubešić, Maja Miličević Petrović, and Tanja Samardžić. 2018. Borders and boundaries in Bosnian, Croatian, Montenegrin and Serbian: Twitter data to the rescue. *Journal of Linguistic Geography*, 6(2):100–124.

Nikola Ljubešić and Peter Rupnik. 2022a. *The news dataset for discriminating between Bosnian, Croatian and Serbian SETimes.HBS 1.0*. Slovenian language resource repository CLARIN.SI.

Nikola Ljubešić and Peter Rupnik. 2022b. *The Twitter user dataset for discriminating between Bosnian, Croatian, Montenegrin and Serbian Twitter-HBS 1.0*. Slovenian language resource repository CLARIN.SI.

Shervin Malmasi, Marcos Zampieri, Nikola Ljubešić, Preslav Nakov, Ahmed Ali, and Jörg Tiedemann. 2016. Discriminating between similar languages and Arabic dialect identification: A report on the third DSL shared task. In *Proceedings of the Third Workshop on NLP for Similar Languages, Varieties and Dialects (VarDial3)*, pages 1–14, Osaka, Japan. The COLING 2016 Organizing Committee.

Fabian Pedregosa, Gaël Varoquaux, Alexandre Gramfort, Vincent Michel, Bertrand Thirion, Olivier Grisel, Mathieu Blondel, Peter Prettenhofer, Ron Weiss, Vincent Dubourg, et al. 2011. Scikit-learn: Machine learning in Python. *the Journal of machine Learning research*, 12:2825–2830.

Liling Tan, Marcos Zampieri, Nikola Ljubešic, and Jörg Tiedemann. 2014. Merging comparable data sources for the discrimination of similar languages: The DSL corpus collection. In *Proceedings of the 7th Workshop on Building and Using Comparable Corpora (BUCC)*, pages 11–15.

Marcos Zampieri, Shervin Malmasi, Nikola Ljubešić, Preslav Nakov, Ahmed Ali, Jörg Tiedemann, Yves Scherrer, and Noëmi Aepli. 2017. Findings of the VarDial evaluation campaign 2017. In *Proceedings of the Fourth Workshop on NLP for Similar Languages, Varieties and Dialects (VarDial)*, pages 1–15, Valencia, Spain. Association for Computational Linguistics.

Marcos Zampieri, Liling Tan, Nikola Ljubešić, and Jörg Tiedemann. 2014. A report on the DSL shared task 2014. In *Proceedings of the first workshop on applying NLP tools to similar languages, varieties and dialects*, pages 58–67.

Marcos Zampieri, Liling Tan, Nikola Ljubešić, Jörg Tiedemann, and Preslav Nakov. 2015. Overview of the DSL shared task 2015. In *Proceedings of the Joint Workshop on Language Technology for Closely Related Languages, Varieties and Dialects*, pages 1–9, Hissar, Bulgaria. Association for Computational Linguistics.

Comparing and Predicting Eye-tracking Data in Mandarin and Cantonese

Junlin Li
The Hong Kong Polytechnic University
junlin.li@connect.polyu.hk

Bo Peng, Yu-Yin Hsu, Emmanuele Chersoni
The Hong Kong Polytechnic University
{bopeng, yyhsu, echers}@polyu.edu.hk

Abstract

Eye-tracking data in Chinese languages present unique challenges due to the non-alphabetic and unspaced nature of the Chinese writing systems. This paper introduces the first deeply-annotated joint Mandarin-Cantonese eye-tracking dataset, from which we achieve a unified eye-tracking prediction system for both language varieties. In addition to the commonly studied first fixation duration and the total fixation duration, this dataset also includes the second fixation duration, expressing fixation patterns that are more relevant to higher-level, structural processing.

A basic comparison of the features and measurements in our dataset revealed variation between Mandarin and Cantonese on fixation patterns related to word class and word position. The test of feature usefulness suggested that traditional features are less powerful in predicting the second-pass fixation, to which the linear distance to root makes a leading contribution in Mandarin. In contrast, Cantonese eye-movement behavior relies more on word position and part of speech.

1 Introduction

Eye-tracking has quickly become one of the most popular methodologies in psycholinguistic studies, as it allows researchers to measure people's real-time processing efforts during a reading task (Attardo and Pickering, 2023). Consequently, more computational models have been proposed to predict eye-fixation patterns in English and many other languages (Hollenstein et al., 2021a,b, 2022; Salicchi et al., 2022).

Chinese languages, being non-alphabetic, are considered unique in eye-tracking research, mainly due to the unspaced nature of the writing conventions, the visual complexity of the characters, and the abundance of homophonic and homographic characters (Hsu and Huang, 2000; Bai et al., 2008). The computational modeling of Chinese eye-movement patterns is still relatively limited, although several traditional psycholinguistic models have been proposed to measure Chinese reading times (Rayner et al., 2007; Li and Pollatsek, 2020; Thierfelder et al., 2020). Such models have focused on factors such as word frequency, word length, and word predictability but have not considered syntactic and semantic processes that may have an equally decisive influence on eye-movement behaviors.

To fill such research gaps, this paper first introduces a deeply-annotated eye-tracking dataset that covers Mandarin texts in simplified characters and Cantonese texts in traditional characters, thus representing two demographically important language varieties. Based on this joint dataset, we implemented a series of statistical tests to investigate the inter-linguistic variance from the perspective of fixation durations. Furthermore, we propose a feature-rich prediction model of basic eye-tracking measurements in Chinese, in addition to an ablation study of the usefulness of features. Our predictors include both traditional and new features, such as syntactic features, local lexical semantic features, and contextual semantic representations. We believe that comparing these features will further broaden our understanding of the differences between Mandarin and Cantonese. The contributions of the present study are as follows:

- we presente the first parallel Mandarin-Cantonese eye-tracking dataset. The dataset is annotated with three eye-tracking features, including the second fixation duration, which reflects higher-level, structural processing of a sentence;
- we explore the similarities and differences between Mandarin and Cantonese, two demographically important varieties within the family of the Sinitic languages, from the perspective of cognitive processing as reflected in eye-tracking measurements.

Tenth Workshop on NLP for Similar Languages, Varieties and Dialects (VarDial 2023), pages 121–132
May 5, 2023 ©2023 Association for Computational Linguistics

- we introduce computational models to approximate and predict the fixation patterns of the two varieties. Specifically, we integrate morphosyntactic features and contextualized semantic representations with traditional lexical features into the modeling of fixation measurements.

2 Related Work

As eye-tracking data are closely linked to real-time cognitive processes, they can reveal the automatic operations in our brains that are related to different linguistic modules, such as lexical access (Clifton Jr et al., 2007), syntactic processing (Van Schijndel and Schuler, 2015), semantic processing (Hwang et al., 2011; De Groot et al., 2016), and pragmatic competence (Gironzetti, 2020). Regarding the modeling of fixation patterns, previous research has highlighted the close relationship between eye-tracking measurements and certain word properties, including word position (Just and Carpenter, 1980), word frequency (Yan et al., 2006; Liversedge et al., 2014), word predictability (Rayner et al., 2005), and word length (Li et al., 2011; Zang et al., 2018). Fixation on a particular word is also sensitive to the cognitive load from the previous word (known as a spill-over effect) (Rayner et al., 1989; Pollatsek et al., 2008).[1]

In addition to these traditional lexical features, morpho-syntactic features, such as part-of-speech categories (POS) and syntactic dependency, also impact fixation patterns. POS have been demonstrated to influence the number of fixations and the fixation duration (Blanchard, 1985). Concerning syntactic dependency, previous studies indicated that cognitive loads from syntactic structure lead to increased refixation probability and duration (Conklin and Pellicer-Sánchez, 2016; Frenck-Mestre, 2005), which is mainly related to the second fixation duration (**SFD**) in this paper and partially reflected on the total fixation duration (**TFD**). Previous research also reported that the sensitivity of first-pass processing to the syntactic agreement increases the first fixation duration (Deutsch, 1998; Deutsch and Bentin, 2001), although there is counter-evidence that syntactic parsing only increases the total fixation duration by affecting the second fixation (Pearlmutter et al., 1999). Despite being crucial for modeling fixation patterns, it should be noted that most of the research that has targeted Chinese languages has not considered POS and syntactic dependency.

Regarding the distinctiveness of the Chinese writing system, most studies have supported the view that words and characters are equally salient units in the cognitive processing of texts written in Chinese characters, as both word properties and character properties influence reading-time measurements and eye-movement behaviors (Bai et al., 2008; Li et al., 2015). Following this assertion, the word-level features widely applied in the reading-time modeling of alphabetic languages are equally applied in Chinese-specific research. Features related to higher-level processing, such as syntactic properties, are also considered in research on Chinese language processing (Lu et al., 2022; Chen and Tsai, 2015; Zang et al., 2020). However, previous studies using syntactic properties have mainly focused on syntactic complexity and the grammatical function of a word without linking the syntactic dependency of the entire sentence to eye-movement modeling.

3 Dataset

This section introduces our eye-tracking dataset's construction procedures and annotation structure.[2] We then present the results of inter-variety comparisons regarding basic eye-tracking measurements in the next section.

3.1 Data Collection and Normalization

This study used two comparable eye-tracking corpora collected by ourselves, one in Mandarin and one in Cantonese, which were recorded using a normal reading paradigm. Each corpus included 30 participants who were native speakers of the target language; the mean age of the Mandarin group was 25.8 years old (22 females) and the Cantonese group was 21.7 years old (20 females). During the recording sessions, the participants read a translated version of *The Little Prince* by Antoine de Saint-Exupéry, in Mandarin, and in Cantonese, respectively. The Mandarin texts were presented in simplified Chinese characters and the Cantonese

[1] According to some studies, another factor affecting fixations is the semantic relatedness of a word with its context, which can be measured via Distributional Semantic Models (Pynte et al., 2008; Mitchell et al., 2010; Salicchi et al., 2023). However, the evidence for the role of semantic relatedness in predicting reading times and eye fixations is controversial (Frank, 2017).

[2] Code and datasets will be made available via Github at the following URL: `https://github.com/CN-Eyetk/MCFIX`.

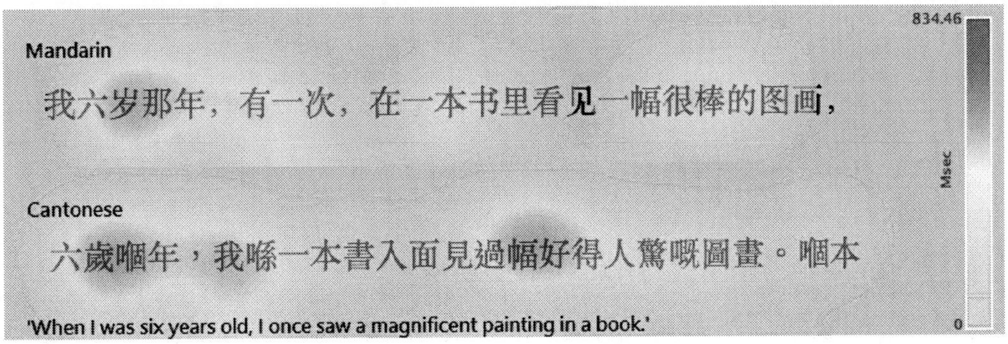

Figure 1: An example heatmaps of fixation duration by Mandarin and Cantonese readers, weighted by the duration of the individual fixations.

texts in traditional Chinese characters. Each corpus contained recordings of two reading tasks using the same texts, i.e., the natural reading (**NR**, only with a reading comprehension task) and the task-specific reading (**TSR**, with the purpose of finding specific information in a given text). Each corpus contained three eye-movement measurements and their standard deviations: first fixation duration (**FFD**), second fixation duration (**SFD**), and total fixation duration (**TFD**). Figure 1 shows the heatmaps of fixation duration recorded from one Mandarin and one Cantonese reader in our data.

We then normalized the raw data as follows: If a word, w, occurs $N_{total} = n + n_{null}$ times, where n is the number of instances with fixation values, and n_{null} is the number of instances with null values, then the normalized value equals the sum of the fixation values of n occurrences divided N_{total} times. Table 2 shows the descriptive statistics for these fixation measurements of the two language varieties in each task. Our datasets show that monosyllabic words were more dominant in Cantonese than in Mandarin, especially for content words such as verbs and nouns, as shown in Figure 2; this tendency is in line with the monosyllabic salience observed in Cantonese (Li et al., 2016).

SENT	WORD	POS	LDR	LDH	DEPTH	Freq	N_{SYL}
1	看见(see)	VERB	0	0	0	260.0	2
1	一(one)	NUM	1	5	2	8489.0	1
1	幅(clf)	DET	2	4	2	103.0	1
1	很(very)	ADV	3	1	3	1755.0	1
1	棒(good)	ADJ	4	2	2	27.0	1
1	的(de)	PART	5	1	3	77946.0	1
1	图画(figure),	NOUN	6	6	1	25.0	2

Table 1: Annotation Example

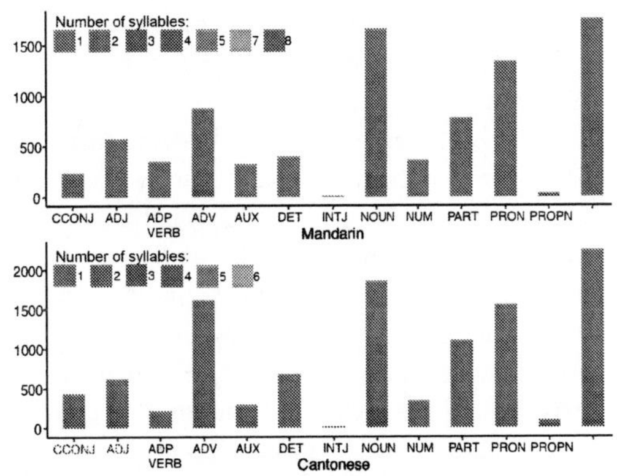

Figure 2: Two-way comparison of syllable number and part-of-speech in Mandarin and Cantonese

3.2 Annotation Structure

In addition to eye-movement measurements, we obtained several linguistic features of our dataset in the annotation: (1) **Word Segmentation**, which inherited the word segmentation marked by native speakers with a Ph.D. in linguistics during the collection of eye-tracking data; (2) **Part-of-speech**, which is derived from `jiagu` toolkit (`https://github.com/ownthink/Jiagu`) for the Mandarin text, and from `pycantonese` (Lee et al., 2022) for the Cantonese text; the results of which were manually checked and aligned by a Mandarin speaker and a Mandarin-Cantonese bilingual speaker; (3) Syntactic distances, including dependency depth (**DEPTH**), linear distance to Head (**LDH**), and linear distance to root (**LDR**); all of these were based on a syntactic analysis derived by the Stanford Dependency Parser (Chang et al., 2009); and (4) Traditional features in eye-tracking modeling, including **word frequency** (obtained from the `cifu` dictionary (Lai and Winterstein, 2020) and the `cncorpus` word-frequency list), and the **syllable number**.

Table 1 provides an illustration of the annotation of linguistic features.

4 Cross-variety Comparison

4.1 One-way Comparison

Concerning the cross-variety variance between the data in the two corpora, we fit a linear model against FFD, SFD, and TFD (all in a log scale). The fixed effects included *LanguageTypes* (Cantonese vs. Mandarin, the former as the treatment), and *WordFrequency*, *POS* and *SyllableCount* ($N_{Syllable}$). The estimation was implemented by `lm` function in `RStudio` (Allaire, 2012).

The result shown in Table 3 (With $N_{syllable}$) highlights the effect of writing system simplification. The tendency indicates that the Mandarin readers consistently had significantly shorter fixation durations for all the FDs of the TSR task and the FFD of the NR task. This finding was consistent with the expectation that lower visual complexity may reduce cognitive effort; thus, Mandarin readers who encountered simplified Chinese texts showed significantly shorter first-past fixation times than Cantonese readers who processed traditional Chinese texts. This tendency extended to all the fixation measures in task-specific reading.

Nonetheless, the tendency caused by the writing system's simplification could be weakened by the fact that Cantonese has more monosyllabic words, thus simpler words, as shown in Figure 2. This was demonstrated by the finding that (1) the exclusion of syllable count from random effect neutralized the significance (See without $N_{syllable}$ in Table 3), and (2) the descriptive statistics of FD levels did not show a significant difference between the two variables (See Table 2).

4.2 FD Variance by POS and Word Position

On par with the general effects of language variety on the word-level fixation duration, this research also implemented a Tukey post hoc test to investigate the FD differences of each POS between the two language varieties. Figure 5 (in the appendix) shows that pronoun fixation and noun fixation (excluding proper names) had significant cross-variety differences, as Mandarin readers tended to fixate more on nouns in both reading tasks, while Cantonese readers were inclined to fixate more on pronouns in TSR. This consistent tendency concerning noun fixation presumably arises from the different distribution of syllabic length between Mandarin and Cantonese, as nouns in Mandarin are more likely to be disyllabic than monosyllabic (see Figure 2). The tendency for pronoun fixation, we assume, arises from the fact that Cantonese pronouns are more ambiguous than those in Mandarin. For example, the singular third-person pronouns of masculine gender "ta1"(他), feminine gender "ta1"(她), and neutral gender "ta1"(它) in Mandarin all correspond to the only singular third-person pronoun "keoi5"(佢) in Cantonese, which may cause Cantonese readers to spend more time on processing pronominal reference. In addition, Cantonese demonstrative pronouns have high-frequency homographs (or pseudo-homographs). The demonstrative pronoun "ni1/nei1" (呢"this") is homographic with the sentence-final particle "ne1" (呢). The demonstrative pronoun "go2" is pseudo-homographic with the classifier "go3" (個). This property presumably induces more efforts for Cantonese readers in the lexical access for demonstrative pronouns.

Apart from POS, we also investigated the similarities and differences between the two language varieties in terms of the effect of word position on fixation durations. For this, we fit the correlation between the word position in the sentence (normalized by sentence length) and the fixation duration with the third-degree polynomial formula (to capture non-linearity). Non-overlapping contours of a confidence interval indicate statistically significant differences. As shown in Figure 3, the final part of each sentence showed significant differences between Mandarin and Cantonese. Cantonese consistently tended to involve a descent of fixation durations in the final quarter of a sentence, while Mandarin was almost the opposite in such a local span, except for TSR's first fixation duration.

5 Methodology

This section introduces the features and the regressors used in the prediction of eye-tracking measurements, derived from the results of the cross-variety comparison drawn from both psycholinguistic and computational studies.

5.1 Prediction Targets

The prediction targets include the subject-wise normalized level (below referred to as *mean level*) of **FFD**, **SFD**, and **TFD** and the *standard deviations*

Mode	Variety	Word Count	FFD_{avg}	FFD_{std}	SFD_{avg}	SFD_{std}	TFD_{avg}	TFD_{std}
NR	Cantonese	5050	108.53	55.56	37.32	41.97	171.37	144.47
	Mandarin	3939	108.98	55.42	40.27	44.91	180.21	160.61
TSR	Cantonese	5047	101.22	52.75	30.29	34.10	145.89	102.89
	Mandarin	3941	101.26	54.45	30.82	34.27	147.30	106.41

Table 2: Descriptive statistics of fixation durations

Mode	Y	With $N_{syllable}$			Without $N_{syllable}$		
		estimates	Pval	Sig	estimates	Pval	Sig
TSR	FFD	+0.031	0.004	**	0.007	0.544	
	SFD	+0.060	0.056		-0.015	0.663	
	TFD	+0.046	0.000	**	0.009	0.515	
NR	FFD	+0.009	0.003	**	-0.01	0.400	
	SFD	+0.002	0.952		-0.064	0.061	
	TFD	+0.017	0.222		-0.016	0.282	

Table 3: Estimates of the effect of *Cantonese* on FDs, with $N_{syllable}$ not placed in random effect (on the left) and placed (on the right).

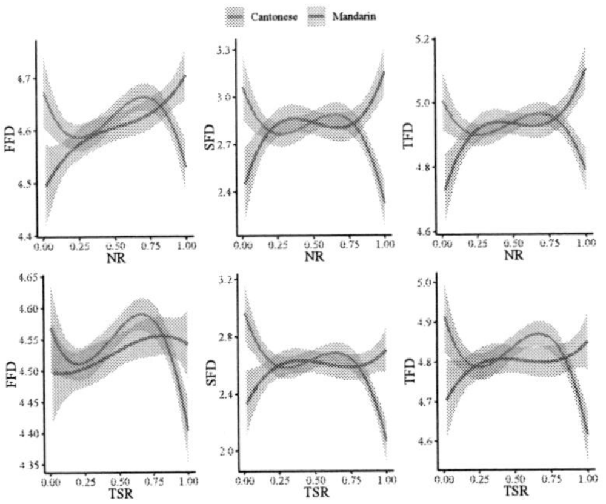

Figure 3: Polynomial contours and their 95% confidence interval of the correlation between normalized word position and FDs (in log scale) in Mandarin and Cantonese.

of **FFD**, **SFD**, and **TFD**, for both Mandarin and Cantonese. We believe that it is important to include the standard deviations in our gold standard: eye-tracking metrics prediction is an example of a task in which predicting only the mean value from a set of measurements typically excludes a large amount of variation existing in the data. For this reason, in the spirit of paving the way for NLP systems that can better deal with human label variation (Plank, 2022), we added this additional challenge to our dataset.

5.2 Features

We used two sets of features in our prediction experiment: Linguistic features and GPT word embeddings.

5.2.1 Linguistic Features

Given the annotation structure in our dataset, we selected nine linguistic features as shown below.

Traditional features based on previous studies included **Frequency** (of the current word and its previous word), **Syllable Number** (of the current word and its previous word), **Word Position**, and **POS**. Specifically, Frequency was extracted from `cifu` dictionary (Lai and Winterstein, 2020) and `cncorpus` word-frequency list[3] and was projected to a log scale; the previous word frequency and syllable number are specified as "-1" for sentence-initial words; word position is the order of a word in a sentence divided by the sentence length (by word).

In addition, we proposed five new features, of which four had not been used in modeling fixation patterns of Chinese languages in natural language processing, and one feature that has recently been shown to be useful in predicting eyemovement patterns: they are **DEPTH**, **LDH** and **LDR**, which are summarized in section 3, **Word Predictability** measured by `GPT2 Surprisal` (Salicchi et al., 2022), and **Orthographic Neighborhood**. The orthographic neighborhood refers to how likely a character cooccurs with other characters in a compound-word, inferring a given character's ambiguity level. We calculated this based on the `cifu` dictionary and `xinhua` wordlist for Cantonese and Mandarin, respectively. To calculate the Orthographic Neighborhood of each word, we divide the word into characters and sum up the number of words containing each single character, treating the summation as the value of the Orthographic Neighborhood. The Surprisal of Mandarin and Cantonese was computed with a simplified Chinese GPT2

[3] `https://github.com/bedlate/cn-corpus`

trained on `CLUE Corpus Small`[4] (hereafter referred to as `clue`), while the Surprisal of Cantonese was additionally calculated with a traditional-Chinese GPT2 finetuned on `cantonese-wikipedia` for 10 epochs [5], which is referred to as `jed351` below. For each round of Cantonese FD modeling, we fed one of the two Surprisals and finally reported the better performance. On account of the character-base tokenization of both `clue` model and `jed351` model, we sum up the Surprisal score of each character c_k^i (the i-th character of the k-th word w_k in a sentence) to represent the exact score of the whole word. More in detail:

suppose $w_k = [c_k^1, c_k^2, ..., c_k^m]$), which means that the k-th word in the current sentence has m characters. Then the surprisal of the whole k-th word is represented as:

$$Surprisal(w_k) = \sum_{i=0}^{m} Surprisal(c_k^i) \quad (1)$$

suppose c_n is the n-th character in the whole sentence, then the surprisal of each character is:

$$Surprisal(c_n) = -\log(P(c_n|c_0, c_1, ..., c_{n-1})) \quad (2)$$

5.2.2 GPT Contextual Word Embeddings

To explore the effectiveness of contextualized word representation in improving eye-tracking prediction, we extracted the last hidden state of each word input from the GPT2 architecture to be concatenated with the linguistic features mentioned above. We used the `clue` model to extract GPT word embedding for both Mandarin and Cantonese. Since `clue` is basically trained on the Mandarin corpus, we equally used the `jed351` model to extract embedding for Cantonese. We separately try one of the two types of Cantonese GPT embedding for each regressor.

All compositions of features tried in this research are summarized below. For each feature composition, we tried both interactions (using the `PolynomialFeatures` module in `scikit-learn`) and non-interaction between linguistic features and reported the best results.

[4] https://huggingface.co/uer/gpt2-chinese-cluecorpussmall.

[5] https://huggingface.co/jed351/gpt2_tiny_zh-hk-wiki

	Gpt Embedding	Other Features
Mandarin	noGpt	Linguistic Features (with clue Surprisal)
	clue	Linguistic Features (with clue Surprisal)
Cantonese	noGpt	Linguistic Features (with clue Surprisal)
		Linguistic Features (with jed351 Surprisal)
	clue	Linguistic Features (with clue Surprisal)
	jed351	Linguistic Features (with jed351 Surprisal)

Table 4: All possible composition of features for Mandarin and Cantonese.

5.3 Regressors

To propose an optimal prediction system, we utilized several regression models to approximate the eye-movement measurements concerned, using the implementations in the `scikit-learn` Python package and `catboost` package (Dorogush et al., 2018) (for GradientBoostDecisionTree only, due to its slow implementation without GPU acceleration). Below in Table 5 we listed the main hyper-parameters.

Regressors	Hyper-Parameters
BRR (BayesianRidge)	alpha=1.0, normalized=True
ELAST (ElastRegressor)	alpha=1.0 , l1_ratio = 0.5 , selection="cyclic"
GBDT (CatBoostRegressor)	num_leaves = 31 , learning_rate =0.03
LGB (LGBMRegressor)	objective='regression' , num_leaves = 31 , learning_rate =0.05
LR (LinearRegression)	fit_intercept=True
MLP (MLPRegressor)	hidden_layer_size=5, activation = identity, solver = adam
PLSR (PLSRegression)	n_components = 5
RF (RandomForestRegressor)	min_samples_split=2, min_samples_leaf =1
RR (Ridge)	alpha=1.0, normalize =True

Table 5: Regressor Parameter Settings

5.4 Metrics

To evaluate and compare the performance of the participating systems, we used the mean absolute error (MAE) in the 5-fold cross-evaluation as the main metric in the **Results and Discussion** section, as it increments linearly with the increases in the error. To complement, the mean squared error (MSE), the R-Square ($R2$), the Pearson correlation ($Pears.$), and the Spearman correlation ($Spear.$) for the 5-fold cross-evaluation are jointly reported for the best prediction system for each of

Y	Lang	Gptvec	brr	elast	gbdt	lgb	lr	mlp	plsr	rf	rr
FFD	Cantonese	-	38.86	38.87	36.19	38.82	38.48	38.99	38.78	**35.64**	38.47
		clue	35.19	36.81	**33.14**	37.81	35.62	35.72	36.27	33.76	35.60
		jed351	35.78	36.46	**33.20**	37.95	35.78	36.22	36.08	33.86	35.78
	Mandarin	-	36.49	36.56	**34.37**	37.20	36.48	36.79	36.69	34.49	36.36
		clue	34.34	35.46	**32.53**	36.64	35.33	35.13	35.02	33.80	35.28
SFD	Cantonese	-	24.54	24.53	**23.48**	24.81	24.49	24.63	24.49	24.98	24.49
		clue	23.39	24.05	**22.58**	24.53	24.06	23.78	23.92	23.73	24.05
		jed351	23.70	23.89	**22.59**	24.56	23.93	23.93	23.86	24.19	23.93
	Mandarin	-	24.38	24.58	**23.81**	25.22	24.38	24.81	24.38	25.38	24.38
		clue	23.84	24.30	**23.39**	24.96	25.08	24.35	24.08	24.64	25.06
TFD	Cantonese	-	74.17	74.03	**70.77**	74.24	74.13	74.55	74.11	74.76	74.11
		clue	68.96	70.31	**66.32**	72.87	71.34	71.34	71.03	68.30	71.29
		jed351	70.27	70.45	**66.41**	72.89	70.91	71.98	70.65	70.22	70.90
	Mandarin	-	73.50	74.07	**71.62**	75.63	73.57	74.46	73.55	77.35	73.56
		clue	70.71	71.60	**69.11**	74.82	74.90	73.61	72.05	73.22	74.84

Table 6: Performance (By MAE, lower is better) of different regressors (with and without GPT2 embeddings) on subject-normalized FFD, SFD, and TFD levels

the 6 FD measurements.

6 Results and Discussion

6.1 Regressor Performance

Table 6 presents the optimal MAE of each regressor in the prediction of the *mean levels* of **FFD**, **SFD**, and **TFD**. Table 7 shows all the metrics for the best system with and without GPT embedding. For the regressor selection, the **GBDT** regressor was dominantly the optimal choice for predicting eye-tracking data for the two Sinitic language varieties. In general, our prediction system is most helpful in approximating a human's first-pass eye-movement behavior, as the best *R2* scores were 44% and 41% for the Mandarin and Cantonese first fixation predictions, respectively (see Table 7). The correlation scores listed in Table 7 ranged between 0.57 and 0.66 for the **FD** mean value prediction and between 0.26 and 0.46 for the **FD** standard deviation prediction, demonstrating the predictability of the **FD** measurements in our dataset and the effectiveness of the features proposed in this research.

The utility of GPT embeddings was evaluated in this study, with Table 7 indicating that they are particularly effective in predicting FFD. Specifically, the performance (by $R2$) on mean level prediction for FFD in Mandarin and Cantonese was reinforced by 6% and 10%, respectively. However, GPT embeddings were found to be less helpful in predicting the mean level of SFD and TFD for both varieties. These results suggest that contextual semantics play a relatively marginal role in predicting non-initial fixation behavior for Mandarin and Cantonese.

The Pears correlation scores listed in Table 7 show a moderate correlation (0.4 - 0.6 for psychology) for most measurements between the ground truth and prediction, except for the standard deviation of Mandarin FFD (Akoglu, 2018).

6.2 Feature Usefulness

To investigate the usefulness of the linguistic features, we performed a series of ablation analyses against each feature in relation to the 6 measurements under discussion and found the change in *MAE* to be a metric suitable for measuring the usefulness. Intending to identify the pure usefulness of each feature, we restricted our ablation analyses to non-interaction **GBDT** regressors to avoid potential confusion due to cross-module interactions and regressor differences. In this paper, we mainly discuss the contribution of each feature to the *MAE* reduction of the mean level prediction.

Figure 4 presents each feature's usefulness (corresponding to positive values and highlighted in color) to the prediction of the mean level of each measurement. To facilitate the discussion, we divided the features into (1) Traditional Features utilized in psycholinguistic research, including **Frequency** (Word Frequency), **N**$_{syl}$ (Syllable Count), **POS** (Part-of-speech), **Word Position**, **Prev Freq** (Previous Word Frequency), and **Prev**N_{syl} (Previous Syllable Number) (2) Newly-introduced features in this research, including **DEPTH**, **LDR** and **LDH**, **Surprisal**, and the **Neighbor** (Orthographical Neighborhood).

6.2.1 Traditional Features

The traditional features widely used in psycholinguistic research indicated the usefulness of all types

Y	Variety	+GPT Embedding						-GPT Embedding				
		Mapper	Gptvec	MAE	R2	Pears	Spear	Mapper	MAE	R2	Pears	Spear
FFD	Cantonese	gbdt-	clue	33.14	0.41	0.64	0.62	rf-	35.64	0.31	0.57	0.53
	Mandarin	gbdt+	clue	32.53	0.44	0.66	0.65	gbdt+	34.37	0.38	0.62	0.60
FFD_{std}	Cantonese	gbdt+	jed351	21.82	0.13	0.37	0.36	gbdt+	22.46	0.08	0.28	0.27
	Mandarin	lgb-	clue	22.03	0.06	0.26	0.28	lgb+	22.22	0.04	0.22	0.23
SFD	Cantonese	gbdt+	clue	22.58	0.32	0.57	0.52	gbdt+	23.48	0.28	0.53	0.45
	Mandarin	gbdt+	clue	23.39	0.33	0.58	0.56	gbdt-	23.81	0.31	0.56	0.54
SFD_{std}	Cantonese	gbdt+	clue	33.09	0.20	0.46	0.46	gbdt-	34.26	0.16	0.40	0.40
	Mandarin	gbdt+	clue	33.21	0.18	0.44	0.48	gbdt-	33.23	0.20	0.45	0.47
TFD	Cantonese	gbdt-	clue	66.32	0.36	0.60	0.60	gbdt-	70.77	0.31	0.56	0.51
	Mandarin	gbdt-	clue	69.11	0.37	0.62	0.66	gbdt-	71.62	0.36	0.60	0.61
TFD_{std}	Cantonese	gbdt+	clue	56.99	0.17	0.43	0.47	gbdt-	58.47	0.16	0.41	0.39
	Mandarin	brr-	clue	62.33	0.20	0.45	0.47	gbdt-	62.50	0.20	0.45	0.47

Table 7: The best model for each language variety on each fixation measurement. The "+" on the mapper denotes the introduction of interaction between linguistic features, while the "-" denotes the contrary.

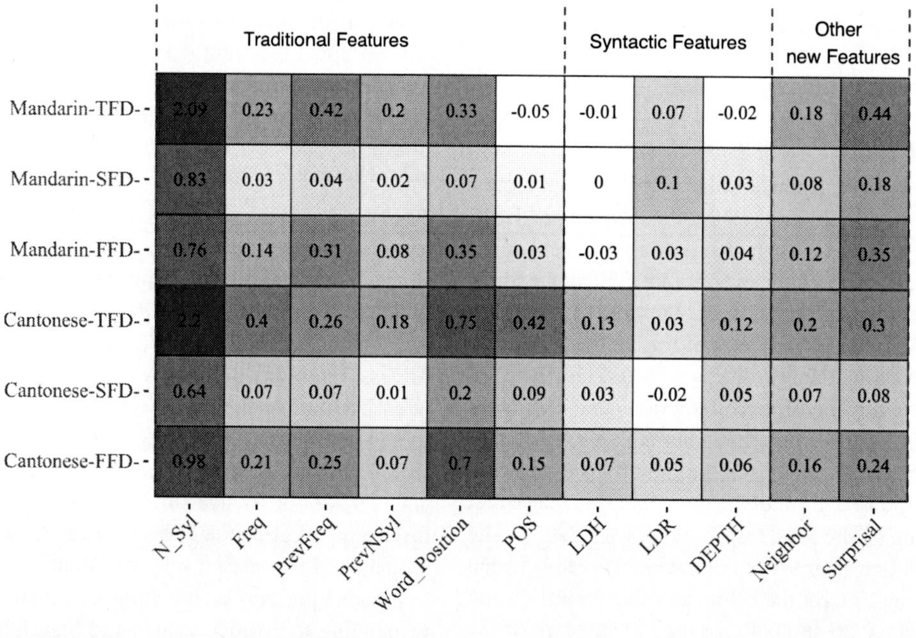

Figure 4: The usefulness of each feature based on ablation analyses of non-interaction models with no GPT embeddings.

of FDs in the two language varieties. In addition, most traditional features showed conspicuously less effectiveness in **SFD** prediction than in **FFD** and **TFD**prediction, except for the current syllabic length (**N**$_{syl}$) for Mandarin, which showed more effectiveness in **SFD** than in **FFD**.

For the cross-variety comparison under discussion, it is worth mentioning that **Word Position** and **POS** are consistently more useful to Cantonese FD predictions. The stronger usefulness of word position in Cantonese is in line with the well-acknowledged typological statement that Cantonese exhibits a more robust canonical SVO order than Mandarin, whose word order shows the property of both SOV and SVO languages (Dryer, 1992, 2003; Liu, 2000).

6.2.2 Newly-introduced Features

Comparing with traditional features (except **N**$_{syl}$), syntactic properties (**Depth**, **LDH**, **LDR**) are a bundle of features whose utility does not bleach as much in second fixation duration, which is consistent with suggestions from psycholinguistic research that second-pass fixation is less dependent on lexical access than syntactic processing(Conklin and Pellicer-Sánchez, 2016)). Specifically, **LDR** stands out as the third most contributive feature in modeling Mandarin's second fixation duration, following **Surprisal** and $\mathbf{N}_{syl}$.

Neighbor and **Surprisal** also display overall effectiveness on all FDs. Specifically, **Surprisal** is the second most useful feature in the prediction of Mandarin **FFD** and **TFD**, following $\mathbf{N}_{syl}$. The finding that the **Surprisal** tends to be more beneficial to Mandarin can be attributed to the specific properties of the GPT models that we applied in this research, both of which take Mandarin text as their dominant training data (to the best of our knowledge, there are no publicly available GPT-like autoregressive Transformer models trained purely on Cantonese texts).

7 Conclusions

In this paper, we introduced an extensively annotated dataset of Mandarin and Cantonese eye-tracking data and shed light on their differences by features, such as word formation, word class, and word order. We also proposed a prediction system of fixation behaviors accompanied by new features from different modules, such as dependency features, the orthographic neighborhood, and GPT word embeddings, which were introduced with the goal of the computational prediction of Chinese eye-tracking data.

Based on a comparison of the regressor performance under different feature compositions, we investigated the usefulness of GPT vectors and linguistic features in reducing prediction errors. The results highlighted the effectiveness of our newly introduced features in modeling fixation patterns in representative Chinese language varieties and the importance of word order, part-of-speech, and syntax in addressing how Mandarin and Cantonese differ in language comprehension.

The findings in our study identify a few possible topics for future studies on language processing and regional syntactic variation of Chinese languages, such as how the syllabic structure, the visual complexity of different writing systems, pronominal resolution, syntactic relations, word order interact with gazing patterns and reading times of Chinese language speakers, especially for native speakers of different varieties. In addition to the varieties we studied here, we also plan to enlarge the dataset by including Mandarin processed through traditional Chinese characters, which is the standard system used in Taiwan. Finally, for future psychological and computational modeling studies, possible refinements of the representations in our experiment could be features targeting orthographic complexity and lexical ambiguity.

Limitations

The current study still has some limitations. For feature introduction, the GPT-based features are probably biased toward Mandarin text due to the position of Cantonese as a low-resource language. For the design of the prediction system, our approach is blind to the sequential properties of word-level fixation measurements. For future exploration, it would be promising to explore a sequential modeling approach.

Acknowledgments

We would like to thank the reviewers for their insightful feedback. This research was made possible by the start-up research funds (1-BE3F, and 1-BD8S) at the Hong Kong Polytechnic University. We also thank Deran Kong, Wenxi Fei, and Ka Keung Leon Lee for assisting with corpus-data collection.

References

Haldun Akoglu. 2018. User's Guide to Correlation Coefficients. *Turkish Journal of Emergency Medicine*, 18(3):91–93.

Joseph J Allaire. 2012. RStudio: Integrated Development Environment for R. *Boston, MA*, 770(394):165–171.

Salvatore Attardo and Lucy Pickering. 2023. *Eye Tracking in Linguistics*. Bloomsbury Publishing.

Xuejun Bai, Guoli Yan, Simon P Liversedge, Chuanli Zang, and Keith Rayner. 2008. Reading Spaced and Unspaced Chinese Text: Evidence from Eye Movements. *Journal of Experimental Psychology: Human Perception and Performance*, 34(5):1277.

Harry E Blanchard. 1985. A Comparison of some Processing Time Measures Based on Eye Movements. *Acta Psychologica*, 58(1):1–15.

Pi-Chuan Chang, Huihsin Tseng, Dan Jurafsky, and Christopher D Manning. 2009. Discriminative Reordering with Chinese Grammatical Relations Features. In *Proceedings of the NAACL-HLT Workshop on Syntax and Structure in Statistical Translation (SSST-3)*.

Po-Heng Chen and Jie-Li Tsai. 2015. The Influence of Syntactic Category and Semantic Constraints on Lexical Ambiguity Resolution: An Eye Movement Study of Processing Chinese Homographs. *Language and Linguistics*, 16(4):555–586.

Charles Clifton Jr, Adrian Staub, and Keith Rayner. 2007. Eye Movements in Reading Words and Sentences. *Eye Movements*, pages 341–371.

Kathy Conklin and Ana Pellicer-Sánchez. 2016. Using Eye-tracking in Applied Linguistics and Second Language Research. *Second Language Research*, 32(3):453–467.

Floor De Groot, Falk Huettig, and Christian NL Olivers. 2016. When Meaning Matters: The Temporal Dynamics of Semantic Influences on Visual Attention. *Journal of Experimental Psychology: Human Perception and Performance*, 42(2):180.

Avital Deutsch. 1998. Subject-predicate Agreement in Hebrew: Interrelations with Semantic Processes. *Language and Cognitive Processes*, 13(5):575–597.

Avital Deutsch and Shlomo Bentin. 2001. Syntactic and Semantic Factors in Processing Gender Agreement in Hebrew: Evidence from ERPs and Eye Movements. *Journal of Memory and Language*, 45(2):200–224.

Anna Veronika Dorogush, Vasily Ershov, and Andrey Gulin. 2018. CatBoost: Gradient Boosting with Categorical Features Support. *arXiv preprint arXiv:1810.11363*.

Matthew S Dryer. 1992. The Greenbergian Word Order Correlations. *Language*, 68(1):81–138.

Matthew S Dryer. 2003. Word Order in Sino-Tibetan Languages from a Typological and Geographical Perspective. *The Sino-Tibetan Languages*, pages 43–55.

Stefan L Frank. 2017. Word Embedding Distance Does not Predict Word Reading Time. In *Proceedings of CogSci*.

Cheryl Frenck-Mestre. 2005. Eye-movement Recording as a Tool for Studying Syntactic Processing in a Second Language: A Review of Methodologies and Experimental Findings. *Second Language Research*, 21(2):175–198.

Elisa Gironzetti. 2020. Eye-tracking Applications for Spanish Pragmatics Research. In *The Routledge Handbook of Spanish Pragmatics*, pages 517–531. Routledge.

Nora Hollenstein, Emmanuele Chersoni, Cassandra L Jacobs, Yohei Oseki, Laurent Prévot, and Enrico Santus. 2021a. CMCL 2021 Shared Task on Eye-tracking Prediction. In *Proceedings of the NAACL Workshop on Cognitive Modeling and Computational Linguistics*.

Nora Hollenstein, Emmanuele Chersoni, Cassandra L Jacobs, Yohei Oseki, Laurent Prévot, and Enrico Santus. 2022. CMCL 2022 Shared Task on Multilingual and Crosslingual Prediction of Human Reading Behavior. In *Proceedings of the ACL Workshop on Cognitive Modeling and Computational Linguistics*.

Nora Hollenstein, Federico Pirovano, Ce Zhang, Lena Jäger, and Lisa Beinborn. 2021b. Multilingual Language Models Predict Human Reading Behavior. In *Proceedings of NAACL*.

Sheng-Hsiung Hsu and Kuo-Chen Huang. 2000. Effects of Word Spacing on Reading Chinese Text from a Video Display Terminal. *Perceptual and Motor Skills*, 90(1):81–92.

Alex D Hwang, Hsueh-Cheng Wang, and Marc Pomplun. 2011. Semantic Guidance of Eye Movements in Real-world Scenes. *Vision Research*, 51(10):1192–1205.

Marcel Adam Just and Patricia A. Carpenter. 1980. A Theory of Reading: From Eye Fixations to Comprehension. *Psychological Review*, 87(4):329–354.

Regine Lai and Grégoire Winterstein. 2020. Cifu: A Frequency Lexicon of Hong Kong Cantonese. In *Proceedings of LREC*.

Jackson L. Lee, Litong Chen, Charles Lam, Chaak Ming Lau, and Tsz-Him Tsui. 2022. PyCantonese: Cantonese Linguistics and NLP in Python. In *Proceedings of LREC*.

David C. S. Li, Cathy S. P. Wong, Wai Mun Leung, and Sam T. S. Wong. 2016. Facilitation of Transference: The Case of Monosyllabic Salience in Hong Kong Cantonese. *Linguistics*, 54(1):1–58.

Xingshan Li, Pingping Liu, and Keith Rayner. 2011. Eye Movement Guidance in Chinese Reading: Is there a Preferred Viewing Location? *Vision Research*, 51(10):1146–1156.

Xingshan Li and Alexander Pollatsek. 2020. An Integrated Model of Word Processing and Eye-movement Control during Chinese Reading. *Psychological Review*, 127(6):1139.

Xingshan Li, Chuanli Zang, Simon P Liversedge, and Alexander Pollatsek. 2015. The Role of Words in Chinese Reading. *The Oxford Handbook of Reading*, page 232.

Danqing Liu. 2000. The Typological Properties of Cantonese Syntax . *Asia Pacific Journal of Language in Education* .

Simon P Liversedge, Chuanli Zang, Manman Zhang, Xuejun Bai, Guoli Yan, and Denis Drieghe. 2014. The Effect of Visual Complexity and Word Frequency on Eye Movements during Chinese Reading. *Visual Cognition*, 22(3-4):441–457.

Zijia Lu, Ying Fu, Manman Zhang, Chuanli Zang, and Xuejun Bai. 2022. Parafoveal Processing of Part-of-speech Information in Chinese Reading. *Acta Psychologica Sinica*, 54(5):441.

Jeff Mitchell, Mirella Lapata, Vera Demberg, and Frank Keller. 2010. Syntactic and Semantic Factors in Processing Difficulty: An Integrated Measure. In *Proceedings of ACL*.

Neal J Pearlmutter, Susan M Garnsey, and Kathryn Bock. 1999. Agreement Processes in Sentence Comprehension. *Journal of Memory and language*, 41(3):427–456.

Barbara Plank. 2022. The 'Problem' of Human Label Variation: On Ground Truth in Data, Modeling and Evaluation. In *Proceedings of EMNLP*.

Alexander Pollatsek, Barbara J Juhasz, Erik D Reichle, Debra Machacek, and Keith Rayner. 2008. Immediate and Delayed Effects of Word Frequency and Word Length on Eye Movements in Reading: A Reversed Delayed Effect of Word Length. *Journal of Experimental Psychology: Human Perception and Performance*, 34(3):726.

Joel Pynte, Boris New, and Alan Kennedy. 2008. On-line Contextual Influences During Reading Normal Text: A Multiple-Regression Analysis. *Vision Research*, 48(21):2172–2183.

Keith Rayner, Xingshan Li, Barbara J Juhasz, and Guoli Yan. 2005. The Effect of Word Predictability on the Eye Movements of Chinese Readers. *Psychonomic Bulletin & Review*, 12:1089–1093.

Keith Rayner, Xingshan Li, and Alexander Pollatsek. 2007. Extending the E-Z Reader Model of Eye Movement Control to Chinese Readers. *Cognitive Science*, 31(6):1021–1033.

Keith Rayner, Sara C. Sereno, Robin K. Morris, A. Réne Schmauder, and Charles Clifton Jr. 1989. Eye Movements and On-line Language Comprehension Processes. *Language and Cognitive Processes*, 4(3-4):SI21–SI49.

Lavinia Salicchi, Emmanuele Chersoni, and Alessandro Lenci. 2023. A Study on Surprisal and Semantic Relatedness for Eye-Tracking Data Prediction. *Frontiers in Psychology*, 14.

Lavinia Salicchi, Rong Xiang, and Yu-Yin Hsu. 2022. HkAmsters at CMCL 2022 Shared Task: Predicting Eye-tracking Data from a Gradient Boosting Framework with Linguistic Features. In *Proceedings of the ACL Workshop on Cognitive Modeling and Computational Linguistics*.

Philip Thierfelder, Gautier Durantin, and Gillian Wigglesworth. 2020. The Effect of Word Predictability on Phonological Activation in Cantonese Reading: a Study of Eye-fixations and Pupillary Response. *Journal of Psycholinguistic Research*, 49:779–801.

Marten Van Schijndel and William Schuler. 2015. Hierarchic Syntax Improves Reading Time Prediction. In *Proceedings of NAACL-HLT*.

Guoli Yan, Hongjie Tian, Xuejun Bai, and Keith Rayner. 2006. The Effect of Word and Character Frequency on the Eye Movements of Chinese Readers. *British Journal of Psychology*, 97(2):259–268.

Chuanli Zang, Hong Du, Xuejun Bai, Guoli Yan, and Simon P Liversedge. 2020. Word Skipping in Chinese Reading: The Role of High-frequency Preview and Syntactic Felicity. *Journal of Experimental Psychology: Learning, Memory, and Cognition*, 46(4):603.

Chuanli Zang, Ying Fu, Xuejun Bai, Guoli Yan, and Simon P Liversedge. 2018. Investigating Word Length Effects in Chinese Reading. *Journal of Experimental Psychology: Human Perception and Performance*, 44(12):1831.

A Appendix

In this appendix, Figure 5 presents each FD's difference between Mandarin and Cantonese ($FD_{Mandarin} - FD_{Cantonese}$) grouped by part-of-speeches. FDs are in log scale. Differences above zero denote longer FD for Mandarin. Part-of-speeches involving significant differences are colored.

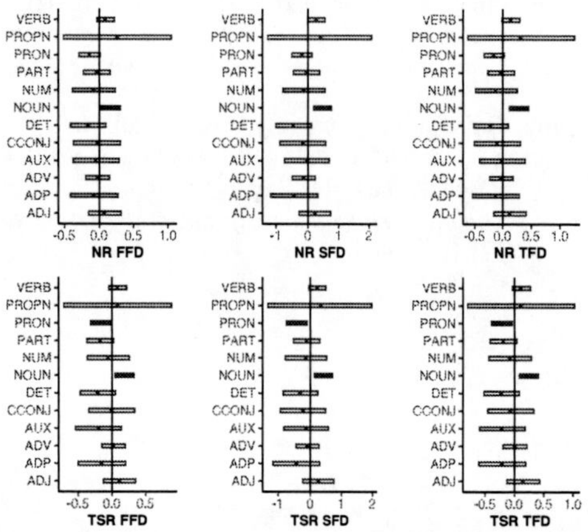

Figure 5: Tukey post hoc test of FD difference between paired part-of-speech in Mandarin and Cantonese (reporting 95%-level confidence intervals of the difference of"Mandarin-Cantonese"). FDs are in log scale. Word classes involving significant variance are colored. Positive difference means longer FD for Mandarin for the corresponding word category.

A Measure for Linguistic Coherence in Spatial Language Variation

Alfred Lameli, Andreas Schönberg
Research Center Deutscher Sprachatlas, Germany
lameli@uni-marburg.de, andreas.schoenberg@uni-marburg.de

Abstract

Based on historical dialect data we introduce a local measure of linguistic coherence in spatial language variation aiming at the identification of regions which are particularly sensitive to language variation and change. Besides, we use a measure of global coherence for the automated detection of linguistic items (e.g., sounds or morphemes) with higher or lesser language variation. The paper describes both the data and the method and provides analyses examples.

1 Introduction

Dialectometric work typically focuses on the co-occurrence of the distribution of variants in different sites (see Goebl 1984). From these co-occurrences, reasonably coherent regions of linguistic similarity can be identified. These regions then provide, for example, clues to the aggregated structuring of higher-level linguistic areas (e.g., within a nation). Alternatively, they show to what extent individual sites of a given corpus are integrated into the region under discussion in terms of their similarity or distance to other sites (e.g., Heeringa 2003). Such analyses, which at the same time constitute the classical field of dialectometry, thus benefit from the aggregation of all linguistic phenomena of a given corpus.

However, if the interest is not in the overall structuring of a region, but in the distribution patterns of individual variants, non-aggregating procedures must be applied. For a single phenomenon, spots of variation may be identified in most cases by visual inspection (see Ormeling 2010 for a critical account). However, in order to capture this variation quantitatively, more recent studies have considered a number of solutions, for example based on resampling techniques (e.g., Wieling & Nerbonne 2015), Kernel Density Estimation (e.g., Rumpf et al. 2009) or the concept of entropy (e.g., Prokić et al. 2009).

This paper presents a diagnostic measure for the detection of coherence or heterogeneity in spatial language variation aimed at identifying those regions that are particularly prone to variation or particularly sensitive to language change. We perform an approach based on nearest neighbor comparison and exemplify the used measure.[1]

In the remainder, we provide information on the data and introduce both a local and a global measure of linguistic coherence and diversity. In what follows we present example analyses based on historical dialect data from southwestern Germany and discuss the introduced procedure.

2 Data

The study makes use of a data set collected by the German linguist Friedrich Maurer during the year 1941 in the Upper German dialect region within the boundaries of the national territory at the time. The survey was based on a questionnaire with 113

[1] The study builds on R programming (R Core Team 2021), using the packages spatstat (Baddeley & Turner 2005) and Rvision (Garnier et al. 2021) mainly. In order to perform our coherence measure more efficiently it has been implemented into a R-package (LinguGeo). The current version of the LinguGeo package can be found at: https://github.com/SchoenbergA/LinguGeo

Tenth Workshop on NLP for Similar Languages, Varieties and Dialects (VarDial 2023), pages 133–141
May 5, 2023 ©2023 Association for Computational Linguistics

individual words (most of them nouns, but also adjectives and verbs) and 10 sentences together with biographic information of the participants. In contrast to both the earlier survey by Wenker (Wenker 2013) and the contemporaneous investigation by Mitzka (cf. Wrede et al. 1926–1956), Maurer focused more strongly on social and biographic information. Thus, in addition to the age of the participants, for example, their gender as well as the origin of their parents or their preferred market towns are documented.

We focus on the Alemannic part of the Maurer data which is mainly related to the southwestern part of nowadays Germany (the Baden region) and the Alsace in France (see Strobel 2021 for further information). In total, the data document 2344 locations, providing a quasi-total coverage of the region under discussion (Figure 1). The hand-written questionnaires of this area have been typewritten and therefore digitalized by student assistants. The data is stored in *.csv files and will be publicly accessible in the future in the data repository of the Research Center Deutscher Sprachatlas.

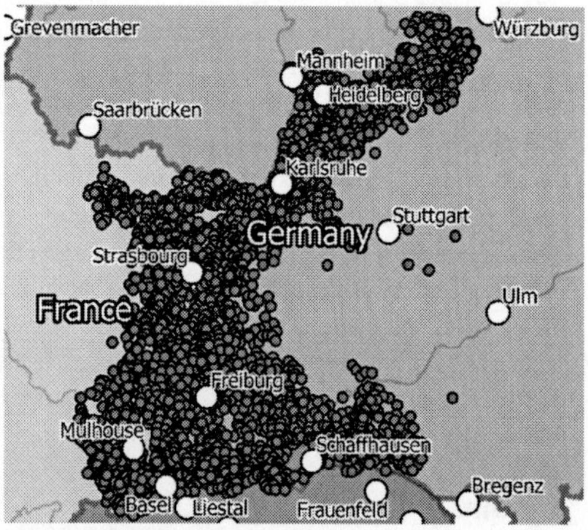

Figure 1: Study area.

3 Method

3.1 Local Measure

In order to analyze the spatial variation of the area under discussion we compare the linguistic realizations of one site with the realizations of its geographic neighbors. Behind the selection of neighborhood relations is the assumption of the so-called "Fundamental Dialectological Postulate" (Nerbonne & Kleiweg 2007), which states that closer objects are linguistically more similar than distant objects.

From a technical point of view, for every site r we compare the linguistic realization of an individual item i of the questionnaire (e.g., a word) with its geographic neighbor s. $Coh_{rs|i}$ is then the number of identities between r and s with $Coh_{rs|i} = 1$ in case of identity and $Coh_{rs|i} = 0$ otherwise.

To obtain a better insight into how the individual sites fit into the language region, the number of compared sites should be $S > 1$. In the present paper, we consider up to 19 neighbors ($0 \leq S \leq 19$), where 0 is used for the rendering of the original data. Coh_{rS} is then the average overlap between r and its set of neighbors S with $0 \leq Coh_{rS} \leq 1$ and $Coh_{rS} = 1$ indicating identity between r and S and $Coh_{rS} = 0$ indicating no identity between r and S. In case a location has several variants for a linguistic variable (e.g., because of several participants or multiple responses), the number of matches between r and s is related to the number of local variants.

An example is provided by Figure 2. The centrally located site is opposed by a total of 5 nearest neighbors, which have a total of 2.5 matches with the central site, resulting in Coh = 2.5/5 = 0.5. The number of variants is irrelevant for this approach but is relevant for the global measure (cf. 3.2)

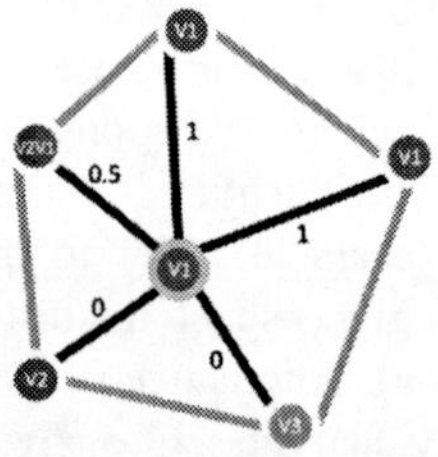

Figure 2: Model of distribution of variants.

Inverting the scale results in a measure of linguistic diversity instead of linguistic coherence which we refer to as Div = 1-Coh. We use this Div measure in order to identify moments of particular dynamics on language maps.

Another point is worth mentioning. The nearest neighbor approach relies heavily on the definition of geographic coordinates and distances. In our approach, the geometric information of the spatial position for each survey site is thus originally stored in the WGS 84 format (longitude and latitude). Due to the ellipsoidal coordinate system, the distances are heavily distorted which directly affects the selection of the nearest neighbors. To use the quasi-exact distances a cartesian coordinate system is required. Therefore, we projected our data to the UTM system related to the ETRS89 ellipsoid.

3.2 Global Measure

While the local measure indicates the integration of individual sites into its nearest spatial neighborhood, it says nothing about the coherence or heterogeneity of an overall map. Various options are available for this purpose. For example, the mean of all local Coh values could be taken as a global measure of coherence (CohG). However, as Figure 3 demonstrates, this measure is dependent on the number of linguistic variants in a data distribution, making it difficult to compare CohG across maps with different numbers of variants. For example, if a map shows two linguistic variants a complete random distribution results in $0.5 \leq CohG \leq 1$ and $0.33 \leq CohG \leq 1$ for three variants etc.

In order to solve this problem, we perform a CohG* correction in which CohG is divided by the number of variants and scaled $0 < CohG^* \leq 1$. As becomes evident by Figure 3, CohG* is robust against the number of variants, while CohG, in contrast, is sensitive to it and converges to CohG* as the number of variants increases. Similar holds for the number of neighbors against which CohG* is robust while CohG is sensitive to it (not reported).

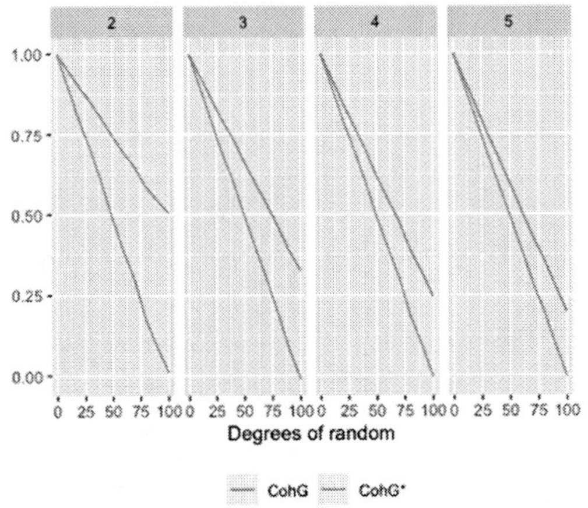

Figure 3: Comparison of CohG and CohG* based on simulated degrees of both spatial coherence and random data filling (0-100 %) for a data distribution with 2 to 5 linguistic variants.

Another view on CohG* is provided in Figure 4 and Figure 5. In these figures, data simulations are performed for the locations of the corpus, generating different degrees of random data distributions. Starting from a uniform distribution, 20 % of the data of each map are successively overwritten with a random distribution.

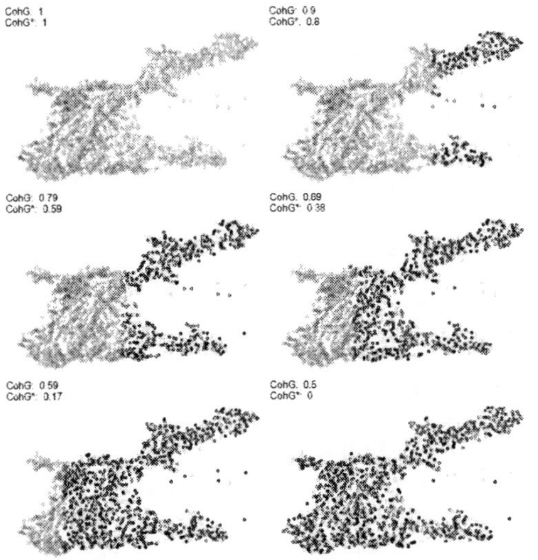

Figure 4: Simulation of different degrees of spatial heterogeneity (0 %, 20 %, 40 %, 60 %, 80 %, 100 %) for a map with two linguistic variables. Variant 1 = purple, variant 2 = yellow, alpha = 1-Coh.

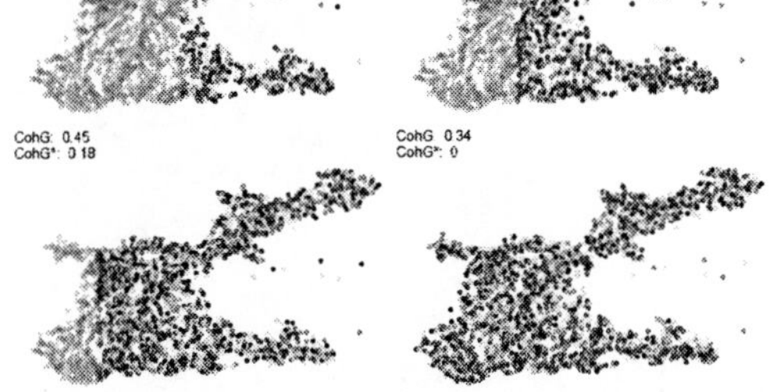

Figure 5: Simulation of different degrees of spatial heterogeneity (0 %, 20 %, 40 %, 60 %, 80 %, 100 %) for a map with three linguistic variables. Variant 1 = purple, variant 2 = yellow, variant 3 = green, alpha = 1-Coh.

While Figure 4 illustrates data simulation with two linguistic variants, Figure 5 illustrates the same procedure based on three linguistic variants. The figures show that while the CohG is related to the amount of variants, the CohG* values describe the same amount of coherence/homogeneity unattached to the number of variants.

Against this background, the Coh measure, and also the CohG* measure, yields plausible results as far as different degrees of coherence or heterogeneity are concerned. However, it is still an open question how the values turn out in concrete use cases and what more detailed conclusions can be drawn from them.

4 Use Cases

4.1 Lambdacism in *Kirche* 'Church'

As a first example we focus on a rather simple spatial pattern provided by the distribution of *-r-* and *-l-* sounds in the word *Kirche* 'church' (*Kirche* vs. *Kilche*) in the southern part of our study area (Figure 6). The phonological process behind this is the so-called lambdacism, which is typical for some regions of the German-speaking area (cf. Lameli 2015).

Figure 6 illustrates the distribution of the variants in the southern part of the study area. At each site one variable is documented, where *Kirche* (blue) occurs 1008 times, *Kilche* (red) 222 times (1230 sites in total). Hence, 81.94 % of the sites in the study area show *-r-*.

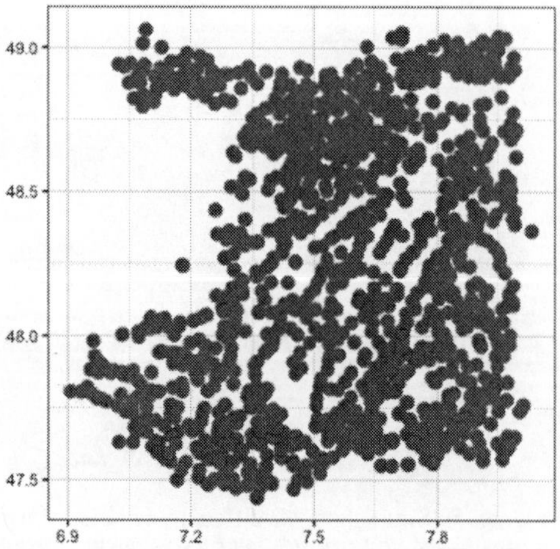

Figure 6: Example of a spatial distribution of linguistic variants *-r-* (blue) and *-l-* (red) in the word *Kirche* 'church'.

In a random distribution the expected probability that a particular site's neighbor shares the same variant is EV = (1008-1) / (1230-1) = 81.94%. For the same distribution we reveal under the consideration of 5 nearest neighbors CohG* = .94 (Coh = .9) indicating that, on average, 94 % of the neighboring 5 sites share the same variant *-r-* as the site under observation. However, the question remains open as to how high CohG* turns out to be in a random distribution when 5 nearest neighbors are considered, as in the present case. For this purpose, 1000 data simulations were performed in which the existing occurrences of *-r-* and *-l-* sounds were randomly distributed among the study sites. The resulting mean of CohG* = .41 indicates that, given a random distribution of data, statistically 41 % of the neighboring five locations share the same variant as a particular site under observation with a range of CohG* = .37–.44.

By CohG* being higher than both the random distribution and the expected value EV, (1) spatial clustering of *-r-* and *-l-* is indicated and, as a consequence, (2) a clear separation of the variants. Indeed, very few locations aside, all variants cluster in contiguous areas as already becomes clear by visual inspection.

Testing the distribution of local Coh values against a normal distribution using a Wilcoxon rank sum test reveals a statistical difference between the expected value EV and the empirically found Coh measure ($z = -4.21$, $p < .001$, $r = .94$). What these measures refer to becomes evident when plotting 1-Coh (= Div) on a map (Figure 7).

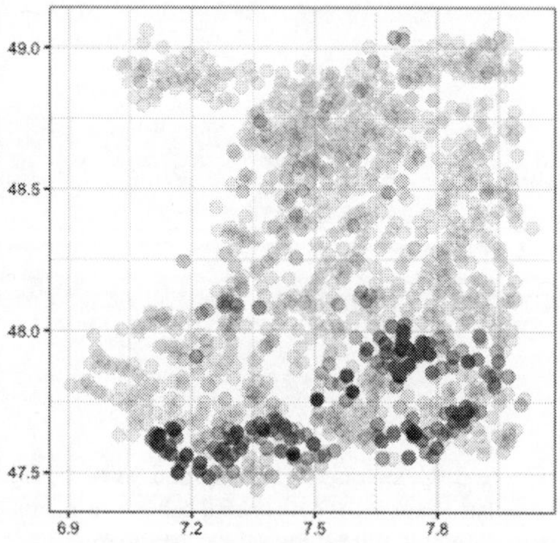

Figure 7: Local measure of linguistic coherence (Div = 1-Coh) applied to the data of Figure 6.

As expected, the highest Div values are at the border zone between the variants. Most interestingly, there are differences depending on the spatial alternation of the variants. For example, on the left, where we find a mix of variants, Div values are high. In contrast, in the center, where we find a separation of *Kirche* and *Kilche*, Div values are low. The spots illustrated by Figure 7 thus allow conclusions to be drawn about zones of increased linguistic dynamics: around the sites with high values (intense colors) there is a high degree of variation, around the sites with low values (pale colors) there is a lower degree of variation. While the former can be expected to be more sensitive to language change regarding the variable under discussion, the latter can be expected to be more robust to language change.

Methodologically, it should be emphasized that, due to the nearest neighbor approach, the described procedure always computes a gradient-like result. Even if there is a sharp separation between variants (Figure 6) a gradient would be computed (Figure 7).

The intensity of this gradient-like effect depends on the number of nearest neighbors. Using the minimum of two nearest neighbors will result in exactly three index values and the resulting map would set a focus on areas which differ from their surroundings (Figure 8/A). This may be useful to detect islands of variation in rather coherent areas. With increasing numbers of nearest neighbors, the amount of possible index values will increase and return much more smoother transitions. This is helpful for the detection of areas with variation in a cluster-like way. Areas with variation in close distances would be smoothed to clusters which would be differentiated from surrounding homogeneous areas (e.g., Figure 8/D). This way of proceeding captures, for example, border regions in a more schematic way and those regions which are most likely unaffected by these border regions.

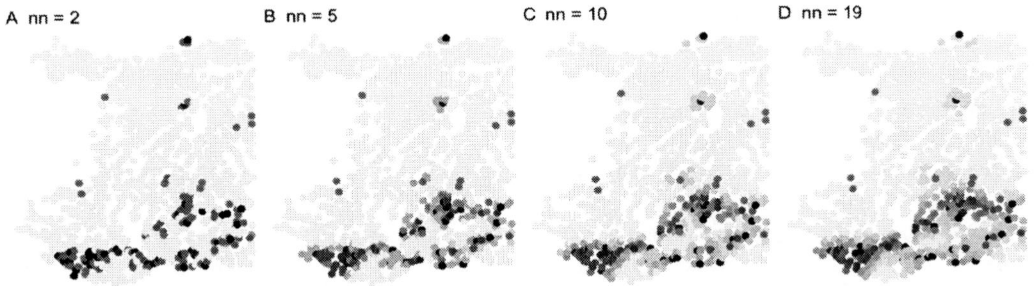

Figure 8: Local measure of linguistic coherence applied to the data of Figure 6 with different number of nearest neighbors and without information on linguistic variants.

4.2 Subtractive Plural in *Hunde* 'Dog-PL'

Another example is provided by Figure 9, which focuses on the whole language area of the Maurer data. The map illustrates the variation of the word ending in *Hunde* ('dog-PL'; CohG* = .87) considering three graphemic variants (<nd>, <ng>, <nn>), of which <nn> (phonologically /n/) and <ng> (phonologically /ŋ/) have been considered as subtractive plurals (Birkenes 2014). While the *Kirche* example considers only two linguistic variants, Figure 9 refers to three linguistic variants. The figure combines three different views. On the left side is the distribution of variants without any preparation, in the middle the representation of the coherence measure (expressed in Div) including information on the variants and on the right side the representation of coherence (Div) without information on the linguistic variants.

Obviously, the coherence map in the middle clearly highlights the spots of linguistic variation. Among them are areas where only two variants interact (e.g., <nd> and <nn> in the South, <nd> and <ng> in the North), but also areas where all three variants meet (in the center). Similar to the previous example the coverage of individual variants is mapped.

The map on the right, on the other hand, emphasizes where generally such patterns of variation are encountered. This map consequently emphasizes the contrast between homogeneous and heterogeneous moments of the spatial data distribution. In this case, too, conclusions can be

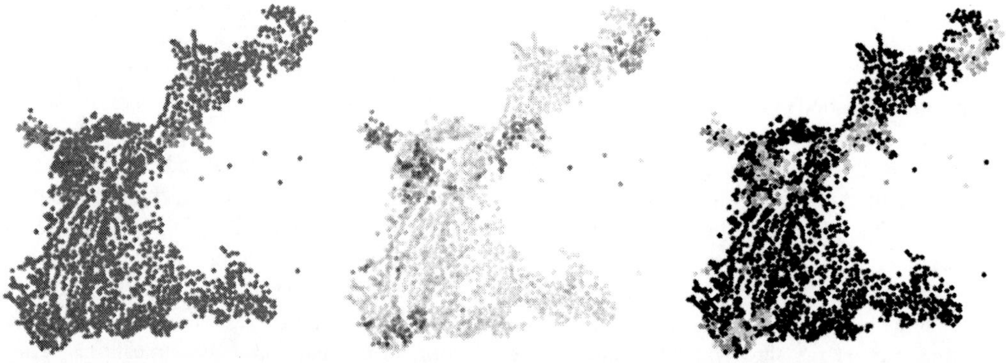

Figure 9: Local measure of linguistic coherence (Div = 1-Coh) for a linguistic variable with three variants (*Hunde* 'dog-PL'); green = <ng>, red = <nd>; blue = <nn>; left: distribution of variants; middle: Div measure with information on linguistic variants; right: Div measure without information on linguistic variants.

drawn (as in the previous example) about the extent of regional variation and possible language change events; it is in the yellow zones where variation is highest and possible language change is most likely.

From a methodological perspective, the following is worth mentioning. By integrating the nearest neighbors, a smoothing effect is created, which shows linguistic variation in places where actually no variation is documented by data collection. The idea behind this is that variation is probably more widespread than what is captured by data collection. For example, if only one person is asked about a particular linguistic variant at each of two surveyed locations (which is very often the case in dialectological studies), it would possibly be wrong to take different answers per se as evidence of strict linguistic differences between those locations. Instead, it must be expected that both variants would be encountered in both localities and would be appropriately documented with other participants if data were repeatedly collected. However, the probability of this decreases with increasing geographical distance. The measure thus provides a prediction for the communicative reach of language variants.

5 Discussion

The Coh measure, as well as the Div measure respectively, reveals spots of local variation, which indicate horizontal (i.e. geographical) or vertical (i.e. social, pragmatic) heterogeneity. As Labov (2004) points out, these spots of increased language variation might be possible starting points of language change. In this regard, Bellmann (1983) considers the model in Figure 10.

Starting from a situation where variant A is the only available realization of a particular linguistic variable, at a certain time variant B becomes an alternative. This is the situation illustrated by Figure 10 for both scenarios (above and below). However, the Coh measure goes beyond local variation by modeling the closest relative area of influence of that alternative.

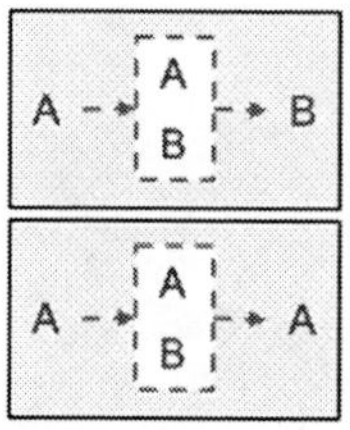

Figure 10: Possible stages in the formation of language variation and/or language change on the example of two variants A and B; above: scenario 1 (language change); below: scenario 2 (temporary language variation).

Obviously, analysis using Coh (like Figure 7) does not specify how long the variative phase will persist. Furthermore, it could be that variant B disappears again (Figure 10 below), and it could just as well be that variant B prevails (Figure 10 above) while A disappears. Consequently, Coh does not allow for a clear prediction of the process of language change, but it does illustrate that, if language change does occur, it is likely to occur at the spots with high Div (= 1-Coh). Against this background, the relevance of the Coh measure is to indicate spots of particular linguistic dynamics. Identifying these spots enables both prediction and explanation of ongoing and/or completed language change.

On the other hand, with CohG* → 1 it can also be shown directly whether a language region has proto-typical variants, which can then be easily identified in the data distribution.

Furthermore, applying the coherence measure to a collection of multiple linguistic phenomena, as shown in Figure 11, leads to a new perspective on the structuring of linguistic space. Instead of highlighting the clusters of linguistic similarity, rather the zones of particular linguistic dynamics are identified. From looking at the coherence values, even without mapping, a first impression is given whether the lemmas in question show a strong spatial clustering or not. This is useful for huge datasets with lots of linguistic variables. At the same time, it becomes evident that the measure is sensitive for outliers (i.e., isolated sites), which are evident by individual points.

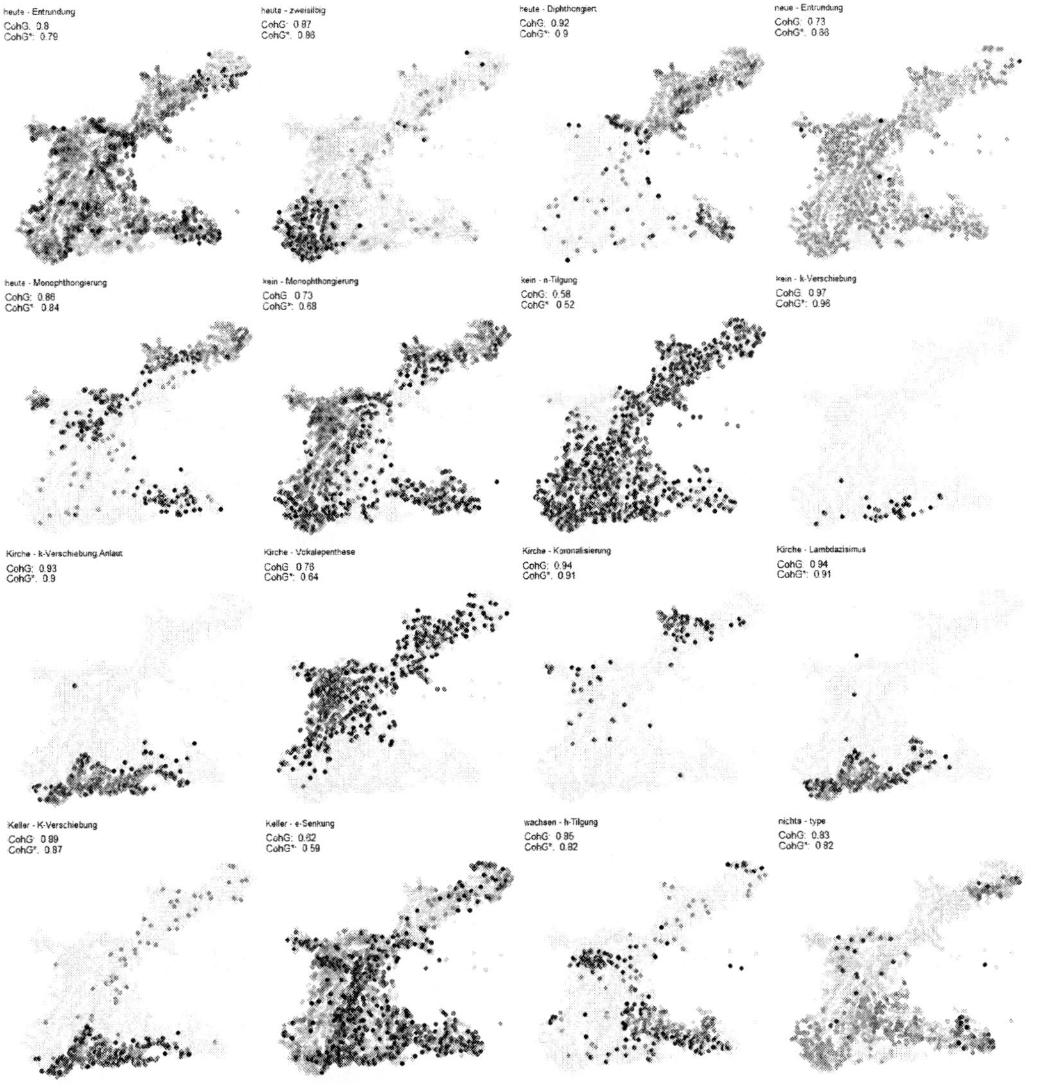

Figure 11: Local measure of linguistic coherence (Div = 1-Coh) for different linguistic variables.

Among the existing dialectometric literature, our coherence measure is comparable to the technique introduced by Rumpf et al. (2009) using Kernel Density Estimation (KDE). Our measure explicitly considers geographical neighborhood, but, in contrast to the KDE approach, it is more focused on local variation. Instead of calculating an adequate bandwith, we choose a certain number of neighbors in order to test for the integration of an individual site into the linguistic area. In this respect, the underlying concept is that linguistic space develops in small-scale communication zones, not in large-scale continua. From a technical perspective, a difference to the KDE approach is that we do not rely on the definition of individual variant-occurrence maps as an intermediate step of analysis, but process the variation given in the data set directly.

Notwithstanding this, there are other studies that work with the notion of coherence or focus on transitional spaces. Nerbonne & Kleiweg (2007), for example, introduce a local measure of incoherence, which, however, focuses on linguistic rather than geographic distances. Our measure thus provides an alternative view of the relationship between spatial and linguistic proximity based on individual maps and not on aggregated data. Goebl (2010), nonetheless, illustrates the importance of skewness as a global statistical measure of the linguistic integration of individual sites into the linguistic area and the assessment of transitional zones. Similar to Nerbonne & Kleiweg (2007), the basis of linguistic measurement is in Goebl's approach not the individual map, but a set of aggregated data. Unlike Goebl (2010), we focus exclusively on concrete geographic neighbors of an individual site with both the local and global measures, which makes our approach, in the case of the local measure, independent from the overall statistical distribution, which is in dialectometric studies typically shaped by linguistic distance or similarity.

6 Conclusion

This paper introduces a nearest neighbor approach as a diagnostic tool in order to find regions which are more sensitive to language variation and change than others. For this purpose, a local measure of coherence is used (Coh). In addition, a global coherence measure (CohG) as well as a corrected global measure (CohG*) was used to quantitatively assess the spatial coherence of more comprehensive data distributions (e.g., on maps) and to automatically identify linguistic items with higher/lesser language variation. Two case studies illustrate the application of the method and the informative quality of the measures.

Limitations

The method works reliably, even if a map contains multiple variants. However, if there are more than, say, 10 or 15 variants, it can happen that no clear spots can be identified on the maps. For this matter, a more probabilistic approach would be desirable, which is currently not implemented.

Another limitation is the distance measure used for the identification of nearest neighbors. Currently, nearest neighbors are defined using Euclidean distance. This is not a problem if the analysis takes place in flat terrain (e.g., the Upper Rhine Plain). In mountainous terrain, however, this can lead to slight biases. To solve this problem, we will implement more realistic distance measures such as travel time in the future.

From a linguistic perspective, a limitation of the method is that even if it informs about the variation spots, it does not provide any information about the direction in which a possible language change could develop. However, such a statement is difficult to make without concrete comparative language data (e.g., diachronic data) or social interpretation. Since the Maurer data allow an analysis in apparent-time, further approaches for investigation will be possible in the future.

Ethics Statement

This work complies with the ACL Ethics Policy.

Acknowledgments

We are grateful to six reviewers for their valuable comments as well as Peter Auer, Michael Cysouw, Alexandra Lieb and Maj-Brit Strobel for discussion. Maj-Brit Strobel was kind enough to provide us with data from her work. This research is funded by the German Research Foundation under the project "Alemannisch variativ" (DFG, grant number 452440801).

References

Adrian Baddeley, Rolf Turner. 2005. spatstat: An R Package for Analyzing Spatial Point Patterns. *Journal of Statistical Software*, 12(6):1-42. URL https://www.jstatsoft.org/v12/i06/.

Günter Bellmann. 1983. Probleme des Substandards im Deutschen. In Klaus J. Mattheier (ed.) *Aspekte der Dialekttheorie*. Niemeyer: Tübingen:105-130.

Magnus Breder Birkenes. 2014. *Subtraktive Nominalmorphologie in den Dialekten des Deutschen. Ein Beitrag zur Interaktion von Phonologie und Morphologie*. Steiner: Stuttgart.

Simon Garnier, Noam Ross, Robert Rudis, Antônio P. Camargo, Marco Sciaini, and Cédric Scherer. 2021. Rvision - Colorblind-Friendly Color Maps for R. R package version 0.6.2. URL https://sjmgarnier.github.io/viridis/.

Hans Goebl. 1984. *Dialektometrische Studien. Anhand italoromanischer und galloromanischer Sprachmaterialien aus AIS und ALF*. Niemeyer: Tübingen:191-193.

Hans Goebl. 2010. Dialectometry and quantitative mapping. In Alfred Lameli et al. (eds.) *Language and Space. An International Handbook of Linguistic Variation. Language Mapping*. Mouton de Gruyter: Berlin, Boston:433-457.

Wilbert Heeringa. 2003. *Measuring Dialect Pronunciation Differences using Levenshtein Distance*. University Press: Groningen.

William Labov. 1994. *Principles of linguistic change. Vol. 1: Internal factors*. Blackwell: Oxford.

Alfred Lameli. 2015. Zur Konzeptualisierung des Sprachraums als Handlungsraum. In Michael Elmentaler et al. (eds.) *Deutsche Dialekte. Konzepte, Probleme, Handlungsfelder*. Steiner: Stuttgart:59-83.

John Nerbonne, Peter Kleiweg. 2008. Toward a dialectological yardstick. Journal of Quantitative Linguistics, 14:148-166.

Ferjan Ormeling. 2010. Visualizing geographic space. The nature of maps. In Alfred Lameli et al. (eds.) *Language and Space. An International Handbook of Linguistic Variation. Language Mapping*. Mouton de Gruyter: Berlin, Boston:21-40.

Jelena Prokić, John Nerbonne, Vladimir Zhobov, Petya Osenova, Kiril Simov, Thomas Zastrow and Erhard Hinrichs. 2009. The computational analysis of Bulgarian dialect pronunciation. *Serdica. Journal of Computing*, 3:269-298.

R Core Team. 2021. R: A language and environment for statistical computing. R Foundation for Statistical Computing, Vienna, Austria. URL https://www.R-project.org/.

Jonas Rumpf, Simon Pickl, Stephan Elspaß, Werner König and Volker Schmidt. 2009. Structural analysis of dialect maps using methods from spatial statistics. *Zeitschrift für Dialektologie und Linguistik*, 76(3):280-308.

Maj-Brit, Strobel. 2021. Die Verschriftungen in der Dialekterhebung Friedrich Maurers in Baden und im Elsass als Evidenz für die Verbreitung der Standardlautung. *Zeitschrift für Germanistische Linguistik*, 49(1):155-188.

Georg Wenker. 2013. *Schriften zum „Sprachatlas des Deutschen Reichs". Gesamtausgabe*. Olms: Hildesheim, New York, Zürich.

Martijn Wieling and John Nerbonne. 2015. Advances in Dialectometry. *Annual Review in Linguistics*, 1(1):243-264.

Ferdinand Wrede, Walther Mitzka and Bernhard Martin. 1926–1956. Deutscher Sprachatlas auf Grund des von Georg Wenker begründeten Sprachatlas des Deutschen Reichs und mit Einschluß. von Luxemburg in vereinfachter Form. Elwert: Marburg.

Dialect and Variant Identification as a Multi-Label Classification Task: A Proposal Based on Near-Duplicate Analysis

Gabriel Bernier-Colborne and **Cyril Goutte** and **Serge Léger**
National Research Council Canada
{Gabriel.Bernier-Colborne | Cyril.Goutte | Serge.Leger}@nrc-cnrc.gc.ca

Abstract

We argue that dialect identification should be treated as a multi-label classification problem rather than the single-class setting prevalent in existing collections and evaluations. In order to avoid extensive human re-labelling of the data, we propose an analysis of ambiguous near-duplicates in an existing collection covering four variants of French. We show how this analysis helps us provide multiple labels for a significant subset of the original data, therefore enriching the annotation with minimal human intervention. The resulting data can then be used to train dialect identifiers in a multi-label setting. Experimental results show that on the enriched dataset, the multi-label classifier produces similar accuracy to the single-label classifier on test cases that are unambiguous (single label), but it increases the macro-averaged F1-score by 0.225 absolute (71% relative gain) on ambiguous texts with multiple labels. On the original data, gains on the ambiguous test cases are smaller but still considerable (+0.077 absolute, 20% relative gain), and accuracy on non-ambiguous test cases is again similar in this case. This supports our thesis that modelling dialect identification as a multi-label problem potentially has a positive impact.

1 Introduction

In this paper, we argue that dialect[1] identification should be treated as a multi-label classification problem unless it can be shown that every text in a given dataset belongs to only one dialect or language variant. This feels like a natural hypothesis, as it seems reasonable that some utterances are equally valid in more than one dialect or variant. However, most datasets for, and evaluations of this task rely on single-label classification, where each utterance is annotated as belonging to a single variant.[2]

Previous work shows that manually identifying the language variety of a text is difficult, and that it is actually easier for native speakers to identify texts that are *not* in their variety (Goutte et al., 2016, sec. 4.4). Accordingly, proper multi-label manual annotation requires multiple annotators with complementary skills, and therefore massive annotation budget, when run at the usual scale of tens-to-hundreds of thousands of utterances.

In this work, we focus instead on analyzing and processing already existing dialect identification data, with minimal annotation need. We argue that automatically assessing differences between two similar texts, as done here, is an easier task. We explore empirically how the data can be enriched with multiple labels, and how switching to the multi-label classification paradigm can potentially improve performance in identifying dialects and variants.

We start by analyzing the duplicates and near-duplicates in an existing dataset built for French dialect identification. We search for instances that are identical or highly similar textually, but are annotated with different labels. We find that a considerable number of near-duplicates have different labels, but no obvious differences that could be considered dialectal in nature.

We further show that near-duplicate analysis is useful in at least two ways. First, it allows us to inspect and refine a dataset, in a manner similar to *measuring data* (Wang et al., 2022; Mitchell et al., 2022, inter alia), by identifying phenomena that might otherwise go unnoticed, e.g. texts that are assigned to different classes but have no actual dialectal differences or spotting artefacts due to the selection of text sources or to the processing

[1] In this paper, we use the terms "dialect" and "language variant" somewhat interchangeably. In the FreCDo dataset, language variants are specifically delimited by national origin, as determined by the top-level domain of the original webpage.

[2] A notable exception is this year's "True Labels" shared task at VarDial (`https://sites.google.com/view/vardial-2023/shared-tasks`).

Tenth Workshop on NLP for Similar Languages, Varieties and Dialects (VarDial 2023), pages 142–151
May 5, 2023 ©2023 Association for Computational Linguistics

pipeline (e.g. boiler plate removal, sentence splitting, etc.). Second, by spotting similar texts that have no obvious dialectal differences, it allows us to convert an existing dataset in single-label format into a multi-label dialect classification format.

Using the results of this analysis, we combine the labels of near-duplicates to create what we argue is a more accurate representation of the data. For further empirical validation of this approach, we use this data to train a multi-label classifier for dialect identification. We compare those results to single-label classification and show that the overall classification performance stays at a similar level, while the performance on the subset of examples that have multiple labels is greatly improved.

The experimental code developed in this work is available at `https://github.com/gbcolborne/vardial2023`.

2 Data

For this project, we used the FreCDo corpus (Găman et al., 2022),[3] which was used for the Cross-Domain French Dialect Identification (FDI) shared task at the VarDial 2022 evaluation campaign (Aepli et al., 2022). It contains 413,522 short texts belonging to one of four varieties of French from Belgium (BE), Canada (CA), Switzerland (CH), and France (FR), cf. Table 1. The data is unbalanced, with a much lower number of CA texts (8.5% overall, $< 1\%$ on Dev). The training, development, and test sets were compiled from several public news websites using different keywords, in order to create a cross-domain split. Furthermore, tokens that are part of a named entity were replaced with the special token "NE".

	BE	CA	CH	FR
Train	121,746	34,003	141,261	61,777
Dev	7,723	171	5,244	4,864
Test	15,235	944	9,824	10,730

Table 1: Number of text segments in the original FreCDO corpus.

We selected this dataset for several reasons. First, we wanted to follow up on the results of the shared task at VarDial 2022 that exploited this dataset. The results of that shared task pointed to various properties of the dataset that could explain some of the errors made by the submitted systems, and the generally low scores of both the baselines and the submitted systems (Bernier-Colborne et al., 2022). These include the presence of duplicates both within classes and across classes. In this work, we extend the analysis of the data to include near-duplicates.

Second, this dataset features four different dialects of French, which seemed promising in terms of identifying texts that belong to more than one dialect. In particular, the four-variant setting seems more flexible than the situation where only two variants are considered (e.g. Portuguese from Brazil and Portugal), in which case the only multi-label configuration is essentially all labels.

Third, the authors of this paper are all fluent in (one or more variants of) French and were therefore able to analyze the texts and identify possible dialectal differences between texts or dialectal markers in a given text.

It is important to note that this dataset was created using methods that are common for dataset compilation for dialect identification tasks (aside from the cross-domain split). These methods include scraping texts from the Internet and assigning them to a language variety based on the top-level domain name of the source. This practice naturally leads to a single-label formulation of the problem, if each unique text is only present in one of the sources.

The limitations of this practice was a motivating factor for the DSL-TL (Discriminating Between Similar Languages - True Labels) shared task at this year's VarDial evaluation campaign:

> The DSLCC was compiled under the assumption that each instance's gold label is determined by where the text is retrieved from. While this is a straightforward (and mostly accurate) practical assumption, previous research has shown the limitations of this problem formulation as some texts may present no linguistic marker that allows systems or native speakers to discriminate between two very similar languages or language varieties.[4]

The solution proposed in DSL-TL was therefore to curate a higher-quality, human-annotated subset of an existing collection of dialect identification data, DSLCC[5], such that some of the resulting examples

[3] `https://github.com/MihaelaGaman/FreCDo`

[4] `https://sites.google.com/view/vardial-2023/shared-tasks`

[5] `http://ttg.uni-saarland.de/resources/DSLCC/`

have multiple labels (Zampieri et al., 2023). This is in line with our proposal to reformulate the problem as a multi-label classification task. However, although DSL-TL provides high-quality annotation on a subset of data, we focus on the use of semi-automatic near-duplicate analysis in order to minimize the annotation burden. Also, as mentioned earlier, the dataset used in this work contains four different dialects of French, whereas the DSL-TL dataset uses only two dialects for each of three different languages: American and British English, Brazilian and European Portuguese, and Argentinian and Peninsular Spanish.

It is also important to note that deduplication is often applied to datasets for dialect identification, although we have observed duplicates both within and across classes in several such datasets. If deduplication is somewhat common, near-duplicate analysis is not a common step in dataset development as far as we can tell.[6] We argue that it is a useful tool in the context of dialect identification. It can be carried out efficiently and provides useful additional information. In fact, our analysis shows that many highly similar near-duplicates vary only in minor aspects that have nothing to do with dialectal variation or lexical choice, such as slight changes in punctuation or formatting (for example the choice of double quotes), which are typically missed by standard deduplication pipelines.

In the following experiments, we used our own, random split of the texts, because the cross-domain nature of the original split was not relevant for our purposes. We also wanted to eliminate the small amount of leakage of texts between the training, development, and test portions of the original dataset. We therefore created an 85/5/10 split, as this was approximately the size of the partitions in the original dataset, by randomly sampling the train/dev/test from the entire original collection.

3 Methods

In this work, we first identify ambiguous near-duplicates that are present in an existing single-label dataset for dialect identification. We perform a light manual inspection (Section 3.2), then create an enriched version of the data by combining the labels of near-duplicate texts. Finally, we train and evaluate classifiers on the resulting data.

[6]We are not aware of a single dataset where such analysis was described in the documentation.

3.1 Identification of Ambiguous Near-duplicates

We used two different text similarity measures to identify near-duplicates. Then, by checking their respective labels, we focus on the near-duplicate pairs that have different label sets.

The first similarity measure is the character-level Levenshtein edit ratio. This is computed by normalizing the Levenshtein distance by the sum of the length of the two texts, and turning that into a similarity by subtracting the result from 1. We used the `Levenshtein` library[7] for Python to compute this, using an arbitrary cutoff at 0.8 to speed up the computation and extract only the most similar text pairs. Given the large size of the pairwise similarity matrix, we used a sparse matrix representation to limit memory usage.[8]

The second similarity measure is what we refer to as the *Manhattan similarity* of the word bigram frequency count vectors of the two texts. This is the absolute difference between the two count vectors divided by the sum of the two vectors, then turned into a similarity again by subtracting from 1. Our motivation for using word bigrams was that these were the most useful features for sparse vector-based classifiers according to the results of the shared task (Aepli et al., 2022; Bernier-Colborne et al., 2022). In order to limit memory requirements, we computed similarities in mini-batches, and kept the 1000 highest similarities for each text.

We are aware that we could integrate additional statistics such as the length of the texts in the similarity measure used to identify interesting near-duplicates. However, we have chosen to explore two text similarities that use very different information, one relying on character sequences and the other on word bigram counts, instead of engineering a more complex measure.

Note that we also considered testing sentence embedding methods, but we prioritised methods that are focused on surface similarity, whereas sentence embedding methods are designed to model semantic similarity beyond surface characteristics.

3.2 Manual Inspection

A sample of the most similar text pairs with different labels, which we will call *ambiguous near-duplicates*, was manually inspected and annotated

[7]`https://github.com/maxbachmann/Levenshtein`

[8]We use `scipy.sparse` for this purpose, (`https://docs.scipy.org/doc/scipy/reference/sparse.html`).

by the authors.[9] The goal was to estimate the proportion of near-duplicates that showed no obvious dialectical differences or markers. We also used the results of this inspection to establish a minimum similarity threshold above which it was unlikely that true dialectal differences were present. For the classification experiments we conduct later, we then assume that all ambiguous text pairs with similarity above that threshold can be considered valid in each of their respective dialects, so we combine their labels (as explained in Section 3.3) before training a multi-label classifier.

The visual inspection was done using an interface that highlights the differences between two similar texts, so that we could quickly locate those differences and assess their nature. We also developed a simple annotation protocol with three possible judgments or categories for each pair of ambiguous near-duplicates. In practice, for each of the two similarity measures, we randomly sampled 260 ambiguous near-duplicates, above an arbitrary threshold on the similarity measure (0.8 for Levenshtein, 0.6 for Manhattan). Out of these 260 examples, 20 were annotated by all human judges, to calibrate their judgments and have a rough estimate of inter-annotator agreement. The other samples were split evenly and annotated by one judge each. We defined a simple annotation protocol for this task, which we refined on one of the common sets of 20 samples. For each sample, the annotator had to pick one of three categories:

1. No lexical differences (e.g. minor changes to punctuation, function words, number of NE tokens, span of NE tokens, numbers, etc.).

2. Minor differences, like something an editor might do to a text, with no potentially dialectal differences.

3. Potentially dialectal differences (including differences in content, such as lexical choice, or addition/removal of entire clauses or sentences).

Examples in the first two categories are very unlikely to present actual dialectal differences or markers, therefore if a pair of texts falls in this category, it is likely justified to combine their label sets, as we do following the method explained in Section 3.3. In the third case, where there *might* be actual dialectal differences between the two texts, combining the labels might introduce noise. Examples are provided in Section 4.1

Note that this simple protocol could likely be improved in the future to ensure higher agreement between annotators.

3.3 Combining Labels

Instead of representing the label of each text as a single integer representing a class identifier, we use a set containing the classes that were observed for that text. So, at first, the vast majority of texts have a single class in their label set. The only exceptions are the texts that appear more than once in the original dataset, and with more than one unique label (i.e. ambiguous *exact* duplicates). This version of the data is referred to as the 'Original' data below. We also initialize a 'Combined' version of the data by copying the Original version.

Once the similarity threshold for near-duplicates has been set, as explained in Section 3.2, we identify all pairs of texts (x_i, x_j) with $i < j$ and a similarity greater or equal to that threshold. For each of these pairs, we add the Original label set of each text in the pair to the Combined label set of the other text.[10]

So, given two texts x_1 and x_2 with Original label sets $\{y_1\}$ and $\{y_2\}$ respectively, if $y_1 \neq y_2$ and the similarity of x_1 and x_2 is above the threshold, then the Combined labels sets of both texts becomes $\{y_1, y_2\}$.

Note that in this process, the same text may receive labels from more than one other text, if it has more than one neighbour given the similarity threshold. So, if text x_3 with Original label set $\{y_3\}$ is also a neighbour of x_1, then the Combined label set of x_1 becomes $\{y_1, y_2, y_3\}$ (assuming $y_2 \neq y_3$, otherwise the label set is unchanged, as y_2 was already in it), and the Combined label set of of x_3 becomes $\{y_1, y_3\}$ (assuming $y_1 \neq y_3$).

3.4 Training and Evaluating Classifiers

We developed a pipeline to train and evaluate single-label and multi-label classifiers.

For the multi-label setting, it takes the source data, a pairwise similarity matrix for the texts, and a minimum similarity threshold, and produces a

[9] All native French speakers, two from Canada and one from France.

[10] A slightly different method would be to first identify sets of neighbouring texts, and assign the combined label set to all of these. This might increase the average number of labels per text, but it would also assume that texts belonging to the same neighbour set should be treated as neighbours even if their similarity measure is below the threshold.

dataset for multi-label classification, by combining the labels of duplicates and near-duplicates that have more than one unique label. It also produces a single-label representation of that data, by creating duplicates both within and across classes, as in the original data. Finally, it creates a single-label version without in-class duplicates. We also create these three representations of the data using the original labels rather than the combined labels.

The texts are randomly split into training, development and test sets (85%, 5% and 10%, respectively). The same split of texts is used for single-label and multi-label settings.

On each of the training sets, we fine-tuned a pre-trained French language model, namely CamemBERT (Martin et al., 2020), which uses the RoBERTa architecture and training procedure (Liu et al., 2019). This was the most successful approach on the FDI shared task at VarDial 2022 (Aepli et al., 2022). We downloaded the `camembert-base` checkpoint from the HuggingFace repository of pre-trained models.[11] This model has 110 million parameters, and was pre-trained on the French portion of the OSCAR corpus (Ortiz Suárez et al., 2019; Ortiz Suárez et al., 2020; Abadji et al., 2021).

Given that we use a transformer architecture, training a multi-label classifier rather than a single-label one only involves a few changes to the output layer (or head) and the representation of the targets.

For the single-label classifiers, we add a randomly initialized softmax output layer and use the cross-entropy loss function. Targets are represented as a single integer class ID for each example.

For the multi-label classifiers, we feed the output logits to a sigmoid activation function and use the binary cross-entropy loss function. Targets are represented as a binary vector indicating which classes a given example belongs to.

The models are fine-tuned using the AdamW optimizer (Loshchilov and Hutter, 2019) with a learning rate of 5×10^{-5} and a batch size of 8 for 3 epochs. These were the hyperparameter settings used by Bernier-Colborne et al. (2022) in the FDI shared task to fine-tune their open run 2 model that achieved the highest score (without ensembling) on the development set.

In the single-label setting, the model produces a probability distribution over all classes, and predicts the most likely class for each example. In the multi-label setting, the model produces a probability for each class, and the predicted labels are all classes for which that probability is greater than 0.5. We do not apply any calibration methods to either the single-label or the multi-label classifiers that we trained.

Both single-label and multi-label models were evaluated on the same test examples, by computing the F1-score of each class, as implemented in `sckikit-learn`.[12] Note that for class-wise F1-scores, the predicted and gold labels are binary, and the score is computed in exactly the same way for single-label and multi-label settings. We also report the macro-averaged F1-score (class-wise average) and weighted F1-score (class-wise average weighted by the support of each class). Macro-averaged F1 is the more common evaluation measure for language identification, but we also report weighted average for completeness.

It is important to note that the scores reported in this paper can not be compared to the scores achieved on the shared task, as our random split of the data is different. In particular, we did not keep the cross-domain split in the original data, because it was not relevant to the problem explored in this paper. As a consequence, our scores are considerably higher.

We evaluate the classifiers both on unambiguous examples, i.e. examples that belong to only one class in the original dataset, and on ambiguous examples, including the near-duplicates with high similarity that belong to more than one class.

Note that training a multi-label classifier incurs no extra cost compared to a single label classifier. However, our procedure for identifying near-duplicate pairs of texts, which we use to enrich an existing dataset, does incur additional cost, as mentioned in the Limitations section below.

4 Results

4.1 Identification of Ambiguous Near-duplicates

Analyzing the exact duplicates in the dataset shows that there are 81 texts that belong to more than one dialect. However, if we extend this analysis to include near-duplicate text pairs, the number of pairs that have different label sets increases sharply. Using the Levenshtein edit ratio with a cutoff at 0.8, we obtain 615,932 near-duplicate text pairs, and

[11] `https://huggingface.co/camembert-base`

[12] `https://scikit-learn.org/stable/modules/generated/sklearn.metrics.f1_score.html`

6044 of those belong to different classes. Using the Manhattan similarity with a cutoff at 0.6, we obtain 576,722 near-duplicates, 3567 of which are ambiguous.

If we look at the most frequent edit operations, using both similarity measures, the most frequent edit operations by far are those that remove/add/replace punctuation or named entity tokens, all of which seem very unlikely to be dialectal in nature.

Manual inspection of a sample of ambiguous near-duplicates resulted in a disagreement rate, between the three annotators, around 15-20% on the common sets (i.e. 3 or 4 examples out of 20).

To illustrate the three categories we established for annotation purposes, consider the following two examples, where additions and deletions are within square brackets, and deletions are striked out.

An example of category 3 (potentially dialectal changes) is shown below. The first text is labelled CH, the second BE, and their edit ratio is 0.919. The first text contains a short phrase at the beginning that is completely absent from the second text. Note that, were this not the case, this example would likely have been annotated as category 1.

> [~~« Nous avons commencé », a-t-il ajouté. « ~~]["]Des collaborateurs (du ministère) sont venus prendre leurs affaires personnelles[~~,~~] mais nous les avons mises sous scellés et nous ne laisseront personne entrer tant que la situation ne se normalise pas dans le pays [~~»~~][""], a indiqué l[~~'~~][']un des militants à [~~NE NE NE~~][l'agence Interfax]. NE[~~,~~] dont le centre est occupé depuis fin novembre par les manifestants pro[-]européens après la volte - face du pouvoir sur un rapprochement avec [~~NE~~][l']NE NE au profit de la NE[~~,~~] est le théâtre de heurts violents entre manifestants radicaux et forces de [~~NE~~][l']ordre depuis dimanche qui ont fait cinq morts.["]

Another example of category 3 is shown below. The first text is labelled CH, and the second BE, and their edit ratio is 0.924.

> [~~Une ~~][L']inconnu[~~e~~] subsiste quant aux réelles intentions de NE NE qui [~~NE ~~][n']a dit mot lundi des troupes russes [~~présent~~][déployé]es aux frontières de [~~NE ~~][l']NE. Il a en revanche une fois encore vilipendé le refus occidental de lui céder sur la fin de la politique d[~~'~~][']élargissement de [~~NE~~][l']NE et le retrait de ses moyens militaires d[~~'NE de l'Est~~]['NE NE NE NE]. La NE a présenté ces exigences comme étant les conditions d[~~'~~][']une désescalade.

An example of category 2, where only the adverb "notamment" was deleted, is shown below. The Manhattan similarity of these texts is 0.973. The first text was labelled CH, and the second BE.

> Ce phénomène météorologique violent touche particulièrement les immenses plaines américaines. Sur des vidéos amateur prises vendredi soir, on voit ces immenses colonnes noires balayant le sol, illuminées par des éclairs intermittents. Le NE a [~~notamment ~~]été balayé sur plus de 200 miles (320 kilomètres) par NE une des plus longues tornades jamais enregistrées aux NE, selon son gouverneur.

The manual annotation of samples of ambiguous near-duplicates indicates that between 6.25% and 11.25% of near-duplicates identified using the Levenshtein edit ratio exhibited *potentially* dialectal differences (i.e. category 3), though most of these were cases where one text had significant additions compared to the other, such that they might *potentially* contain dialectal markers. As noted above, the examples in category 3 might introduce some level of noise when we combine the labels of near-duplicates. As for "editorial" type changes (i.e. category 2), they represent between 0 and 8.75% of the samples.

As for the Manhattan similarity, the number of texts containing potentially dialectal differences was much higher, 36.25% and 46.25%. Additions with potential dialectal markers account for the vast majority of these. The number of "editorial" type changes was between 0 and 2.5%.

The two similarity measures identified different kinds of differences. The edit ratio was more effective for identifying slight, character-level changes between texts. The Manhattan similarity identified a large number of text pairs where one text had an additional trailing or leading sentence, which might indicate that the data should be split at sentence level rather than paragraph level, or that the paragraph splitting method could be improved.

The classification tests described in the next section were only carried out using the Levenshtein edit ratio as similarity measure, because there was a much higher proportion of potentially dialectal differences in the samples we annotated for the Manhattan similarity, and therefore a higher likelihood of introducing noise in the enriched dataset. We set the minimum similarity threshold at 0.8, which was the cutoff used when the near-duplicates were initially computed.

Using the Levenshtein edit ratio with a minimum of 0.8, we identified 615,932 pairs of similar texts. 6044 of these near-duplicate pairs had different sets of unique labels, and were therefore ambiguous. Among these 6044 pairs of ambiguous near-duplicates, there are 2901 unique texts. 74% of these have only one neighbour (i.e. they appear in only one pair), but the number of neighbours reaches as high as 241 for one of the texts. As for the number of new, unique labels each text will receive from its neighbours, 85% of texts receive only one new, unique label, but almost 15% receive two, and 10 texts (0.34%) receive three. There are also 8 texts (0.28%) that receive no new, unique labels.[13]

The distribution of the number of unique labels in the original dataset and the one we created by combining the labels of near-duplicates are shown in Table 2.

Labels/Text	Original	Combined
1	325,182	322,297
2	77	2,516
3	4	439
4	0	11

Table 2: Distribution of label counts according to the original labels and the combined labels.

The number of texts for each of the training, development, and test partitions we created using the original labels and the combined labels is shown in Table 3.

The most frequently confused pairs of dialects in the training sets, according to the original labels and our combined labels, are shown in Table 4.

Partition	Subset	Original	Combined
Train	Unambig	276,408	273,929
	Ambig	66	2545
Dev	Unambig	16,256	16,132
	Ambig	7	131
Test	Unambig	32,518	32,236
	Ambig	8	290

Table 3: Number of texts using original labels and combined labels.

Pairs	Original	Combined
(BE, FR)	54	1377
(CH, FR)	13	531
(BE, CH)	11	1381
(CA, FR)	0	19
(CA, CH)	0	18
(BE, CA)	0	13

Table 4: Most frequently confused classes in the training sets, using the original labels and the combined labels.

4.2 Classification

The classifiers were compared in the following ways. Using either the original labels of the dataset or the enriched (combined) labels resulting from our analysis of near-duplicates, we train classifiers on all the training data, and evaluate them on two subsets of the test data: ambiguous texts, that belong to more than one dialect, and unambiguous texts. In the single-label setting, ambiguous texts in the training set are represented by duplicating the text for each of its labels.[14] In this case, the model is evaluated on a test set that contains no in-class duplicates, as evaluating on in-class duplicates serves no purpose. In the multi-label setting, both the training and test data is represented in a multi-label format.

It is important to note that, on ambiguous test cases, single-label classifiers are obviously at a disadvantage, as they can only predict one class for a given text.

The results of this experiment are shown in Table 5 and Table 6 for the original labels and the combined labels respectively. When inspecting these results, it is important to remember that there

[13]These are texts that had *exact* duplicates with different labels. If such a text is in an ambiguous near-duplicate pair, and the other text's label set is a subset of this text's label set, then it will "give" one or more new labels to it, but will not receive any.

[14]We also tried training single-label classifiers without any in-class duplicates in the training data, but this made very little differences to the scores. We do not report these scores to avoid unnecessary confusion.

Test Set	Classifier	BE	CA	CH	FR	Average	Weighted
Unambig	Single-label	0.891	0.722	0.898	0.817	0.832	0.877
	Multi-label	0.894	0.670	0.903	0.826	0.823	0.882
Ambig	Single-label	0.533	-	0.571	0.400	0.376	0.490
	Multi-label	0.727	-	0.800	0.286	0.453	0.575

Table 5: Results using original labels: class-wise F1 scores, macro-average and weighted average. Note that there were no CA examples in the ambiguous test set.

Test Set	Classifier	BE	CA	CH	FR	Average	Weighted
Unambig	Single-label	0.891	0.644	0.901	0.818	0.813	0.878
	Multi-label	0.895	0.690	0.895	0.814	0.824	0.877
Ambig	Single-label	0.519	0.000	0.399	0.357	0.319	0.438
	Multi-label	0.815	0.000	0.800	0.561	0.544	0.739

Table 6: Results using combined labels: class-wise F1 scores, macro-average and weighted average.

are only 8 unique texts in the ambiguous test set using the original labels. None of these were labelled as CA, so the F1-score for this class is actually undefined.

On the enriched dataset (produced by combining labels of near-duplicates), the multi-label classifier produces similar accuracy to the single-label classifier on test cases that are unambiguous. The only class that displays significant difference is CA (up from 0.644 to 0.690), but that class is much smaller so it hardly makes a difference overall. On ambiguous examples, however, the macro-averaged F1-score increases from 0.319 to 0.544, for a 0.225 absolute gain (71% relative gain) on the combined data. Results on the original data are similar. Gains on the ambiguous test cases are smaller but still sizeable (+0.077 absolute, 20% relative gain), and accuracy on non-ambiguous test cases is hardly changed overall. To summarize, on unambiguous texts, the single-label and multi-label classifiers achieve similar accuracy, but on ambiguous texts, the multi-label classifier is considerably more accurate.

Note that we do not report overall performance (on both unambiguous and ambiguous examples), because it is almost identical to the performance on unambiguous examples, given that there is only around 1% of ambiguous examples with multiple labels. The main finding we want to highlight here is that multi-label classification improves accuracy on ambiguous examples without sacrificing accuracy on unambiguous ones, and at no extra cost in terms of modelling.[15]

[15]The only extra costs involved here are those of creating the enriched dataset, by combining labels of near-duplicates.

It is important to note that the multi-label classifiers sometimes predict no dialects at all. Knowing that the test set contains no examples that belong to no classes, we could force the classifier to at least predict the most probable label, but we did not do this. The other option is simply to accept that the classifier does not assign sufficient probability to any dialect.

These results show that multi-label classifiers provide additional predictive information about ambiguous cases without degrading performance on unambiguous ones.

5 Discussion

Based on our analysis and experimental results, we argue that the analysis of near-duplicates and particularly ambiguous near-duplicates, should be an integral part of a dataset creation and validation pipeline, and should be described in the documentation for the collection. In the case of French variant identification, this analysis uncovered a number of features and issues with the dataset, such as differing formatting and typological conventions, which evade traditional deduplication, and may cause further problems, such as inconsistent named entity tagging, especially in terms of span. Another issue is that the segmentation of the original news stories into text fragments may differ between similar instances. This suggests that we may improve the near-duplicate detection and analysis by integrating sentence splitting into the processing, i.e. further split segments into individual sentences to detect more duplicates or near-duplicates.

It is important to remember that we do not believe that the ambiguity of duplicate text pairs and near-duplicates is unique to this dataset. In fact, we have observed similar issues in several datasets used for dialect identification in the past. However, further testing, e.g. on datasets in other languages, may be required to better establish the validity of the proposed approach.

Although we show that modelling dialect identification as a multi-label problem is useful, the proportion of ambiguous near-duplicates identified by our methods may seem small and therefore of little significance. If another dataset contained more ambiguous near-duplicates, or if a better method of identifying them were to be developed, the utility of this proposal would only be heightened. Note that in the dataset developed for the "True Labels" shared task at this year's VarDial evaluation campaign (Zampieri et al., 2023), the number of ambiguous examples was between 12% and 32%, which is much higher than the $\sim 1\%$ proportion we identified in the FreCDo dataset using near-duplicate analysis. In the proof of concept presented here, we limited ourselves to semi-automatic methods that exploit a sampling-based re-annotation protocol that is simple and inexpensive. Note also that further refinements to this protocol could reduce the number of disagreements between annotators on the sampled cases.

6 Conclusion

This contribution is motivated by the hypothesis that dialect identification is best addressed as a multi-label problem. By analyzing the similarity between instances in a four-class, French-language variant identification collection, we showed that there are a significant number of duplicates or near-duplicates with essentially the same surface representation and content, but differing reference labels. This is likely an artefact of the data acquisition pipeline, which focuses on the source of the data and provides a single label. By leveraging this finding, we were able to re-label some instances with multiple labels, and show that taking those into account by training a multi-label classifier produces a large increase in performance on the instances with multiple labels, while maintaining the performance on instances with a single label.

We argue that the analysis of ambiguous near-duplicates should be a standard in dataset creation and validation efforts, hopefully producing data that is labelled in a more informative way than by provenance alone.

Additional investigations may provide more insight on how to best represent dialect and variant classification. For example, we could encode multiple labels in a single-label model by encoding combinations of dialects as classes. Another possibility would be to formulate dialect identification as a word-level sequence tagging problem, identifying parts of a sentence that are dialectal markers, and parts that are not specific. This would likely require much more labelling, modelling and training effort.

Limitations

It must be acknowledged that identifying near-duplicates is a computationally intensive task, as it involves pairwise comparisons of a potentially large number of texts. For instance, processing 350K texts, as we did in this work, involves well over 100B comparisons. It took us about two days to compute the Levenshtein edit ratio matrix on this dataset, using a cutoff of 0.8 to speed up the dynamic program. This was done on a CPU server with large amounts of memory. Scaling this to larger datasets may require more efficient methods.

Furthermore, we have only experimented on dialects of the French language. Our method uses no tools that are specific to French, so that we believe that it may be useful on other dialect identification collections. However we cannot guarantee that any findings will generalize to all or any specific language or language families that have different properties.

Acknowledgements

We would like to thank the anonymous reviewers for their helpful suggestions, which we hope have improved this paper.

References

Julien Abadji, Pedro Javier Ortiz Suárez, Laurent Romary, and Benoît Sagot. 2021. Ungoliant: An optimized pipeline for the generation of a very large-scale multilingual web corpus. In *Proceedings of the Workshop on Challenges in the Management of Large Corpora (CMLC-9) 2021. Limerick, 12 July 2021 (Online-Event)*, pages 1 – 9, Mannheim. Leibniz-Institut für Deutsche Sprache.

Noëmi Aepli, Antonios Anastasopoulos, Adrian-Gabriel Chifu, William Domingues, Fahim Faisal, Mihaela Găman, Radu Tudor Ionescu, and Yves Scherrer. 2022. Findings of the VarDial evaluation campaign 2022. In *Proceedings of the Ninth Workshop on NLP for Similar Languages, Varieties and Dialects*, pages 1–13, Gyeongju, Republic of Korea. Association for Computational Linguistics.

Gabriel Bernier-Colborne, Serge Léger, and Cyril Goutte. 2022. Transfer learning improves French cross-domain dialect identification: NRC @ VarDial 2022. In *Proceedings of the Ninth Workshop on NLP for Similar Languages, Varieties and Dialects*, pages 109–118, Gyeongju, Republic of Korea. Association for Computational Linguistics.

Cyril Goutte, Serge Léger, Shervin Malmasi, and Marcos Zampieri. 2016. Discriminating similar languages: Evaluations and explorations. In *Proceedings of the Tenth International Conference on Language Resources and Evaluation (LREC'16)*, pages 1800–1807, Portorož, Slovenia. European Language Resources Association (ELRA).

Mihaela Găman, Adrian-Gabriel Chifu, William Domingues, and Radu Tudor Ionescu. 2022. FreCDo: A large corpus for french cross-domain dialect identification. ArXiv:2212.07707.

Yinhan Liu, Myle Ott, Naman Goyal, Jingfei Du, Mandar Joshi, Danqi Chen, Omer Levy, Mike Lewis, Luke Zettlemoyer, and Veselin Stoyanov. 2019. RoBERTa: A robustly optimized BERT pretraining approach. ArXiv:1907.11692.

Ilya Loshchilov and Frank Hutter. 2019. Decoupled weight decay regularization. In *7th International Conference on Learning Representations, ICLR 2019, New Orleans, LA, USA, May 6-9, 2019*.

Louis Martin, Benjamin Muller, Pedro Javier Ortiz Suárez, Yoann Dupont, Laurent Romary, Éric de la Clergerie, Djamé Seddah, and Benoît Sagot. 2020. CamemBERT: a tasty French language model. In *Proceedings of the 58th Annual Meeting of the Association for Computational Linguistics*, pages 7203–7219, Online. Association for Computational Linguistics.

Margaret Mitchell, Alexandra Sasha Luccioni, Nathan Lambert, Marissa Gerchick, Angelina McMillan-Major, Ezinwanne Ozoani, Nazneen Rajani, Tristan Thrush, Yacine Jernite, and Douwe Kiela. 2022. Measuring data. ArXiv:2212.05129.

Pedro Javier Ortiz Suárez, Laurent Romary, and Benoît Sagot. 2020. A monolingual approach to contextualized word embeddings for mid-resource languages. In *Proceedings of the 58th Annual Meeting of the Association for Computational Linguistics*, pages 1703–1714, Online. Association for Computational Linguistics.

Pedro Javier Ortiz Suárez, Benoît Sagot, and Laurent Romary. 2019. Asynchronous pipelines for processing huge corpora on medium to low resource infrastructures. In *Proceedings of the Workshop on Challenges in the Management of Large Corpora (CMLC-7) 2019. Cardiff, 22nd July 2019*, pages 9 – 16, Mannheim. Leibniz-Institut für Deutsche Sprache.

Chengwen Wang, Qingxiu Dong, Xiaochen Wang, Haitao Wang, and Zhifang Sui. 2022. Statistical dataset evaluation: Reliability, difficulty, and validity. ArXiv:2212.09272.

Marcos Zampieri, Kai North, Tommi Jauhiainen, Mariano Felice, Neha Kumari, Nishant Nair, and Yash Bangera. 2023. Language variety identification with true labels. ArXiv:2303.01490.

Fine-Tuning BERT with Character-Level Noise for Zero-Shot Transfer to Dialects and Closely-Related Languages

Aarohi Srivastava and **David Chiang**
University of Notre Dame, USA
{asrivas2,dchiang}@nd.edu

Abstract

In this work, we induce character-level noise in various forms when fine-tuning BERT to enable zero-shot cross-lingual transfer to unseen dialects and languages. We fine-tune BERT on three sentence-level classification tasks and evaluate our approach on an assortment of unseen dialects and languages. We find that character-level noise can be an extremely effective agent of cross-lingual transfer under certain conditions, while it is not as helpful in others. Specifically, we explore these differences in terms of the nature of the task and the relationships between source and target languages, finding that introduction of character-level noise during fine-tuning is particularly helpful when a task draws on surface level cues and the source-target cross-lingual pair has a relatively high lexical overlap with shorter (i.e., less meaningful) unseen tokens on average.

1 Introduction

Contemporary NLP methods such as BERT (Devlin et al., 2019), with the large amount of knowledge contained within their parameters, paired with the relatively low computational power required to fine-tune them for a downstream task, have taken over many NLP applications. Indeed, several monolingual and multilingual BERT models are available that encompass a number of languages (Devlin et al., 2019). However, the strength of these models is tied to the availability of data, and the large amounts of data required to pre-train such models exclude some languages for which it is difficult to collect large amounts of written text.

The scarcity of data becomes more severe with dialects and language varieties. In fact, the very nature of dialects as an evolving form of the language, often spoken rather than written, with various social and cultural nuances, can make it difficult to develop systems tailored to specific dialects. In many applications, users may span a continuum of idiolects, some falling into established dialects and others not. It may therefore be impossible to train a system on even a small amount of data in every idiolect. In this paper, we consider *zero-shot cross-lingual transfer*, which we define strictly as any scenario in which the test data is of a language variety not included in any stage of training. For instance, we may fine-tune a standard Italian BERT model on standard Italian sentiment analysis data, and then perform inference on Neapolitan (a variety closely related to standard Italian). We call standard Italian the *source* language, and Neapolitan the *target* language.

The mismatch in BERT's performance when evaluating on the source versus target language can arise for a variety of reasons depending on the properties of the target language. For example, some language varieties may have similar morphology but different vocabulary, so that BERT may encounter completely new words when tested on the dialect. An example of this is the use of "soda" in some regions of the United States and "pop" in others to refer to a carbonated beverage; a model trained only on the "soda" varieties may have difficulty identifying the meaning of "pop" if it appears in test data.

In other cases, language varieties may have similar vocabulary, but phonological, morphological, or orthographic differences may throw off the subword tokenization method used by the model. A simple example is the distinction in spelling between "color" (American English) and "colour" (British English); if a model were trained exclusively on American English and "colour" was not part of its vocabulary, at test time, "colour" would be tokenized differently than "color," possibly resulting in a different interpretation by the model.

In this work, we focus on the second type of dialectal variation. Following Aepli and Sennrich (2022), we study how introducing character-level noise in training can improve performance for zero-shot cross-lingual transfer between closely-related

Tenth Workshop on NLP for Similar Languages, Varieties and Dialects (VarDial 2023), pages 152–162
May 5, 2023

languages. Aepli and Sennrich's (2022) method is a two-step process. The first step is *continued pre-training* of BERT on three types of data: target language data, un-noised source language data, and noised source language data. The second step is *fine-tuning* on noised task data in the source language. Here, we only use fine-tuning, and we only use source-language data, making our method strictly zero-shot. We explore the next questions: which techniques of character-level noising help cross-lingual transfer the most, and in which situations should one expect character-level noising to work best?

To explore these questions, we fine-tune monolingual BERT models on three sentence-level classification tasks: intent classification, topic identification, and sentiment analysis. We introduce multiple variations on the method of noising in order to optimize cross-lingual transfer. We test our methods on an assortment of unseen languages, some closely-related and some more distant relatives. For the intent classification task, our systems work almost perfectly, that is, they perform nearly as well on the target language as on the source language. We also boost task performance in less closely-related languages (in the same and different families). Furthermore, we find that we can obtain even bigger improvements by using more noise, and we find that exposing the model to more variations of the data during fine-tuning also helps. Finally, we explore the conditions for cross-lingual transfer needed for our method to be successful.

2 Background and Related Work

2.1 Fine-tuning BERT for Dialectal NLP

There are many previous findings that fine-tuning a BERT model on a specific task involving dialectal data leads to high performance on the task with dialectal test data. Examples include sentiment analysis on Arabic dialects (Abdel-Salam, 2022; Fsih et al., 2022; Husain et al., 2022), hate speech detection for Egyptian-Arabic (Ahmed et al., 2022), part-of-speech tagging for North-African Arabizi (Srivastava et al., 2019), and sentiment analysis for Hong Kong Chinese (Li et al., 2022). The success in diverse applications of the general method informs our decision to stay within the paradigm of BERT fine-tuning; however, without task-labeled fine-tuning data available in the test dialect/language, we must do something else in the fine-tuning step (in our case, inducing character-level noise) in order to facilitate zero-shot cross-lingual transfer.

2.2 Adversarial Learning

Adversarial learning has been employed in the space of zero-shot cross-lingual transfer with success (Ponti et al., 2018; Huang et al., 2019; He et al., 2020; Dong et al., 2020). However, this line of work draws on additional learning techniques and/or model architectures (e.g., BiLSTMs and GANs), expending extra computation for training, rather than working within the scope of fine-tuning; additionally, adversarial attacks are often done in the embedding space rather than to the words themselves. At the same time, it provides an intuition that inclusion of adversarial examples in training can be an effective tool in various applications.

2.3 Zero-Shot Cross-Lingual Transfer

In Section 1, we gave a narrow definition of zero-shot transfer as using no target-language data at all during training. For example, fine-tuning standard Italian BERT on standard Italian, then testing on Neapolitan, would meet our definition. Note that it is possible for the pre-training data of Italian BERT to contain Neapolitan text given that the pre-training data is constructed by scraping various online sources (Devlin et al., 2019); however, because the presence of Neapolitan text would likely be accidental in the pre-training, we do not control for this. In contrast, if the source language is Italian and the target language is Spanish, and we were to use multilingual BERT as the pre-trained model, we would not consider this zero-shot cross-lingual transfer, as multilingual BERT includes Spanish as one of the intentional training languages.

All past work in zero-shot cross-lingual transfer that we are aware of has used some target-language data during training, whether by using a multilingual model or by introducing new data from the target language at some stage. Approaches involving meta-learning (Nooralahzadeh et al., 2020) and adapter layers (Vidoni et al., 2020; Parović et al., 2022) add a component to the model and train it specifically to the target language. Under the BERT-based paradigm, Wang et al. (2019) learn contextual word alignments to align the contextualized embeddings in the source and target language, which requires parallel text in the source and target languages. Tian et al. (2021) fine-tune BERT in the source language, then generate "silver labels" in the target language and iteratively fine-tune on those; although this doesn't require parallel data, it still requires target-language data. Huang et al. (2021) employ adversarial training and randomized smoothing for zero-shot cross-lingual transfer; though their method does not introduce additional data from the target language during training, they work with multilingual models that include the target languages in the pre-training. As described above (Section 1), the method Aepli and Sennrich (2022) use is directly related to ours, but is not strictly zero-shot, because continued pre-training uses target-language data.

3 Methods

Our experiments focus on fine-tuning monolingual language models on same-language data, and testing for zero-shot cross-lingual transfer to other languages, inducing noise in the fine-tuning data to facilitate this transfer. Building on Aepli and Sennrich's (2022) promising finding that character-level noise can be used as a conduit for cross-lingual transfer between closely-related languages, we introduce a range of options for applying character noise in order to explore how we can better leverage the benefits of character-level noise for zero-shot cross-lingual transfer.

3.1 Model

The models we use in our experiments are all BERT-type models (Devlin et al., 2019) with one additional fine-tuning layer for sentence-level classification. We use the base size (12 Transformer encoder layers) of the relevant monolingual BERT models for our tasks, topped with a linear classifier which maps the start-of-sentence `CLS` token to a sentence-level class. In our setup, the pre-trained model is fine-tuned on one of three sentence-level classification tasks: intent classification, topic identification, and sentiment analysis. All models used are the uncased versions for simplicity and consistency. In an effort to minimize computation and stick to the zero-shot case, a distinction we make from Aepli and Sennrich's (2022) work is to limit experiments to fine-tuning only (no continued pre-training).

3.2 Noising Technique

Our noising technique is similar to that of Aepli and Sennrich (2022). We begin with raw text, and we define a word to be any continuous substring of letters (identified using Python's `isalpha` function). For each word, with probability p we apply noise to the word, and with probability $1 - p$ we leave the word unchanged. We leave non-words (for example, numbers, symbols, and punctuation) unchanged, as we expect variation between closely related languages to primarily affect words. We express p as a percentage and refer to it as the *noise level*. Noise is applied at a single, randomly selected character position in the word, meaning that noise can only be applied to a word up to one time.

We include four possible types of character-level noise in the fine-tuning data. Three are in common with Aepli and Sennrich (2022): *insertion*, *deletion*, and *replacement*. We also add *swapping* between adjacent letters. We describe the noising technique below (Section 3.3). All four of these operations are present in cases of dialectal variation. For example, American English spells words like *color* with an *or* ending, while the British English spelling has an insertion of *u* as in *colour* (or vice versa, there is a deletion from British to American English). Metathesis results in swapping adjacent sounds (sometimes realized in orthography), such as *ask* in standard English and *aks* in some varieties.

As insertion and replacement require inclusion of an additional character outside those in the word, the character is chosen from the alphabet of the language of the noised text. For example, if the text to apply noise to is in English, the alphabet would consist of letters *a* through *z*, while for German, the alphabet would also consist of umlaut vowels (*ä*, *ö*, *ü*) and the eszett (*ß*). All random selections are uniform within the set of possibilities. Below, we exemplify how each type of noise may be applied by taking the example of the word *straw*:

- *Insert* a randomly selected alphabet letter ("j") at a randomly selected index of the word (index 1): *sjtraw*.
- *Delete* the letter at a randomly selected index of the word (index 2): *staw*.
- *Replace* the letter at a randomly selected index of the word (index 3) with a randomly selected alphabet letter ("o"): *strow*.
- *Swap* the letter at a randomly selected index of the word (not including the final index of the word) with the subsequent letter of the word: *strwa*.

3.3 Noising Variations

Aepli and Sennrich (2022) used 10–15% character-level noise in their fine-tuning data and found their method to be effective in promoting cross-lingual transfer. Given the promise of their result, we introduce two dimensions along which to vary the noise application: noise level and composition of fine-tuning data. In addition to the baseline (0% noise level), we employ higher levels of noise: 25%, 50%, 75%, and 100% of words.

Because the goal is to expose BERT to different spellings and tokenizations of the same word during fine-tuning, we include multiple copies of the fine-tuning data, each with some difference in noise. The more copies we include, the more we might expect the model to adapt to surface-level variation in the context of the task.

We tried two possible compositions: *joint* and *stacked*. In the *joint* composition, we include two copies of the fine-tuning data: the first copy is the original data without noise, and the second copy is noised using all four types of noise in equal proportion. In the *stacked* composition, we include five copies of the fine-tuning data: the first copy is, once again, the original data without noise, and the remaining copies are noised with each of the four types of noise, respectively. Including multiple copies allows the model to see the same sentences during fine-tuning with variations in spelling (and thereby the token sequence).

For reference, assuming a noise level of 50%, the compositions would appear as follows:

- Joint-composition:
  1. Original data (0% noise level)
  2. Noised data: 12.5% each of insertion, deletion, replacement, and swapping noise.
- Stacked-composition:
  1. Original data (0% noise level)
  2. Insertion-noised data (50% noise level)
  3. Deletion-noised data (50% noise level)
  4. Replacement-noised data (50% noise level)
  5. Swapping-noised data (50% noise level)

4 Experiments

In order to evaluate the effectiveness of inducing character-level noise for zero-shot cross-lingual transfer under the various settings described in Section 3.3, we test on three tasks: intent classification, topic identification, and sentiment analysis. All three tasks are sentence-level classification tasks; however, each task has unique challenges that can bolster or break compatibility with our approach. We are interested in seeing how noise can help in each of these scenarios.

4.1 Tasks

The intent classification task we use is xSID (van der Goot et al., 2021), a benchmark for cross-lingual slot and intent detection that includes parallel labeled data in 13 languages. The xSID dataset was drawn from the English Snips (Coucke et al., 2018) and cross-lingual Facebook (Schuster et al., 2019) datasets and translated to the other languages. We take German (de) and Italian (it) to be the source languages in our experiments; the training data consists of 10,000 sentences each, and the validation data consists of 300 sentences each. We do not use any data from the target languages until inference; the test data for each language consists of 300 sentences. There are 18 total intent labels for classification. For the most part, each sample is a simple imperative or interrogative (e.g., "Remind me to wake up around 6 am tomorrow."). Our intent classification system is included in the 2023 VarDial Evaluation Campaign (Aepli et al., 2023).

The topic identification task we use is MOROCO (Butnaru and Ionescu, 2019), a Moldavian (ro-MD) and Romanian (ro) dialectal corpus which consists of news text from these two language varieties labeled by topic. There are five possible topic labels: culture, finance, politics, science, sports, and tech. There are 21,719 training samples and close to 6,000 validation and test samples each. In contrast to the intent classification data, MOROCO samples contain much longer multi-sentence text. In addition, Butnaru and Ionescu (2019) remove named entities from the data in order to minimize the ability to use surface level cues to solve the task. We take Romanian to be the source language and Moldavian to be the target language for our experiments.

The sentiment analysis task we use is TASS 2020 (Garciá-Vegaa et al., 2020), a Spanish dialectal corpus which consists of tweets from five varieties of Spanish: Spain (es), Costa Rica (es-CR), Mexico (es-MX), Peru (es-PE), and Uruguay (es-UY). Given that much of the pre-training data for Spanish BERT (Cañete, 2019; Cañete et al., 2020) comes from European sources, we take the Spain subset to be the source language, and the remaining four varieties to be the target languages. There are three possible sentiment analysis labels:

positive, neutral, and negative. The Spain training subset contains 1126 examples. For each variety, the test data contains close to 1000 examples.

4.2 Fine-Tuning

For each task, we fine-tune the relevant BERT model on task data from a single source language, and test on other related target languages. We fine-tune each model five times with a different random initialization each time, and report the average across the five trials. For intent classification, we take German and Italian to be the source languages, fine-tuning German BERT[1] on the German subset of xSID and Italian BERT[2] on the Italian subset of xSID. For topic identification, we take Romanian to be the source of transfer and fine-tune Romanian BERT[3] (Dumitrescu et al., 2020) on the Romanian subset of MOROCO. For sentiment analysis, we take Spain Spanish to be the source of transfer and fine-tune Spanish BERT (Cañete et al., 2020) on the corresponding subset of TASS 2020.

We fine-tune the baseline model, as well as eight variations to facilitate zero-shot cross-lingual transfer for each task. Recall that the baseline model is fine-tuned only on data from the source language, and the possible variations are in terms of noise level and composition of fine-tuning data. The eight variations all involve fine-tuning with noise – we test all combinations of noise level (25%, 50%, 75%, or 100%) and composition of fine-tuning data (joint vs. stacked). Because the stacked composition includes more copies of the fine-tuning data, we adjust the number of epochs so that each variation is trained for the same number of steps. Thus, the intent classification and sentiment analysis joint-composition models are fine-tuned for 5 epochs, while the stacked composition models are fine-tuned for 2 epochs. However, in the topic identification task, we find that training for 2 epochs in the joint-classification model yields better validation performance than 5 epochs, so we train for 2 epochs in both settings of topic identification.

4.3 Testing

We evaluate each model on test data from multiple target languages in order to determine each model's effectiveness in supporting zero-shot cross-lingual transfer. We also test on the source language to ensure that performance is maintained despite the introduction of noise. Note that tests are restricted to languages that share the same script as the fine-tuning data.

For the German intent classification models, we test on 2 dialects of German: Swiss German (de-CH) and South Tyrolean (de-IT); 3 Germanic languages (phylogenically closest to farthest): Dutch (nl), English (en), and Danish (da), and 1 non-Germanic language: Italian (it). For the Italian intent classification models, we test on one dialect of Italian (Neapolitan, it-NA) and one non-Romance language (German, de). For the Romanian topic identification models, we test on Moldavian. For the Spanish sentiment analysis models, we test on the four Latin American varieties of Spanish included in the TASS 2020 dataset: Costa Rica, Mexico, Peru, and Uruguay.

The results for our experiments (Section 4) are presented in Table 1 (German intent classification), Table 2 (Italian intent classification), Table 3 (topic identification), and Table 4 (sentiment analysis). Each reported score is the average of five trials and accompanied by the 95% confidence interval. Our results demonstrate that our character-level noise intervention boosts performance anywhere from 11 to 40 percentage points across all language pairs tested for intent classification (except English), while maintaining or even raising performance on the source language. We suspect that the approach did not work well for English due to the fact that, unlike the other target languages, English has much more of a loan-word culture, commonly using words from several languages of origin. Curiously, our results also show that the character-level noise intervention was not helpful for the topic identification and sentiment analysis tasks. Below, we investigate the reasons behind the performance boosts in intent classification as they relate to our noise settings (noise level and composition of fine-tuning data), as well as the differences in the tasks (nature of the task and cross-lingual transfer pairs) that result in such a sharp contrast in the utility of character-level noise.

5 Results

5.1 Level of Noise

Our intent classification results demonstrate that noise can be an extremely effective tool in promot-

[1] https://huggingface.co/dbmdz/bert-base-german-uncased

[2] https://huggingface.co/dbmdz/bert-base-italian-uncased

[3] https://huggingface.co/dumitrescustefan/bert-base-romanian-uncased-v1

Noise Level	Comp-osition	de	de-CH	de-IT	nl	en	da	it	Average
0%	N/A	98.2 ±0.6	74.9 ±7.4	59.5 ±8.8	37.0 ±3.9	78.0 ±1.4	38.8 ±4.8	21.3 ±1.3	58.2 ±1.7
25%	Joint	97.9 ±0.4	71.2 ±7.7	67.3 ±8.0	37.1 ±3.9	74.1 ±2.6	39.2 ±4.4	25.3 ±4.1	58.9 ±1.6
50%	Joint	98.2 ±0.8	89.3 ±2.6	85.7 ±3.3	67.6 ±2.0	77.3 ±1.9	62.5 ±4.2	34.9 ±5.6	73.6 ±1.6
75%	Joint	98.7 ±0.3	92.7 ±1.3	89.9 ±2.0	68.5 ±2.2	**79.3** ±1.0	61.9 ±4.2	34.5 ±4.9	75.1 ±1.7
100%	Joint	98.4 ±0.5	94.6 ±2.5	90.4 ±3.9	73.1 ±1.3	78.2 ±1.3	**65.5** ±2.2	**44.5** ±5.0	77.8 ±1.0
25%	Stacked	98.8 ±0.4	91.4 ±4.5	86.3 ±1.8	58.1 ±5.6	77.9 ±1.4	56.0 ±5.6	28.9 ±3.5	71.0 ±2.5
50%	Stacked	**99.0** ±0.4	93.6 ±2.7	**91.7** ±2.2	66.4 ±1.4	78.0 ±3.2	60.4 ±2.9	37.1 ±3.5	75.2 ±1.2
75%	Stacked	98.7 ±0.2	94.1 ±2.2	90.3 ±2.6	71.2 ±5.1	78.0 ±1.7	64.2 ±3.8	41.9 ±4.7	76.9 ±2.0
100%	Stacked	**99.0** ±0.5	**95.3** ±1.7	90.5 ±2.9	**77.0** ±2.8	77.5 ±1.3	63.5 ±2.3	44.4 ±2.7	**78.2** ±1.1

Table 1: Intent classification results for German BERT with 95% confidence interval measured for five trials. Bold numbers indicate the highest results (by absolute comparison).

Noise Level	Comp-osition	it	it-NA	de	Average
0%	N/A	97.5 ±0.6	79.9 ±0.7	31.7 ±5.5	69.7 ±1.7
25%	Joint	98.1 ±0.3	79.9 ±0.4	33.7 ±6.0	70.6 ±1.8
50%	Joint	98.0 ±0.7	90.3 ±0.2	37.0 ±2.2	75.1 ±0.8
75%	Joint	97.7 ±0.3	91.3 ±1.4	42.3 ±6.4	77.1 ±2.1
100%	Joint	97.9 ±0.5	93.1 ±0.5	**45.2** ±3.1	**78.8** ±1.1
25%	Stacked	**98.3** ±0.3	90.0 ±1.0	34.3 ±4.1	74.2 ±1.6
50%	Stacked	97.6 ±0.8	93.2 ±1.2	43.7 ±1.8	78.2 ±1.0
75%	Stacked	97.7 ±0.5	**93.4** ±0.5	42.3 ±3.3	77.8 ±1.2
100%	Stacked	96.6 ±0.8	91.0 ±1.1	44.7 ±2.5	77.4 ±0.8

Table 2: Intent classification results for Italian BERT with 95% confidence interval measured for five trials. Bold numbers indicate the highest results (by absolute comparison).

Noise Level	Comp-osition	ro	ro-MD	Average
0%	N/A	77.7 ±0.6	**85.7** ±0.8	**81.7** ±0.5
25%	Joint	77.8 ±0.7	82.2 ±4.5	80.0 ±2.5
50%	Joint	77.2 ±0.7	84.9 ±1.9	81.1 ±1.3
75%	Joint	77.7 ±0.7	83.1 ±2.5	80.4 ±1.1
100%	Joint	**77.9** ±0.8	81.6 ±3.8	79.7 ±2.1
25%	Stacked	75.1 ±0.5	80.0 ±3.5	77.5 ±1.9
50%	Stacked	76.3 ±0.5	83.5 ±1.6	79.9 ±0.9
75%	Stacked	77.0 ±0.5	83.8 ±1.5	80.4 ±0.9
100%	Stacked	77.3 ±0.5	82.6 ±3.7	79.9 ±1.7

Table 3: Topic identification results for Romanian BERT with 95% confidence interval measured for five trials.

ing zero-shot cross-lingual transfer. While Aepli and Sennrich (2022) use noise levels of 10% and 15% in their experiments, we use higher noise levels (25%, 50%, 75%, and 100%). Across our intent classification experiments, we find a trend towards "the more, the better" when it comes to character-level noise – 100% noise is the best (comparing the average scores across all languages). In German intent classification, for transfer to closely-related varieties (de-CH) and de-IT), our intervention is capable of boosting performance very close to the German performance itself. We also nearly double performance for the other, less closely-related languages tested, including the non-Germanic language tested, Italian, though there is still a big distance to the German performance. Similarly, in Italian intent classification, we are able to bring Neapolitan performance close to the Italian source performance, and we even raise accuracy for German, a non-Romance language.

These takeaways from the intent classification task show that character-level noise can be an extremely effective agent for cross-lingual transfer for both close (dialects) and more distant (different families) language pairs. However, while it is nearly enough to bring about comparable performance for closely related languages, it is of course not enough to do the same for more distant language pairs.

5.2 Composition of Fine-tuning Data

In conjunction with using higher levels of noise, we also experiment with two methods of composing the fine-tuning data, which integrate the noise differently (joint vs. stacked composition). Recall that under both compositions, one copy of the original fine-tuning data is included; in the joint composition, we include one additional copy that contains four types of character-level noise, while

Noise Level	Comp-osition	es	es-CR	es-MX	es-PE	es-UY	Average
0%	N/A	66.9 ±2.2	62.6 ±1.9	66.6 ±2.3	49.6 ±3.0	**64.4** ±1.9	**61.5** ±1.6
25%	Joint	**67.3** ±0.7	62.7 ±1.3	66.9 ±0.6	47.6 ±2.0	63.0 ±1.0	61.2 ±0.5
50%	Joint	65.8 ±1.5	**63.4** ±1.3	66.9 ±1.0	49.4 ±2.6	64.1 ±1.9	61.4 ±0.7
75%	Joint	67.0 ±1.7	61.7 ±1.8	66.1 ±2.7	48.7 ±3.0	63.6 ±2.0	61.0 ±0.7
100%	Joint	66.3 ±1.8	62.5 ±1.8	66.0 ±1.7	**49.9** ±3.0	63.3 ±0.8	61.3 ±0.6
25%	Stacked	66.3 ±1.2	61.8 ±1.4	66.9 ±1.8	49.1 ±2.0	63.7 ±1.7	61.2 ±0.6
50%	Stacked	66.7 ±1.0	62.7 ±2.2	66.9 ±0.9	47.5 ±1.8	63.7 ±1.9	61.1 ±1.2
75%	Stacked	66.0 ±1.9	63.2 ±1.1	66.0 ±1.6	48.9 ±1.8	64.2 ±1.5	61.2 ±0.6
100%	Stacked	67.2 ±1.1	61.3 ±2.3	**68.4** ±0.7	45.3 ±3.0	62.7 ±0.9	60.7 ±1.1

Table 4: Sentiment analysis results for Spanish BERT with 95% confidence interval measured for five trials. Bold numbers indicate the highest results (by absolute comparison).

Source	Target	Lexical Overlap (%)	Average Length of OOV Tokens
de	de	92.5	5.3
	de-CH	84.7	4.4
	de-IT	89.1	4.8
	nl	83.7	4.2
	en	79.4	4.3
	da	83.7	4.2
	it	84.1	4.3
it	it	93.2	5.7
	it-NA	90.2	5.2
	de	87.7	4.4
ro	ro	100.0	N/A
	ro-MD	97.3	6.3
es	es	62.8	5.9
	es-CR	63.0	6.0
	es-MX	61.5	5.9
	es-PE	60.7	6.0
	es-UY	61.2	5.8

Table 5: Lexical overlap measures based on the appropriate test data.

the stacked composition includes *four* additional copies, each with a distinct type of noise. Having more copies of the data, each with varied spelling and tokenization, allows the model to build robustness to such variation. In addition, though the noise level within each copy of the data is the same, including more copies with noise increases the proportion of noise in the data as a whole (over all the copies). We find that the stacked-composition models perform better on average than the joint-composition models for the intent classification task (+4 points in German, +1 point in Italian).

5.3 Lexical Overlap

We introduce a *lexical overlap* metric in order to aid our analysis when comparing results for source-target pairs. We measure lexical overlap in terms of the overlap of the distinct tokens in the fine-tuning data of the source language and the test data of the target language. To do so, we apply the subword tokenizer of the source language BERT to the source fine-tuning data and the target test data to obtain the source and target vocabulary sets, and take the intersection. Given S, the vocabulary of the source *fine-tuning* data, and T, the vocabulary of the target *test* data, we define lexical overlap as $|S \cap T| \ / \ |T|$. The lexical overlap measures are found in Table 5. Romanian and Moldavian have the highest lexical overlap in the topic identification data, while the Spanish varieties have the lowest lexical overlap in the sentiment analysis data. Moreover, while the overlap between the fine-tuning and test data in the source language is high for German and a complete match for Romanian, it is low for Spain Spanish, indicating that the sentiment analysis task poses an additional challenge of high lexical variation within the corpus.

To strengthen our comparison of the source and target language, we also introduce a measurement to understand what kinds of tokens are present in the target vocabulary but absent from the source vocabulary. We calculate the average length (in characters) of the out of vocabulary target language tokens. A shorter average length indicates that the tokens from the target data that are not present in the source data are short subwords, while a longer average length indicates that the target data includes longer, more meaningful subwords that are not in the source data. An example from the data would be the use of "Alarm" in German text and "Wecker" in Swiss German text; both are in the vocabulary of German BERT; however, because the former is seen more often in association with alarm-related intent labels during fine-tuning, it can be difficult for the model to recognize "Wecker" in this context during inference. However, character-level noise clearly does not address the "Alarm" vs. "Wecker" case as there is no surface-level resemblance, so we would not expect to see improvement for language pairs with a longer average length of out-of-vocabulary tokens. We do expect to see improvement for language pairs with a shorter average length of out-of-vocabulary tokens.

5.4 Nature of the Task

The nature of the task seems to dictate the extent to which boosting unseen language performance via noise in fine-tuning is possible. As described above, success in the intent classification task often comes down to lexical pattern recognition. For example, sentences in the data might explicitly include "set alarm to..." when the intent label is set-alarm. As a result, we are able to reach near-perfect accuracy in the baseline for German (98%). However, when it comes to related varieties like Swiss German and South Tyrolean, despite the variations often being small in key intent-related words, the baseline is not able to perform well as it is not robust to such variation. By including noise in the data, as the results show, we are able to make the model more robust to such variation and see large boosts in performance for all languages. An illustrative example from xSID (van der Goot et al., 2021) is as follows:

English: Is it going to be sunny today?

German: Wird es heute sonnig?

Swiss German: Isches hüt sunnig?

The word "sunny" is likely enough to cue the model to weather-related intent labels. In German, it is "sonnig," while in Swiss German, it is "sunnig." This small one-character replacement is enough to change German BERT's subword tokens from "sonn" and "ig" to "sun" and "nig," and because embeddings are tied to tokens, this small difference in spelling can propagate and lead to downstream errors. Including random character-level noise in fine-tuning helps the model deal with small variations like this.

In contrast, the topic identification and sentiment analysis tasks are difficult to solve simply by surface-level cues. The baseline performances are indicative of this difficulty: Romanian baseline performance is 77.7%, and es baseline performance is 66.9% (as opposed to the near-perfect German and Italian intent classification baseline scores). Recall that the authors of the MOROCO dataset (Butnaru and Ionescu, 2019) replace all named entities with NE placeholders, so it is intentionally made difficult to use surface-level cues for topic identification. Moreover, the low lexical overlap between the fine-tuning and test data for the source Spanish variety (es) is indicative of higher lexical variation within the data, meaning surface-level patterns learned during fine-tuning would not be as helpful at inference. Though noise makes the model more robust to seeing variations at the *surface* level, these two task settings require deeper cues, so other techniques may be required to further facilitate cross-lingual transfer in such cases.

5.5 Source-Target Pairs

The utility of character-level noise for German and Italian intent classification but not Romanian-Moldavian topic identification or Spanish sentiment analysis can be explained in part by the nature of the tasks themselves. However, we can learn even more by examining the differences in the source-target language pairs. Examining the lexical overlap measures for the language pairs (Table 5), we see that the pairs with the highest lexical overlap are Romanian-Moldavian and Italian-Neapolitan, followed closely by the other German- and Italian-sourced pairs. The Spanish pairs have the lowest lexical overlap. Lexical overlap leaves open the question of what does not overlap – we measure this in terms of the average length of the target language tokens that are out of the vocabulary of the source language, as described in Section 5.3. Romanian- and Spanish-sourced pairs have higher average lengths, while German- and Italian-sourced pairs have lower average lengths.

Lower lexical overlap paired with high average length suggests that not only does the test data differ substantially from the fine-tuning data, but the differences are in the form of longer subword tokens that could contribute greatly to the meaning of the sentence as a whole. As described in Section 5.3, character-level noise can only do so much to help when the differences are on the order of long subword tokens. As a result, a case where there is lower lexical overlap as well as high average length of out-of-vocabulary (OOV) tokens would not be a good candidate for character-level noise to be used to promote cross-lingual transfer; the example in our experiments is the Spanish sentiment analysis task.

In contrast, the Romanian-Moldavian pair has an extremely high lexical overlap of 97.3%, meaning that only 2.7% of the tokens in the Moldavian test data are out of the vocabulary of the fine-tuning data. As a result, though this pair also has the

Noise Level	Comp-osition	de	de-CH	de-IT	nl	en	da	it	Average
0%	N/A	97.6 ±0.5	70.7 ±3.0	91.5 ±2.3	90.9 ±1.6	**91.3** ±3.1	82.0 ±3.6	73.3 ±3.9	85.3 ±2.0
25%	Joint	97.1 ±0.8	73.7 ±4.0	91.7 ±2.5	88.2 ±2.4	88.4 ±0.4	82.3 ±2.7	71.8 ±4.1	84.7 ±1.4
50%	Joint	97.8 ±0.6	82.1 ±2.1	94.0 ±2.0	91.2 ±1.0	86.1 ±4.1	80.3 ±2.0	**76.4** ±1.9	86.9 ±1.2
75%	Joint	98.7 ±0.4	83.2 ±1.7	95.4 ±1.3	**92.3** ±1.3	89.4 ±2.4	82.3 ±3.0	73.4 ±3.2	87.8 ±0.8
100%	Joint	98.5 ±0.6	83.5 ±5.4	96.3 ±2.7	89.4 ±2.4	89.5 ±4.0	82.4 ±1.3	74.7 ±3.4	87.7 ±1.2
25%	Stacked	98.1 ±0.4	80.9 ±2.6	95.9 ±1.1	91.1 ±1.1	90.1 ±5.6	85.5 ±4.1	69.9 ±3.1	87.4 ±2.3
50%	Stacked	98.5 ±0.9	86.9 ±1.6	96.1 ±1.4	88.4 ±3.0	87.3 ±1.9	**87.1** ±0.8	72.1 ±1.5	**88.0** ±0.4
75%	Stacked	**98.9** ±0.3	**87.3** ±1.8	**96.4** ±1.1	87.9 ±3.4	86.5 ±2.7	83.5 ±2.9	70.3 ±1.9	87.2 ±1.3
100%	Stacked	98.8 ±0.6	85.7 ±3.0	95.5 ±1.3	86.6 ±3.7	86.1 ±3.0	82.9 ±3.0	62.5 ±7.8	85.4 ±2.0

Table 6: German intent classification results for mBERT with 95% confidence interval measured for five trials. Bold numbers indicate the highest results (by absolute comparison).

highest average length of OOV tokens, it does not pose the same issue as for Spanish because of the low presence of OOV tokens.

The German- and Italian-sourced pairs strike a happy balance in terms of having a mid- to high-range lexical overlap comparatively, while having the lowest OOV token lengths. Thus, in addition to the nature of the intent classification task itself being compatible with the character-level noising technique, these specific language pairs possess the ideal properties to see improvement by applying character-level noise.

5.6 Monolingual vs. Multilingual

We focus on the monolingual models for our analysis, as those are the cases in which we truly have zero-shot cross-lingual transfer (target language is not included in the pre-training data for monolingual models). However, we acknowledge that mBERT can be an effective tool to promote cross-lingual transfer and test our methods on the German intent classification task (one of our success cases) with mBERT for comparison. We find that multilingual BERT (Table 6) has a higher baseline score than monolingual German BERT (Table 1) for all languages except Swiss German. German, Dutch, English, Danish, and Italian are all included in mBERT's pre-training, contributing to their higher baseline performance. However, the monolingual German model has a higher baseline score for Swiss German than mBERT.

For intent classification, our noise intervention boosts the mBERT baseline scores for all language pairs (except English, once again). The trend of the more noise the better applies here as well; the mBERT model fine-tuned with 100% noise under the joint composition performs the best across the languages. Though mBERT achieves better performance on seen languages than German BERT, the Swiss German results demonstrate that German BERT may be better for related but *unseen* varieties.

6 Conclusion

In this work, we explore two questions: first, when is it a good idea to use character-level noise in fine-tuning as an agent for zero-shot cross-lingual transfer, and second, in cases where inducing character-level noise is helpful, which noising techniques work the best? We fine-tune monolingual BERT models on three sentence-level classification tasks, each with a different source language, introducing several variations in the method of noising for the fine-tuning data. We test on a medley of unseen dialects, closely-related languages, and distant relatives. We find that one of our test settings lends itself particularly well to our method, while the other two do not. This distinction comes down to the nature of the task and the relationship (in terms of lexical overlap) between the cross-lingual source-target pair tested. Our extensions in the space of noising variations allow us to optimize zero-shot cross-lingual transfer to the unseen target languages for the the success case, yielding a boost in performance not only for closely-related pairs, but also for more distant pairs.

Limitations

Though we make an effort to maintain the rigor of our methods and analysis, there are some limitations in our approach which could be addressed in future work. First, beyond the nature of the task data itself, a possible reason that character-level noise would not be appropriate for the Spanish sentiment analysis task is that the TASS 2020 dataset contains considerably fewer training examples than the other two tasks' datasets, so we may not be able to achieve the optimal performance on this task under the BERT fine-tuning paradigm. In addition, to stay authentic to the raw data, we do not apply any special preprocessing (like removing mentions or hashtags from the Spanish Twitter data); however, it is possible that such factors contribute to success in the task. Furthermore, our analysis involves three dimensions of comparison: the nature of the task, lexical overlap, and average length of out of vocabulary words. To validate our analysis, we would have liked to expand the experiments to incorporate all possible combinations of the three factors; however, we were unable to due to limited availability of task-labeled dialect data. Similarly, though we test several variations of the noising scheme, there are many more possible and we can't say definitively whether some other character-level noising scheme would work well for the topic identification and sentiment analysis tasks. Finally, we are able to offer anecdotal insight into why introduction of noise contributes to improvements; however, without a formal error analysis we cannot say for sure. We would like to conduct a thorough error analysis in future.

Ethics Statement

Because our project deals with existing datasets and models, and our method involves synthetic generation of noise, our research process itself does not inherently involve ethical concerns. However, as with any new development, there can always be potential implications of the work that raise ethical concerns. For instance, we discuss methods of applying synthetic noise to text, which could also be used in adversarial attacks. Our method is intended for a zero-shot setting in which a user is using a nonstandard variety related to some standard language. This can be a valuable tool; however, one can imagine a scenario in which a code language is developed un-monitored online communication, but with extensions of our method, performance for a variety of tasks could improve on the code language, enabling undesired monitoring.

Acknowledgements

This material is based upon work supported by the US National Science Foundation under Grant No. IIS-2125948.

References

Reem Abdel-Salam. 2022. Dialect & sentiment identification in nuanced Arabic tweets using an ensemble of prompt-based, fine-tuned, and multitask BERT-based models. In *Proceedings of the The Seventh Arabic Natural Language Processing Workshop (WANLP)*, pages 452–457.

Noëmi Aepli, Çağrı Çöltekin, Rob van der Goot, Tommi Jauhiainen, Mourhaf Kazzaz, Nikola Ljubešić, Kai North, Barbara Plank, Yves Scherrer, and Marcos Zampieri. 2023. Findings of the VarDial evaluation campaign 2023. In *Proceedings of the Tenth Workshop on NLP for Similar Languages, Varieties and Dialects (VarDial)*.

Noëmi Aepli and Rico Sennrich. 2022. Improving zero-shot cross-lingual transfer between closely related languages by injecting character-level noise. In *Findings of the Association for Computational Linguistics: ACL 2022*, pages 4074–4083.

Ibrahim Ahmed, Mostafa Abbas, Rany Hatem, Andrew Ihab, and Mohamed Waleed Fahkr. 2022. Fine-tuning Arabic pre-trained transformer models for Egyptian-Arabic dialect offensive language and hate speech detection and classification. In *Proceedings of the 20th International Conference on Language Engineering (ESOLEC)*, volume 20, pages 170–174.

Andrei Butnaru and Radu Tudor Ionescu. 2019. MOROCO: The Moldavian and Romanian dialectal corpus. In *Proc. ACL*, pages 688–698.

José Cañete. 2019. Compilation of large Spanish unannotated corpora. Zenodo.

José Cañete, Gabriel Chaperon, Rodrigo Fuentes, Jou-Hui Ho, Hojin Kang, and Jorge Pérez. 2020. Spanish pre-trained BERT model and evaluation data. In *Proceedings of the Workshop on Practical Machine Learning for Developing Countries (PML4DC)*.

Alice Coucke, Alaa Saade, Adrien Ball, Théodore Bluche, Alexandre Caulier, David Leroy, Clément Doumouro, Thibault Gisselbrecht, Francesco Caltagirone, Thibaut Lavril, Maël Primet, and Joseph Dureau. 2018. Snips voice platform: an embedded spoken language understanding system for private-by-design voice interfaces. In *Proc. Workshop on Privacy in Machine Learning and Artificial Intelligence*.

Jacob Devlin, Ming-Wei Chang, Kenton Lee, and Kristina Toutanova. 2019. BERT: Pre-training of deep bidirectional transformers for language understanding. In *Proc. NAACL HLT*, pages 4171–4186.

Xin Dong, Yaxin Zhu, Yupeng Zhang, Zuohui Fu, Dongkuan Xu, Sen Yang, and Gerard De Melo. 2020. Leveraging adversarial training in self-learning for cross-lingual text classification. In *Proceedings of the 43rd International ACM SIGIR Conference on Research and Development in Information Retrieval*, pages 1541–1544.

Stefan Dumitrescu, Andrei-Marius Avram, and Sampo Pyysalo. 2020. The birth of Romanian BERT. In *Findings of the Association for Computational Linguistics: EMNLP 2020*, pages 4324–4328.

Emna Fsih, Sameh Kchaou, Rahma Boujelbane, and Lamia Hadrich-Belguith. 2022. Benchmarking transfer learning approaches for sentiment analysis of Arabic dialect. In *Proceedings of the The Seventh Arabic Natural Language Processing Workshop (WANLP)*, pages 431–435.

Manuel Garciá-Vegaa, Manuel Carlos Diáz-Galiano, Miguel Á. Garciá-Cumbreras, Flor Miriam Plaza del Arco, Arturo Montejo-Raéz, Salud María Jiménez-Zafra, Eugenio Martínez Cámara, César Antonio Aguilar, Marco Antonio Sobrevilla Cabezudo, Luis Chiruzzo, and Daniela Moctezuma. 2020. Overview of TASS 2020: Introducing emotion detection. In *Proceedings of the Iberian Languages Evaluation Forum (IberLEF 2020)*, pages 163–170.

Keqing He, Yuanmeng Yan, and Weiran Xu. 2020. Adversarial cross-lingual transfer learning for slot tagging of low-resource languages. In *2020 International Joint Conference on Neural Networks (IJCNN)*, pages 1–8. IEEE.

Kuan-Hao Huang, Wasi Ahmad, Nanyun Peng, and Kai-Wei Chang. 2021. Improving zero-shot cross-lingual transfer learning via robust training. In *Proc. EMNLP*, pages 1684–1697.

Lifu Huang, Heng Ji, and Jonathan May. 2019. Cross-lingual multi-level adversarial transfer to enhance low-resource name tagging. In *Proc. NAACL HLT*, pages 3823–3833.

Fatemah Husain, Hana Al-Ostad, and Halima Omar. 2022. A weak supervised transfer learning approach for sentiment analysis to the Kuwaiti dialect. In *Proceedings of the The Seventh Arabic Natural Language Processing Workshop (WANLP)*, pages 161–173.

Guanrong Li, Ziwei Wang, Minzhu Zhao, Yunya Song, and Liang Lan. 2022. Sentiment analysis of political posts on Hong Kong local forums using fine-tuned mBERT. In *Proceedings of the IEEE International Conference on Big Data*, pages 6763–6765.

Farhad Nooralahzadeh, Giannis Bekoulis, Johannes Bjerva, and Isabelle Augenstein. 2020. Zero-shot cross-lingual transfer with meta learning. In *Proc. EMNLP*, pages 4547–4562.

Marinela Parović, Goran Glavaš, Ivan Vulić, and Anna Korhonen. 2022. BAD-X: Bilingual adapters improve zero-shot cross-lingual transfer. In *Proc. NAACL HLT*, pages 1791–1799.

Edoardo Maria Ponti, Ivan Vulić, Goran Glavaš, Nikola Mrkšić, and Anna Korhonen. 2018. Adversarial propagation and zero-shot cross-lingual transfer of word vector specialization. In *Proc. EMNLP*, pages 282–293.

Sebastian Schuster, Sonal Gupta, Rushin Shah, and Mike Lewis. 2019. Cross-lingual transfer learning for multilingual task oriented dialog. In *Proc. NAACL HLT*, pages 3795–3805.

Abhishek Srivastava, Benjamin Muller, and Djamé Seddah. 2019. Unsupervised Learning for Handling Code-Mixed Data: A Case Study on POS Tagging of North-African Arabizi Dialect. Poster presented at First Annual EurNLP Summit.

Lin Tian, Xiuzhen Zhang, and Jey Han Lau. 2021. Rumour detection via zero-shot cross-lingual transfer learning. In *Machine Learning and Knowledge Discovery in Databases: Research Track (ECML PKDD 2021)*, volume 12975 of *LNCS*, pages 603–618. Springer.

Rob van der Goot, Ibrahim Sharaf, Aizhan Imankulova, Ahmet Üstün, Marija Stepanović, Alan Ramponi, Siti Oryza Khairunnisa, Mamoru Komachi, and Barbara Plank. 2021. From masked language modeling to translation: Non-English auxiliary tasks improve zero-shot spoken language understanding. In *Proc. NAACL HLT*, pages 2479–2497.

Marko Vidoni, Ivan Vulić, and Goran Glavaš. 2020. Orthogonal language and task adapters in zero-shot cross-lingual transfer. arXiv:2012.06460.

Yuxuan Wang, Wanxiang Che, Jiang Guo, Yijia Liu, and Ting Liu. 2019. Cross-lingual BERT transformation for zero-shot dependency parsing. In *Proc. EMNLP-IJCNLP*, pages 5721–5727.

Lemmatization Experiments on Two Low-Resourced Languages: Low Saxon and Occitan

Aleksandra Miletić
University of Helsinki
Department of Digital Humanities
aleksandra.miletic@helsinki.fi

Janine Siewert
University of Helsinki
Department of Digital Humanities
janine.siewert@helsinki.fi

Abstract

We present lemmatization experiments on the unstandardized low-resourced languages Low Saxon and Occitan using two machine-learning-based approaches represented by MaChAmp and Stanza. We show different ways to increase training data by leveraging historical corpora, small amounts of gold data and dictionary information, and discuss the usefulness of this additional data. In the results, we find some differences in the performance of the models depending on the language. This variation is likely to be partly due to differences in the corpora we used, such as the amount of internal variation. However, we also observe common tendencies, for instance that sequential models trained only on gold-annotated data often yield the best overall performance and generalize better to unknown tokens.

1 Introduction

Lemmatization consists in finding the base form of a given inflected form. The definition of the base-form for a grammatical category can vary across languages. It can include, e.g., finding the masculine singular for an adjective (*bèlas* 'beautiful.F.PL' > *bèu* 'beautiful.M.SG), or finding the infinitive for a verb (*atten* 'eat.3PL.IND.PRES' > *eaten* 'eat.INF'). The main benefit of lemmatization lies in reducing data sparsity by grouping together all surface forms stemming from the same lemma. It is especially useful for morphologically rich languages, for which the high number of surface forms leads to lower token – type ratios. For such languages, lemmatization is systematically used as a preprocessing step for downstream tasks such as parsing, and it is essential for building efficient corpus querying systems.

We approach this task from the perspective of two low-resourced, non standardized minority languages: Occitan and Low Saxon. In the case of non standardized varieties, acquiring even minimal amounts of manually lemmatized data can be difficult. One of the reasons is the definition of lemmatization itself: in the absence of a common standard, which approach to lemmatization should be adopted? Should lemmatization respect different levels of variation (lexical, morphological, orthographic) which are present in multi-dialect datasets? Or should one variety be chosen for lemmatization purposes and used across all dialects? The former solution allows for the preservation of dialectal differences, but limits the positive impact of lemmatization on data sparsity. The latter is more effective in this respect but it compounds lemmatization and normalization, arguably making the task more difficult. Furthermore, it can be deemed problematic by the speakers of the language in question.

In this paper, we explore both of these approaches: our Low Saxon dataset adopts an interdialectal lemmatization approach, whereas the Occitan dataset's lemmas are dialect-specific. We evaluate the effects of using small, manually annotated datasets for training lemmatization models vs relying on a larger, automatically preannotated corpus. We investigate the utility of developing one general model for all dialects vs training dialect-specific models. Since lemmatization typically relies on PoS information to aid the processing of ambiguous tokens, we look into different ways of using this annotation layer in our corpora by evaluating two learning paradigms: joint learning and classical, sequential learning for PoS-tagging and lemmatization.

2 Related Work

Lemmatization methods based on machine learning can be divided into edit tree-based approaches and string transduction methods. The edit tree-based algorithms (ges; Grzegorz Chrupala and van Genabith, 2008; Müller et al., 2015) derive the sequence of edit operations needed to transform the inflected form into the lemma. The edit tree is

Tenth Workshop on NLP for Similar Languages, Varieties and Dialects (VarDial 2023), pages 163–173
May 5, 2023 ©2023 Association for Computational Linguistics

used as a label for each wordform – lemma pair. The model learns to predict the edit tree and not the lemma itself, thus treating lemmatization as a classification task.

With the advent of neural methods, lemmatization has been recast as a string-transduction task (e.g. Bergmanis and Goldwater, 2018; Manjavacas et al., 2019). Currently, the main contribution of these approaches to the state of the art seems to be better generalization capacities, measured as the model's ability to correctly lemmatize unseen wordforms. Bergmanis and Goldwater (2018) report an important improvement on unknown tokens over non-neural approaches, and similar observations are made by Manjavacas et al. (2019). However, both works remark that the neural networks do not seem to outperform edit tree-based approaches on ambiguous tokens. In general, the capacity to deal with ambiguous tokens is believed to depend on the availability of contextual information, which is supposed to facilitate disambiguation. Bergmanis and Goldwater (2018) use a sliding character window as context, and Manjavacas et al. (2019) condition the decoder on sentence-level embeddings. These efforts to include contextual information do not seem sufficient to beat the edit-based methods on this type of tokens.

The well-suitedness of one type of lemmatization algorithm over the other may also depend on the linguistic properties of a given language. Manjavacas et al. (2019) note that, when evaluating on modern languages, the edit tree-based method outperforms the neural model on both West European and Uralic languages, whereas for Slavic languages the neural model yields better results. These results would, however, need to be confirmed, since Ljubešić and Dobrovoljc (2019) find that the edit tree-based approach beats the neural model on South Slavic languages they investigate.

Lemmatization is often paired with PoS (Part of Speech) tagging. Since inflected forms can be ambiguous as to their lemma, relying on PoS-tags can help the disambiguation process. This information can be exploited as part of joint multi-task learning (Kondratyuk et al., 2018; Manjavacas et al., 2019; van der Goot et al., 2021) or, more traditionally, in a sequential approach, in which the models for two tasks are learned separately, but the lemmatizer relies on the morphological information during training and prediction (e.g. Qi et al., 2020). Vatri and McGillivray (2020) compare lemmatizers for Ancient Greek based on dictionary lookup that exploit PoS information to distinguish ambiguous tokens. Alternatively, some approaches do not rely on this type of information at all (e.g. Bergmanis and Goldwater, 2018), which may simplify lemmatization for low-resource languages.

More generally, lemmatization in the low-resource setting has also received attention in recent work. Bergmanis and Goldwater (2018) evaluate their models both on the full amount of available data and on 10k samples. Saunack et al. (2021) explore the lower bound for training data size on Indian languages: they compare a standard setting with low-resource settings with only 500 and 100 training instances, in which they rely on data augmentation techniques. Saurav et al. (2020) investigate cross-lingual approaches for lemmatizing low-resourced Indian languages.

In this work, we are particularly interested in the low-resource setting, since the gold standard datasets available for Low Saxon and Occitan are limited in size. We also experiment with the cross-lingual and cross-lectal approach by using historical data and related languages. We opt for neural models since we expect a high proportion of unknown tokens in our datasets due to the fact that we are dealing with non standardized languages. We examine both the joint and sequential learning in an attempt to identify the optimal approach to exploit the PoS tagging information present in our datasets.

3 Languages

3.1 Low Saxon

Low Saxon is a West Germanic language spoken by approximately 4.8 million people primarily in the north-eastern Netherlands and northern Germany (Moseley, 2010). Despite official recognition in both countries, no interdialectal standard variety has been established so far.

Dialect classification of Low Saxon is normally more finegrained than the three-fold subdivision we use here. Dutch Low Saxon is traditionally divided into Gronings, Stellingwerfs, Drents, Sallands, Twents, Veluws, Achterhoeks and Urkers (Bloemhoff et al., 2019, 20), but due to scarcity of data we treat it as one group. The traditional classification of German Low Saxon (see for instance Schröder, 2004 and Stellmacher, 1983) assumes an East-West division based on, among others, the history of settlement and the plural suffix of verbs in the present tense. However, we have not found this traditional division to correspond to overall dialect similarity in our previous dialectometric experiments. Therefore, we instead adopt a north-south division following Lameli (2016) and our own observations. The northern group consists of North Saxon and Mecklenburgish - West Pomeranian, and the southern group of Westphalian and Eastphalian. We excluded Brandenburgish, East Pomeranian and Low Prussian due to data scarcity.

Compared with Middle Low Saxon, the number of inflectional categories has decreased, and there is dialectal variation in the number of categories preserved. For instance, while nouns in Middle Low Saxon inflected for four cases, nominative, genitive, dative and accusative (Lasch, 1974), only a few of the southern varieties in Westphalia and Eastphalia still distinguish the dative and accusative (Lindow et al., 1998). Most Low Saxon varieties in Germany distinguish the nominative and the accusative, whereas Dutch Low Saxon typically does not. Usage of the genitive is very restricted in all Low Saxon varieties.

At the phonological level, we find noticeable variation in the number of distinct vowel phonemes preserved and in the ways vowel phonemes have merged. A typical example is the merger of Proto-Germanic *â and lengthened *a[1] that has occurred outside of Westphalia (Niebaum, 2008; Bloemhoff et al., 2019). As a result, we find the same phoneme in *Spraak*[2] 'language' and *Water* 'water' in the north-western dialects, while Westphalian, here Münsterlandic, shows distinct phonemes in *Spraoke* and *Water*.

In addition to the dialectal variation, there is considerable orthographic variation as most Low Saxon writers follow regional writing traditions to different degrees or might devise their own spelling systems. These regional or personal spellings often draw some inspiration from the majority language orthographies. This can be seen, e.g., in the frequent capitalization of nouns by German Low Saxon writers and in the representation of the voiced sibilant /z/ with the grapheme <z> by Dutch Low Saxon writers, while German Low Saxon writers commonly use <s> for the same phoneme.

Our corpus reflects this orthographic and dialectal variation that poses significant challenges to NLP.

[1]This lengthening happened relatively regularly in open syllables.

[2]Notice the apocope of final *-e* that has occurred in most northern dialects. Vowel length is often marked by doubling the letter in closed syllables.

3.2 Occitan

Occitan is Romance language which belongs to the Gallo-Romance group. It is closest to Catalan, with which it forms a subgroup called occitano-roman (Bec, 1970). It is spoken in southern France (except in the Basque and Catalan areas), in several valleys of the Italian Piedmont and in the Val d'Aran in Spain. When it comes to its linguistic properties, Occitan is a null subject language with tense, person and number inflection marks on finite verbs. Number and gender are marked on all components of the noun phrase in many dialects.

The most widely accepted classification proposed by Bec (1995) includes 6 major dialectal groups: Auvernhat, Gascon, Lengadocian, Lemosin, Provençau and Vivaroaupenc[3], each of them with areas of greater or lesser variation. Geographic variation affects all levels of linguistic structure. In this paper we focus on Lengadocian, Gascon, Provençau and Lemosin, due to the availability of annotated material for these dialect groups. Geographical variation affects all levels of linguistic structure. Different phonological processes have resulted in series of wordforms specific to each dialect group, e.g. the word *son* translates to *hilh* in Gascon, *filh* in Lengaodcian and Lemosin, and *fiu* in Provençau. On the lexical level, the word *potato* corresponds to *mandòrra*, whereas it is *trufa/trufet* or *patana/patanon* in Lengadocian. On the morpho-syntactic level, verb inflection varies from one dialect to another, and there is also an important degree of intra-dialectal variation. To illustrate, *we are* corresponds to *èm* in Gascon, *sem* in Lemosin, *sèm* in Lengadocian and *siam* in Provençau based on the most frequent paradigm for each dialect group.

This situation is further complicated by the existence of several orthographic norms, out of which two seem to dominate today: the so-called *Mistralian* orthography, inspired by French writing conventions, and the *classical* orthography, closer to the medieval troubadours' spelling (Sibille, 2002). The data used in our experiments is limited to the classical orthography.

		Dataset	Sent.	Tok.	Types	Sent. len.
Low Saxon	SMALL	All dialects	904	19258	6000	21.30
		Dutch LS	310	6716	2297	21.66
		North Ger. LS	265	5415	1961	20.43
		South Ger. LS	326	7127	2635	21.86
	LARGE	All dialects	126359	2431944	166625	19.25
Occitan	SMALL	All dialects	1522	26122	6196	17.16
		Gascon	255	4170	1429	16.35
		Lengadocian	1113	19315	4499	17.35
		Lemosin	77	1344	596	17.45
		Provençau	77	1293	583	16.79
	LARGE	-	100000	2037723	147070	20.38

Table 1: SMALL and LARGE dataset information for Low Saxon and Occitan

4 Datasets

For both languages, we use two basic datasets: the SMALL dataset is manually annotated and it was available for both languages at the beginning of the experiments reported here. The LARGE datasets are an order of magnitude greater than their SMALL counterparts, but contain only automatic preannotation with PoS-tags and lemmas. In the experiments presented here, the SMALL datasets were used for initial training of our models, and we make use of their dev and test splits for training and for evaluation. The LARGE datasets were used as additional training material in various setups in an attempt to improve model accuracies. In the remainder of this section, we provide some quantitative details and descriptions of each dataset. Note that the LARGE datasets were not annotated at the beginning of our work. The strategies used to palliate this are described in Section 6.

In the case of Low Saxon, both the SMALL and the LARGE dataset stem from the same corpus, described in Siewert et al. (2020), and contain several genres, for instance fiction texts such as fairytales or novels, and non-fiction texts such as letters, announcements or political speeches. The Low Saxon dataset is roughly split into two time periods: 1800–1939 and 1980–2022. The distribution within the dialect groups is as follows: Dutch Low Saxon 20% and 80%, North German Low Saxon 87% and 13%, South German Low Saxon 44% and 56%.

For Occitan, the SMALL dataset is based on the treebank presented in Miletic et al. (2020) and contains predominantly literary texts. The LARGE Occitan corpus contains Occitan Wikipedia articles from 2021, taken from the Leipzig Corpora Collection[4].

For both languages, the gold dataset has also been stratified into dialect groups in order to examine the usefulness of dialect-specific training data and evaluate model performance for different dialects. The gold sets are split into train, test and development sets (except in the case of Occitan, for which two dialect groups do not have a dev set, the total amount of annotated data being too small)[5]. A quantitative overview of gold splits is given in Table 2. The unknown and ambiguous tokens are defined in relation to the gold annotated train set including all dialects.

5 Tools

We make use of two training paradigms: multi-task learning applied to PoS-tagging and lemmatization, in which both tasks are learned as part of the same model, and traditional sequential learning, in which a separate model is trained for each task. We explore the former with MaChAmp (van der Goot et al., 2021) and use the Stanza NLP pipeline (Qi et al., 2020) for the latter.

5.1 MaChAmp

MaChAmp is a toolkit that allows for easy finetuning and joint learning of a wide range of NLP tasks, including PoS-tagging, lemmatization, parsing, masked language modelling and text generation. MaChAmp takes a pretrained contextualized model as the initial encoder and fine-tunes it according to a given set of downstream tasks. Each task has its own decoder for task-specific predictions. The tool also allows an initial round of training on a specific task, and then fine-tune it in a second round of training. We put this functionalty to test in our lemmatization experiments. As the default embeddings, MaChAmp uses mBERT (Devlin et al., 2019). For a detailed description of the tool and the model it is based on, the reader is referred to van der Goot et al. (2021)

5.2 Stanza

Stanza is a Python NLP pipeline currently supporting 66 languages (which do not include Occitan and Low Saxon). The tool supports tokenization,

[3]Names of dialects are given in Occitan (each one in its dialect) as there is no standardized orthographic form for those names in English.

[4]`https://corpora.uni-leipzig.de/en?corpusId=oci_wikipedia_2021`

[5]Since the original corpus did not have *dev* splits, the corpus was re-split into *train*, *dev* and *test* for the needs of the experiments we describe.

	Dataset	train			test					dev				
		Sent.	Tok.	Types	Sent.	Tok.	Types	Unk. (%)	Amb. (%)	Sent.	Tok.	Types	Unk. (%)	Amb. (%)
Low Saxon	All dialects	723	15346	5083	91	1972	1020	26.88	36.76	90	1940	930	26.29	32.84
	Dutch LS	249	5072	1878	31	925	469	24.54	37.73	30	719	410	23.5	32.55
	North German LS	213	4447	1683	26	391	241	24.3	37.6	26	577	352	25.12	33.62
	South German LS	262	5827	2220	32	656	407	31.71	34.91	32	644	406	30.43	32.45
Occitan	All dialects	1196	20551	5292	202	3179	1054	22.11	28.18	124	2392	1009	16.39	31.77
	Gascon	195	3258	1173	35	421	230	26.37	23.28	25	491	267	19.35	33.60
	Lengadocian	884	15494	3937	130	1920	577	19.64	27.50	99	1901	814	15.62	31.30
	Lemosin	56	919	434	16	413	211	27.76	31.76	-	-	-	-	-
	Provençau	61	880	424	16	413	211	23.49	32.69	-	-	-	-	-

Table 2: SMALL dataset split into train, dev and test

multi-word token expansion, lemmatization, PoS and morphological feature tagging, dependency parsing, and named entity recognition. In this work, we utilize its PoS-tagger, based on a biLSTM model, and its lemmatizer, a neural seq2seq model. For more details, please see Qi et al. (2020).

6 Strategies for Creating Large(r) Amounts of Annotated Data

One of the dimensions of lemmatization we explored in this work relates to the size and the nature of the training material. Specifically, we compared the performance of tools trained on small amounts of gold-annotated data with using larger corpora that were automatically preannotated. As mentioned in Section 1, the corpora we used as our LARGE datasets were not annotated at the outset of the experiments presented here. There were, to the best of our knowledge, no freely available models based on neural approaches for the PoS-taggging and the lemmatization of Low Saxon and Occitan. The first round of our experiments was therefore dedicated to creating initial models for both tasks which would allow us to produce reliable automatic preannotation. For Low Saxon, we leveraged an existing historical corpus of Middle Low Saxon to train models that were then transferred to Modern Low Saxon. This had the advantage of using a corpus that was larger than the available gold standard in Modern Low Saxon. For Occitan, no comparable historical corpus was available. We therefore relied on bootstrapping using the SMALL dataset.

6.1 Leveraging a Historical Corpus for the Preannotation of Modern Text

The initial preannotation of the Low Saxon lemmas was done with MaChAmp and the reference corpus Middle Low German[6] / Low Rhenish (Peters, 2017). The reference corpus uses a tagset specifically designed for the needs of Middle Low Saxon. Therefore, we instead made use of the automatic PoS annotation provided by Siewert et al. (2022).

The reference corpus consists of two parts: an annotated part that comes with supradialectal lemmatization following primarily the *Mittelniederdeutsches Handwörterbuch* by Lasch et al. and the one by Lübben (1995 - 1888) and a transcribed part without annotation. We converted the annotated part to the ConLLU-format required by the tools we used. The MaChAmp lemmatization model achieved an accuracy of 89.9% on this data. This model was subsequently finetuned on a small set of manually annotated modern data in order to annotate the rest of the corpus.

Our modern Low Saxon gold annotated dataset does not employ the Middle Low Saxon dictionary spelling, but the *Nysassiske Skryvwyse*[7] 'New Saxon spelling', an interregional spelling based on historical sound correspondences and used by, for instance, the Dutch Low Saxon Wikipedia. As this spelling does not reduce all dialectal variation, the lemma form is, as far as possible, chosen based on the Middle Low Saxon dictionary form, attested Old Saxon forms or Proto-Germanic reconstructions. For future comparisons with the historical corpus, it would be desirable to add a Middle Low Saxon lemmatization layer to the modern data.

The final pretrained MaChAmp model for modern Low Saxon achieved a lemma accuracy of 87%, and a PoS accuracy of 94% on the manually annotated development set. These relatively good results (compared with our later experiments) might be explained by some overfitting as we used the same development set in two consecutive training steps: Original lemmatization finetuning and later joint training of lemmatization and PoS tagging.

[6]Called "Middle Low German" in the official English name of the reference corpus; We otherwise refer to this language as "Middle Low Saxon".

[7]`https://skryvwyse.eu`

6.2 Bootstrapping Using a Small Gold Standard Corpus and a Lexicon

For Occitan, we used MaChAmp in order to train a PoS-tagger and a lemmatizer which would allow us to preprocess the LARGE dataset. Since this was a preliminary experiment with the tool on this language, we opted for training independent models for each of the tasks in order to evaluate the baseline performance for each task on gold data. In this scenario, we did a single training run on the full SMALL dataset, using the default embeddings.

The PoS-tagger achieved global accuracy of 92.26% on the test set comprised of all dialects, the highest being 92.97% on Lengadocian and the lowest 89.10% on Provençau.

The lemmatizer's global accuracy reached 89.30%, ranging from 88.6% on Gascon to 93.33 on Lengadocian and Lemosin (detailed results for the global evaluation are available in Table 6, and for the dialect-specific evaluation in Table 7).

These models were ensembled with the morphological lexicon Loflòc (Vergez-Couret, 2016; Bras et al., 2020). If a wordform was present in the lexicon and only had one entry, it was annotated with information found in the lexicon. Otherwise, the models' predictions were used. Around a third of the wordforms received lexicon-based annotations.

The preannotated corpus was used as the LARGE dataset in the experiments described in the sections below.

7 Large Preannotated Corpora and Small Gold Datasets

Following the creation of additional annotated material, we trained new models with both MaChAmp and Stanza.

With MaChAmp, we used the LARGE datasets for the initial round of training, and the SMALL dataset for the fine-tuning of the model. The fine-tuning was done both with the full SMALL dataset and using dialect-specific subsets of it. We trained for lemmatization and PoS-tagging jointly, resulting in one model capable of performing both tasks.

With Stanza, we trained lemmatizers both on the SMALL dataset on its own and on a combined dataset, concatenating SMALL and LARGE datasets. This approach was chosen because the current version of Stanza does not support retraining. We leveraged the available morphological information in the training process. We also trained the corresponding PoS-tagging models: they are used to approximate a pipeline setup and evaluate the Stanza lemmatizers on predicted PoS-tags.

Additionally, we trained a lemmatizer that does not rely on morphological annotation with both tools. These models were intended as a baseline, but they also correspond to a real-life usecase in which a lemmatized corpus for a given language is available, but contains no PoS tags.

The global lemmatization results are given in Table 6, whereas the dialect-specific results are available in Tables 7 and 8. We report mean accuracy and standard deviation over three training runs on the test set[8]. In addition to results on the full evaluation set, we also report performance on unknown and ambiguous tokens. We consider as unknown tokens those that do not appear in any of the training material. We define as ambiguous all tokens having more than one possible lemma in the training material. In the case of dialect-specific evaluations, we evaluate the dialect-specific model trained using MaChAmp along with the general models trained with both tools. Our goal is to assess if dialect-specific training is useful even if it entails using less training data than for the general model.

7.1 General results

As an overall tendency, Occitan seems to be easier to lemmatize than Low Saxon, with the former's accuracy ranging often around 10% higher than the latter's. In case of the unknown tokens, the difference is even bigger. Given the greater orthographic variation in our Low Saxon dataset, this does not come as a surprise.

The sequential approach of the Stanza pipeline most of the time yields the best results for both Low Saxon and Occitan. Surprisingly, we found the MaChAmp base model[9] to perform best for Low Saxon, with an almost 5% advantage over the finetuned model. On Occitan, finetuning the MaChAmp model does bring an improvement, albeit a small one (around 1.5%)

Large automatically annotated corpora seem to bring some benefit for the overall accuracy but they do not generally outperform the smaller Stanza models which have access to the PoS information. In the case of unknown tokens in particular, we see that the Stanza model trained only on gold data with gold PoS performs best.

[8] The results on the *dev* set are available in Appendix A.

[9] Only trained on a large corpus of automatically annotated data, no finetuning on gold data.

	Tool	Training set	Task	Train cond.	Test cond.	ALL	UNK	AMB
Occitan	MaChAmp	SMALL	LEM	no POS, gold LEM	no POS	91.28$^{\pm 0.42}$	72.22$^{\pm 1.55}$	96.23$^{\pm 0.37}$
		LARGE	POS+LEM	pred. POS+LEM	no POS	91.77$^{\pm 0.23}$	68.54$^{\pm 1.86}$	92.19$^{\pm 0.14}$
		L+S	POS+LEM	pred. POS+LEM	no POS	92.16$^{\pm 0.25}$	67.2$^{\pm 0.33}$	93.05$^{\pm 0.45}$
	Stanza	SMALL	LEM	no POS	no POS	90.35$^{\pm 0.42}$	66.86$^{\pm 1.85}$	95.78$^{\pm 0.0}$
		SMALL	LEM	gold POS+LEM	pred. POS	**93.21** $^{\pm 0.09}$	**78.43** $^{\pm 0.41}$	**96.69** $^{\pm 0.0}$
		COMB	LEM	pred. POS+LEM	pred. POS	92.49$^{\pm 0.08}$	68.4$^{\pm 0.98}$	92.63$^{\pm 0.0}$
Low Saxon	MaChAmp	SMALL	LEM	no POS, gold LEM	no POS	70.74$^{\pm 0.09}$	17.47$^{\pm 0.48}$	88.63$^{\pm 0.26}$
		LARGE	POS+LEM	pred. POS+LEM	no POS	**83.42** $^{\pm 0.21}$	30.19$^{\pm 1.33}$	85.19$^{\pm 0.47}$
		L+S	POS+LEM	pred. POS+LEM	no POS	78.14$^{\pm 0.31}$	20.44$^{\pm 1.18}$	81.2$^{\pm 0.22}$
	Stanza	SMALL	LEM	no POS	no POS	75.33$^{\pm 0.11}$	36.41$^{\pm 0.42}$	82.03$^{\pm 0.0}$
		SMALL	LEM	gold POS+LEM	pred. POS	80.52$^{\pm 0.43}$	**45.66** $^{\pm 1.59}$	**89.42** $^{\pm 0.0}$
		COMB	LEM	pred. POS+LEM	pred. POS	81.31$^{\pm 0.05}$	20.12$^{\pm 0.89}$	82.16$^{\pm 0.0}$

Table 3: Global Lemmatization Accuracy for Occitan and Low Saxon

		Gascon					Lemosin		
Tool	Train	ALL	UNK	AMB	Tool	Train	ALL	UNK	AMB
MaChAmp	L+S	89.66$^{\pm 0.52}$	57.01$^{\pm 1.24}$	90.28$^{\pm 0.57}$	MaChAmp	L+S	**90.91** $^{\pm 0.2}$	**74.42** $^{\pm 1.9}$	94.35$^{\pm 0.46}$
MaChAmp	L+GAS	88.86$^{\pm 0.41}$	54.38$^{\pm 1.24}$	89.58$^{\pm 0.98}$	MaChAmp	L+LEM	87.64$^{\pm 0.57}$	64.34$^{\pm 1.1}$	92.66$^{\pm 0.8}$
Stanza	SMALL	**90.71** $^{\pm 0.75}$	**77.78** $^{\pm 2.79}$	**91.49** $^{\pm 0.0}$	Stanza	SMALL	90.59$^{\pm 0.41}$	72.6$^{\pm 0.8}$	**99.22** $^{\pm 0.0}$
Stanza	COMB	90.06$^{\pm 0.11}$	67.54$^{\pm 1.24}$	89.58$^{\pm 0.0}$	Stanza	COMB	89.79$^{\pm 0.23}$	66.67$^{\pm 1.09}$	92.66$^{\pm 0.0}$

		Lengadocian					Provençau		
Tool	Train	ALL	UNK	AMB	Tool	Train	ALL	UNK	AMB
MaChAmp	L+S	93.08$^{\pm 0.48}$	69.91$^{\pm 0.33}$	92.76$^{\pm 0.69}$	MaChAmp	L+S	91.67$^{\pm 0.0}$	54.67$^{\pm 1.89}$	95.14$^{\pm 0.44}$
MaChAmp	L+LEN	92.56$^{\pm 0.6}$	68.29$^{\pm 0.33}$	92.29$^{\pm 0.8}$	MaChAmp	L+PRO	86.6$^{\pm 0.11}$	52.0$^{\pm 0.0}$	89.55$^{\pm 0.25}$
Stanza	SMALL	**94.42** $^{\pm 0.13}$	**81.35** $^{\pm 0.9}$	**96.54** $^{\pm 0.0}$	Stanza	SMALL	**92.81** $^{\pm 0.31}$	**74.92** $^{\pm 1.28}$	**98.51** $^{\pm 0.0}$
Stanza	COMB	93.72$^{\pm 0.11}$	71.53$^{\pm 1.5}$	92.98$^{\pm 0.0}$	Stanza	COMB	92.08$^{\pm 0.12}$	54.67$^{\pm 1.89}$	93.51$^{\pm 0.0}$

Table 4: Dialect-Specific Lemmatization Accuracy on Occitan

7.2 Dialect-Specific Results

When testing on individual dialects, too, the sequential approach of the Stanza model most often yields a higher accuracy for both Low Saxon and Occitan. As in case of the general tests, we do not find the automatically annotated data to benefit the model performance on Occitan. However, for both North and South German Low Saxon, we observed an improvement of the overall accuracy. Furthermore, we find MaChAmp to generalise particularly well to Lemosin.

When comparing the performance of the general and the dialect-specific MaChAmp models, the finetuning on a small dialect-specific dataset does not bring any improvement except for unknown tokens in German North Low Saxon. The MaChAmp models in fact consistently show a better overall accuracy when finetuned on the general gold train data. Since the general gold train data combines all the dialect-specific train sets, it is reasonable to suppose that these results are driven by the size difference between the finetuning datasets.

For Stanza, a more focused approach – here exclusive training on gold data without adding automatically annotated data – leads to a higher accuracy for lemmatizing unknown tokens. This holds true for both Low Saxon and Occitan, with the exception of Lemosin.

8 Discussion and Conclusion

The overall accuracy results for Low Saxon are noticeably lower than for Occitan, around 10% on average. One possible explanation could be the greater orthographic variation that is likely the reason behind the higher percentages of unknown and ambiguous tokens in Low Saxon seen in Table 2. While our Occitan corpus makes use of the same spelling convention throughout, the Low Saxon corpus contains various writing systems even within the same dialect group. Furthermore, we trained the models for Occitan on major dialects, whereas we used groups of major dialects for Low Saxon. Another reason might be found in the different diachronic structure of the datasets: Whereas the Occitan data mostly comes from the 20th and 21st century, the Low Saxon dataset covers the period

Dutch Low Saxon

Tool	Train	All	Unk	Amb
MaChAmp	L+S	$77.46^{\pm 0.24}$	$11.11^{\pm 1.13}$	$82.39^{\pm 0.22}$
MaChAmp	L+DLS	$76.31^{\pm 0.23}$	$10.65^{\pm 0.66}$	$81.16^{\pm 0.08}$
Stanza	SMALL	**80.41** $^{\pm 0.81}$	**21.3** $^{\pm 4.72}$	**84.45** $^{\pm 0.66}$
Stanza	COMB	$78.93^{\pm 0.11}$	$14.35^{\pm 1.31}$	$81.98^{\pm 0.0}$

(German) North Low Saxon

Tool	Train	All	Unk	Amb
MaChAmp	L+S	$86.77^{\pm 0.8}$	$30.55^{\pm 3.93}$	**90.35** $^{\pm 0.62}$
MaChAmp	L+NLS	$82.65^{\pm 0.32}$	**33.33** $^{\pm 6.81}$	$85.35^{\pm 0.79}$
Stanza	SMALL	$84.79^{\pm 0.92}$	**33.33** $^{\pm 6.81}$	$89.01^{\pm 1.08}$
Stanza	COMB	**89.6** $^{\pm 0.12}$	$30.55^{\pm 3.93}$	$89.01^{\pm 0.0}$

(German) South Low Saxon

Tool	Train	All	Unk	Amb
MaChAmp	L+S	$73.97^{\pm 0.22}$	$45.45^{\pm 0.00}$	$74.49^{\pm 0.26}$
MaChAmp	L+SLS	$72.74^{\pm 0.54}$	$42.42^{\pm 4.29}$	$73.57^{\pm 0.62}$
Stanza	SMALL	$78.15^{\pm 0.56}$	**46.97** $^{\pm 2.14}$	**79.42** $^{\pm 1.22}$
Stanza	COMB	**79.68** $^{\pm 0.08}$	$33.33^{\pm 2.14}$	$78.44^{\pm 0.0}$

Table 5: Dialect-Specific Lemmatization Accuracy for Low Saxon

from the 19th century to the 21st.

This greater variation might be the reason why a sequential approach proves particularly useful for Low Saxon. As a result of the dialectal and orthographic variation, there are many ambiguous tokens that need to be lemmatized differently depending on the writing system and dialect. For instance, the character string *doe* typically refers to the feminine or masculine definite article in eastern Westphalian, where it should be lemmatized as *de*, whereas it should be lemmatized as *du* in Gronings, where it represents the pronoun of the second person singular. In addition, this string can stand for the 1st person singular in the present tense of the verb *doon* ‘to do’ in many dialects throughout the language area. PoS-tagging effectively disambiguates these three usages.

When it comes to Occitan, we noted that the Stanza model trained only on the gold data performs better than its counterpart trained on both preannotated and gold data. This may be due to the genre mismatch between the gold corpus (which is predominantly literary) and the automatically annotated corpus (which is extracted from Wikipedia). MaChAmp's finetuning approach seems to be more robust to this, since the model trained on both preannotated and gold data achieves better general results than the the one limited to the gold dataset.

The different model behaviour we have observed in our two low-resourced languages also warrants a more general question: How faithfully can low-resource scenarios be simulated by using small amounts of data from standardized high-resource languages? As this seems to be a relatively common practice, it would be worth investigating how this approach actually compares to the task it is supposed to simulate.

In conclusion, we found that the sequential approach implemented by Stanza was a good fit for both languages. The amount of training data also seemed to have more of an impact than dialect-level specificity, given that the MaChAmp models finetuned on the full gold dataset systematically outperformed the dialect-specific models.Another common tendency for both languages is the positive effect of using only gold data for training on the performance of the Stanza model over unknown tokens. This is a particularly interesting finding because it could be expected that a larger amount of training would make the model generalize better. It seems that in our case the reliability of the training data was more important.

Data Access

The new annotated corpora created as part of this work are distributed on Zenodo.

The datasets for Low Saxon are available here: `https://doi.org/10.5281/zenodo.7777282`.

The large dataset for Occitan is available here: `https://doi.org/10.5281/zenodo.7777340`.

Limitations

The MaChAmp and Stanza results are not fully comparable as we did not present the performance of dialect-specific Stanza models here. Since Stanza does not allow finetuning, we do not expect the small individual dialect-specific train sets to have a strong effect compared with the much larger amount of automatically annotated data. We defer testing this hypothesis to future work.

Acknowledgements

This work has been supported by the Academy of Finland through project No. 342859 “CorCoDial – Corpus-based computational dialectology”.

References

Pierre Bec. 1970. *Manuel pratique de philologie romane*, volume Vol. 1. Picard.

Pierre Bec. 1995. *La langue occitane*, 6th edition. PUF.

Toms Bergmanis and Sharon Goldwater. 2018. Context sensitive neural lemmatization with Lematus. In *Proceedings of the 2018 Conference of the North American Chapter of the Association for Computational Linguistics: Human Language Technologies, Volume 1 (Long Papers)*, pages 1391–1400, New Orleans, Louisiana. Association for Computational Linguistics.

Henk Bloemhoff, Philomèle Bloemhoff de Bruijn, Jan Nijen Twilhaar, Henk Nijkeuter, and Harrie Scholtmeijer. 2019. *Nedersaksisch in een notendop – Inleiding in de Nedersaksische taal en literatuur.* Koninklijke Van Gorcum, Assen.

Myriam Bras, Marianne Vergez-Couret, Nabil Hathout, Jean Sibille, Aure Séguier, and Benazet Dazéas. 2020. Loflòc : Lexic obèrt flechit occitan. In *Fidélités et dissidences (Actes du XIIe congrès de l'Association Internationale d'Études Occitanes)*, Albi. Centre d'Etude de la Littérature Occitane.

Jacob Devlin, Ming-Wei Chang, Kenton Lee, and Kristina Toutanova. 2019. BERT: Pre-training of deep bidirectional transformers for language understanding. In *Proceedings of the 2019 Conference of the North American Chapter of the Association for Computational Linguistics: Human Language Technologies, Volume 1 (Long and Short Papers)*, pages 4171–4186, Minneapolis, Minnesota. Association for Computational Linguistics.

Georgiana Dinu Grzegorz Chrupala and Josef van Genabith. 2008. Learning morphology with morfette. In *Proceedings of the Sixth International Conference on Language Resources and Evaluation (LREC'08)*, Marrakech, Morocco. European Language Resources Association (ELRA). Http://www.lrec-conf.org/proceedings/lrec2008/.

Daniel Kondratyuk, Tomáš Gavenčiak, Milan Straka, and Jan Hajič. 2018. LemmaTag: Jointly tagging and lemmatizing for morphologically rich languages with BRNNs. In *Proceedings of the 2018 Conference on Empirical Methods in Natural Language Processing*, pages 4921–4928, Brussels, Belgium. Association for Computational Linguistics.

Alfred Lameli. 2016. Raumstrukturen im Niederdeutschen. Eine Re-Analyse der Wenkerdaten. *Niederdeutsches Jahrbuch. Jahrbuch des Vereins für niederdeutsche Sprachforschung*, 139:131–152.

Agathe. Lasch. 1974. *Mittelniederdeutsche Grammatik.* Sammlung kurzer Grammatiken germanischer Dialekte ; 9. Niemeyer, Halle a. S.

Agathe Lasch, Conrad Borchling, Gerhard Cordes, Dieter Möhn, Ingrid Schröder, Jürgen Meier, and Sabina Tsapaeva. *Mittelniederdeutsches Handwörterbuch.*

Wolfgang Lindow, Dieter Möhn, Hermann Niebaum, Dieter Stellmacher, Hans Taubken, and Jan Wirrer. 1998. *Niederdeutsche Grammatik.* Schuster, Leer.

Nikola Ljubešić and Kaja Dobrovoljc. 2019. What does neural bring? analysing improvements in morphosyntactic annotation and lemmatisation of Slovenian, Croatian and Serbian. In *Proceedings of the 7th Workshop on Balto-Slavic Natural Language Processing*, pages 29–34, Florence, Italy. Association for Computational Linguistics.

August. Lübben. 1995 - 1888. *Mittelniederdeutsches Handwörterbuch.* Wissenschaftliche Buchgesellschaft, Darmstadt.

Enrique Manjavacas, Ákos Kádár, and Mike Kestemont. 2019. Improving lemmatization of non-standard languages with joint learning. In *Proceedings of the 2019 Conference of the North American Chapter of the Association for Computational Linguistics: Human Language Technologies, Volume 1 (Long and Short Papers)*, pages 1493–1503, Minneapolis, Minnesota. Association for Computational Linguistics.

Aleksandra Miletic, Myriam Bras, Marianne Vergez-Couret, Louise Esher, Clamença Poujade, and Jean Sibille. 2020. A four-dialect treebank for Occitan: Building process and parsing experiments. In *Proceedings of the 7th Workshop on NLP for Similar Languages, Varieties and Dialects*, pages 140–149, Barcelona, Spain (Online). International Committee on Computational Linguistics (ICCL).

Christopher Moseley, editor. 2010. *Atlas of the World's Languages in Danger*, 3 edition. UNESCO Publishing, Paris. Online version: `http://www.unesco.org/culture/en/endangeredlanguages/atlas`.

Thomas Müller, Ryan Cotterell, Alexander Fraser, and Hinrich Schütze. 2015. Joint lemmatization and morphological tagging with lemming. In *Proceedings of the 2015 Conference on Empirical Methods in Natural Language Processing*, pages 2268–2274, Lisbon, Portugal. Association for Computational Linguistics.

Hermann Niebaum. 2008. Het Nederduits. In Henk Bloemhoff, Jurjen van der Kooi, Hermann Niebaum, and Siemon Reker, editors, *Handboek Nedersaksische Taal- en Letterkunde*, pages 430–447. Koninklijke Van Gorcum, Assen.

Robert Peters. 2017. Das referenzkorpus mittelniederdeutsch/ niederrheinisch (1200–1650). *Niederdeutsches Jahrbuch. Jahrbuch des Vereins für niederdeutsche Sprachforschung*, 140:35–42.

Peng Qi, Yuhao Zhang, Yuhui Zhang, Jason Bolton, and Christopher D. Manning. 2020. Stanza: A Python natural language processing toolkit for many human languages. In *Proceedings of the 58th Annual Meeting of the Association for Computational Linguistics: System Demonstrations*.

Kumar Saunack, Kumar Saurav, and Pushpak Bhattacharyya. 2021. How low is too low? a monolingual take on lemmatisation in Indian languages. In *Proceedings of the 2021 Conference of the North American Chapter of the Association for Computational Linguistics: Human Language Technologies*, pages 4088–4094, Online. Association for Computational Linguistics.

Kumar Saurav, Kumar Saunack, and Pushpak Bhattacharyya. 2020. Analysing cross-lingual transfer in lemmatisation for Indian languages. In *Proceedings of the 28th International Conference on Computational Linguistics*, pages 6070–6076, Barcelona, Spain (Online). International Committee on Computational Linguistics.

Ingrid Schröder. 2004. Niederdeutsch in der Gegenwart: Sprachgebiet – Grammatisches – Binnendifferenzierung. In Dieter Stellmacher, editor, *Niederdeutsche Sprache und Literatur der Gegenwart*, pages 35–97. Georg Olms Verlag, Hildesheim, Zürich and New York.

Jean Sibille. 2002. Ecrire l'occitan : essai de présentation et de synthèse. In *Les langues de France et leur codification. Ecrits divers – Ecrits ouverts*, Paris, France. Inalco / Association Universitaire des Langues de France, L'Harmattan.

Janine Siewert, Yves Scherrer, and Martijn Wieling. 2022. Low Saxon dialect distances at the orthographic and syntactic level. In *Proceedings of the 3rd Workshop on Computational Approaches to Historical Language Change*, pages 119–124, Dublin, Ireland. Association for Computational Linguistics.

Janine Siewert, Yves Scherrer, Martijn Wieling, and Jörg Tiedemann. 2020. LSDC - a comprehensive dataset for low Saxon dialect classification. In *Proceedings of the 7th Workshop on NLP for Similar Languages, Varieties and Dialects*, pages 25–35, Barcelona, Spain (Online). International Committee on Computational Linguistics (ICCL).

Dieter Stellmacher. 1983. Neuniederdeutsche Grammatik – Phonologie und Morphologie. In Gerhard Cordes and Dieter Möhn, editors, *Handbuch zur niederdeutschen Sprach- und Literaturwissenschaft*, pages 238–278. Erich Schmidt Verlag, Berlin, Germany.

Rob van der Goot, Ahmet Üstün, Alan Ramponi, Ibrahim Sharaf, and Barbara Plank. 2021. Massive choice, ample tasks (MaChAmp): A toolkit for multitask learning in NLP. In *Proceedings of the 16th Conference of the European Chapter of the Association for Computational Linguistics: System Demonstrations*, pages 176–197, Online. Association for Computational Linguistics.

Alessandro Vatri and Barbara McGillivray. 2020. Lemmatization for ancient greek: An experimental assessment of the state of the art. *Journal of Greek linguistics*, 20(2):179–196.

Marianne Vergez-Couret. 2016. Description du lexique Loflòc. Research report, CLLE-ERSS.

A Complementary Evaluation Results

	Tool	Training set	Task	Train cond.	Test cond.	ALL	UNK	AMB
Occitan	MaChAmp	SMALL	LEM	no POS, gold LEM	no POS	$93.57^{\pm0.06}$	$78.74^{\pm1.14}$	$95.08^{\pm0.28}$
		LARGE	POS+LEM	pred. POS+LEM	no POS	$93.32^{\pm0.09}$	$76.07^{\pm0.5}$	$91.94^{\pm0.15}$
		L+S	POS+LEM	pred. POS+LEM	no POS	$94.24^{\pm0.17}$	$73.49^{\pm0.74}$	$93.47^{\pm0.29}$
	Stanza	SMALL	LEM	no POS	no POS	$92.84^{\pm0.14}$	$75.43^{\pm0.84}$	$93.1^{\pm0.0}$
		SMALL	LEM	gold POS+LEM	pred. POS	$94.68^{\pm0.03}$	$83.16^{\pm0.21}$	$94.86^{\pm0.0}$
		COMB	LEM	pred. POS+LEM	pred. POS	$93.53^{\pm0.06}$	$74.01^{\pm1.11}$	$91.19^{\pm0.0}$
Low Saxon	MaChAmp	SMALL	LEM	no POS, gold LEM	no POS	$74.72^{\pm0.62}$	$25.48^{\pm1.67}$	$91.84^{\pm0.44}$
		LARGE	POS+LEM	pred. POS+LEM	no POS	$86.69^{\pm0.31}$	$52.01^{\pm0.89}$	$89.14^{\pm0.46}$
		L+S	POS+LEM	pred. POS+LEM	no POS	$81.64^{\pm0.43}$	$56.74^{\pm0.58}$	$83.41^{\pm0.38}$
	Stanza	SMALL	LEM	no POS	no POS	$78.7^{\pm0.23}$	$42.38^{\pm0.9}$	$85.09^{\pm0.0}$
		SMALL	LEM	gold POS+LEM	pred. POS	$82.4^{\pm0.16}$	$47.64^{\pm0.61}$	$92.15^{\pm0.0}$
		COMB	LEM	pred. POS+LEM	pred. POS	$83.54^{\pm0.17}$	$55.79^{\pm2.34}$	$83.95^{\pm0.0}$

Table 6: Global Lemmatization Accuracy for Occitan and Low Saxon. *Dev* set.

		Gascon					**Lengadocian**		
Tool	Train	ALL	UNK	AMB	Tool	Train	ALL	UNK	AMB
MaChAmp	L+S	$93.6^{\pm0.36}$	$69.1^{\pm1.15}$	$93.55^{\pm1.11}$	MaChAmp	L+S	$94.4^{\pm0.14}$	$75.58^{\pm0.95}$	$93.45^{\pm0.1}$
MaChAmp	L+GAS	$92.83^{\pm0.1}$	$69.1^{\pm2.3}$	$92.14^{\pm0.22}$	MaChAmp	L+LEN	$94.12^{\pm0.13}$	$74.03^{\pm1.09}$	$93.25^{\pm0.11}$
Stanza	SMALL	$94.29^{\pm0.2}$	$79.65^{\pm0.99}$	$96.15^{\pm0.0}$	Stanza	SMALL	$94.78^{\pm0.02}$	$84.29^{\pm0.16}$	$94.51^{\pm0.0}$
Stanza	COMB	$90.4^{\pm0.0}$	$68.29^{\pm0.0}$	$87.26^{\pm0.0}$	Stanza	COMB	$94.33^{\pm0.08}$	$76.75^{\pm1.65}$	$92.16^{\pm0.0}$

Table 7: Dialect-Specific Lemmatization Accuracy on Occitan. *Dev* set (there are no dialect-specific *dev* sets for Lemosin and Provençau.)

		Dutch Low Saxon					**(German) North Low Saxon**		
Tool	Train	All	Unk	Amb	Tool	Train	All	Unk	Amb
MaChAmp	L+S	$83.64^{\pm0.75}$	$60.0^{\pm1.26}$	$86.57^{\pm0.61}$	MaChAmp	L+S	$84.49^{\pm0.46}$	$60.49^{\pm1.74}$	$86.7^{\pm0.49}$
MaChAmp	L+DLS	$81.35^{\pm0.13}$	$52.31^{\pm0.00}$	$84.77^{\pm0.35}$	MaChAmp	L+NLS	$80.96^{\pm0.22}$	$60.49^{\pm3.49}$	$83.42^{\pm0.37}$
Stanza	SMALL	$84.2^{\pm0.5}$	$50.26^{\pm2.62}$	$87.55^{\pm0.11}$	Stanza	SMALL	$83.97^{\pm0.46}$	$45.68^{\pm1.75}$	$87.39^{\pm0.95}$
Stanza	COMB	$84.11^{\pm0.35}$	$55.9^{\pm3.84}$	$84.52^{\pm0.0}$	Stanza	COMB	$87.96^{\pm0.08}$	$65.43^{\pm1.75}$	$88.08^{\pm0.0}$

		(German) South Low Saxon		
Tool	Train	All	Unk	Amb
MaChAmp	L+S	$76.82^{\pm0.07}$	$50.34^{\pm0.96}$	$77.63^{\pm0.11}$
MaChAmp	L+SLS	$74.25^{\pm0.71}$	$48.3^{\pm1.92}$	$74.68^{\pm0.88}$
Stanza	SMALL	$78.96^{\pm0.34}$	$42.86^{\pm0.0}$	$81.41^{\pm0.49}$
Stanza	COMB	$78.91^{\pm0.15}$	$50.34^{\pm1.92}$	$79.82^{\pm0.0}$

Table 8: Dialect-Specific Lemmatization Accuracy for Low Saxon. *Dev* set.

The Use of Khislavichi Lect Morphological Tagging to Determine its Position in the East Slavic Group

Ilia Afanasev
National Research University Higher School of Economics
ilia.afanasev.1997@gmail.com

Abstract

The study of low-resourced East Slavic lects is becoming increasingly relevant as they face the prospect of extinction under the pressure of standard Russian while being treated by academia as an inferior part of this lect. The Khislavichi lect, spoken in a settlement on the border of Russia and Belarus, is a perfect example of such an attitude.

We take an alternative approach and study East Slavic lects (such as Khislavichi) as separate systems. The proposed method includes the development of a tagged corpus through morphological tagging with the models trained on the bigger lects. Morphological tagging results may be used to place these lects among the bigger ones, such as standard Belarusian or standard Russian.

The implemented morphological taggers of standard Russian and standard Belarusian demonstrate an accuracy higher than the accuracy of multilingual models by 3 to 15%. The study suggests possible ways to adapt these taggers to the Khislavichi dataset, such as tagset unification and transcription closer to the actual sound rather than the standard lect pronunciation. Automatic classification supports the hypothesis that Khislavichi is a border East Slavic lect that historically was Belarusian but got russified: the algorithm places it either slightly closer to Russian or to Belarusian.

1 Introduction

Automatic classification of lects that are both closely related and low-resourced has been the target of dialectology studies for the last two decades, because it provides insights on the linguistic variation, used both for developing language tools and language studies (Nerbonne et al., 1999) (Gooskens and Heeringa, 2004) (Snoek, 2013) (Campos et al., 2020b). However, the morphological tagging results were rarely considered to be the basis for automatic classification. The main goal of this research is to develop a morphological tagger for a low-resourced East Slavic lect of Khislavichi with the help of the lects that possess significantly more resources, standard Russian and standard Belarusian. After the tagger is built, the morphological variation becomes the main subject of study: what differences between standard Russian, standard Belarusian, and Khislavichi stop the tagger from the correct cross-prediction between these lects? The automatic classification of standard Russian, standard Belarusian, and Khislavichi lects with distance-tree matrix (Bapat, 2010) demonstrates how it is possible to specify the position of a low-resourced lect in the context of much bigger lects that are phylogenetically connected to it.

The neutral term *lect* is used instead of *dialect* and/or *language* because the latter often imply a hierarchy of subjugation and one lect being considered as an inferior part of the other. The distinction between a language and a dialect is significantly more connected to the sphere of sociolinguistics rather than pure linguistic variation (Otheguy and Stern, 2011). As language classification studies operate in terms of language distance and not language hierarchy, all three lects are studied as equal.

Avoiding the language/dialect distinction, particularly in the study of the Khislavichi lect, is a requisite, as its current research is heavily influenced by extralinguistic factors. By now, it is safe to assume that Khislavichi is an East Slavic lect, phylogenetically more closely connected to standard Belarusian while being heavily influenced by standard Russian as a part of the process of an intense russification (Bączkowski, 1958). This process continues now and affects lesser Russian lects (Daniel et al., 2019), East Slavic lects (Naza-Accent, 2023), and the lects of ethnic groups of diverse origins in Russia (Liberty, 2023). Even the very name Khislavichi is transcribed into English as *Khislavièi* (IPA: [hɪsɫavʲɪʨɪ]), with the letters *ch* representing the Russian voiceless alveolo-palatal affricate *č* and not the native voiceless postalveolar

Tenth Workshop on NLP for Similar Languages, Varieties and Dialects (VarDial 2023), pages 174–186
May 5, 2023

affricate *č* which is more similar to Belarusian.

In this paper, which deals with the issue of linguistic variation and classification in relation to morphological tagging, Khislavichi lect is treated as a separate entity equally connected to standard Belarusian and standard Russian. Therefore, automatic language classification will provide data on its possible grouping with the other two, not its position within the language hierarchy or its inclusion into either standard Russian or standard Belarusian. However, while making conclusions, we should not ignore the historical context, mainly the intensive russification the Khislavichi lect has undergone.

Treating Khislavichi as a separate lect opens the road to its fully independent study, as it will no longer be considered a part of the Russian language (Zaharova and Orlova, 2004), contrary to its placement within the Russian lect in the earlier research. This study requires the development of natural language processing tools (NLP). The first tool in this pipeline is generally a morphological tagger. Morphological tagging is a process (and a product of this process) that includes assigning universal part-of-speech tags and morphological features to the tokens (Toleu et al., 2022). Morphological tagging is employed to get basic information on the grammar structure of the lect under study. Afterwards, it is utilised in both further processing, such as lemmatisation or masked language modelling, and the research of a lect, for instance, in the creation of a lect grammar. Some studies suggest that the results of lect automatic processing may also be used for its classification (Campos et al., 2020b). Morphological tagging was not considered to be the best candidate in comparison with perplexity (Campos et al., 2020a). However, morphological tagging seems to be useful for the preliminary classification that presents general information on the relationship between a small lect and the larger ones that surround it or influence it.

The classification of lects is a process of grouping lects by some meaningful characteristics. Among such characteristics may be the historical differentiation (Gooskens and Heeringa, 2004) or typological similarities (Hammarström and O'Connor, 2013) (McGregor, 2013) (Wälchli and von Waldenfels, 2013). The classification may give some insights into the development of a language or signal of a currently occurring intense language change. In this paper, the suggestion is to classify the lects based on the differences that cause problems in the work of a morphological tagger. The optimal algorithm is a distance-tree matrix (Bapat, 2010). To build a tree from a triangular distance matrix collected from the models accuracy scores we use a statistical method, UPGMA(Sokal and Michener, 1958), implemented via *biopython* package (Cock et al., 2009). It is generally used in evolutionary biology, and probably may be successfully adapted for language study, as the whole idea of tree classification had been (Schleicher, 1863).

The second section is dedicated to the previous research on the topics of morphological tagging, Khislavichi lect studies, and classification methods, including the automatic ones. The third section details the methods of morphological tagging (biLSTM neural network) and automatic classification (a distance matrix-based tree) that are going to be implemented in the experiments. The fourth section contains information about the datasets used for training, evaluation, and tests of taggers. The fifth section presents experiments and their analysis, performed on Russian, Belarusian, and Khislavichi material. The conclusion wraps up the research with the final analysis of the morphological tagger prediction efficiency and provides an outline for future research of the Khislavichi lect and the classification methods.

2 Related Work

The variation within the low-resourced closely-related territorially close lects, often joined under the term dialect, has been intensely studied for the last two decades (Nerbonne et al., 1999) (Arhangel'skij, 2021). Different methods have been used to study the lect variation. The most frequent, though heavily criticised (Prokić and Moran, 2013), is the edit distance group of methods (Kosmajac and Keselj, 2020), mainly represented by using Levenshtein distance on a certain list of words (Nerbonne and Heeringa, 1997) (Nerbonne et al., 1999) (Gooskens and Heeringa, 2004), generally the Swadesh list items (Nerbonne and Heeringa, 1997). Recent years, however, witnessed some changes in this situation. The Swadesh list items are no longer the ultimate solution, some other, topic-restricted, wordlists are used (Saxena and Borin, 2013) (Snoek, 2013). The methods changed as well: phonetical approach (Saxena et al., 2022), the perplexity of large language models on the task of masked language modelling (Campos et al., 2020b), sequence alignment approach (List, 2011), linguacultural approach (Lewandowska–Tomaszczyk, 2021), information theory approach (Wettig et al., 2013), and interdisciplinary approach (Carling et al., 2013). Morphological taggers generally were not used to measure language variation, but most were claimed to benefit from it (Magistry et al., 2019). This article inquires about the possible reverse situation when language variation is measured by the results of morphological tagging.

Automatic morphological tagging is an NLP task that has existed for a long time (Spyns, 1996) (Aduriz et al., 1996) (Branco and Silva, 2003) (Berdičevskis et al., 2016) (Sierra Martínez et al., 2018) (Ljubešić and Dobrovoljc, 2019). There are different approaches to it, especially when low-resourced lects are considered. Currently, the dominating approaches are the rule-based, adjusted for the needs of a particular language (Gambäck, 2012), and the more universal one based on recurrent neural networks (Straka et al., 2016). The current shift into the direction of language-independent morphological tagging (Toleu et al., 2022) leads to the development of taggers that can deal with close lects (Obeid et al., 2022), which is an essential problem, for instance, for Arabic (Inoue et al., 2022) (Fashwan and Alansary, 2022). Low-resourced morphological tagging is gaining increasing recognition (ImaniGooghari et al., 2022) (Wiemerslage et al., 2022). Now a lot of attention is paid to the selection of data to train, evaluate, and test a tagger on (Muradoglu and Hulden, 2022). The old models (Qi et al., 2018) (Qi et al., 2020) are adjusted (Scherrer, 2021) to meet the new requirements of efficient training on low-resourced closely-related lects.

Low-resourced closely-related East Slavic lects are currently undergoing extinction (Daniel et al., 2019), with Khislavichi being no exception (Ryko and Spiricheva, 2022). The Khislavichi lect is a lect of the Khislavichi settlement, which is located on the border between Russia and Belarus. It used to be a part of Belarusian territories until the beginning of the XX century, but became a part of Russia in 1924 (Ryko and Spiricheva, 2020). Its study began at the beginning of the XX century when it was characterised as a Northern Belarusian dialect (Karskij, 1903) (Durnovo et al., 1915) (though it is important to state that the Belarusian language itself was then considered a dialect of Russian by the "colonial scientists" from the Russian Empire). Since the 1960s Khislavichi was considered to be a Russian dialect with Belarusian elements becoming less and less prominent (Zaharova and Orlova, 2004). The current consensus is that the Khislavichi lect is a borderline lect between Russian and Belarusian, sharing key features with both these languages (Ryko and Spiricheva, 2022). Yet the Russian features are mostly borrowed or inflicted upon this lect, and Belarusian features form its historical core (Ryko and Spiricheva, 2022). The question of its classification remains uncertain. For a review of the historical and contemporary state of the Khislavichi lect and its overall linguistic description, one should refer to Ryko and Spiricheva (2022).

There are different ways to produce a classification of lects (Holman et al., 2008). The idea of splitting lects into non-hierarchical groups by performing hierarchical clustering became prevalent during the last decade (Buch et al., 2013). The clustering is made automatically, as recent years have witnessed an increasing use of quantitative methods for classification (Pastorelli, 2017) (Mironova, 2018). The algorithms that provide visualisations for the clusters were developed as well (Korkiakangas and Lassila, 2018). Some clustering solutions are distance-based (Rama and Kolachina, 2013).

3 Method

The research is split into three parts. The models for Russian and Belarusian are prepared via training and evaluation on the respective language datasets to get a general picture of their performance. After that, a cross-evaluation is performed to see the ability of both models to generalise based on the knowledge they have previously acquired. Next, the predictions on the Khislavchi lect material are made and evaluated manually. The final stage includes the automatic classification of the lects based on the results of the tagging evaluation.

There are different models, including the multilingual pre-trained ones, that are used for the morphological tagging of heterogeneous lects (Straka and Straková, 2017) (Kondratyuk, 2019) (Kanerva et al., 2021). However, for this experiment, the model for training should be as unaware of the potential structure of Russian, Belarusian, or Khislavichi as possible. At the same time, after training on one lect, it should still not know the others while possessing the ability to generalise its previous findings for their tagging. One more requirement is that the model should preserve some level of consistency while being trained on the corpora that are not significantly low-resourced but yet do not achieve the old national corpus standard of 1 million words. The models stated previously are either universal or underprepared for the low-resource scenario. One possible pick that satisfies all the requirements is the Stanza tagger, developed at Stanford for Universal Dependencies tagging (Qi et al., 2018) (Qi et al., 2020). It was recently modified to use bidirectional character-level LSTM by default, and specifically adjusted to the aims of part-of-speech tagging, the starting point for low-resource NLP (Scherrer, 2021). This fork is used in this paper.

After the model is chosen, the training phase begins. It consists of two subsequent runs of the code, yielding two trained models, one for Russian, and one for Belarusian respectively. These models should satisfy the requirements for overall accuracy, overcoming the basic threshold of 50%, and, optimistically, getting close to the threshold of 85 – 90% overall accuracy. To exclude overfitting, the additional evaluation of the model on the previously chosen part of the dataset is performed. The models are also compared to the previous results of morphological tagging for the Russian and Belarusian languages to check whether their ability to tag is not significantly lower. In the latter case, the shift to the other language model is probably going to be necessary.

When the conditions are met, the models are cross-evaluated. The model that was trained on the Russian material is evaluated on the Belarusian material, and vice versa. This helps to evaluate the ability of both models to generalise before the final run is performed. There can be no expectations at this stage, as both the Russian and the Belarusian models are going to be trained on the monolingual corpora. However, as both lects are East Slavic, the models are probably going to demonstrate at least a 20 to 30 per cent level of accuracy. At this stage, a manual analysis by the researcher must be performed to highlight some common mistakes that can be made by the model that switches from Russian to Belarusian tagging and the other way around as well.

The final run of both models is going to be performed on the Khislavichi material. As it is with cross-evaluation runs, there is no particular threshold that the models are expected to overcome. And for Khislavichi tagging there is an additional obstacle of the gold dataset absence. So, the evaluation is performed only by overall accuracy, and both models are getting the easiest possible treatment: they may not guess all the tags, however, if the tags they assign are correct, they get a point. Their performance, thus, may seem to get significantly boosted, though, in fact, it is going to remain at the same level as in the cross-evaluation stage. The main expectation here is that predictions of both models demonstrate a close accuracy score, as Khislavichi lect is generally supposed to be located just in the middle of the spectre between standard Russian and standard Belarusian. If the expectation is not met, the reasons should be provided. This leads to the analysis of the errors the models make on the Khislavichi material, as well as to possible explanations of the most common mistakes. And if one of the models performs abnormally well (getting close to the monolingual evaluation level of accuracy, or dealing particularly well with some classes of units), or abnormally bad (getting close to the bilingual evaluation level of accuracy, or coping particularly badly with some classes of units) the rationale is also going to be given. If the results of the two models contrast in some meaningful manner, clarification is expected. The analysis should provide recommendations for developing future datasets and taggers for the Khislavichi dataset.

After all the accuracy scores are acquired, the overall analysis for the whole picture of Russian-Belarusian continuum morphological tagging should be provided.

The research finishes with an attempt to automatically classify the three lects of standard Russian, standard Belarusian, and Khislavichi. For this, the standard method of distance-tree matrix (Bapat, 2010) is applied. This method has been previously successfully used in phylogenetic studies in biology (Fitch and Margoliash, 1967) (Gilbert and Parker, 2022) (de Vienne et al., 2011). The borrowing of the automatic classification method from biology is justified, as the evolution of language and the evolution of life share a lot of similarities (Pasquini et al., 2023), which have been highlighted recently (Ladoukakis et al., 2022), and the concept of linguistic phylogeny tree is borrowed from biology (Schleicher, 1863). This may lead to a new potential way of lect classification, a possibility to clusterise lects with the same computational methods as species (Wattel, 1996) (Bapat, 2010). When the classification is performed, the resulting trees are drawn by a Python script that employs these methods. The resulting trees demonstrate the clusterisation of the standard Russian, standard Belarusian, and Khislavichi lects predicted through morphological tagging.

4 Data

Three datasets are employed for the experiments. The first one is the corpus of the Khislavichi lect (Ryko and Spiricheva, 2020). The second one is the Belarusian-HSE corpus, the Belarusian Universal Dependencies one (Shishkina and Lyashevskaya, 2021). The third one is the Taiga corpus, one of the Russian Universal Dependencies datasets (Lyashevskaya et al., 2017) (Shavrina and Shapovalova, 2017).

As the Khislavichi lect and its relationship to standard Russian and standard Belarusian form the centre of the research, the entirety of the currently available data should be investigated. These data in the corpus have been collected and digitised by A. Ryko and M. Spiricheva (Ryko and Spiricheva, 2020). These are transcribed recordings of the interviews with the native speakers of this lect, all born between the late 1920s and the late 1960s.

The Khislavichi data is heterogeneous. Not all texts are presented as transcriptions, most of them are edited into a cross between a transcription and a standard Russian text: only the differentiating lexemes are given in parentheses. For instance, in как (як) 'how', как is a standard Russian form, and як is a Khislavichi form. For some texts, however, transcription is available as well. Additional complications arise from the fact that the lect was under the process of intense russification during the Soviet period, which manifests in the speakers born in the late 1920s and the late 1960s speaking in different manners. The common features persist (such as using č, more similar to Belarusian, and not č̀, more similar to Russian, in words like Хиславичах 'Khislavichi'), however, some radical changes in lexis start manifesting (for example, using лук instead of цыбуля for onion). The texts are interviews, with interviewers speaking in standard Russian.

With these issues in mind, the Khislavichi dataset is additionally preprocessed. The latter issue is resolved by the exclusion of the interviewers' lines from the final dataset. The issue of an in-lect heterogeneity is treated as a matter of fact, no additional splits are performed. Where the transcriptions are available, they are taken. If a pair of standard Russian lexemes and a differentiating Khislavichi lexeme in parentheses is met in the texts made to resemble standard Russian, only the differentiating Khislavichi lexeme is taken. The resulting set of texts is transferred into the CoNLL-U format, which turns it into a corpus of nearly 100 000 tokens. This corpus is split into the training, evaluation, and test datasets (80 000, 10 000, and 10 000 tokens respectively). As the research does not imply training the model for the Khislavichi lect, only the test dataset is going to be used for the later evaluation of the models trained on the Belarusian and Russian material.

The Belarusian-HSE corpus (Shishkina and Lyashevskaya, 2021) is chosen to get the model able to perform morphological tagging for Belarusian. While there are some much larger corpora, for instance, Belarusian N-corpus (N-corpus, 2023), their tagging is not disambiguated and thus is impossible to be used for training. Additionally, these corpora are not in open access. The Belarusian-HSE corpus, in turn, is available in CoNLL-U format from the start and was designed with the tagger training in mind, as this is the requirement for the Universal Dependencies corpora. This corpus consists of different text genres, from the newspapers to the Telegram messages and community posts, so it may safely be called a balanced representation of the modern Belarusian language (Shishkina and Lyashevskaya, 2021). The size of the corpus is 305 000 tokens, which makes it sufficient for the modern taggers to be trained on, especially for the ones that are well-adjusted for the Universal Dependencies low-resourced datasets (Qi et al., 2018). The corpus is split into the training, evaluation, and test parts in 80/10/10% proportion, as is generally the case with the Universal Dependencies datasets. In contrast to the Khislavichi dataset, training and evaluation parts are going to be used in the training phase to get the model for tagging Belarusian texts. The test part is going to be used for the final evaluation of this model, as well as for testing the ability of the model trained for the tagging of Russian texts, which subsequently will aid the automatic classification of standard Russian, standard Belarusian, and Khislavichi lects.

The Russian corpus, in its turn, should meet one, but a very strict condition. It should match the Belarusian-HSE corpus in size, the precision of manual tagging, and adjustment for the taggers that are designed for the data in Universal Dependencies (CoNLL-U) format. Again, there are giant corpora, consisting of billions of words, such as the Russian National Corpus (Corpus, 2023), but they are not in open access, and, what is much more important, their tagging is not fully disambiguated. There is even a big Universal Dependencies corpus, 1.5 million words SynTagRus (Droganova et al., 2018). However, its use is going to give an advantage to the Russian model. It is going to train better on a significantly bigger corpus. So, a smaller corpus should be used. The Taiga corpus (Lyashevskaya et al., 2017) (Shavrina and Shapovalova, 2017), with an overall size of 197 000 tokens, is proposed as a suitable candidate. This corpus is prepared in a Universal Dependencies format and designed specifically for tagging tasks. It is smaller, though not greatly, than the Belarusian-HSE corpus. It is also balanced, and quite representative of modern Russian, containing blog texts, news texts, fiction (including poetry) texts, Wikipedia articles, as well as different texts from social media (Lyashevskaya et al., 2017). It is split into the training (80%), evaluation (10%), and test (10%) parts. As with Belarusian, the model is going to be trained with the use of the training and the evaluation parts of the dataset. After this, the test part of the dataset will be used for the evaluation of the trained model as well as the model trained on the Belarusian dataset, supplying the data for the automatic classification of the lects.

Both Belarusian-HSE and Taiga contain a significant amount of texts from social media, a genre that is as close to the main Khislavichi corpus genres, everyday talks and events retelling. This should eliminate genre elements from affecting accuracy scores of the models.

5 Experiments and Analysis

The starting point is testing the models in the languages they were trained on. Thus, the first experiment includes testing the model that was trained on the standard Russian Taiga corpus on the test subset of this corpus, and testing the model that was trained on the standard Belarusian corpus on the test subset of its corpus.

After that, cross-evaluation is performed: the model that was trained in standard Russian is tested on the test dataset from the Belarusian corpus, and vice versa. The evaluation highlights the main difficulties the models face while tagging a closely-related lect.

Model	PoS + Feats	PoS	UFeats
UD	63.0%	86.4%	69.2%
Stanza(m)	**92.99%**	**96.96%**	**83.81%**

Table 1: Comparison of morphological tagging for Belarusian-HSE by UDPipe (Straka and Straková, 2017) and modified Stanza (Scherrer, 2021). The best results, here and afterwards, are given in **bold**.

In the last experiment, both these models are tested on the restricted test dataset from the Khislavichi lect, with an in-depth analysis of the reasons why each of the models succeeds in tagging of particular language units and fails in others. Some preliminary predictions on how the classification may look like are made at this stage.

The final analysis includes the comparison and the discussion of the experiments results, putting each of them in the general context of the research. Two possible ways for the following automatic classification of lects, based on the morphological tagging evaluation results, are suggested and realised. The *pro et contra* for both of them is given.

5.1 Monolingual Experiments

The first model to train was a Belarusian one. It achieved an almost perfect part-of-speech tagging accuracy of 97% and morphological features tagging accuracy of close to 85%. The results of the model run on the test part of the dataset were compared to UDPipe, a multilingual morphological tagging model presented in Straka and Straková (2017). The comparison is performed by PoS + Feats (both morphological features tagging and part-of-speech match), PoS (part-of-speech match), and UFeats (morphological tagging exact match). The summary of this comparison is presented in Table 1.

A modified Stanza tagger provides a more effective tagging than UDPipe. However, UDPipe is a multilingual model, and this Stanza version was specifically trained for Belarusian, so it is incorrect to make a direct comparison. For this research, it is enough to state that the model is sufficiently trained, and does not overfit.

The next model to train was a Russian one. It achieved the part-of-speech tagging accuracy of 94%, and 76% accuracy for morphological features. The results for the Russian model were compared to the results of the UDPipe model on the Taiga

Model	PoS + Feats	PoS	UFeats
UD	86.4%	75.8%	74.0%
Stanza(m)	**87.98%**	**93.63%**	**76.45%**

Table 2: Comparison of morphological tagging for Russian-Taiga by UDPipe (Straka and Straková, 2017) and modified Stanza (Scherrer, 2021).

Direction	PoS + Feats	PoS	UFeats	OOV
Ru > Bel	56.47%	67.46%	43.83%	73.84%
Bel > Ru	**58.9%**	**68.07%**	**51.63%**	60.8%

Table 3: Comparison of morphological tagging for Belarusian-HSE by the model trained on Taiga (Ru > Bel) and morphological tagging for Taiga by the model trained on Belarusian-HSE (Bel > Ru). The architecture of both models is the modified Stanza (Scherrer, 2021).

corpus. The comparison is given in Table 2.

The modified Stanza tagger again outperformed the UDPipe one (and proved its ability to efficiently operate under the lacking lect resources - both Taiga and Belarusian-HSE are not particularly big corpora), though this time not by a huge margin. This may be due to the fact that the training material for UDPipe run on Russian included more data than the training material for UDPipe run on Belarusian, or to the inner workings of the modified Stanza tagger, which was unable to train on the Taiga corpus. In any case, as this tagger beat the multilingual one, its results for Russian may also be called sufficient for further experiments.

5.2 Cross-evaluation between Russian and Belarusian

The next experiment was the run of the Belarusian-HSE-trained model on the test set of Taiga, and the run of the Taiga-trained model on the test set of Belarusian-HSE. This was conducted to evaluate the generalisation ability of the models and to detect whether some specific factors make cross-prediction between the lects easier or harder. The results are presented in Table 3.

The out-of-vocabulary (OOV) rate of the Belarusian model is smaller than the out-of-vocabulary rate of the Russian model, which is probably due to the Russian influence on Belarusian, and overall heterogeneuity of the Belarusian corpus. The size of the corpus hardly matters: the model, trained on downsampled Belarusian corpus, showed the same results in cross-evaluation experiments. In each possible category of comparison this model is slightly better, which is especially obvious in morphological features tagging. However, its accuracy falls more significantly (for instance, 34.09% against 31.41% in the exact morphological tagging category), which may indicate that it is overfitting for the Belarusian language.

Not all the errors that the Belarusian model makes support this theory. There are some strange ones, like tagging *)* as a punctuation mark and not a symbol when it is used as a smile. This is clearly an annotation schema difference. Sometimes not all glosses are used: for instance, *Tense=Pres* (the one that denotes present tense) is missing from the tagging of verb решается 'solve-PRES.3SG.REFL'.

However, most errors are connected to the fact that the model was trained on the monolingual dataset. There are cases of words unknown in Belarusian but very frequent in Russian, such as отлично 'excellently' consistently tagged as nouns. Words that end with ть are often verbs in Belarusian, yet in Russian, there are words like пусть 'let it be', which are not verbs but particles, and this confuses the model. One more type of error that is connected with language interference: the model tags да 'and' as a preposition 'to', which it is in Belarusian.

The errors that the Russian model makes while tagging the Belarusian dataset are of the similar type. For instance, it incorrectly adds glosses like *NameType=Geo* 'geographical proper name' to the words like Еўрасаюза'European Union.-GEN.SG'. A lot of mistakes are connected to the difference in the alphabets. Thus, Belarusian і and Russian и both mean 'and', which are pronounced in basically the same way, but due to the graphic differences і is not tagged as a coordinative conjunction and is tagged as a noun instead.

The errors of the Russian model put the errors of the Belarusian model in context. The bigger vocabulary of the Belarusian model leads to a higher level of language interference in this model, and thus its generalisation ability seemed to be worse than that of the Russian one. In fact, though, the generalisation ability of both the models is not great, both models fail in tagging a completely different lect in comparison to tagging the lect they were trained on. However, they retain a level of accuracy in which it is preferable to use them instead of the

Direction	Accuracy
Ru > Khi	**70.06%**
Bel > Khi	54.75

Table 4: Comparison of morphological tagging for the Khislavichi dataset by the models trained on Taiga (Ru > Khi) and Belarusian-HSE (Bel > Khi). The architecture of both models is the modified Stanza (Scherrer, 2021).

random assignment of parts of speech and morphological features (which would get 40 to 60% accuracy score). It is true for all the cases of the Belarusian model; the Russian model fails in the exact morphological features match task, yet it is often due to the tagset differences. Russian model tends to overtag, assigning more tags than there are in the original dataset. Sometimes it may be even treated as a correct assignment: *PronType=Dem*, demonstrative pronoun tag, for гэта 'that'. Thus, the Russian and the Belarusian models both may be used for preliminary tagging of closely-related East Slavic lects. The Khislavichi lect is a suitable candidate due to its strong connection to both standard Russian and standard Belarusian.

5.3 Evaluation on the Khislavichi Dataset

The last run of the models was conducted on the test part of the Khislavichi dataset, consisting of nearly 8000 tokens.

The issue with the Khislavichi dataset is that there are no gold data for it, and thus the evaluation had to be done manually, which may have led to some errors and inconsistencies, as any kind of human validation is going to. The only criterion of the evaluation was the total accuracy. As these models were previously proven to not perform efficiently on the lects they had not been trained on, the criterion is made to be very soft. It is enough for a model to not make an overt error to score. A model may not guess all the glosses, due to the annotation schema differences, but if all the glosses that model predicted are correct, it scores. The results of the experiments on Belarusian and Russian models are presented in Table 4.

These results seemingly differ from the ones that were acquired previously. Here, the Russian model demonstrates a much higher level of accuracy than the Belarusian. Its score is closer to its part-of-speech score in Belarusian, while the Belarusian model score is closer to its joined part-of-speech and morphological feature tagging score in Russian. What does this mean?

Input / Target lect	Russian	Belarusian	Khislavichi
Russian	0.88		
Belarusian	0.59	0.93	
Khislavichi	0.55	0.7	0

Table 5: Russian-centred distance matrix

Input / Target lect	Belarusian	Russian	Khislavichi
Belarusian	0.93		
Russian	0.57	0.88	
Khislavichi	0.7	0.55	0

Table 6: Belarusian-centred distance matrix

The models do not perform in an unusual way for them, even statistically. The ability of the Russian model to generalise is enough to get 70% of part-of-speech tags correctly in at least some East Slavic lects. The Belarusian model may meet a higher concentration of its *faux amis* in the dataset, as it has a bigger vocabulary. The Russian model, however, also meets a lot of language interference. Thus, both models are confused with the aforementioned word да. In the Khislavichi dataset, it mostly takes an interjection role and the meaning 'yes'. The Russian model treats it as a coordinative conjunction, and the Belarusian one – as a preposition. Both are mistaken.

Both models are sometimes fined due to the features of the Khislavichi dataset. Thus, //, which is meant to be a punctuation mark of a big pause in the speech, is consistently tagged by both models as a symbol. The same may be said about all the fragmentary tokens, denoted with the = sign at the end of the word. They should be tagged as X, non-word, yet the datasets the models were trained on do not possess examples of such cases, so the models fail in tagging these particular units.

Nearly 80% of the Khislavichi dataset is presented not as a transcription, but almost as a translation into the Russian language, so it is significantly easier for the Russian model to tag. When it meets raw transcribed tokens, such as захочыть 'want-FUT.3.SG' (which it tags as an infinitive), it often does not score. In contrast with the Russian model, the Belarusian one, while facing these transcribed tokens of Khislavichi origin, successfully tags them: the transcription often makes

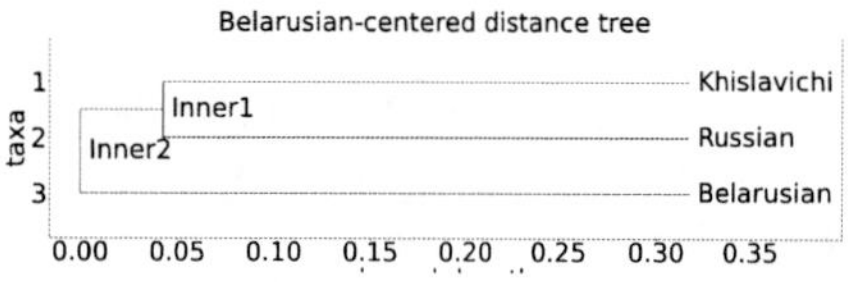

Figure 1: Belarusian-centered distance tree, built with UPGMA (Sokal and Michener, 1958)

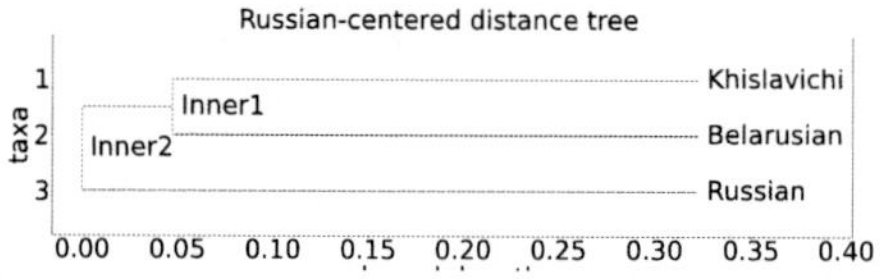

Figure 2: Russian-centered distance tree, built with UPGMA (Sokal and Michener, 1958)

Khislavichi tokens look more similar to Belarusian.

The Belarusian model meets the same kind of issues with the words that contain <w> (the labio-velar approximant transcription, designated as <ў> in Belarusian. It does not correctly tag these words due to the alphabet differences. The same may be said for the items like иГ 'them', which is written as ix and их in Belarusian and Russian respectively.

There are few mistakes connected to the systemic differences between Russian or Belarusian and Khislavichi. They are mostly sparse and hidden by writing system-based errata. There are, however, some common issues. Belarusian-trained model often predicts nouns like боль 'pain' as masculine, which they are in Belarusian. Russian-trained model assigns *Aspect=Perf* to words like ляжыт in the contexts where they are *Aspect=Cont*. This preference probably comes from the perfective contexts being more frequent in Russian.

Contrarily to the first impression, the attempt at tagging Khislavichi did not create an anomaly. There are two key reasons for the Russian-trained model performance boost, and the Belarusian-trained model performance remaining at the same level: the Khislavichi dataset transcription is forced to a form resembling standard Russian, and the sounds that Khislavichi and Belarusian share are transcribed differently in the dataset. It produces a lot of noise that interferes in the actual results.

5.4 Automatic Classification

The experiments results are grouped into the two possible distance matrices, presented in Table 5 and Table 6. The first matrix is centred around the standard Russian model, and the second one - around the standard Belarusian one. The per cent values of accuracy are replaced by a floating-point value. Khislavichi do not have gold data, so the accuracy score of the model, trained on it, is 0.

Using these two matrices, two distance trees are built with UPGMA (Sokal and Michener, 1958). They are presented in figures 1 (Belarusian-centered) and 2 (Russian-centered). The trees are very similar. When the focus is on the failures of a model trained on one of the standard Russian and standard Belarusian lects, it shifts the other one closer to the Khislavichi lect. For the classification to be more precise, grapholinguistic issues should be resolved and an additional model should be trained on the Khislavichi material.

6 Conclusion

The models for morphological tagging of Russian and Belarusian, based on the architecture provided in Scherrer (2021), beat the previous results set by the multilingual models by a significant margin for both Belarusian and Russian. Both models demonstrated the ability to perform a moderately successful tagging of the closely-related lects.

The cross-evaluation results and the results of evaluation on the Khislavichi dataset show that the Russian and Belarusian models may be used for the preliminary tagging of closely related low-resourced East Slavic lects. The classification by the results of morphological tagging retains the same uncertainty level of the Khislavichi lect position among the other East Slavic lects as the classifications reviewed in Ryko and Spiricheva (2022). In the current dataset orthography state, the reasonable conclusion is the Khislavichi dataset being classified as borderline between Russian and Belarusian datasets, not the Khislavichi lect - as borderline between Russian and Belarusian (the same notion for Italian presents Davis (2017)).

We are going to modify and implement the presented automatic classification method for the bigger number of lects, and use the transformed and tagged Khislavichi corpus for the further Khislavichi lect processing. The corpus probably will later become a Universal Dependencies part.

7 Acknowledgements

We thank the anonymous reviewers for their comments on the proposed method and datasets, which greatly aided the final paper. The remaining errata are, of course, ours.

References

Itziar Aduriz, Izaskun Aldezabal, Iñaki Alegria, Xabier Artola, Nerea Ezeiza, and Ruben Urizar. 1996. Euslem: A lemmatiser/tagger for basque. In *Proceedings of the 7th EURALEX International Congress*, pages 27–35, Göteborg, Sweden. Novum Grafiska AB.

Timofei A. Arhangel'skij. 2021. Primenenie dialektometricheskogo metoda k klassifikacii udmurtskih dialektov. *Uralo-altajskie issledovaniya*, 2(41):7–20.

Włodzimierz Bączkowski. 1958. *Russian colonialism: the Tsarist and Soviet empires*. Frederick A. Praeger, New York.

R. B. Bapat. 2010. Distance matrix of a tree. In *Graphs and Matrices*, pages 95–109, London. Springer London.

Aleksandrs Berdičevskis, Hanna Eckhoff, and Tatiana Gavrilova. 2016. The beginning of a beautiful friendship: rule-based and statistical analysis of middle russian. In *Komp'yuternaya lingvistika i intellektual'nye tekhnologii. Trudy mezhdunarodnoj konferencii «Dialog»*, pages 99–111, Moscow, Russia. RSSU.

Antònio Branco and Jõao Silva. 2003. Portuguese specific issues in the rapid development of state of the art taggers. In *Proceedings of the Workshop on Language Technology for Normalisation of Less-Resourced Languages (SALTMIL8/AfLaT2012)*, pages 7–9, Paris. European Language Resources Association.

Armin Buch, David Erschler, Gerhard Jäger, and Andrei Lupas. 2013. Towards automated language classification: A clustering approach. In *Approaches to Measuring Linguistic Differences*, pages 303–328, Berlin, Boston. De Gruyter Mouton.

José Campos, Pablo Gamallo, Iñaki Alegria, and Marco Neves. 2020a. A methodology to measure the diachronic language distance between three languages based on perplexity. *Journal of Quantitative Linguistics*, 28:1–31.

José Ramom Pichel Campos, Pablo Gamallo Otero, and Iñaki Alegria Loinaz. 2020b. Measuring diachronic language distance using perplexity: Application to english, portuguese, and spanish. *Natural Language Engineering*, 26(4):433–454.

Gerd Carling, Love Eriksen, Arthur Holmer, and Joost van de Weijer. 2013. Contrasting linguistics and archaeology in the matrix model: Gis and cluster analysis of the arawakan languages. In *Approaches to Measuring Linguistic Differences*, pages 29–56, Berlin, Boston. De Gruyter Mouton.

Peter JA Cock, Tiago Antao, Jeffrey T Chang, Brad A Chapman, Cymon J Cox, Andrew Dalke, Iddo Friedberg, Thomas Hamelryck, Frank Kauff, Bartek Wilczynski, et al. 2009. Biopython: freely available python tools for computational molecular biology and bioinformatics. *Bioinformatics*, 25(11):1422–1423.

The Russian National Corpus. 2023. The russian national corpus.

Michael Daniel, Ruprecht von Waldenfels, Aleksandra Ter-Avanesova, Polina Kazakova, Ilya Schurov, Ekaterina Gerasimenko, Daria Ignatenko, Ekaterina Makhlina, Maria Tsfasman, Samira Verhees, and et al. 2019. Dialect loss in the russian north: Modeling change across variables. *Language Variation and Change*, 31(3):353–376.

Joseph Davis. 2017. The semantic difference between Italian vi and ci. *Lingua*, 200:107–121.

Damien M. de Vienne, Gabriela Aguileta, and Sébastien Ollier. 2011. Euclidean Nature of Phylogenetic Distance Matrices. *Systematic Biology*, 60(6):826–832.

Kira Droganova, Olga Lyashevskaya, and Daniel Zeman. 2018. Data conversion and consistency of monolingual corpora: Russian ud treebanks. In *Proceedings of the 17th International Workshop on Treebanks and Linguistic Theories (TLT 2018), December 13–14, 2018, Oslo University, Norway*, 155, pages 52–65. Linköping University Electronic Press.

Nikolaj N. Durnovo, Nikolaj N. Sokolov, and Dmitrij N. Ushakov. 1915. *Opyt dialektologicheskoj karty russkogo jazyka v Evrope s prilozheniem Ocherka russkoj dialektologii*. Sinodal'naja tipografija, Moscow.

Amany Fashwan and Sameh Alansary. 2022. Developing a tag-set and extracting the morphological lexicons to build a morphological analyzer for Egyptian Arabic. In *Proceedings of the The Seventh Arabic Natural Language Processing Workshop (WANLP)*, pages 142–160, Abu Dhabi, United Arab Emirates (Hybrid). Association for Computational Linguistics.

Walter M. Fitch and Emanuel Margoliash. 1967. Construction of phylogenetic trees. *Science*, 155(3760):279–284.

Björn Gambäck. 2012. Tagging and verifying an amharic news corpus. In *Proceedings of the Workshop on Language Technology for Normalisation of Less-Resourced Languages (SALTMIL8/AfLaT2012)*, pages 79–84, Paris. European Language Resources Association.

Gregory S. Gilbert and Ingrid M. Parker. 2022. Phylogenetic distance metrics for studies of focal species in communities: Quantiles and cumulative curves. *Diversity*, 14(7).

Charlotte Gooskens and Wilbert Heeringa. 2004. Perceptive evaluation of levenshtein dialect distance measurements using norwegian dialect data. *Language Variation and Change*, 16:189 – 207.

Harald Hammarström and Loretta O'Connor. 2013. Dependency-sensitive typological distance. In *Approaches to Measuring Linguistic Differences*, pages 329–352, Berlin, Boston. De Gruyter Mouton.

Eric W. Holman, Søren Wichmann, Cecil H. Brown, Viveka Velupillai, André Müller, and Dik Bakker. 2008. Explorations in automated language classification. *Folia Linguistica*, 42(3-4):331–354.

Ayyoob ImaniGooghari, Silvia Severini, Masoud Jalili Sabet, François Yvon, and Hinrich Schütze. 2022. Graph-based multilingual label propagation for low-resource part-of-speech tagging. In *Proceedings of the 2022 Conference on Empirical Methods in Natural Language Processing*, pages 1577–1589, Abu Dhabi, United Arab Emirates. Association for Computational Linguistics.

Go Inoue, Salam Khalifa, and Nizar Habash. 2022. Morphosyntactic tagging with pre-trained language models for Arabic and its dialects. In *Findings of the Association for Computational Linguistics: ACL 2022*, pages 1708–1719, Dublin, Ireland. Association for Computational Linguistics.

Jenna Kanerva, Filip Ginter, and Tapio Salakoski. 2021. Universal lemmatizer: A sequence-to-sequence model for lemmatizing universal dependencies treebanks. *Natural Language Engineering*, 27(5):545–574.

Yefim F. Karskij. 1903. *Belorusy. Vol. I. Vvedenie v izuchenie jazyka i narodnoj slovesnosti*. Warsaw Academic County Publishing, Warsaw.

Dan Kondratyuk. 2019. Cross-lingual lemmatization and morphology tagging with two-stage multilingual BERT fine-tuning. In *Proceedings of the 16th Workshop on Computational Research in Phonetics, Phonology, and Morphology*, pages 12–18, Florence, Italy. Association for Computational Linguistics.

Timo Korkiakangas and Matti Lassila. 2018. Visualizing linguistic variation in a network of Latin documents and scribes. *Journal of Data Mining & Digital Humanities*, Numéro spécial sur le traitement assisté par ordinateur de l'intertextualité dans les langues anciennes.

Dijana Kosmajac and Vlado Keselj. 2020. Language distance using common n-grams approach. In *2020 19th International Symposium INFOTEH-JAHORINA (INFOTEH)*. IEEE.

Manolis Ladoukakis, Dimitris Michelioudakis, and Elena Anagnostopoulou. 2022. Toward an evolutionary framework for language variation and change. *BioEssays*, 44:210–216.

Barbara Lewandowska–Tomaszczyk. 2021. Comparing languages and cultures: Parametrization of analytic criteria. *Russian Journal of Linguistics*, 25(2):343–368.

Radio Free Europe/Radio Liberty. 2023. In Russia, there are 40% fewer Komi-Permyaks, 35% fewer Mordovians (Erzya and Moksha), 30% fewer Udmurts, and more than 20% fewer Chuvash and Mari. *Radio Free Europe/Radio Liberty*.

Johann-Mattis List. 2011. Multiple sequence alignment in historical linguistics: A sound class based approach. In *Proceedings of ConSOLE XIX*, page 241–260.

Nikola Ljubešić and Kaja Dobrovoljc. 2019. What does neural bring? analysing improvements in morphosyntactic annotation and lemmatisation of Slovenian, Croatian and Serbian. In *Proceedings of the 7th Workshop on Balto-Slavic Natural Language Processing*, pages 29–34, Florence, Italy. Association for Computational Linguistics.

Olga Lyashevskaya, Victor Bocharov, Alexey Sorokin, Tatiana Shavrina, Dmitry Granovsky, and Svetlana Alexeeva. 2017. Text collections for evaluation of Russian morphological taggers. *Journal of Linguistics/Jazykovedný casopis*, 68:258–267.

Pierre Magistry, Anne-Laure Ligozat, and Sophie Rosset. 2019. Exploiting languages proximity for part-of-speech tagging of three French regional languages. *Language Resources and Evaluation*, 53:865–888.

William B. McGregor. 2013. Comparing linguistic systems of categorisation. In *Approaches to Measuring Linguistic Differences*, pages 387–428, Berlin, Boston. De Gruyter Mouton.

Dina M. Mironova. 2018. *Avtomatizirovannaja klassifikacija drevnih rukopisej : na materiale 525 spiskov slavjanskogo Evangelija ot Matfeja XI - XVI vv. : avtoreferat dis. ... kandidata filologicheskih nauk : 10.02.21*. SPbU, Saint-Petersbourg.

Saliha Muradoglu and Mans Hulden. 2022. Eeny, meeny, miny, moe. how to choose data for morphological inflection. In *Proceedings of the 2022 Conference on Empirical Methods in Natural Language Processing*, pages 7294–7303, Abu Dhabi, United Arab Emirates. Association for Computational Linguistics.

Belarusian N-corpus. 2023. Belarusian N-corpus.

NazaAccent. 2023. Rosstat: From 2010 to 2021, There are One Million Fewer Ukrainians in Russia. *NazaAccent*.

J. Nerbonne and Wilbert Heeringa. 1997. Measuring dialect distance phonetically. In *Computational Phonology. Third Meeting of the ACL Special Interest Group in Computational Phonolby.*, pages 11 – 18. Association for Computational Linguistics (ACL).

John Nerbonne, Wilbert Heeringa, and Peter Kleiwig. 1999. Edit distance and dialect proximity. In *Time Warps, String Edits and Macromolecules: The Theory and Practice of Sequence Comparison, 2nd Ed.*, pages i–xviii. CSLI, Stanford, CA.

Ossama Obeid, Go Inoue, and Nizar Habash. 2022. Camelira: An Arabic multi-dialect morphological disambiguator. In *Proceedings of the The 2022 Conference on Empirical Methods in Natural Language Processing: System Demonstrations*, pages 319–326, Abu Dhabi, UAE. Association for Computational Linguistics.

Ricardo Otheguy and Nancy Stern. 2011. On so-called Spanglish. *International Journal of Bilingualism - INT J BILING*, 15:85–100.

Michele Pasquini, Maurizio Serva, and Davide Vergni. 2023. Gradual modifications and abrupt replacements: Two stochastic lexical ingredients of language evolution. *Computational Linguistics*, pages 1–23.

David Pastorelli. 2017. A Classification of Manuscripts Based on A New Quantitative Method. The Old Latin Witnesses of John's Gospel as Text Case. *Journal of Data Mining & Digital Humanities*, Numéro spécial sur le traitement assisté par ordinateur de l'intertextualité dans les langues anciennes.

Jelena Prokić and Steven Moran. 2013. Black box approaches to genealogical classification and their shortcomings. In *Approaches to Measuring Linguistic Differences*, pages 429–446, Berlin, Boston. De Gruyter Mouton.

Peng Qi, Timothy Dozat, Yuhao Zhang, and Christopher D. Manning. 2018. Universal Dependency parsing from scratch. In *Proceedings of the CoNLL 2018 Shared Task: Multilingual Parsing from Raw Text to Universal Dependencies*, pages 160–170, Brussels, Belgium. Association for Computational Linguistics.

Peng Qi, Yuhao Zhang, Yuhui Zhang, Jason Bolton, and Christopher D. Manning. 2020. Stanza: A python natural language processing toolkit for many human languages. In *Proceedings of the 58th Annual Meeting of the Association for Computational Linguistics: System Demonstrations*, pages 101–108, Online. Association for Computational Linguistics.

Taraka Rama and Sudheer Kolachina. 2013. Distance-based phylogenetic inference algorithms in the subgrouping of dravidian languages. In *Approaches to Measuring Linguistic Differences*, pages 141–174, Berlin, Boston. De Gruyter Mouton.

Anastasiia Ryko and Margarita V. Spiricheva. 2020. *Corpus of the Russian dialect spoken in Khislavichi district*. Linguistic Convergence Laboratory, HSE University, Moscow.

Anastasiia Ryko and Margarita V. Spiricheva. 2022. The degree of preservation of dialectal features in different generations (khislavichi district of the smolensk region). *RSUH/RGGU Bulletin. "Literary Theory. Linguistics. Cultural Studies" Series*, 5:121–141.

Anju Saxena and Lars Borin. 2013. Carving tibeto-kanauri by its joints: Using basic vocabulary lists for genetic grouping of languages. In *Approaches to Measuring Linguistic Differences*, pages 175–198, Berlin, Boston. De Gruyter Mouton.

Anju Saxena, Anna Sjöberg, Padam Sagar, and Lars Borin. 2022. 4 linguistic variation: a challenge for describing the phonology of kanashi. In *Synchronic and Diachronic Aspects of Kanashi*, pages 131–144, Berlin, Boston. De Gruyter Mouton.

Yves Scherrer. 2021. Adaptation of morphosyntactic taggers. In *Similar Languages, Varieties, and Dialects: A Computational Perspective*, Studies in Natural Language Processing, page 138–166. Cambridge University Press.

August Schleicher. 1863. *Die Darwinsche Theorie und die Sprachwissenschaft – offenes Sendschreiben an Herrn Dr. Ernst Haeckel*. H. Boehlau, Weimar.

Tatiana Shavrina and Olga Shapovalova. 2017. To the methodology of corpus construction for machine learning: «Taiga» syntax tree corpus and parser. In *Proceedings of the International Conference "CORPORA 2017", Saint-Petersbourg, Russia*, pages 78–84. Linköping University Electronic Press.

Yana Shishkina and Olga Lyashevskaya. 2021. Sculpting enhanced dependencies for Belarusian. In *Analysis of Images, Social Networks and Texts: 10th International Conference, AIST 2021, Tbilisi, Georgia, December 16–18, 2021, Revised Selected Papers*, page 137–147, Berlin, Heidelberg. Springer-Verlag.

Luz Sierra Martínez, Carlos Cobos, Juan Corrales, Tulio Curieux, Enrique Herrera-Viedma, and Diego Peluffo-Ordóñez. 2018. Building a Nasa Yuwe language corpus and tagging with a metaheuristic approach. *Computacion y Sistemas*, 22:881–894.

Conor Snoek. 2013. Using semantically restricted wordlists to investigate relationships among Athapaskan languages. In *Approaches to Measuring Linguistic Differences*, pages 231–248, Berlin, Boston. De Gruyter Mouton.

R. R. Sokal and C. D. Michener. 1958. A statistical method for evaluating systematic relationships. *University of Kansas Science Bulletin*, 38:1409–1438.

Peter Spyns. 1996. A tagger/lemmatiser for Dutch medical language. In *Proceedings of the 16th Conference on Computational Linguistics - Volume 2*, COLING '96, page 1147–1150, USA. Association for Computational Linguistics.

Milan Straka, Jan Hajič, and Jana Straková. 2016. UDPipe: Trainable pipeline for processing CoNLL-U files performing tokenization, morphological analysis, POS tagging and parsing. In *Proceedings of the Tenth International Conference on Language Resources and Evaluation (LREC'16)*, pages 4290–4297, Portorož, Slovenia. European Language Resources Association (ELRA).

Milan Straka and Jana Straková. 2017. Tokenizing, POS tagging, lemmatizing and parsing UD 2.0 with UDPipe. In *Proceedings of the CoNLL 2017 Shared Task: Multilingual Parsing from Raw Text to Universal Dependencies*, pages 88–99, Vancouver, Canada. Association for Computational Linguistics.

Alymzhan Toleu, Gulmira Tolegen, and Rustam Mussabayev. 2022. Language-independent approach for morphological disambiguation. In *Proceedings of the 29th International Conference on Computational Linguistics*, pages 5288–5297, Gyeongju, Republic of Korea. International Committee on Computational Linguistics.

Evert Wattel. 1996. Clustering stemmatological trees. In M. van Mulken P. van Reenen, editor, *Studies in Stemmatology*, page 123 - 134. John Benjamins Publishing Company, Amsterdam, Philadelphia.

Hannes Wettig, Javad Nouri, Kirill Reshetnikov, and Roman Yangarber. 2013. Information-theoretic modeling of etymological sound change. In *Approaches to Measuring Linguistic Differences*, pages 507–532, Berlin, Boston. De Gruyter Mouton.

Adam Wiemerslage, Miikka Silfverberg, Changbing Yang, Arya McCarthy, Garrett Nicolai, Eliana Colunga, and Katharina Kann. 2022. Morphological processing of low-resource languages: Where we are and what's next. In *Findings of the Association for Computational Linguistics: ACL 2022*, pages 988–1007, Dublin, Ireland. Association for Computational Linguistics.

Bernhard Wälchli and Ruprecht von Waldenfels. 2013. Measuring morphosemantic language distance in parallel texts. In *Approaches to Measuring Linguistic Differences*, pages 475–506, Berlin, Boston. De Gruyter Mouton.

Kapitolina F. Zaharova and Varvara G. Orlova. 2004. *Dialektnoe chlenenie russkogo yazyka*. URSS, Moscow.

DIATOPIT: A Corpus of Social Media Posts for the Study of Diatopic Language Variation in Italy

Alan Ramponi, **Camilla Casula**
alramponi@fbk.eu, ccasula@fbk.eu

Fondazione Bruno Kessler (FBK), Italy
University of Trento, Italy

Abstract

We introduce DIATOPIT, the first corpus specifically focused on diatopic language variation in Italy for language varieties other than Standard Italian. DIATOPIT comprises over 15K geolocated social media posts from Twitter over a period of two years, including regional Italian usage and content fully written in local language varieties or exhibiting code-switching with Standard Italian. We detail how we tackled key challenges in creating such a resource, including the absence of orthography standards for most local language varieties and the lack of reliable language identification tools. We assess the representativeness of DIATOPIT across time and space, and show that the density of *non*-Standard Italian content across areas correlates with actual language use. We finally conduct computational experiments and find that modeling diatopic variation on highly multilingual areas such as Italy is a complex task even for recent language models.[1]

(a)	chiov' tutt a jurnat', ce serv' o mbrell' **en.** *it's raining all day, we need an umbrella*
(b)	ho così sonno che me bala l'oeucc **en.** *I'm so sleepy that my eye trembles*
(c)	da caruso anche io ci andavo spesso! **en.** *I used to go there often as a kid too!*

Table 1: Examples from DIATOPIT, with *non*-Standard Italian content in green. (a) posts fully written in local language varieties (here, Neapolitan [nap]); (b) posts code-switched with Standard Italian (here, Lombard [lmo]); (c) posts including regional Italian usage (here, "*caruso*" from the Sicilian [scn] "*carusu*"). Posts have been slightly redacted to preserve users' anonymity.

1 Introduction

Italy is one of the most linguistically-diverse countries in Europe. Despite its relatively small geographical area, it exhibits a notable profusion of linguistic variation, "*hold[ing] especial treasures for linguists*" (Maiden and Parry, 1997). Therefore, the study of diatopic linguistic variation in Italy has constantly been a focal point in linguistics (Bartoli et al., 1995; Jaberg et al., 1987, *inter alia*).

On the other hand, little attention has been given so far to this matter in the natural language processing community. Indeed, most work in NLP still focuses on Standard Italian (`ita`; the official national language), considering it as a "monolithic language". However, a large number of local languages, dialects, and regional varieties of Standard Italian (i.e., *regional Italian*)[2] shape the Italian linguistic landscape (Ramponi, 2022). Computational studies of diatopic variation can ultimately help to enrich and complement linguistic atlases, as well as to provide insights on actual use of local language varieties (e.g., adherence to orthography standards) and their vitality (e.g., code-switching as a sign of language replacement (Cerruti and Regis, 2005)). The ever-growing number of people who interact on social media offers opportunities in this direction, since user-generated texts are indeed informal, featuring linguistic patterns from spoken language (Eisenstein, 2013; van der Goot et al., 2021).

In this paper we introduce DIATOPIT, the first corpus of geolocated social media posts from Twitter with a focus on diatopic variation in Italy for language varieties[3] other than Standard Italian. DIATOPIT comprises 15,039 posts with content fully written in local language varieties (cf. Figure 1, *(a)*), exhibiting code-switching with Standard Italian (cf. Figure 1, *(b)*), or including regional Italian (cf. Figure 1, *(c)*). Compared to other existing datasets with geolocation information (Han et al., 2016; Gaman et al., 2020; Chakravarthi et al.,

[1] Repository: `https://github.com/dhfbk/diatopit`

[2] Geographical differentiation of Standard Italian due to influences by languages and dialects of Italy (Avolio, 2009).

[3] For brevity, we use "language varieties" to refer to local languages and dialects of Italy as well as regional Italian, whereas we add "local" to specifically refer to the former.

Tenth Workshop on NLP for Similar Languages, Varieties and Dialects (VarDial 2023), pages 187–199
May 5, 2023 ©2023 Association for Computational Linguistics

2021), DIATOPIT is focused on Italy and on non-standard language use. We describe how we tackled challenges in the corpus creation process, such as the lack of reliable, variation-informed language identification tools and the absence of orthography standards for most local varieties (Section 2), and provide detailed analyses over time and space, also highlighting the density and function of *non*-Standard Italian content across Italian regions (Section 3). Finally, we show that modeling diatopic language variation is a difficult task even for state-of-the-art language models (Section 4).

The corpus is meant to encourage research on diatopic variation in Italy, study code-switching and divergences in orthography for local language varieties, and serve as a basis for responsible development of annotated resources for Italy's varieties.

2 Corpus Creation

Building a corpus of social media posts written in language varieties of Italy other than Standard Italian is a tough task, especially in the absence of reliable language identification tools.[4] Most languages and dialects of Italy – see Ramponi (2022) for an overview – are primarily oral and have no established orthography, and standards that have been proposed for a fraction of them are rarely adopted by their speakers. Indeed, when those language varieties are transposed into writing, speakers typically write "the way words sound" (Ramponi, 2022). The language functions of those varieties – most of which are endangered (Moseley, 2010) – are increasingly restricted, resulting in frequent code-switching with Standard Italian, a sign of language replacement (Cerruti and Regis, 2005).

In this section we describe how we tackle these challenges to build the DIATOPIT corpus. We detail all stages, from data collection (Section 2.1) and sampling for *non*-Standard Italian content (Section 2.2), to content curation and data augmentation of under-represented speaking areas (Section 2.3). Data statements (Bender and Friedman, 2018) for DIATOPIT are presented in Appendix A.

2.1 Collection of Geolocated Posts in Italy

For our initial collection, we use the Twitter APIs to retrieve geolocated tweets in Italy over a period of two years, from `2020-07-01` to `2022-06-30`. This ensures that coordinates of tweets fall within the Italian territory, and thus that content exhibiting linguistic variation is relevant to Italy. Moreover, the large time frame mitigates potential biases in the corpus about exceptional or occasional events, whereas the presence of the same number of months across years avoids over-representing recurring events, both local (e.g., the *Italian Song Festival*, February) and global (e.g., Christmas).

We then sample posts that have been classified as "`it`" by Twitter, due to the frequent code-switching of local language varieties with Standard Italian (cf. Section 2) and the absence of dedicated language classifiers. In addition, we observed that content (partially and even fully) written in language varieties of Italy is typically classified as `it` by the Twitter language identifier.[5] We obtain over 10 million geolocated tweets for further filtering.

2.2 Sampling *Non*-Standard Italian Posts

To construct a representative sample of social media posts written in language varieties of Italy other than Italian, we take our initial collection (Section 2.1) and further filter it to contain *non*-Standard Italian content. We deliberately avoid using predefined lexicons for sampling, since *(i)* their coverage is typically low in terms of both vocabulary and representation of local variants, and *(ii)* using them for sampling could bias our corpus towards standard orthographies, thus excluding variation due to speakers' lack of knowledge of written conventions (if any). We instead adopt a complementary approach in which lexical units for sampling naturally emerge from their actual use on social media.

We analyze the whole collection of tweets, computing frequencies of out-of-vocabulary (OOV) tokens.[6] We consider a token as OOV if it is not a special token (i.e., hashtag, punctuation, number, emoji) nor is part of the Aspell dictionary for Italian.[7] Additionally, we do not consider as OOV all tokens that are part of the English dictionary[8] to avoid including international discourse in our corpus. We inspect the resulting token frequencies and further exclude common interjections (e.g., *boh*, en: *I don't know*), elongated words (e.g., *ciaoo*, en: *helloo*), words in Italian with wrong diacritics

[4]Language identification tools for (a subset of) language varieties of Italy are mostly trained on Wikipedia, a very specific domain that does not reflect how those languages and dialects are typically used by their speakers (Ramponi, 2022).

[5]Nonetheless, in future work we plan to extend the corpus with the fraction of relevant content classified as non-`it`, too.

[6]Tokenization of posts has been performed by using the `it_core_news_sm` model by spaCy (`https://spacy.io`).

[7]`http://aspell.net: aspell6-it-2.2_20050523-0`.

[8]`http://aspell.net: aspell6-en-2020.12.07-0`.

(e.g., *perchè*; en: *why/because*), youth language and slang words (e.g., *xke*, en: *why/because* [ABBR.]; *buongiornissimo*, en: *good morning* [SUP.]), tokenization errors (e.g., *∼il*, en: *∼the*), tokens in foreign languages (e.g., *gracias*, en: *thank you*), tokens in Italian or English that are not included in Aspell dictionaries (e.g., *quest'*, en: *this* [CONTR.]; *t-shirt*), and tokens that explicitly refer to named entities (e.g., soccer players, singers, brands, cities).

We use tokens $t \in T_{oov}$ with a frequency $F(t) \geq k$ as our search keywords, and retain from the collection all tweets that contain at least one of such terms. To avoid including social media posts with tokenization errors and rare typos, we empirically set $k = 48$, which corresponds to an average token frequency of 2 occurrences per month. We obtain over 100K tweets with 953 search tokens. Search tokens are made available in our repository.

2.3 Corpus Curation and Augmentation

Posts that match at least one OOV token do not necessarily contain lexical items of local language varieties or signal of interest for diatopic studies. Indeed, our initial exploration revealed that a fraction of matched posts were spam messages or still contained no signal due to the ambiguity of some search terms. Moreover, we found occasional mismatches between the geolocation attached to posts and the language varieties used within them.[9]

Motivated by these factors, we focus on the subset of posts matching at least 2 OOV tokens (i.e., roughly 20K tweets) and conduct a manual curation process. Two curators with good knowledge of language varieties of Italy and background in NLP and sociolinguistics identified all user IDs whose posts contain *(i)* spam content or *(ii)* content in language varieties that are not spoken in the area of the geolocated position (e.g., due to tourism or relocation). We then removed all the tweets posted by spam users, the subset of posts with clearly incongruous content and geolocation, as well as matched tweets exhibiting no diatopic signals.

To mitigate the under-representation in our corpus of some areas in which local language varieties are scarcely spoken, we additionally conducted two steps of data augmentation. In the first step, the curators manually checked the remaining subset of posts with just a single matched OOV token for all regions with $\leq 1\%$ posts over the total.[10] During the whole process, cases of doubt were managed by the curators by consulting dictionaries and asking native speakers for clarification. Posts containing content in *non*-Standard Italian were then added to the corpus. In the second step, we took the set of tweets from all regions except the over-represented ones (i.e., Lazio and Campania; cf. Figure 2a) and employed the lexical artifacts package (Ramponi and Tonelli, 2022) to compute a ranking of the highly-discriminative tokens for each region in a *one-vs-rest* scheme. A list comprising the top 50 OOV tokens of each region, totalling 820 unique keywords, was then used to sample additional tweets from the initial collection (Section 2.1). The curators then manually checked these sets, adding relevant tweets to the corpus. Finally, we deduplicated the corpus by removing tweets that had the same content and author ID.[11]

3 Corpus Analysis

In this section we present detailed analyses on the DIATOPIT corpus. We first provide summary statistics (Section 3.1). Then, we discuss the corpus distribution across time and space (Section 3.2). Lastly, we show that the density of *non*-Standard Italian tokens across regions correlates with the actual use of languages varieties in Italy, and that language functions of the most indicative tokens per region are good indicators of vitality (Section 3.3).

3.1 Summary Statistics

In Table 2 we present summary statistics and density information about the corpus. DIATOPIT comprises 15,039 posts with geolocation information across all 20 administrative regions of Italy, accounting for a total of 388,069 tokens, 54,635 of which are OOV (i.e., 14.1%). Posts have an average length of 25.8 tokens and have been written by 3,672 authors (i.e., 4.1 posts per author on average).

By a closer look, Lazio (LAZ) and Campania (CAM) are the most represented regions in the corpus, with 39.2% and 21.5% instances, respectively. All other regions comprise from 0.1% to 5.9% posts, with those with $\leq 1.5\%$ instances representing territories with a small population or in which local language varieties are little spoken.

[9]Although language and mobility is an interesting topic, it goes beyond the purpose of this work. We leave the study of this phenomenon as future direction for research.

[10]We refer the reader to Appendix B for additional details.

[11]Indeed, we do not consider a tweet with the same content but posted by different authors as a duplicate, but rather a useful signal for diatopic studies and language vitality assessments, especially if posted from different locations.

	Instances		Tokens				Authors	Density		
	I (#)	I (%)	T_{all}	T_{all}^{unique}	T_{oov}	T_{oov}^{unique}	A	T_{all}/I	I/A	$\frac{T_{oov}}{T_{all}}$ (%)
ABR	166	1.1%	3,939	1,495	523	370	86	23.7	1.9	13.3%
BAS	49	0.3%	1,166	575	164	141	30	23.8	1.6	14.1%
CAL	336	2.2%	7,683	2,626	1,399	872	101	22.9	3.3	18.2%
CAM	3,240	21.5%	78,233	11,627	13,185	3,889	645	24.2	5.0	16.9%
EMI	395	2.6%	9,861	2,902	1,020	589	173	25.0	2.3	10.3%
FRI	270	1.8%	6,851	2,360	1,008	652	83	25.4	3.3	14.7%
LAZ	5,895	39.2%	162,532	19,379	19,031	4,635	987	27.6	6.0	11.7%
LIG	273	1.8%	6,378	1,853	819	434	82	23.4	3.3	12.8%
LOM	803	5.3%	20,966	5,125	3,139	1,535	327	26.1	2.5	15.0%
MAR	197	1.3%	5,035	1,821	679	432	96	25.6	2.1	13.5%
MOL	35	0.2%	692	364	111	90	21	19.8	1.7	16.0%
PIE	288	1.9%	6,498	2,094	750	434	127	22.6	2.3	11.5%
PUG	320	2.1%	8,000	2,558	1,254	733	157	25.0	2.0	15.7%
SAR	440	2.9%	11,711	3,513	2,665	1,504	129	26.6	3.4	22.8%
SIC	720	4.8%	16,780	4,355	3,050	1,444	240	23.3	3.0	18.2%
TOS	506	3.4%	13,640	3,449	1,459	700	194	27.0	2.6	10.7%
TRE	61	0.4%	1,434	670	153	111	37	23.5	1.6	10.7%
UMB	150	1.0%	4,129	1,425	512	284	49	27.5	3.1	12.4%
VAL	14	0.1%	420	260	44	42	14	30.0	1.0	10.5%
VEN	881	5.9%	22,121	5,093	3,670	1,593	252	25.1	3.5	16.6%
ALL	15,039	100.0%	388,069	40,744	54,635	16,482	3,672	25.8	4.1	14.1%

Table 2: Summary statistics for the DIATOPIT corpus. Region names (*left*) are presented with their first three letters (see Figure 2a for full names and location). Columns (*top*). I: instances (#: raw number; %: percentage); T_{all}: tokens; T_{all}^{unique}: unique tokens; T_{oov}: OOV tokens; T_{oov}^{unique}: unique OOV tokens; A: authors; T_{all}/I: average tokens per instance; I/A: average instances per author; T_{oov}/T_{all} (%): average density of OOV tokens within posts.

Regions vary a lot in terms of average density of OOV tokens within posts (T_{oov}/T_{all}). Sardinia (SAR), Sicilia (SIC), Calabria (CAL), Campania (CAM) and Veneto (VEN) are the regions in which lexical items of language varieties of Italy other than Standard Italian are used more frequently.[12] Lastly, LAZ, CAM, and VEN are the regions in which the ratio of instances per author (I/A) is higher, a sign of a more confident use of local language varieties by their speakers.

3.2 Distribution Across Time and Space

In order to assess the potential presence of temporal biases in our corpus, we examine the distribution of social media posts across time, and compare it with that of the initial collection (cf. Section 2.1). Figure 1 shows the percentage of tweets for each month within the 2-year time span for the DIATOPIT corpus and the reference (i.e., the initial collection). We observe that the number of posts in DIATOPIT closely follows the distribution of the reference, with the only exception for the period from `2021-10` to `2021-12`. We examined tweets posted within this time span and we positively found that the small peak is due to some users posting more than average about a wide range of topics rather than due to period-specific biases.

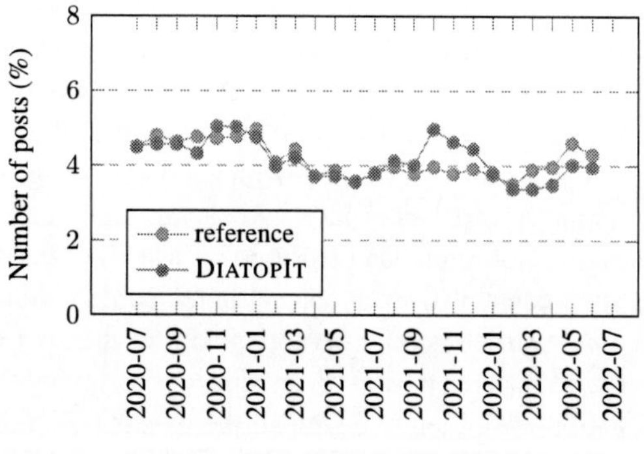

Figure 1: Distribution of social media posts over time in both DIATOPIT and the initial collection (*reference*).

As regards the spatial dimension, in Figure 2

[12]Note that multiple local languages and dialects are often spoken within a region, and they often cross administrative borders. Refer to Pellegrini (1977) for a linguistic map.

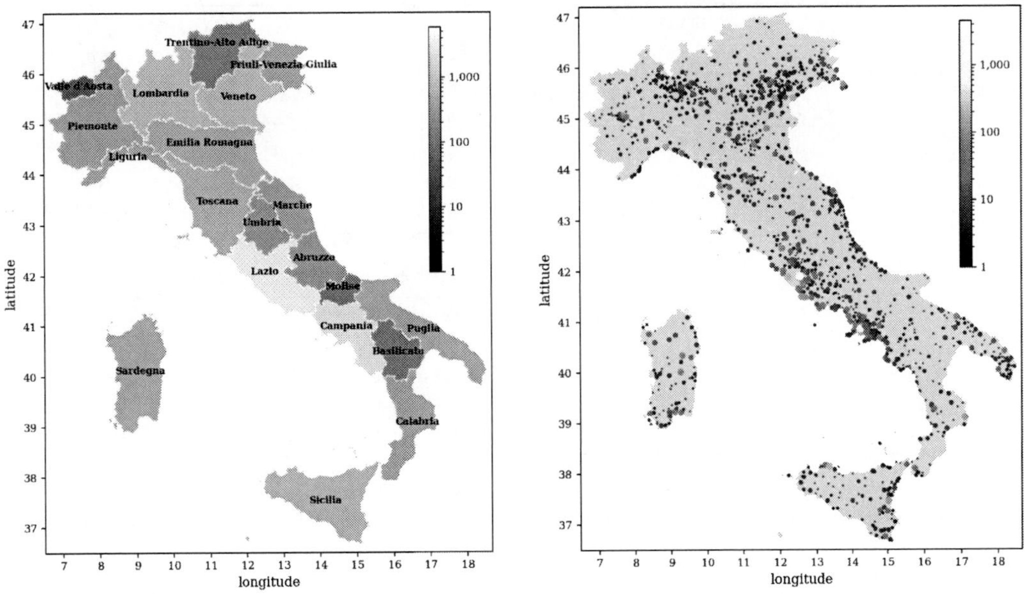

(a) Tweets by administrative region.

(b) Tweets by geographical coordinates.

Figure 2: Distribution of social media posts in the DIATOPIT corpus by administrative region and coordinates.

we present the distribution of tweets in our corpus. While Figure 2a contextualizes across space the per-region instances presented in Table 2, Figure 2b shows a fine-grained distribution of social media posts by geographical coordinates. As expected, a large number of posts comes from densely-populated cities and coastal and lowlands areas. Rural and mountain areas are instead weakly represented. Although the resident population is a good indicator for the amount of content that is posted online within a particular area, the density of *non*-Standard Italian content can diverge a lot between regions (cf. Section 3.1). Moreover, densely-populated areas do not always exhibit a high proportion of tweets. This is the case of e.g., Piemonte (PIE), a region of northwest Italy (cf. Figure 2a) with a population of > 4.2M, for which there exists a relatively low number of tweets containing *non*-Standard Italian content (1.9%, cf. Table 2) due to the limited use of local varieties (Figure 3).

3.3 Density and Functions of OOV Tokens

We hypothesize that geographical areas in which local language varieties are spoken the most are likely to exhibit a lower degree of mixing with Standard Italian compared to areas in which those are gradually disappearing. Indeed, the less a variety is used, the more lexical items that belong to Standard Italian would be employed.

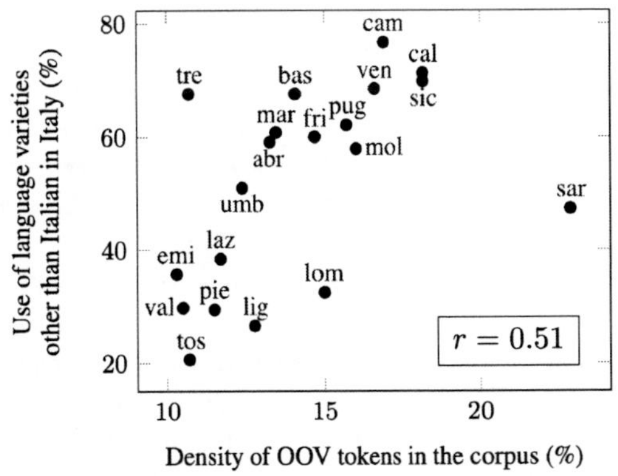

Figure 3: Pearson correlation coefficient (r) between the density of OOV tokens (T_{oov}/T_{all}) for each region and the actual usage of language varieties other than Standard Italian in those regions (ISTAT, 2017).

To test this hypothesis and assess the representativeness of DIATOPIT, we take the results of the most recent national survey on the actual use of languages and dialects in Italy divided by region (ISTAT, 2017) and check if the proportion of OOV tokens (T_{oov}/T_{all}) in our corpus for those regions correlates with it (cf. Appendix C). We calculated the Pearson correlation coefficient r and found a substantial correlation ($r = 0.51$). As shown in Figure 3, there is a high correlation for most regions, with the exception of Trentino-Alto Adige (TRE)

CAL		CAM		EMI		LAZ		LOM	
token	*score*	*token*	*score*	*token*	*score*	*token*	*score*	*token*	*score*
u	1.00	o*	1.00	soccia	1.00	na	1.00	i*	1.00
ccu	0.91	e*	1.00	cinno	0.96	de	0.97	el	0.99
i*	0.90	tutt	0.94	maroni	0.94	pe	0.97	ratt	0.99
frica	0.85	nun	0.90	cagher	0.91	je	0.94	ciapa	0.96
ca	0.84	stu	0.88	mond	0.85	er	0.89	insci̇̀	0.93
PUG		**SAR**		**SIC**		**TOS**		**VEN**	
token	*score*	*token*	*score*	*token*	*score*	*token*	*score*	*token*	*score*
lu	1.00	su*	1.00	u	1.00	diaccio	0.96	ghe	1.00
sule	0.83	sa	0.99	bonu	0.93	pigliá	0.91	xe	1.00
ientu	0.82	tottu	0.97	ca	0.89	tope	0.89	el	0.96
trmon	0.74	itte	0.95	cu	0.88	gliè	0.88	no*	0.83
trimone	0.72	unu	0.93	semu	0.87	boja	0.86	ga	0.81

Table 3: Top-5 most indicative tokens and associated scores (in $[0, 1]$) for regions with $\geq 2\%$ instances in the DIATOPIT corpus. Tokens marked with * are those that are typically included in stopword lists for Standard Italian.

and Sardegna (SAR). While results for TRE can be justified by highly-spoken German varieties in the South Tyrol province that are little represented in our corpus (cf. Limitations section), we argue that results for SAR are due to the long-established speakers' awareness of the prestige status of their varieties (i.e., Sardinian: srd, Sassarese: sdc, and Gallurese: sdn). Indeed, the survey by ISTAT (2017) mostly framed questions using the word "*dialect*", a term that historically carries negative connotations in Italy (Avolio, 2009).

Besides the raw density of *non*-Standard Italian content, the function of the most indicative OOV tokens for each region can give insights into language use and vitality, too. Intuitively, the more language varieties are spoken in a region, the higher is the likelihood that non-content tokens that are necessary to form articulated sentences (e.g., articles, prepositions and conjunctions) are used.

To the goal, we employ the lexical artifacts package (Ramponi and Tonelli, 2022) and compute the most discriminative tokens for each region in a *one-vs-rest* scheme, i.e., unveiling lexical items that are more frequently used in the region of interest compared to all other regions. We present the top-5 most indicative tokens for all regions with $\geq 2\%$ instances over the total[13] in Table 3.

Regions in which local varieties are spoken the most (i.e., CAL, CAM, SIC, VEN; cf. Figure 3, *top*) mostly present non-content tokens as the most informative, confirming our hyphothesis. Both CAL and SIC have "*u*" (en: *the* [M. SG.]) and "*ccu/cu*" (en: *with*) among the most indicative terms, as well as "*i*" (CAL; en: *the* [M. PL.]), and "*semu*" (SIC; en: *we are*), amongst others. Relevant examples for CAM and VEN also include "o" and "el" (en: *the* [M. SG.]), "stu" (CAM; en: *this*), "ghe" (VEN; en: *there is*), and "xe" (VEN; en: *is*). SAR also shows non-content tokens as the most informative, e.g., "*su*" (en: *the* [M. SG.]), "*sa*" (en: *the* [F. SG.]) and "*unu*" (en: *a/an/one*), confirming that the high density of OOV terms for this region is due to a confident use of local varieties by their speakers.

On the other hand, regions from Table 3 in which languages and dialects are spoken the least (i.e., EMI, LOM, TOS; cf. Figure 3, *bottom*) show a higher fraction of non-content tokens, a sign of the increasingly restricted function of language varieties. As prototypical examples, we can find "*cinno*" (EMI; en: *kid*), "*ratt*" (LOM; en: *rat(s)*), and "*diaccio*" (TOS; en: *icy/frozen/very cold*).

Exceptions on the ends are represented by PUG and LAZ (cf. Figure 3, *mid-top* and *mid-bottom*, respectively). PUG exhibits both content and non-content tokens, e.g., "*lu*" (en: *the* [M. SG.]), "*ientu*" (en: *wind*), and "*trmon*" (en: *stupid*), whereas LAZ only comprises non-content tokens, e.g., "*na*" (en: *a/an* [F. SG.]), "*de*" (en: *of*), and "*pe*" (en: *for*). While for PUG this can be ascribable to the small size of its subset and thus to the diversity of language included in it, the situation of LAZ is to be considered an outlier. Specifically, varieties spoken in LAZ are highly used indeed, but they

[13]This allows us to ground the discussion based on the subsets for which the PMI-based computation (Fano, 1961) behind the lexical artifacts package is more reliable.

are considered "ways of speaking" or "accents" of Standard Italian rather than proper language varieties (De Mauro, 1989). This has probably had an impact on the results of the aforementioned survey by ISTAT (2017) and justifies this divergence.

4 Experiments

In this section we present our experiments on the DIATOPIT corpus. Our objective is to understand how difficult it is to model diatopic language variation in Italy, i.e., by identifying coarse- and fine-grained geographical areas of a post based solely on its textual content.[14] Ultimately, this will help in building tools to reliably identify content for language varieties of Italy from social media, and thus to better represent them in NLP. We first introduce the experimental setup (Section 4.1) and the baselines we employed (Section 4.2). Then, we present the results and provide a discussion (Section 4.3).

4.1 Experimental Setup

Tasks We cast the problem of identifying the area from which a tweet has been posted into two tasks of increasing complexity: *(i) coarse-grained geolocation* (CG), i.e., predict the administrative region from which a tweet has been posted (classification task), and *(ii) fine-grained geolocation* (FG), i.e., predict latitude and longitude coordinates for the post (double-regression task). For each task we provide several experimental baselines (Section 4.2).

Data splits For training and testing the models, we divide the corpus into `train`, `dev`, and `test` sets. Given the highly-unbalanced distribution of instances across regions (cf. Table 2), for `dev` and `test` sets we draw a number of posts per region according to a smoothed distribution. Specifically, for each region r we take its raw number of instances I_r and we calculate a smoothed value $\sqrt{I_r}$, further adjusted by a multiplication factor λ to control the proportional size of the resulting `dev` and `test` sets.[15] This ensures a more reliable evaluation due to a higher percentage of instances in `dev` and `test` sets for under-represented regions. Moreover, we deliberately avoid sampling those instances at random, since this process could lead to a limited coverage of linguistic phenomena and microvariation in `dev` and `test`. We instead ask curators to manually select `dev` and `test` instances from a 50% random sample for each region[16] to be as representative as possible of a wide range of linguistic phenomena and microvariation. Additionally, we also ask them not to include instances that explicitly cite others (e.g., *"as my grandma says: 'X'"*) to focus our evaluation on actual language use. Once the predefined smoothed value for each region was reached, we added the rest of the examples to the remaining 50% (i.e., `train`). Due to the very low number of instances for some regions, and thus scarcity of data for properly evaluating those, we decided to keep posts for the top-13 regions (≥ 200 instances) for development and the top-17 regions (≥ 50 instances) for testing (cf. Table 2), while leaving all 20 regions for training. This led to 13,669 examples for `train`, 552 examples for `dev`, and 818 examples for `test`, distributed as shown in Appendix D.

Evaluation metrics Since the distribution of instances per region is highly imbalanced, for the CG task we use macro-averaged scores so that each region in the evaluation set (either `dev` or `test`) is factored equally into the metric. Specifically, we employ macro-averaged precision (P), recall (R), and F_1 score. For the FG task, we instead use the mean error of the predicted coordinates from actual coordinates in kilometers (km), calculated using the Haversine formula.[17]

4.2 Baseline Models

We use several baseline models in order to provide reference points for future work using our corpus.

Naïve baselines For task CG we use a most-frequent baseline that always predicts the most frequent region in the training set (i.e., LAZ). For the FG task we instead employ a centroid baseline that computes the center point from training instances and predicts it for all test instances.

[14] This is in contrast to standard language/dialect identification tasks, in which the goal is to categorize texts into uniform language/dialect categories rather than identify areas where those are spoken – thus taking microvariation into account. Our formulation also differs from the Italy's language and dialect identification task (Aepli et al., 2022), in that we also deal with naturally occurring code-switched content and regional varieties of Standard Italian. Moreover, we model language from social media which is more spontaneous and does not necessarily adhere to orthography standards.

[15] We use $\lambda = 1.50$ and $\lambda = 2.25$ for `dev` and `test`, respectively, i.e., making the size of the `test` 3/2 that of `dev`. For regions for which instances are extremely scarce, we simply draw the same number of `dev` instances for the `test` portion.

[16] This further ensures that `train` is not deprived of important signal since it was left untouched in this process.

[17] https://github.com/mapado/haversine

Machine learning models For both tasks we train two traditional models: for the CG task, we train a logistic regression (LR) and a support vector machine (SVM) classifier, whereas for FG we train a regression model based on k-nearest neighbors (kNN) and a decision tree (DT) regressor. We use the `scikit-learn`[18] count vectorizer for feature extraction and employ default hyperparameters.

Pretrained language models We fine-tune two monolingual and two multilingual transformer-based (Vaswani et al., 2017) models for each task. The monolingual models we use are AlBERTo (Polignano et al., 2019), a BERT-based (Devlin et al., 2019) model pre-trained on Italian text data from Twitter, and UmBERTo (Parisi et al., 2020), a RoBERTa-based (Liu et al., 2019) model pre-trained on the Italian portion of the OSCAR web-crawled corpus (Suárez et al., 2019). While DIATOPIT comprises *non*-Standard Italian content, we hypothesize that the pre-training material that has been used by those models (i.e., social media texts and raw data) may include content in language varieties of Italy due to the over-prediction of Italian of current language identifiers (cf. Section 2.1).

The multilingual models we use are instead multilingual BERT base (mBERT; Devlin et al., 2019), which is pre-trained on Wikipedia texts in 104 languages, and XLM-Roberta base (XLM-R; Conneau et al., 2020), which is pre-trained on the filtered CommonCrawl raw corpus in 100 languages. In addition to Italian, mBERT pre-training material includes Wikipedia content for some language varieties represented in DIATOPIT, i.e., Lombard [`lmo`], Piedmontese [`pms`] and Sicilian [`scn`], albeit it reflects an artificial use of language (Ramponi, 2022).

We use default Huggingface (Wolf et al., 2020) `TrainingArguments` hyperparameters, setting the learning rate to $5e^{-5}$ and training models for 10 epochs. For the CG task we use a batch size of 32 and cross-entropy loss, whereas for the FG task we train models using a batch size of 64 and mean squared error (MSE) loss. We use MSE loss instead of mean absolute error (MAE) loss as it assigns higher penalties to large errors.

4.3 Results and Discussion

In this section we report the results obtained by our baselines for both tasks. Results are averaged across 5 runs using different random seeds for shuffling the data and initializing the models.

[18] `https://scikit-learn.org/stable/index.html`

Method	**P**	**R**	**F_1**
Most frequent	$4.47_{\pm 0.0}$	$21.15_{\pm 0.0}$	$7.38_{\pm 0.0}$
LR	$60.36_{\pm 0.0}$	$45.92_{\pm 0.0}$	$49.29_{\pm 0.0}$
SVM	$63.83_{\pm 0.0}$	$51.04_{\pm 0.0}$	$53.95_{\pm 0.0}$
AlBERTo	$62.52_{\pm 2.3}$	$56.98_{\pm 1.2}$	$\mathbf{58.43}_{\pm 1.5}$
UmBERTo	$58.97_{\pm 2.4}$	$55.86_{\pm 2.2}$	$56.19_{\pm 2.2}$
mBERT	$59.71_{\pm 3.1}$	$56.48_{\pm 2.2}$	$57.29_{\pm 2.4}$
XLM-R	$57.73_{\pm 3.0}$	$51.35_{\pm 1.3}$	$51.86_{\pm 1.9}$

Table 4: Test set results for the CG task. We report average precision (P), recall (R), and macro F_1 scores across 5 runs (±: std dev). Best results are in bold.

4.3.1 Coarse-Grained Geolocation

Results on the CG task are presented in Table 4. The best-performing baseline is AlBERTo, with a macro F_1 score of 58.43, while – besides the most frequent baseline – the lowest score is obtained by LR, with a macro F_1 score of 49.29. Interestingly, the SVM classifier is a strong baseline even though it is far less computationally expensive than transformer-based models, performing better (+2.09) than XLM-R. A potential reason for traditional models to be competitive against large language models (LLMs) is that the variation of lexical items across varieties makes them very informative features. Furthermore, LLMs could suffer from suboptimal subword tokenization, given that tokenizers for these models are not optimized for the language varieties in our corpus. Overall, it appears that transformer-based models might benefit from being trained on in-domain data (i.e., Twitter for AlBERTo) or data containing a subset of the varieties represented in DIATOPIT (e.g., mBERT).

The CG task is generally challenging, not only because it represents a very unbalanced multi-class classification problem (cf. Table 2), but also because there are some language varieties that are very close across regions, especially in border areas. In Figure 4 we present the confusion matrix for our best-performing baseline (i.e., AlBERTo), showing the effect of these challenges on model predictions. For instance, the high class imbalance causes the model to perform better (especially with regards to recall) on highly represented regions (e.g., LAZ and CAM), while regions with a lower percentage of instances in the corpus tend to be predicted less frequently. Specifically, regions that are scarcely represented in training data are often confused with neighboring regions and/or regions where a simi-

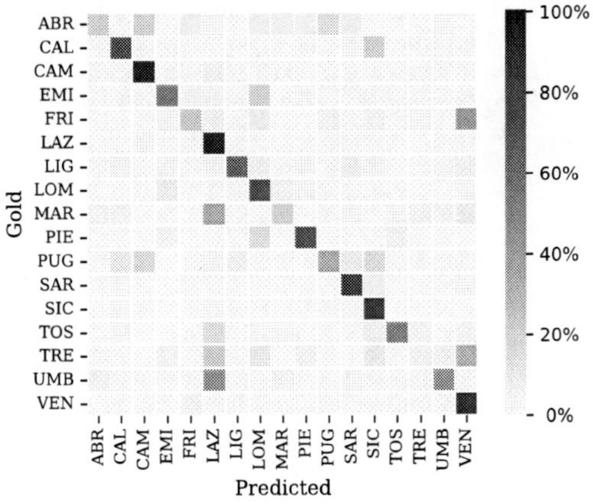

Figure 4: Confusion matrix for AlBERTo on the CG test set. Each row is normalized so that its sum is 100%.

lar variety is spoken. This is the case of e.g., FRI and TRE, in which varieties of Venetian [vec] are spoken (amongst others), and thus instances are often misclassified as VEN, the region in which vec is predominantly used. Similarly, PUG is often confused with CAM, but also with SIC, despite not being near to it. This is because of language varieties spoken in the southern part of PUG (i.e., *Salentino* varieties), which are close to those of SIC, being both part of extreme southern varieties (cf. Pellegrini (1977) for more details). Results by region for all methods are in Appendix D.

Despite the aforementioned challenges, in part due to the simplification entailed in framing diatopic variation across space as a classification task in which the labels are administrative regions, the error analysis shows that models tend to confound regions that actually share common linguistic traits. This seems to indicate that DIATOPIT does reflect the actual distribution of language varieties in Italy.

4.3.2 Fine-Grained Geolocation

Results on the FG task for all baselines are presented in Table 5. Similarly to the coarse-grained geolocation task, the best-performing model is AlBERTo, with a mean average error of 151.54 km. Interestingly, DT performs similarly to AlBERTo (152.45 km; +0.91), even though it requires a fraction of the computational cost. Other transformer-based models have much higher error rates than AlBERTo, as well as a very large standard deviation across runs. This indicates that they are not sufficiently robust for modeling fine-grained geolocation. We hypothesize that the stability of results by AlBERTo compared to UmBERTo, mBERT, and XLM-R is due to the in-domain nature of textual data used during pre-training. Moreover, the good results obtained by DT suggest that current transformer-based models are rather limited for modeling language variation over space in highly multilingual areas such as Italy due to an insufficient vocabulary coverage. In future work we plan to experiment with token-free models (Xue et al., 2022; Clark et al., 2022; Tay et al., 2022) to assess if the vocabulary issue can be mitigated.

Method	Avg dist (km)
Centroid	$281.04_{\pm 0.0}$
*k*NN	$245.60_{\pm 0.0}$
DT	$152.45_{\pm 1.4}$
AlBERTo	$\mathbf{151.54}_{\pm 7.8}$
UmBERTo	$207.65_{\pm 41.3}$
mBERT	$211.51_{\pm 39.4}$
XLM-R	$266.32_{\pm 23.8}$

Table 5: Test set results for the FG task. We report the average distance in kilometers across 5 runs (±: std dev). Best results are in bold (the lower, the better).

More generally, the improvement achieved by our best baseline over the centroid baseline for the FG task is comparable or better than the improvements obtained by the best-performing models in the Social Media Variety Geolocation (SMG) task at the 2020 VarDial Evaluation Campaign (Gaman et al., 2020), focused on the geolocation of social media posts in different geographical areas. While our best model's mean error improves by 46.08% over the centroid baseline, the models in the SMG task showed mean error improvements over the centroid baselines of 40.41%, 16,96%, and 47.97%.

5 Conclusion

We present DIATOPIT, the first corpus focused on diatopic variation in Italy for language varieties other than Standard Italian. Our analyses and experiments show that DIATOPIT is highly representative of actual use of Italy's language varieties, and can thus be used to advance research in the area. We plan to study divergences in orthography and code-switching in future work, in order to further assess vitality across varieties. Data and relevant materials (e.g., search terms) are available to the research community at `https://github.com/dhfbk/diatopit`.

Ethics Statement and Limitations

We release the corpus in the form of tweet IDs to be hydrated, in compliance to the Twitter developer policy. The corpus contains content that may be offensive or upsetting due to the occasional use of swear words by users. Latitude and longitude coordinates do not correspond to specific places within cities, but instead represent cities as a whole (i.e., posts within the same city have the same coordinates). Curators are part of the authors of this paper, and did the curation as part of their work. The corpus is meant to study diatopic language variation in Italy and can be used for research purposes only.

DIATOPIT includes content in regional varieties of Standard Italian as well as content written in the following local language varieties (ISO 639-3): `egl`, `fur`, `lij`, `lmo`, `nap`, `pms`, `rgn`, `scn`, `sdc`, `sdn`, `srd`, and `vec`, albeit with different amounts of data. Rare instances for `aae`, *Algherese Catalan* and *Calabrian Greek* are also present. Germanic varieties (e.g., `cim`, `mhn`, `wae`, *South Tyrolean*), `frp`, `lld`, and `svm` are instead mostly absent due to either the very low number of speakers or the sampling procedure. As regards to the latter, we plan to further extend the corpus with relevant samples classified as other than `it` by the Twitter language identifier to further mitigate under-representation of certain language varieties due to orthographic reasons or language branch.

References

Noëmi Aepli, Antonios Anastasopoulos, Adrian-Gabriel Chifu, William Domingues, Fahim Faisal, Mihaela Gaman, Radu Tudor Ionescu, and Yves Scherrer. 2022. Findings of the VarDial evaluation campaign 2022. In *Proceedings of the Ninth Workshop on NLP for Similar Languages, Varieties and Dialects*, pages 1–13, Gyeongju, Republic of Korea. Association for Computational Linguistics.

Francesco Avolio. 2009. *Lingue e Dialetti d'Italia*. Le Bussole. Carocci, Roma, Italy.

Matteo Bartoli, Ugo Pellis, and Lorenzo Massobrio. 1995. *Atlante Linguistico Italiano*. Istituto Poligrafico e Zecca dello Stato, Roma, Italy.

Emily M. Bender and Batya Friedman. 2018. Data statements for natural language processing: Toward mitigating system bias and enabling better science. *Transactions of the Association for Computational Linguistics*, 6:587–604.

Massimo Cerruti and Riccardo Regis. 2005. 'Code switching' e teoria linguistica: La situazione italoromanza. *Italian Journal of Linguistics*, 17(1):179.

Bharathi Raja Chakravarthi, Gaman Mihaela, Radu Tudor Ionescu, Heidi Jauhiainen, Tommi Jauhiainen, Krister Lindén, Nikola Ljubešić, Niko Partanen, Ruba Priyadharshini, Christoph Purschke, Eswari Rajagopal, Yves Scherrer, and Marcos Zampieri. 2021. Findings of the VarDial evaluation campaign 2021. In *Proceedings of the Eighth Workshop on NLP for Similar Languages, Varieties and Dialects*, pages 1–11, Kiyv, Ukraine. Association for Computational Linguistics.

Jonathan H. Clark, Dan Garrette, Iulia Turc, and John Wieting. 2022. Canine: Pre-training an efficient tokenization-free encoder for language representation. *Transactions of the Association for Computational Linguistics*, 10:73–91.

Alexis Conneau, Kartikay Khandelwal, Naman Goyal, Vishrav Chaudhary, Guillaume Wenzek, Francisco Guzmán, Edouard Grave, Myle Ott, Luke Zettlemoyer, and Veselin Stoyanov. 2020. Unsupervised cross-lingual representation learning at scale. In *Proceedings of the 58th Annual Meeting of the Association for Computational Linguistics*, pages 8440–8451, Online. Association for Computational Linguistics.

Tullio De Mauro. 1989. *Il romanesco ieri e oggi*. Bulzoni, Roma, Italy.

Jacob Devlin, Ming-Wei Chang, Kenton Lee, and Kristina Toutanova. 2019. BERT: Pre-training of deep bidirectional transformers for language understanding. In *Proceedings of the 2019 Conference of the North American Chapter of the Association for Computational Linguistics: Human Language Technologies, Volume 1 (Long and Short Papers)*, pages 4171–4186, Minneapolis, Minnesota. Association for Computational Linguistics.

Jacob Eisenstein. 2013. What to do about bad language on the internet. In *Proceedings of the 2013 Conference of the North American Chapter of the Association for Computational Linguistics: Human Language Technologies*, pages 359–369, Atlanta, Georgia. Association for Computational Linguistics.

Robert M Fano. 1961. Transmission of information: A statistical theory of communications. *American Journal of Physics*, 29:793–794.

Mihaela Gaman, Dirk Hovy, Radu Tudor Ionescu, Heidi Jauhiainen, Tommi Jauhiainen, Krister Lindén, Nikola Ljubešić, Niko Partanen, Christoph Purschke, Yves Scherrer, and Marcos Zampieri. 2020. A report on the VarDial evaluation campaign 2020. In *Proceedings of the 7th Workshop on NLP for Similar Languages, Varieties and Dialects*, pages 1–14, Barcelona, Spain (Online). International Committee on Computational Linguistics (ICCL).

Bo Han, Afshin Rahimi, Leon Derczynski, and Timothy Baldwin. 2016. Twitter geolocation prediction shared task of the 2016 workshop on noisy user-generated text. In *Proceedings of the 2nd Workshop on Noisy*

User-generated Text (WNUT), pages 213–217, Osaka, Japan. The COLING 2016 Organizing Committee.

ISTAT. 2017. L'uso della lingua italiana, dei dialetti e di altre lingue in Italia. https://www.istat.it/it/archivio/207961. Accessed: 2023-02-01.

Karl Jaberg, Jakob Jud, and Glauco Sanga. 1987. *Atlante Linguistico ed Etnografico dell'Italia e della Svizzera Meridionale*, Italian edition. Unicopli, Milano, Italy.

Yinhan Liu, Myle Ott, Naman Goyal, Jingfei Du, Mandar Joshi, Danqi Chen, Omer Levy, Mike Lewis, Luke Zettlemoyer, and Veselin Stoyanov. 2019. RoBERTa: A robustly optimized BERT pretraining approach. *arXiv preprint arXiv:1907.11692.*

Martin Maiden and Mair Parry. 1997. *The Dialects of Italy.* Routledge, London, England.

Christopher Moseley. 2010. *Atlas of the World's Languages in Danger*, 3rd edition. Memory of Peoples. UNESCO Publishing, Paris, France.

Loreto Parisi, Simone Francia, and Paolo Magnani. 2020. UmBERTo: an Italian language model trained with whole word masking. https://github.com/musixmatchresearch/umberto. Accessed: 2023-02-01.

Giovan Battista Pellegrini. 1977. *Carta dei Dialetti d'Italia.* Profilo dei Dialetti Italiani. Pacini, Pisa, Italy.

Marco Polignano, Pierpaolo Basile, Marco de Gemmis, Giovanni Semeraro, and Valerio Basile. 2019. AlBERTo: Italian BERT language understanding model for NLP challenging tasks based on tweets. In *Proceedings of the Sixth Italian Conference on Computational Linguistics (CLiC-it 2019)*, volume 2481. CEUR.

Alan Ramponi. 2022. NLP for language varieties of Italy: Challenges and the path forward. *arXiv preprint arXiv:2209.09757.*

Alan Ramponi and Sara Tonelli. 2022. Features or spurious artifacts? data-centric baselines for fair and robust hate speech detection. In *Proceedings of the 2022 Conference of the North American Chapter of the Association for Computational Linguistics: Human Language Technologies*, pages 3027–3040, Seattle, United States. Association for Computational Linguistics.

Pedro Javier Ortiz Suárez, Benoît Sagot, and Laurent Romary. 2019. Asynchronous pipeline for processing huge corpora on medium to low resource infrastructures. In *7th Workshop on the Challenges in the Management of Large Corpora (CMLC-7)*. Leibniz-Institut für Deutsche Sprache.

Yi Tay, Vinh Q Tran, Sebastian Ruder, Jai Gupta, Hyung Won Chung, Dara Bahri, Zhen Qin, Simon Baumgartner, Cong Yu, and Donald Metzler. 2022. Charformer: Fast character transformers via gradient-based subword tokenization. In *The Tenth International Conference on Learning Representations, ICLR 2022*, Virtual.

Rob van der Goot, Alan Ramponi, Arkaitz Zubiaga, Barbara Plank, Benjamin Muller, Iñaki San Vicente Roncal, Nikola Ljubešić, Özlem Çetinoğlu, Rahmad Mahendra, Talha Çolakoğlu, Timothy Baldwin, Tommaso Caselli, and Wladimir Sidorenko. 2021. MultiLexNorm: A shared task on multilingual lexical normalization. In *Proceedings of the Seventh Workshop on Noisy User-generated Text (W-NUT 2021)*, pages 493–509, Online. Association for Computational Linguistics.

Ashish Vaswani, Noam Shazeer, Niki Parmar, Jakob Uszkoreit, Llion Jones, Aidan N Gomez, Łukasz Kaiser, and Illia Polosukhin. 2017. Attention is all you need. *Advances in neural information processing systems*, 30.

Thomas Wolf, Lysandre Debut, Victor Sanh, Julien Chaumond, Clement Delangue, Anthony Moi, Pierric Cistac, Tim Rault, Remi Louf, Morgan Funtowicz, Joe Davison, Sam Shleifer, Patrick von Platen, Clara Ma, Yacine Jernite, Julien Plu, Canwen Xu, Teven Le Scao, Sylvain Gugger, Mariama Drame, Quentin Lhoest, and Alexander Rush. 2020. Transformers: State-of-the-art natural language processing. In *Proceedings of the 2020 Conference on Empirical Methods in Natural Language Processing: System Demonstrations*, pages 38–45, Online. Association for Computational Linguistics.

Linting Xue, Aditya Barua, Noah Constant, Rami Al-Rfou, Sharan Narang, Mihir Kale, Adam Roberts, and Colin Raffel. 2022. ByT5: Towards a token-free future with pre-trained byte-to-byte models. *Transactions of the Association for Computational Linguistics*, 10:291–306.

Appendix

A Data Statements

We present the data statements (Bender and Friedman, 2018) for DIATOPIT in the following.

CURATION RATIONALE. DIATOPIT consists of social media posts (partially and fully) written in language varieties of Italy other than Standard Italian, and is thus meant to encourage research on diatopic variation in Italy, study code-switching and divergences in orthography for local language varieties, and serve as a basis for responsible development of annotated resources for Italy's varieties. Details on corpus creation are given in Section 2.

LANGUAGE VARIETIES. The corpus includes content in regional varieties of Standard Italian (`ita`), as well as content written in the following local language varieties (ISO 639-3 codes, wherever available): `egl`, `fur`, `lij`, `lmo`, `nap`, `pms`, `rgn`, `scn`, `sdc`, `sdn`, `srd`, and `vec`, albeit with different amounts of data. Rare instances for `aae`, *Algherese Catalan* and *Calabrian Greek* are also present. Orthographic variation is common due to the spontaneous written speech of social media posts and the lack of standardization of most language varieties.

SPEAKER DEMOGRAPHIC. The corpus consists of anonymized social media posts, and thus user demographics are not known.

ANNOTATOR DEMOGRAPHIC. Two curators native to Italy with good knowledge of Italy's language varieties and background in NLP and sociolinguistics. They identify themselves as a woman and a man, with age ranges 20–30 and 30–40, and native speakers of `ita`, `srd`, and `vec`. Additional native speakers who have been consulted during curation in the presence of doubtful cases greatly vary in terms of demographic characteristics.

SPEECH SITUATION AND TEXT CHARACTERISTICS. The interaction is mainly asynchronous and the intended audience is everyone. The modality is (spontaneous) written text, the genre is social media without any particular topical focus due to the sampling procedure (cf. Section 2). Social media posts have been produced between `2020-07-01` and `2022-06-30`, and collected in September 2022.

PREPROCESSING AND DATA FORMATTING. All posts have been anonymized by replacing user mentions, email addresses and URLs with placeholders (i.e., `[USER]`, `[EMAIL]` and `[URL]`, respectively). Additionally, explicit location mentions derived from cross-posting have been replaced with the `[LOCATION]` placeholder. Newline characters have been replaced with single spaces. Latitude and longitude coordinates have been computed by taking the central point from the 4-point bounding box of city areas as provided by the Twitter APIs.

B Corpus Augmentation

Step 1 Data augmentation for geographical regions with $\leq 1\%$ instances I over the total has been carried out based on their initial amount of data (cf. Table 6, *top*). For regions with $I < 0.5\%$ posts (i.e., severely under-represented), all the posts matching at least an OOV token have been manually curated for inclusion (N = 4,606). For regions with $0.5\% \leq I \leq 1.0\%$ posts (i.e., moderately under-represented), a random 10% of the posts matching at least an OOV token have been manually curated for inclusion (N = 6,107). This led to 718 extra posts across all those regions, and notably an increment of more than $2\times$ instances for some regions (e.g., EMI: $0.99\% \rightarrow 2.41\%$; FRI: $0.70\% \rightarrow 1.70\%$; LIG: $0.62\% \rightarrow 1.37\%$).

Step 2 All regions except the over-represented LAZ and CAM (i.e., those with $I \leq 20.0\%$ posts over the total) were used to calculate highly-discriminative tokens for further sampling of posts (cf. Table 6, *bottom*). This led to N = 4,384 social media posts, 1,961 of which have been included in the final corpus after curation.

C Details about the Correlation Analysis

For the correlation analysis in Section 3.3 we took data from Table 1 of the survey by ISTAT (2017) on the usage of languages and dialects across Italy's administrative regions. Specifically, for our calculation we relied on percentages indicating the use of languages and dialects with friends, which is typically the case for spontaneous and informal social media content that includes local language varieties of Italy. Nevertheless, we found a similar correlation when considering the family context.

D Additional Details on the Experiments

The distribution of instances for the experiments is in Table 7, whereas results for the CG task divided by region and method are presented in Table 8.

Step	I (%)	Regions (relative percentage)
1	[0.5%, 1.0%]	Emi (0.99%), Mar (0.90%), Abr (0.85%), Pie (0.82%), Fri (0.70%), Lig (0.62%)
	< 0.5%	Tre (0.23%), Bas (0.19%), Mol (0.15%), Val (0.03%)
2	$\leq$ 20.0%	Ven (4.19%), Lom (3.79%), Sic (3.08%), Tos (2.56%), Emi (2.41%), Pug (1.86%), Fri (1.70%), Cal (1.57%), Sar (1.51%), Pie (1.49%), Lig (1.37%), Mar (1.35%), Abr (1.11%), Umb (1.09%), Tre (0.39%), Bas (0.35%), Mol (0.25%), Val (0.09%)

Table 6: Geographical regions (and their relative percentages at the beginning of each stage) that have been selected for the two steps of data augmentation, i.e., step 1 (*top*) and step 2 (*bottom*).

Abr	**Bas**	**Cal**	**Cam**	**Emi**	**Fri**	**Laz**
151 / – / 15	49 / – / –	282 / 27 / 27	3,027 / 85 / 128	320 / 30 / 45	220 / 25 / 25	5,607 / 115 / 173
Lig	**Lom**	**Mar**	**Mol**	**Pie**	**Pug**	**Sar**
223 / 25 / 25	696 / 43 / 64	181 / – / 16	35 / – / –	238 / 25 / 25	266 / 27 / 27	362 / 31 / 47
Sic	**Tos**	**Tre**	**Umb**	**Val**	**Ven**	
620 / 40 / 60	421 / 34 / 51	52 / – / 9	136 / – / 14	14 / – / –	769 / 45 / 67	

Table 7: Distribution of `train` / `dev` / `test` instances by region for the sake of computational experiments.

Region		Method					
Abbr.	Full name	LR	SVM	AlBERTo	UmBERTo	mBERT	XLM-R
Abr	*Abruzzo*	$0.00_{\pm0.0}$	$21.05_{\pm0.0}$	$27.28_{\pm14.7}$	$31.06_{\pm12.4}$	$44.28_{\pm10.1}$	$15.95_{\pm4.7}$
Cal	*Calabria*	$61.90_{\pm0.0}$	$57.14_{\pm0.0}$	$67.22_{\pm2.2}$	$56.98_{\pm8.5}$	$58.08_{\pm5.0}$	$41.42_{\pm6.7}$
Cam	*Campania*	$80.14_{\pm0.0}$	$81.75_{\pm0.0}$	$89.52_{\pm1.7}$	$91.02_{\pm1.1}$	$89.68_{\pm1.5}$	$89.73_{\pm1.4}$
Emi	*Emilia Romagna*	$47.06_{\pm0.0}$	$55.26_{\pm0.0}$	$62.04_{\pm6.4}$	$63.18_{\pm2.6}$	$56.60_{\pm4.9}$	$56.88_{\pm2.7}$
Fri	*Friuli-Venezia Giulia*	$36.36_{\pm0.0}$	$30.00_{\pm0.0}$	$28.62_{\pm4.5}$	$36.81_{\pm5.0}$	$25.24_{\pm4.9}$	$24.78_{\pm8.5}$
Laz	*Lazio*	$72.29_{\pm0.0}$	$78.47_{\pm0.0}$	$87.47_{\pm0.5}$	$88.95_{\pm1.4}$	$85.87_{\pm0.8}$	$87.01_{\pm1.3}$
Lig	*Liguria*	$48.65_{\pm0.0}$	$66.67_{\pm0.0}$	$68.95_{\pm4.8}$	$69.72_{\pm5.2}$	$76.84_{\pm2.6}$	$78.22_{\pm1.8}$
Lom	*Lombardia*	$59.84_{\pm0.0}$	$60.80_{\pm0.0}$	$70.06_{\pm1.7}$	$72.44_{\pm4.8}$	$71.97_{\pm1.9}$	$70.70_{\pm3.2}$
Mar	*Marche*	$26.09_{\pm0.0}$	$25.00_{\pm0.0}$	$20.96_{\pm5.0}$	$21.57_{\pm10.5}$	$25.75_{\pm5.7}$	$14.21_{\pm5.8}$
Pie	*Piemonte*	$75.56_{\pm0.0}$	$74.51_{\pm0.0}$	$73.21_{\pm3.7}$	$65.46_{\pm5.6}$	$71.70_{\pm1.5}$	$65.48_{\pm6.8}$
Pug	*Puglia*	$40.00_{\pm0.0}$	$38.89_{\pm0.0}$	$41.33_{\pm5.3}$	$39.97_{\pm6.0}$	$37.13_{\pm7.6}$	$29.07_{\pm5.3}$
Sar	*Sardegna*	$78.16_{\pm0.0}$	$80.95_{\pm0.0}$	$80.91_{\pm3.8}$	$80.19_{\pm2.5}$	$80.45_{\pm3.1}$	$76.53_{\pm2.6}$
Sic	*Sicilia*	$74.38_{\pm0.0}$	$74.80_{\pm0.0}$	$78.42_{\pm2.3}$	$79.76_{\pm2.6}$	$82.13_{\pm3.8}$	$78.82_{\pm3.2}$
Tos	*Toscana*	$62.50_{\pm0.0}$	$74.23_{\pm0.0}$	$67.36_{\pm3.4}$	$70.71_{\pm1.1}$	$69.28_{\pm3.4}$	$68.37_{\pm4.5}$
Tre	*Trentino-Alto Adige*	$0.00_{\pm0.0}$	$0.00_{\pm0.0}$	$4.72_{\pm6.5}$	$0.00_{\pm0.0}$	$10.30_{\pm15.1}$	$0.00_{\pm0.0}$
Umb	*Umbria*	$0.00_{\pm0.0}$	$23.53_{\pm0.0}$	$46.75_{\pm7.2}$	$5.17_{\pm7.1}$	$10.20_{\pm11.8}$	$7.11_{\pm10.2}$
Ven	*Veneto*	$75.00_{\pm0.0}$	$74.17_{\pm0.0}$	$78.38_{\pm2.4}$	$82.32_{\pm2.3}$	$78.35_{\pm3.6}$	$77.29_{\pm1.5}$

Table 8: Test set results for the CG task by region. We report average macro F_1 scores across 5 runs ($\pm$: std dev).

Dialect Representation Learning with Neural Dialect-to-Standard Normalization

Olli Kuparinen and **Yves Scherrer**
Department of Digital Humanities
University of Helsinki
olli.kuparinen@helsinki.fi, yves.scherrer@helsinki.fi

Abstract

Language label tokens are often used in multilingual neural language modeling and sequence-to-sequence learning to enhance the performance of such models. An additional product of the technique is that the models learn representations of the language tokens, which in turn reflect the relationships between the languages. In this paper, we study the learned representations of dialects produced by neural dialect-to-standard normalization models. We use two large datasets of typologically different languages, namely Finnish and Norwegian, and evaluate the learned representations against traditional dialect divisions of both languages. We find that the inferred dialect embeddings correlate well with the traditional dialects. The methodology could be further used in noisier settings to find new insights into language variation.

1 Introduction

Starting with Johnson et al. (2017), multilingual neural models have become increasingly popular for both language modeling and sequence-to-sequence learning tasks. The most common type of multilingual model makes use of language labels that are prepended to the training and test instances to inform the model about the language being processed. The embeddings of the language models can then be analyzed to find emerging properties of the relationships between the languages (Östling and Tiedemann, 2017).

In this paper, we apply the same idea to a smaller granularity of linguistic variation, namely dialectal variation within a language area, and we use dialect-to-standard normalization as the modeling task. Focusing on two typologically different languages, we experiment with large datasets of Finnish and Norwegian dialects. We study the inferred dialect embeddings with different dimensionality reduction algorithms to see whether the neural normalization models learn dialectal differences. We find that the learned representations correlate well with the traditional dialect classifications.

2 Related Work

2.1 Representation Learning in Multilingual and Multidialectal Settings

Johnson et al. (2017) present a simple approach to multilingual machine translation that relies on additional input tokens signalling the model which target language it is supposed to generate. While they find interesting benefits of this approach (e.g., zero-shot translation), they do not specifically analyze the internal representations of the language labels. In contemporary work, Östling and Tiedemann (2017) analyze the structure of the language embedding space obtained from a multilingual language model. They find for example that the inferred clustering of Germanic languages corresponds closely to the established genetic relationships.

Abe et al. (2018) combine these two lines of research and apply them to dialectal data. Their training material includes texts from 48 Japanese dialects, each of which is aligned with the standard variety. They introduce a multi-dialectal neural machine translation model translating between the dialects and standard Japanese. Besides the practical benefits of dialect-to-standard and standard-to-dialect translation, the induced dialect label embeddings can be used for dialectometric analyses. For instance, they find that the clusters inferred from the dialect embeddings correspond to the major dialect areas of Japan. In this work, we apply a similar method to Finnish and Norwegian dialects.

Instead of training multi-dialectal translation or language models, Hovy and Purschke (2018) use a topic modelling approach to learn continuous document representations of cities in a large corpus of online posts from the German-speaking area. These city embeddings reflect the major German dialect areas according to earlier dialectological

Tenth Workshop on NLP for Similar Languages, Varieties and Dialects (VarDial 2023), pages 200–212
May 5, 2023

research.

2.2 Dialect-to-Standard Normalization

The dialect-to-standard translation task, often also referred to as dialect normalization, has been independently researched for a number of dialect areas, e.g., Swiss German (Scherrer and Ljubešić, 2016; Honnet et al., 2018), Finnish (Partanen et al., 2019) or Estonian (Hämäläinen et al., 2022). Most commonly, statistical or neural character-level machine translation models are used for this task.

Methodologically, dialect normalization is closely related to historical text normalization, and recent work in this field has notably investigated the optimal word segmentation strategies and hyperparameters (Bollmann, 2019; Wu et al., 2021; Bawden et al., 2022). We take these recent findings into account in our experiments.

2.3 Finnish and Norwegian Dialects

Both Finnish and Norwegian boast differing dialects which are used in everyday speech. There is also a long dialectological tradition for both languages, which is visible in the amount of available dialect corpora. In addition to the datasets used in this work (see Section 3), there are, for instance, the LiA corpus of historical dialect recordings in Norwegian (Hagen et al., 2021) and the Finnish Dialect Syntax archive (University of Turku and Institute for the Languages of Finland, 1985).

The dialects of Finnish are traditionally divided into Eastern and Western dialects (see Figure 1) and to eight more fine-grained dialect areas. The division is mostly based on Kettunen (1940) and explicitly defined in e.g., Itkonen (1989). We use this eight-dialect division for the evaluation of our representation learning.

The dialects of Norwegian are divided into four dialect areas: Western, Eastern, Central (or Trøndersk) and Northern dialects (Hanssen, 2010 - 2014), which in turn have several subgroups. We use the four-dialect division for evaluation. The dialect divisions for both languages are presented in Figure 1.

3 Data

3.1 Samples of Spoken Finnish

The Samples of Spoken Finnish corpus (fi. *Suomen kielen näytteitä*, SKN) is a collection of interviews conducted mostly in the 1960s (Institute for the Languages of Finland, 2021).[1] The corpus includes 99 interviews from 50 locations (2 for each location, with one exception) and presents the dialects of Finnish comprehensively. The key figures of the dataset are described in Table 1.

The interviews have been transcribed with the Uralic Phonetic Alphabet (UPA) on two levels of precision: a detailed transcription with diacritics and a simplified version which relies mostly on standard Finnish characters. We use the simplified transcriptions and only the utterances of the interviewees, not the interviewers. The transcriptions have been manually normalized to standard Finnish. The detailed transcriptions have been used for dialect-to-standard normalization in Partanen et al. (2019).

3.2 Norwegian Dialect Corpus

The Norwegian Dialect Corpus (Johannessen et al., 2009) consists of interviews and informal conversations recorded in Norway between 2006 and 2010.[2] The corpus was collected as part of a larger study focusing on the dialectal variation of the North Germanic languages. The recordings come from 111 locations, with 438 speakers appearing in total. The same speakers appear in interviews and conversations with each other. We use the utterances of both contexts. The size of the dataset is described in Table 1.

The recordings have been phonetically transcribed and normalized to Bokmål (one of the standard languages for Norwegian). The normalization has been conducted semi-automatically: first with an automatic tool and thereafter manually checked.

The publicly available transcriptions and normalizations are not well aligned: the number of utterances is not identical, only one of the two layers contains quotation marks, and the orthographic transcriptions for some utterances are missing. We automatically re-align the transcriptions and normalizations before using them in our experiments.[3]

4 Experimental Setup

4.1 Preprocessing

We remove punctuation and pause markers from the transcriptions and normalizations, and exclude

[1] http://urn.fi/urn:nbn:fi:lb-2021112221, Licence: CC-BY

[2] http://www.tekstlab.uio.no/scandiasyn/download.html, Licence: CC BY-NC-SA 4.0.

[3] The re-aligned version of NDC is available at https://github.com/Helsinki-NLP/ndc-aligned.

		Speakers	Locations	Texts	Sentences	Words
SKN	(Samples of Spoken Finnish)	99	50	99	41,407	630,665
NDC	(Norwegian Dialect Corpus)	438	111	684	126,460	1,684,059

Table 1: The sizes of our two datasets.

Dialect	mie poikain kans olen kahen teäl
Standard	minä poikani kanssa olen kahden täällä
Dialect-BPE	<SKN34_Markkova> mi@@ e po@@ i@@ ka@@ in kan@@ s ol@@ en ka@@ h@@ en te@@ ä@@ l
Standard-BPE	minä po@@ i@@ ka@@ ni kan@@ ssa ol@@ en ka@@ hd@@ en tä@@ ä@@ llä
English gloss	'Me and my son are alone here.'

Table 2: An example sentence from the Finnish dataset, with the source and target on top, preprocessed source and target (i.e. BPE-encoded and source label added) in the middle, and an English gloss below. The label in the beginning of the source identifies the speaker, and the embeddings learned on these label tokens are used for the analyses.

utterances that only include filler words (such as *mm, aha*, for instance). For NDC, we substitute all anonymized name tags with a capital X. The names in SKN are not anonymized, and we thus leave them as they are. Each speaker's utterances are split so that 80% of sentences are used for training, 10% of sentences are used for the development, and 10% of sentences are set aside for testing.

Following recent findings in historical text normalization (e.g., Tang et al., 2018; Bawden et al., 2022), we work on subword tokens instead of characters. We segment our data with the byte-pair encoding (BPE; Sennrich et al., 2016) algorithm. The number of merge operations is set to 200, following Gutierrez-Vasques et al. (2021). The vocabulary is shared between the source and the target. This results in a vocabulary of 336 tokens for SKN and 360 tokens for NDC. The vocabularies were evaluated qualitatively and they include meaningful units such as case markers and other morphological units for Finnish, as well as frequent words such as pronouns for both languages. Further tuning of the vocabulary size could anyhow enhance the results.

We add a speaker label at the beginning of each utterance. Note that labels generally indicate the target variety, whereas in our setup they represent the source variety. The target variety is fixed to be the standard. Therefore, the labels are not necessary for successful normalization, but we use them here to infer the speaker representations. An example of our preprocessing is shown in Table 2.

4.2 NMT Model Setup

Our NMT model is a classical Transformer with 6 encoder and decoder layers, vector size 512, and 8 attention heads each (Vaswani et al., 2017). We enabled position representation clipping because we found it to be beneficial in preliminary experiments. The models were trained for 100,000 steps with a batch size of 5000 tokens and gradient accumulation over 8 batches, and an initial learning rate of 4. The models were trained with the OpenNMT-py (Klein et al., 2017) toolkit with the default settings for all other parameters.[4]

4.3 Dimensionality Reduction

After training the NMT model, we obtain the embedding vectors for each of the speaker labels. This results in a matrix with 99 (SKN) or 438 (NDC) rows and 512 columns.

We run three dimensionality reduction methods on the matrices: a principal component analysis (PCA; Hotelling 1933), a k-means clustering (MacQueen, 1967), and hierarchical agglomerative clustering with Ward linkage (Ward, 1963). All methods are run on the scikit-learn toolkit (Pedregosa et al., 2011).

The PCA is used to visualize the dialect continuum (see 4.4). Because the visualization relies on three color channels (red, green, and blue), the PCA is run with three components, each being represented by one color. Both k-means and Ward clustering are run with the number of clusters ranging from 2 to 20, and the clusterings are evaluated

[4]We did initial testing with an RNN-based model as well, but the results were considerably better with the Transformer.

with the methodology described in Section 4.5. The number of clusters was defined by preliminary experiments, which showed that increasing the number above 20 did not enhance the results. K-means clustering is averaged over five runs, since it is known to fluctuate.

4.4 Visualization

The PCA weights are normalized to values between 0 and 1 and used to present the red, green and blue colors in a map visualization (Nerbonne et al., 1999). For example, having values such as 0.5 for PC1, 0.25 for PC2, and 0.75 for PC3 would translate to 128 on the red channel, 64 on the green channel, and 192 on the blue channel, since the maximum value per color is 256. Having a color channel for each of the three components therefore translates to a single color (purple in the example case). The method is used to create Figure 2. A similar approach has been presented in Hovy and Purschke (2018), and an often used technique in dialectometry called multidimensional scaling (MDS) functions on the same principle but with distance matrices (Nerbonne et al., 1999; Leinonen et al., 2016).

The best clustering results are also presented on maps. The map visualizations are created with QGIS (QGIS Development Team, 2023). For the Ward clustering results, we present the dendrograms (see Figure 6), which show the relations between clusters. The dendrograms are created with scipy (Virtanen et al., 2020) and matplotlib (Hunter, 2007) toolkits.

4.5 Evaluation

We evaluate the normalization performance on the development sets to ensure that our models are working as expected. We compare our results to Partanen et al. (2019), who produce a good baseline for the SKN dataset, even though they use the detailed transcriptions and different preprocessing[5] in their work. Since they evaluate their model performance on word error rate (WER), we use the same metric for the comparison.[6]

We evaluate the clusters produced by k-means and Ward primarily with V-measure (Rosenberg and Hirschberg, 2007). V-measure is the harmonic mean of homogeneity (how homogeneous the produced clusters are in terms of predefined classes) and completeness (how well the predefined classes stay complete in the clustering). Completeness is typically higher with fewer clusters (there are less clusters for the classes to spread out into) and homogeneity with a higher number of clusters (the clusters do not include as many classes). V-measure can thus be seen as an equivalent of F_1-score and homogeneity and completeness as precision and recall. The difference is that V-measure does not expect there to be an exact right number of clusters. The V-measure score is between 0 and 1, with 1 being a perfect match between the gold labels and the clustering solution.

As a more traditional metric, we also present the adjusted Rand index (Rand, 1971). As V-measure, the adjusted Rand index tries to compute the similarity between the gold labels and the predicted labels of a clustering algorithm. Mathematically, Rand index presents the probability that a randomly chosen pair of elements from the gold labels and the predicted labels will agree. The adjusted Rand index (ARI) is typically used instead of the plain version, as it is corrected for chance. The ARI score is between -1 and 1, with 0 being a random prediction and 1 being a perfect match. Scores below 0 are worse than the random baseline. Both V-measure and ARI are computed with the scikit-learn toolkit (Pedregosa et al., 2011).

We evaluate the clusterings against traditional dialect divisions. For Finnish, we use the eight-way classification presented in Itkonen (1989). For Norwegian, the ground truth is the four-way divide presented in Hanssen (2010 - 2014). The dialect divisions are presented in Figure 1. We compare our results to a geographically and administratively defined baseline, namely the regional units of Finland (NUTS3 in European Union Nomenclature), and the counties used in Norway from 1972 to 2018.[7]

5 Results

5.1 Normalization Performance

The word error rates for our models and for Partanen et al. (2019) are presented in Table 3. Our SKN model produces a similar, albeit slightly worse, score than in their work. As far as we are aware, there is no existing work on the normalization of

[5]On top of the different transcriptions, they use a character-level neural machine translation model with an RNN-architecture, and split the data to chunks of three words (non-overlapping trigrams).

[6]We use `https://github.com/nsmartinez/WERpp` for calculating the WER, as do Partanen et al. (2019).

[7]The number of counties was reduced from 19 to 11 in 2018.

	SKN	NDC
Partanen et al. (2019)	5.73	—
This work	6.11	4.89

Table 3: Word error rates (↓) for Partanen et al. (2019), our SKN model, and our NDC model.

the NDC dataset, and thus the score can not be compared. Achieving a similar score as Partanen et al. (2019) for Finnish, and a lower one for Norwegian, does not indicate issues with the model performance, and the learned representations of the speakers can therefore be used for further analysis.

5.2 Principal Component Analysis

Dialects create a continuum, with either subtle transitions from one area to another, or stronger borders between them. For instance in Finnish dialectology, a strong border is seen between the Western and Eastern dialects and smaller differences inside these large areas. To analyze whether the neural models have learned such differences, we run a three-component principal component analysis on the learned speaker embeddings.

Three components are chosen for visualization purposes, as each of the three components are presented with their own color on a map visualization. The speakers' locations are plotted on the map, and the degree of each component in each speakers' interview is presented as red, green, and blue colors, as explained in Section 4.4. Thus, similar hues indicate linguistic similarity of the speakers, and the degree of color change from one area to another indicates the degree of linguistic difference. The results of the principal component analysis are presented in Figure 2. The Finnish and Norwegian results are presented in the same figure for convenience, but the analysis is separate for both languages.

The explained variance of the principal component analysis model is low for both languages (14% for Finnish and 9% for Norwegian). We hypothesize this is due to the used data: we are working on the embedding space of the normalization model, which may include manifold variation, for example relating to the actual normalization task. The explained variance may thus not be as good a measure here as it is for multi-dimensional scaling, for instance, which works on distance matrices. Limiting the model to three components due to visualization might also affect the explained variance.

We commence with an analysis of the Finnish speakers in Figure 2. There are clearly differing areas in the South-West (bright green), South-East (light green), South-East Häme (blue), and Savo (red). The South-West, South-East, and Savo are traditional dialect areas, but South-East Häme has been traditionally seen as a part of a larger Häme area (dark blue in Figure 2). The shade of the blue thus indicates that South-East Häme, although related to the rest of Häme, is somewhat different from it. Regarding the transitions from one area to another, there is a clear difference between East and West in the South and center of the country (from blue to red), but not as big a difference in the North. This reflects the understanding that the Northern dialects are a combination of Western and Eastern influence (e.g., Leino et al. 2006).

For Norwegian, the color changes in Figure 2 are more subtle than for Finnish, indicating transitional areas between the dialects. There is a clearly red area (PC1) around Oslo, a purple cluster (PC1 and PC3) in the center of the country and dark hues in the West. The Trøndersk area in the middle has a cyan quality (PC2 and PC3), which turns green (PC2) in the North and yellow in the far North (Finnmark). Regarding the four-way division of Eastern, Western, Trøndersk, and Northern dialects, the map shows that there is internal variation in the areas.

5.3 Clustering Evaluation

We run k-means clustering and agglomerative clustering with Ward linkage on the learned speaker representations to examine whether the methodology captures similar divisions as in traditional dialectology. We evaluate each clustering with the number of clusters ranging from 2 to 20, and compare them to dialect divisions presented in the past, as explained in Section 4.5. We use V-measure and adjusted Rand index as metrics, and a geographically and administratively defined baseline against which to compare the clustering performance. The results for both methods and datasets are presented in Figure 3 and Figure 4. In case of ambiguity between the V-measure and adjusted Rand index, we prefer the V-measure.

Figure 3 and Figure 4 show that agglomerative clustering with Ward linkage outperforms k-means on both datasets, with the difference being clearer for Finnish. Similar findings have been reported before (Heeringa, 2004; Prokić and Nerbonne, 2008;

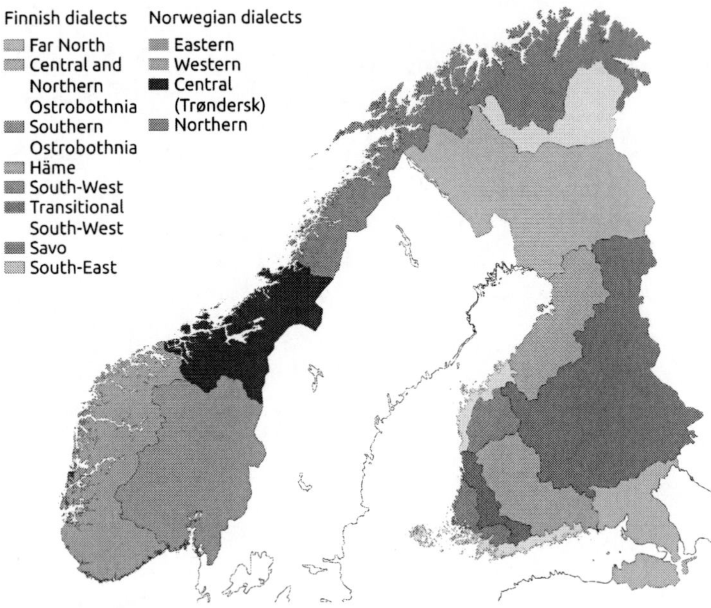

Figure 1: The dialect areas used as gold labels. The Norwegian division is based on Hanssen (2010 - 2014) and the Finnish one on Itkonen (1989).

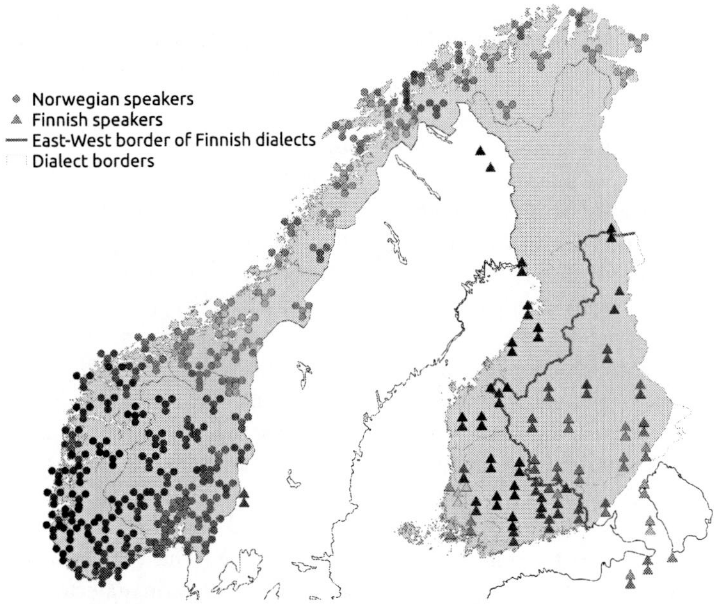

Figure 2: Visualization of a three-component principal component analysis. The Norwegian speakers are presented with circles and Finnish speakers with triangles. The dialect areas that are used as ground truth are presented with thin grey lines. The first principal component is presented as red, second as green, and third as blue. The color shade of each speaker is thus a combination of these three colors. Note that the PCA is different for both languages, and they are presented side by side because of geographical proximity. Also note that there are two locations of Finnish in Sweden (in the North and in the far West, close to the Norwegian border.)

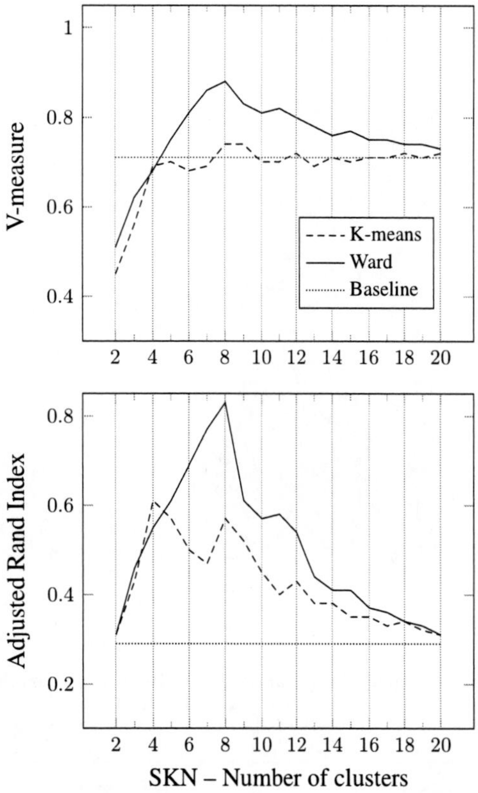

Figure 3: Evaluation of the clustering methods on the SKN dataset. K-means averaged over five runs. Baseline is presented as a horizontal line.

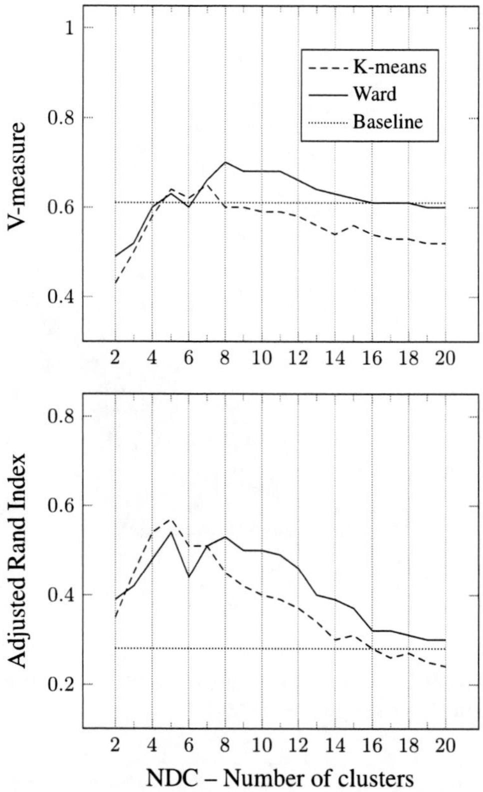

Figure 4: Evaluation of the clustering methods on the NDC dataset. K-means averaged over five runs. Baseline is presented as a horizontal line.

Hovy and Purschke, 2018). The scores are also generally worse for Norwegian, with the models barely outperforming the V-measure baseline. The best V-measure scores are achieved with Ward having 8 clusters for both languages. For Finnish, the 8-cluster solution also achieves the clearly best Rand index score. For Norwegian, the 8-cluster solution is on par with a 5-cluster solution on the adjusted Rand index. The 8-cluster solutions with Ward for both languages are presented in Figure 5.

For k-means, the scores differ between the two metrics: best scores are achieved with 5 (Rand) or 7 (V-measure) clusters for Norwegian, and with 4 (Rand) or 8 (V-measure) clusters for Finnish. Since the k-means scores are generally worse, they are presented in Appendix A in Figure 7.

5.4 Ward Clustering

The 8-cluster solutions for agglomerative clustering with Ward linkage are presented on a map in Figure 5 and as dendrograms in Figure 6. The colors and cluster labels are shared between the figures.

The 8-cluster solution for Finnish presented in Figure 5 manages to capture five of the eight traditional dialect areas completely. The South-Western dialects are presented in cluster number 3 (hereafter C3; presented in purple), Southern Ostrobothnia in C5 (brown), Central and Northern Ostrobothnia in C6 (pink), Savo in C0 (orange[8]) and South-East in C4 (green). The Far North is also homogeneously presented in C1 (yellow), but some speakers from the South are in the same cluster. Häme is divided, with the South-East Häme generating its own cluster (C2 / red; rest of Häme in C7 / grey). The division of Häme seemed apparent also in Figure 2 and has been reported in dialectometry before (Leino and Hyvönen, 2008). Overall, the learned representations correspond to the traditional dialects of Finnish very well, which was evident in the V-measure and ARI scores in Figure 3.

The dendrogram in Figure 6 further presents the

[8]Värmland in Western Sweden was inhabited by immigrants from Savo.

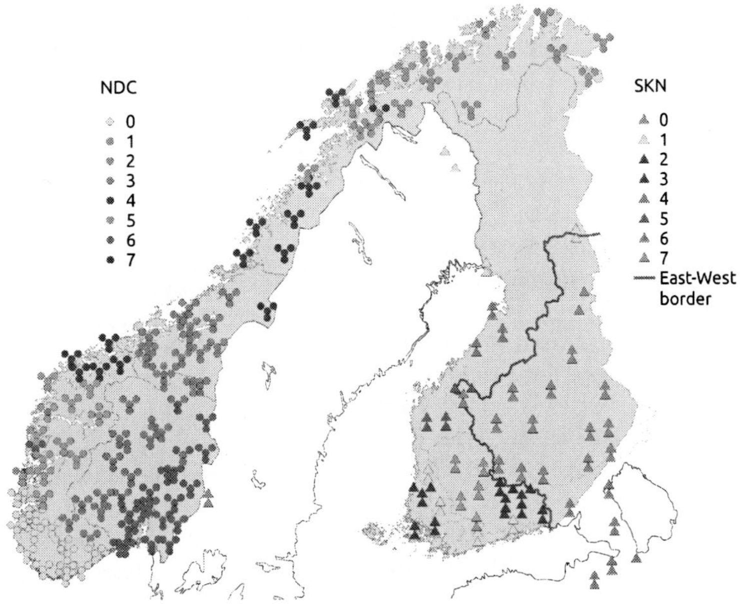

Figure 5: Agglomerative clustering (Ward linkage) based on highest V-measure. Eight clusters for both languages. Norwegian speakers are presented with circles and Finnish speakers with triangles.

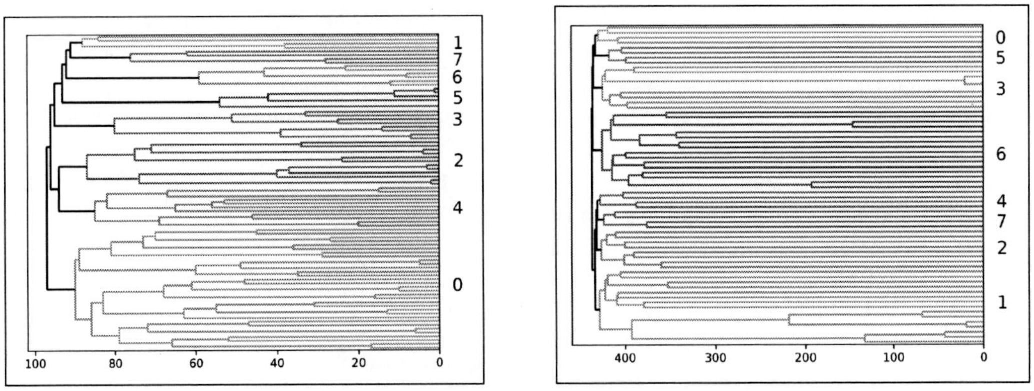

Figure 6: Dendrograms for the agglomerative clustering (Ward linkage). SKN on the left and NDC on the right. The dendrogram for NDC has been truncated for clarity. Cluster labels and colors match those of Figure 5.

relations between the clusters. The first division happens between Savo (C0 / orange) and all other dialects. Further divisions are between South-East (C4 / green and C2 / red) and the Western dialects, which in turn split up one dialect area at a time (in order: South-West (C3 / purple), Southern Ostrobothnia (C5 / brown), Central and Northern Ostrobothnia (C6 / pink) and finally Häme (C7 / grey) and the Far North (C1 / yellow)).

The clusters for Norwegian in Figure 5 are also quite distinct. The central Trøndersk area is mostly presented in cluster number 2 (hereafter C2; presented in green color), but the three other dialect areas are divided, with two clusters in Eastern (C3 / pink and C6 / brown) and Northern (C1 / orange and C7 / red) dialects, and three clusters in the Western (C0 / yellow, C5 / grey and C4 / purple) dialects. The clusters tend to stay inside the traditional dialect areas, apart from some Western speakers belonging to cluster number 3 (pink) and the municipality of Lierne (in the central Trøndersk area, near the Swedish border) belonging completely to cluster number 4 (purple).

The Norwegian Eastern dialects are moreover divided into mountain communities (*fjellbygdmål*) and lower elevation communities (*flatbygdmål*) (Hanssen, 2010 - 2014), and our clusters number 3 (pink) and 6 (brown) follow this division quite well. Likewise, the Northern dialects have a subdivision into Nordland and Troms-Finnmark, which is also reflected in clusters number 7 (red) and 1 (orange). The Western dialects have three subgroups, as do our clusters, but the areas are not as clear. The clustering is thus quite faithful to the subdivisions of the major dialect areas.

The dendrogram for NDC in Figure 6 presents the relations between the clusters. The first division is between North and South, as C2 (green), C4 (purple), C7 (red), and C1 (orange), presenting the Central and Northern dialects, are divided from the Western and Eastern dialects, presented in C5 (grey), C0 (yellow), C3 (pink) and C6 (brown). This is somewhat unexpected, as a two-way division is typically seen to be between East and West.

In the North, C1 (orange; the area of Finnmark) is divided from the three others, and C2 (green; Trøndersk) is further divided from C4 (purple) and C7 (red). In the South, C6 (brown) around Oslo (*flatbygdmål*) is first divided from the others, followed by C3 (pink; *fjellbygdmål*). This is to be expected, as both C3 and C6 clusters belong to the Eastern dialects.

All in all, it is apparent that the learned representations of the neural normalization models reflect dialect divisions. For Finnish, the clustering produced by Ward in Figure 5 is very close to the gold labels. For Norwegian, it is likely that using a more fine-grained division as gold standard could produce even higher V-measure scores, since in our clustering the four major dialect areas are divided in a way that reflects traditional understanding of dialectal subgroups.

6 Conclusions

In this paper, we apply neural dialect-to-standard normalization models to two typologically different languages and use the learned speaker representations to study the dialect continuum and division of the languages. We use large datasets of Norwegian and Finnish dialects, which have been manually transcribed and manually or semi-automatically normalized to a standard form. We add speaker labels to each dialect utterance (source) and normalize to the standard language, using byte-pair encoded data.

The model learns representations of the speakers based on the speaker labels added to the dialect utterances. The learned representations are further studied with principal component analysis, agglomerative clustering with Ward linkage, and k-means clustering. The results are evaluated against gold standard divisions of the dialects using V-measure and adjusted Rand index as metrics. Agglomerative clustering with Ward linkage outperforms k-means clustering for both languages on V-measure.

We find that the learned representations of the speakers correspond well to traditional dialect divisions. We also show that some dialect areas, such as the Häme dialect in Finnish are not as homogenic as could be assumed by the traditional division. The methodology could be further used with noisier data from social media for instance, which could reveal new insights into areal variation.

Limitations

We use clean, systematically transcribed and normalized datasets. Further evaluation of the methodology on noisier data is left for future work. We focus on two typologically different languages, but our work is still tied to the linguistic and dialectal practices of Northern Europe.

The used neural normalization model has not gone through extensive hyperparameter tuning, since the aim of the paper is not in the best possible normalization quality. It is however possible that the learned representations would perform even better if such tuning was to be executed. This also applies to the chosen dimensionality reduction methodology: using different methods might offer better results.

There are multiple ways to divide the Finnish and Norwegian dialects. We have chosen one such division for both languages, and used them as the gold standards. Using different divisions could result in different models achieving the highest scores. One could also try to avoid using gold labels altogether to find new insights into areal variation. It is anyhow apparent that the models learn dialectal differences between speakers, and that the selection of the gold standard only affects which models are deemed to perform best.

Acknowledgements

This work has been supported by the Academy of Finland through project No. 342859 "CorCoDial – Corpus-based computational dialectology".

References

Kaori Abe, Yuichiroh Matsubayashi, Naoaki Okazaki, and Kentaro Inui. 2018. Multi-dialect neural machine translation and dialectometry. In *Proceedings of the 32nd Pacific Asia Conference on Language, Information and Computation*, Hong Kong. Association for Computational Linguistics.

Rachel Bawden, Jonathan Poinhos, Eleni Kogkitsidou, Philippe Gambette, Benoît Sagot, and Simon Gabay. 2022. Automatic normalisation of Early Modern French. In *Proceedings of the Language Resources and Evaluation Conference*, pages 3354–3366, Marseille, France. European Language Resources Association.

Marcel Bollmann. 2019. A large-scale comparison of historical text normalization systems. In *Proceedings of the 2019 Conference of the North American Chapter of the Association for Computational Linguistics: Human Language Technologies, Volume 1 (Long and Short Papers)*, pages 3885–3898, Minneapolis, Minnesota. Association for Computational Linguistics.

Ximena Gutierrez-Vasques, Christian Bentz, Olga Sozinova, and Tanja Samardzic. 2021. From characters to words: the turning point of BPE merges. In *Proceedings of the 16th Conference of the European Chapter of the Association for Computational Linguistics: Main Volume*, pages 3454–3468, Online. Association for Computational Linguistics.

Kristin Hagen, Gjert Kristoffersen, Øystein A. Vangsnes, and Tor A. Åfarli, editors. 2021. *Språk i arkiva: Ny forsking om eldre talemål frå LIA-prosjektet*. Novus forlag.

Mika Hämäläinen, Khalid Alnajjar, and Tuuli Tuisk. 2022. Help from the neighbors: Estonian dialect normalization using a Finnish dialect generator. In *Proceedings of the Third Workshop on Deep Learning for Low-Resource Natural Language Processing*, pages 61–66, Hybrid. Association for Computational Linguistics.

Eskil Hanssen. 2010 - 2014. *Dialekter i Norge*, 3. opplag. edition. LNUs skriftserie ; nr. 184. Fagbokforlaget, Bergen.

Wilbert Jan Heeringa. 2004. *Measuring Dialect Pronunciation Differences using Levenshtein Distance*. Ph.D. thesis, University of Groningen.

Pierre-Edouard Honnet, Andrei Popescu-Belis, Claudiu Musat, and Michael Baeriswyl. 2018. Machine translation of low-resource spoken dialects: Strategies for normalizing Swiss German. In *Proceedings of the Eleventh International Conference on Language Resources and Evaluation (LREC 2018)*, Miyazaki, Japan. European Language Resources Association (ELRA).

Harold Hotelling. 1933. Analysis of a complex of statistical variables into principal components. *Journal of Educational Psychology*, 24:498–520.

Dirk Hovy and Christoph Purschke. 2018. Capturing regional variation with distributed place representations and geographic retrofitting. In *Proceedings of the 2018 Conference on Empirical Methods in Natural Language Processing*, pages 4383–4394, Brussels, Belgium. Association for Computational Linguistics.

J. D. Hunter. 2007. Matplotlib: A 2d graphics environment. *Computing in Science & Engineering*, 9(3):90–95.

Institute for the Languages of Finland. 2021. Samples of Spoken Finnish, VRT Version.

Terho Itkonen. 1989. *Nurmijärven murrekirja*. Kotiseudun murrekirjoja ; 10. Suomalaisen kirjallisuuden seura, Helsinki.

Janne Bondi Johannessen, Joel James Priestley, Kristin Hagen, Tor Anders Åfarli, and Øystein Alexander Vangsnes. 2009. The Nordic Dialect Corpus – an advanced research tool. In *Proceedings of the 17th Nordic Conference of Computational Linguistics (NODALIDA 2009)*, pages 73–80, Odense, Denmark. Northern European Association for Language Technology (NEALT).

Melvin Johnson, Mike Schuster, Quoc V. Le, Maxim Krikun, Yonghui Wu, Zhifeng Chen, Nikhil Thorat, Fernanda Viégas, Martin Wattenberg, Greg Corrado, Macduff Hughes, and Jeffrey Dean. 2017. Google's multilingual neural machine translation system: Enabling zero-shot translation. *Transactions of the Association for Computational Linguistics*, 5:339–351.

Lauri Kettunen. 1940. *Suomen murteet. 3, A, Murrekartasto.* Suomalaisen Kirjallisuuden Seuran toimituksia ; 188. Osa. Suomalaisen kirjallisuuden seura, Helsinki.

Guillaume Klein, Yoon Kim, Yuntian Deng, Jean Senellart, and Alexander Rush. 2017. OpenNMT: Open-source toolkit for neural machine translation. In *Proceedings of ACL 2017, System Demonstrations*, pages 67–72, Vancouver, Canada. Association for Computational Linguistics.

Antti Leino and Saara Hyvönen. 2008. Comparison of component models in analysing the distribution of dialectal features. *International Journal of Humanities and Arts Computing*, 2(1-2):173–187.

Antti Leino, Saara Hyvönen, and Marko Salmenkivi. 2006. Mitä murteita suomessa onkaan? murresanaston levikin kvantitatiivista analyysiä. *Virittäjä*, 110(1):26.

Therese Leinonen, Çağrı Çöltekin, and John Nerbonne. 2016. Using gabmap. *Lingua*, 178:71–83. Linguistic Research in the CLARIN Infrastructure.

J. MacQueen. 1967. Some methods for classification and analysis of multivariate observations. In *5th Berkeley Symposium on Mathematical Statistics and Probability.* University of California Press.

John Nerbonne, Wilbert Heeringa, and Peter Kleiweg. 1999. *Edit Distance and Dialect Proximity*, pages 433–464. CSLI Press, Stanford.

Robert Östling and Jörg Tiedemann. 2017. Continuous multilinguality with language vectors. In *Proceedings of the 15th Conference of the European Chapter of the Association for Computational Linguistics: Volume 2, Short Papers*, pages 644–649, Valencia, Spain. Association for Computational Linguistics.

Niko Partanen, Mika Hämäläinen, and Khalid Alnajjar. 2019. Dialect text normalization to normative standard Finnish. In *Proceedings of the 5th Workshop on Noisy User-generated Text (W-NUT 2019)*, pages 141–146, Hong Kong, China. Association for Computational Linguistics.

F. Pedregosa, G. Varoquaux, A. Gramfort, V. Michel, B. Thirion, O. Grisel, M. Blondel, P. Prettenhofer, R. Weiss, V. Dubourg, J. Vanderplas, A. Passos, D. Cournapeau, M. Brucher, M. Perrot, and E. Duchesnay. 2011. Scikit-learn: Machine learning in Python. *Journal of Machine Learning Research*, 12:2825–2830.

Jelena Prokić and John Nerbonne. 2008. Recognizing groups among dialects. *International Journal for Humanities and Arts Computing*, 2(Special Issue on Language Variation):153–172.

QGIS Development Team. 2023. *QGIS Geographic Information System.* QGIS Association.

William M. Rand. 1971. Objective criteria for the evaluation of clustering methods. *Journal of the American Statistical Association*, 66(336):846–850.

Andrew Rosenberg and Julia Hirschberg. 2007. V-measure: A conditional entropy-based external cluster evaluation measure. In *Proceedings of the 2007 Joint Conference on Empirical Methods in Natural Language Processing and Computational Natural Language Learning (EMNLP-CoNLL)*, pages 410–420, Prague, Czech Republic. Association for Computational Linguistics.

Yves Scherrer and Nikola Ljubešić. 2016. Automatic normalisation of the Swiss German ArchiMob corpus using character-level machine translation. In *Proceedings of the 13th Conference on Natural Language Processing (KONVENS)*, Bochumer Linguistische Arbeitsberichte 16, Bochum.

Rico Sennrich, Barry Haddow, and Alexandra Birch. 2016. Neural machine translation of rare words with subword units. In *Proceedings of the 54th Annual Meeting of the Association for Computational Linguistics (Volume 1: Long Papers)*, pages 1715–1725, Berlin, Germany. Association for Computational Linguistics.

Gongbo Tang, Fabienne Cap, Eva Pettersson, and Joakim Nivre. 2018. An evaluation of neural machine translation models on historical spelling normalization. In *Proceedings of the 27th International Conference on Computational Linguistics*, pages 1320–1331, Santa Fe, New Mexico, USA. Association for Computational Linguistics.

University of Turku and Institute for the Languages of Finland. 1985. The Finnish Dialect Corpus of the Syntax Archive, Downloadable Version.

Ashish Vaswani, Noam Shazeer, Niki Parmar, Jakob Uszkoreit, Llion Jones, Aidan N Gomez, Ł ukasz Kaiser, and Illia Polosukhin. 2017. Attention is all you need. In *Advances in Neural Information Processing Systems*, volume 30. Curran Associates, Inc.

Pauli Virtanen, Ralf Gommers, Travis E. Oliphant, Matt Haberland, Tyler Reddy, David Cournapeau, Evgeni Burovski, Pearu Peterson, Warren Weckesser, Jonathan Bright, Stéfan J. van der Walt, Matthew Brett, Joshua Wilson, K. Jarrod Millman, Nikolay Mayorov, Andrew R. J. Nelson, Eric Jones, Robert Kern, Eric Larson, C J Carey, İlhan Polat, Yu Feng, Eric W. Moore, Jake VanderPlas, Denis Laxalde, Josef Perktold, Robert Cimrman, Ian Henriksen, E. A. Quintero, Charles R. Harris, Anne M. Archibald, Antônio H. Ribeiro, Fabian Pedregosa, Paul van Mulbregt, and SciPy 1.0 Contributors. 2020. SciPy 1.0: Fundamental Algorithms for Scientific Computing in Python. *Nature Methods*, 17:261–272.

Joe H. Ward. 1963. Hierarchical grouping to optimize an objective function. *Journal of the American Statistical Association*, 58:236–244.

Shijie Wu, Ryan Cotterell, and Mans Hulden. 2021. Applying the transformer to character-level transduction. In *Proceedings of the 16th Conference of the European Chapter of the Association for Computational Linguistics: Main Volume*, pages 1901–1907, Online. Association for Computational Linguistics.

A K-means Clustering

Figure 7 presents the best k-means clustering results (evaluated by the V-measure). This results in 7 clusters for Norwegian and 8 or 9 clusters for Finnish. Note that while we averaged over 5 runs when evaluating, we only present the single best run with the said number of clusters. Therefore we present the 8-cluster solution for Finnish, since it achieved a higher single run score than a 9-cluster solution.

The Finnish division achieves to capture the South-Eastern (C4 / green), Southern Ostrobothnian (C5 / brown), Northern Ostrobothnian (C7 / grey), Häme (C1 / yellow), and South-Western (C2 / red) dialects for the most part. The traditional dialect areas of South-West transitional, Far North, and Savo are however divided into several clusters. This results in a lower V-measure score than for the Ward clustering in Figure 5.

The Norwegian clusters produced by the k-means are reminiscent of the Ward clustering, presented in Figure 5. The central dialects (Trøndersk) are mostly presented in C3 (pink). The Eastern dialects are divided into mountain community (C1 / orange) and lower elevation (C5 / grey), Western dialects are divided into three groups (C2, C6, C4), and the Northern dialects into two groups (C4 / purple and C0 / yellow). There are however considerably more outliers, with some speakers belonging to different clusters than their surrounding speakers. This results in low V-measure when evaluated against the dialect areas.

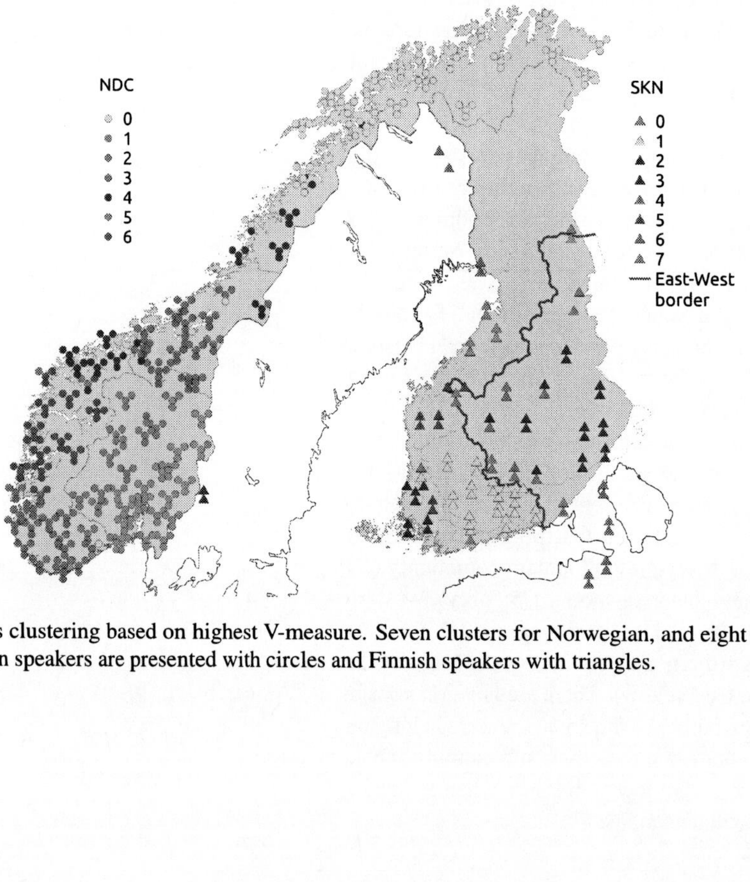

Figure 7: K-means clustering based on highest V-measure. Seven clusters for Norwegian, and eight clusters for Finnish. Norwegian speakers are presented with circles and Finnish speakers with triangles.

VarDial in the Wild: Industrial Applications of LID Systems for Closely-Related Language Varieties

Fritz Hohl
Sony Europe B.V., Stuttgart, Germany
fritz.hohl@sony.com

Soh-Eun Shim
Sony Europe B.V., Stuttgart, Germany
soh-eun.shim@sony.com

Abstract

This report describes first an industrial use case for identifying closely related languages, e.g. dialects, namely the detection of languages of movie subtitle documents. We then present a 2-stage architecture that is able to detect macrolanguages in the first stage and language variants in the second. Using our architecture, we participated in the DSL-TL Shared Task of the VarDial 2023 workshop. We describe the results of our experiments. In the first experiment we report an accuracy of 97.8% on a set of 460 subtitle files. In our second experiment we used DSL-TL data and achieve a macro-average F1 of 76% for the binary task, and 54% for the three-way task in the dev set. In the open track, we augment the data with named entities retrieved from Wikidata and achieve minor increases of about 1% for both tracks.

1 Introduction

In the NLP community the problem of identifying languages of documents is often perceived as being solved (Zampieri et al., 2023), also due to the good accuracy of this function in tools like Google Translate. This is especially true for many users as they apply this method in cases where they want to understand text that is not their field of native speaker expertise. However, when applying state of the art language identification tools to applications where an accurate distinction of closely related languages, e.g. dialects is important, it soon becomes clear that these tools often either do not offer variants in their list of covered languages or confuse them regularly. One of these application areas are movie subtitles. As we will see in the next section, although these texts are typically not too small for language identification, they often differ from news domain content, which is the source of the shared task data. Section 3 will describe the architecture of our system. Using this architecture, we participated in the DSL-TL Shared Task of the VarDial 2023 workshop. We describe this Shared Task briefly in Section 4. Our experiments of our system on this Shared Task and other data can be found in Section 5, while Section 6 presents a manual oracle experiment that aims at finding out how much an extended NER-like mechanism can reduce errors. Finally, Section 7 conclude our findings.

Format Title	File Extension
DCTitle format	xml
TTML	xml
Flashplayer TTAF	xml
SMPTE-TT (extension of TTML)	xml
TTML	dxfp
TTML	itt
CAP	cap
STL	stl
Scenarist_SCC V1.0	scc
SRT	srt
WEBVTT	vtt

Table 1: Example subtitle file formats.

2 LID for Subtitles

Subtitle files contain the Closed Captions or Subtitles of movies and similar video content. These files come in a variety of different, partially proprietary formats (see Table 1 for some of them).

The content consists typically of a mix of time stamps, dialogue lines, textual descriptions of visual content, and symbols, e.g. for music (see Fig. 1 for an example extract of such content).

In order to cope with the diversity of formats, and to extract the textual parts in the target language, a preprocessing stage is needed. Afterwards, UTF-8-encoded text can be fed into the Language Identification stage. In our experience the resulting subtitle text documents have a median file size of about 25 kbytes. Subtitles and Closed Captions

Tenth Workshop on NLP for Similar Languages, Varieties and Dialects (VarDial 2023), pages 213–221
May 5, 2023 ©2023 Association for Computational Linguistics

are meant to be displayed over the video for a certain amount of time (hence the time stamps). The displayed text for this period can contain either single words, parts of sentences, or multiple sentences. These text portions are reflected by line breaks in the document, i.e. line breaks separate different time periods. Apart from textual descriptions and symbols, texts transcribe mainly the spoken dialogue. DVD and BluRay releases of video content often come with a number of subtitles in different languages and language variants.[1] Also, releases of these media in different regions or countries come with different sets of subtitle languages. As a result, for a single piece of video content, many different subtitle documents exist. If one imagines that e.g. for a single movie, different versions of that movie are needed even in a single language (realizing different ratings, different cuts, or being trailer versions), the number of subtitles documents over an entire catalogue of movies is very large. Ideally, a digital asset management system denotes the language of a single subtitle file. However, in reality, movie studios have a very large catalogue of content that partially predates the widespread availability of low-threshold asset management platforms. This means that there are many subtitle files on many disks in many drawers of which no exact metadata is known. This is where Language Identification really helps as it avoids the need of re-creating subtitle files for existing movies if they are about to be re-released. Also, it helps to verify existing language metadata as these might be incorrect. The user of such a tool will be typically a technician, not a linguist. Also, the user will probably have to face a lot of different languages, some of which will be very foreign to the user. Finally, it will be very difficult for the user to get a gold language label for a file using standard tools. Subtitles are relatively mono-lingual; they might contain a moderate amount of code-switching and the occasional sentence in another language.

3 System Architecture

The requirements for the use case mentioned in Section 2 asked for a system that could not only recognize macrolanguages, but also language variants. An earlier internal language identification system implementation based purely on character n-grams and perplexity proved to be especially

```
7
00:01:30,904 -> 00:01:32,839
ANIMATED MUSIC PLAYS ON TV
8
00:01:37,443 -> 00:01:39,578
♪♪♪
9
00:01:41,014 -> 00:01:44,645
[ON TV IN JAPANESE] ANNOUNCER: The boom slang was
stolen from the zoo last night.
10
00:01:44,729 -> 00:01:47,398
It's extremely dangerous.
11
00:01:47,754 -> 00:01:49,689
[RHYTHMIC BEEPING AND WHOOSHING CONTINUE]
```

Figure 1: Subtitle file extract.

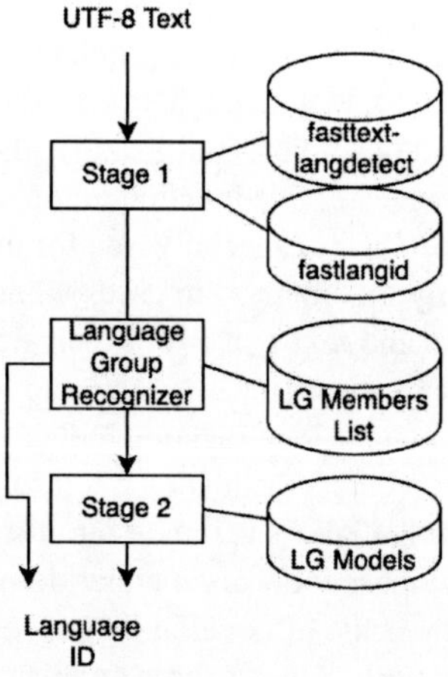

Figure 2: Overall architecture.

[1]For four releases of the movie "Bullet Train" from 2022 alone, we counted 30 different subtitle languages.

weak when it comes to closely-related languages and dialects. Consulting the literature (Goutte et al., 2014; Zampieri et al., 2015) we decided in favor of a two-stage system, where the first stage aims at recognizing a "language group". For us, Language Groups are groups of closely related languages that are difficult to distinguish in the first stage. Language Groups can be macrolanguages that contain e.g. different language variants, or simply a set of languages that are hard to tell apart for a stage 1 algorithm. If the language in stage 1 is marked in a list as being a member of a certain Language Group, a stage 2 takes over and aims at determining the concrete member of the language group. Using this architecture, not all language group member languages need to be recognized in stage 1. Let's now have a closer look at the two stages (see Figure 2).

3.1 Stage 1

For stage 1, our system follows the general approach of Goutte et al. (2014); Zampieri et al. (2015). More concretely, we use the 126 MB-model of fasttext-langdetect (Joulin et al. (2016a,b)) directly. This package uses pretrained fastText embeddings for language identification and provides support for 176 languages. The only difference is that we additionally use the model from fastlangid[2] in order to cure the inexplicable weakness of fasttext-langdetect not to distinguish traditional and simplified Chinese.

3.2 Stage 2

Our second stage utilizes an SVM with 1- to 4-character n-gram features, along with word unigram features. SVMs have been shown in prior work to have strong baselines, which have consistently outperformed RNNs in prior experiments (Çöltekin et al., 2018). All n-gram features are weighted with sub-linear tf-idf scaling. The SVM models are trained with scikitlearn (Pedregosa et al., 2011).

4 The DSL-TL Shared Task at VarDial 2023

The Shared Task on "Discriminating Between Similar Languages - True Labels" (DSL-TL) aims at examining the effects of a data set for identifying sentences in similar languages that have been gold-labelled in a new way. Previously, the gold labels for such sentences have been derived from

Language code	# of files	Language code	# of files
bg	2	ms	1
da	3	no	3
de	5	pl	6
el	1	PT-PT	9
en	225	PT-BR	13
es	103	ru	7
fi	3	sr	1
fr	14	sv	3
hu	3	th	4
is	3	tr	4
it	9	zh-hans	6
ja	23	zh-hant	2
mr	7		

Table 2: Subtitle evaluation data.

the country (and therefore the language variant) association of the source of a sentence, e.g. a newspaper that is primarily published in a certain country. This method is problematic if e.g these sentences do not contain a variant-specific markers and, thus, do not help an automatic mechanism to determine a language variant. The new way to label sentences is using multiple human annotators to determine a variant label while offering a labeller to also specify that a sentence is not variant-specific. The subject of this labelling campaign has been nearly 13k sentences in a number of language varieties, namely English (American and British), Portuguese (Brazilian and European), and Spanish (Argentinian and Peninsular). The DSL-TL webpage[3] explains the Shared Task in more detail and contains a link to the data used in the Shared Task. (Zampieri et al., 2023) explains the new dataset, the annotation process that led to this dataset, and the performance of baseline algorithms on the dataset. The results of all teams and the shared tasks will be explained in (Aepli et al., 2023).

5 Experiments on Subtitle Files

One of the original use cases for our system is subtitle file language identification.

5.1 Data

Stage 1 was used out of the box; no further training was used. The Language Group models of Stage 2 were trained on prior years of DSLCC data (Tan

[2] https://github.com/currentslab/fastlangid

[3] https://sites.google.com/view/vardial-2023/shared-tasks#h.klf8c6mlh0zk

et al., 2014) for the internal system. The evaluation data set consists of 460 subtitle files that have been converted to UTF-8 text. Table 2 shows the distribution of these files to Gold labels. Gold labels have been raised mainly by a single person taking into account the content of the files, language hints in the filenames that sometimes occur (but which are sometimes also wrong), and existing language identification tools. As most of the labels denote languages which can be easily distinguished, these labels are expected to be correct. One group of labels, though, posed quite a challenge. 22 files belong to the Language Group "Portuguese" with the two members pt-PT and pt-BR. These files were labelled by a native Brazilian Portuguese speaker who expressed doubts on the reliability of his judgments on these files.

5.2 Results

The content in the files was concatenated, then processed by the system as described in Section 4. We also limited the set of language groups and variants to those we expected to be contained in the test data set (because in our experience, the probability to correctly identify the standard variant in a language group is smaller than to identify the macrolanguage). From the 460 files, 451 (or 98.0%) were recognized correctly. The 9 error cases can be divided as follows:

- 7 cases confused pt-PT with pt-BR. In 6 of these cases the file name hints to the possibility that these files might have been indeed created as pt-BR.
- 2 cases were extremely short files (in fact these were the smallest files of the evaluation set).

So, on this evaluation set our system seems to perform quite well as long as the content size is not too small.

6 Experiments on DSL-TL Data

Now we will describe our experiments for the DSL-TL Shared Task. Until mentioned otherwise, all stages have been trained on DSL-TL training data. In Section 6.2 the system will be tested on the DSL-TL dev set, in Section 6.3 on the DSL-TL test set.

6.1 Predicting Macrolanguages for DSL-TL

Regarding stage 1 of our architecture, we wondered with respect to the DSL-TL task whether our existing stage 1 trained on 177 languages (i.e. with data outside the DSL-TL datasets) would perform worse than a stage 1 trained purely on the three language families of the Shared Task using only DSL-TL training data.

In our experiment, applied to the combined DSL-TL dev set data of all languages, the only difference was that our existing stage 1 incorrectly predicted one Argentinian Spanish sentence as Italian (this sentence was "`19. Lucas di Grassi (BRA/Virgin-Cosworth): 1min24s547`)", which, considering the Italian origin of the last name, arguably constitutes a reasonable error. All other stage 1 predictions (also from the DSL-TL-only stage 1) were correct.

6.2 Results on DSL-TL Dev Data

In observance of the influence Named Entities potentially have upon the task, we ran two experiments on the DSL-TL data. First, for the closed task, we varied the number of maximum word n-grams added to observe the difference in performance. Second, we also experimented with adding named entities as retrieved from a linked open database (Vrandečić and Krötzsch, 2014) to the data as our submission to the open task, which allows for the usage of external data. We observe a consistent improvement in both the binary and three-way task by way of this method.

6.2.1 Word n-gram Features

Table 3 shows our results of increasing the maximum number of word n-gram features on the dev data in the binary task. Table 4 shows our results per class. Table 5 and Table 6 show the same results for the three-way classification task. Our results replicate the conclusion made by Çöltekin et al. (2018): increasing the number of word n-gram features becomes useful up to a certain point, after which the effect either levels out or starts hurting performance. We hypothesize that this is due to higher n-gram numbers capturing named entities, but once the granularity exceeds what is typical for a named entity, the features start to lose predictive power.

6.2.2 Adding Named Entities

Our second approach experiments with using additional NER data as retrieved from Wikidata (Vrandečić and Krötzsch, 2014). This NER data consists of 10k person names per country associated with the 6 language variants (i.e. the US, the UK, Spain,

	0	1	2	3
pt	0.66	0.66	**0.68**	0.68
en	0.80	0.81	**0.82**	0.82
es	0.74	**0.76**	0.75	0.75

Table 3: Macro averaged F1 on dev data binary classification task, where the columns indicate the maximum number of word n-gram features used.

	0	1	2	3
PT-BR	0.83	0.82	**0.84**	0.84
PT-PT	0.48	0.5	**0.52**	0.52
ES-ES	0.84	**0.85**	0.85	0.85
ES-AR	0.65	**0.67**	0.66	0.65
EN-GB	0.75	0.77	**0.79**	0.79
EN-US	0.84	0.85	**0.86**	0.86

Table 4: Per class F1 on dev data binary classification task, where the columns indicate the maximum number of word n-gram features used.

Argentina, Portugal, and Brazil). From these lists we selected a number of names randomly per sentence per language variant and added these names as training features to the sentence. Our results for the binary task are listed in Table 7, and the three-way results are noted down in Table 9. Table 8 and Table 10 shows our per class results. We observe that in the binary case, Spanish sees an improvement of 2% while Portuguese and English deteriorate in performance; in the three-way case however, the opposite phenomenon is observed, where considerable improvements are seen for both Portuguese and English, but not Spanish.

6.3 Results on DSL-TL Test Data

The results of our system on Open and Closed Tasks, on Task 1 (three-way labels) and Task 2 (binary labels) as macro averages per language and per single label, as well as the rank of our result among the baselines and the other teams can be found in Table 11. Our results can be found under the team name "SSL" in (Zampieri et al., 2023).

	0	1	2	3
pt	**0.42**	0.42	0.42	0.42
en	0.52	0.54	**0.55**	0.54
es	**0.52**	0.51	0.52	0.52

Table 5: Macro averaged F1 on dev data three-way classification task, where the columns indicate the maximum number of word n-gram features used.

	0	1	2	3
PT	0.04	**0.05**	0.03	0.03
PT-BR	0.78	0.77	**0.79**	0.79
PT-PT	0.43	**0.45**	0.44	0.45
ES	**0.40**	0.39	0.39	0.39
ES-ES	**0.69**	0.67	0.68	0.68
ES-AR	0.46	**0.48**	0.48	0.48
EN	0.07	**0.13**	0.12	0.10
EN-GB	0.70	0.71	**0.74**	0.73
EN-US	0.78	**0.79**	0.79	0.79

Table 6: Per class F1 on dev data three-way classification task, where the columns indicate the maximum number of word n-gram features used.

7 Country-Informed NER Oracle Performance

We were wondering how much a slightly different approach would fare using an NER-like system that could tell one the country a Named Entity is typically associated with. One (probably inefficient) way to implement this system would be to google a maximum-length Named Entity candidate (the English DSL-TL data is very consistently capitalized in terms of Named Entities) and to take the first country reference that is found in the results (maybe normalizing the result, e.g. from "English" to "UK"). When a Knowledge Panel appears in the results, this information should first be taken into account. As we cared only about oracle performance, we did this process manually.

In order to reduce the English dev set sentences to manually label this way, we only looked at the 92 sentences (from 599) our automatic method from above incorrectly predicted.

For each of these sentences, we marked the capitalized Proper Nouns and then started a Google search. We also looked at mentioned currencies. An example of this data can be found in Table 12.

When comparing the labels from the Oracle mechanism to the DSL-TL labels, we found four groups:

- In 32 cases (34.8%) the Oracle mechanism found the TL label.
- In 25 cases (27.2%) the Oracle mechanism did not come to a conclusion as either no usable Named Entities were found or there was no majority for a country of the found Named Entity (e.g. there were two names associated with the US and two with the UK).

	0	1	2	3	4	5	6	7	8	9
pt	**0.68**	0.67	0.64	0.59	0.57	0.58	0.52	0.51	0.47	0.48
en	**0.82**	0.81	0.82	0.81	0.78	0.77	0.75	0.75	0.74	0.69
es	0.75	**0.77**	0.77	0.77	0.75	0.77	0.77	0.77	0.76	0.77

Table 7: Macro averaged F1 on dev data binary classification task, where the columns indicate the number of person names appended to each training instance.

	0	1	2	3	4	5	6	7	8	9
pt-pt	**0.53**	0.5	0.45	0.34	0.3	0.33	0.22	0.19	0.13	0.14
pt-br	**0.84**	0.83	0.83	0.83	0.83	0.83	0.82	0.82	0.82	0.82
en-gb	**0.79**	0.78	0.79	0.76	0.73	0.71	0.67	0.67	0.65	0.58
en-us	0.85	0.85	**0.86**	0.85	0.84	0.83	0.83	0.83	0.82	0.81
es-es	**0.85**	0.85	0.85	0.85	0.84	0.84	0.84	0.84	0.82	0.83
es-ar	0.66	0.68	0.69	0.69	0.67	0.7	0.7	0.7	0.7	**0.71**

Table 8: Per class F1 on dev data binary classification task, where the columns indicate the number of person names appended to each training instance.

	0	1	2	3	4	5	6	7	8	9
pt	0.42	**0.46**	0.46	0.38	0.30	0.24	0.19	0.15	0.13	0.10
en	0.55	0.58	**0.62**	0.57	0.53	0.45	0.36	0.30	0.24	0.20
es	**0.53**	0.49	0.40	0.33	0.28	0.22	0.20	0.19	0.18	0.18

Table 9: Macro averaged F1 on dev data three-way classification task, where the columns indicate the number of person names appended to each training instance.

	0	1	2	3	4	5	6	7	8	9
pt	0.03	0.16	0.28	**0.28**	0.26	0.26	0.25	0.24	0.24	0.24
pt-pt	**0.45**	0.43	0.34	0.17	0.09	0.06	0.03	0.01	0.02	0.01
pt-br	**0.78**	0.78	0.76	0.68	0.54	0.41	0.28	0.2	0.13	0.07
en	0.14	0.2	**0.33**	0.31	0.32	0.29	0.26	0.25	0.24	0.24
en-gb	**0.73**	0.73	0.73	0.66	0.55	0.38	0.24	0.12	0.05	0.04
en-us	**0.8**	0.8	0.79	0.75	0.71	0.67	0.58	0.52	0.42	0.34
es	0.0	0.0	0.0	0.0	0.0	0.43	0.48	**0.5**	0.5	0.5
es-es	0.71	0.71	**0.72**	0.72	0.71	0.69	0.6	0.46	0.33	0.21
es-ar	0.5	**0.52**	0.52	0.51	0.49	0.47	0.39	0.25	0.16	0.13

Table 10: Per class F1 on dev data three-way classification task, where the columns indicate the number of person names appended to each training instance.

Type	Track	Results for	Recall	Precisio	F1-score	Rank
Closed	Track 1	Macro Average	0.4978	0.4734	0.4817	12 of 13
Closed	Track 1	"en" label	0	0	0	14 of 14
Closed	Track 1	"en-GB" label	0.7807	0.7063	0.7417	9 of 14
Closed	Track 1	"en-US" label	0.8462	0.763	0.8024	6 of 14
Closed	Track 1	"es" label	0.3205	0.3623	0.3401	13 of 14
Closed	Track 1	"es-AR" label	0.4135	0.5046	0.4545	10 of 14
Closed	Track 1	"es-ES" label	0.767	0.6371	0.696	5 of 14
Closed	Track 1	"pt" label	0	0	0	11 of 14
Closed	Track 1	"pt-PT" label	0.8997	0.7079	0.7923	1 of 14
Closed	Track 1	"pt-BR" label	0.4526	0.5794	0.5082	7 of 14
Closed	Track 2	Macro Average	0.7521	0.7885	0.7604	8 of 15
Closed	Track 2	"en-GB" label	0.7895	0.7895	0.7895	10 of 15
Closed	Track 2	"en-US" label	0.8526	0.8471	0.8498	10 of 15
Closed	Track 2	"es-AR" label	0.5789	0.828	0.6814	10 of 15
Closed	Track 2	"es-ES" label	0.9223	0.7724	0.8407	5 of 15
Closed	Track 2	"pt-PT" label	0.9097	0.7861	0.8434	1 of 15
Closed	Track 2	"pt-BR" label	0.4599	0.7079	0.5575	11 of 15
Open	Track 1	Macro Average	0.4937	0.5068	0.4889	1/1
Open	Track 1	"en" label	0.1333	0.1481	0.1404	1/1
Open	Track 1	"en-GB" label	0.693	0.7248	0.7085	1/1
Open	Track 1	"en-US" label	0.8205	0.7711	0.795	1/1
Open	Track 1	"es" label	0.4038	0.3772	0.3901	1/1
Open	Track 1	"es-AR" label	0.3609	0.4948	0.4174	1/1
Open	Track 1	"es-ES" label	0.7379	0.658	0.6957	1/1
Open	Track 1	"pt" label	0.322	0.1473	0.2021	1/1
Open	Track 1	"pt-PT" label	0.7525	0.7401	0.7463	1/1
Open	Track 1	"pt-BR" label	0.219	0.5	0.3046	1/1
Open	Track 2	Macro Average	0.7647	0.7951	0.7729	2 of 2
Open	Track 2	"en-GB" label	0.7544	0.8037	0.7783	2 of 2
Open	Track 2	"en-US" label	0.8718	0.8293	0.85	2 of 2
Open	Track 2	"es-AR" label	0.6917	0.8288	0.7541	2 of 2
Open	Track 2	"es-ES" label	0.9078	0.8202	0.8618	2 of 2
Open	Track 2	"pt-PT" label	0.9097	0.7839	0.8421	1 of 2
Open	Track 2	"pt-BR" label	0.4526	0.7045	0.5511	2 of 2

Table 11: Results on DSL-TL Test data.

sentence	TL label	Oracle label
The **Grenfell Tower** fire shifted the tectonic plates of **British** society, triggering a wave of investigations and renewing a national conversation about social housing. One year on, **Jack Hardy** reviews the major episodes from a traumatic year.	EN-GB	EN-GB
EASTLEIGH'S rapidly rising star **Luke Coulson** is putting club before country. The **Spitfires**' 22-year-old league top scorer will sacrifice his place in the **England** C squad in order to play in Tuesday's **FA Cup** first round replay at **Swindon Town**.	EN-US	EN-GB
GOOD Samaritans cornered three loose ponies which galloped through oncoming traffic on the A31 on Monday night.	EN-GB	None

Table 12: Example oracle data.

- In 31 cases (33.7%) the Oracle mechanism found a label different from the TL label, but we would have labeled the sentence differently. Our opinion was mainly informed by the subject matter and the country of the Named Entities as we are of the opinion that it would be only of local interest and therefore could have been published only by a local newspaper.

  Sometimes we could also trace the sentence to a newspaper from a certain country. This opinion is obviously based on our belief of the intention-based criteria for documents of a language variant. Therefore, the reader might either count this group as errors or as correct cases. We discussed our suspicion that the labelers are heavily using their knowledge of the country of Named Entities in order to come to a label. For this group, we basically claim that the labelers did not follow that suspicion.

- In 4 cases (4.3%) the Oracle mechanism found the wrong label and we agree that the TL label is correct.

8 Conclusion

We reported on our use case for Language Identification, namely movie subtitles. For movie subtitles there is a need to also recognize close languages and variants.

We presented the 2-stage architecture of our Language Identification system that uses a second stage if a language is identified in the first stage that is marked as being a member of a "language group". We reported on the results of our experiments. In the first experiment we reported an accuracy of 97.8% on a set of 460 subtitle files. In our second experiment we used DSL-TL data and achieved for the dev set a macro-averaged F1 of 54% in the three-way classification task, and 76% in the binary classification task, where we see an increase in performance by adding Named Entities retrieved from a knowledge base. On the DSL-TL test set for the closed task we achieved a macro-averaged F1 of 48% in the three-way classification task, and 76% in the binary classification task. On the open task, we achieved 49% for the three-way, and 77% on the binary task.

We reported on a small experiment using a manually executed "country-informed" NER on those sentences of the English DSL-TL dev set that were incorrectly predicted by our system. We did this in order to see how much head room remains in the NER-based approach to identify DSL-TL data as some sort of oracle data. As it turns out, this mechanism can reduce the number of errors by at least a third. As future work we intend to examine the question whether it is better to keep language group languages separated for training stage 1 or whether the data for a language group should be mixed together before training in order to achieve a better stage 1 performance.

There are two aspects that are not clear to us when it comes to the DSL-TL dataset, and that might lead to future research. First, how strongly influence named entities the human labellers and is this detrimental to the label accuracy? To quote (Goutte et al., 2016)

> [...] named entities [...] can influence [...] also the performance of human annotators.

Second, again (Goutte et al., 2016) mentions that a

> general tendency we observed is that it is easier to identify an instance that is not from the speaker's own language than the opposite. Our results indicate that humans are better in telling what is not a text written in their own language or variety than telling what it is.

We understand from the description of the new annotation process that a labeller could annotate sentences in his/her own, or another variant. As the ratio of native speakers for the corresponding variants seems not to be mentioned, it is hard to assess the influence of this aspect on the results. Maybe it would be worthwhile to trying to evaluate the accuracy of the new labels. This is, of course, not easy as then another, more accurate process would be needed to come to "platinum" labels.

Limitations

The NER-based extensions to our base 2-stage algorithm increase the accuracy only for documents that contain enough Named Entities. Such documents can be found in news domains, but not in all other domains. Depending on the implementation, the extensions might additionally rely on a correct capitalization in the document. Basically, all Language Identification systems assume that a document is using the written version of a variant. If a document is transcribing the spoken variant, it will have problems to be processed.

Acknowledgements

We would like to thank the reviewers who provided us with valuable comments. We also want to thank Sony's Culver City Laboratory (CCL) for the collaboration in this area, and to Sony Pictures Entertainment and Sony Music Publishing for the provided data.

References

Noëmi Aepli, Çağrı Çöltekin, Rob van der Goot, Tommi Jauhiainen, Mourhaf Kazzaz, Nikola Ljubešić, Kai North, Barbara Plank, Yves Scherrer, and Marcos Zampieri. 2023. Findings of the VarDial evaluation campaign 2023. In *Proceedings of the Tenth Workshop on NLP for Similar Languages, Varieties and Dialects*, Dubrovnik, Croatia. Association for Computational Linguistics.

Çağrı Çöltekin, Taraka Rama, and Verena Blaschke. 2018. Tübingen-Oslo team at the VarDial 2018 evaluation campaign: An analysis of n-gram features in language variety identification. In *Proceedings of the Fifth Workshop on NLP for Similar Languages, Varieties and Dialects (VarDial 2018)*, pages 55–65, Santa Fe, New Mexico, USA. Association for Computational Linguistics.

Cyril Goutte, Serge Léger, and Marine Carpuat. 2014. The NRC system for discriminating similar languages. In *Proceedings of the First Workshop on Applying NLP Tools to Similar Languages, Varieties and Dialects*, pages 139–145, Dublin, Ireland. Association for Computational Linguistics and Dublin City University.

Cyril Goutte, Serge Léger, Shervin Malmasi, and Marcos Zampieri. 2016. Discriminating similar languages: Evaluations and explorations. In *Proceedings of the Tenth International Conference on Language Resources and Evaluation (LREC'16)*, pages 1800–1807, Portorož, Slovenia. European Language Resources Association (ELRA).

Armand Joulin, Edouard Grave, Piotr Bojanowski, Matthijs Douze, Hérve Jégou, and Tomas Mikolov. 2016a. Fasttext.zip: Compressing text classification models. *arXiv preprint arXiv:1612.03651*.

Armand Joulin, Edouard Grave, Piotr Bojanowski, and Tomas Mikolov. 2016b. Bag of tricks for efficient text classification. *arXiv preprint arXiv:1607.01759*.

F. Pedregosa, G. Varoquaux, A. Gramfort, V. Michel, B. Thirion, O. Grisel, M. Blondel, P. Prettenhofer, R. Weiss, V. Dubourg, J. Vanderplas, A. Passos, D. Cournapeau, M. Brucher, M. Perrot, and E. Duchesnay. 2011. Scikit-learn: Machine learning in Python. *Journal of Machine Learning Research*, 12:2825–2830.

Liling Tan, Marcos Zampieri, Nikola Ljubešić, and Jörg Tiedemann. 2014. Merging comparable data sources for the discrimination of similar languages: The dsl corpus collection. In *Proceedings of the BUCC Workshop*.

Denny Vrandečić and Markus Krötzsch. 2014. Wikidata: A free collaborative knowledgebase. *Commun. ACM*, 57(10):78–85.

Marcos Zampieri, Kai North, Tommi Jauhiainen, Mariano Felice, Neha Kumari, Nishant Nair, and Yash Bangera. 2023. Language variety identification with true labels. *arXiv preprint arXiv:2303.01490*.

Marcos Zampieri, Liling Tan, Nikola Ljubešić, Jörg Tiedemann, and Preslav Nakov. 2015. Overview of the DSL shared task 2015. In *Proceedings of the Joint Workshop on Language Technology for Closely Related Languages, Varieties and Dialects*, pages 1–9, Hissar, Bulgaria. Association for Computational Linguistics.

Two-stage Pipeline for Multilingual Dialect Detection

Ankit Vaidya and **Aditya Kane**
Pune Institute of Computer Technology, Pune
{ankitvaidya1905, adityakane1}@gmail.com

Abstract

Dialect Identification is a crucial task for localizing various Large Language Models. This paper outlines our approach to the VarDial 2023 DSL-TL shared task. Here we have to identify three or two dialects from three languages each which results in a 9-way classification for Track-1 and 6-way classification for Track-2 respectively. Our proposed approach consists of a two-stage system and outperforms other participants' systems and previous works in this domain. We achieve a score of 58.54% for Track-1 and 85.61% for Track-2. Our codebase is available publicly[1].

1 Introduction

Language has been the primary mode of communication for humans since the pre-historic ages. Studies have explored the evolution of language and outlined mathematical models that govern the intricacies of natural language (Nowak and Krakauer, 1999; Hauser et al., 2014). Inevitably, as humans established civilization in various parts of the world, this language was modified by, and for the group of people occupied by that particular geographical region. This gave rise to multiple national dialects of the same language.

The VarDial workshop (Aepli et al., 2023) (co-located with EACL 2023) explores various dialects and variations of the same language. We participated in the Discriminating Between Similar Languages - True Labels (DSL-TL) shared task. In this task, the participants were provided with data from three languages, with each language having three varieties. This shared task consisted of two tracks – Track-1 featuring nine-way classification and Track-2 featuring six-way classification. The second track included two particular national dialects of each language (eg. American English and British English), and the first track had one general label (English) in addition to the aforementioned two.

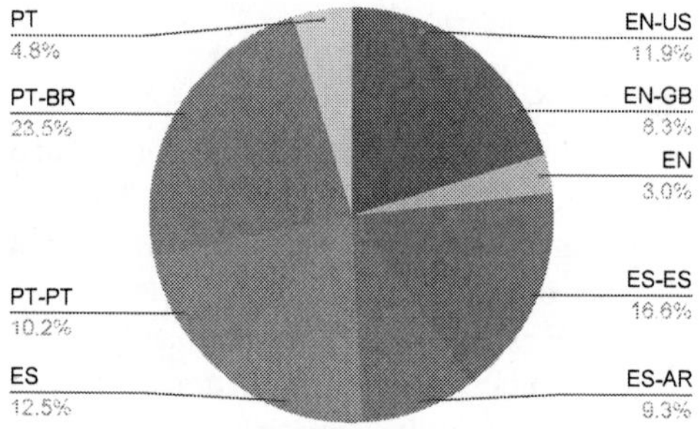

Figure 1: Class distribution of dialects

We ranked 1st in both of the tracks. Moreover, we beat the next best submission by a margin of 4.5% in the first task and 5.6% in the second task.We were the only team to surpass the organizer baseline scores. We present our winning solution in this paper. We used an end-to-end deep learning pipeline which consisted of a language identification model and three language-specific models, one for each language. We converged upon the best combination by doing an elaborate analysis of various models available. Furthermore, in this work we also analyze the performance of the pipeline as a whole and also provide an ablation study. Lastly, we provide some future directions in this area of research.

2 Related Work

The present literature encompasses various aspects of dialect identification. We study this from three perspectives: large language models, language identification and dialect classification problems.

2.1 Large Language Models

The success of transformers and BERT (Devlin et al., 2019) based models was inevitable since the initial boom of the transformer (Vaswani et al.,

[1] https://github.com/ankit-vaidya19/EACL_VarDial2023

Tenth Workshop on NLP for Similar Languages, Varieties and Dialects (VarDial 2023), pages 222–229

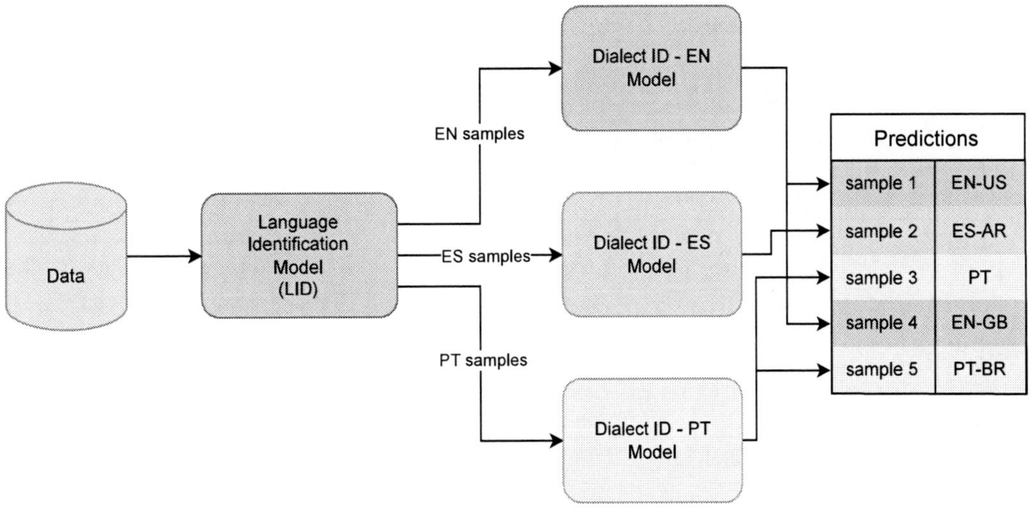

Figure 2: System diagram for dialect classification.The LID classifies the input into one of 3 languages.The sample is then further classified into dialects by language specific models.

2017) model. In recent years, many other architectures like RoBERTa (Liu et al., 2019) and ELECTRA (Clark et al., 2020) have further pushed the state-of-the-art in this domain. Moreover, autoregressive models like GPT (Radford and Narasimhan, 2018) and GPT-2 (Radford et al., 2019) have also shown their prowess. Multilingual versions of RoBERTA, namely XLM-RoBERTa (Conneau et al., 2020) are also available. Lastly, language specific models like Spanish BERT (la Rosa y Eduardo G. Ponferrada y Manu Romero y Paulo Villegas y Pablo González de Prado Salas y María Grandury, 2022) and Portuguese BERT (Souza et al., 2020) are available as well. Our winning solution makes use of these large language models trained on specific languages.

2.2 Language Identification Models

Many multilingual language identification models have been developed in order to classify the language of the input sentence beforehand. Even though the initial works used n-gram models and generative mixture models (Lui et al., 2014; Baldwin and Lui, 2010; Al-Badrashiny and Diab, 2016; Bernier-Colborne et al., 2021; Bestgen, 2021) or even conditional random fields (Al-Badrashiny and Diab, 2016) and other classical machine learning methods like naive bayes (Jauhiainen et al., 2020, 2022, 2021), modern methods have shifted to the use of deep learning for language identification (Mathur et al., 2017; Thara and Poornachandran, 2021; Romero et al., 2021; Bernier-Colborne et al., 2022). Recent works have focused on deep learning based methods, where handling codemixed data is a big challenge in the domain. For our experiments, we use a version of XLM-RoBERTa finetuned on a language identification dataset[2]. This model has near-perfect test accuracy of 99.6%.

2.3 Dialect Classification

Dialect classification has been previously solved using statistical methods like Gaussian Mixture Models and Frame Selection Decoding or Support Vector Machines (SVM) (Lei and Hansen, 2011; Tillmann et al., 2014). It has been explored relatively sparsely, mostly in the case for local languages (Hegde et al., 2020). Deep learning approaches have been explored in previous editions of the VarDial workshop shared tasks (Rebeja and Cristea, 2020) and otherwise (Lin et al., 2020). Dialect classification was also explored previously as a part of other shared tasks (Khered et al., 2022). We want to stress that given the multilingual nature of the dataset, using the present methods directly was not an option. In our work, although we take inspiration from the previous works, we propose a novel system that surpasses the performance of the previous systems by a large margin.

3 Data

The dataset (Zampieri et al., 2023) contained a total of 11,610 sentences belonging to 3 languages:

[2]This model is available here and dataset is available here

Model-EN	Model-ES	Model-PT	Validation F1	Test F1
RoBERTa$_{base}$	Spanish RoBERTa$_{base}$	XLM-RoBERTa$_{base}$	60.74%	-
RoBERTa$_{base}$	Spanish BERT$_{base}$	XLM-RoBERTa$_{base}$	60.05%	-
BERT$_{base}$	Spanish RoBERTa$_{base}$	XLM-RoBERTa$_{base}$	59.08%	-
BERT$_{base}$	Spanish BERT$_{base}$	Portuguese BERT$_{base}$	60.17%	-
BERT$_{base}$	Spanish BERT$_{base}$	XLM-RoBERTa$_{base}$	58.40%	-
BERT$_{base}$	**Spanish RoBERTa$_{base}$**	**Portuguese BERT$_{base}$**	**60.85%**	**58.54%**
RoBERTa$_{base}$	Spanish RoBERTa$_{base}$	Portuguese BERT$_{base}$	62.51%	58.09%
RoBERTa$_{base}$	Spanish BERT$_{base}$	Portuguese BERT$_{base}$	61.83%	57.03%

Table 1: Our complete results for Track-1 using the two-stage dialect detection pipeline. Model-* denotes the language of the models used for the experiments.

Model-EN	Model-ES	Model-PT	Validation F1	Test F1
RoBERTa$_{base}$	XLM-RoBERTa$_{base}$	Portuguese BERT$_{base}$	80.84%	-
RoBERTa$_{base}$	XLM-RoBERTa$_{base}$	XLM-RoBERTa$_{base}$	79.16%	-
BERT$_{base}$	Spanish RoBERTa$_{base}$	XLM-RoBERTa$_{base}$	82.22%	-
BERT$_{base}$	XLM-RoBERTa$_{base}$	Portuguese BERT$_{base}$	80.55%	-
BERT$_{base}$	XLM-RoBERTa$_{base}$	XLM-RoBERTa$_{base}$	78.87%	-
RoBERTa$_{base}$	**Spanish RoBERTa$_{base}$**	**Portuguese BERT$_{base}$**	**84.19%**	**85.61%**
BERT$_{base}$	Spanish RoBERTa$_{base}$	Portuguese BERT$_{base}$	83.90%	85.11%
RoBERTa$_{base}$	Spanish RoBERTa$_{base}$	XLM-RoBERTa$_{base}$	82.51%	83.68%

Table 2: Our complete results for Track-2 using the two-stage dialect detection pipeline. Model-* denotes the language of the models used for the experiments.

English (EN), Spanish (ES), Portuguese (PT) and each language had 3 corresponding varieties. The varieties for English were: American English ($EN-US$), British English ($EN-GB$) and Common English Instances (EN). Similarly varieties corresponding to Spanish and Portuguese were: European/Peninsular Spanish ($ES-ES$), Argentine Spanish ($ES-AR$), Common Spanish Instances (ES) and European Portuguese ($PT-PT$), Brazilian Portuguese ($PT-BR$), Common Portuguese Instances (PT). These were divided into a training set containing 8,745 sentences and the validation set containing 2,865 sentences. The system was evaluated on a separate testing set containing 1,290 sentences. This dataset has acute class imbalance. We observed that the class PT-BR had the most number of samples (2,724) and the class EN had the least number of samples (349), and thus the imbalance ratio was almost 1:8. We have illustrated the data distribution in Figure 1. We tried to mitigate this imbalance using over-sampling and weighted sampling methods. However, the improved data sampling method did not affect the performance.

4 System Description

This was a problem of multi-class classification having 9 classes for Track-1 and 6 classes for Track-2. The samples were belonging to 3 languages having 3 varieties each, so the classification pipeline was made in 2 stages. The Language Identification (LID) model which is the first stage classifies the sentence into 3 languages: English (EN), Spanish (ES) and Portuguese (PT). The LID is a pretrained XLM-RoBERTa that is fine-tuned for the task of language identification. It is able to classify the input sentence into 20 languages. We classify and separate the samples according to their language. The samples corresponding to the specific languages are then fed into the language specific models for dialect identification. For dialect identification we have used models like BERT and RoBERTa with a linear layer connected to the pooler output of the models. Then fine-tuning is done on the models for dialect identification using the samples corresponding to the specific languages. For the task of dialect identification we experimented with several pretrained models

Lg	Model	Train F1	Val F1
EN	**RoBERTa**	**79.74%**	**71.34%**
EN	BERT	80.71%	70.19%
EN	ELECTRA	65.02%	66.60%
EN	XLM-RoBERTa	71.64%	66.12%
EN	GPT-2	56.78%	49.74%
ES	**Spanish RoBERTa**	**74.36%**	**62.96%**
ES	XLM-RoBERTa	59.46%	61.58%
ES	Spanish BERT	67.40%	60.76%
ES	Spanish GPT-2	34.33%	46.11%
PT	**Portuguese BERT**	**67.63%**	**55.15%**
PT	XLM-RoBERTa	64.33%	48.46%
PT	Portuguese ELECTRA	62.11%	46.34%
PT	Portuguese GPT-2	38.52%	34.19%

Table 3: Performance on Track-1 validation dataset of individual models used in the two-stage pipeline. "Lg" stands for language of the model used.

Lg	Model	Train F1	Val F1
EN	**RoBERTa**	**91.70%**	**88.75%**
EN	BERT	94.24%	88.32%
EN	XLM-RoBERTa	87.61%	84.68%
ES	**Spanish RoBERTa**	**96.05%**	**87.05%**
ES	XLM-RoBERTa	89.25%	80.29%
PT	**Portuguese BERT**	**89.49%**	**79.21%**
PT	XLM-RoBERTa	81.61%	75.91%

Table 4: Performance on Track-2 validation dataset of individual models used in the two-stage pipeline. "Lg" stands for language of the model used.

like XLM-RoBERTa, BERT, ELECTRA, GPT-2 and RoBERTa. All models were fine-tuned for 20 epochs with a learning rate of 1e-6 and weight decay 1e-6 with a batch size of 8. The best performing model checkpoint was chosen according to the epoch-wise validation macro-F1 score.

5 Experiments and Results

5.1 Experiments Using Large Language Models

For the task of Dialect Identification we have tried various language specific models like XLM-RoBERTa, BERT, ELECTRA, RoBERTa and GPT-2. The base variant of all these models were used and all the models were used through the HuggingFace (Wolf et al., 2020) library. The pooler output of these models was passed through a linear layer and the models were fine-tuned. First, we experimented with different models for Track-1. All the models were trained for 20 epochs with learning rate 1e-6, weight decay 1e-6 and a batch size of 8. We used XLM-RoBERTa as the baseline for all 3 languages. The best performing models for the English language were RoBERTa and BERT whereas GPT-2 was the worst performing. Similarly the language specific versions of RoBERTa and BERT performed well for the Spanish and Portuguese respectively. Overall the worst performing model was GPT-2 across all 3 languages. The validation F1 scores are present in Table 3. The two best-performing models for every language were chosen for Track-2. The same procedure as specified above was used and the F1 scores are present in Table 4. The train and validation F1 scores for 2-class classification are higher for all models as compared to the F1 score of the same models for 3-class classification. This was mainly due to the poor representation and accuracy of classification of the third class. We observed symptoms of overfitting in all models after 12-15 epochs and the best validation F1 score was obtained in the range of 4-8 epochs.

Lg	Model	Adapted F1	F.T. F1
EN	RoBERTa	85.20%	88.75%
EN	BERT	83.21%	88.32%
EN	XLM-RoBERTa	81.21%	84.68%
ES	Spanish RoBERTa	78.45%	87.05%
ES	XLM-RoBERTa	66.89%	80.29%
PT	Portuguese BERT	72.17%	79.21%
PT	XLM-RoBERTa	71.89%	75.91%

Table 5: Comparative results of two-way classification using the finetuned (F.T.) predictions and predictions adapted from three-way classification models.

5.2 LID Experiments

The pipeline for dialect identification is divided into two parts as the sentences in the dataset belong to different languages. The stages are described in Section 4. The XLM-RoBERTa we have used for language classification has a test accuracy of 99.6% meaning it correctly classifies all input sentences and hence, can be considered as a perfect classifier. For the final pipeline we experimented using the two best performing models for each language in

Track-1 and Track-2. For both the tracks we experimented with all 8 (2^3) possible combinations of models and calculated the validation F1 score for the combined validation dataset which had sentences belonging to all languages. The validation scores for Track-1 and Track-2 are shown in Table 1 and Table 2 respectively. For both the tracks, the three pipelines with the best validation F1 scores were chosen for submission.

5.3 Using 3-way Classifier as a 2-way Classifier

In Track-1, participants are expected to train a classifier which classifies amongst 9 classes, and in Track-2, participants are expected to train a classifier which classifies amongst 6 classes. These 6 classes are a proper subset of the 9 classes from Track-1. Thus, an intuitive baseline for Track-2 is to use the model finetuned for Track-1, whilst considering only the relevant classes for the latter task. The classes EN, ES and PT, i.e. the classes without any national dialect associated with them are not included in Track-2 as compared to Track-1. Thus, we calculate the predictions for the Track-2 validation dataset using the models for Track-1 and exclude the metrics for Track-1 specific classes to get the metrics for this "adapted" 2-way classification. We show the results of this experiment in Table 5 and observe that, as expected, the adapted 2-way classification performs worse compared to the explicitly finetuned variant.

5.4 Results for Track-1 and Track-2

We now present our experiments and their performance for both tracks. Our experiments for Track-1 are described in Table 1 and our experiments for Track-2 are described in Table 2. The participants were allowed three submissions for evaluation on the test set, so we submitted predictions using the three systems which performed the best on the validation set. As mentioned in Section 5.2, we performed 2^3, i.e. a total of 8 experiments using the two best models for each language. We observed that RoBERTa$_{base}$ on English, Spanish BERT$_{base}$ on Spanish and Portuguese BERT$_{base}$ performed the best on the testing set for Track-1. The same combination, with RoBERTa$_{base}$ for English, worked best for Track-2. All of our submissions were the top submissions for each track, which surpassed the next best competitors by a margin of 4.5% and 5.6% for Track-1 and Track-2 respectively.

5.5 Ablation of Best Submissions

We hereby make some observations of our submissions and other experiments. To assist this, we plot the confusion matrices of our best submissions for Track-1 and Track-2 in Figures 3 and 4 respectively. Note that these confusion matrices have their rows (i.e. true labels axes) normalized according to the number of samples in the class. Here are observations from our experiments:

1. **BERT-based models outperform other models across all languages:** We observe that BERT-based models outperform ELECTRA-based and GPT-2-based models, as shown in Table 3. We speculate this is because of the inherent architecture of BERT, which combines semantic learning with knowledge retention. This combination of traits is particularly useful for this task.

2. **Common labels perform the worst across all languages:** We observe that the common labels EN, ES and PT perform the worst, both in the individual as well as the two-stage setup. We hypothesize this is because of the absence of dialect specific words, or words that are specific to the geographical origin of the national dialect (for example, "Yankees" for EN-US and "Oxford" for EN-GB).

3. **English models work better than models of other languages:** It can be noted from Figures 4 and 3 that the English models have the best performance across all classes. This can be attributed to two reasons: absence of national dialect specific words and lesser pretraining data in the case of Portuguese.

4. **British English is most correctly classified class:** We can observe that the Spanish or Portuguese models make equal number of mistakes in the case of either national dialect, in the case of Track-2 (see Figure 4). However, in the case of English, the label $EN - GB$ is correctly classified for more than 95% of the cases. We speculate this is because British English involves slightly distinctive grammar and semantics, which help the model separate it from other classes.

5. **The proposed 2-step method is scalable for multiple language dialect classification:** We can strongly assert that the novel 2-step deep

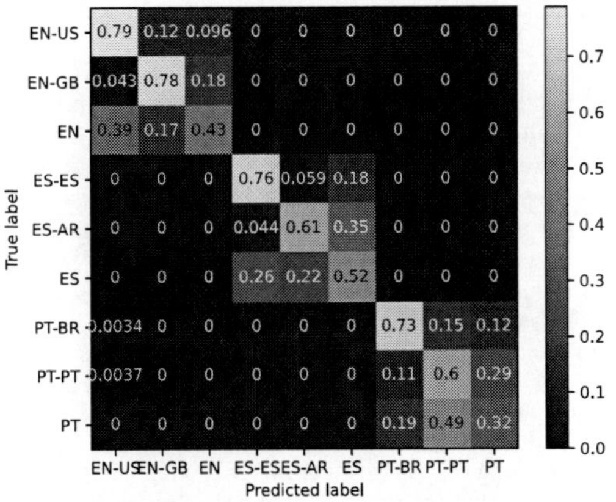

Figure 3: Confusion matrix of 9-way classification. Note that rows are normalized according to the number of samples is that class.

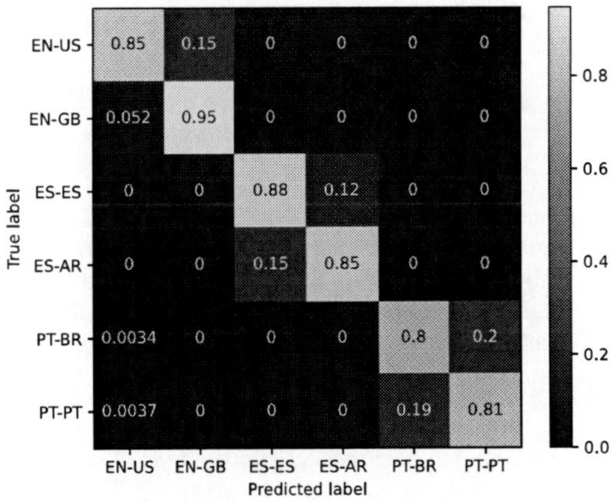

Figure 4: Confusion matrix of 6-way classification. Note that rows are normalized according to the number of samples is that class.

learning method for multilingual dialect classification is a scalable method for the task due to two specific reasons: firstly, the multilingual models (like XLM-RoBERTa) might not have the vocabulary as well as the learning capabilities to learn the minute differences between individual dialects. Secondly, this system can be quickly expanded for a new language by simply adding a language specific dialect classifier, provided the language identification model supports that particular language.

6 Conclusion

In this paper we propose a two-stage classification pipeline for dialect identification for multilingual corpora. We conduct thorough ablations on this setup and provide valuable insights. We foresee multiple future directions for this work. The first is to expand this work to many languages and dialects. Secondly, it is a worthwhile research direction to distill this multi-model setup into a single model with multiple prediction heads.

Limitations

The obvious limitation of this system is the excessive memory consumption due to the usage of language specific models. For low resource languages this system is difficult to train and scale. We hope that these problems will be addressed by researchers in future works.

References

Noëmi Aepli, Çağrı Çöltekin, Rob van der Goot, Tommi Jauhiainen, Mourhaf Kazzaz, Nikola Ljubešić, Kai North, Barbara Plank, Yves Scherrer, and Marcos Zampieri. 2023. Findings of the VarDial evaluation campaign 2023. In *Proceedings of the Tenth Workshop on NLP for Similar Languages, Varieties and Dialects*, Dubrovnik, Croatia. Association for Computational Linguistics.

Mohamed Al-Badrashiny and Mona Diab. 2016. LILI: A simple language independent approach for language identification. In *Proceedings of COLING 2016, the 26th International Conference on Computational Linguistics: Technical Papers*, pages 1211–1219, Osaka, Japan. The COLING 2016 Organizing Committee.

Timothy Baldwin and Marco Lui. 2010. Language identification: The long and the short of the matter. In *Human Language Technologies: The 2010 Annual Conference of the North American Chapter of the Association for Computational Linguistics*, pages 229–237, Los Angeles, California. Association for Computational Linguistics.

Gabriel Bernier-Colborne, Serge Leger, and Cyril Goutte. 2021. N-gram and neural models for uralic language identification: NRC at VarDial 2021. In *Proceedings of the Eighth Workshop on NLP for Similar Languages, Varieties and Dialects*, pages 128–134, Kiyv, Ukraine. Association for Computational Linguistics.

Gabriel Bernier-Colborne, Serge Leger, and Cyril Goutte. 2022. Transfer learning improves French cross-domain dialect identification: NRC @ VarDial 2022. In *Proceedings of the Ninth Workshop on NLP for Similar Languages, Varieties and Dialects*, pages 109–118, Gyeongju, Republic of Korea. Association for Computational Linguistics.

Yves Bestgen. 2021. Optimizing a supervised classifier for a difficult language identification problem. In *Proceedings of the Eighth Workshop on NLP for Similar Languages, Varieties and Dialects*, pages 96–101, Kiyv, Ukraine. Association for Computational Linguistics.

Kevin Clark, Minh-Thang Luong, Quoc V. Le, and Christopher D. Manning. 2020. ELECTRA: pre-training text encoders as discriminators rather than generators. *CoRR*, abs/2003.10555.

Alexis Conneau, Kartikay Khandelwal, Naman Goyal, Vishrav Chaudhary, Guillaume Wenzek, Francisco Guzmán, Edouard Grave, Myle Ott, Luke Zettlemoyer, and Veselin Stoyanov. 2020. Unsupervised cross-lingual representation learning at scale. In *Proceedings of the 58th Annual Meeting of the Association for Computational Linguistics*, pages 8440–8451, Online. Association for Computational Linguistics.

Jacob Devlin, Ming-Wei Chang, Kenton Lee, and Kristina Toutanova. 2019. BERT: Pre-training of deep bidirectional transformers for language understanding. In *Proceedings of the 2019 Conference of the North American Chapter of the Association for Computational Linguistics: Human Language Technologies, Volume 1 (Long and Short Papers)*, pages 4171–4186, Minneapolis, Minnesota. Association for Computational Linguistics.

Marc D. Hauser, Charles Yang, Robert C. Berwick, Ian Tattersall, Michael J. Ryan, Jeffrey Watumull, Noam Chomsky, and Richard C. Lewontin. 2014. The mystery of language evolution. *Frontiers in Psychology*, 5.

Pradyoth Hegde, Nagaratna B. Chittaragi, Siva Krishna P. Mothukuri, and Shashidhar G. Koolagudi. 2020. Kannada dialect classification using cnn. In *Mining Intelligence and Knowledge Exploration*, pages 254–259, Cham. Springer International Publishing.

Tommi Jauhiainen, Heidi Jauhiainen, and Krister Lindén. 2021. Naive Bayes-based experiments in Romanian dialect identification. In *Proceedings of the Eighth Workshop on NLP for Similar Languages, Varieties and Dialects*, pages 76–83, Kiyv, Ukraine. Association for Computational Linguistics.

Tommi Jauhiainen, Heidi Jauhiainen, and Krister Lindén. 2022. Italian language and dialect identification and regional French variety detection using adaptive naive Bayes. In *Proceedings of the Ninth Workshop on NLP for Similar Languages, Varieties and Dialects*, pages 119–129, Gyeongju, Republic of Korea. Association for Computational Linguistics.

Tommi Jauhiainen, Heidi Jauhiainen, Niko Partanen, and Krister Lindén. 2020. Uralic language identification (ULI) 2020 shared task dataset and the wanca 2017 corpora. In *Proceedings of the 7th Workshop on NLP for Similar Languages, Varieties and Dialects*, pages 173–185, Barcelona, Spain (Online). International Committee on Computational Linguistics (ICCL).

Abdullah Salem Khered, Ingy Yasser Hassan Abdou Abdelhalim, and Riza Batista-Navarro. 2022. Building an ensemble of transformer models for Arabic dialect classification and sentiment analysis. In *Proceedings of the The Seventh Arabic Natural Language Processing Workshop (WANLP)*, pages 479–484, Abu Dhabi, United Arab Emirates (Hybrid). Association for Computational Linguistics.

Javier De la Rosa y Eduardo G. Ponferrada y Manu Romero y Paulo Villegas y Pablo González de Prado Salas y María Grandury. 2022. Bertin: Efficient pre-training of a spanish language model using perplexity sampling. *Procesamiento del Lenguaje Natural*, 68(0):13–23.

Yun Lei and John H. L. Hansen. 2011. Dialect classification via text-independent training and testing for arabic, spanish, and chinese. *IEEE Transactions on Audio, Speech, and Language Processing*, 19(1):85–96.

Wanqiu Lin, Maulik Madhavi, Rohan Kumar Das, and Haizhou Li. 2020. Transformer-based arabic dialect identification.

Yinhan Liu, Myle Ott, Naman Goyal, Jingfei Du, Mandar Joshi, Danqi Chen, Omer Levy, Mike Lewis, Luke Zettlemoyer, and Veselin Stoyanov. 2019. Roberta: A robustly optimized bert pretraining approach. *ArXiv*, abs/1907.11692.

Marco Lui, Jey Han Lau, and Timothy Baldwin. 2014. Automatic detection and language identification of multilingual documents. *Transactions of the Association for Computational Linguistics*, 2:27–40.

Priyank Mathur, Arkajyoti Misra, and Emrah Budur. 2017. LIDE: language identification from text documents. *CoRR*, abs/1701.03682.

Martin A. Nowak and David C. Krakauer. 1999. The evolution of language. *Proceedings of the National Academy of Sciences*, 96(14):8028–8033.

Alec Radford and Karthik Narasimhan. 2018. Improving language understanding by generative pre-training.

Alec Radford, Jeff Wu, Rewon Child, David Luan, Dario Amodei, and Ilya Sutskever. 2019. Language models are unsupervised multitask learners.

Petru Rebeja and Dan Cristea. 2020. A dual-encoding system for dialect classification. In *Proceedings of the 7th Workshop on NLP for Similar Languages, Varieties and Dialects*, pages 212–219, Barcelona, Spain (Online). International Committee on Computational Linguistics (ICCL).

David Romero, Luis Fernando D'Haro, and Christian Salamea. 2021. Exploring Transformer-based Language Recognition using Phonotactic Information. In *Proc. IberSPEECH 2021*, pages 250–254.

Fábio Souza, Rodrigo Nogueira, and Roberto Lotufo. 2020. BERTimbau: pretrained BERT models for Brazilian Portuguese. In *9th Brazilian Conference on Intelligent Systems, BRACIS, Rio Grande do Sul, Brazil, October 20-23 (to appear)*.

S. Thara and Prabaharan Poornachandran. 2021. Transformer based language identification for malayalam-english code-mixed text. *IEEE Access*, 9:118837–118850.

Christoph Tillmann, Saab Mansour, and Yaser Al-Onaizan. 2014. Improved sentence-level Arabic dialect classification. In *Proceedings of the First Workshop on Applying NLP Tools to Similar Languages, Varieties and Dialects*, pages 110–119, Dublin, Ireland. Association for Computational Linguistics and Dublin City University.

Ashish Vaswani, Noam Shazeer, Niki Parmar, Jakob Uszkoreit, Llion Jones, Aidan N Gomez, Ł ukasz Kaiser, and Illia Polosukhin. 2017. Attention is all you need. In *Advances in Neural Information Processing Systems*, volume 30. Curran Associates, Inc.

Thomas Wolf, Lysandre Debut, Victor Sanh, Julien Chaumond, Clement Delangue, Anthony Moi, Pierric Cistac, Tim Rault, Remi Louf, Morgan Funtowicz, Joe Davison, Sam Shleifer, Patrick von Platen, Clara Ma, Yacine Jernite, Julien Plu, Canwen Xu, Teven Le Scao, Sylvain Gugger, Mariama Drame, Quentin Lhoest, and Alexander Rush. 2020. Transformers: State-of-the-art natural language processing. In *Proceedings of the 2020 Conference on Empirical Methods in Natural Language Processing: System Demonstrations*, pages 38–45, Online. Association for Computational Linguistics.

Marcos Zampieri, Kai North, Tommi Jauhiainen, Mariano Felice, Neha Kumari, Nishant Nair, and Yash Bangera. 2023. Language variety identification with true labels. *arXiv preprint arXiv:2303.01490*.

Using Ensemble Learning in Language Variety Identification

Mihaela Găman
Department of Computer Science
University of Bucharest
14 Academiei, Bucharest, Romania
mp.gaman@gmail.com

Abstract

The present work describes the solutions proposed by the UnibucNLP team to address the closed format of the DSL-TL task featured in the tenth VarDial Evaluation Campaign. The DSL-TL organizers provided approximately 11 thousand sentences written in three different languages and manually tagged with one of 9 classes. Out of these, 3 tags are considered *common label* and the remaining 6 tags are *variety-specific*. The DSL-TL task features 2 subtasks: *Track 1* - a three-way and *Track 2* - a two-way classification per language. In *Track 2* only the variety-specific labels are used for scoring, whereas in *Track 1* the common label is considered as well. Our team participated in both tracks, with three ensemble-based submissions for each. The meta-learner used for *Track 1* is XGBoost and for *Track 2*, Logistic Regression. With each submission, we are gradually increasing the complexity of the ensemble, starting with two shallow, string-kernel based methods. To the first ensemble, we add a convolutional neural network for our second submission. The third ensemble submitted adds a fine-tuned BERT model to the second one. In *Track 1*, ensemble three is our highest ranked, with an $F1 - score$ of 53.18%; 5.36% less than the leader. Surprisingly, in *Track 2* the ensemble of shallow methods surpasses the other two, more complex ensembles, achieving an $F1 - score$ of 69.35%.

1 Introduction

Discriminating between Similar Languages using a manually annotated data set of True Labels (Zampieri et al., 2023) was included on the list of shared tasks in the tenth VarDial evaluation campaign (Aepli et al., 2023), under the DSL-TL acronym. The topic of discriminating among language varieties and similar languages has been addressed in previous VarDial editions (Zampieri et al., 2017; Malmasi et al., 2016; Zampieri et al., 2015, 2014). However, we find the DSL-TL task compelling as it introduces qualitative human-annotations from multiple sources.

In DSL-TL organizers provide a set of sentences coming from news reports[1] written in either English, Spanish or Portuguese and split in a train, development and test subsets. The test split represents a collection of unlabelled sentences, with labels being subject to further submissions from participants. The examples in the train and development sets are tagged with one of nine labels, namely *EN-GB*, *EN-US*, *EN*, *ES-ES*, *ES-AR*, *ES*, *PT-PT*, *PT-BR* and *PT*. Six of the labels provided, aside from the language itself, also specify the language variety, marked with the initials of the country (i.e. *GB* – Great Britain, *US* – USA, *ES* – Spain, *AR* – Argentine, *PT* – Portugal, *BR* – Brazil). These are referenced to, by the organizers, as *variety-specific* labels. The remaining three tags, i.e. *EN*, *ES* and *PT*, are considered *common* labels. Based on this terminology, the task features two subtasks:

- *Track 1* - a nine-way classification, where both the variety-specific (e.g. *EN-GB* or *EN-US*) as well as the common label (e.g. *EN*) are considered for scoring.
- *Track 2* - evaluates a six-way classification setup, considering only the variety-specific labels.

The DSL-TL task is presented in both the open and closed formats for each of the two aforementioned tracks. Three submissions are allowed for each pair $(subtask, format)$, which amounts to a total of maximum 12 different sets of predictions that can be submitted by each team.

Our team chose the closed format and participated in both tracks, with three submissions for each subtask. All the models submitted are powered by ensemble learning. For *Track 1*, the meta-learning is based on Extreme Gradient Boosting

[1] https://github.com/LanguageTechnologyLab/DSL-TL

Tenth Workshop on NLP for Similar Languages, Varieties and Dialects (VarDial 2023), pages 230–240
May 5, 2023 ©2023 Association for Computational Linguistics

(XGBoost) (Chen and Guestrin, 2016), while for *Track 2* we employ Multinomial Logistic Regression (Peng et al., 2002) as our meta-classifier. The same subset of individual learners is used for each set of ensembles submitted , independent of its meta-learner (i.e. XGBoost or Logistic Regression) and destination (i.e. subtask).

With each submission, we gradually increase the complexity of the models plugged into the aforementioned ensembles. We start by combining the powers of two shallow methods, namely Support Vector Machines (SVM) (Cortes and Vapnik, 1995) and Kernel Ridge Regression (KRR) (Hoerl and Kennard, 1970), both using string kernels - a feature extraction technique that proved useful in previous endeavours of identifying language varieties (Ionescu and Popescu, 2016). For our second submission, we augment the ensemble of shallow models with a Character-level Convolutional Neural Network (Char-CNN) (Zhang et al., 2015), which adds depth to the ensemble and a new way of regarding the data (i.e. at the character level). The third ensemble submitted for each track contains the two string kernel based shallow methods, the Char-CNN and also a fine-tuned BERT (Devlin et al., 2019) as individual learners.

We fine-tuned and evaluated all of the individual models and meta-learners previously mentioned using the development set provided by Zampieri et al. (2023). Our final submissions include the development subset in the training routine. Moreover, our preference for only submitting ensemble models reflect the best results obtained locally with models trained on the training split and tested on the development data.

The rest of the present paper is structured as follows. In Section 2 we present related work in the space of language varieties identification. We describe in detail our approach for the DSL-TL task in Section 3. The experiments conducted and the empirical results obtained are discussed across Section 4. A set of conclusions will be drawn in Section 5.

2 Related Work

Usually modeled as a text classification problem and tackled using supervised learning approaches (Jauhiainen et al., 2019b), Language Identification (LI) research dates from the mid-60's (Mustonen, 1965), with periodic updates until the early 2000s (Takcı and Soğukpınar, 2004; Sibun, 1996; Grefenstette, 1995). Initially focused on dissimilar languages, LI has reached a peak when McNamee (2005) achieved a nearly-perfect outcome using character n-grams based models to discriminate among different languages in samples collected online.

In the last decade, language identification research has regained momentum, with social media becoming a rich and resourceful source of data. User-generated content (Tromp and Pechenizkiy, 2011) and free-form short texts (Anand, 2014) can be counted among the reasons why the research in the area of language identification was resumed. New challenges have arisen - e.g. mixing two or more different languages in social media content (Molina et al., 2016). Moreover, the idea of discriminating among similar languages or language varieties started gathering an entire community around it, especially in the VarDial evaluation campaign (Aepli et al., 2022; Chakravarthi et al., 2021; Gaman et al., 2020).

The problem of discriminating among similar languages has been tackled, to date, using a variety of ML-powered techniques practicing both shallow (Ljubešic and Kranjcic, 2014), as well as deep-learning (Li et al., 2018) with an accuracy surpassing a 95% threshold.

For language varieties on the other hand, we can observe fluctuations in performance as shown in the VarDial reports to date (Aepli et al., 2022; Chakravarthi et al., 2021; Gaman et al., 2020). For instance, Goutte et al. (2014) applies a common approach to three different language varieties: European vs Brazilian Portuguese, Castilian vs Argentine Spanish and British vs American English. The same model achieves an accuracy above 90% for the first 2 varieties and just below 53% for the third. In the Arabic dialect identification task (Malmasi et al., 2016), the highest ranking systems were based either on ensemble learning or on single SVMs trained on character and word-level n-grams (Malmasi and Zampieri, 2016; Eldesouki et al., 2016) and achieved accuracies of around 50%. Recent shared tasks (Aepli et al., 2022; Chakravarthi et al., 2021; Gaman et al., 2020; Zampieri et al., 2019, 2018, 2017) continued the work in the space of language varieties, with multiple different languages targeted over the years. Among these, we count German (Malmasi and Zampieri, 2017b), Chinese (Jauhiainen et al., 2019a) and Italian Jauhiainen et al. (2022) dialects, Dutch vs Flemish (Çöltekin and Rama, 2017), Romanian vs Moldavian (Çöltekin, 2020), etc. Performance was consistent with the results in earlier campaigns (2014 - 2016) – the highest ranked results varied greatly from task to task, with n-gram based shallow models often outperforming other approaches. These works show that language identification is not a resolved problem, as we still see a struggle in performance in automatically identifying certain dialects and language varieties.

Among the most recent works on language identification, we should mention the one on which the current DSL-TL shared task is based. Zampieri et al. (2023) introduce DSL-TL as the first human-annotated multilingual data set for language variety classification. DSL-TL uses instances from DSLCC (Tan et al., 2014) - an extensive collection of samples for LI, introduced and enhanced in prior VarDial evaluation campaigns (Zampieri et al., 2017; Malmasi et al., 2016; Zampieri et al., 2014). DSL-TL also uses news reports from Zellers et al. (2019). The authors label the data from multiple human sources using a crowdsourcing platform. Moreover, alongside the qualitative data set, the authors train multiple models on these samples. The approaches used count Naive Bayes, Adaptive Naive Bayes and deep learning based methods such as mBERT, XLM-R, and XLM-R-LD and are employed as baselines in the shared task referred in the present paper. Intriguing perhaps, the authors observe similar performance across the shallow and deep learning based methods. Additionally, in some cases, the shallow methods even surpass the deep ones - an observation consistent with prior findings (Jauhiainen et al., 2019b; Medvedeva et al., 2017).

Analyzing the baselines introduced by Zampieri et al. (2023), we consider appropriate to tackle the classification problem posed by the DSL-TL task from both angles. Thus, as previously mentioned, we are combining shallow and deep learning techniques in our ensemble-powered solutions. Our choice is encouraged by prior research in the space of LI, which shows good results obtained by stacking ensembles (Malmasi and Zampieri, 2017b,a). Moreover, we choose most of the individual learners used based on their prior impact in language identification tasks: SVM with string kernels (Kruengkrai et al., 2005), CNNs (Jaech et al., 2016) and BERT (Zaharia et al., 2020). From our perspective, prior success in LI is an indication that these methods have a high chance of being suitable for the DSL-TL use-case as well. Additionally, each of the two choices of meta-learners were also used before in language variety identification: Logistic Regression (Porta and Sancho, 2014; Chen and Maison, 2003) and XGBoost (Barbaresi, 2016).

3 Methods

Our team submitted three distinct ensemble-based systems for each of the two tracks of the DSL-TL task. The choice of architecture for the meta-learner represents the one difference between the ensembles submitted for each track. For the first subtask, we use an XGBoost-based meta-learner, whereas for the second one, we rely on Logistic Regression. As mentioned in both Section 1 and Section 2, we gradually increase the complexity of the ensemble used in each submission. Figure 1 displays the prediction pipeline of the third and most complex system submitted, which is similar with a system that we used in a previous VarDial geo-location challenge (Gaman et al., 2021). From left to right, also in Figure 1, we can infer how the other pipelines are composed: the first system submitted only uses two shallow models (i.e. SVM and KRR) and the second submission adds a char-level CNN to the first system. In the continuation of this section, we briefly describe each individual machine learning technique used in the ensembles submitted, as well as the meta-learners.

3.1 Shallow Learning based on String Kernels

String Kernels. Introduced by Lodhi et al. (2001), string kernels represent an effective method (Cozma et al., 2018; Ionescu and Butnaru, 2018; Giménez-Pérez et al., 2017; Ionescu et al., 2014) of comparing two textual samples. String kernels use the inner product generated by all the character n-grams in a given document. We observe good performance of string kernel-based systems in dialect identification, with emphasis on previous VarDial editions (Butnaru and Ionescu, 2018; Ionescu and Popescu, 2016).

Using the technique introduced by Popescu et al. (2017), we obtain a kernel matrix X where the element X_{ij} measures the similarity between two documents x_i and x_j. The similarity function used is the presence bits string kernel (Popescu and Ionescu, 2013), which is defined as follows:

$$k^{0/1}(x_i, x_j) = \sum_{g \in S^n} \#(x_i, g) \cdot \#(x_j, g), \quad (1)$$

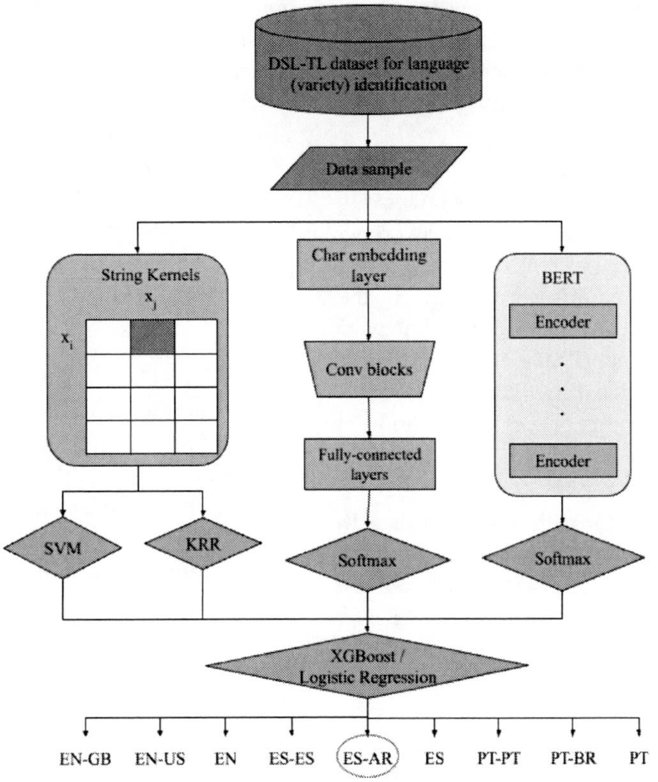

Figure 1: Full ensemble (submission 3) proposed by UnibucNLP for the DSL-TL shared task. Best viewed in color.

where S is a set of characters; x_i and x_j are the strings to be compared; n is the length of the char n-grams used and $\#(x, g)$ is a function with binary outcome that returns 1 when n-gram g occurs at least once in x.

Support Vector Machines – SVM(s). The goal in SVMs (Cortes and Vapnik, 1995) is to find the best hyperplane that separates the training data points in their respective classes. At the same time, in order to achieve better generalization, SVM tries to maximize the margin that separates the two classes, using *support vectors* (i.e. the points closest to the decision boundary). An advantage of SVM is the kernel trick (Shawe-Taylor and Cristianini, 2004) - a technique used to map the non-linearly separable data in a higher-dimensional space, where it becomes separable through a hyperplane. Although designed with 2-way classification in mind, SVMs can be used in the multi-class setup through the training of multiple models in a one-vs-one or one-vs-rest scheme. In our current experiments, we use the one-vs-one technique. Moreover, instead of using a standard kernel, we employ the SVMs with the custom n-gram based string kernel defined in Equation 1.

Kernel Ridge Regression (KRR). Considered a generalization of Ridge Regression (Hoerl and Kennard, 1970), KRR is obtained by combining L2 linear regression with the kernel trick (Saunders et al., 1998). Thus, KRR presents the same two big advantages as is the case with SVM - (1) it can model non-linearly separable data and (2) we can use a custom kernel function. For the DSL-TL task, we employ the presence bits kernel from Equation 1. We also follow two steps to repurpose the trained regressor for multi-class classification: (1) we round the continuous predictions to match the values in $\{-1, 1\}$ and (2) we use the one-versus-rest scheme.

3.2 Deep Learning

Character-level Convolutional Neural Network (Char-CNN). Regarded as the base unit in any given vocabulary, characters represent a popular (Al-Rfou et al., 2019; Kim et al., 2016; Zhang et al., 2015; Sutskever et al., 2011) non-pretentious source of features for text-based ML models. When working at character level, we remove dependencies of syntax and semantic structure (Ballesteros et al., 2015). Given that in DSL-TL we have multiple languages mixed in the same data set, the aforementioned property represents a welcomed advantage for the present use-case.

CNNs are a type of neural network that joins convolutions and pooling operations in convolutional blocks. Towards the end of the network we usually add a sequence of fully connected layers, followed by a terminal prediction layer. In this work, we employ a convolutional neural network operating at char level (Zhang et al., 2015) with squeeze-and-excitation (SE) blocks, introduced and successfully used in dialect identification by Butnaru and Ionescu (2019).

Transformers (BERT). With an encoder-decoder based architecture, transformers (Vaswani et al., 2017) are among the most important advancements in NLP in the past decade. Widely used since its release, BERT (Devlin et al., 2019) is a special type of transformer, which pre-trains deep bidirectional representations of language in a self-supervised fashion. For downstream tasks, such as our current language varieties identification problem, it is straightforward to fine-tune a pretrained BERT model. BERT is our last choice of individual learner given the good results obtained in similar dialect / language variety identification setups (Zaharia et al., 2020).

3.3 Ensemble Learning

XGBoost. XGBoost is a tree-based ensemble model (Chen and Guestrin, 2016; Friedman, 2001), effectively employed in both academic research (Li, 2010; Burges, 2010; Bennett et al., 2007) as well as the industry (He et al., 2014). In our experiments, XGBoost is the chosen meta-learner for *Track 1*. We train XGBoost over the predictions of each individual models previously described in the current section.

Logistic Regression (LR). Multinomial Logistic Regression is a generalization of LR (Peng et al., 2002) to multi-class classification problems. Logistic Regression has been historically employed in language identification tasks (Porta and Sancho, 2014; Chen and Maison, 2003). Moreover, in our experiments, the ensembles that used multinomial Logistic Regression as meta-learner achieved similar performance when compared to the XGBoost meta-learner. Thus, we decided to also submit the predictions of the set of ensembles based on LR. We should mention that we trained the LR-based ensembles on all of the tags available, including the common labels (i.e. GB, ES and PT). No language-variety specifics were enforced for this ensemble whose predictions were submitted for *Track 2*.

4 Experiments

4.1 Data Set

The DSL-TL data set (Zampieri et al., 2023) is targeted towards the task of discriminating between language varieties. Consistent with its purpose, the data set contains a total of $12,900$ instances written in either English (EN), Spanish (ES) or Portuguese (PT) and manually labelled from multiple sources. DSL-TL makes a distinction among two different varieties for each of the three languages included. Thus, we observe the following six composed labels in the data set: *EN-GB* - British English, *EN-US* - American English, *ES-ES* - Castilian Spanish, *ES-AR* - Argentine Spanish, *PT-PT* - European Portuguese and *PT-BR* - Brazilian Portuguese. Moreover, we also have 3 common labels, namely *EN*, *ES* and *PT*, for the samples not containing any variety specific markers.

DSL-TL provides three splits for training, development and the final testing of the solutions proposed to address the task. The split was performed following the $70/20/10$ rule. The training and development textual samples are provided alongside their respective language labels. The test set only contains the textual samples, pending further submission of predictions such that the organizers can evaluate them against the ground truth.

4.2 Hyperparameter Tuning

SVM. In our experiments, we use SVM with a pre-computed string kernel and the regularization parameter $C = 10$. We select the best regularization value via grid search from a range of values from 10^{-4} to 10^{4}, with a multiplication step of 10. For the string kernel used, we experiment with multiple presence-bits string kernels based on various n-gram lengths, from 3 to 6 characters long. The best performance in terms of accuracy and macro $F1 - score$ was achieved by a string kernel based on the blended spectrum of 3 to 5 character n-grams.

KRR. For KRR, we tune the regularization λ using a set of values that range from 10^{-6} to 10^{-1}, and a multiplication step of 10. The best value for λ

in our 9-way classfication setup was 10^{-2}. Similar with the SVMs, the string kernel used in KRR is based on a blended spectrum of 3 to 5 character n-grams.

CharCNN. The third individual learner used is a character-level CNN (Zhang et al., 2015), operating on an input window of maximum 256 characters in each sample, as indicated by a closer inspection of the data. The architecture used is very similar with the one employed by Butnaru and Ionescu (2019) in Romanian dialect identification. Each of the maximum 256 characters considered in the input layer is embedded into a vector of size 128, selected from a set of powers of 2 as potential embedding sizes, ranging from 16 up until 256. Three convolutional blocks follow, each having a convolutional layer with 128 filters, a stride of 1 and filter sizes 7, 5 and 3. We use max pooling with a filter of size 3 to downsample the output of the convolutional layer. Each convolutional block is followed by a Squeeze-and-Excitation (SE) block with a reduction ratio $r = 64$. The sequence of convolutional blocks is followed by one fully connected layer with 128 neural units, out of which we drop neurons with a probability of 0.5. The neural network is also equipped with a final Softmax-activated prediction layer, of size 9 to retrieve a probability for each of the classes in DSL-TL. We use a learning rate of 10^{-4} and train the network for 100 epochs on mini-batches of 128 samples. Early stopping is used with a tolerance of 10 consecutive epochs for stalled performance.

Fine-tuned BERT. Our fourth and last individual learner consists in a fine-tuned multilingual BERT model (Devlin et al., 2019). Prior to fine tuning the model, we use the multilingual BERT tokenizer to encode each example into a list of token IDs. Then, each token is translated into a 768-dimensional embedding vector. Furthermore, the architecture is augmented with a global average pooling layer to achieve a Continuous Bag-of-Words (CBOW) representation of the data. In the end, a Softmax output layer predicts the likeliness of a sample being marked with each of the nine language tags provided. We fine-tune the model described above for 30 epochs with early stopping. We train on mini-batches of 32 samples and optimize using Adam with decoupled weight decay (AdamW) (Loshchilov and Hutter, 2019), a learning rate of $5 \cdot 10^{-5}$ and an ϵ equal to 10^{-8}. We tuned the learning rate using a few different values in the range of 10^{-5} and 10^{-4} and tested two loss options, cross-entropy vs. negative log-likelihood. In the end, we opted for the cross-entropy loss.

XGBoost. We fine-tune the XGBoost meta-learner separately, for each of the three submissions. The set of values considered for the maximum depth of a tree is $[3, 5, 7, 9, 10]$. We fine-tuned the learning rate in a range starting from 10^{-4} up to 10^{-1}, with a multiplying step of 10. The subsample ratio of columns when constructing each tree was picked from $[0.1, 0.3, 0.5, 0.7]$. The number of estimators is gradually initialized with values ranging from 50 and up to 400 with an additive step of 50. For each submission, a different set of parameters was deemed optimal. Thus, for the ensemble composed of shallow models, the best parameters were: max_depth=5, learning_rate=10^{-1}, n_estimators=50 and colsample_bytree=0.5. When adding the character-level CNN into the mix of shallow models, the best choice of hyper parameters changes slightly: max_depth and learning_rate remain the same as previously mentioned; however, in this case, n_estimators=100 and colsample_bytree=0.7. With BERT included in the ensemble of shallow and deep models, all the optimal parameters change as follows: max_depth=7, learning_rate=10^{-3}, n_estimators=200 and colsample_bytree=0.5.

Logistic Regression. In the case of the Logistic Regression based meta-learner, we use L2 regularization and only fine tune the inverse of the regularization strength parameter, noted as C. The range of values tested starts with 10^{-5} and ends with 10^5. Different optimal values are observed for each run, as we gradually increase the number of learners and their respective depths. For the ensemble of shallow methods, we observe that a C=10^3 gives the best scores both in terms of accuracy, as well as for the $macroF1-score$. The optimal value for C decreases to 10^2 when we combine the Char-CNN with the two shallow models. We observe a further decrease in the best value for C, i.e. 10^1, when we add the BERT model to the second ensemble.

4.3 Results

Track 1 For *Track 1* we submitted 3 XGBoost stacking ensembles, gradually adding more complex individual learners to the ensemble as follows. For the first run, we combine only the powers of two shallow models, namely SVM and KRR. In the second run, we add a character-level CNN to the ensemble of shallow models. Finally, in the third run, we add a fine tuned BERT model to the second run. In our local testing, the performance on the development set increased with the addition of each individual learner. Thus, we deemed our first run, *UnibucNLP-run-1*, as being the weakest of the three submissions for this track, followed by the second run, *UnibucNLP-run-2* and with *UnibucNLP-run-3* being the top performing system that we have submitted.

Method	Rank	F1-score
VaidyaKane-run-3	1	0.5854
baseline-mBERT	4	0.54
baseline-XLM-R	5	0.536
UnibucNLP-run-3	6	0.5318
baseline-XLM-R-LD	7	0.529
baseline-NB	8	0.503
UnibucNLP-run-1	11	0.4875
UnibucNLP-run-2	13	0.4572

Table 1: The final results for the closed format of *Track 1* obtained by our XGBoost based ensembles on the DSL-TL test set. For simplicity, we compare ourselves only against the baseline and the top scoring method. In bold are the methods that we submitted and described in the current work.

Table 1 partially confirms our intuition, as our third run is indeed out-performing the other two ensemble-based systems. Surprisingly perhaps, the ensemble that combines the predictions of the Char-CNN and the ones of SVM and KRR falls behind the model that employs only the shallow individual models. Our best performing submission is situated just below two of the best performing baselines provided for Track 1, and immediately above the worst-performing baselines in this subtask. The 9-way classification proved to be a difficult problem, as most of the submissions are below the worst performing baseline provided by the organizers. Three submissions of the same team (i.e. *VaidyaKane*) are above all of the baselines, then our best performing system is right in the middle, ranking sixth if we consider the baselines and fourth if we don't, then, below the baselines we can see the scores of all the other systems submitted (including ours - run 1 and run 2).

Table 2 shows the ranking and score of our best performing method for each of the 9 classes considered. We achieve a good position in classifying the samples that are written in English - ranking first for *EN-US*, second for the common label *EN* and fourth for *EN-GB*. Although for the common Spanish tag we rank second, for the Castilian and Argentine language varieties, we only achieve the seventh and ninth positions respectively. The common label for Portuguese seems to bring ourselves and everyone other participant down, with the best model not being able to obtain an $F1 - score$ greater than 0.1633. The results for European Portuguese are better, and with values very close to each other across all of the systems submitted. In these conditions, for *PT-PT* we achieve an $F1 - score$ of 0.7618. In the end, as shown in the final rows of Table 2, all of our systems achieve the worst results for Brazilian Portuguese.

Tag	Method	Rank	F1-score
EN	VaidyaKane-run-3	1	0.3333
EN	**UnibucNLP-run-3**	2	0.32
EN	baseline-mBERT	3	0.303
EN-GB	VaidyaKane-run-1	1	0.8148
EN-GB	**UnibucNLP-run-3**	4	0.8034
EN-GB	baseline-XLM-R	5	0.793
EN-US	**UnibucNLP-run-3**	1	0.8454
EN-US	baseline-mBERT	3	0.829
ES	VaidyaKane-run-2	1	0.4738
ES	**UnibucNLP-run-3**	2	0.4573
ES	baseline-mBERT	3	0.455
ES-AR	VaidyaKane-run-1	1	0.6204
ES-AR	baseline-mBERT	4	0.518
ES-AR	**UnibucNLP-run-3**	9	0.4884
ES-ES	VaidyaKane-run-1	1	0.7692
ES-ES	baseline-XLM-R	3	0.719
ES-ES	**UnibucNLP-run-1**	7	0.6858
PT	VaidyaKane-run-2	1	0.1633
PT	baseline-NB	4	0.126
PT	**UnibucNLP-run-3**	7	0.1165
PT-PT	ssl-run-1	1	0.7923
PT-PT	baseline-XLM-R	5	0.769
PT-PT	**UnibucNLP-run-3**	7	0.7618
PT-BR	baseline-XLM-R	1	0.562
PT-BR	**UnibucNLP-run-1**	12	0.4683
PT-BR	**UnibucNLP-run-2**	13	0.378
PT-BR	**UnibucNLP-run-3**	14	0.3575

Table 2: The performance per class reported on the test set for the closed format of *Track 1* obtained by our best performing ensemble compared to the baseline and the top scoring method. We mark in bold our own work.

Track 2 *Track 2* tests a six-way classification, using only the variety-specific tags and ignoring the common labels. For this subtask, we submit three stacking ensembles, following the same logic as for the submissions in *Track 1*, the only difference being that we use Logistic Regression as meta-learner. We do not perform any variety-specific transformations and we do not exclude the common labels at training for the three runs submitted for *Track 2*. Thus, our expectations are consistent with the results obtained and displayed in Table 3.

Method	Rank	F1-score
VaidyaKane-run-1	1	0.8561
baseline-ANB	4	0.799
baseline-NB	5	0.794
baseline-XLM-R	6	0.78
baseline-XLM-R-LD	7	0.772
baseline-mBERT	9	0.755
UnibucNLP-run-1	13	0.6935
UnibucNLP-run-3	14	0.6855
UnibucNLP-run-2	15	0.6182

Table 3: The final results for the closed format of *Track 2* obtained by our Logistic Regression based ensembles on the DSL-TL test set. For simplicity, we compare ourselves only against the baselines and the top scoring method. In bold are the methods that we submitted and described in the current work.

One interesting fact observed in Table 3 is that our first run - an ensemble of string kernel based shallow models, outperforms our other two runs, based on more complex models such as the Char-CNN and BERT models.

5 Conclusions

In this work we propose six ensemble models to address the problem of language-variety identification in news reports. To tackle the two tracks proposed by the DSL-TL task, we employ two similar sets of ensembles which differ only in the choice of meta-learner: XGBoost for the 9-way classification in the first track, and Logistic Regression for the 6-way classification in the second one. By the definition of *Track 2*, our Logistic Regression based systems are evaluated only on the variety-specific labels provided. However, we have trained these LR powered ensembles also on the common labels, in hopes that the model will learn additional useful representations. For each set of ensembles submitted, we follow a similar strategy: increase the number of models and individual models' complexity for each run. Thus, our first submission only combines predictions from KRR and SVM - two shallow models. In the second ensemble we add a CNN working at character level, and in the third one, we augment the second ensemble with a fine tuned multilingual BERT model.

For the 9-way classification, our best performing model achieves a macro F1-score of 53.18%, 5% less than the top scoring submission. Overall, our model ranks fourth out of 9 total submissions and surpasses two of the four strong baselines proposed by the organizers. In the variety-specific, 6-way classification of Track 2, most of the models submitted by participants (including ours) fall behind the proposed baselines. Interestingly, our best performing submission in this case is the ensemble of shallow models, which obtains a score of 69.35%, surpassing the other 2, more complex ensembles, that we submitted.

Given the final results, we conclude that in future similar endeavours we should not underestimate the power of shallow models, as they consistently seem to achieve good results in language identification setups. Moreover, we intend on performing a closer analysis of the baselines proposed in Zampieri et al. (2023) - the paper that introduces DSL-TL, try to replicate and perhaps enhance the already impressive methods that the authors used for this task.

Limitations

Limitations of the present work and results include tackling the closed format of the DSL-TL task. As shown in Zampieri et al. (2023) using additional data, from the broader DSLCC corpus (Tan et al., 2014), would have likely helped both the 9-way as well as the 6-way classification attempted in our submissions.

Hardware limitations represent another disadvantage, due to which a better, broader fine-tuning of the deep learning based models could not be fully achieved in time.

Acknowledgements

The authors would like to kindly thank reviewers for their suggestions, which were deemed to be very helpful in improving the present writing.

References

Noëmi Aepli, Antonios Anastasopoulos, Adrian-Gabriel Chifu, William Domingues, Fahim Faisal, Mihaela Gaman, Radu Tudor Ionescu, and Yves Scherrer. 2022. Findings of the VarDial evaluation campaign 2022. In *Proceedings of VarDial*, pages 1–13.

Noëmi Aepli, Çağrı Çöltekin, Rob van der Goot, Tommi Jauhiainen, Mourhaf Kazzaz, Nikola Ljubešić, Kai North, Barbara Plank, Yves Scherrer, and Marcos Zampieri. 2023. Findings of the VarDial evaluation campaign 2023. In *Proceedings of VarDial*.

Rami Al-Rfou, Dokook Choe, Noah Constant, Mandy Guo, and Llion Jones. 2019. Character-Level Language Modeling with Deeper Self-Attention. In *Proceedings of AAAI*, pages 3159–3166.

Supriya Anand. 2014. Language identification for transliterated forms of indian language queries. In *Proceedings of FIRE*.

Miguel Ballesteros, Chris Dyer, and Noah A. Smith. 2015. Improved Transition-Based Parsing by Modeling Characters instead of Words with LSTMs. In *Proceedings of EMNLP*, pages 349–59.

Adrien Barbaresi. 2016. An unsupervised morphological criterion for discriminating similar languages. In *Proceedings of VarDial*, pages 212–220.

James Bennett, Stan Lanning, et al. 2007. The Netflix Prize. In *Proceedings of KDD*, volume 2007, page 35.

Christopher J.C. Burges. 2010. From RankNet to LambdaRank to LambdaMART: An Overview. *Learning*, 11(23-581):81.

Andrei Butnaru and Radu Tudor Ionescu. 2018. UnibucKernel Reloaded: First Place in Arabic Dialect Identification for the Second Year in a Row. In *Proceedings of VarDial*, pages 77–87.

Andrei M. Butnaru and Radu Tudor Ionescu. 2019. MOROCO: The Moldavian and Romanian Dialectal Corpus. In *Proceedings of ACL*, pages 688–698.

Bharathi Raja Chakravarthi, Gaman Mihaela, Radu Tudor Ionescu, Heidi Jauhiainen, Tommi Jauhiainen, Krister Lindén, Nikola Ljubešić, Niko Partanen, Ruba Priyadharshini, Christoph Purschke, Eswari Rajagopal, Yves Scherrer, and Marcos Zampieri. 2021. Findings of the VarDial evaluation campaign 2021. In *Proceedings of VarDial*, pages 1–11.

Stanley Chen and Benoît Maison. 2003. Using place name data to train language identification models.

Tianqi Chen and Carlos Guestrin. 2016. Xgboost: A scalable tree boosting system. In *Proceedings of SIGKDD*, page 785–794.

Çağrı Çöltekin. 2020. Dialect identification under domain shift: Experiments with discriminating Romanian and Moldavian. In *Proceedings of VarDial*, pages 186–192.

Çağrı Çöltekin and Taraka Rama. 2017. Tübingen system in VarDial 2017 shared task: experiments with language identification and cross-lingual parsing. In *Proceedings of VarDial*, pages 146–155.

Corinna Cortes and Vladimir Vapnik. 1995. Support-vector networks. *Machine Learning*, 20(3):273–297.

Mădălina Cozma, Andrei Butnaru, and Radu Tudor Ionescu. 2018. Automated essay scoring with string kernels and word embeddings. In *Proceedings of ACL*, pages 503–509.

Jacob Devlin, Ming-Wei Chang, Kenton Lee, and Kristina Toutanova. 2019. BERT: Pre-training of Deep Bidirectional Transformers for Language Understanding. In *Proceedings of NAACL*, pages 4171–4186.

Mohamed Eldesouki, Fahim Dalvi, Hassan Sajjad, and Kareem Darwish. 2016. QCRI @ DSL 2016: Spoken Arabic dialect identification using textual features. In *Proceedings of VarDial*, pages 221–226.

Jerome H Friedman. 2001. Greedy function approximation: a gradient boosting machine. *Annals of statistics*, pages 1189–1232.

Mihaela Gaman, Sebastian Cojocariu, and Radu Tudor Ionescu. 2021. UnibucKernel: Geolocating Swiss German jodels using ensemble learning. In *Proceedings of VarDial*, pages 84–95.

Mihaela Gaman, Dirk Hovy, Radu Tudor Ionescu, Heidi Jauhiainen, Tommi Jauhiainen, Krister Lindén, Nikola Ljubešić, Niko Partanen, Christoph Purschke, Yves Scherrer, and Marcos Zampieri. 2020. A report on the VarDial evaluation campaign 2020. In *Proceedings of VarDial*, pages 1–14.

Rosa M. Giménez-Pérez, Marc Franco-Salvador, and Paolo Rosso. 2017. Single and Cross-domain Polarity Classification using String Kernels. In *Proceedings of EACL*, pages 558–563.

Cyril Goutte, Serge Léger, and Marine Carpuat. 2014. The NRC system for discriminating similar languages. In *Proceedings of VarDial*, pages 139–145.

Gregory Grefenstette. 1995. Comparing two language identification schemes. In *Proceedings of JADT*, volume 95.

Xinran He, Junfeng Pan, Ou Jin, Tianbing Xu, Bo Liu, Tao Xu, Yanxin Shi, Antoine Atallah, Ralf Herbrich, Stuart Bowers, et al. 2014. Practical lessons from predicting clicks on ads at facebook. In *Proceedings of ADKDD*, pages 1–9.

Arthur E. Hoerl and Robert W. Kennard. 1970. Ridge regression: Biased estimation for nonorthogonal problems. *Technometrics*, 12(1):55–67.

Radu Tudor Ionescu and Andrei Butnaru. 2018. Improving the results of string kernels in sentiment analysis and Arabic dialect identification by adapting them to your test set. In *Proceedings of EMNLP*, pages 1084–1090.

Radu Tudor Ionescu and Marius Popescu. 2016. UnibucKernel: An Approach for Arabic Dialect Identification based on Multiple String Kernels. In *Proceedings of VarDial*, pages 135–144.

Radu Tudor Ionescu, Marius Popescu, and Aoife Cahill. 2014. Can characters reveal your native language? A language-independent approach to native language identification. In *Proceedings of EMNLP*, pages 1363–1373.

Aaron Jaech, George Mulcaire, Shobhit Hathi, Mari Ostendorf, and Noah Smith. 2016. Hierarchical character-word models for language identification. In *Proceedings of SocialNLP*, pages 84–93.

Tommi Jauhiainen, Heidi Jauhiainen, and Krister Lindén. 2022. Italian language and dialect identification and regional French variety detection using adaptive naive Bayes. In *Proceedings of VarDial*, pages 119–129.

Tommi Jauhiainen, Krister Lindén, and Heidi Jauhiainen. 2019a. Discriminating between Mandarin Chinese and Swiss-German varieties using adaptive language models. In *Proceedings of VarDial*, pages 178–187.

Tommi Jauhiainen, Marco Lui, Marcos Zampieri, Timothy Baldwin, and Krister Lindén. 2019b. Automatic language identification in texts: A survey. 65(1):675–682.

Yoon Kim, Yacine Jernite, David Sontag, and Alexander M. Rush. 2016. Character-Aware Neural Language Models. In *Proceedings of AAAI*, pages 2741–2749.

C. Kruengkrai, P. Srichaivattana, V. Sornlertlamvanich, and H. Isahara. 2005. Language identification based on string kernels. In *Proceedings of IEEE*, volume 2, pages 926–929.

Ping Li. 2010. Robust Logitboost and Adaptive Base Class (ABC) Logitboost. In *Proceedings of UAI*, pages 302–311.

Yitong Li, Timothy Baldwin, and Trevor Cohn. 2018. What's in a domain? learning domain-robust text representations using adversarial training. In *Proceedings of NAACL*, pages 474–479.

Nikola Ljubešic and Denis Kranjcic. 2014. Discriminating between very similar languages among twitter users. In *Proceedings of LTC*, pages 90–94.

Huma Lodhi, John Shawe-Taylor, Nello Cristianini, and Christopher J.C.H. Watkins. 2001. Text Classification Using String Kernels. In *Proceedings of NIPS*, pages 563–569.

Ilya Loshchilov and Frank Hutter. 2019. Decoupled Weight Decay Regularization. In *Proceedings of ICLR*.

Shervin Malmasi and Marcos Zampieri. 2016. Arabic dialect identification in speech transcripts. In *Proceedings of VarDial*, pages 106–113.

Shervin Malmasi and Marcos Zampieri. 2017a. Arabic dialect identification using iVectors and ASR transcripts. In *Proceedings of VarDial*, pages 178–183.

Shervin Malmasi and Marcos Zampieri. 2017b. German dialect identification in interview transcriptions. In *Proceedings of VarDial*, pages 164–169.

Shervin Malmasi, Marcos Zampieri, Nikola Ljubešić, Preslav Nakov, Ahmed Ali, and Jörg Tiedemann. 2016. Discriminating between similar languages and Arabic dialect identification: A report on the third DSL shared task. In *Proceedings of VarDial*, pages 1–14.

Paul McNamee. 2005. Language identification: A solved problem suitable for undergraduate instruction. *J. Comput. Sci. Coll.*, 20(3):94–101.

Maria Medvedeva, Martin Kroon, and Barbara Plank. 2017. When sparse traditional models outperform dense neural networks: the curious case of discriminating between similar languages. In *Proceedings of VarDial*, pages 156–163.

Giovanni Molina, Fahad AlGhamdi, Mahmoud Ghoneim, Abdelati Hawwari, Nicolas Rey-Villamizar, Mona Diab, and Thamar Solorio. 2016. Overview for the second shared task on language identification in code-switched data. In *Proceedings of CodeSwitch*, pages 40–49.

Seppo Mustonen. 1965. Multiple discriminant analysis in linguistic problems. *Statistical Methods in Linguistics*, 4:37–44.

Joanne Peng, Kuk Lee, and Gary Ingersoll. 2002. An introduction to logistic regression analysis and reporting. *Journal of Educational Research - J EDUC RES*, 96:3–14.

Marius Popescu, Cristian Grozea, and Radu Tudor Ionescu. 2017. HASKER: An efficient algorithm for string kernels. Application to polarity classification in various languages. In *Proceedings of KES*, pages 1755–1763.

Marius Popescu and Radu Tudor Ionescu. 2013. The Story of the Characters, the DNA and the Native Language. In *Proceedings of BEA-8*, pages 270–278.

Jordi Porta and José-Luis Sancho. 2014. Using maximum entropy models to discriminate between similar languages and varieties. In *Proceedings of VarDial*, pages 120–128.

Craig Saunders, Alexander Gammerman, and Volodya Vovk. 1998. Ridge Regression Learning Algorithm in Dual Variables. In *Proceedings of ICML*, pages 512–521.

John Shawe-Taylor and Nello Cristianini. 2004. *Kernel Methods for Pattern Analysis*. Cambridge University Press.

Penelope Sibun. 1996. Language identification: Examining the issues. In *Proceedings of SDAIR*.

Ilya Sutskever, James Martens, and Geoffrey Hinton. 2011. Generating Text with Recurrent Neural Networks. In *Proceedings of ICML*, pages 1017–1024.

Hidayet Takcı and İbrahim Soğukpınar. 2004. Centroid-based language identification using letter feature set. In *Proceedings of CICLing*, pages 640–648. Springer.

Liling Tan, Marcos Zampieri, Nikola Ljubešic, and Jörg Tiedemann. 2014. Merging comparable data sources for the discrimination of similar languages: The dsl corpus collection. In *Proceedings of the 7th Workshop on Building and Using Comparable Corpora (BUCC)*, pages 11–15.

Erik Tromp and Mykola Pechenizkiy. 2011. Graph-based n-gram language identification on short texts. In *Proceedings of BeNeLearn*, pages 27–34.

Ashish Vaswani, Noam Shazeer, Niki Parmar, Jakob Uszkoreit, Llion Jones, Aidan N. Gomez, Łukasz Kaiser, and Illia Polosukhin. 2017. Attention is all you need. In *Proceedings of NIPS*, pages 5998–6008.

George-Eduard Zaharia, Andrei-Marius Avram, Dumitru-Clementin Cercel, and Traian Rebedea. 2020. Exploring the power of Romanian BERT for dialect identification. In *Proceedings of VarDial*, pages 232–241.

Marcos Zampieri, Shervin Malmasi, Nikola Ljubešić, Preslav Nakov, Ahmed Ali, Jörg Tiedemann, Yves Scherrer, and Noëmi Aepli. 2017. Findings of the VarDial evaluation campaign 2017. In *Proceedings of VarDial*, pages 1–15.

Marcos Zampieri, Shervin Malmasi, Preslav Nakov, Ahmed Ali, Suwon Shon, James Glass, Yves Scherrer, Tanja Samardžić, Nikola Ljubešić, Jörg Tiedemann, Chris van der Lee, Stefan Grondelaers, Nelleke Oostdijk, Dirk Speelman, Antal van den Bosch, Ritesh Kumar, Bornini Lahiri, and Mayank Jain. 2018. Language identification and morphosyntactic tagging: The second VarDial evaluation campaign. In *Proceedings of VarDial*, pages 1–17.

Marcos Zampieri, Shervin Malmasi, Yves Scherrer, Tanja Samardžić, Francis Tyers, Miikka Silfverberg, Natalia Klyueva, Tung-Le Pan, Chu-Ren Huang, Radu Tudor Ionescu, Andrei M. Butnaru, and Tommi Jauhiainen. 2019. A report on the third VarDial evaluation campaign. In *Proceedings of VarDial*, pages 1–16.

Marcos Zampieri, Kai North, Tommi Jauhiainen, Mariano Felice, Neha Kumari, Nishant Nair, and Yash Bangera. 2023. Language variety identification with true labels. *arXiv preprint arXiv:2303.01490*.

Marcos Zampieri, Liling Tan, Nikola Ljubešić, and Jörg Tiedemann. 2014. A report on the DSL shared task 2014. In *Proceedings of VarDial*, pages 58–67.

Marcos Zampieri, Liling Tan, Nikola Ljubešić, Jörg Tiedemann, and Preslav Nakov. 2015. Overview of the DSL shared task 2015. In *Proceedings of VarDial*, pages 1–9.

Rowan Zellers, Ari Holtzman, Hannah Rashkin, Yonatan Bisk, Ali Farhadi, Franziska Roesner, and Yejin Choi. 2019. *Defending against Neural Fake News*.

Xiang Zhang, Junbo Zhao, and Yann LeCun. 2015. Character-level Convolutional Networks for Text Classification. In *Proceedings of NIPS*, pages 649–657.

Zero-Shot Slot and Intent Detection in Low-Resource Languages

Sang Yun Kwon[1,*] **Gagan Bhatia** [1,*] **El Moatez Billah Nagoudi**[1]
Alcides Alcoba Inciarte[1] **Muhammad Abdul-Mageed**[1,2]
[1]Deep Learning & Natural Language Processing Group, The University of British Columbia
[2]Department of Natural Language Processing & Department of Machine Learning, MBZUAI
{skwon01@student.,gagan30@student.,moatez.nagoudi@,alcobaaj@mail.,muhammad.mageed@}ubc.ca

Abstract

Intent detection and slot filling are critical tasks in spoken and natural language understanding for task-oriented dialog systems. In this work we describe our participation in the slot and intent detection for low-resource language varieties (SID4LR; Aepli et al. (2023)). We investigate the slot and intent detection (SID) tasks using a wide range of models and settings. Given the recent success of multitask-prompted finetuning of large language models, we also test the generalization capability of the recent encoder-decoder model mT0 (Muennighoff et al., 2022) on new tasks (i.e., SID) in languages they have never intentionally seen. We show that our best model outperforms the baseline by a large margin (up to +30 F_1 points) in both SID tasks.

1 Introduction

Digital conversational assistants have become increasingly pervasive. Examples of popular virtual assistants include Siri, Alexa, and Google. A crucial factor in the effectiveness of these systems is their capacity to understand user input and respond or act accordingly to fulfill particular requirements. Most of these applications are voice-based and hence need spoken language understanding (SLU). SLU typically starts with automatic speech recognition (ASR), taking the sound of spoken language and transcribing it into text. Then, it handles natural language understanding (NLU) tasks to extract semantic features from the text including question answering, dialogue management, intent detection, and slot filling.

The intent detection task aims to recognize the speaker's desired outcome from a given utterance. And slot filling focuses on identifying the main arguments or the spans of words in the utterance that contain semantic information relevant to the intent. Table 1 shows four utterances in different languages: English, Swiss German (GSW), South

Lang.	Annotation
EN	Set an alarm for 6 am on Wed
GSW	Du em Mittwuch e Wecker dry fürem sächsi em Morge .
ST	Stell an Wecker firn Mittig af 6 in der friah
NAP	Imposta 'na sveglia 'e 6 'e matina 'e miercurì

Table 1: Examples of xSID annotations in our target languages from the validation set with intents (alarm / set_alarm) and slots (location , datetime). **EN**: English, **GSW**:Swiss German **ST**: South Tyrolean, **NAP**: Neapolitan

Tyrolean (ST), and Neapolitan (NAP). The English example has the intent *set_alarm* and two individual spans *Set an alarm* and *6 am on Wed* are labeled with their slot tags *location* and *datetime*, respectively, using the Inside, Outside, Beginning (IOB) (Ramshaw and Marcus, 1995) tagging format.

In this work, we present our participation in the slot and intent detection for low-resource language varieties (SID4LR; Aepli et al. (2023)) shared task. The shared task takes as its target three low resources languages– Swiss German (GSW), South Tyrolean (ST), and Neapolitan (NAP). The main objective of the SID4LR shared task is to find the most effective approach for transferring knowledge to less commonly spoken languages that have limited resources and lack a standard writing system, in the zero-shot setting (i.e., without use of any training data). In the context of the shared task, we target the following four main research questions:

Q1: Can successful models on English SID tasks be generalizable to new unseen languages (i.e., the zero-shot setting)?

Q2: How do models trained on a language from the given language family fare on a low-resource variety from the same family under the zero-shot setting (i.e., with no access to training data from these low-resource varieties). For

Tenth Workshop on NLP for Similar Languages, Varieties and Dialects (VarDial 2023), pages 241–250
May 5, 2023 ©2023 Association for Computational Linguistics

example, in our case, we ask how do models trained on German perform on Swiss German or South Tyrolean, and how do models trained on Italian perform on Neapolitan.

Q3: What impact does exploiting data augmentation techniques such as paraphrasing and machine translation have on the SID tasks in the zero-shot context?

Q4: Are the existing large multilingual models, trained using multitask-prompted fine-tuning, able to achieve zero-shot generalization to SID tasks in languages that they have never intentionally seen?

The rest of this paper is organized as follows: Section 2 is a literature review on intent and slot detection tasks. The shared task, the source data provided in SID4LR, and the external parallel data we exploit to build our models are described in Section 3. In Section 4, we provide information about datasets, baselines, and data preprocessing. The baseline, and multilingual pre-trained language models we used are described in Section 5. We present our experimental settings and our training procedures in Section 6. Section 7 is an analysis and discussion of our results. And we conclude in Section 8.

2 Related Work

The problem of low-resource slot and intent detection for languages with limited training data has been the focus of several recent research works. In this section, we discuss some of the most relevant and recent works, including datasets, benchmarks, and models that aim to address this challenge.

2.1 SID Benchmarks and Corpus

The table below provides an overview of various datasets used for NLU tasks. These datasets cover a range of languages, domains, intents, and slots, and are widely used to evaluate the performance of NLU models. Some of the prominent datasets include MASSIVE, SLURP, NLU Evaluation Data, ATIS, MultiATIS++, Snips, TOP, MTOP, Cross-lingual Multilingual Task-Oriented Dialog, Microsoft Dialog Challenge, and Fluent Speech Commands. These datasets have been used for tasks such as intent classification, slot filling, and semantic parsing. Overall, these datasets provide a useful resource for researchers to benchmark their models and develop better NLU systems.

2.2 SID Approaches and Models

The are many works devoted to the SID tasks. Most of these works are categorized into three approaches: *(1) single model for intent detection, (2) single model for slot filling, and (3) joint model.*

(1) Single Model for Intent Detection refers to developing a single model that can identify the intent behind a user's spoken or written input. This approach involves training a neural network or other machine learning model on a large dataset of labeled examples. Each example consists of user input and its corresponding intent label. The model then uses this training data to learn patterns and features that can accurately predict the intent of new user inputs. For instance, Ravuri and Stolcke (2015) proposed a recurrent neural network and LSTM models for intent detection in spoken language understanding. In this work, the authors first discuss the limitations of traditional intent detection approaches that rely on handcrafted features and propose using deep learning models to learn features directly from the data. Zhang et al. (2021) investigate the robustness of pre-trained transformers-based models such as BERT and RoBERTa for intent classification in spoken language understanding. They conduct experiments on two datasets, ATIS (Upadhyay et al., 2018) and SNIPS (Coucke et al., 2018), showing that pre-trained transformers perform well on in-scope intent detection.

(2) Single Model for Slot Filling is an approach that aims to develop a single model capable of identifying slots in spoken language understanding. The model takes a sentence as input and predicts the slot labels for each word in the sentence. Various recurrent neural network (RNN) architectures such as Elman-type (Mesnil et al., 2015) and Jordan-type (Mesnil et al., 2015) networks and their variants have been explored to find the most effective architecture for slot filling. Incorporating word embeddings has also been studied and found to improve slot-filling performance significantly. For example, Yao et al. (2014) use LSTM networks with word embeddings for slot filling on the ATIS (Upadhyay et al., 2018) dataset and achieve state-of-the-art (SOTA) results at the time. Goo et al. (2018) propose a bi-directional LSTM (BLSTM) with an attention mechanism for slot filling on the ATIS (Upadhyay et al., 2018) and SNIPS (Coucke et al., 2018) datasets.

(3) Joint Model is an approach that aims to jointly

Name	# Langs	Utt. per Lang (K)	Domains	Intents	Slots
Airline Travel Information System (ATIS) (Price, 1990)	1	5.8	1	26	129
ATIS with Hindi and Turkish (Upadhyay et al., 2018)	3	1.3-5.8	1	26	129
Cross-lingual Multilingual Task Oriented Dialog (Schuster et al., 2019)	3	5.08-43.3	3	12	11
Fluent Speech Commands (FSC) (Lugosch et al., 2019)	1	30	-	31	-
MASSIVE (FitzGerald et al., 2022)	51	19.5	18	60	55
Microsoft Dialog Challenge (Li et al., 2018)	1	38.2	3	11	29
MultiATIS++ (Xu et al., 2020)	9	1.4-5.8	1	21-26	99-140
Multilingual Task-Oriented Semantic Parsing (MTOP) (Li et al., 2021)	6	15.1-22.2	11	104-113	72-75
NLU Evaluation Data (Liu et al., 2019)	1	25, 7	18	54	56
SLURP (Bastianelli et al., 2020)	1	16, 5	18	60	55
SNIPS (Coucke et al., 2018)	1	14.4	-	7	53
Task Oriented Parsing (TOP) (Gupta et al., 2018)	1	44.8	2	25	36
xSID (van der Goot et al., 2021)	13	10	7	16	33

Table 2: SID benchmark and datasets with the number of languages covered, number of utterances per language, domain, intent count, and slot count.

model the intent detection and slot-filling tasks in spoken language understanding. This approach trains a single model to predict both the intent and slot labels simultaneously. The model uses the context of the input sentence to predict these labels. Joint models have been shown to achieve SOTA performance on several spoken language understanding datasets. Xu and Sarikaya (2013) propose a joint convolutional neural network (CNN) and RNN model for intent detection and slot filling on the ATIS (Upadhyay et al., 2018) dataset. They achieved SOTA results at the time. In the same context, Liu and Lane (2016) proposed an attention-based neural network for joint intent detection and slot filling. The model uses an attention mechanism to weigh the importance of different parts of the input sentence for predicting the intent label and slot labels. Chen et al. (2019) explore the use of the BERT model for joint intent detection and slot filling on ATIS (Upadhyay et al., 2018) and SNIPS (Coucke et al., 2018). They report SOTA results on both datasets.

3 SID4LR Shared Task

Task Formulation. Intent detection and slot-filling are critical NLP tasks where, given an utterance, a system is responsible for parsing the user's intent and extracting relevant information to act or reply appropriately. While many neural-based models have achieved SOTA performance for these tasks, their success often depends on large amounts of labeled data. However, many real-world datasets are limited to specific domains and are only available in English or a few other languages. As a result, it is important to reuse existing data in high-resource languages to develop models for low-resource languages, especially since tasks like intent classification and slot-filling require abundant labeled data.

Shared Task Problem Statement. This shared task of SID aims to address the challenges of performing SID for low-resource language varieties for the following languages: Swiss German, South Tyrolean, and Neapolitan. The training data provided consists of the Cross-lingual Slot and Intent Detection ($xSID_{0.4}$) corpus (van der Goot et al., 2021), a cross-lingual spoken language understanding dataset, covering 12 languages (Arabic, Chinese, Dutch, Danish, English, German, Indonesian, Italian, Japanese, Kazakh, Serbian, Turkish) from six language families with English training. The task allowed the use of pre-trained models and external data including data from the target language.

Evaluation Metric. The primary evaluation metric for slot filling is the span F_1 score, where both span and label must match exactly, and accuracy is used to evaluate intent detection where it is calculated through the ratio of the number of correct predictions of intent to the total number of sentences. More details regarding the shared task can be found in Aepli et al. (2023).

4 Data

Shared Task Data. The $xSID_{0.4}$ (van der Goot et al., 2021) corpus comprises cross-lingual SLU evaluation datasets covering 13 languages from six language families. The training dataset contains 43,605 sentences, the development set contains 300 sentences, and the test set contains 500 sentences. The corpus contains sentences from Snips and Facebook, which were translated into all 13 target languages, resulting in a cross-lingual SLU evaluation dataset. All examples are annotated with

Language	# Train	# Valid	# Test
ar	42, 157	300	500
da	43, 605	300	500
de	43, 605	300	500
en	43, 605	300	500
id	42, 157	300	500
it	43, 605	300	500
ja	29, 073	150	250
kk	42, 157	300	500
nl	43, 605	300	500
sr	43, 605	300	500
tr	43, 605	300	500
zh	42, 157	300	500

Table 3: Number of samples in the train, validation, and test sets for each language in the multilingual dataset $xSID_{0.4}$, where the language codes are represented by two-letter ISO codes. The dataset includes 12 languages: Arabic (ar), Danish (da), German (de), English (en), Indonesian (id), Italian (it), Japanese (ja), Kazakh (kk), Dutch (nl), Serbian (sr), Turkish (tr), and Chinese (zh).

their intent and corresponding slots. Listing 1 provides examples of annotations with intent and slots. We converted the dataset into a JSON format that includes intents and slots. This JSON file was then converted to HuggingFace Dataset format for easy use with our transformer models. A sample of the resulting JSON format is shown in Listing 2.

```
# text: show all reminders
# intent: reminder/show_reminders
# slots: 5:8:reminder/reference,
         9:18:reminder/noun
1 show      reminder/show_reminders O
2 all       reminder/show_reminders B-reference
3 reminders reminder/show_reminders O
```

Listing 1: Example of the dataset format

```
{'text':'show all reminders',
 'slots': 'reference:all',
 'intent': 'reminder/show_reminders',
 '__index_level_0__': 0}
```

Listing 2: Example of the preprocessed dataset

External Data. As mentioned, Swiss German, South Tyrolean, and Neapolitan are low-resource languages with limited available labeled data. To address this challenge, we incorporate unlabeled data from different sources to augment our training data. We describe these external sources next.

SwissCrawl (Linder et al., 2020), a corpus of over 500, 000 Swiss German sentences gathered from web crawling between September and November 2019. The sentences are representative of how native speakers write in forums and social media and may contain slang and ascii emojis.

DiDi Corpus (Frey et al., 2016) is a multilingual language corpus of 600, 000 tokens from Facebook users in South Tyrol, Italy. It includes CMC texts, socio-demographic data, and linguistic annotations on thread, text, and token level. The corpus is mainly German and Italian, with English also present, and has been manually anonymized and annotated.

OSCAR Corpus (Caswell et al., 2021) is a large multilingual corpus created by scraping the web and includes texts in more than 200 languages. The OSCAR Corpus includes texts in Neapolitan, which is a Romance language spoken in the southern part of Italy, particularly in the region of Campania. The Neapolitan texts in the corpus consist of around 4.4 million tokens, making it one of the largest resources available for this language.

5 Pre-trained Language Models

In this study, we evaluate several popular multilingual Transformer-based language models, including mBERT, XLM-R, SBERT, LaBSE, LASER, and mT0. These models are capable of effectively capturing cross-lingual embeddings, enabling transfer learning across multiple languages. Below we provide a description of each model used in our experiments on the training dataset.

mBERT. is the multilingual version of BERT (Devlin et al., 2019), which is an encoder model with bidirectional representations from Transformers trained with a denoising objective. mBERT is trained on Wikipedia for 104 languages including German and Italian.

XLM-R. (Conneau et al., 2020) is a transformer-based multilingual masked language model pre-trained on more than 2TB of filtered CommonCrawl data in 100 languages, including languages including German and Italian. XLM-R uses a Transformer model (Vaswani et al., 2017) trained with a multilingual masked language model XLM (Conneau and Lample, 2019).

sBERT. Sentence-BERT (SBERT) (Reimers and Gurevych, 2019), is a modification of the pretrained

BERT (Devlin et al., 2019) model that uses siamese and triplet network structures to derive semantically meaningful sentence embeddings that can be compared using cosine-similarity. As we work under a multilingual context, we use the multilingual versions from previously monolingual SBERT models (Reimers and Gurevych, 2020) which is trained for sentence embedding in 50+ languages from various language families.

LaBSE. Language-agnostic BERT Sentence Encoder (LaBSE) (Feng et al., 2020a) is a BERT-based model trained to generate sentence embeddings in 109 different languages. The model's pre-training approach involves a combination of masked language modeling and translation language modeling. The pre-training process combines masked language modeling with translation language modeling. LaBSE is useful for producing sentence embeddings in multiple languages and performing bi-text retrieval.

LASER. Language-Agnostic Sentence Representations (LASER) (Feng et al., 2020b) is a contextualized language model based on a BiLSTM encoder trained on parallel data from OPUS website (Tiedemann, 2012) using a translation objective. The LASER model can handle 200 different languages.

mT0. (Muennighoff et al., 2022) is a group of sequence-to-sequence models that come with different sizes from 300M to 13B parameters trained to investigate the cross-lingual generalization through multitask finetuning. mT0 can execute human instructions in many languages without any prior training. The models are fine-tuned from pre-existing mT5 (Xue et al., 2020) multilingual language models using a cross-lingual task mixture called xP3. These refined models are capable of cross-lingual generalization to unseen languages.

6 Experiments and Settings

Training on English Data. As a baseline setting, we train all the pre-trained models described in Section 5 on the English part of the multilingual dataset $\text{xSID}_{0.4}$ (van der Goot et al., 2021) and evaluate them on Swiss German, South Tyrolean, and Neapolitan under a zero-shot setting.

Training on German/Italian Data. Our second approach aims to train all the pre-trained models on the language family of low-resource languages (i.e., German for Swiss German and South Tyrolean, and Italian for Neapolitan, respectively) under the zero-shot setting. So, we extract the German and Italian SID data from $\text{xSID}_{0.4}$, and then fine-tune all our models on both datasets. Then, we evaluate the German models on GSW and ST tasks and the Italian models on the NAP task.

Training on Multilingual Dataset. Next, we explore a third training approach that involves the full multilingual $\text{xSID}_{0.4}$ dataset. To do so, we combine all the 12 available languages in the $\text{xSID}_{0.4}$ dataset and fine-tune our pre-trained models on this combined dataset. We then evaluate each target using a zero-shot setting. This approach allows us to train on larger and more diverse datasets. In total, we generate $502,936$ training sentences across all languages in the dataset.

Paraphrase and Machine Translation. To improve the performance of our pretrained models, we also explore the impact of data augmentation techniques such as paraphrasing and machine translation. Specifically, we aime to examine how these techniques can enhance the performance of our models on cross-lingual SLU tasks. To this end, we experiment with different data augmentation strategies, including paraphrasing and machine translation. Paraphrasing is performed using the quality-guided controlled paraphrase generation (QCPG) model (Bandel et al., 2022), resulting in a total of $130,815$ sentences in English. These sentences are then translated into German and Italian using the OPUS-MT model (Tiedemann and Thottingal, 2020), creating cross-lingual datasets for our experiment.

To further augment our training data for low-resource languages, we leverage Meta AI's No Language Left Behind (NLLB), which provides open-source models capable of high-quality translations between 200 languages (including low-resource languages (NLLB Team et al., 2022)). To create our new training data using the NLLB model, we first use FastText to detect the language codes of our target languages. Next, we utilize NLLB models to translate the English training data into the predicted language codes. The language codes identified for our target languages are *deu_latn* for Swiss German, *est_latn* for South Tyrolean, and *ita_Latn* for Neapolitan. We generate $43,605$ sentences for each of the three languages. It is worth noting that we ensure that the labels for each sentence remain the same throughout the paraphrasing and machine translation process to maintain the integrity of the data.

Training on External Data. Since the language

models we employ do not have a strong representation of the low-resource languages used on the task, we leverage large corpora of each of the low-resource languages into the training process. By incorporating external datasets, the models are exposed to more comprehensive information about the semantics of each low-resource language, enabling them to better capture the nuances and complexities of the target languages.

Training MT0 As discussed in Section 5, the MT0 models share the same architecture as MT5/T5 models, i.e., they are encoder-decoder models. Therefore, we train them for intent classification and slot detection using the data preprocessing approach described in Section 4. We utilize the PEFT library provided by Huggingface (Sourab Mangrulkar, 2022) to train the mT0-small, mT0-Base, and mt0-Large models. Our approach involves using LORA (Hu et al., 2021), which allows us to achieve SOTA performance while consuming significantly less memory. For the mT0-xxl models, we utilize DeepSpeed (Rasley et al., 2020) with CPU offloading to train a model with 13B parameters on a 40GB A100 GPU.

Combining Models. In recent studies, joint learning techniques that combine multiple classification approaches have produced promising results (Bilat et al., 2020). These approaches involve concatenating the outputs of individual models and passing the resulting output through multiple neural network layers, allowing the resulting network to be trained jointly. In this part of our experiments, we investigate the effectiveness of this approach in zero-shot settings by combining multilingual models. Specifically, we combine LASER embeddings, from the LASER model, with other multilingual models including mBERT, sBERT, LaBSE and XLMR.

7 Results and Discussions

Evaluation on Validation Data. We present the accuracy scores of all our models across various settings. Table 4 presents the evaluation results for the intent classification task on the validation set. Our transformer-based models, with different experimental settings, outperform the baseline on all the target languages. For instance, **mT0-base** outperforms the baseline (mBERT) with an average of +16.49, +22.93, +17.90 for GSW, ST, and NAP, respectively. Notably, our best combination was the mT0-xxl model under the multilingual setting. It achieves the best results of 89.00, 94.00, and 87.00, improving the baseline with +29.30, +33.30, and +25.70 Accuracy point in the three target languages.

The results of the slot filling task on the validation set are shown in Table 5. Our transformer-based models perform better than the baseline across all target languages when tested under different experimental settings. Our best-performing model, mT0-large, achieves the most outstanding results using the Multilingual settings with F_1 scores of 60.30, 55.00, and 52.30 in the three target languages. These results represent a notable improvement over the baseline, with an increase of +30.88, +4.65, and +0.90 F_1 points in the three target languages.

Our results on the validation data suggest that larger models generally achieve better performance, implying that higher parameter counts result in better cross-lingual and zero-shot setting performance. Moreover, as the mT0 models are fine-tuned from pre-existing mT5 multilingual language models, they are capable of performing cross-lingual generalization on unseen languages. This capability may be a possible reason for the mT0 models outperforming other models in zero-shot settings.

Official Shared Task (Test) Results. Our findings regarding the performance of larger models are also observed in the test set. Table 6 presents the evaluation results for both slot filling and intent classification tasks across all three target languages. Our mT0 models strongly outperform the baseline models. Specifically, our mT0 models outperformed the baseline models in all target languages for the intent classification task, highlighting the effectiveness of larger models for intent classification. Moreover, our mT0 models also outperform the baseline models in two of the target languages for slot filling task, further indicating the superiority of larger models for sentence-level classification tasks. The improvement in scores for intent classification is more evident than for slot filling. The larger improvement in scores for intent classification may be correlated with the fact that for our data augmentation experiment on paraphrasing and machine translation, we were only able to augment data for intent classification, resulting in a larger improvement in performance for this task compared to slot filling.

It is worth noting that we use the validation set for model selection, which resulted in higher scores than those achieved on the test set. This is because

Setting	Lang.	mBert	LS	LL	LX	mT0-small	mT0-base	mT0-large	mT0-xxl
English	GSW	51.67	45.30	52.70	48.30	69.20	70.20	69.00	80.00
	ST	61.00	58.00	66.70	61.70	74.50	76.20	79.10	89.00
	NAP	61.00	55.30	56.00	67.0	71.30	72.00	75.00	76.33
German	GSW	59.00	74.00	68.00	80.70	69.30	73.33	80.33	84.33
	ST	59.70	55.70	59.00	51.00	83.33	88.33	84.66	92.00
Italian	NAP	65.30	63.30	63.70	55.70	77.66	84.66	83.33	86.00
Multilingual	GSW	59.70	62.70	59.70	53.30	75.00	76.33	84.00	89.00
	ST	60.70	54.70	58.00	56.30	88.33	85.66	90.66	94.00
	NAP	61.30	55.70	59.00	60.30	82.66	84.66	86.00	87.00
Paraphrase+MT	GSW	45.30	37.30	58.00	64.00	79.00	83.00	84.33	**91.00**
	ST	61.70	61.30	60.70	60.70	90.66	93.00	90.00	**95.66**
	NAP	63.70	60.00	58.70	60.00	85.66	**89.00**	87.33	88.33

Table 4: Accuracy results for intent classification on the validation set. **Baseline:** mBERT (Devlin et al., 2019). **LS:** LASER (Feng et al., 2020b)+sBERT (Reimers and Gurevych, 2019). **LL:** LASER+LaBSE (Feng et al., 2020a). **LX:** LASER+XLM-R (Conneau and Lample, 2019). **Underline:** Best-performing models for each setting. **Bold:** Best F_1 score across all the experiments and settings.

Setting	Lang.	Baseline	mt0-small	mt0-base	mt0-large
English	GSW	26.23	25.42	34.00	**40.32**
	ST	44.61	32.40	44.00	**54.30**
	NAP	48.01	42.20	47.90	**49.00**
Multi-langl	GSW	29.42	28.90	42.30	**60.30**
	ST	50.35	43.40	53.40	**55.00**
	NAP	51.40	49.00	50.30	**52.30**

Table 5: Slot-f1 results for Slot Filling on the validation set. Bold entries are the best-performing models for each experiment and setting.

Task	Lang.	Baseline	mT0-large
Slots	ST	44.61	**46.41**
	GSW	26.23	**27.39**
	NAP	**48.01**	38.82
Intents	ST	61.00	**89.40**
	GSW	51.67	**81.60**
	NAP	61.00	**85.40**

Table 6: Results on the test set for both SID tasks. **Bold** entries indicate the model's performance compared to the baseline model.

the validation data is similar to the data used during training, while the test data is entirely new and unseen. As a result, the test scores may be lower due to differences in the distribution of data between the training and test sets. Nevertheless, our mT0 models consistently outperform the baseline models on the test set, providing further evidence for the effectiveness of larger models in SID tasks.

8 Conclusion

We described our contribution to the SID4LR (Aepli et al., 2023) shared tasks. Our models target both the slot and intent sub-task in three proposed low-resource languages, namely, Swiss German, South Tyrolean, and Neapolitan. We test the utility of existing pretrained language models such as mT0 (Muennighoff et al., 2022) on the intent detection and slot filling tasks. We show that such models can lead to improving the results of the baseline with an average of +27 F_1 points. In the future, we intend to use mT0 to jointly model the intent detection and slot filling tasks for improving overall performance.

References

Noëmi Aepli, Çağrı Çöltekin, Rob van der Goot, Tommi Jauhiainen, Mourhaf Kazzaz, Nikola Ljubešić, Kai North, Barbara Plank, Yves Scherrer, and Marcos Zampieri. 2023. Findings of the VarDial evaluation campaign 2023. In *Proceedings of the Tenth Workshop on NLP for Similar Languages, Varieties and Dialects*, Dubrovnik, Croatia. Association for Computational Linguistics.

Elron Bandel, Ranit Aharonov, Michal Shmueli-Scheuer, Ilya Shnayderman, Noam Slonim, and Liat Ein-Dor. 2022. Quality controlled paraphrase generation. In *Proceedings of the 60th Annual Meeting of the Association for Computational Linguistics (Volume 1: Long Papers)*, pages 596–609, Dublin, Ireland. Association for Computational Linguistics.

Emanuele Bastianelli, Andrea Vanzo, Pawel Swietojanski, and Verena Rieser. 2020. SLURP: A spoken language understanding resource package. In *Proceedings of the 2020 Conference on Empirical Methods in Natural Language Processing (EMNLP)*, pages 7252–7262, Online. Association for Computational Linguistics.

Loïs Bilat, Georgiana Dinu, and Mark Cieliebak. 2020. Cross-lingual toxicity detection. pages 50–55.

Isaac Caswell, Julia Kreutzer, Lisa Wang, Ahsan Wahab, Daan van Esch, Nasanbayar Ulzii-Orshikh, Allahsera Tapo, Nishant Subramani, Artem Sokolov, Claytone Sikasote, Monang Setyawan, Supheakmungkol Sarin, Sokhar Samb, Benoît Sagot, Clara Rivera, Annette Rios, Isabel Papadimitriou, Salomey Osei, Pedro Javier Ortiz Suárez, Iroro Orife, Kelechi Ogueji, Rubungo Andre Niyongabo, Toan Q. Nguyen, Mathias Müller, André Müller, Shamsuddeen Hassan Muhammad, Nanda Muhammad, Ayanda Mnyakeni, Jamshidbek Mirzakhalov, Tapiwanashe Matangira, Colin Leong, Nze Lawson, Sneha Kudugunta, Yacine Jernite, Mathias Jenny, Orhan Firat, Bonaventure F. P. Dossou, Sakhile Dlamini, Nisansa de Silva, Sakine Çabuk Ballı, Stella Biderman, Alessia Battisti, Ahmed Baruwa, Ankur Bapna, Pallavi Baljekar, Israel Abebe Azime, Ayodele Awokoya, Duygu Ataman, Orevaoghene Ahia, Oghenefego Ahia, Sweta Agrawal, and Mofetoluwa Adeyemi. 2021. Quality at a Glance: An Audit of Web-Crawled Multilingual Datasets. *arXiv e-prints*, page arXiv:2103.12028.

Qian Chen, Zhu Zhuo, and Wen Wang. 2019. BERT for joint intent classification and slot filling. *CoRR*, abs/1902.10909.

Alexis Conneau, Kartikay Khandelwal, Naman Goyal, Vishrav Chaudhary, Guillaume Wenzek, Francisco Guzmán, Edouard Grave, Myle Ott, Luke Zettlemoyer, and Veselin Stoyanov. 2020. Unsupervised cross-lingual representation learning at scale. In *Proceedings of the 58th Annual Meeting of the Association for Computational Linguistics*, pages 8440–8451, Online. Association for Computational Linguistics.

Alexis Conneau and Guillaume Lample. 2019. Cross-lingual language model pretraining. *Advances in neural information processing systems*, 32.

Alice Coucke, Alaa Saade, Adrien Ball, Théodore Bluche, Alexandre Caulier, David Leroy, Clément Doumouro, Thibault Gisselbrecht, Francesco Caltagirone, Thibaut Lavril, Maël Primet, and Joseph Dureau. 2018. Snips voice platform: an embedded spoken language understanding system for private-by-design voice interfaces.

Jacob Devlin, Ming-Wei Chang, Kenton Lee, and Kristina Toutanova. 2019. BERT: Pre-training of Deep Bidirectional Transformers for Language Understanding. In *Proceedings of the 2019 Conference of the North American Chapter of the Association for Computational Linguistics: Human Language Technologies, Volume 1 (Long and Short Papers)*, pages 4171–4186.

Fangxiaoyu Feng, Yinfei Yang, Daniel Cer, Naveen Arivazhagan, and Wei Wang. 2020a. Language-agnostic bert sentence embedding.

Fangxiaoyu Feng, Yinfei Yang, Daniel Cer, Naveen Arivazhagan, and Wei Wang. 2020b. Language-agnostic bert sentence embedding. *arXiv preprint arXiv:2007.01852*.

Jack FitzGerald, Christopher Hench, Charith Peris, Scott Mackie, Kay Rottmann, Ana Sanchez, Aaron Nash, Liam Urbach, Vishesh Kakarala, Richa Singh, Swetha Ranganath, Laurie Crist, Misha Britan, Wouter Leeuwis, Gokhan Tur, and Prem Natarajan. 2022. Massive: A 1m-example multilingual natural language understanding dataset with 51 typologically-diverse languages.

Jennifer Frey, Aivars Glaznieks, and Egon Stemle. 2016. The didi corpus of south tyrolean cmc data: A multilingual corpus of facebook texts.

Chih-Wen Goo, Guang Gao, Yun-Kai Hsu, Chih-Li Huo, Tsung-Chieh Chen, Keng-Wei Hsu, and Yun-Nung Chen. 2018. Slot-gated modeling for joint slot filling and intent prediction. In *Proceedings of The 16th Annual Conference of the North American Chapter of the Association for Computational Linguistics: Human Language Technologies*.

Sonal Gupta, Rushin Shah, Mrinal Mohit, Anuj Kumar, and Mike Lewis. 2018. Semantic parsing for task oriented dialog using hierarchical representations. In *Proceedings of the 2018 Conference on Empirical Methods in Natural Language Processing*, pages 2787–2792, Brussels, Belgium. Association for Computational Linguistics.

Edward J. Hu, Yelong Shen, Phillip Wallis, Zeyuan Allen-Zhu, Yuanzhi Li, Shean Wang, and Weizhu Chen. 2021. Lora: Low-rank adaptation of large language models. *CoRR*, abs/2106.09685.

Haoran Li, Abhinav Arora, Shuohui Chen, Anchit Gupta, Sonal Gupta, and Yashar Mehdad. 2021. MTOP: A comprehensive multilingual task-oriented semantic parsing benchmark. In *Proceedings of the 16th Conference of the European Chapter of the Association for Computational Linguistics: Main Volume*, pages 2950–2962, Online. Association for Computational Linguistics.

Xiujun Li, Yu Wang, Siqi Sun, Sarah Panda, Jingjing Liu, and Jianfeng Gao. 2018. Microsoft dialogue challenge: Building end-to-end task-completion dialogue systems.

Lucy Linder, Michael Jungo, Jean Hennebert, Claudiu Cristian Musat, and Andreas Fischer. 2020. Automatic creation of text corpora for low-resource languages from the internet: The case of swiss german. In *Proceedings of The 12th Language Resources and Evaluation Conference*, pages 2706–2711, Marseille, France. European Language Resources Association.

Bing Liu and Ian R. Lane. 2016. Attention-based recurrent neural network models for joint intent detection and slot filling. *CoRR*, abs/1609.01454.

Xingkun Liu, Arash Eshghi, Pawel Swietojanski, and Verena Rieser. 2019. Benchmarking natural language understanding services for building conversational agents.

Loren Lugosch, Mirco Ravanelli, Patrick Ignoto, Vikrant Singh Tomar, and Yoshua Bengio. 2019. Speech Model Pre-Training for End-to-End Spoken Language Understanding. In *Proc. Interspeech 2019*, pages 814–818.

Grégoire Mesnil, Yann Dauphin, Kaisheng Yao, Yoshua Bengio, Li Deng, Dilek Hakkani-Tur, Xiaodong He, Larry Heck, Gokhan Tur, Dong Yu, and Geoffrey Zweig. 2015. Using recurrent neural networks for slot filling in spoken language understanding. *IEEE/ACM Transactions on Audio, Speech, and Language Processing*, 23(3):530–539.

Niklas Muennighoff, Thomas Wang, Lintang Sutawika, Adam Roberts, Stella Biderman, Teven Le Scao, M Saiful Bari, Sheng Shen, Zheng-Xin Yong, Hailey Schoelkopf, et al. 2022. Crosslingual generalization through multitask finetuning. *arXiv preprint arXiv:2211.01786*.

NLLB Team, Marta R. Costa-jussà, James Cross, Onur Çelebi, Maha Elbayad, Kenneth Heafield, Kevin Heffernan, Elahe Kalbassi, Janice Lam, Daniel Licht, Jean Maillard, Anna Sun, Skyler Wang, Guillaume Wenzek, Al Youngblood, Bapi Akula, Loic Barrault, Gabriel Mejia-Gonzalez, Prangthip Hansanti, John Hoffman, Semarley Jarrett, Kaushik Ram Sadagopan, Dirk Rowe, Shannon Spruit, Chau Tran, Pierre Andrews, Necip Fazil Ayan, Shruti Bhosale, Sergey Edunov, Angela Fan, Cynthia Gao, Vedanuj Goswami, Francisco Guzmán, Philipp Koehn, Alexandre Mourachko, Christophe Ropers, Safiyyah Saleem, Holger Schwenk, and Jeff Wang. 2022. No language left behind: Scaling human-centered machine translation.

P. J. Price. 1990. Evaluation of spoken language systems: the ATIS domain. In *Speech and Natural Language: Proceedings of a Workshop Held at Hidden Valley, Pennsylvania, June 24-27,1990*.

Lance Ramshaw and Mitch Marcus. 1995. Text chunking using transformation-based learning. In *Third Workshop on Very Large Corpora*.

Jeff Rasley, Samyam Rajbhandari, Olatunji Ruwase, and Yuxiong He. 2020. Deepspeed: System optimizations enable training deep learning models with over 100 billion parameters. In *Proceedings of the 26th ACM SIGKDD International Conference on Knowledge Discovery Data Mining*, KDD '20, page 3505–3506, New York, NY, USA. Association for Computing Machinery.

Suman Ravuri and Andreas Stolcke. 2015. Recurrent neural network and lstm models for lexical utterance classification. pages 135–139.

Nils Reimers and Iryna Gurevych. 2019. Sentence-bert: Sentence embeddings using siamese bert-networks. *arXiv preprint arXiv:1908.10084*.

Nils Reimers and Iryna Gurevych. 2020. Making monolingual sentence embeddings multilingual using knowledge distillation. *arXiv preprint arXiv:2004.09813*.

Sebastian Schuster, Sonal Gupta, Rushin Shah, and Mike Lewis. 2019. Cross-lingual transfer learning for multilingual task oriented dialog. In *Proceedings of the 2019 Conference of the North American Chapter of the Association for Computational Linguistics: Human Language Technologies, Volume 1 (Long and Short Papers)*, pages 3795–3805, Minneapolis, Minnesota. Association for Computational Linguistics.

Lysandre Debut Younes Belkada Sayak Paul Sourab Mangrulkar, Sylvain Gugger. 2022. Peft: State-of-the-art parameter-efficient fine-tuning methods. `https://github.com/huggingface/peft`.

Jörg Tiedemann. 2012. Parallel data, tools and interfaces in opus. In *Lrec*, volume 2012, pages 2214–2218. Citeseer.

Jörg Tiedemann and Santhosh Thottingal. 2020. OPUS-MT — Building open translation services for the World. In *Proceedings of the 22nd Annual Conferenec of the European Association for Machine Translation (EAMT)*, Lisbon, Portugal.

Shyam Upadhyay, Manaal Faruqui, Gokhan Tür, Hakkani-Tür Dilek, and Larry Heck. 2018. (almost) zero-shot cross-lingual spoken language understanding. In *2018 IEEE International Conference on Acoustics, Speech and Signal Processing (ICASSP)*, pages 6034–6038.

Rob van der Goot, Ibrahim Sharaf, Aizhan Imankulova, Ahmet Üstün, Marija Stepanović, Alan Ramponi, Siti Oryza Khairunnisa, Mamoru Komachi, and Barbara Plank. 2021. From masked language modeling to translation: Non-English auxiliary tasks improve zero-shot spoken language understanding. In *Proceedings of the 2021 Conference of the North American Chapter of the Association for Computational Linguistics: Human Language Technologies*, pages 2479–2497, Online. Association for Computational Linguistics.

Ashish Vaswani, Noam Shazeer, Niki Parmar, Jakob Uszkoreit, Llion Jones, Aidan N Gomez, Łukasz Kaiser, and Illia Polosukhin. 2017. Attention is all you need. In *Advances in Neural Information Processing Systems*, pages 6000–6010.

Puyang Xu and Ruhi Sarikaya. 2013. Convolutional neural network based triangular crf for joint intent detection and slot filling. pages 78–83.

Weijia Xu, Batool Haider, and Saab Mansour. 2020. End-to-end slot alignment and recognition for cross-lingual NLU. In *Proceedings of the 2020 Conference on Empirical Methods in Natural Language Processing (EMNLP)*, pages 5052–5063, Online. Association for Computational Linguistics.

Linting Xue, Noah Constant, Adam Roberts, Mihir Kale, Rami Al-Rfou, Aditya Siddhant, Aditya Barua, and Colin Raffel. 2020. mt5: A massively multilingual pre-trained text-to-text transformer. *arXiv preprint arXiv:2010.11934*.

Kaisheng Yao, Baolin Peng, Geoffrey Zweig, Dong Yu, Xiaolong Li, and Feng Gao. 2014. Recurrent conditional random field for language understanding. In *2014 IEEE International Conference on Acoustics, Speech and Signal Processing (ICASSP)*, pages 4077–4081.

Jianguo Zhang, Kazuma Hashimoto, Yao Wan, Ye Liu, Caiming Xiong, and Philip S. Yu. 2021. Are pre-trained transformers robust in intent classification? A missing ingredient in evaluation of out-of-scope intent detection. *CoRR*, abs/2106.04564.

Findings of the VarDial Evaluation Campaign 2023

Noëmi Aepli[1], Çağrı Çöltekin[2], Rob van der Goot[3], Tommi Jauhiainen[4]
Mourhaf Kazzaz[2], Nikola Ljubešić[5,6], Kai North[7], Barbara Plank[8]
Yves Scherrer[4], Marcos Zampieri[7]

[1]University of Zurich, [2]University of Tübingen, [3]IT University of Copenhagen,
[4]University of Helsinki, [5]Jožef Stefan Institute, [6]University of Zagreb,
[7]George Mason University, [8]LMU Munich

Abstract

This report presents the results of the shared tasks organized as part of the VarDial Evaluation Campaign 2023. The campaign is part of the tenth workshop on Natural Language Processing (NLP) for Similar Languages, Varieties and Dialects (VarDial), co-located with EACL 2023. Three separate shared tasks were included this year: Slot and intent detection for low-resource language varieties (SID4LR), Discriminating Between Similar Languages – True Labels (DSL-TL), and Discriminating Between Similar Languages – Speech (DSL-S). All three tasks were organized for the first time this year.

1 Introduction

The workshop series on *NLP for Similar Languages, Varieties and Dialects* (VarDial), traditionally co-located with international conferences, has reached its tenth edition. Since the first edition, VarDial has hosted shared tasks on various topics such as language and dialect identification, morphosyntactic tagging, question answering, and cross-lingual dependency parsing. The shared tasks have featured many languages and dialects from different families and data from various sources, genres, and domains (Aepli et al., 2022; Chakravarthi et al., 2021; Gaman et al., 2020; Zampieri et al., 2019, 2018, 2017; Malmasi et al., 2016; Zampieri et al., 2015, 2014).

As part of the VarDial Evaluation Campaign 2023, we offered three shared tasks which we present in this paper:

- **SID4LR:** Slot and intent detection for low-resource language varieties[1]
- **DSL-TL:** Discriminating Between Similar Languages – True Labels[2]
- **DSL-S:** Discriminating Between Similar Languages – Speech[3]

DSL-TL and DSL-S continue the long line of language and dialect identification (Jauhiainen et al., 2019) shared tasks at VarDial, whereas the SID4LR features a task novel to the evaluation campaigns.

This overview paper is structured as follows: in Section 2, we briefly introduce the three shared tasks. Section 3 presents the teams that submitted systems to the shared tasks. Each task is then discussed in detail, focusing on the data, the participants' approaches, and the obtained results. Section 4 is dedicated to SID4LR, Section 5 to DSL-TL, and Section 6 to DSL-S.

2 Shared Tasks at VarDial 2023

The evaluation campaign took place in January – February 2023. Due to the ACL placing the workshop at the EACL conference in early May, the schedule from the shared tasks' first announcement to completion was relatively tight. The call for participation in the shared tasks was first published in early January, the training data sets for the shared tasks were released on January 23rd, and the results were due to be submitted on February 27th.[4]

2.1 SID for Low-resource Language Varieties (SID4LR)

The SID4LR shared task focused on Slot and Intent Detection (SID) for digital assistant data in three low-resource language varieties: Swiss German (GSW) from the city of Bern, South Tyrolean (DE-ST), and Neapolitan (NAP). Intent detection is the task of automatically classifying the intent of an utterance and slot detection aims at finding the relevant (labeled) span. Figure 1 illustrates these two tasks with an example. The objective of this shared

[1]Task organizers: Noëmi Aepli, Rob van der Goot, Barbara Plank, Yves Scherrer.

[2]Task organizers: Marcos Zampieri, Kai North, Tommi Jauhiainen.

[3]Task organizers: Çağrı Çöltekin, Mourhaf Kazzaz, Tommi Jauhiainen, Nikola Ljubešić.

[4]https://sites.google.com/view/vardial-2023/shared-tasks

Tenth Workshop on NLP for Similar Languages, Varieties and Dialects (VarDial 2023), pages 251–261
May 5, 2023 ©2023 Association for Computational Linguistics

English (EN)	Remind me to go to the dentist next Monday
Italian (IT)	Ricordami di andare dal dentista lunedì prossimo
Neapolitan (NAP)	**Ricuordam' 'e 'i addo dentista lunnerì prossimo**
German (DE)	Erinnere mich am nächsten Montag zum Zahnarzt zu gehen
Swiss German (GSW)	**Du mi dra erinnere nöchscht Mänti zum Proffumech zga**
South Tyrolean (DE-ST)	**Erinner mi in negschtn Muntig zin Zohnorzt zu gian**

Figure 1: Example of the SID tasks. The **three target languages (NAP, GSW, DE-ST)** are in bold, the corresponding high-resource languages (DE and IT) and the translation (EN) are included for comparison. The *slot* annotations are coloured: datetime and reminder/todo. The *intent* for this sentence is `reminder/set_reminder`.

task is to address the following question: *How can we best do zero-shot transfer to low-resource language varieties without standard orthography?*

The xSID-0.4 corpus[5], which includes data from both Snips (Coucke et al., 2018) and Facebook (Schuster et al., 2019), constitutes the training data, providing labeled information for slot and intent detection in 13 different languages. The original training data is in English, but we also provided automatic translations of the training data into German, Italian, and other languages. These translations are obtained with the Fairseq library (Ott et al., 2019), using spoken data for training (more details in van der Goot et al. (2021a)). Bleu scores (Papineni et al., 2002) were 25.93 and 44.73 for respectively German and Italian. Slot label annotations were transferred using the attention weights. Participants were allowed to use other data to train on as long as it was not annotated for SID in the target languages. Specifically, the following resources were allowed:

1. annotated data from other (related and unrelated) languages in the xSID-0.4 corpus;

2. raw text data from the target languages, if available (e.g., Wikipedia, web crawls);

3. pre-trained language models containing data from the target languages.

It was not mandatory for the participants to provide systems for all tasks and languages; they had the option to only take part in a specific subset. We used the standard evaluation metrics for these tasks, namely the span F1 score for slots and accuracy for intents.

2.2 Discriminating Between Similar Languages – True Labels (DSL-TL)

Discriminating between similar languages (e.g., Croatian and Serbian) and national language varieties (e.g., Brazilian and European Portuguese) has been a popular topic at VarDial since its first edition. The DSL shared tasks organized from 2014 to 2017 (Zampieri et al., 2017; Malmasi et al., 2016; Zampieri et al., 2015, 2014) have addressed this issue by providing participants with the DSL Corpus Collection (DSLCC) (Tan et al., 2014), a collection of journalistic texts containing texts written in groups of similar languages (e.g., Indonesian and Malay) and language varieties (e.g., Brazilian and European Portuguese).[6] The DSLCC was compiled assuming each instance's gold label is determined by where the text is retrieved from. While this is a straightforward and primarily accurate practical assumption, previous research (Goutte et al., 2016) has shown the limitations of this problem formulation as some texts may present no linguistic marker that allows systems or native speakers to discriminate between two very similar languages or language varieties.

At VarDial 2023, we tackle this important limitation by introducing the DSL True Labels (DSL-TL) shared task. DSL-TL provided participants with the DSL-TL dataset (Zampieri et al., 2023), the first human-annotated language variety identification dataset where the sentences can belong to several varieties simultaneously. The DSL-TL dataset contains newspaper texts annotated by multiple native speakers of the included language and language varieties, namely English (American and British varieties), Portuguese (Brazilian and European varieties), and Spanish (Argentinian and Peninsular varieties). More details on the DSL-TL shared task and dataset are presented in Section 5.

[5]https://bitbucket.org/robvanderg/sid4lr

[6]http://ttg.uni-saarland.de/resources/DSLCC/

Team	SID4LR	DSL-TL	DSL-S	System Description Paper
UBC	✓			Kwon et al. (2023)
Notre Dame	✓			Srivastava and Chiang (2023)
VaidyaKane		✓		Vaidya and Kane (2023)
ssl		✓		Hohl and Shim (2023)
UnibucNLP		✓		Gaman (2023)
SATLab		✓		

Table 1: The teams that participated in the VarDial Evaluation Campaign 2023.

2.3 Discriminating Between Similar Languages – Speech (DSL-S)

In the DSL-S 2023 shared task, participants were using the training, and the development sets from the Mozilla Common Voice (CV, Ardila et al., 2020) to develop a language identifier for speech.[7] The nine languages selected for the task come from four different subgroups of Indo-European or Uralic language families (Swedish, Norwegian Nynorsk, Danish, Finnish, Estonian, Moksha, Erzya, Russian, and Ukrainian).

The 9-way classification task was divided into two separate tracks. Only the training and development data from the CV dataset were allowed in the closed track, and no other data were to be used. This prohibition included systems and models trained (unsupervised or supervised) on any other data. On the open track, the use of any openly available (available to any possible shared task participant) datasets and models not including or trained on the Mozilla Common Voice test set was allowed. The evaluation measure used was the Macro F1 score over the nine languages.

3 Participating Teams

A total of six teams submitted runs to the SID4LR and DSL-TL tasks. Two teams registered for the DSL-S shared task, but neither provided any submissions. In Table 1, we list the teams that participated in the shared tasks, including references to the system description papers, which are published as parts of the VarDial workshop proceedings. Detailed information about the submissions is included in the task-specific sections below.

4 SID for Low-resource Language Varieties

4.1 Dataset

The xSID-0.4 corpus[8] makes up the training data and provides labeled information for slot and intent detection in 13 different languages. The xSID dataset consists of sentences from the English Snips (Coucke et al., 2018) and cross-lingual Facebook (Schuster et al., 2019) datasets, which were manually translated into 12 other languages (van der Goot et al., 2021a). There are 43,605 sentences in the English training data. The evaluation data contains 500 test sentences and 300 validation sentences per language. For the test data, we took the existing South Tyrolean (DE-ST) part of xSID (van der Goot et al., 2021a) and two novel translations created for this shared task: Bernese Swiss German (GSW) and Neapolitan (NAP). The new translations were done by native speakers of the two language varieties. They translated directly from English without seeing the Italian or German source sentences. The translations were then processed and annotated by the shared task organizers (who have passive knowledge of the two language varieties). The two steps were done according to the guidelines from the original paper by van der Goot et al. (2021a).

4.2 Participants and Approaches

UBC: Team UBC (Kwon et al., 2023) participated in both subtasks: slot and intent detection. They used several multilingual Transformer-based language models, including mBERT, XLM-R, SBERT, LaBSE, LASER, and mT0. Furthermore, they experimented with a variety of settings to improve performance: varying the source languages, combining different language models, data augmentation via paraphrasing and machine trans-

[7]Further information available at: https://dsl-s.github.io.

[8]https://bitbucket.org/robvanderg/sid4lr

lation, and pre-training on the target languages. For the latter, they made use of additional external data from various sources for all three target languages for the training.

Notre Dame: Team Notre Dame (Srivastava and Chiang, 2023) submitted a research paper to the VarDial workshop, within which they also described their participation in the intent detection subtask. The team applied zero-shot methods, i.e., they did not use any data from the target language in the training process. They fine-tuned monolingual language models[9] with noise-induced data. The noising technique they applied is similar to that of Aepli and Sennrich (2022) with three main differences: they 1) add an additional noise type: *swapping* between adjacent letters; 2) they employ higher levels of noise and include multiple copies of the fine-tuning data; and 3) remove the step of continued pre-training to avoid using any target language data.

Baseline: The baseline we provided is the same as in the original xSID paper, trained on the English data, with an updated version of MaChAmp (van der Goot et al., 2021b). The model uses an mBERT encoder and a separate decoder head for each task, one for slot detection (with a CRF layer) and one for intent classification.

4.3 Results

We evaluated the submitted systems according to accuracy for intents and according to the span F1 score for slots (where both span and label must match exactly). Table 2 contains the scores.

For intent classification, the winner for all three languages is the team Notre Dame. Both teams beat the baseline by a large margin. All systems reached the highest scores on DE-ST and the lowest scores on GSW, but both participating teams managed to significantly close the gaps between the languages compared to the baseline.

For slot detection, the UBC team outperformed the baseline for DE-ST and GSW but not for NAP. Again, GSW turned out to be the most difficult language variety of the three. We must note, however, that the UBC submission contained a large amount of ill-formed slots. Between 13% (DE-ST, NAP) and 28% (GSW) of predicted slots start with an `I-` label instead of `B-`; the evaluation script simply ignores such slots. Furthermore, a small number of predicted spans have inconsistent labels (e.g., `I-datetime` immediately followed by `I-location`). This suggests that the model architecture chosen by the UBC team was not appropriate for span labeling tasks and that a different architecture could have led to further improvements compared to the baseline. The baseline system, which uses a CRF prediction layer, did not produce any such inconsistencies.

		Baseline	UBC	Notre Dame
Intent detection	**DE-ST**	0.6160	0.8940	**0.9420**
	GSW	0.4720	0.8160	**0.8860**
	NAP	0.5900	0.8540	**0.8900**
Slot detection	**DE-ST**	0.4288	**0.4692**	–
	GSW	0.2530	**0.2899**	–
	NAP	**0.4457**	0.4215	–

Table 2: Results for intent classification (accuracy) and slot detection (Span-F1 score). UBC submitted several models for intent detection, and here we report their best-performing system for each language.

4.4 Summary

The UBC submissions are based on a pre-trained multilingual language model (mT0), which was fine-tuned on the 12 languages of the xSID dataset. Among these languages are Italian and German, but all training sets except the English one have been produced by machine translation. This setup worked better than using only the related languages of xSID (IT and DE) or only English. Also, further data augmentation with paraphrasing and machine translation did not have any positive effect. These findings suggest that task-specific knowledge is more important than having access to linguistic material in the target languages (or even in related high-resource languages).

The Notre Dame participation provides a somewhat contrasting result. They start with a monolingual BERT model of the related high-resource language (IT or DE) and use fine-tuning to make the model more robust to character-level noise. The possibility of including unrelated languages was not explored here.

The contributions proposed by the participants are thus largely complementary, and it would be interesting to see if their combination leads to further improvements on the task. For instance, task-specific fine-tuning (using all of the xSID data)

[9]German BERT: `https://huggingface.co/dbmdz/bert-base-german-uncased` and Italian BERT: `https://huggingface.co/dbmdz/bert-base-italian-uncased`

could be combined with language-specific fine-tuning (based on the noise induction task) and complemented with the baseline's CRF architecture to provide consistent slot labels.

A striking finding of this shared task are the poor results on Swiss German compared to the other two low-resource varieties, Neapolitan and South-Tyrolean German. This may be due to the particular Swiss German dialect used in this dataset and/or to some translator-specific preferences or biases. Further analysis will be required to fully explain these differences.

5 Discriminating Between Similar Languages – True Labels

The DSL-TL shared task contained two tracks:

- **Track 1 – Three-way Classification:** In this track, systems were evaluated with respect to the prediction of all three labels for each language, namely the variety-specific labels (e.g., PT-PT or PT-BR) and the common label (e.g., PT).

- **Track 2 – Binary Classification:** In this track, systems were scored only on the variety-specific labels (e.g., EN-GB, EN-US).

In addition to the two tracks mentioned above, we provided participants with the option of using external data sources (open submission) or only the DSL-TL dataset (closed submission).

5.1 Dataset

Data DSL-TL contains 12,900 instances split between three languages and six national language varieties, as shown in Table 3. Instances in the DSL-TL are short extracts (1 to 3 sentences long) from newspaper articles randomly sampled from two sources (Zellers et al., 2019; Tan et al., 2014). Considering the source's ground truth label, the DSL-TL creators randomly selected 2,500 instances for each Portuguese and Spanish variety and 1,500 instances for each English variety.

Annotation DSL-TL was annotated using crowd-sourcing through Amazon Mechanical Turk (AMT).[10] The annotation task was restricted to annotators based on the six national language variety countries, namely Argentina, Brazil, Portugal, Spain, United Kingdom, and the United States. The annotators were asked to label each instance with what they believed to be the most representative variety label, namely European (pt-PT) or Brazilian Portuguese (pt-BR), Castilian (es-ES) or Argentine Spanish (es-AR), and British (en-GB) or American English (en-US). The label distributions are shown in Table 3. The annotators were presented with three choices: (1) language variety A, (2) language variety B, or (3) both or neither for cases in which no clear language variety marker (either linguistic or named entity) was present in the text. The annotator agreement calculations and filtering carried out after the annotation stage are described in detail in the dataset description paper (Zampieri et al., 2023). Finally, the instances in DSL-TL have been split into training, development, and testing partitions, as shown in Table 4.

5.2 Participants and Approaches

Four teams provided submissions to the shared task.

VaidyaKane: All submissions from the team VaidyaKane used a pre-trained multilingual XLM-RoBERTa fine-tuned to language identification[11] to classify the language of the sentence (Conneau et al., 2020b). After the initial language identification, they experimented with several language-specific BERT models to identify the exact variety. Their best submission on track one used "bert-base-uncased"[12] for English (Devlin et al., 2019), "bertin-project/bertin-roberta-base-spanish"[13] for Spanish (la Rosa et al., 2022), and "neuralmind/bert-base-portuguese-cased"[14] for Portuguese (Souza et al., 2020). On track two, the models for Spanish and Portuguese were the same, but "roberta-base"[15] was used for English (Liu et al., 2019).

ssl: Team ssl submitted one submission to each of the four track combinations. For the closed tracks, they trained an SVM classifier using TF-IDF weighted character n-grams from one to four and word n-grams from one to two. On the open

[10] https://www.mturk.com/

[11] https://huggingface.co/papluca/xlm-roberta-base-language-detection

[12] https://huggingface.co/bert-base-uncased

[13] https://huggingface.co/bertin-project/bertin-roberta-base-spanish

[14] https://huggingface.co/neuralmind/bert-base-portuguese-cased

[15] https://huggingface.co/roberta-base

Language	Variety A	Variety B	Both/Neither	Total
Portuguese	1,317 (pt-PT)	3,023 (pt-BR)	613 (pt)	4,953
Spanish	2,131 (es-ES)	1,211 (es-AR)	1,605 (es)	4,947
English	1,081 (en-GB)	1,540 (en-US)	379 (en)	3,000
Total				**12,900**

Table 3: DSL-TL's class splits and the total number of instances.

Variety	Train	Dev	Test	Total
Portuguese	3,467	991	495	4,953
Spanish	3,467	985	495	4,947
English	2,097	603	300	3,000
Total				12,900

Table 4: DSL-TL's train, dev, and test splits are 70/20/10% of the total number of instances, respectively.

tracks, they also used names of people obtained from Wikidata (Vrandečić and Krötzsch, 2014).

UnibucNLP: On track one, the UnibucNLP team submitted a run using an XGBoost stacking ensemble (Chen and Guestrin, 2016). The classifier stack for the ensemble consisted of one SVM and one KRR classifier. For track two, the stack classifiers were the same, but Logistic Regression was used for the stacking ensemble.

SATLab: On both tracks, the SATLab team used a Logistic Regression classifier from the LIBLinear package with character n-grams from one to five weighted by BM25 and L2 normalization. The n-grams had to appear in at least two different sentences in the training data. The system was very similar to the one used by Bestgen (2021) in the Dravidian Language Identification (DLI) shared task in 2021 (Chakravarthi et al., 2021).

5.3 Results

Tables 5 to 8 show the recall, precision, and F1 scores for the baselines and best submissions for all track combinations.

Rank	Model	R	P	F1
	baseline-mBERT	0.5490	0.5450	0.5400
	baseline-XLM-R	0.5280	0.5490	0.5360
1	run-3-UnibucNLP	0.5291	0.5542	0.5318
	baseline-NB	0.5090	0.5090	0.5030
2	run-1-SATLab	0.4987	0.4896	0.4905
3	run-1-ssl	0.4978	0.4734	0.4817

Table 5: The macro average scores of the best run for each team on **closed track 1**.

Rank	Model	R	P	F1
	baseline-ANB	0.8200	0.7990	0.7990
	baseline-NB	0.8110	0.7920	0.7940
	baseline-XLM-R	0.7830	0.7820	0.7800
1	run-1-ssl	0.7521	0.7885	0.7604
	baseline-mBERT	0.7600	0.7530	0.7550
2	run-2-SATLab	0.7520	0.7430	0.7452
3	run-1-UnibucNLP	0.6502	0.7756	0.6935

Table 6: The macro average scores of the best run for each team on **closed track 2**.

Rank	Model	R	P	F1
1	run-3-VaidyaKa	0.5962	0.5866	0.5854
2	run-1-ssl	0.4937	0.5068	0.4889

Table 7: The macro average scores of the best run for **open track 1**.

Rank	Model	R	P	F1
1	run-1-VaidyaKa	0.8705	0.8523	0.8561
	baseline-NB	0.8200	0.8030	0.8030
2	run-1-ssl	0.7647	0.7951	0.7729

Table 8: The macro average scores of the best run for each team on **open track 2**.

Team UnibucNLP (Gaman, 2023) achieved the first place out of nine submissions on the closed version of track one. Their XGBoost stacking ensemble attained an F1 score of 0.5318. The results were still slightly worse than the multilingual BERT[16] (mBERT) (Devlin et al., 2019) and the XLM-RoBERTa[17] (XLM-R) (Liu et al., 2019) baselines. All other submissions achieved slightly worse F1 scores. In the second place, team SATLab's logistic regressor obtained an F1 score of 0.4905. In third place, team ssl's SVM produced an F1 score of 0.4817. The similarity between the top three F1 scores shows that automatically differentiating between similar language varieties is a challenging task, especially when taking into consideration neutral labels (EN, ES, or PT), as well as only using the provided data.

[16]mBERT: `https://huggingface.co/bert-base-multilingual-cased`

[17]XLM-R: `https://huggingface.co/xlm-roberta-base`

Team ssl (Hohl and Shim, 2023) achieved the best performance out of ten submissions on the closed version of track two. Their SVM was able to more effectively differentiate between six labels that did not include the aforementioned neutral labels (en-GB, en-US, es-AR, es-ES, pt-PT, or pt-BR). They achieved an F1 score of 0.7604. Their results were closely followed by the performance of SATLab's logistic regressor, having attained an F1 score of 0.7452, and UnibucNLP's XGBoost stacking ensemble with an F1 score of 0.6935. All submissions were clearly behind the adaptive and traditional Naive Bayes baselines, which were identical to the systems winning the Identification of Languages and Dialects of Italy (ITDI) shared task in 2022 (Jauhiainen et al., 2022a; Aepli et al., 2022). SVMs are well-known to perform well when there is a clear distinction between class boundaries. This likely explains why team ssl's SVM has outperformed UnibucNLP's ensemble since neutral labels that contained features of both classes were no longer considered.

Team VaidyaKane's (Vaidya and Kane, 2023) submission to the open version of track 1 outperformed all other open and closed submissions for this track. Their two-stage transformer-based model achieved an F1 score of 0.5854. Team ssl was the only other team to submit predictions for open tracks 1 and 2. Their open submission for track 1 achieved an F1 score of 0.4889 which surpassed that of their closed submission for this track. The use of additional data was, therefore, found to improve overall performances.

Team VaidyaKane produced the highest F1 score on the open version of track 2. They achieved an F1 score of 0.8561, which was greater than all other open and closed submissions for either track. Team ssl also saw a further improvement in their SVM's model performance when using additional data for track 2. Their SVM model produced an F1 score of 0.7729, which was superior to their closed-track submission. These performances show that the use of additional data is beneficial and further proves that the classification of language varieties is an easier task than the classification of language varieties with neutral labels.

5.4 Summary

The DSL-TL shared task introduced a novel problem formulation in language variety identification. The new human-annotated dataset with the presence of the 'both or neither' class represent a new way of looking at the problem. Given the similarity between language varieties, we believe this new problem formulation constitutes a fairer way of evaluating language identification systems, albeit rather challenging in terms of performance as demonstrated in this shared task.

6 Discriminating Between Similar Languages – Speech

6.1 Dataset

The DSL-S shared task uses Mozilla Common Voice data (version 12 released in Dec 2022) in 9 languages from two language families. The data comes from volunteers reading a pre-selected set of sentences in each language. The audio is recorded through a web-based interface. For training and development sets, we follow the training and development set of the source data. Even though the test data used in this task comes from the Common Voice test data for the nine languages, we do not use the entire test set of the CV release but sample 100 audio files for each language. There is no overlap of sentences and speakers between the data sets. Table 9 presents the test set's statistics. The total amount of unpacked speech data is around 15 gigabytes. The data includes severe class imbalance, as well as substantial differences in the number of speakers. Generalization from a small number of speakers is a known challenge in similar speech data sets, including earlier VarDial evaluation campaigns.[18] The CV data set makes this task further challenging since the variety of speakers in the test set is much larger than the training and the development sets.

Similar to the earlier VarDial shared tasks with audio data (Zampieri et al., 2017, 2018, 2019), we provided 400-dimensional i-vector and 512-dimensional x-vector features, both extracted using Kaldi (Povey et al., 2011). Unlike earlier tasks, however, the raw audio data was also available to the potential participants.

6.2 Participants and Approaches

Two teams registered for the shared task, but neither provided any submissions. In this section, we briefly introduce the baselines we provided. For the closed track, we provided a linear SVM baseline with x-vectors features (Snyder et al., 2018). The

[18]See Jauhiainen et al. (2018) and Wu et al. (2019) for earlier approaches to this problem.

	Train			Dev			Test		
	n	spk	duration	n	spk	duration	n	spk	duration
DA	2734	3	3:17:38	2105	10	2:50:46	100	48	0:07:50
ET	3137	221	5:49:04	2638	167	4:57:54	100	88	0:11:12
FI	2121	3	2:43:47	1651	13	1:59:23	100	63	0:07:46
MDF	173	2	0:15:39	54	1	0:04:39	100	7	0:08:40
MYV	1241	2	1:58:26	239	1	0:22:55	100	9	0:09:07
NO	314	3	0:22:43	168	4	0:13:28	100	18	0:07:35
RU	26043	252	37:16:50	10153	394	15:23:17	100	98	0:09:15
SV	7421	22	8:11:54	5012	73	5:32:33	100	89	0:07:24
UK	15749	28	18:38:31	8085	103	10:58:25	100	28	0:08:22

Table 9: Number of instances (n), number of speakers (spk) and total duration (hour:minute:seconds) for each split of the DSL-S shared task. The speaker numbers are approximated based on client id detection by CV.

System	P	R	F1
SVM + x-vectors	0.0914	0.1189	0.0876
XLS-R	0.6736	0.5953	0.5856
XLS-R + NB	0.7331	0.7167	0.7031

Table 10: Baseline scores of the DSL-S shared task.

SVM baseline was implemented using scikit-learn (Pedregosa et al., 2011), and tuned only for the SVM margin parameter 'C'. The open track baseline uses two baselines - the XLS-R multilingual pre-trained transformer speech model (Conneau et al., 2020a)[19] with a classification head for direct speech classification, and a multilingual speech recognition system [20] based on XLS-R (Babu et al., 2021) to transcribe the speech, and uses Naive Bayes (Jauhiainen et al., 2022a,b) to identify the language.[21]

6.3 Results

The scores for the baselines are presented in Table 10. The SVM baseline performs particularly badly on the test set (the development precision, recall, and F1 scores are 0.4088, 0.4011, 0.3777, respectively). The reason behind this is likely due to the fact that, although they were used for language identification in earlier research, the x-vectors are designed for speaker identification. Given the variability of speaker features in the test set, any classifier relying on speaker features are likely to fail. The baselines relying on pre-trained transformer models perform substantially better, with the direct speech classifier being more than 10 points behind the transcription and text classification approach. While the direct speech classification approach could be further improved through hyperparameter optimisation (currently we fine-tune for 3 epochs with a batch size of 24 and a learning rate of 1e-04) and a selection of the layer from which the features are extracted (related work suggests that lower transformer layers are more informative for discriminating between languages (Bartley et al., 2023)), these baseline results show that transcription and text classification might still be a shorter path to a reasonably performing system for discriminating between similar languages than direct speech classification.

6.4 Summary

Although we did not have any submissions for this shared task, we believe that the task includes many interesting challenges. Based only on our baseline results, identifying languages from a limited amount of data (without pre-trained speech models) seems challenging, yet this is particularly interesting for low-resource settings and for investigating differences and similarities for closely related language varieties. We hope to see more interest in the community for language/dialect identification from speech.

7 Conclusion

This paper presented an overview of the three shared tasks organized as part of the VarDial Evaluation Campaign 2023: Slot and intent detection for low-resource language varieties (SID4LR), Discriminating Between Similar Languages – True La-

[19] https://huggingface.co/facebook/wav2vec2-large-xlsr-53

[20] https://huggingface.co/voidful/wav2vec2-xlsr-multilingual-56

[21] https://github.com/tosaja/TunPRF-NADI

bels (DSL-TL), and Discriminating Between Similar Languages – Speech (DSL-S).

Acknowledgements

We thank all the participants for their interest in the shared tasks.

The work related to the SID4LR shared task has received funding from the Swiss National Science Foundation (project nos. 191934 and 176727) and ERC Grant 101043235. The work related to the DSL-TL and DSL-S shared tasks has received partial funding from the Academy of Finland (funding decision no. 341798). The work related to the DSL-S shared task has received funding from the Slovenian Research Agency within the research project J7-4642 and the research programme P6-0411.

References

Noëmi Aepli, Antonios Anastasopoulos, Adrian-Gabriel Chifu, William Domingues, Fahim Faisal, Mihaela Gaman, Radu Tudor Ionescu, and Yves Scherrer. 2022. Findings of the VarDial evaluation campaign 2022. In *Proceedings of the Ninth Workshop on NLP for Similar Languages, Varieties and Dialects*, pages 1–13, Gyeongju, Republic of Korea. Association for Computational Linguistics.

Noëmi Aepli and Rico Sennrich. 2022. Improving zero-shot cross-lingual transfer between closely related languages by injecting character-level noise. In *Findings of the Association for Computational Linguistics: ACL 2022*, pages 4074–4083, Dublin, Ireland. Association for Computational Linguistics.

Rosana Ardila, Megan Branson, Kelly Davis, Michael Kohler, Josh Meyer, Michael Henretty, Reuben Morais, Lindsay Saunders, Francis Tyers, and Gregor Weber. 2020. Common voice: A massively-multilingual speech corpus. In *Proceedings of the 12th Language Resources and Evaluation Conference*, pages 4218–4222, Marseille, France. European Language Resources Association.

Arun Babu, Changhan Wang, Andros Tjandra, Kushal Lakhotia, Qiantong Xu, Naman Goyal, Kritika Singh, Patrick von Platen, Yatharth Saraf, Juan Pino, et al. 2021. XLS-R: Self-supervised cross-lingual speech representation learning at scale. *arXiv preprint arXiv:2111.09296*.

Travis M. Bartley, Fei Jia, Krishna C. Puvvada, Samuel Kriman, and Boris Ginsburg. 2023. Accidental learners: Spoken language identification in multilingual self-supervised models.

Yves Bestgen. 2021. Optimizing a supervised classifier for a difficult language identification problem. In *Proceedings of the Eighth Workshop on NLP for Similar Languages, Varieties and Dialects*, pages 96–101, Kiyv, Ukraine. Association for Computational Linguistics.

Bharathi Raja Chakravarthi, Gaman Mihaela, Radu Tudor Ionescu, Heidi Jauhiainen, Tommi Jauhiainen, Krister Lindén, Nikola Ljubešić, Niko Partanen, Ruba Priyadharshini, Christoph Purschke, Eswari Rajagopal, Yves Scherrer, and Marcos Zampieri. 2021. Findings of the VarDial evaluation campaign 2021. In *Proceedings of the Eighth Workshop on NLP for Similar Languages, Varieties and Dialects*, pages 1–11, Kiyv, Ukraine. Association for Computational Linguistics.

Tianqi Chen and Carlos Guestrin. 2016. Xgboost: A scalable tree boosting system. In *Proceedings of the 22nd ACM SIGKDD International Conference on Knowledge Discovery and Data Mining*, KDD '16, page 785–794, New York, NY, USA. Association for Computing Machinery.

Alexis Conneau, Alexei Baevski, Ronan Collobert, Abdelrahman Mohamed, and Michael Auli. 2020a. Unsupervised cross-lingual representation learning for speech recognition.

Alexis Conneau, Kartikay Khandelwal, Naman Goyal, Vishrav Chaudhary, Guillaume Wenzek, Francisco Guzmán, Edouard Grave, Myle Ott, Luke Zettlemoyer, and Veselin Stoyanov. 2020b. Unsupervised cross-lingual representation learning at scale. In *Proceedings of the 58th Annual Meeting of the Association for Computational Linguistics*, pages 8440–8451, Online. Association for Computational Linguistics.

Alice Coucke, Alaa Saade, Adrien Ball, Théodore Bluche, Alexandre Caulier, David Leroy, Clément Doumouro, Thibault Gisselbrecht, Francesco Caltagirone, Thibaut Lavril, et al. 2018. Snips voice platform: an embedded spoken language understanding system for private-by-design voice interfaces. *arXiv preprint arXiv:1805.10190*.

Jacob Devlin, Ming-Wei Chang, Kenton Lee, and Kristina Toutanova. 2019. BERT: Pre-training of deep bidirectional transformers for language understanding. In *Proceedings of the 2019 Conference of the North American Chapter of the Association for Computational Linguistics: Human Language Technologies, Volume 1 (Long and Short Papers)*, pages 4171–4186, Minneapolis, Minnesota. Association for Computational Linguistics.

Mihaela Gaman. 2023. Using ensemble learning in language variety identification. In *Proceedings of the Tenth Workshop on NLP for Similar Languages, Varieties and Dialects*, Dubrovnik, Croatia. Association for Computational Linguistics.

Mihaela Gaman, Dirk Hovy, Radu Tudor Ionescu, Heidi Jauhiainen, Tommi Jauhiainen, Krister Lindén, Nikola Ljubešić, Niko Partanen, Christoph Purschke, Yves Scherrer, and Marcos Zampieri. 2020. A report on the VarDial evaluation campaign 2020. In

Proceedings of the 7th Workshop on NLP for Similar Languages, Varieties and Dialects, pages 1–14, Barcelona, Spain (Online). International Committee on Computational Linguistics (ICCL).

Cyril Goutte, Serge Léger, Shervin Malmasi, and Marcos Zampieri. 2016. Discriminating similar languages: Evaluations and explorations. In *Proceedings of the Tenth International Conference on Language Resources and Evaluation (LREC'16)*, pages 1800–1807, Portorož, Slovenia. European Language Resources Association (ELRA).

Fritz Hohl and Soh-Eun Shim. 2023. Vardial in the wild: Industrial applications of lid systems for closely-related language varieties. In *Proceedings of the Tenth Workshop on NLP for Similar Languages, Varieties and Dialects*, Dubrovnik, Croatia. Association for Computational Linguistics.

Tommi Jauhiainen, Heidi Jauhiainen, and Krister Lindén. 2018. HeLI-based experiments in Swiss German dialect identification. In *Proceedings of the Fifth Workshop on NLP for Similar Languages, Varieties and Dialects (VarDial 2018)*, pages 254–262, Santa Fe, New Mexico, USA. Association for Computational Linguistics.

Tommi Jauhiainen, Heidi Jauhiainen, and Krister Lindén. 2022a. Italian language and dialect identification and regional French variety detection using adaptive naive Bayes. In *Proceedings of the Ninth Workshop on NLP for Similar Languages, Varieties and Dialects*, pages 119–129, Gyeongju, Republic of Korea. Association for Computational Linguistics.

Tommi Jauhiainen, Heidi Jauhiainen, and Krister Lindén. 2022b. Optimizing naive Bayes for Arabic dialect identification. In *Proceedings of the The Seventh Arabic Natural Language Processing Workshop (WANLP)*, pages 409–414, Abu Dhabi, United Arab Emirates (Hybrid). Association for Computational Linguistics.

Tommi Jauhiainen, Marco Lui, Marcos Zampieri, Timothy Baldwin, and Krister Lindén. 2019. Automatic Language Identification in Texts: A Survey. *Journal of Artificial Intelligence Research*, 65:675–782.

Sang Yun Kwon, Gagan Bhatia, ElMoatez Billah Nagoudi, Alcides Alcoba Inciarte, and Muhammad Abdul-Mageed. 2023. Sidlr: Slot and intent detection models for low-resource language varieties. In *Proceedings of the Tenth Workshop on NLP for Similar Languages, Varieties and Dialects*, Dubrovnik, Croatia. Association for Computational Linguistics.

Javier De la Rosa, Eduardo G. Ponferrada, Manu Romero, Paulo Villegas, Pablo González de Prado Salas, and María Grandury. 2022. Bertin: Efficient pre-training of a spanish language model using perplexity sampling. *Procesamiento del Lenguaje Natural*, 68(0):13–23.

Yinhan Liu, Myle Ott, Naman Goyal, Jingfei Du, Mandar Joshi, Danqi Chen, Omer Levy, Mike Lewis, Luke Zettlemoyer, and Veselin Stoyanov. 2019. Roberta: A robustly optimized BERT pretraining approach. *CoRR*, abs/1907.11692.

Shervin Malmasi, Marcos Zampieri, Nikola Ljubešić, Preslav Nakov, Ahmed Ali, and Jörg Tiedemann. 2016. Discriminating between similar languages and Arabic dialect identification: A report on the third DSL shared task. In *Proceedings of the Third Workshop on NLP for Similar Languages, Varieties and Dialects (VarDial3)*, pages 1–14, Osaka, Japan. The COLING 2016 Organizing Committee.

Myle Ott, Sergey Edunov, Alexei Baevski, Angela Fan, Sam Gross, Nathan Ng, David Grangier, and Michael Auli. 2019. fairseq: A fast, extensible toolkit for sequence modeling. In *Proceedings of the 2019 Conference of the North American Chapter of the Association for Computational Linguistics (Demonstrations)*, pages 48–53, Minneapolis, Minnesota. Association for Computational Linguistics.

Kishore Papineni, Salim Roukos, Todd Ward, and Wei-Jing Zhu. 2002. Bleu: a method for automatic evaluation of machine translation. In *Proceedings of the 40th Annual Meeting of the Association for Computational Linguistics*, pages 311–318, Philadelphia, Pennsylvania, USA. Association for Computational Linguistics.

F. Pedregosa, G. Varoquaux, A. Gramfort, V. Michel, B. Thirion, O. Grisel, M. Blondel, P. Prettenhofer, R. Weiss, V. Dubourg, J. Vanderplas, A. Passos, D. Cournapeau, M. Brucher, M. Perrot, and E. Duchesnay. 2011. Scikit-learn: Machine learning in Python. *Journal of Machine Learning Research*, 12:2825–2830.

Daniel Povey, Arnab Ghoshal, Gilles Boulianne, Lukas Burget, Ondrej Glembek, Nagendra Goel, Mirko Hannemann, Petr Motlicek, Yanmin Qian, Petr Schwarz, Jan Silovsky, Georg Stemmer, and Karel Vesely. 2011. The kaldi speech recognition toolkit. In *IEEE 2011 Workshop on Automatic Speech Recognition and Understanding*. IEEE Signal Processing Society.

Sebastian Schuster, Sonal Gupta, Rushin Shah, and Mike Lewis. 2019. Cross-lingual transfer learning for multilingual task oriented dialog. In *Proceedings of the 2019 Conference of the North American Chapter of the Association for Computational Linguistics: Human Language Technologies, Volume 1 (Long and Short Papers)*, pages 3795–3805, Minneapolis, Minnesota. Association for Computational Linguistics.

David Snyder, Daniel Garcia-Romero, Gregory Sell, Daniel Povey, and Sanjeev Khudanpur. 2018. X-Vectors: Robust DNN embeddings for speaker recognition. In *2018 IEEE International Conference on Acoustics, Speech and Signal Processing (ICASSP)*, pages 5329–5333.

Fábio Souza, Rodrigo Nogueira, and Roberto Lotufo. 2020. BERTimbau: pretrained BERT models for Brazilian Portuguese. In *9th Brazilian Conference on Intelligent Systems, BRACIS, Rio Grande do Sul, Brazil, October 20-23 (to appear)*.

Aarohi Srivastava and David Chiang. 2023. Fine-tuning bert with character-level noise for zero-shot transfer to dialects and closely-related languages. In *Proceedings of the Tenth Workshop on NLP for Similar Languages, Varieties and Dialects*, Dubrovnik, Croatia. Association for Computational Linguistics.

Liling Tan, Marcos Zampieri, Nikola Ljubesic, and Jörg Tiedemann. 2014. Merging comparable data sources for the discrimination of similar languages : The dsl corpus collection. In *International Conference on Language Resources and Evaluation*.

Ankit Vaidya and Aditya Kane. 2023. Two-stage pipeline for multilingual dialect detection. In *Proceedings of the Tenth Workshop on NLP for Similar Languages, Varieties and Dialects*, Dubrovnik, Croatia. Association for Computational Linguistics.

Rob van der Goot, Ibrahim Sharaf, Aizhan Imankulova, Ahmet Üstün, Marija Stepanović, Alan Ramponi, Siti Oryza Khairunnisa, Mamoru Komachi, and Barbara Plank. 2021a. From masked language modeling to translation: Non-English auxiliary tasks improve zero-shot spoken language understanding. In *Proceedings of the 2021 Conference of the North American Chapter of the Association for Computational Linguistics: Human Language Technologies*, pages 2479–2497, Online. Association for Computational Linguistics.

Rob van der Goot, Ahmet Üstün, Alan Ramponi, Ibrahim Sharaf, and Barbara Plank. 2021b. Massive choice, ample tasks (MaChAmp): A toolkit for multi-task learning in NLP. In *Proceedings of the 16th Conference of the European Chapter of the Association for Computational Linguistics: System Demonstrations*, pages 176–197, Online. Association for Computational Linguistics.

Denny Vrandečić and Markus Krötzsch. 2014. Wikidata: A free collaborative knowledgebase. *Commun. ACM*, 57(10):78–85.

Nianheng Wu, Eric DeMattos, Kwok Him So, Pin-zhen Chen, and Çağrı Çöltekin. 2019. Language discrimination and transfer learning for similar languages: Experiments with feature combinations and adaptation. In *Proceedings of the Sixth Workshop on NLP for Similar Languages, Varieties and Dialects*, pages 54–63, Ann Arbor, Michigan. Association for Computational Linguistics.

Marcos Zampieri, Shervin Malmasi, Nikola Ljubešić, Preslav Nakov, Ahmed Ali, Jörg Tiedemann, Yves Scherrer, and Noëmi Aepli. 2017. Findings of the VarDial evaluation campaign 2017. In *Proceedings of the Fourth Workshop on NLP for Similar Languages, Varieties and Dialects (VarDial)*, pages 1–15, Valencia, Spain. Association for Computational Linguistics.

Marcos Zampieri, Shervin Malmasi, Preslav Nakov, Ahmed Ali, Suwon Shon, James Glass, Yves Scherrer, Tanja Samardžić, Nikola Ljubešić, Jörg Tiedemann, Chris van der Lee, Stefan Grondelaers, Nelleke Oostdijk, Dirk Speelman, Antal van den Bosch, Ritesh Kumar, Bornini Lahiri, and Mayank Jain. 2018. Language identification and morphosyntactic tagging: The second VarDial evaluation campaign. In *Proceedings of the Fifth Workshop on NLP for Similar Languages, Varieties and Dialects (VarDial 2018)*, pages 1–17, Santa Fe, New Mexico, USA. Association for Computational Linguistics.

Marcos Zampieri, Shervin Malmasi, Yves Scherrer, Tanja Samardžić, Francis Tyers, Miikka Silfverberg, Natalia Klyueva, Tung-Le Pan, Chu-Ren Huang, Radu Tudor Ionescu, Andrei M. Butnaru, and Tommi Jauhiainen. 2019. A report on the third VarDial evaluation campaign. In *Proceedings of the Sixth Workshop on NLP for Similar Languages, Varieties and Dialects*, pages 1–16, Ann Arbor, Michigan. Association for Computational Linguistics.

Marcos Zampieri, Kai North, Tommi Jauhiainen, Mariano Felice, Neha Kumari, Nishant Nair, and Yash Bangera. 2023. Language variety identification with true labels. *arXiv preprint arXiv:2303.01490*.

Marcos Zampieri, Liling Tan, Nikola Ljubešić, and Jörg Tiedemann. 2014. A report on the DSL shared task 2014. In *Proceedings of the First Workshop on Applying NLP Tools to Similar Languages, Varieties and Dialects*, pages 58–67, Dublin, Ireland. Association for Computational Linguistics and Dublin City University.

Marcos Zampieri, Liling Tan, Nikola Ljubešić, Jörg Tiedemann, and Preslav Nakov. 2015. Overview of the DSL shared task 2015. In *Proceedings of the Joint Workshop on Language Technology for Closely Related Languages, Varieties and Dialects*, pages 1–9, Hissar, Bulgaria. Association for Computational Linguistics.

Rowan Zellers, Ari Holtzman, Hannah Rashkin, Yonatan Bisk, Ali Farhadi, Franziska Roesner, and Yejin Choi. 2019. Defending against neural fake news. *Advances in neural information processing systems*, 32.

Author Index

Association for Computational Linguistics
209 N. Eighth Street
Stroudsburg, Pennsylvania 18360

ISBN 978-1-7138-7389-1

CURRAN ASSOCIATES INC.
proceedings.com